ALTERNATIVE INVESTMENTS AND FIXED INCOME

CFA® PROGRAM CURRICULUM
2013 • Level II • Volume 5

WILEY

John Wiley & Sons, Inc.

Please visit our website at
www.WileyGlobalFinance.com.

MIX
Paper from
responsible sources
FSC® C101537

Contents

🅞 indicates an optional segment

○ indicates an optional segment

○ indicates an optional segment

Ⓞ indicates an optional segment

◙ indicates an optional segment

How to Use the CFA Program Curriculum

Congratulations on passing Level I of the Chartered Financial Analyst (CFA®) Program. This exciting and rewarding program of study reflects your desire to become a serious investment professional. You are embarking on a program noted for its high ethical standards and the breadth of knowledge, skills, and abilities it develops. Your commitment to the CFA Program should be educationally and professionally rewarding.

The credential you seek is respected around the world as a mark of accomplishment and dedication. Each level of the program represents a distinct achievement in professional development. Successful completion of the program is rewarded with membership in a prestigious global community of investment professionals. CFA charterholders are dedicated to life-long learning and maintaining currency with the ever-changing dynamics of a challenging profession. The CFA Program represents the first step towards a career-long commitment to professional education.

The CFA examination measures your mastery of the core skills required to succeed as an investment professional. These core skills are the basis for the Candidate Body of Knowledge (CBOK™). The CBOK consists of four components:

- A broad topic outline that lists the major top-level topic areas (CBOK Topic Outline)
- Topic area weights that indicate the relative exam weightings of the top-level topic areas
- Learning outcome statements (LOS) that advise candidates about the specific knowledge, skills, and abilities they should acquire from readings covering a topic area (LOS are provided in candidate study sessions and at the beginning of each reading)
- The CFA Program curriculum, readings, and end-of-reading questions, which candidates receive upon exam registration

Therefore, the keys to your success on the CFA exam is studying and understanding the CBOK™. The following sections provide background on the CBOK, the organization of the curriculum, and tips for developing an effective study program.

CURRICULUM DEVELOPMENT PROCESS

The CFA Program is grounded in the practice of the investment profession. Using the Global Body of Investment Knowledge (GBIK) collaborative website, CFA Institute performs a continuous practice analysis with investment professionals around the world to determine the knowledge, skills, and abilities (competencies) that are relevant to the profession. Regional expert panels and targeted surveys are conducted annually to verify and reinforce the continuous feedback from the GBIK collaborative website. The practice analysis process ultimately defines the CBOK. The CBOK contains the competencies that are generally accepted and applied by investment professionals. These competencies are used in practice in a generalist context and are expected to be demonstrated by a recently qualified CFA charterholder.

A committee consisting of practicing charterholders, in conjunction with CFA Institute staff, designs the CFA Program curriculum in order to deliver the CBOK to candidates. The examinations, also written by practicing charterholders, are designed to allow you to demonstrate your mastery of the CBOK as set forth in the CFA Program curriculum. As you structure your personal study program, you should emphasize mastery of the CBOK and the practical application of that knowledge. For more information on the practice analysis, CBOK, and development of the CFA Program curriculum, please visit www.cfainstitute.org.

ORGANIZATION OF THE CURRICULUM

The Level II CFA Program curriculum is organized into 10 topic areas. Each topic area begins with a brief statement of the material and the depth of knowledge expected.

Each topic area is then divided into one or more study sessions. These study sessions—18 sessions in the Level II curriculum—should form the basic structure of your reading and preparation.

Each study session includes a statement of its structure and objective, and is further divided into specific reading assignments. An outline illustrating the organization of these 18 study sessions can be found at the front of each volume.

The reading assignments are the basis for all examination questions, and are selected or developed specifically to teach the knowledge, skills, and abilities reflected in the CBOK. These readings are drawn from CFA Institute-commissioned content, textbook chapters, professional journal articles, research analyst reports, and cases. All readings include problems and solutions to help you understand and master the topic areas.

Reading-specific Learning Outcome Statements (LOS) are listed at the beginning of each reading. These LOS indicate what you should be able to accomplish after studying the reading. The LOS, the reading, and the end-of-reading questions are dependent on each other, with the reading and questions providing context for understanding the scope of the LOS.

You should use the LOS to guide and focus your study, as each examination question is based on an assigned reading and one or more LOS. The readings provide context for the LOS and enable you to apply a principle or concept in a variety of scenarios. The candidate is responsible for the entirety of all of the required material in a study session, the assigned readings as well as the end-of-reading questions and problems.

We encourage you to review the material on LOS (http://www.cfainstitute.org/cfaprogram/courseofstudy/Pages/cfa_los.aspx), including the descriptions of LOS "command words," (www.cfainstitute.org/Documents/cfa_and_cipm_los_command_words.pdf).

FEATURES OF THE CURRICULUM

OPTIONAL
SEGMENT

- **Required vs. Optional Segments** - You should read all of an assigned reading. In some cases, however, we have reprinted an entire chapter or article and marked certain parts of the reading as "optional." The CFA examination is based only on the required segments, and the optional segments are included only when they might help you to better understand the required segments (by seeing the required material in its full context). When an optional segment begins, you will see text and a dashed vertical bar in the outside margin that will continue until the optional segment ends, accompanied by another icon. *Unless the material is specifically marked as optional, you should assume it is required.* You should rely on the required segments and the reading-specific LOS in preparing for the examination.

END OPTIONAL
SEGMENT

- **Problems/Solutions** - *All questions and problems in the readings as well as their solutions (which are provided directly following the problems) are part of the curriculum and are required material for the exam.* When appropriate, we have included problems within and after the readings to demonstrate practical application and reinforce your understanding of the concepts presented. The questions and problems are designed to help you learn these concepts and may serve as a basis for exam questions. Many of these questions are adapted from past CFA examinations.

- **Margins** - The wide margins in each volume provide space for your note-taking.

- **Six-Volume Structure** - For portability of the curriculum, the material is spread over six volumes.

- **Glossary and Index** - For your convenience, we have printed a comprehensive glossary and index in each volume. Throughout the curriculum, a **bolded blue** word in a reading denotes a term defined in the glossary.

- **Source Material** - The authorship, publisher, and copyright owners are given for each reading for your reference. We recommend that you use this CFA Institute curriculum rather than the original source materials because the curriculum may include only selected pages from outside readings, updated sections within the readings, and contains problems and solutions tailored to the CFA Program.

- **LOS Self-Check** - We have inserted checkboxes next to each LOS that you can use to track your progress in mastering the concepts in each reading.

DESIGNING YOUR PERSONAL STUDY PROGRAM

Create a Schedule - An orderly, systematic approach to examination preparation is critical. You should dedicate a consistent block of time every week to reading and studying. Complete all reading assignments and the associated problems and solutions in each study session. Review the LOS both before and after you study each reading to ensure that you have mastered the applicable content and can demonstrate the knowledge, skill, or ability described by the LOS and the assigned reading. Use the LOS self-check to track your progress and highlight areas of weakness for later review.

As you prepare for your exam, we will e-mail you important exam updates, testing policies, and study tips. Be sure to read these carefully. Curriculum errata are periodically updated and posted on the study session page at www.cfainstitute.org. You may also sign up for an RSS feed to alert you to the latest errata update.

Successful candidates report an average of over 300 hours preparing for each exam. Your preparation time will vary based on your prior education and experience. For each level of the curriculum, there are 18 study sessions, so a good plan is to devote 15–20 hours per week, for 18 weeks, to studying the material. Use the final four to six weeks before the exam to review what you've learned and practice with sample and mock exams. This recommendation, however, may underestimate the hours needed for appropriate examination preparation depending on your individual circumstances, relevant experience, and academic background. You will undoubtedly adjust your study time to conform to your own strengths and weaknesses, and your educational and professional background.

You will probably spend more time on some study sessions than on others, but on average you should plan on devoting 15-20 hours per study session. You should allow ample time for both in-depth study of all topic areas and additional concentration on those topic areas for which you feel least prepared.

Online Sample Examinations - CFA Institute online sample examinations are intended to assess your exam preparation as you progress toward the end of your study. After each question, you will receive immediate feedback noting the correct response and indicating the relevant assigned reading, so you will be able to identify areas of weakness for further study. The 120-minute sample examinations reflect the question formats, topics, and level of difficulty of the actual CFA examinations. Aggregate data indicate that the CFA examination pass rate was higher among candidates who took one or more online sample examinations than among candidates who did not take the online sample examinations. For more information on the online sample examinations, please visit www.cfainstitute.org.

Online Mock Examinations - In response to candidate requests, CFA Institute has developed mock examinations that mimic the actual CFA examinations not only in question format and level of difficulty, but also in length and topic weight. The three-hour online mock exams simulate the morning and afternoon sessions of the actual CFA exam, and are intended to be taken after you complete your study of the full curriculum, so you can test your understanding of the CBOK and your readiness for the exam. The mock exams are available in a printable PDF format with feedback provided at the end of the exam, rather than after each question as with the sample exams. CFA Institute recommends that you take these mock exams at the final stage of your preparation toward the actual CFA examination. For more information on the online mock examinations, please visit www.cfainstitute.org.

Preparatory Providers - After you enroll in the CFA Program, you may receive numerous solicitations for preparatory courses and review materials. When considering a prep course make sure the provider is in compliance with the CFA Institute Prep Provider Guidelines Program (www.cfainstitute.org/partners/examprep/Pages/cfa_prep_provider_guidelines.aspx). Just remember, there are no shortcuts to success on the CFA examinations; reading and studying the CFA curriculum is the key to success on the examination. The CFA examinations reference only the CFA Institute assigned curriculum—no preparatory course or review course materials are consulted or referenced.

SUMMARY

Every question on the CFA examination is based on the content contained in the required readings and on one or more LOS. Frequently, an examination question is based on a specific example highlighted within a reading or on a specific end-of-reading question and/or problem and its solution. To make effective use of the CFA Program curriculum, please remember these key points:

1. All pages printed in the curriculum are required reading for the examination except for occasional sections marked as optional. You may read optional pages as background, but you will not be tested on them.

2. All questions, problems, and their solutions - printed at the end of readings - are part of the curriculum and are required study material for the examination.

3. You should make appropriate use of the online sample/mock examinations and other resources available at www.cfainstitute.org.

4. You should schedule and commit sufficient study time to cover the 18 study sessions, review the materials, and take sample/mock examinations.

5. **Note:** Some of the concepts in the study sessions may be superseded by updated rulings and/or pronouncements issued after a reading was published. Candidates are expected to be familiar with the overall analytical framework contained in the assigned readings. Candidates are not responsible for changes that occur after the material was written.

FEEDBACK

At CFA Institute, we are committed to delivering a comprehensive and rigorous curriculum for the development of competent, ethically grounded investment professionals. We rely on candidate and member feedback as we work to incorporate content, design, and packaging improvements. You can be assured that we will continue to listen to your suggestions. Please send any comments or feedback to curriculum@cfainstitute.org. Ongoing improvements in the curriculum will help you prepare for success on the upcoming examinations, and for a lifetime of learning as a serious investment professional.

Alternative Investments

TOPIC LEVEL LEARNING OUTCOME

The candidate should be able to analyze and evaluate real estate and private equity using appropriate valuation concepts and techniques.

13

Alternative Investments

This study session discusses the following categories of alternative investments; real estate, private equity, and hedge funds. Real estate investments, both private investment and investment through publicly traded securities, are described and methods for analysis and evaluation are presented. Private equity, including venture capital and leveraged buyouts, is examined from the perspectives of a private equity firm evaluating equity investments for its portfolio and an investor evaluating participation in a private equity fund. Finally, investing in hedge funds is surveyed.

READING ASSIGNMENTS

Reading 38 *Private Real Estate Investments*
by Jeffery D. Fisher and Bryan D. MacGregor

Reading 39 *Publicly Traded Real Estate Securities*
by Anthony Paolone, CFA, Ian Rossa O'Reilly, CFA, and David Kruth, CFA

Reading 40 *Private Equity Valuation*
by Yves Courtois, CFA, and Tim Jenkinson

Reading 41 *Investing in Hedge Funds: A Survey*
The Research Foundation of CFA Institute Literature Review, by Keith H. Black, CFA

38

Private Real Estate Investments

by Jeffrey D. Fisher and Bryan D. MacGregor

LEARNING OUTCOMES

Mastery	The candidate should be able to:
☐	**a** classify and describe basic forms of real estate investments;
☐	**b** describe the characteristics, the classification, and basic segments of real estate;
☐	**c** explain the role in a portfolio, the major economic value determinants, investment characteristics, and principal risks of private real estate;
☐	**d** describe commercial property types, including their distinctive investment characteristics;
☐	**e** compare the income, cost, and sales comparison approaches to valuing real estate properties;
☐	**f** estimate and interpret the inputs (for example, net operating income, capitalization rate, and discount rate) to the direct capitalization and discounted cash flow valuation methods;
☐	**g** calculate the value of a property using the direct capitalization and discounted cash flow methods;
☐	**h** compare the direct capitalization and discounted cash flow methods;
☐	**i** calculate the value of a property using the cost and sales comparison approaches;
☐	**j** describe due diligence in private equity real estate investment;
☐	**k** discuss private equity real estate investment indices, including their construction and potential biases;
☐	**l** explain the role in a portfolio, the major economic value determinants, investment characteristics, principal risks, and due diligence of private real estate debt investment; and
☐	**m** calculate and interpret financial ratios used to analyze and evaluate private real estate investments.

INTRODUCTION

Real estate investments comprise a significant part of the portfolios of many investors, so understanding how to analyze real estate investments and evaluate the role of real estate investments in a portfolio is important. Real estate investments can take a variety of forms, from private equity investment in (ownership of) real estate properties (real estate properties, hereafter, may simply be referred to as real estate) to publicly traded debt investment, such as mortgage-backed securities. While this reading discusses the basic forms of real estate investments and provides an overview of the real estate market, its focus is private equity investment in commercial (or income-producing) real estate.

Private equity investment in real estate is sometimes referred to as direct ownership, in contrast to indirect ownership of real estate through publicly traded equity securities, such as real estate investment trusts (REITs). Similarly, lending in the private market, such as mortgage lending by banks or insurance companies, is sometimes referred to as direct lending. **Mortgages** are loans with real estate serving as collateral for the loan. Publicly traded debt investment, such as mortgage-backed securities (MBSs), are sometimes referred to as indirect lending. Each form of real estate investment has characteristics that an investor should be aware of when considering and making a real estate investment. Also, real estate has characteristics that differentiate it from other asset classes.

Private real estate investments—equity and debt—are often included in the portfolios of investors with long-term investment horizons and with the ability to tolerate relatively lower liquidity. Examples of such investors are endowments, pension funds, and life insurance companies. Other real estate investors may have short investment horizons, such as a real estate developer who plans to sell a real estate property to a long-term investor once the development of the property is complete. Publicly traded, pooled-investment forms of real estate investments, such as REITs, may be suitable for investors with short investment horizons and higher liquidity needs.

Valuation of commercial real estate properties constitutes a significant portion of this reading. Regardless of the form of real estate investment, the value of the underlying real estate is critical to its value. The concepts and valuation techniques described in this reading are generally applicable to global real estate markets. Valuation of the underlying real estate is of importance to private real estate equity and debt investors because the value of each type of investment is inextricably tied to the value of the underlying real estate. Also, because real estate properties do not transact frequently and are unique, we rely on estimates of value or appraisals rather than transaction prices to assess changes in value over time. However, transaction prices of similar properties can be useful in estimating value. In creating real estate indices that serve as benchmarks for performance evaluation, appraised values—rather than transaction prices—are often used. In recent years, several indices based on actual transactions have been developed. Both types of indices are discussed in this reading.

The reading is organized as follows: Section 2 describes basic forms of real estate investment, covering equity and debt investments and public and private investments. Section 3 discusses characteristics of real estate and classifications of real estate properties. Section 4 focuses on private equity investment in real estate. It discusses benefits of and risks associated with investing in real estate. The main types of commercial real estate markets and characteristics of each are covered. Section 5 introduces the appraisal (valuation) process and the main approaches used by appraisers to estimate value. Section 6 discusses the income approach, and Section 7 discusses the cost and sales comparison approaches. Section 8 discusses reconciling the results from these three approaches. Section 9 discusses the due diligence process typically followed when acquiring real estate investments. Section 10 presents a brief international perspective. Section 11 considers real estate market indices. Section 12 discusses some aspects of private market real estate debt. A summary and practice problems complete the reading.

REAL ESTATE INVESTMENT: BASIC FORMS   **2**

Investment in real estate has been defined from a capital market perspective in the context of quadrants, or four main areas through which capital can be invested. The quadrants are a result of two dimensions of investment. The first dimension is whether the investment is made in the private or public market. The private market often involves investing directly in an asset (for example, purchasing a property) or getting a claim on an asset (for example, through providing a mortgage to the purchaser). The investment can made indirectly through a number of different investment vehicles, such as a partnership or commingled real estate fund (CREF). In either case, the transactions occur in the private market. The public market does not involve such direct investment; rather, it involves investing in a security with claims on the underlying position(s)—for example, through investments in a real estate investment trust (REIT), a real estate operating company (REOC), or a mortgage-backed security.

The second dimension, as illustrated in the examples above, is whether the investment is structured as equity or debt. An "equity" investor has an ownership interest: Such an investor may be the owner of the real estate property or may invest in securities of a company or a REIT that owns the real estate property. The owner of the real estate property controls such decisions as whether to obtain a mortgage loan on the real estate, who should handle property management, and when to sell the real estate. In the case of a REIT, that control is delegated to the managers of the REIT by the shareholders. A "debt" investor is in a position of lender: Such an investor may loan funds to the "entity" acquiring the real estate property or may invest in securities based on real estate lending. Typically, the real estate property is used as collateral for a mortgage loan. If there is a loan on the real estate (mortgage), then the mortgage lender has a priority claim on the real estate. The value of the equity investor's interest in the real estate is equal to the value of the real estate less the amount owed to the mortgage lender.

Combining the two dimensions, we have four quadrants: private equity, public equity, private debt, and public debt, as illustrated in Exhibit 1.

Exhibit 1	**Examples of the Basic Forms of Real Estate Investment**	
	Equity	**Debt**
Private	Direct investments in real estate. This can be through sole ownership, joint ventures, real estate limited partnerships, or other forms of commingled funds.	Mortgages
Publicly traded	Shares of real estate operating companies and shares of REITs	Mortgage-backed securities (residential and commercial)

Each of the basic forms of real estate investment has its own risks, expected returns, regulations, legal structures, and market structures. Private real estate investment, compared with publicly traded real estate investment, typically involves larger investments because of the indivisibility of real estate property and is more illiquid. Publicly traded real estate investment allows the real estate property to remain undivided but the ownership or claim on the property to be divided. This leads to more liquidity and allows investors to diversify by purchasing ownership interests in more properties than if an entire property had to be owned by a single investor and/or to diversify by having claims against more properties than if an entire mortgage had to be funded and retained by a single lender.

Real estate requires management. Private equity investment (ownership) in real estate properties requires property management expertise on the part of the owner or the hiring of property managers. Real estate owned by REOCs and REITs is professionally managed and requires no real estate management expertise on the part of an investor in shares of the REOCs and REITs.

Equity investors generally expect a higher rate of return than lenders (debt investors) because they take on more risk. The lenders' claims on the cash flows and proceeds from sale must be satisfied before the equity investors can receive anything. As the amount of debt on a property, or financial leverage, increases, risk increases for both debt and equity and an investor's—whether debt or equity—return expectations will increase. Of course, the risk is that the higher return will not materialize, and the risk is even higher for an equity investor.

Debt investors in real estate, whether through private or public markets, expect to receive their return from promised cash flows and typically do not participate in any appreciation in value of the underlying real estate. Thus, debt investments in real estate are similar to other fixed-income investments, such as bonds. The returns to equity real estate investors have two components: an income stream resulting from such activities as renting the property and a capital appreciation component resulting from changes in the value of the underlying real estate. If the returns to equity real estate investors are less than perfectly positively correlated with the returns to stocks and/or bonds, then adding equity real estate investments to a traditional portfolio will potentially have diversification benefits.

Real estate markets in each of the four quadrants in Exhibit 1 have evolved and matured to create relatively efficient market structures for accessing all types of capital for real estate (i.e., public and private debt and equity). Such structures are critical for the success of the asset class for both lenders and equity investors. The categorization of real estate investment into the four quadrants helps investors identify the form(s) that best fit(s) their objectives. For example, some investors may prefer to own and manage real estate. Other investors may prefer the greater liquidity and professional management associated with purchasing publicly traded REITs. Other investors may prefer mortgage lending because it involves less risk than equity investment or unsecured lending; the mortgage lender has a priority claim on the real estate used as collateral for the mortgage. Still other investors may want to invest in each quadrant or allocate more capital to one quadrant or another over time as they perceive shifts in the relative value of each. Each quadrant offers differences in risk and expected return, including the impact of taxes on the return. So investors should explore the risk and return characteristics of each quadrant as part of their investment decisions. The balance of this reading focuses on private investment in real estate—particularly, equity investment.

Example 1

Form of Investment

An investor is interested in adding real estate to her portfolio for the first time. She has no previous real estate experience but thinks adding real estate will provide some diversification benefits. She is concerned about liquidity because she may need the money in a year or so. Which form of investment is *most likely* appropriate for her?

A. Shares of REITs

B. Mortgage-backed securities

C. Direct ownership of commercial real estate property

Solution:

A is correct. She is probably better-off investing in shares of publicly traded REITs, which provide liquidity, have professional management, and require a lower investment than direct ownership of real estate. Using REITs, she may be able to put together a diversified real estate investment portfolio. Although REITs are more correlated with stocks than direct ownership of real estate, direct ownership is much less liquid and a lot of properties are needed to have a diversified real estate portfolio. Also, adding shares of REITs to her current portfolio should provide more diversification benefits than adding debt in the form of mortgage-backed securities and will allow her to benefit from any appreciation of the real estate. Debt investments in real estate, such as MBSs, are similar to other fixed-income investments, such as bonds. The difference is that their income streams are secured on real estate assets, which means that the risks are default risks linked to the performance of the real estate assets and the ability of mortgagees to pay interest. In contrast, adding equity real estate investments to a traditional portfolio will potentially have diversification benefits.

REAL ESTATE: CHARACTERISTICS AND CLASSIFICATIONS

3

Regardless of the form of investment, the value of the underlying real estate property is critical to the performance of the investment. If the property increases in value, the equity investor will benefit from the appreciation and the debt investor is more likely to receive the promised cash flows. If the property declines in value, however, the equity investor and even the debt investor may experience a loss.

3.1 Characteristics

Real estate has characteristics that distinguish it from the other main investment asset classes and that complicate the measurement and assessment of performance. These include the following:

- *Heterogeneity and fixed location*: Whereas all bonds of a particular issue and stocks of a particular type in a specific company are identical, no two properties are the same. Even identically constructed buildings with the same tenants and leases will be at different locations. Buildings differ in use, size, location, age, type of construction, quality, and tenant and leasing arrangements. These factors are important in trying to establish value and also in the amount of specific risk in a real estate investment.

- *High unit value*: The unit value of a real estate property is much larger than that of a bond or stock because of its indivisibility. The amount required to make a private equity investment in real estate limits the pool of potential private equity investors and the ability to construct a diversified real estate portfolio.

This factor is important in the development of publicly traded securities, such as REITs, which allow partial ownership of an indivisible asset.

■ *Management intensive*: An investor in bonds or stocks is not expected to be actively involved in managing the company, but a private real estate equity investor or direct owner of real estate has responsibility for management of the real estate, including maintaining the properties, negotiating leases, and collecting rents. This active management, whether done by the owner or by hired property managers, creates additional costs that must be taken into account.

■ *High transaction costs*: Buying and selling of real estate is also costly and time consuming because others, such as appraisers, lawyers, and construction professionals, are likely to be involved in the process until a transaction is completed.

■ *Depreciation*: Buildings depreciate as a result of use and the passage of time. A building's value may also change as the desirability of its location and its design changes from the perspective of end users.

■ *Need for debt capital*: Because of the large amounts required to purchase and develop real estate properties, the ability to access funds and the cost of funds in the credit markets are important. As a result, real estate values are sensitive to the cost and availability of debt capital. When debt capital is scarce or interest rates are high, the value of real estate tends to be lower than when debt capital is readily available or interest rates are low.

■ *Illiquidity*: As a result of several of the above factors, real estate properties are relatively illiquid. They may take a significant amount of time to market and to sell at a price that is close to the owner's perceived fair market value.

■ *Price determination*: As a result of the heterogeneity of real estate properties and the low volume of transactions, estimates of value or appraisals rather than transaction prices are usually necessary to assess changes in value or expected selling price over time. However, the transaction prices of similar properties are often considered in estimating the value of or appraising a property. The limited number of participants in the market for a property, combined with the importance of local knowledge, makes it harder to know the market value of a property. In a less efficient market, those who have superior information and skill at evaluating properties may have an advantage. This is quite different from stocks in publicly traded companies, where many buyers and sellers value and transact in the shares in an active market.

The above factors fundamentally affect the nature of real estate investment. To overcome some of these problems, markets in securitized real estate, most notably through REITs, have expanded. REITs are a type of publicly traded equity investment in real estate. The REIT provides or hires professional property managers. Investing in shares of a REIT typically allows exposure to a diversified portfolio of real estate. The shares are typically liquid, and active trading results in prices that are more likely to reflect market value. A separate reading discusses REITs in greater detail.

Example 2

Investment Characteristics

An investor states that he likes investing in real estate because the market is less efficient. Why might an investor prefer to invest in a less efficient market rather than a more efficient market?

Solution:

In a less efficient market, an investor with superior knowledge and information and/or a better understanding of the appropriate price to pay for properties (superior valuation skills) may earn a higher return, provided that market prices adjust to intrinsic values, by making more informed investment decisions.

3.2 Classifications

There are many different types of real estate properties. One simple classification distinguishes between residential and non-residential properties. Another potential classification is single-family residential, commercial, farmland, and timberland.

Residential properties include *single-family houses* and *multi-family properties*, such as apartments. In general, residential properties are properties that provide housing for individuals or families. Single-family properties may be owner-occupied or rental properties, whereas multi-family properties are rental properties even if the owner or manager occupies one of the units. Multi-family housing is usually differentiated by location (urban or suburban) and shape of structure (high-rise, low-rise, or garden apartments). Residential real estate properties, particularly multi-family properties, purchased with the intent to let, lease, or rent (in other words, produce income) are typically included in the category of **commercial real estate properties** (sometimes called income-producing real estate properties).

Non-residential properties include commercial properties other than multi-family properties, farmland, and timberland. Commercial real estate is by far the largest class of real estate for investment and is the focus of this reading. Commercial real estate properties are typically classified by end use. In addition to multi-family properties, commercial real estate properties include office, industrial and warehouse, retail, and hospitality properties. However, the same *building* can serve more than one end use. For example, it can contain both office and retail space. In fact, the same building can contain residential as well as non-residential uses of space. A property that has a combination of end users is usually referred to as a *mixed-use development.* Thus, the classifications should be viewed mainly as a convenient way of categorizing the use of space for the purpose of analyzing the determinants of supply and demand and economic performance for each type of space.

- *Office* properties range from major multi-tenant office buildings found in the central business districts of most large cities to single-tenant office buildings. They are often built to suit or considering the needs of a specific tenant or tenants. An example of a property developed and built considering the needs of prospective tenants would be a medical office building near a hospital.

- *Industrial and warehouse* properties include property used for light or heavy manufacturing as well as associated warehouse space. This category includes special purpose buildings designed specifically for industrial use that would be difficult to convert to another use, buildings used by wholesale distributors, and combinations of warehouse/showroom and office facilities. Older buildings that originally had one use may be converted to another use. For example, office space may be converted to warehouse or light industrial space and warehouse or light industrial space may be converted to residential or office space. Frequently, the conversion is based on the desirability of the area for the new use.

- *Retail* properties vary from large shopping centers with several stores, including large department stores, as tenants to small stores occupied by individual tenants. As indicated earlier, it is also common to find retail space combined with office space, particularly on the ground floor of office buildings in major cities, or residential space.

- ▪ _Hospitality_ properties vary considerably in size and amenities available. Motels and smaller hotels are used primarily as a place for business travelers and families to spend a night. These properties may have limited amenities and are often located very close to a major highway. Hotels designed for tourists who plan to stay longer usually have a restaurant, a swimming pool, and other amenities. They are also typically located near other attractions that tourists visit. Hotels at "destination resorts" provide the greatest amount of amenities. These resorts are away from major cities, where the guests usually stay for several days or even several weeks. Facilities at these resort hotels can be quite luxurious, with several restaurants, swimming pools, nearby golf courses, and so on. Hotels that cater to convention business may be either in a popular destination resort or located near the center of a major city.

- ▪ _Other types_ of commercial real estate that can be owned by investors include parking facilities, restaurants, and recreational uses, such as country clubs, marinas, sports complexes, and so on. Retail space that complements the recreational activity (such as gift and golf shops) is often associated with, or part of, these recreational real estate properties. Dining facilities and possibly hotel or residential facilities may also be present. A property might also be intended for use by a special institution, such as a hospital, a government agency, or a university. The physical structure of a building intended for a specific use may be similar to the physical structure of buildings intended for other uses. For example, government office space is similar to other office space. Some buildings intended for one use may not easily be adapted for other uses. For example, buildings used by universities and hospitals may not easily be adapted to other uses.

Some commercial property types are more management intensive than others. Of the main commercial property types, hotels require the most day-to-day management and are more like operating a business than multi-family, office, or retail space. Shopping centers (shopping malls) are also relatively management intensive because it is important for the owner to maintain the right tenant mix and promote the mall. Many of the "other" property types, such as recreational facilities, can also require significant management. Usually, investors consider properties that are more management intensive as riskier because of the operational risks. Therefore, investors typically require a higher rate of return on these management-intensive properties.

Farmland and timberland are unique in that each can be used to produce a saleable commodity. Farmland can be used to produce crops or as pastureland for livestock, and timberland can be used to produce timber (wood) for use in the forest products industry. While crops and livestock are produced annually, timber has a much longer growing cycle before the product is saleable. Also, the harvesting of timber can be deferred if market conditions are perceived to be unfavorable. Sales of the commodities or leasing the land to another entity generate income. Harvest quantities and commodity prices are the primary determinants of revenue. These are affected by many factors outside of the control of the producer and include weather and population demographics. In addition to income-generating potential, both farmland and timberland have potential for capital appreciation.

Example 3

Commercial Real Estate Segments

Commercial real estate properties are *most likely* to include:

A. residential, industrial, hospitality, retail, and office.

B. multi-family, industrial, warehouse, retail, and office.

C. multi-family, industrial, hospitality, retail, and timberland.

Solution:

B is correct. Commercial real estate properties include multi-family, industrial, warehouse, retail, and office as well as hospitality and other. Residential properties include single-family, owner-occupied homes as well as income-producing (commercial) residential properties. Timberland is a unique category of real estate.

PRIVATE MARKET REAL ESTATE EQUITY INVESTMENTS

4

There are many different types of equity real estate investors, ranging from individual investors to large pension funds, sovereign wealth funds, and publicly traded real estate companies. Hereafter, for simplicity, the term *investor* refers to an equity investor in real estate. Although there may be some differences in the motivations for each type of investor, they all hope to achieve one or more of the following benefits of equity real estate investment:

- *Current income*: Investors may expect to earn current income on the property through letting, leasing, or renting the property. Investors expect that market demand for space in the property will be sufficient to produce net income after collecting rents and paying operating expenses. This income constitutes part of an investor's return. The amount available to the investor will be affected by taxes and financing costs.

- *Price appreciation (capital appreciation)*: Investors often expect prices to rise over time. Any price increase also contributes to an investor's total return. Investors may anticipate selling properties after holding them for a period of time and realizing the capital appreciation.

- *Inflation hedge*: Investors may expect both rents and real estate prices to rise in an inflationary environment. If rents and prices do in fact increase with inflation, then equity real estate investments provide investors with an inflationary hedge. This means that the real rate of return, as opposed to the nominal rate of return, may be less volatile for equity real estate investments.

- *Diversification*: Investors may anticipate diversification benefits. Real estate performance has not typically been highly correlated with the performance of other asset classes, such as stocks, bonds, or money market funds, so adding real estate to a portfolio may lower the risk of the portfolio (that is, the volatility of returns) relative to the expected return.

Exhibit 2 shows correlations of returns, for the period 1978–2009, between several asset classes in the United States based on various reported indices. The indices used are the National Council of Real Estate Investment Fiduciaries (NCREIF) Property Index for private real estate equity investments, the S&P 500 Index for stocks, the Barclays Capital Government Bond for bonds, the National Association of Real Estate

Investment Trusts (NAREIT) Equity REIT Index for publicly traded real estate investments, 90-day T-bills, and the all items U.S. Consumer Price Index for All Urban Consumers (CPI-U).

Note that the correlation between the NCREIF index and the S&P 500 is relatively low and the correlation between the NCREIF index and bonds is negative. This indicates the potential for diversification benefits of adding private equity real estate investment to a stock and bond portfolio. Also note that publicly traded REITs have a higher correlation with stocks and bonds than private real estate, which suggests that public and private real estate do not necessarily provide the same diversification benefits. When real estate is publicly traded, it tends to behave more like the rest of the stock market than the real estate market. However, some argue that because the NCREIF index is appraisal based and lags changes in the transactions market, its correlation with stock indices that are based on transactions is dampened. This issue is discussed in more detail later in the reading. As a final note on the correlations, note that the NCREIF index had a higher correlation with the CPI-U than the other alternatives with the exception of T-bills. This suggests that private equity real estate investments may provide some inflation protection.

Although the correlations discussed above are based on U.S. data, evidence suggests that real estate provides similar diversification benefits in other countries.

Exhibit 2	**Correlation among Returns on Various Asset Classes (1978–2009)**					
	CPI-U	**Bonds**[a]	**S&P 500**	**T-Bills**	**NCREIF**[b]	**REITs**[c]
CPI-U	1					
Bonds	−0.2423	1				
S&P 500	0.0114	0.0570	1			
T-bills	0.4885	0.1586	0.0953	1		
NCREIF	0.3214	−0.0978	0.1363	0.3911	1	
REITs	0.1135	0.1258	0.5946	0.0602	0.2527	1

[a] Barclays Capital Government Bond
[b] National Council of Real Estate Investment Fiduciaries Property Index (NPI)
[c] National Association of Real Estate Investment Trusts Equity REIT Index

▪ *Tax Benefits*: A final reason for investing in real estate, which may be more important to some investors in certain countries than others, is the preferential tax benefits that may result. Private real estate investments may receive a favorable tax treatment compared with other investments. In other words, the same before-tax return may result in a higher after-tax return on real estate investments compared with the after-tax return on other possible investments. The preferential tax treatment in the United States comes from the fact that real estate can be depreciated for tax purposes over a shorter period than the period over which the property actually deteriorates. Although some real estate investors, such as pension funds, do not normally pay taxes, they compete with taxable investors who might be willing to pay more for the same property. Publicly traded REITs also have some tax benefits in some countries. For example, in the United States, there is no corporate income tax paid by the REIT. That is, by qualifying for REIT status, the corporation is exempt from corporate taxation as long as it follows certain guidelines required to maintain REIT status.

Example 4

Motivations for Investing in Real Estate

Why would an investor want to include real estate equity investments in a portfolio that already has a diversified mixture of stocks and bonds?

Solution:

Real estate equity offers diversification benefits because it is less than perfectly correlated with stocks and bonds; this is particularly true of direct ownership (private equity investment). In other words, there are times when stocks and bonds may perform poorly but private equity real estate investments perform well and vice versa. Thus, adding real estate equity investments to a portfolio may reduce the volatility of the portfolio.

4.1 Risk Factors

Investors want to have an expected return that compensates them for incurring risk. The higher the risk, the higher should be the expected return. In this section, we consider risk factors associated with investing in commercial real estate. Most of the risk factors listed affect the value of the real estate property and, therefore, the investment—equity or debt—in the property. Leverage affects returns on investments in real estate but not the value of the underlying real estate property. Following are characteristic sources of risk or risk factors of real estate investment.

- *Business conditions*: Fundamentally, the real estate business involves renting space to users. The demand for space depends on a myriad of international, national, regional, and local economic conditions. GDP, employment, household income, interest rates, and inflation are particularly relevant to real estate. Changes in economic conditions will affect real estate investments because both current income and real estate values may be affected.

- *Long lead time for new development*: New development projects typically require a considerable amount of time from the point the project is first conceived until all the approvals are obtained, the development is complete, and it is leased up. During this time, market conditions can change considerably from what was initially anticipated. If the market has weakened, rents can be lower and vacancy higher than originally expected, resulting in lower returns to the developer. Alternatively, the demand can be greater than was anticipated, leading to a shortage of space to meet current demand. These dynamics tend to result in wide price swings for real estate over the development period.

- *Cost and availability of capital*: Real estate must compete with other assets for debt and equity capital. The willingness of investors to invest in real estate depends on the availability of debt capital and the cost of that capital as well as the expected return on other investments, such as stocks and bonds, which affects the availability of equity capital. A shortage of debt capital and high interest rates can significantly reduce the demand for real estate and lower prices. Alternatively, an environment of low interest rates and easy access to debt capital can increase the demand for real estate investments. These capital market forces can cause prices to increase or decrease regardless of any changes in the underlying demand for real estate from tenants.

- *Unexpected inflation*: Inflation risk depends on how the income and price of an asset is affected by unexpected inflation. Fixed-income securities are usually negatively affected by inflation because the purchasing power of the income decreases with inflation and the face value is fixed at maturity. Real estate may offer some inflation protection if the leases provide for rent increases due to inflation or the ability to pass any increases in expenses due to inflation on to tenants. Construction costs for real estate also tend to increase with inflation, which puts upward pressure on real estate values. Thus, real estate equity investments may not have much inflation risk depending on how net operating income (NOI) and values respond to inflation being higher than expected. In a weak market with high vacancy rates and low rents, when new construction is not feasible, values may not increase with inflation.

■ *Demographics*: Linked to the above factors are a variety of demographic factors, such as the size and age distribution of the population in the local market, the distribution of socio-economic groups, and rates of new household formation. These demographic factors affect the demand for real estate.

■ *Lack of liquidity*: Liquidity is the ability to convert an asset to cash quickly without a significant price discount or loss of principal. Real estate is considered to have low liquidity (high liquidity risk) because of the large value of an individual investment and the time and cost it takes to sell a property at its current value. Buyers are unlikely to make large investments without conducting adequate due diligence, which takes both time and money. Therefore, buyers are not likely to agree to a quick purchase without a significant discount to the price. Illiquidity means both a longer time to realize cash and also a risk that the market may move against the investor.

■ *Environmental*: Real estate values can be affected by environmental conditions, including contaminants related to a prior owner or an adjacent property owner. Such problems can significantly reduce the value because of the costs incurred to correct them.

■ *Availability of information*: Of increasing importance to investors, especially when investing globally, is having adequate information to make informed investment decisions. A lack of information to do the property analysis adds to the risk of the investment. The amount of data available on real estate space and capital markets has improved considerably. While some countries have much more information available to investors than others, in general, the availability of information has been increasing on a global basis because real estate investment has become more global and investors want to evaluate investment alternatives on a comparable basis. Real estate indices have become available in many countries around the world. These indices allow investors to benchmark the performance of their properties against that of peers and also provide a better understanding of the risk and return for real estate compared with other asset classes. Indices are discussed in more detail in Section 11.

■ *Management*: Management involves the cost of monitoring an investment. Investment management can be categorized into two levels: asset management and property management. Asset management involves monitoring the investment's financial performance and making changes as needed. Property management is exclusive to real estate investments. It involves the overall day-to-day operation of the property and the physical maintenance of the property, including the buildings. Management risk reflects the ability of the property and asset managers to make the right decisions regarding the operation of the property, such as negotiating leases, maintaining the property, marketing the property, and doing renovations when necessary.

■ *Leverage*: Leverage affects returns on investments in real estate but not the value of the underlying real estate property. Leverage is the use of borrowed funds to finance some of the purchase price of an investment. The ratio of borrowed funds to total purchase price is known as the loan-to-value

(LTV) ratio. Higher LTV ratios mean greater amounts of leverage. Real estate transactions can be more highly leveraged than most other types of investments. But increasing leverage also increases risk because the lender has the first claim on the cash flow and on the value of the property if there is default on the loan. A small change in NOI can result in a relatively large change in the amount of cash flow available to the equity investor after making the mortgage payment.

■ *Other risk factors*: Many other risk factors exist, such as unobserved physical defects in the property, natural disasters (for example, earthquakes and hurricanes), and acts of terrorism. Unfortunately, the biggest risk may be one that was unidentified as a risk at the time of purchasing the property. Unidentified risks can be devastating to investors.

Risks that are identified can be planned for to some extent. In some cases, a risk can be converted to a known dollar amount through insurance. In other cases, risk can be reduced through diversification or shifted to another party through contractual arrangements. For example, the risk of expenses increasing can be shifted to tenants by including expense reimbursement clauses in their leases. The risk that remains must be evaluated and reflected in contractual terms (for example, rental prices) such that the expected return is equal to or greater than the required return necessary to make the investment.

Example 5

Commercial Real Estate Risk

An investor is concerned about interest rates rising and decides that she will pay all cash and not borrow any money to avoid incurring any risk due to interest rate changes. This strategy is *most likely* to:

A. reduce the risk due to leverage.

B. eliminate the risk due to inflation.

C. eliminate the risk due to interest rate changes.

Solution:

A is correct. If less money is borrowed, there is less risk due to the use of financial leverage. There is still risk related to changes in interest rates. If interest rates rise, the value of real estate will likely be affected even if the investor did not borrow any money. Higher interest rates mean investors require a higher rate of return on all assets. The resale price of the property will likely depend on the cost of debt to the next buyer, who may be more likely to obtain debt financing. Furthermore, the investor may be better off getting a loan at a fixed interest rate before rates rise. There is still risk of inflation, although real estate tends to have a low amount of inflation risk. But borrowing less money doesn't necessarily mean the property is less affected by inflation.

4.2 Real Estate Risk and Return Relative to Stocks and Bonds

The characteristics of real estate and the risk factors described above ultimately affect the risk and return of equity real estate investments. The structure of leases between the owner and tenants also affects risk and return. More will be discussed about the nature of real estate leases later in this reading, but in general, leases can be thought of as giving equity real estate investment a bond-like characteristic because the tenant has a legal agreement to make periodic payments to the owner. At the end of the lease term, however, there will be uncertainty as to whether the tenant will renew the lease and what the rental rate will be at that time. These issues will depend on the availability of competing space and also on factors that affect the profitability of the companies leasing the space and the strength of the overall economy in much the same way that stock prices are affected by the same factors. These factors give a stock market characteristic to the risk of real estate. On balance, because of these two influences (bond-like and stock-like characteristics), real estate, as an asset class, tends to have a risk and return (based on historical data) profile that falls between the risk and return profiles of stocks and bonds. By this, we mean the risk and return characteristics of a portfolio of real estate versus a portfolio of stocks and a portfolio of bonds. An individual real estate investment could certainly have risk that is greater or less than that of an individual stock or bond. Exhibit 3 illustrates the basic risk–return relationships of stocks, bonds, and private equity real estate. In Exhibit 3, risk is measured by the standard deviation of expected returns.

Exhibit 3	Returns and Risks of Private Equity Real Estate Compared with Stocks and Bonds

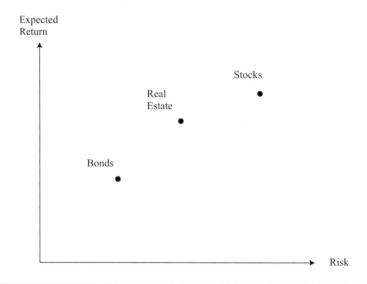

Example 6

Investment Risk

Which is a riskier investment, private equity real estate or bonds? Explain why.

Solution:

Empirical evidence suggests that private equity real estate is riskier than bonds. Although real estate leases offer income streams somewhat like bonds, the income expected when leases renew can be quite uncertain and depend on market conditions at that time, which is unlike the more certain face value of a bond at maturity.

4.3 Commercial Real Estate

In this section, the main economic factors that influence demand for each commercial real estate property type and typical lease terms are discussed. It is important to discuss lease terms because they affect a property's value. The main property types included in institutional investors' portfolios are office, industrial and warehouse, retail, and multi-family (apartments). These property types are often considered the *core* property types used to create a portfolio that is relatively low risk, assuming the properties are in good locations and well leased (fiscally sound and responsible tenants, low vacancies, and good rental terms). Another type of property that might be held by an institutional investor is hospitality properties (for example, hotels). Hotels are usually considered riskier because there are no leases and their performance may be highly correlated with the business cycle—especially if there is a restaurant and the hotel depends on convention business.

For each property type, location is a critical factor in determining value. Properties with the highest value per unit of space are in the best locations and have modern features and functionality. Moderately valued properties are typically in adequate but not prime locations and/or have slightly outdated features. Properties with the lowest values per unit of space are in poor locations and have outdated features.

4.3.1 *Office*

The demand for office properties depends heavily on employment growth—especially in those industries that use large amounts of office space, such as finance and insurance. The typical amount of space used per employee is also important because it tends to increase when the economy is strong and decline when the economy is weak. There also has been a tendency for the average amount of space per employee to decrease over time as technology has allowed more employees to spend more time working away from the office and less permanent space is needed.

The average length of an office building lease varies globally. For example, leases on office space average 3–5 years in the United States and around 10 years in the United Kingdom. However, lease lengths may vary based on a number of factors, including the desirability of the property and the financial strength of the tenant as well as other terms in the lease, such as provisions for future rent changes and whether there are options to extend the lease.

An important consideration in office leases is whether the owner or tenant incurs the risk of operating expenses, such as utilities, increasing in the future. A "net lease" requires the tenant to be responsible for paying operating expenses, whereas a "gross lease" requires the owner to pay the operating expenses. The rent for a net lease is lower than that for an equivalent gross lease because the tenant must bear the operating expenses as well as the risk of expenses being higher than expected.

Not all office leases are structured as net or gross leases. For example, a lease may be structured so that in the first year of the lease, the owner is responsible for paying the operating expenses and for every year of the lease after that, the owner pays for expenses up to the amount paid in the first year. Any increase in expenses above that amount is "passed through" to the tenant as an "expense reimbursement." That is, the tenant bears the risk of any increase in expenses, although the owner benefits from any decline in expenses. In a multi-tenant building, the expenses may be prorated among the tenants on the basis of the amount of space they are leasing. While having a small number of tenants can simplify managing a property, it increases risk. If one tenant gets into financial difficulties or decides not to renew a lease, it can have a significant effect on cash flows.

There are differences in how leases are structured over time and in different countries. It is important to have an understanding of how leases are typically structured in a market and to stay informed about changes in the typical structure. Lease terms will affect the return and risk to the investor. For example, in the United Kingdom, until the early 1990s, lease terms averaged about 20 years in length, but they have now fallen by nearly half. Rents are typically fixed for five years and then set at the higher of the then market rent or contract rent upon review; these are known as upward-only rent reviews. Leases are typically on a full repairing and insuring (FRI) basis; the tenant is responsible for most costs. Therefore, detailed cost (expense) analysis is much less important in deriving net operating income—a critical measure in estimating the value of a commercial property—in the United Kingdom than in markets where operating costs are typically the responsibility of the owner.

Example 7

Net and Gross Leases

What is the net rent equivalent for an office building where the gross rent is $20 per square foot and operating expenses are $8 per square foot?

Solution:

On a gross lease, the owner pays the operating expense, whereas on a net lease the tenant pays. So we might expect the rent on a net lease to be $20 − $8 or $12 per square foot. Because the risk of change in operating expenses is borne by the tenant rather than the owner, the rent might even be lower than $12.

4.3.2 Industrial and Warehouse

The demand for industrial and warehouse space is heavily dependent on the overall strength of the economy and economic growth. The demand for warehouse space is also dependent on import and export activity in the economy. Industrial leases are often net leases, although gross leases or leases with expense reimbursements, as described above for office properties, also occur.

4.3.3 Retail

The demand for retail space depends heavily on trends in consumer spending. Consumer spending, in turn, depends on the health of the economy, job growth, population growth, and savings rates.

Retail lease terms, including length of leases and rental rates, vary not only on the basis of the quality of the property but also by the size and the importance of the tenant. For example, in the United States, the length of leases for the smaller tenants in a shopping center are typically three to five years and are longer for larger "anchor" tenants, such as a department store. Anchor tenants may be given rental terms designed to attract them to the property. The quality of anchor tenants is a factor in attracting other tenants.

A unique aspect of many retail leases is the requirement that the tenants pay additional rent once their sales reach a certain level. This type of lease is referred to as a "percentage lease." The lease will typically specify a "minimum rent" that must be paid regardless of the tenant's sales and the basis for calculating percentage rent once the tenant's sales reach a certain level or breakpoint. For example, the lease may specify a minimum rent of $30 per square foot plus 10 percent of sales over $300 per square foot. Note that at the breakpoint of $300 per square foot in sales, we obtain the same rent per square foot based on either the minimum rent of $30 or 10 percent of $300. This is a typical way of structuring the breakpoint, and the sales level of $300 would be referred to as a "natural breakpoint."

Example 8

Retail Rents

A retail lease specifies that the minimum rent is $40 per square foot plus 5 percent of sales revenue over $800 per square foot. What would the rent be if the tenant's sales are $1,000 per square foot?

Solution:

The rent per square foot will be $40 plus 5% × ($1,000 − $800) or $40 + $10 = $50. We get the same answer by multiplying 5% × $1,000 (= $50) because $800 is the "natural breakpoint," meaning that 5 percent of $800 results in the minimum rent of $40. A lease may not have the breakpoint set at this natural level, in which case it is important that the lease clearly defines how to calculate the rent.

4.3.4 *Multi-Family*

The demand for multi-family space depends on population growth, especially for the age segment most likely to rent apartments. In other words, population demographics are important. The relevant age segment can be very broad or very narrow depending on the propensity to rent in the culture. Homeownership rates vary from country to country. The relevant age segment for renters can also vary by type of property being rented out or by locale. For example, in the United States, the typical renter has historically been between 25 and 35 years old. However, the average age of a renter of property in an area attractive to retirees may be higher.

Demand also depends on how the cost of renting compares with the cost of owning—that is, the ratio of home prices to rents. As home prices rise and become less affordable, more people will rent. Similarly, as home prices fall, there may be a shift from renting to owning. Higher interest rates will also make homeownership more expensive because for owners that partially finance the purchase with debt, the financing cost will be higher and for other homeowners, the opportunity cost of having funds tied up in a home will increase. This increase in the cost of ownership may cause a shift toward renting. If interest rates decrease, there may be a shift toward homeownership.

Multi-family properties typically have leases that range from six months to two years, with one year being most typical. The tenant may or may not be responsible for paying expenses, such as utilities, depending on whether there are separate meters for each unit. The owner is typically responsible for the upkeep of common property, insurance, and repair and maintenance of the property. The tenant is typically responsible for cleaning the space rented and for insurance on personal property.

Example 9

Economic Value Determinants

1. The primary economic driver of the demand for office space is *most likely*:
   A. job growth.
   B. population growth.
   C. growth in savings rates.

2. The demand for which of the following types of real estate is likely *most* affected by population demographics?
   A. Office
   B. Multi-family
   C. Industrial and warehouse

Solution to 1:

A is correct. Job growth is the main economic driver of office demand, especially jobs in industries that are heavy users of office space, such as finance and insurance. As jobs increase, companies need to provide office space for the new employees. Population growth may indirectly affect the demand for office space because it affects demand and job growth. Growth in savings rates affects consumer spending and the demand for retail space.

Solution to 2:

B is correct. Population demographics are a primary determinant of the demand for multi-family space.

5   OVERVIEW OF THE VALUATION OF COMMERCIAL REAL ESTATE

Regardless of the form of real estate investment, the value of the underlying real estate is critical because the value of any real estate investment is inextricably tied to the value of the underlying real estate. Commercial real estate properties do not transact frequently, and each property is unique. Therefore, estimates of value or appraisals, rather than transaction prices, are used to assess changes in value or expected selling price over time. Appraisals are typically done by individuals with recognized expertise in this area. These can be independent experts hired to do the appraisals or in-house experts.

5.1 Appraisals

Appraisals (estimates of value) are critical for such infrequently traded and unique assets as real estate properties. For publicly traded assets, such as stocks and bonds, we have frequent transaction prices that reflect the value that investors are currently placing on these assets. In contrast, commercial real estate, such as an apartment or office building, does not trade frequently. For example, a particular building might sell once in a 10-year period. Thus, we cannot rely on transactions activity for a particular property to indicate how its value is changing over time.

There are companies, such as real estate investment trusts, that invest primarily in real estate and have publicly traded shares. REITs are available in many countries around the world. REIT prices can be observed as with any publicly traded share. REITs are businesses that buy and sell real estate; often do development; decide how properties are to be financed, when to refinance, and when to renovate properties; and make many other ongoing management decisions that determine the success of the REIT. Therefore, the prices of REIT shares reflect both the performance of the management of the company that owns the real estate and the value of the underlying properties.

Thus, although it is useful to know how the values of REIT shares are changing over time as an indicator of changing conditions in the real estate market, it does not substitute for the need to estimate the value of individual properties. In fact, knowing the appraised value of properties held by REITs is helpful in estimating the value of the REIT, although, as suggested above, many other factors can affect REIT share prices over time.

Appraisals can be used to evaluate the performance of the investment or to determine an estimate of price or value if a transaction is anticipated. Even if there has been a recent transaction of the property, because it is only one transaction between a particular buyer and seller, the transaction price at which the property sold may not reflect the value a typical investor might place on the property at that time.[1] There may be circumstances under which a buyer may be willing to pay more than a typical buyer would pay or a seller may be willing to accept less than a typical seller would accept. Thus, even when there is a transaction, an appraisal is often used as a basis for estimating the value of the property rather than just assuming that the agreed upon transaction price equals the value. For example, an appraisal is likely to be required if the purchaser of the property wants to finance a portion of the purchase with debt. The lender will typically require an independent appraisal of the property to estimate the value of the collateral for the loan. Even if the purchaser is not borrowing to finance a portion of the purchase, the purchaser may have an appraisal done to help establish a reasonable offer price for the property. Similarly, the seller may have an appraisal done to help establish the asking price for the property.

Properties are also appraised for other reasons. Another important use of appraisals is for performance measurement—that is, to measure the performance of real estate that is managed for a client. For example, a pension fund may have decided to invest in real estate in addition to stocks and bonds to diversify its portfolio. It may have invested directly in the real estate or through an investment manager that acquires and manages the real estate portfolio. In either case, the pension fund wants to know how its real estate investments are performing. This performance can be evaluated relative to the performance of stocks and bonds and against a benchmark that measures the performance of the relevant real estate asset class. The benchmark is used in the same way that a stock index might be used as a benchmark for measuring the performance of a stock portfolio.

Measuring the performance of a real estate portfolio requires estimating property values on a periodic basis, such as annually. Although more frequent measures may be desirable, it may not be practical because appraising property values is a time-consuming and costly process. It may involve an independent appraisal by a firm that specializes in appraising investment properties, or it may be done by an appraiser who works for the investment management firm. In either case, the appraiser is tasked with estimating the value of the property.

5.1.1 *Value*

The focus of an appraisal is usually on what is referred to as the *market value* of the property. The market value can be thought of as the most probable sale price. It is what a *typical* investor is willing to pay for the property. There are other definitions of value that differ from market value. For example, *investment value* (sometimes called worth) is the value to a *particular* investor. It could be higher or lower than market value depending on the particular investor's motivations and how well the property fits into the investor's portfolio, the investor's risk tolerance, the investor's tax circumstances, and so on. For example, an investor who is seeking to have a globally well-diversified portfolio of real estate that does not already have any investments in New York City and Shanghai may place a higher value on acquiring a property in either of those locations than an investor who already has New York City and Shanghai properties in his or her portfolio.

There are other types of value that are relevant in practice, such as *value in use*, which is the value to a particular user—for example, the value of a manufacturing plant to the company using the building as part of its business. For property tax purposes, the relevant value is the assessed value of the property, which may differ from market

---

1 The term special purchaser is used in some countries, such as the United Kingdom, to refer to purchasers who are not typical.

value because of the way the assessor defines the value. In most cases, the focus of an appraisal is on market value.

Potential sellers and buyers care about market value because it is useful to know when negotiating price. The market value may differ from the value that the potential buyer or seller originally placed on the property and from the price that is ultimately agreed upon.[2] A seller in distressed circumstances may be willing to accept less than market value because of liquidity needs, and a particular buyer (investor) may be willing to pay more than market value because the worth (investment value) to that buyer exceeds the value to a typical investor.

Lenders usually care about market value because if a borrower defaults on a mortgage loan, the market value less transaction costs is the maximum that the lender can expect to receive from the sale of the property. But there are some exceptions. In some cases, the lender may ask for a more conservative value, which can be referred to as a *mortgage lending value*. For example, in Germany the mortgage lending value is the value of the property which, based on experience, may throughout the life of the loan be expected to be generated in the event of sale, irrespective of temporary (e.g., economically induced) fluctuations in value on the relevant property market and excluding speculative elements. In determining the mortgage lending value, the future saleability of the property is to be taken as a basis within the scope of a "prudent valuation," taking into consideration the long-term, permanent features of the property, the normal regional market situation, and the present and possible alternative uses. Some have argued that over the decades in which it has been applied, the mortgage lending value has helped mortgage lending in Germany to have a stabilizing effect on the German real estate market by evening out current, possibly exaggerated market expectations. The mortgage lending value contrasts with the notion of "mark-to-market" or "fair value" accounting, which would value an asset at its market value at the time the loan is made.

Example 10

Market Value

A property that was developed two years ago at a cost of ¥60.0 million, including land, is put on the market for that price. It sells quickly for ¥50.0 million. After the closing, the purchaser admits he would have paid up to ¥65.0 million for the property because he owned vacant land next to the property purchased. A very similar property (approximately the same size, age, etc.) recently sold for ¥55.0 million.

1. The purchaser is *most likely* a:
   A. typical investor.
   B. particular investor.
   C. short-term investor.

2. The market value of the property is *closest* to:
   A. ¥50.0 million.
   B. ¥55.0 million.
   C. ¥65.0 million.

---

2 For further discussion of the various definitions of value, refer to such publications as the "Uniform Standards of Professional Appraisal Practice," the Royal Institution of Chartered Surveyors (RICS) *Red Book*, and "The International Valuation Standards."

3. The investment value of the property to the buyer is *closest* to:

    A. ¥50.0 million.

    B. ¥60.0 million.

    C. ¥65.0 million.

Solution to 1:

B is correct. This investor may be willing to pay more than the typical investor because of his particular circumstances.

Solution to 2:

B is correct. The purchaser paid ¥50.0 million rather than the ¥65.0 million he was willing to pay for the property. However, we have to be careful about using a transaction price as an indication of market value because the market may have been thin and the seller may have been distressed and willing to accept less than the property would have sold for if it had been kept on the market for a longer period of time. The quick sale suggests that the price may have been lower than what a typical investor may be willing to pay. There was a comparable property that sold for ¥55.0 million. Combining these facts and based only on this information, it is reasonable to assume that the market value is closest to ¥55.0 million. Note that what it cost to develop the property two years ago is not particularly relevant. Markets may have deteriorated since that time, and new construction may not be feasible.

Solution to 3:

C is correct. The investment value of the property is ¥65.0 million. The purchaser was willing to pay up to ¥65.0 million, suggesting that his investment value was higher than the amount paid. He paid only as much as he had to, based on negotiations with the seller.

5.2 Introduction to Valuation Approaches

In general, there are three different approaches that appraisers use to estimate value: the **income approach**, the **cost approach**, and the **sales comparison approach**. The income approach considers what price an investor would pay based on an expected rate of return that is commensurate with the risk of the investment. The value estimated with this approach is essentially the present value of the expected future income from the property, including proceeds from resale at the end of a typical investment holding period. The concept is that value depends on the expected rate of return that investors would require to invest in the property.

The cost approach considers what it would cost to buy the land and construct a new property on the site that has the same utility or functionality as the property being appraised (referred to as the *subject property*). Adjustments are made if the subject property is older or not of a modern design, if it is not feasible to construct a new property in the current market, or if the location of the property is not ideal for its current use. The concept is that you should not pay more for a property than the cost of buying vacant land and developing a comparable property.

The sales comparison approach considers what similar or *comparable properties* (comparables) transacted for in the current market. Adjustments are made to reflect comparables' differences from the subject property, such as size, age, location, and condition of the property and to adjust for differences in market conditions at the times of sale. The concept is that you would not pay more than others are paying for similar properties.

These approaches are unlikely to result in the same value because they rely on different assumptions and availability of data to estimate the value. The idea is to try to triangulate on the market value by approaching the estimate three different ways. The appraiser may have more confidence in one or more of the approaches depending on the availability of data for each approach. Part of the appraisal process is to try to *reconcile* the differences in the estimates of value from each approach and come up with a final estimate of value for the subject property.

5.2.1 *Highest and Best Use*

Before we elaborate on the three approaches to estimating value, it is helpful to understand an important concept known as *highest and best use*. The highest and best use of a vacant site is the use that would result in the highest value for the land. This concept is best illustrated with an example. Suppose you are trying to determine the highest and best use of a vacant site. Three alternative uses—apartment, office, and retail—have been identified as consistent with zoning regulations and are financially feasible at the right land value. The physical characteristics of the site make construction of buildings consistent with each of these uses possible. Exhibit 4 summarizes relevant details for each potential use:

Exhibit 4	Highest and Best Use		
	Apartment	**Office**	**Retail**
Value after construction	$2,500,000	$5,000,000	$4,000,000
Cost to construct building	(2,000,000)	(4,800,000)	(3,000,000)
Implied land value	$500,000	$200,000	$1,000,000

The value after construction is what the property would sell for once it is constructed and leased. The cost to construct the building includes an amount for profit to the developer. The profit compensates the developer for handling the construction phase and getting the property leased. Subtracting the cost to construct from the value after construction gives the amount that could be paid for the land. In this case, the retail use results in the highest price that can be paid for the land. So retail is the highest and best use of the site, and the land value would be $1 million.

The idea is that the price would be bid up to that amount by investors or developers who are competing for the site, including several bidders planning to develop retail. Note that the highest and best use is not the use with the highest total value, which in this example is office. Even though office has a higher value if it is built, the higher construction costs result in a lower amount that can be paid for the land. A developer cannot pay $1 million for the land and build the office building. If they did, they would have a $5.8 million total investment in the land and construction cost but the value would be only $5 million. So that would result in an $800,000 loss in value because an office building is not the highest and best use of the site.

The theory is that the land value is based on its highest and best use *as if vacant* even if there is an existing building on the site. If there is an existing building on the site that is not the highest and best use of the site, then the value of the building—not the land—will be lower. For example, suppose that a site with an old warehouse on it would sell for $1.5 million as a warehouse (land and building). If vacant, the land is worth $1 million. Thus, the value of the existing building (warehouse) is $500,000 (= $1,500,000 – $1,000,000). As long as the value under the existing use is more than the land value, the building should remain on the site. If the value under the existing use falls below the land value, any building(s) on the site will likely be demolished so the building that represents the highest and best use of the site can be constructed. For example, if the value as a warehouse is only $800,000, it implies a building value of negative $200,000. The building should be demolished, assuming the demolition costs are less than $200,000.

Example 11

Highest and Best Use

Two uses have been identified for a property. One is an office building that would have a value after construction of $20 million. Development costs would be $16 million, which includes a profit to the developer. The second use is an apartment building that would have a value after construction of $25 million. Development costs, including a profit to the developer, would be $22 million. What is the highest and best use of the site and the implied land value?

Solution:

	Office	Apartment
Value on completion	$20,000,000	$25,000,000
Cost to construct building	(16,000,000)	(22,000,000)
Implied land value	$4,000,000	$3,000,000

An investor/developer could pay up to $4 million for the land to develop an office building but only $3 million for the land to develop an apartment building. The highest and best use of the site is an office building with a land value of $4 million. Of course, this answer assumes a competitive market with several potential developers who would bid for the land to develop an office building.

We will now discuss each of the approaches to estimating value in more detail and provide examples of each.

THE INCOME APPROACH TO VALUATION

6

The **direct capitalization method** and **discounted cash flow method** (DCF) are two income approaches used to appraise a commercial (income-producing) property. The direct capitalization method estimates the value of an income-producing property based on the level and quality of its net operating income. The DCF method discounts future projected cash flows to arrive at a present value of the property. Net operating income, a measure of income and a *proxy for cash flow*, is a focus of both approaches.

6.1 General Approach and Net Operating Income

The income approach focuses on net operating income[3] generated from a property. There are two income approaches, each of which considers growth. The first, the direct capitalization method, capitalizes the current NOI using a growth implicit **capitalization rate**. When the capitalization rate is applied to the forecasted first-year NOI

---

[3] NOI in this real estate property context is similar to earnings before interest, taxes, depreciation, and amortization (EBITDA) in a financial reporting context.

for the property, the implicit assumption is that the first-year NOI is representative of what the typical first-year NOI would be for similar properties. The second, the DCF method, applies an explicit growth rate to construct an NOI stream from which a present value can be derived. As we will see, there is some overlap because, even for the second method, we generally estimate a terminal value by capitalizing NOI at some future date.

Income can be projected either for the entire economic life of the property or for a typical holding period with the assumption that the property will be sold at the end of the holding period. We will see that there are many different ways of applying the income approach depending on how complex the income is for the property being valued. But no matter how the approach is applied, the concept is that the value is based on discounting the cash flows, typically represented by NOI in real estate contexts. The discount rate should reflect the risk characteristics of the property. It can be derived from market comparisons or from specific analysis; we will examine both cases.

When the property has a lot of different leases with different expiration dates and complex lease provisions, the income approach is often done with spreadsheets or software.[4] At the other extreme, when simplifying assumptions can be made about the pattern of future income, simple formulas often can be used to estimate the value.

To value a property using an income approach, we need to calculate the **net operating income** for the property. NOI is a measure of the income from the property after deducting operating expenses for such items as property taxes, insurance, maintenance, utilities, repairs, and insurance but before deducting any costs associated with financing and before deducting federal income taxes. This is not to suggest that financing costs and federal income taxes are not important to an investor's cash flows. It simply means that NOI is a before-tax unleveraged measure of income.[5]

There may be situations where the lease on a property requires the tenants to be responsible for some or all of the expenses so that they would not be deducted when calculating NOI. Or they might be deducted, but then the additional income received from the tenants due to reimbursement of these expenses would be included when calculating the NOI. Of course, when the tenant must pay the expenses, we might expect the rent to be lower. It is necessary to consider specific lease terms when estimating NOI. As mentioned before, typical lease terms vary from country to country.

A general calculation of NOI is shown in Exhibit 5.

Exhibit 5	Calculating NOI

Rental income at full occupancy

+ Other income (such as parking)

= *Potential gross income (PGI)*

− Vacancy and collection loss

= *Effective gross income (EGI)*

− Operating expenses (OE)

= *Net operating income (NOI)*

---

4 One example is a software package called ARGUS Valuation DCF, which was initially used primarily in the United States. There are now versions in many other languages, including Japanese, Chinese, German, and Spanish. See www.argussoftware.com for further information.

5 Cash flows may also be affected by capital expenditures for such items as a roof replacement. Sometimes such items are accounted for by including a "reserve allowance" as one of the expenses. The reserve allowance spreads the cost of the capital expenditure over time. At other times, the expenditure may be deducted from NOI in the year it is expected to occur.

Example 12

Net Operating Income

A 50-unit apartment building rents for $1,000 per unit per month. It currently has 45 units rented. Operating expenses, including property taxes, insurance, maintenance, and advertising, are typically 40 percent of effective gross income. The property manager is paid 10 percent of effective gross income. Other income from parking and laundry is expected to average $500 per rented unit per year. Calculate the NOI.

Solution:

Rental income at full occupancy	50 × $1,000 × 12 =	$600,000
Other income	50 × $500 =	+25,000
Potential gross income		$625,000
Vacancy loss	5/50 or 10% × $625,000 =	−62,500
Effective gross income		$562,500
Property management	10% of $562,500 =	−56,250
Other operating expenses	40% of $562,500 =	−225,000
Net operating income		$281,250

6.2 The Direct Capitalization Method

The direct capitalization method capitalizes the current NOI at a rate known as the capitalization rate, or cap rate for short. If we think about the inverse of the cap rate as a multiplier, the approach is analogous to an income multiplier. The direct capitalization method differs from the DCF method, in which future operating income (a proxy for cash flow) is discounted at a discount rate to produce a present value.

6.2.1 *The Capitalization Rate and the Discount Rate*

The cap and discount rates are closely linked but are not the same. Briefly, the discount rate is the return required from an investment and comprises the risk-free rate plus a risk premium specific to the investment. The cap rate is lower than the discount rate because it is calculated using the current NOI. So, the cap rate is like a current yield for the property whereas the discount rate is applied to current and future NOI, which may be expected to grow. In general, when income and value are growing at a constant compound growth rate, we have:

Cap rate = Discount rate − Growth rate   **(1)**

The growth rate is implicit in the cap rate, but we have to make it explicit for a DCF valuation.

6.2.2 *Defining the Capitalization Rate*

The capitalization rate is a very important measure for valuing income-producing real estate property. The cap rate is defined as follows:

Cap rate = NOI/Value   **(2)**

where the NOI is usually based on what is expected during the current or first year of ownership of the property. Sometimes the term *going-in cap rate* is used to clarify that it is based on the first year of ownership when the investor is *going into* the deal. (Later, we will see that the *terminal cap rate* is based on expected income for the year after the anticipated sale of the property.)

The value used in the above cap rate formula is an estimate of what the property is worth at the time of purchase. If we rearrange the above equation and solve for value we see that:

Value = NOI/Cap rate (3)

So, if we know the appropriate cap rate, we can estimate the value of the property by dividing its first-year NOI by the cap rate.

Where does the cap rate come from? That will be an important part of our discussion. A simple answer is that it is based on observing what other similar or comparable properties are selling for. Assuming that the sale price for a comparable property is a good indication of the value of the subject property, we have:

Cap rate = NOI/Sale price of comparable (4)

We would not want to rely on the price for just one sale to indicate what the cap rate is. We want to observe several sales of similar properties before drawing conclusions about what cap rates investors are willing to accept for a property. As we will discuss later, there are also reasons why we would expect the cap rate to differ for different properties, such as what the future income potential is for the property—that is, how it is expected to change after the first year. This is important because the cap rate is only explicitly based on the first-year income. But the cap rate that investors are willing to accept depends on how they expect the income to change in the future and the risk of that income. These expectations are said to be implicit in the cap rate.

The cap rate is like a snapshot at a point in time of the relationship between NOI and value. It is somewhat analogous to the price–earnings multiple for a stock except that it is the reciprocal.[6] The reciprocal of the cap rate is price divided by NOI. Just as stocks with greater earnings growth potential tend to have higher price–earnings multiples, properties with greater income growth potential have higher ratios of price to current NOI and thus lower cap rates.

It is often necessary to make adjustments based on specific lease terms and characteristics of a market. For example, a similar approach is common in the United Kingdom, where the term fully let property is used to refer to a property that is leased at market rent because either it has a new tenant or the rent has just been reviewed. In such cases, the appraisal is undertaken by applying a capitalization rate to this rent rather than to NOI because leases usually require the tenant to pay all costs. The cap rate derived by dividing rent by the recent sales prices of comparables is often called the all risks yield (ARY). Note that the term "yield" in this case is used like a "current yield" based on first-year NOI. It is a cap rate and will differ from the total return that an investor might expect to get from future growth in NOI and value. If it is assumed, however, that the rent will be level in the foreseeable future (like a perpetuity), then the cap rate will be the same as the return and the all risks yield will be an internal rate of return (IRR) or yield to maturity.

In simple terms, the valuation is:

Market value = Rent/ARY (5)

Again, this valuation is essentially the same as dividing NOI by the cap rate as discussed earlier except the occupant is assumed to be responsible for all expenses so the rent is divided by the ARY.[7] ARY is a cap rate and will differ from the required total return (the discount rate) an investor might expect to get by future growth in NOI and value. If rents are expected to increase after every rent review, then the investor's expected return will be higher than the cap rate. If rents are expected to

---

6 In the United Kingdom, the reciprocal of the cap rate is called the "years purchase" (YP). It is the number of years that it would take for income at the current level to be equal to the original purchase price.
7 In practice, management costs should also be considered, although operating costs falling on the landlord are typically much lower than in the United States.

increase at a constant compound rate, then the investor's expected return (discount rate) will equal the cap rate plus the growth rate.

Example 13

Capitalizing NOI

A property has just been let at an NOI of £250,000 for the first year, and the capitalization rate on comparable properties is 5 percent. What is the value of the property?

Solution:

Value = NOI/Cap rate = £250,000/0.05 = £5,000,000

Suppose the rent review for the property in Example 13 occurs every year and rents are expected to increase 2 percent each year. An approximation of the IRR would simply be the cap rate plus the growth rate; in this case, a 5 percent cap rate plus 2 percent rent growth results in a 7 percent IRR. Of course, if the rent review were less frequent, as in the United Kingdom where it is typically every five years, then we could not simply add the growth rate to the cap rate to get the IRR. But it would still be higher than the cap rate if rents were expected to increase.

6.2.3 *Stabilized NOI*

When the cap rate is applied to the forecasted first-year NOI for the property, the implicit assumption is that the first-year NOI is representative of what the typical first-year NOI would be for similar properties. In some cases, the appraiser might project an NOI to be used to estimate value that is different from what might actually be expected for the first year of ownership for the property if what is actually expected is not typical.

An example of this might be when a property is undergoing a renovation and there is a temporarily higher-than-typical amount of vacancy until the renovation is complete. The purpose of the appraisal might be to estimate what the property will be worth once the renovation is complete. A cap rate will be used from properties that are not being renovated because they are more typical. Thus, the appraiser projects what is referred to as a **stabilized NOI**, which is what the NOI would be if the property were not being renovated—in other words, what the NOI will be once the renovation is complete. This NOI is used to estimate the value. Of course, if the property is being purchased before the renovation is complete, a slightly lower price will be paid because the purchaser has to wait for the renovation to be complete to get the higher NOI. Applying the cap rate to the lower NOI that is occurring during the renovation will understate the value of the property because it implicitly assumes that the lower NOI is expected to continue.[8]

Example 14

Value of a Property to be Renovated

A property is being purchased that requires some renovation to be competitive with otherwise comparable properties. Renovations satisfactory to the purchaser will be completed by the seller at the seller's expense. If it were already renovated,

---

8 Some readers may correctly think that, rather than use a stabilized NOI, a lower cap rate could be used to reflect the fact that the NOI will be higher in the future. The problem is that it is not easy to know how much lower the cap rate should be if there are no sales of comparable properties intended for renovation.

it would have NOI of ¥9 million next year, which would be expected to increase by 3 percent per year thereafter. Investors would normally require a 12 percent IRR (discount rate) to purchase the property after it is renovated. Because of the renovation, the NOI will only be ¥4 million next year. But after that, the NOI is expected to be the same as it would be if it had already been renovated at the time of purchase. What is the value of or the price a typical investor is willing to pay for the property?

Solution:

If the property was already renovated (and the NOI stabilized), the value would be:

Value if renovated = ¥9,000,000/(0.12 − 0.03) = ¥100,000,000

But because of the renovation, there is a loss in income of ¥5 million during the first year. If for simplicity we assume that this would have been received at the end of the year, then the present value of the lost income at a 12 percent discount rate is as follows:

Loss in value = ¥5,000,000/(1.12) = ¥4,464,286

Thus, the value of the property is as follows:

Value if renovated	¥100,000,000
Less loss in value	− ¥4,464,286
= Value	¥95,535,714

An alternative approach is to get the present value of the first year's income and the value in a year when renovated.

{¥4,000,000 + [¥9,000,000(1.03)]/(0.12− 0.03)]}/(1.12) = ¥95,535,714

6.2.4 *Other Forms of the Income Approach*

Direct capitalization usually uses NOI and a cap rate. However, there are some alternatives to the use of NOI and a cap rate. For example, a *gross income multiplier* might be used in some situations. The gross income multiplier is the ratio of the sale price to the gross income expected from the property in the first year after sale. It may be obtained from comparable sales in a similar way to what was illustrated for cap rates. The problem with using a gross income multiplier is that it does not explicitly consider vacancy rates and operating expenses. Thus, it implicitly assumes that the ratio of vacancy and expenses to gross income is similar for the comparable and subject properties. But if, for example, expenses were expected to be lower on one property versus another because it was more energy efficient, an investor would pay more for the same rent. Thus, its gross income multiplier should be higher. Use of a gross rent multiplier is also considered a form of direct capitalization but is generally not considered as reliable as using a capitalization rate.

6.3 The Discounted Cash Flow (DCF) Method

The direct capitalization method typically estimates value by capitalizing the first-year NOI at a cap rate derived from market evidence.[9]

---

9 The DCF method (sometimes referred to as a yield capitalization method) involves projecting income beyond the first year and discounting that income at a discount rate (yield rate). The terms *yield rate* and *discount rate* are being used synonymously in this discussion, as are the terms *yield capitalization* and *discounted cash flow* analysis.

6.3.1 *The Relationship between Discount Rate and Cap Rate*

If the income and value for a property are expected to change over time at the same compound rate—for example, 3 percent per year—then the relationship between the cap rate and discount rate is the same as in Equation 1:

Cap rate = Discount rate – Growth rate

To see the intuition behind this, let us solve for the discount rate, which is the return that is required to invest in the property.

Discount rate = Cap rate + Growth rate

Recall that the cap rate is based on first-year NOI. The growth rate captures how NOI will change in the future along with the property value. Thus, we can say that the investor's return (discount rate) comes from the return on first-year income (cap rate) plus the growth in income and value over time (growth rate). Although income and value may not always change at the same compound rate each year, this formula gives us insight into the relationship between the discount rate and the cap rate. Essentially, the difference between the discount and cap rates has to do with growth in income and value.

Intuitively, given that both methods start from the same NOI in the first year, you would pay more for an income stream that will grow than for one that will be constant. So, the price is higher and the cap rate is lower when the NOI is growing. This is what is meant by the growth being *implicit* in the cap rate. If the growth rate is constant, we can extend Equation 3 using Equation 1 to give:

$$V = NOI/(r - g) \qquad\qquad (6)$$

where:

r is the discount rate (required return)
g is the growth rate for income (given constant growth in income, value will grow at the same rate)

This equation is analogous to the dividend growth model applied to stocks. If NOI is not expected to grow at a constant rate, then NOIs are projected into the future and each period's NOI is discounted to arrive at a value of the property. Rather than project NOIs into infinity, typically, NOIs are projected for a specified holding period and a terminal value (estimated sale price) at the end of the holding period is estimated.

Example 15

Growth Explicit Appraisal

NOI is expected to be $100,000 the first year, and after that, NOI is expected to increase at 2 percent per year for the foreseeable future. The property value is also expected to increase by 2 percent per year. Investors expect to get a 12 percent IRR given the level of risk, and therefore, the value is estimated using a 12 percent discount rate. What is the value of the property today (beginning of first year)?

Solution:

$$V = NOI/(r - g)$$
$$= \$100,000/(0.12 - 0.02)$$
$$= \$100,000/0.10$$
$$= \$1,000,000$$

6.3.2 *The Terminal Capitalization Rate*

When a DCF methodology is used to value a property, generally, one of the important inputs is the estimated sale price of the property at the end of a typical holding period. This input is often referred to as the estimated terminal value. Estimating the terminal value of a property can be quite challenging in practice, especially given that the purpose of the analysis is to estimate the value of the property today. But if we do not know the value of the property today, how can we know what it will be worth in the future when sold to another investor? This means we must also use some method for estimating what the property will be worth when sold in the future.

In theory, this value is based on the present value of income to be received by the *next* investor. But we usually do not try to project NOI for another holding period beyond the initial one. Rather, we rely on the direct capitalization method using the NOI of the first year of ownership for the next investor and a cap rate. The cap rate used to estimate the resale price or terminal value is referred to as a *terminal cap rate* or *residual cap rate*. It is a cap rate that is selected at the time of valuation to be applied to the NOI earned in the first year after the property is expected to be sold to a new buyer.

Selecting a terminal cap rate is challenging. Recall that the cap rate equals the discount rate less the growth rate when income and value are growing constantly at the same rate. Whether constant growth is realistic or not, we know that the cap rate will be higher (lower) if the discount rate is higher (lower). Similarly, the cap rate will be lower if the growth rate is expected to be higher, and vice versa. These relationships also apply to the terminal cap rate as well as the going-in cap rate.

The terminal cap rate could be the same, higher, or lower than the going-in cap rate depending on expected discount and growth rates at the time of sale. If interest rates are expected to be higher in the future, pushing up discount rates, then terminal cap rates might be higher. The growth rate is often assumed to be a little lower because the property is older at the time of sale and may not be as competitive. This situation would result in a slightly higher terminal cap rate. Uncertainty about what the NOI will be in the future may also result in selecting a higher terminal cap rate. The point is that the terminal cap rate is not necessarily the same as the going-in cap rate at the time of the appraisal.

Example 16

Appraisal with a Terminal Value

Net operating income (NOI) is expected to be level at $100,000 per year for the next five years because of existing leases. Starting in Year 6, the NOI is expected to increase to $120,000 because of lease rollovers and increase at 2 percent per year thereafter. The property value is also expected to increase at 2 percent per year after Year 5. Investors require a 12 percent return and expect to hold the property for five years. What is the current value of the property?

Solution:

Exhibit 6 shows the projected NOI for this example. Because NOI and property value are expected to grow at the same constant rate after Year 5, we can calculate the cap rate at that time based on the discount rate less the growth rate. That gives us a terminal cap rate that can be used to estimate the value that the property could be sold for at the end of Year 5 (based on the income a buyer would get after that). We can then discount this value along with the income for Years 1–5 to get the present value.

Exhibit 6 **Projected Income**

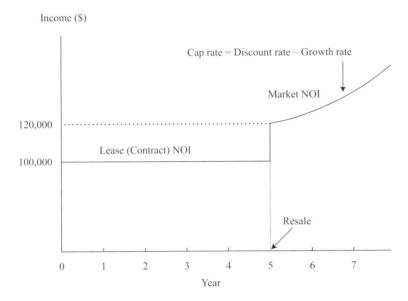

Step 1. Estimate resale price after five years.
Resale (residual) or "terminal" cap rate = 12% − 2% = 10%
Apply this to NOI in Year 6:
Resale = $120,000/0.10 = $1,200,000
Note: The value that can be obtained by selling the property at some point in the future is often referred to as the "*reversion.*"

Step 2. Discount the level NOI for the first five years and the resale price.[10]

PMT = $100,000

FV = $1,200,000

$n = 5$

$i = 12\%$

Solving for PV, the current value of the property is estimated to be $1,041,390. Note that the implied going-in cap rate is $100,000/$1,041,390 = 9.60%.

In Example 16, the going-in cap rate is lower than the terminal cap rate. An investor is willing to pay a higher price for the current NOI because he or she knows that it will increase when the lease is renewed at market rents in five years. The expected rent jump on lease renewal is implicit in the cap rate.

As noted earlier, we often expect the terminal cap rate to be higher than the going-in cap rate because it is being applied to income that is more uncertain. Also, the property is older and may have less growth potential. Finding a lower implied going-in cap rate in this example is consistent with this. However, there are times when we would expect the terminal cap rate to be lower than the going-in cap rate—for example, if we thought that interest rates and thus discount rates would be lower when the property is sold in the future or we expected that markets would be a lot stronger in the future with expectations for higher rental growth than in the current market.

---

10 The solution is shown as if it were obtained with either a financial calculator or Microsoft Excel functions.

Example 17

Appraisal with Level NOI

Suppose the NOI from a property is expected to be level at $600,000 per year for a long period of time such that, for all practical purposes, it can be assumed to be a perpetuity. What is the value of the property assuming investors want a 12 percent rate of return?

Solution:

In this case, the growth rate is zero, so we have:

Value = NOI/Discount rate

Value = $600,000/0.12 = $5,000,000

Note that in this case the cap rate will be the same as the discount rate. This is true when there is no expected change in income and value over time.

6.3.3 *Adapting to Different Lease Structures*

Lease structures vary across locales and can have an effect on the way value is typically estimated in a specific locale. For example, in the United Kingdom, lease structures have influenced the development of specific approaches to appraisal. In the United Kingdom, the term valuation is typically used rather than the term appraisal. A valuation, like an appraisal, is usually an assessment of "the most likely selling price" of a property or its market value (MV). While the cost approach (discussed in Section 7.1) is used in particular circumstances and the sales comparison approach dominates the single-family home market, the most common approach to valuing commercial property combines elements of direct capitalization (often with implicit discounted cash flow analysis) and explicit discounted cash flow analysis. This combination has been developed in response to the typical structure of U.K. leases.

In Section 6.2.2, we discussed the use of a cap rate called the all risks yield to value a fully let property (a property fully leased at current market rents with the tenant[s] paying all operating expenses) in the United Kingdom. If the appraisal date falls between the initial letting (or the last rent review) and the next rent review, adjustments have to be made because the contract rent (referred to as passing rent) is not equal to the current market rent (referred to as the open market rent). If the current market rent is greater than the contract rent, then the rent is likely to be adjusted upward at the time of the rent review and the property has what is referred to in the United Kingdom as a "*reversionary potential*" because of the higher rent at the next rent review.[11] This expected increase in rent has to be included in the appraisal.

There are several ways of dealing with this expected change in rent, but each should result in a similar valuation. One way, which is referred to as the "term and reversion approach" in the United Kingdom, simply splits the income into two components. The *term rent* is the fixed passing (current contract) rent from the date of appraisal to the next rent review, and the *reversion* is the estimated rental value (ERV). The values of the two components of the income stream are appraised separately by the application of different capitalization rates.

The capitalization rate used for the reversion is derived from sales of comparable fully let properties, on the basis that the reversion is equivalent to a fully let property,

---

11 The term *reversion* is used in the United States to refer to the proceeds from the sale of a property that may or may not be at the end of a lease. Reversion and reversionary potential are similar in that they both refer to expected future benefits.

because both have potential for income growth every five years due to rent review.[12] However, the capitalized reversionary income is a future value, so it has to be discounted from the time of the rent review to the present. By convention, the rate used to discount this future reversionary value to the present is the same as the capitalization rate used to calculate the reversionary value, although they do not have to be the same.

The discount rate applied to the term rent is typically lower than that for the reversion because the term rent is regarded as less risky because it is secured by existing leases and tenants are less likely to default when they have leases with below-market-rate rents. Example 18 illustrates estimating the value of a property with term rent and reversion.

Example 18

A Term and Reversion Valuation

A property was let for a five-year term three years ago at £400,000 per year. Rent reviews occur every five years. The estimated rental value (ERV) in the current market is £450,000, and the all risks yield (cap rate) on comparable fully let properties is 5 percent. A lower rate of 4 percent is considered appropriate to discount the term rent because it is less risky than market rent (ERV). Exhibit 7 shows the assumed cash flows for this example. Estimate the value of the property.

Exhibit 7	Assumed Cash Flows

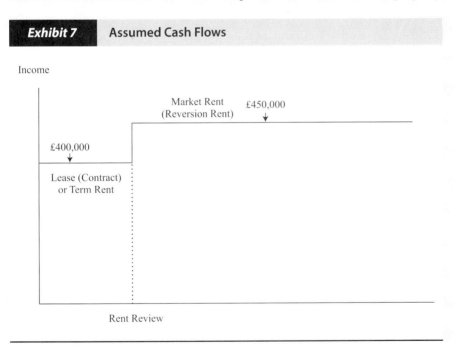

Solution:

The first step is to find the present value of the term rent of £400,000 per year for two years. At a 4 percent discount rate, the present value of £400,000 per year for two years is £754,438. The second step is to estimate the present value of the £450,000 ERV at the time of the rent review. At a 5 percent capitalization rate, this value is £9,000,000 (= £450,000/0.05). This value is at the time of rent review and must be discounted back for two years to the present. Using a

---

12 This assumes capitalization rates will not change significantly between the time of the appraisal and the time of the rent review.

discount rate that is the same as the capitalization rate of 5 percent results in a present value of £8,163,265. Adding this to the value of the term rent of £754,438 results in a total value of £8,917,703. In summary:

Term rent	£400,000	
PV 2 years at 4%	× 1.8860947	
Value of term rent		= £754,438
Reversion to ERV	£450,000	
PV perpetuity at 5%	÷ 0.05	
Value at rent review	= £9,000,000	
PV 2 years at 5%	× 0.9070295	
Value of reversion		= £8,163,265
Total capital value		£8,917,703

Note that despite the differences in terminology, this example is similar to Example 16, in which there was level income for five years and an assumed resale at the end of the fifth year. Recall that the value associated with resale of the property in the future is often referred to as the reversion value. It is the same concept as in this example. The value of the property is equal to the value of the income received for a period of time plus the expected value from sale in the future (at the end of the period) regardless of whether the property is actually sold or not. In Example 18, the property could be sold at the time of rent review for £9 million. So the total value is equal to the present value of the income until the rent review plus the present value of what the property could be sold for at rent review.

A variation of the above method that is sometimes used in the United Kingdom is referred to as the "layer method." The only difference is that it deals with the higher income expected from the rent review in a different way mathematically. It assumes that one source of income is the current contract rent as if it would continue indefinitely (perpetuity) and then adds to the value of this income the value from the incremental rent expected to be received after the rent review. A cap rate close to or equal to the all risks yield is normally applied to the contract rent because it is regarded as secure income—rent reviews are upward only in the United Kingdom and rental growth should ensure that the rent from the new lease will be at least as high as the current rent. The additional income expected after the rent review is often capitalized at a higher rate than the all risks yield because it is regarded as more risky although it could increase even more after subsequent rent reviews, and as we have seen, a higher growth rate for income results in a lower cap rate. Example 19 illustrates the use of the layer method.

Example 19

The Layer Method

Consider the same property as in Example 18. The cash flow is shown in Exhibit 8. The current contract (term) rent is to be discounted at 5 percent, and the incremental rent is to be discounted at 6 percent. Estimate the value of the property using the layer method.

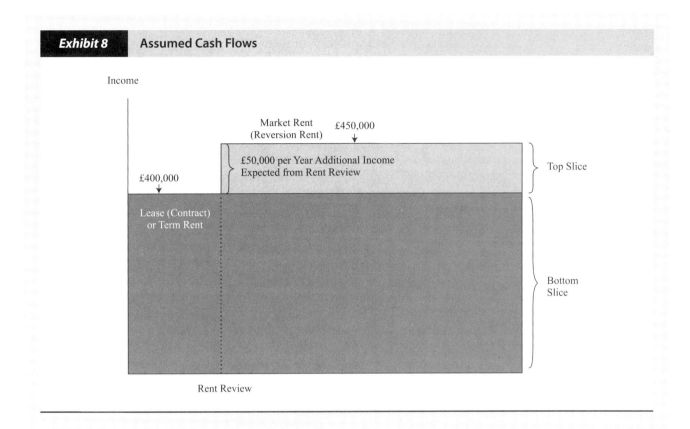

Exhibit 8   Assumed Cash Flows

Solution:

Using the layer method, the valuation is as follows:

Term rent	£400,000	
PV in perpetuity at 5%	÷ 0.05	
Value of bottom slice		= £8,000,000
Reversion to ERV	£450,000	
Less bottom slice	− £400,000	
Top slice rent =	£50,000	
PV perpetuity at 6%	× 16.6666667	
PV 2 years at 6%	× 0.8899964	
Value of top slice		= £741,664
Total capital value		£8,741,664

This method produces a slightly different answer from that shown in Example 18. In theory, the cap rates could have been adjusted to produce the same answer as in Example 18; in practice, adjustments involve both market convention and subjectivity.

6.3.4 *The Equivalent Yield*

In Examples 18 and 19, different cap rates were applied to the two different sources of income (current contract rent versus market rent to be received at rent review). There is a single discount rate that could be applied mathematically to both income streams that would result in the same value. This rate is referred to as the "equivalent yield." Again, we must be careful about terminology because this rate will not be an IRR unless one assumes there will not be any increase in rent after the first rent review. Otherwise, the equivalent yield is simply an average of the two separate cap rates—although not a simple average because of the mathematics of discounting. A concept proposed by Investment Property Databank (IPD) in the United Kingdom is to show the "effective yield" for a property being valued, where the effective yield is an IRR calculation based on reasonable assumptions for future rent reviews beyond the first one. The concept of an effective yield would be the same as the discount rate that would be used to value a property using discounted cash flow analysis, and an effective yield can be calculated regardless of how the value was estimated. That is, based on the value being estimated by the appraiser, what would the investor expect to earn as an IRR based on projected future cash flows either to perpetuity or with a resale at the end of a holding period? In theory, the holding period would not matter because the resale price represents the present value of income beyond the holding period. So having a holding period assumption is more for convenience and being realistic about how far into the future cash flows can be estimated.

6.4 Advanced DCF: Lease-by-Lease Analysis

The use of a DCF approach for real estate income-producing properties, especially when there are lots of tenants and more complex leases, is intuitively appealing. The general steps to a DCF analysis are as follows:

- Project income from existing leases
- Make assumptions about lease renewals
- Make assumptions about operating expenses
- Make assumptions about capital expenditures
- Make assumptions about absorption of any vacant space
- Estimate resale value (reversion)
- Select discount rate to find PV of cash flows

6.4.1 *Project Income from Existing Leases*

This step involves capturing the start and end dates for each lease and the various determinants of rent under the lease, such as the base rent, projected increases in the base rent (steps), and adjustments that may occur because the lease is linked to an index (such as a CPI adjustment). The projected income from existing leases would include income from expense reimbursements on leases that provide for the tenant being billed for some portion of the operating expenses because either it is a net lease or it is a gross lease but has a provision for pass-through of expenses to the tenant if they exceed a certain amount.

6.4.2 *Make Assumptions about Lease Renewals*

Assumptions also have to be made about what will happen when a lease comes up for renewal—often referred to as market leasing assumptions. That is, does the appraiser think it will be renewed or not? These assumptions are usually not as simple as saying it will be renewed or will not be renewed but involve estimating a probability that the lease will be renewed, which is referred to as the renewal probability. For example, for a particular tenant or group of tenants, it might be assumed that there is a 70 percent chance that the lease will be renewed and a 30 percent chance that it will not be renewed. Estimating this probability obviously involves some judgment, but the estimate will be based on historical experience with different types of tenants as well as consideration of economic conditions likely to exist at the time of the lease renewal.

The assumption about lease renewal probabilities affects cash flows in several ways. First, the assumption about the rent that would be received from an existing tenant that renews a lease may be lower than that expected from a new tenant found to lease the space if the existing tenant does not renew. This is because the owner may be willing to accept a lower rent from an existing tenant that is already in place and has been paying rent on time, and the space will not be vacant until a new tenant is found. Second, a new tenant is more likely to ask the owner to spend money to fix up the tenant's space—so-called tenant improvements (TIs). Third, finding a new tenant is likely to involve paying leasing commissions to a broker, whereas the commissions might be avoided or be less if an existing tenant renews.

In conjunction with making assumptions about the lease renewal probability, the analyst would also indicate how many months it will take to lease the space if the lease is not renewed. This is usually done by specifying the number of months vacant if a lease is not renewed. Combining assumptions about the renewal probability, the number of months vacant, and the length for a new lease is one way to estimate a vacancy rate for the property. For example, a 60 percent renewal probability with 10 months vacant if not renewed suggests that there is a 40 percent chance the lease will not be renewed, so on average there would be 40% × 10 months or 4 months vacancy when the lease comes up for renewal. If the typical lease is 3 years or 36 months, then this suggests a vacancy rate due to this lease of 4 months every 40 months (36 + 4) or a 10 percent vacancy rate.

6.4.3 *Make Assumptions about Operating Expenses*

Operating expenses involve items that must be paid by the owner, such as property taxes, insurance, maintenance, management, marketing, and utilities. Even if the tenant is responsible for paying some or all of the expenses, they often must first be paid by the owner, and then the owner is reimbursed by the tenant. So they would be included as an expense, and there would be additional reimbursement income from the tenant for those expenses that are the tenant's responsibility.

Operating expenses are often categorized as fixed, variable, or a hybrid of the two. By variable expenses, we mean that they depend on the level of occupancy, whereas fixed expenses do not depend on the level of occupancy. Fixed expenses can still change over time—for example, they may increase with inflation. Most expenses change over time because of inflation. But some expenses also depend on the occupancy of the property, such as the management fee, which is often a percentage of income collected from tenants. Insurance and property taxes are more likely to be fixed and not vary with occupancy. Utilities may be a hybrid. With more tenants, there will be higher utility expenses, but there is usually some fixed amount of utility expense even for a building that is almost empty; common areas (lobbies, hallways, and so on) must be heated/air conditioned and adequately lit. The temperature of unoccupied spaces may be kept within a certain range to prevent damage. Thus, utilities might be considered to be partially fixed and partially variable.

Example 20

Utility Expenses

Utilities are assumed to be 25 percent fixed and 75 percent variable. If a 200,000 square foot building was fully occupied, the utility expense would be $4 per square foot. Assuming that all utility expenses are allocated to occupied space, what is the utility expense per occupied square foot if the building is 80 percent occupied?

Solution:

The fixed portion is ($4 × 0.25 × 200,000)/(0.80 × 200,000) = $1.25 per occupied square foot.
The variable portion is $4 × 0.75 = $3.00 per occupied square foot.
The total utility expense is $4.25 per occupied square foot.

6.4.4 *Make Assumptions about Capital Expenditures*

In addition to the operating expenses discussed above, there may be additional expenditures that have to be paid for items that are not ordinary annual expenses, such as a new heating and air conditioning system or replacing a roof. These items are referred to as capital expenditures (or capex), and they affect cash flows. Funds used to fix up a tenant's space for a new lease are also considered capital expenditures, as are funds spent to renovate the building. These capital expenditures are deducted from the NOI to calculate cash flow that would be discounted when doing a DCF analysis. Note that these expenditures will differ in most years, and in some years there may not be any. They are lumpy by nature. In some cases, analysts estimate on average what the annual amount of capital expenditures will be and have a deduction each year for capital expenditures rather than project exactly in which year(s) they might spend the money. In such cases, capex should still be a deduction from NOI, although some analysts include it along with other operating expenses and call it a "replacement reserve." Regardless of how the capex is handled, the present value of the cash flows should be essentially the same.

6.4.5 *Make Assumptions about Absorption of Any Vacant Space*

The property being valued may also have some space that is currently vacant and needs to be leased up. Accounting for currently vacant space involves making an assumption as to when the space is likely to be leased, which could involve several leases starting at different points in time in the future. Until the space is leased, it will be reflected in the vacancy rate for the property, as will space that is vacant as a result of the lease renewal assumptions discussed above.

6.4.6 *Estimate Resale Value (Reversion)*

When doing a DCF analysis, the usual practice is to make an assumption as to how long the property will be held by the initial investor. For example, it might be assumed that the property will be held for 10 years and then sold to a second investor. An alternative would be to project cash flows for the entire economic life of the property, although there would still normally be value to the land after the building is ready for demolition.

Obviously, it is harder to project cash flows the further we go in the future, so for practical purposes, a holding period of about 10 years is typically used. This allows us to capture the details of existing leases and what will happen when most if not all of them renew if the lease term of the longest lease is 10 years or less. Having a holding period that goes beyond when existing leases expire can make it easier to estimate the resale price at the end of the holding period because all leases will be at market rents and have normal rent growth thereafter. In contrast, if there were unexpired leases that had unusually low (or high) contract rent, they could bias the estimate of the resale price if not properly accounted for when estimating the resale price.

The way the resale price is often estimated is to use the concept of a terminal cap rate that was discussed earlier. The idea is that, although we want to capture the details of the leases for the next 10 years or so of the holding period, to get the resale price we will revert to a more simple direct capitalization approach. If the holding period is 10 years, the expected NOI in Year 11 would be used to estimate the resale price because this is the first year of NOI for the next buyer.

Recall our earlier discussion of the terminal cap rate and the relationship between the cap rate, the discount rate, and expected future growth in NOI and value. The terminal cap rate will capture how income and value is projected to change for a new investor. We could say that the resale price will be the present value of cash flows expected after that. So even though we select a holding period when the property will be sold, we are still implicitly considering all future cash flows for the property. We only try to capture the detail on a year-by-year basis up until the end of the holding period plus one year.

Note that, in theory, the length of the holding period does not matter because the resale price reflects the present value of cash flows expected after the holding period. So the choice of a holding period is somewhat arbitrary, and it is more important to pick one that goes beyond the term of existing leases for the reasons discussed above. To elaborate, if there was a major lease that had significantly below-market rent under the contract terms of the lease, its income would be expected to increase when the lease ends, which should result in higher income from that point forward. The analyst would want to capture this in his or her analysis. But if the income used to estimate the resale price is before the lease expires, applying a cap rate to that income may underestimate the resale price because it would not capture the growth in income and value when this lease renews.

6.4.7 *Select Discount Rate to Find PV of Cash Flows*

Ultimately, the purpose of a DCF analysis is to discount the projected future cash flows, including the resale price, to get a present value. This requires selection of an appropriate discount rate to capture the riskiness of the cash flows. Knowing what the discount rate should be can be a challenge because it is not directly observable. That is, analysts do not know what the investor projected as cash flows in the future and what return was expected at the time a property was purchased—although analysts could ask the buyer, which is one of the ways, analysts try to determine what discount rate to use. That is, analysts can survey buyers of properties in the market to find out what return they expected when they purchased the property. Some companies and organizations publish the results of investor surveys.

The discount rate should be higher than what the mortgage rate would be for a loan on the property—regardless of whether the investor plans to actually get a loan. This is because investing in the property is usually considered riskier than making a loan on the property. The lender gets repaid before the investor receives any cash flow, and thus the lender bears less risk than the investor. So the discount rate should have a risk premium beyond that reflected in the mortgage rate.

Some argue that more than one discount rate is applicable because some cash flows expected from a property are riskier than others. For example, a lower discount rate might be used to find the present value of the income from existing leases, but a higher discount rate might be used for the income from lease renewals and resale. That said, even if a single discount rate is used, it can be thought of as an average of the different rates that might be applied to different components of the cash flow. So, the important thing is to use a discount rate that reflects, on average, how risky the investment is compared with alternatives.

Example 21

Direct Capitalization and Discounted Cash Flow

What is the main difference between direct capitalization and discounted cash flow (DCF) analysis?

Solution:

Direct capitalization applies a capitalization rate or an income multiplier to the forecasted first-year NOI. Thus, expected increases (growth) in NOI in the future must be implicit in the multiplier or cap rate. In contrast, when doing a DCF, the future cash flows are projected each year until sale of the property. Then each year's cash flow and the expected resale proceeds are discounted using a discount rate. Thus, the future income pattern, including the effect of growth, is explicit in a DCF. Furthermore, DCF often considers other cash flows that might occur in the future that are not reflected in NOI, such as capital expenditures.

6.5 Advantages and Disadvantages of the Income Approach

We have seen that there are many ways of applying the income approach, ranging from a relatively simple use of a cap rate with direct capitalization to more advanced DCF analysis that involves projecting cash flows over a holding period and capturing the details of the leases for each year of the holding period.

The *advantage* of the more complex DCF approach is that it captures the cash flows that investors actually care about. And this approach does not depend on current transactions from comparable sales as long as we feel that we can select an appropriate discount rate.

The *disadvantage* is the amount of detailed information that is needed and the need to forecast what will happen in the future even if it is just forecasting a growth rate for the NOI and not doing a detailed lease-by-lease analysis. Selecting an appropriate discount rate is critical, as is selecting an appropriate terminal cap rate. Small variations in assumptions can have a significant impact on the value.

Because it can be tedious to capture all the details of existing leases, specialized software is often used to do DCF analysis.

6.6 Common Errors

Discounted cash flow analysis requires a lot of assumptions, and analysts may knowingly or otherwise make assumptions that are not consistent with reality. The following are some of the more common erroneous assumptions:

- The discount rate does not reflect the risk.
- Income growth is greater than expense growth.
- The terminal cap rate is not logical compared with the implied going-in cap rate.
- The terminal cap rate is applied to an income that is not typical.
- The cyclical nature of real estate markets is not recognized.

Example 22

Disadvantages of and Errors in Discounted Cash Flow Analysis

A property is being valued using an 8 percent discount rate. A terminal capitalization rate of 5.5 percent was used to estimate the resale price. After solving for value, the appraiser calculates the implied going-in capitalization rate to be 6 percent. Market rents and property values have been increasing about 1 percent per year, and that is expected to continue in the foreseeable future. Current mortgage rates for a loan on the property would be 7.5 percent. Do the assumed discount and terminal capitalization rates seem reasonable?

Solution:

There are several "red flags" or warning signs. First, the discount rate is only 50 basis points above the mortgage rate. Whether this is a sufficient risk premium for an equity investor is questionable. Second, the terminal capitalization rate is less than the going-in capitalization rate, which suggests either interest rates will fall in the future or NOI and property values will increase at an even faster rate in the future. Usually, terminal capitalization rates are the same as or slightly higher than going-in capitalization rates to reflect the fact that the property will be older when sold, and older properties usually have less NOI growth.

Finally, the difference between the discount rate of 8 percent and the going-in capitalization rate of 6 percent implies 2 percent per year growth. Yet NOI and property values are expected to increase only about 1 percent per year. Overall, it appears that the appraiser may be overvaluing the property.

THE COST AND SALES COMPARISON APPROACHES TO VALUATION

7

We now turn to two other approaches to valuation: the cost approach and the sales comparison approach. The cost approach is typically used for unusual properties or those with specialized use for which market comparables are difficult to obtain. The sales comparison approach is most commonly used for single-family homes, where income is not relevant and sales data for reasonable comparables is available.

7.1 The Cost Approach

The cost approach involves estimating the value of the building(s) based on adjusted replacement cost. The estimated value of the land (usually from a sales comparison approach) is added to the estimated value of the building to arrive at the estimated total value of the property. To determine the value of the building, the **replacement cost**, assuming it was built today using current construction costs and standards, is first estimated.[13] The replacement cost is adjusted for different types of depreciation (loss in value) to arrive at a **depreciated replacement cost**.[14]

The first type of depreciation is for **physical deterioration**, which is generally related to the age of the property because components of the property wear out over time. There are two types of physical deterioration: curable and incurable. Curable means that fixing the problem will add value that is at least as great as the cost of the cure. For example, replacing a roof might increase the value of the property by at least as much as the cost of doing so and, therefore, is curable. Fixing a structural problem with the foundation of the building may cost more to cure than the amount that it would increase the value of the property if cured and would be considered incurable deterioration.

The replacement cost estimate for the property assumes it is a new building that has no obsolescence. That is, it is the value assuming nothing needs cured. Thus, the cost of fixing any curable items would have to be deducted from the replacement cost. A prospective purchaser would not pay as much for a property that had items that need to be fixed and would likely deduct the cost of fixing them from the purchase price.

After deducting the cost of fixing curable items from the replacement cost of the property, a deduction still has to be made for incurable depreciation. A buyer would pay less for a building that is older and has wear and tear. Because incurable depreciation by definition would not be feasible to fix because it does not increase

---

13 There is sometimes a distinction made between "replacement cost" and "reproduction cost," where reproduction cost refers to the cost of creating an exact replica of the building using the original building materials. In contrast, replacement cost refers to creating a building that provides the same utility to users but is constructed with modern building materials. Reproduction cost may be higher than replacement cost because it is not economical to construct the building using the original materials. Thus, replacement cost is more relevant as a starting point to estimate value using the cost approach.

14 It should be noted that the depreciation being estimated for the cost approach may have little relationship to the amount of depreciation that would be used on financial statements using a historical cost approach to accounting.

value as much as the cost to fix, we would not deduct the cost of fixing it from the replacement cost. Rather, appraisers try to estimate how a property's age is likely to affect its value. A simple way that is often used to estimate this depreciation is to base it on the effective age of the property relative to its economic life. The effective age can differ from the actual age if it has more or less than the normal amount of wear and tear. For example, if the property has an effective age of 10 years and its economic life is usually 50 years, then the physical depreciation is assumed to be 10/50 or 20 percent. This ratio is applied to the value calculated above, which is after subtracting the curable depreciation from the replacement cost so as to not double count. That is, we have already accounted for the loss in value do to curable depreciation.

The second type of depreciation is referred to as **functional obsolescence**. It is a loss in value due to a design that is different from that of a new building constructed with an appropriate design for the intended use of the property. This could result from changes in design standards since the building was constructed or because the building had a poor design to start, even if it were a relatively new building. Functional obsolescence usually results in the building generating less NOI than it otherwise would because the building may be less efficient and have a higher operating expense or may not command as much rent as a building with the proper design. The amount of functional obsolescence is often estimated by the present value of the income loss due to the obsolescence. For example, suppose an office has a poorly designed elevator system such that there tends to be unusually long waiting times for tenants and visitors to use them. This situation affects the types of tenants that are willing to rent space in the building, and the rent is less than it would be if the elevators had greater capacity. The appraiser determines that this design flaw likely reduces NOI by about $25,000 per year. An 8 percent cap rate is considered appropriate to estimate the value of the property. This cap rate can be applied to the $25,000 loss in NOI due to the poor elevator design to arrive at a $312,500 loss in value due to functional obsolescence. This amount is deducted from the replacement cost.

Finally, there is depreciation that is external to the property. This *external obsolescence* is due to either the location of the property or economic conditions. **Locational obsolescence** results when the location is not optimal for the property. It usually occurs because something happens after the building was constructed that changes the desirability of the location for the existing use; the existing use may no longer be the highest and best use of the site.

For example, a luxury apartment building is on a site where the highest and best use when it was first developed was to construct the luxury apartment. But perhaps after the apartment was constructed, a manufacturing plant that was allowed by the zoning was built on a nearby site, and this made the location much less desirable for a luxury apartment building. That is, a luxury apartment building is no longer the highest and best use of the site. Perhaps now the highest and best use is an apartment building that would have lower rents and appeal to people working at the manufacturing plant.

After the manufacturing plant was built, rents had to be lowered on the apartment building currently on the site. Thus, its value is lower than it would be on a site where the highest and best use is still a luxury apartment building. Suppose the decline in the value of the apartment building (land and building) is $200,000. This amount is the total loss in value due to the manufacturing plant. But some of this loss in value would show up in the land value being lower, which would be reflected in comparable land sales taking place after the manufacturing plant was built being lower than before it was built and lower at better locations. For example, a vacant site near the manufacturing plant would have sold for $100,000 before the manufacturing plant was built but would now sell for $75,000 to be used for low-income housing. Thus, some of the loss in value of the property would already be reflected in the lower land value, and this portion does not have to be deducted from the replacement cost of the building.

The land value for the existing luxury office building near the manufacturing plant would be $75,000 based on its use for lower-income apartments if vacant. Because the land value reflects a $25,000 loss in value, the amount of locational obsolescence attributed to the building would be the $200,000 total decline in value less the $25,000 attributed to the land or $175,000. Thus, $175,000 is deducted from the replacement cost of the building in the cost approach.

Economic obsolescence results when new construction is not feasible under current economic conditions. This usually occurs when rent levels are not sufficiently high to generate a value for a newly constructed property that is at least equal to the development costs (including a profit to the developer). Thus, the replacement cost of the new property exceeds what it would really be worth if it were developed. In this situation, even a new building would have a loss in value.

In Exhibit 9, the cost approach is illustrated for a small office building. The building has a replacement cost of $16 million plus a developer's profit of $750,000. This is what it would cost to build a brand new building that has the same utility as the property being valued. The land value of $4 million is based on comparable sales of other parcels of land. The subject property is not new and has some deferred maintenance that is curable; spending money to fix these items (such as replacing the roof) will add at least as much value as the cost of curing the problem. The cost to cure the building amounts to $1 million. It has to be deducted from replacement cost because the subject property needs these repairs whereas the replacement cost assumes everything is new.

An older building will also have additional physical deterioration (wear and tear) due to age that is not curable but must be accounted for. As discussed previously, a common way of doing this is to use the ratio of the effective age of the property to its economic life. Effective age could be higher or lower than the actual age, depending on how well maintained the property is or whether it has unusually large or small deterioration. In this case, the effective age is 10 years and the economic life is 50 years, which means it is 10/50 or 20 percent worn out. This ratio is applied to the amount we arrived at after deducting the curable depreciation from the replacement cost.[15] This results in a deduction of $3,150,000 [= (16,750,000 − 1,000,000)0.20] for wear and tear that is not curable.

Next, functional obsolescence, which has to do with design problems, is considered. In this case, the property is deemed to have a poor floor plan compared with a modern building. It also has higher-than-average energy consumption. Keep in mind that we are estimating the value of the property "as is" with its existing design flaws. The deduction for this functional obsolescence is estimated at $1.75 million.

Locational obsolescence also has to be considered. The construction of roads in an adjacent park reduced the amenity value compared with a typical office building in this market. In other words, the location is not the most desirable location for this office building. This lowers the market rent for the property, which is estimated to lower the value by $1 million. Finally, there is some economic obsolescence, which is due to recent construction of competing properties that has resulted in a higher vacancy rate than would be typical for a new building. It results in a loss in value of $1 million. Subtracting all of the depreciation discussed above results in a depreciated building value of $8.85 million. Finally, adding the land value of $4 million results in a value estimate of $12.85 million.

---

15 To not deduct the curable items before applying the 20 percent to account for incurable items would be double-counting. If the curable items were fixed, they would be brand new. We are trying to capture the additional depreciation on the portions of the building that cannot be cured.

Exhibit 9	The Cost Approach			

Market value of the land (from comparables)				$4,000,000
Replacement cost, including constructor's profit				
Building costs (psf)	$200			
Total area (sf)	80,000			
			$16,000,000	
Developer's profit		$750,000		
			$16,750,000	
Reduction for curable deterioration		$1,000,000		
			$15,750,000	
Reduction for incurable deterioration				
Total economic life	50			
Remaining economic life	40			
Effective age	10			
Ratio of effective to total	20%			
Reduction for incurable deterioration		$3,150,000		
			$12,600,000	
Reduction for functional obsolescence (poor floor plan and substandard energy efficiency)		$1,750,000		
			$10,850,000	
Reduction for locational obsolescence (recent construction of roads in park land thus reducing amenity)		$1,000,000		
			$9,850,000	
Reduction for economic obsolescence (recent construction of competing properties thus increasing supply and vacancy rates)		$1,000,000		
Building value		$8,850,000		
Final appraised value (building and land)				**$12,850,000**

Example 23

The Cost Approach

A 12-year-old industrial property is being valued using the cost approach. The appraiser feels that it has an effective age of 15 years based on its current condition. For example, there are cracks in the foundation that are not feasible to repair (incurable physical depreciation). That is, it would cost more to try to repair these problems than the value that would be created in the property. The appraiser believes that it has a 60-year remaining economic life (75-year total economic life).

The building was constructed using a greater ceiling height than users require in the current market (superadequacy). It would cost $27 million to reproduce (reproduction cost) the building with the same ceiling height but $25 million to construct a replacement property (replacement cost) with the same utility but a normal ceiling height.

The higher ceiling results in increased heating and air-conditioning costs of $50,000 per year. A cap rate that would be used to value the property would be 10 percent.

The building was designed to include a cafeteria that is no longer functional (functional obsolescence). This area can be converted to usable space at a conversion cost of $25,000, and it is believed that the value of the property would increase by at least this amount (curable functional obsolescence).

The roof needs to be replaced at a cost of $250,000, and other necessary repairs amount to $50,000. The costs of these repairs will increase the value of the building by at least their $300,000 cost (curable physical depreciation).

The road providing access to the property is a two-lane road, whereas newer industrial properties are accessible by four-lane roads. This has a negative impact on rents (locational obsolescence), which is estimated to reduce NOI by $100,000 per year.

Based on comparable sales of vacant land, the land is estimated to be worth $5 million. Estimate the value using the cost approach.

Solution:

Preliminary Calculations:

Replacement cost (built to current standards)					$25,000,000
Physical depreciation					
Roof	$250,000				
Other	50,000				
Total curable physical depreciation	$300,000				$300,000
Replacement cost after curable physical depreciation					$24,700,000
Ratio of effective age to total economic life		= 15/75 = 20%			
Incurable physical depreciation	20.00%	x	$24,700,000	=	$4,940,000
Curable functional obsolescence					
Conversion of cafeteria					$25,000
Incurable functional obsolescence					
Extra HVAC costs	$50,000	/	10.00%	=	$500,000
Locational obsolescence	$100,000	/	10.00%	=	$1,000,000

Cost Approach Summary:

Replacement Cost		$25,000,000
Physical deterioration:		
Curable	$300,000	
Incurable	$4,940,000	
Functional obsolescence		
Curable	$25,000	
Incurable	$500,000	
Locational obsolescence	$1,000,000	
Total depreciation	$6,765,000	$6,765,000
Depreciated cost		$18,235,000
Plus: Land value		5,000,000
Estimated value from cost approach		$23,235,000

7.2 The Sales Comparison Approach

The sales comparison approach implicitly assumes that the value of a property depends on what other comparable properties are selling for in the current market. Ideally, the comparables would be exactly the same as the subject property in terms of size, age, location, quality of construction, amenities, view, and so on, and would be sold on the same date as the date of the appraised value. Obviously, this is impossible, so adjustments have to be made to each of the comparables for differences from the "subject" property due to these factors. The idea is to determine what the comparables would have sold for if they were like the subject property.

Exhibit 10 shows the sales comparison approach applied to a subject property. There have been sales of five comparable properties within the last year. They are similar to the subject property, but there are always some differences that need to be accounted for. The idea is to determine how much each of the comparables would have sold for if they were exactly the same as the subject property. Calculating the price per square foot (or square meter) is often a good way to account for differences in size, although other measures of size may be appropriate in some cases, such as cubic feet (or cubic meters) for a warehouse or number of units in an apartment building.

Next, the price per square foot is adjusted for each of the comparables. For example, Comparable 1 is in good condition. The subject property is in only average condition. Thus, we lower the price per square foot of the comparable to determine what it would have sold for if it were in only average condition like the subject property. Each comparable is adjusted to what it would sell for if its location, condition, age, and time of sale were the same as the subject property. Notice that after these adjustments, the range in price per square foot is tighter across the five comparables.

In this example, we average the price per square foot for each of the comparables, although in many cases more weight may be given to comparables that the appraiser feels are more similar to the subject property or where they feel more confident in the adjustments. We multiply this price per square foot by the square feet of the subject property to arrive at our estimate of value using the sales comparison approach.

Exhibit 10	The Sales Comparison Approach

| Variable | Subject Property | Comparables | | | | |
		1	2	3	4	5
Size (square feet)	15,000	25,000	20,000	10,000	16,000	12,500
Age (years)	10	1	5	10	15	20
Condition	Average	Good	Good	Good	Average	Poor
Location	Prime	Prime	Secondary	Secondary	Secondary	Prime
Date of sale (months ago)		3	9	6	7	12
Sale price		$5,500,000	$3,000,000	$1,300,000	$1,750,000	$1,300,000
Sale price psf		$220	$150	$130	$109	$104
Adjustments						
Age (years)		−22.5%	−12.5%	0.0%	12.5%	25.0%
Condition		−10.0%	−10.0%	−10.0%	0.0%	10.0%
Location		0.0%	20.0%	20.0%	20.0%	0.0%
Date of sale (months ago)		1.5%	4.5%	3.0%	3.5%	6.0%

Exhibit 10	Continued						

Adjustments

Adjusted price psf			$151.80	$153.00	$146.90	$148.24	$146.64
Average price psf		$149.30					

Appraised value	**$2,239,500**

The following indicates how the adjustments were made to the comparables to reflect the characteristics of the subject property. The adjustments to Comparable 1 are discussed to help clarify the process.

1. Depreciated at 2.5 percent per annum. Because the subject property is nine years older, a depreciation adjustment of –22.5% (= 9 × 2.5%) reduces the value of Comparable 1.
2. Condition adjustment after average depreciation is taken into account: Good, none; Average, 10%; Poor, 20%. Because Comparable 1 is in good condition and the subject property is in only average condition, a condition adjustment of –10 percent reduces the value of Comparable 1.
3. Location adjustment: Prime, none; Secondary, 20%. Comparable 1 and the subject property are both in prime locations, so no location adjustment is made.
4. Market has been rising by 0.5 percent per month. Thus, an adjustment of 1.5 percent is made to the sale price of Comparable 1 because the sale occurred three months ago.

Example 24

The Sales Comparison Approach

Referring to Exhibit 10, suppose there is a sixth comparable that sold one month ago for $2.686 million. It is 15,000 square feet, eight years old, in good condition, and in a prime location. What is the adjusted price per square foot based on this comparable?

Solution:

The sale price per square foot is $2,686,000/15,000 = $179. This price must be adjusted downward by 5 percent because it is two years newer than the subject, down by 10 percent because the condition is better than that of the subject property, and up by 1/2 percent because prices have increased since this comparable sold. This results in an adjusted price per square foot of $153.05.

7.3 Advantages and Disadvantages of the Cost and Sales Comparison Approaches

The cost approach to valuation is sometimes said to set an upper limit on the value. It is assumed that an investor would never pay more than the cost to buy land and develop a comparable building. This assumption may be somewhat of an overstatement because it can take time and effort to develop another building and find tenants. Furthermore, there may not be the demand for another building of the same type in the market. That said, one would question a value that is much higher than implied by the cost approach. The main disadvantage of the cost approach is that it can be difficult to estimate the depreciation for a property that is older and/or has much obsolescence. So the cost approach will be most reliable for newer properties that have a relatively modern design in a stable market.

The sales comparison approach relies on a reasonable number of comparable sales to be able to gauge what investors are expected to be willing to pay for the subject property. When the market is active, the sales comparison approach can be quite reliable. But when the market is weak, there tends to be fewer transactions, which makes it difficult to find comparable properties at a location reasonably close to the subject property. Even in an active market, there may be limited comparable sales for some properties, such as regional malls or special purpose properties.

Finally, the sales comparison approach assumes the investors who are buying properties are behaving rationally. That is, it assumes that the prices paid by investors in the current market are representative of market values. However, as mentioned in Section 5.1.1, the investment value to a particular investor may result in that investor being willing to pay a price in excess of market value. Also, there are times when investors in general are overly exuberant and there is a "bubble" in prices being paid for properties. This raises the question of whether these prices still represent "market value" because it seems likely that prices will eventually fall back to a more normal level. It is often argued that the appraiser's job is to measure what investors are willing to pay whether they think it is rational or not because market value is a most probable selling price.

8   RECONCILIATION

We have discussed three different approaches to valuation: the income, cost, and sales comparison approaches. It would be highly unusual to get the same answer from all three approaches. They rely on different sources of data and different assumptions, and although in theory they should produce the same answer, in practice, this would be unlikely because of imperfections in the data and inefficiencies in the market. Thus, the appraiser needs to *reconcile* the differences and arrive at a final conclusion about the value.

Some approaches may be more applicable than others, depending on the property types and market conditions. The purpose of reconciliation is to decide which approach or approaches you have the most confidence in and come up with a final estimate of value. In an active market with lots of transactions, the appraiser may have more confidence in the sales comparison approach. This may be the case for apartment buildings in many markets. When there are fewer transactions, as might be the case during weak markets or for property types that do not transact as frequently, the appraiser may have more confidence in the income approach. For example, there may be only one large regional mall in a smaller town, so there are no comparable sales of regional malls to rely on. But the appraiser may have all the details of the existing leases and be pretty confident in what investors want as a rate of return for regional malls around the country because they have similar kinds of tenants.

Example 25

Choosing among the Three Approaches

Suppose it is a weak market with hardly any transactions taking place and no new construction during the past year. Investors indicate that they will purchase properties if they can get an adequate return for the risk. What does this suggest about the reliability of the three approaches?

Solution:

The sales comparison approach relies on having transactions to use as comparables. Therefore, in a weak market with few transactions, it is difficult to apply this approach. The replacement cost of a building could be calculated, but if new construction is not feasible, then there is economic depreciation that can be hard to estimate. There is a loss in value because market rents are not high enough to provide an adequate return on new construction. Assuming the property being appraised is generating income, a value can always be calculated using the income approach as long as the appraiser can determine an appropriate discount rate that reflects what the typical investor would require to invest in the property. Thus, in this kind of market, the income approach is likely to be the most reliable.

DUE DILIGENCE

9

The property value is usually estimated as part of the process of a property transaction, whether done by a hired appraiser[16] or by the investor. In addition, investors—both private debt and equity investors—will normally go through a process of "due diligence" to verify other facts and conditions that might affect the value of the property and that might not have been identified by the appraiser. The following is an example of items that are usually part of this process:

- Review the leases for the major tenants and review the history of rental payments and any defaults or late payments.
- Get copies of bills for operating expenses, such as utility expenses.
- Look at cash flow statements of the previous owner for operating expenses and revenues.
- Have an environmental inspection to be sure there are no issues, such as a contaminant material on the site.
- Have a physical/engineering inspection to be sure there are no structural issues with the property and to check the condition of the building systems, structures, foundation, and adequacy of utilities.
- Have an attorney or appropriate party review the ownership history to be sure there are no issues related to the seller's ability to transfer free and clear title that is not subject to any previously unidentified liens.
- Review service and maintenance agreements to determine whether there are recurring problems.
- Have a property survey to determine whether the physical improvements are in the boundary lines of the site and to find out if there are any easements that would affect the value.
- Verify that the property is compliant with zoning, environmental regulations, parking ratios, and so on.
- Verify that property taxes, insurance, special assessments, and so on, have been paid.

When an investor decides to acquire commercial real estate, they will often sign a contract or "letter of intent" that states the investor's intent to acquire the property at a specified price but subject to due diligence. If problems are found during the due diligence period, the investor is likely to try to renegotiate the price or back out of the deal, which he or she can do because either the contract contains a conditional

---

16 Terminology may vary among locales. For example, an appraiser is called a "valuer" in the United Kingdom and other parts of Europe.

clause or a letter of intent was used. A contract that contains a conditional clause or a letter of intent is not a binding contract. The prospective buyer may have to forfeit a deposit depending on the terms of the conditional contract or the letter of intent. In some countries, it may not be customary to use a conditional contract or a letter of intent as a first step. In such countries, some due diligence should be done before entering into a contract that will be binding. Conducting due diligence can be costly but lowers the risk of acquiring a property or lending funds on a property with unexpected legal or physical problems.

Example 26

Due Diligence

What is the primary purpose of due diligence?

Solution:

Due diligence is done to identify legal, environmental, physical, and other unanticipated problems that have not been disclosed by the seller that could be quite costly to remediate or that could negatively affect value. If identified, an issue or issues could result in negotiating a lower price or allow the investor to walk away from the transaction.

---

10 VALUATION IN AN INTERNATIONAL CONTEXT

As mentioned earlier in the reading, different lease structures and conventions can result in slightly different approaches to valuation in different countries, but the underlying principles are very similar and tending to converge with increasing amounts of cross-border investment in real estate and the need for standardized ways of analyzing properties. This is especially evident in the increasing use of DCF analysis—especially for properties that are institutionally owned.

We have discussed the different approaches and techniques that are used to value properties, such as the sales comparison, cost, and income approaches. And we have discussed several ways of applying the income approach because variations in its application tend to occur depending on the lease structure of the property and tradition in the country. Differences across countries will mainly be based on which approaches are emphasized and which of the ways of applying the approach is used.

As an example, Germany has a tradition of valuing the land and building separately even when using the income approach. The land is valued using a sales comparison approach because the government has good data on land sales. So when using the income approach, it is simply assumed that the land is being leased. That is, the land is assumed to be owned by an entity other than the entity that owns the building. Thus, an assumed land lease payment is deducted from the NOI. The resulting cash flow represents income to the building and can be discounted or a cap rate can be applied to it in the same way we have illustrated in this reading. The resulting value will be for the building, and this value can then be added to the value of the land from the sales comparison approach to get the total value. This same approach is used in the United States when the land is actually being leased from a third party. The point is that this is just a slight variation in applying the concepts and techniques illustrated in this reading.

We now set out some general international comparisons. In different international markets, professionals operate in different regulatory environments, have different training, may use specific definitions of the key concepts, may apply different interpretations of common concepts, use variations of basic methods, and have differing availability of key data. These issues affect the local practices of appraisal to different extents in different countries.

Although there has been a progressive extension of international standards and common approaches,[17] it is always useful to be aware of local approaches.[18] However, it is important to bear in mind that the general concepts are the same and that value should have the same bases in any market, that is, it is derived from an income stream that has a risk associated with it. Any appraisal method, however much it may appear otherwise, is simply a way to establish an appropriate value for that income.

Some key differences among countries are summarized in Exhibit 11.

Exhibit 11	Summary of International Valuation Methodologies[19]				
Country	Valuation Framework	Valuation Approaches	Lease Structure and Rent Reviews	Landlord vs. Tenant Expense Responsibility	Globalization
China	People's Republic of China and Regulations for Urban Land Valuation	Sales Comparison, Cost, and Income Approaches	2- to 3-year terms Upon expiry	Landlord: structure Tenant: interior, maintenance, insurance	DCF methodology gaining popularity
France	La Charte de l'Expertise en Évaluation Immobilière, [Le COB]	Sales Comparison and Cost Approaches, Comparative Implicit Capitalization	3-, 6-, 9-year terms Upon expiry, rental changes tie to INSEE Index	Landlord: structure Tenant: interior, maintenance, insurance	DCF gaining popularity with international investments/ valuations
Germany	WertV, WertR BelWertV	Sales Comparison, Cost, and Income Approaches	5-, 10-year terms Upon expiry, rental changes tie to cost of living index	Landlord: structure *'Dach und Fach'* Tenant: interior	DCF gaining popularity with international investments/ valuations
Japan	Ministry of Land, Infrastructure, Transport and Tourism	Sales Comparison, Cost, and Income Approaches	3-, 5-year terms 6 months prior to lease expiration	Landlord: repair Tenant: inside maintenance, insurance	DCF used as an analysis tool and widely used in international investments/ valuations

(continued)

---

17 The quest for international standards in valuation has a long history. The RICS in the United Kingdom has for many years produced its valuation standards rules and guidance in the form of the *Red Book* and has been expanding internationally as the main international professional body for appraisers. In Europe, since the early 1980s, the European Group of Valuers' Associations has produced its *Blue Book* of valuation standards. The International Valuation Standards Council (ISVC) produces the "International Valuation Standards."

18 For those interested in the differences within Europe, the European Mortgage Federation in 2009 produced a study titled "EMF Study on the Valuation of Property for Lending Purposes." It analyzes 16 separate European markets according to a number of criteria, including the regulatory framework, methods, and the training of valuers.

19 An excellent reference on differences in appraisal practices across countries can be found in *Real Estate Valuation in Global Markets*, 2nd edition, edited by Howard Gelbtuch, MAI, and published by the Appraisal Institute in 2011.

Exhibit 11   *Continued*

Country	Valuation Framework	Valuation Approaches	Lease Structure and Rent Reviews	Landlord vs. Tenant Expense Responsibility	Globalization
United Kingdom	Royal Institution of Chartered Surveyors (RICS) *Red Book*	Sales Comparison and Cost Approaches, Implicit Capitalization	Recently changed from 25 years to 10, 15 years 5-year upward only	Landlord: minimal Tenant: all repairs, insurance	DCF used as an analysis tool and widely used in international investments/ valuations
United States	Universal Standards of Professional Appraisal Practice (USPAP)	Sales Comparison and Cost Approaches, Implicit Capitalization, DCF	3-, 5-year terms 10+ years Upon expiry	Depends on lease structure	DCF used extensively by institutional investors

11   INDICES

An investor will find a variety of real estate indices to choose from and may find one that seems representative of the market of interest to them. However, the investor should be aware of how the index is constructed and the inherent limitations resulting from the construction method. Investors should also be aware that the apparent low correlation of real estate with other asset classes may be due to limitations in real estate index construction.

11.1 Appraisal-Based Indices

Many indices rely on appraisals to estimate how the value of a portfolio of properties or the real estate market in general is changing over time. Real estate indices often rely on appraisals to estimate values because there usually are not sufficient transactions of the same property to rely on transactions to indicate value. Even though there may be real estate transactions occurring, it is not the same property; differences in sale prices (transaction prices) can be due to changes in the market or differences in the characteristics of the property (size, age, location, and so on). Appraisal-based indices combine valuation information from individual properties and provide a measure of market movements.

A well-known index that measures the change in values of real estate held by institutional investors in the United States is the NCREIF Property Index (NPI).[20] Members of NCREIF, who are investment managers and pension fund plan sponsors, contribute information on the appraised value along with the NOI, capital expenditures, and other information, such as occupancy, to NCREIF every quarter. This information is then used to create an index that measures the performance of these properties quarterly. The return for all the properties is calculated as follows:[21]

$$\text{Return} = \frac{\text{NOI} - \text{Capital expenditures} + (\text{Ending market value} - \text{Beginning market value})}{\text{Beginning market value}} \qquad (7)$$

---

20 See www.ncreif.org for further information. NCREIF provides a variety of indices based on different factors, such as property type and location.

21 The actual formula used by NCREIF differs slightly to capture the fact that the NOI and capital expenditures may occur throughout the quarter and not just at the very end. But the differences between the NPI calculation and the simplified formula shown in Equation 7 are not significant.

In Equation 7, the beginning and ending market values are based on the appraisals of the properties.

The return calculated with this formula is commonly known as the holding period return and is equivalent to a single-period IRR (the IRR if the property were purchased at the beginning of the quarter at its beginning market value and sold at the end of the quarter at its ending market value). A similar equation is used to calculate the returns on stocks and bonds, but in those cases an actual transaction price is typically used. Because this is not possible for real estate, the appraised value is used.

The above return is first calculated for each individual property and then value weighted to get the return for all properties in the index. An alternative would be to equal weight each property, but value weighing gives the return for the portfolio of properties because properties with more value do affect the portfolio more than properties with less value (and less income).

We saw earlier that taking the NOI and dividing by the beginning market value gives the cap rate for the property, which is also referred to as the income return for the property or for the index when it is for all properties. The remaining component in the equation ([Ending market value – Beginning market value – Capital expenditures]/Beginning market value) is referred to as the capital return. It is the change in value net of capital expenditures. To have a positive capital return, the value must increase by more than any funds invested in the property for capital expenditures. That is, replacing the roof may increase the market value but results in a positive rate of return only if the value increases by more than what was spent to replace the roof.

It should also be noted that the income return is not the same as cash flow because cash flow is calculated after capital expenditures. That is, the amount of cash flow available each quarter is NOI – Capital expenditures. Thus, we can also think of the total return in the above formula as measuring the cash flow (NOI – Capital expenditures) plus the change in value (Ending market value – Beginning market value).

Having an index like the one described above is important because it allows us to compare the performance of real estate with other asset classes, such as stocks and bonds. The quarterly returns are also important for measuring risk, which is often measured as the volatility or standard deviation of the quarterly returns. The index is also a benchmark to which the returns for individual funds can be compared. For example, an investment manager may have a fund of properties that a pension fund or wealthy investor has invested in, and the pension fund or investor may want to know if that investment manager has done better or worse than a benchmark that reflects how the broader market has performed.

Appraisal-based indices, such as the NCREIF Property Index, are also available in many other countries. Many of them are available from Investment Property Databank (IPD), which produces indices for 23 countries.[22] The IPD indices are calculated in a similar manner to the NPI.[23]

Example 27

Appraisal-Based Indices

Why are appraisals often used to create real estate performance indices?

---

[22] Australia, Austria, Belgium, Canada, Denmark, Finland, France, Germany, Ireland, Italy, Japan, South Korea, the Netherlands, New Zealand, Norway, Poland, Portugal, South Africa, Spain, Sweden, Switzerland, the United Kingdom, and the United States.
[23] See www.ipd.com for further information.

Solution:

Because properties do not transact very frequently, it is more difficult to create transaction-based indices as is done for publicly traded securities. Appraisal-based indices can be constructed even when there are no transactions by relying on quarterly or annual appraisals of the property. Of course when there are no transactions, it is also difficult for appraisers to estimate value.

11.2 Transaction-Based Indices

In recent years, indices have been created that are based on actual transactions rather than appraised values. These indices have been made possible by companies that collect information on enough transactions to create an index based only on transactions. In fact, both NCREIF and IPD have transaction information that can be used for this purpose. When creating a transaction-based index, the fact that the same property does not sell very frequently is still an issue. So, to develop an index that measures changes in value quarterly as discussed above for the appraisal index, the fact that there are different properties selling every quarter needs to be controlled for. Some econometric technique, usually involving a regression analysis, is used to address the issue and to create the index. There are two main ways this is done. One is to create what is referred to as a repeat sales index, and the other is to create what is referred to as a hedonic index.

A repeat sales index, as the name implies, relies on repeat sales of the same property. A particular property may sell only twice during the entire period of the index. But if there are at least some properties that have sold each quarter, the repeat sales regression methodology can use this information to create an index. Of course, the more sales, the more reliable is the index. In general, the idea of this type of index is that, because it is the same property that sold twice, the change in value between the two sale dates indicates how market conditions have changed over time. The regression methodology allocates this change in value to each time period—that is, each quarter based on the information from sales that occurred that quarter. The details of how the regression works is beyond the scope of this reading. An example of a repeat sales index for commercial real estate in the United States is the Moody's REAL index.[24]

A hedonic index does not require repeat sales of the same property. It requires only one sale. The way it controls for the fact that different properties are selling each quarter is to include variables in the regression that control for differences in the characteristics of the property, such as size, age, quality of construction, and location. These independent variables in the regression reflect how differences in characteristics cause values to differ so that they can be separated from the differences in value due to changes in market conditions from quarter to quarter. Again, the details of this regression are beyond the scope of this reading. The point is that there are ways of constructing indices that are based only on transactions. But they require a lot of data and are usually most reliable at the national level for the major property types, but sometimes they are reliable at the regional level of a country if sufficient transactions are available.

Example 28

Transaction-Based Indices

Describe two main ways of creating transaction-based indices.

---

24 See www.realindices.com for further information.

Solution:

The two main ways are (1) a repeat sales index and (2) a hedonic index. A repeat sales index requires repeat sales of the same property; because it is the same property, controls for differences in property characteristics, such as its size and location, are not required. A hedonic index requires only one sale of a property and thus can usually include more properties than a repeat sales index, but it must control for "hedonic" characteristics of the property, such as its size and location.

11.3 Advantages and Disadvantages of Appraisal-Based and Transaction-Based Indices

All indices, whether appraisal- or transaction-based, have advantages and disadvantages. Appraisal-based indices are often criticized for having appraisal lag, which results from appraised values tending to lag when there are sudden shifts in the market. In an upward market, transaction prices usually start to rise first, and then as these higher prices are reflected in comparable sales and investor surveys, they are captured in appraised values. Thus, appraisal-based indices may not capture the price increase until a quarter or more after it was reflected in transactions. The same lag would also occur in a down market, with appraised values not falling as soon as transaction prices. Another cause of appraisal lag is that all properties in an appraisal-based index may not be appraised every quarter. A manager may assume the value has stayed the same for several quarters until he or she goes through the appraisal process to estimate a new value. This causes a lag in the index. That being said, if the investment managers are all using appraised values to measure returns and if the index is based on appraised values, then it is an "apples to apples" comparison.

If the purpose of the index is for comparison with other asset classes that are publicly traded, however, appraisal lag is more of an issue. Appraisal lag tends to "smooth" the index, meaning that it has less volatility. It behaves somewhat like a moving average of what an index would look like if it were based on values obtained from transactions rather than appraisals. Thus, appraisal-based indices may underestimate the volatility of real estate returns. Because of the lag in appraisal-based real estate indices, they will also tend to have a lower correlation with other asset classes. This is problematic if the index is used in asset allocation models to determine how much of a portfolio should be allocated to real estate versus other asset classes. The allocation to real estate would likely be overestimated.

There are two general ways of adjusting for the appraisal lag. The first is to "unsmooth" the appraisal-based index. Several techniques have been developed to do this, although they are beyond the scope of this reading. In general, these techniques attempt to adjust for the appraisal lag; the resulting unsmoothed index will have more volatility and more correlation with other asset classes. The second way of adjusting for the appraisal lag is to use a transaction-based index when comparing real estate with other asset classes.

Transaction-based indices tend to lead appraisal-based indices for the reasons discussed above but can be noisy (that is, they include random elements in the observations) because of the need to use statistical techniques to estimate the index. So, there may be upward or downward movements from quarter to quarter that are somewhat random even though in general (viewed over a year or more) the index is capturing the correct movements in the market. The challenge for those creating these indices is to try to keep the noise to a minimum through use of appropriate statistical techniques and collecting as much data as possible.

Example 29

Comparing Appraisal-Based and Transaction-Based Indices

What are the main differences between the performance of appraisal-based and transaction-based indices?

Solution:

An appraisal-based index will tend to have less volatility and lag a transaction-based index, resulting in a lower correlation with other asset classes being reported for an appraisal-based index.

12   PRIVATE MARKET REAL ESTATE DEBT

Thus far, our focus has been on analyzing a property without considering whether there would be debt financing on the property or it would be purchased on an all-cash basis. This is because the way a property is financed should not affect the property's value. This does not mean that the overall level of interest rates and availability of debt in the market do not affect values. It means that, for a given property, the investor paying all cash should be paying the same price as one who decides to use some debt financing. Of course, investors who do use debt financing will normally expect to earn a higher rate of return on their equity investment. This is because they expect to earn a greater return on the property than what they will be paying the lender. Thus, there will be positive financial leverage. By borrowing money, the investor is taking on more risk in anticipation of a higher return on equity invested. The risk is higher because with debt there will be more uncertainty as to what return the investor will actually earn on equity because the investor gets what is left over after paying the lender. A small drop in property value can result in a large decrease in the investor's return if a high amount of debt was used to finance the property. When a property is valued without explicitly considering financing, the discount rate can be thought of as a weighted average of the rate of return an equity investor would want and the interest rate on the debt.

The maximum amount of debt that an investor can obtain on commercial real estate is usually limited by either the ratio of the loan to the appraised value of the property (loan to value or LTV) or the debt service coverage ratio (DSCR), depending on which measure results in the lowest loan amount. The debt service coverage ratio is the ratio of the first-year NOI to the loan payment (referred to as debt service for commercial real estate). That is,

$$\text{DSCR} = \text{NOI/Debt service} \tag{8}$$

The debt service includes both interest and principal payments on the mortgage. The principal payments are the portion of the loan payment that amortizes the loan over the loan term. An "interest-only" loan would be one that has no principal payments, so the loan balance would remain constant over time. Interest-only loans typically either revert to amortizing loans at some point or have a specified maturity date. For example, an interest-only loan might be made that requires the entire balance of the loan to be repaid after 7–10 years (referred to as a "balloon payment"). Lenders typically require a DSCR of 1.2 or greater to provide a margin of safety that the NOI from the property can cover the debt service.

Example 30

Loans on Real Estate

A property has been appraised for $5 million and is expected to have NOI of $400,000 in the first year. The lender is willing to make an interest-only loan at an 8 percent interest rate as long as the loan-to-value ratio does not exceed 80 percent and the DSCR is at least 1.25. The balance of the loan will be due after seven years. How much of a loan can be obtained?

Solution:

Based on the loan-to-value ratio, the loan would be 80 percent of $5 million or $4 million. With a DSCR of 1.25, the maximum debt service would be $400,000/1.25 = $320,000. This amount is the mortgage payment that would result in a 1.25 DSCR for an interest-only loan.

If the loan is interest only, then we can obtain the loan amount by simply dividing the mortgage payment by the interest rate. Therefore, the loan amount would be $320,000/0.08 = $4,000,000.

In this case, we obtain the same loan amount based on either the LTV or DSCR requirements of the lender. If one ratio had resulted in a lower loan amount, that would normally be the maximum that could be borrowed.

When financing is used on a property, equity investors often look at their first-year return on equity or "equity dividend rate" as a measure of how much cash flow they are getting as a percentage of their equity investment. This is sometimes referred to as a "cash-on-cash" return because it measures how much cash they are receiving as a percentage of the cash equity they put into the investment.

Example 31

Equity Dividend Rate

Using the information in Example 30, what is the equity dividend rate or cash-on-cash return assuming the property is purchased at its appraised value?

Solution:

The first-year cash flow is the NOI less the mortgage payment.

NOI	$400,000
DS	$320,000
Cash flow	$80,000

The amount of equity is the purchase price less the loan amount.

Price	$5,000,000
Mortgage	$4,000,000
Equity	$1,000,000

The equity yield rate is the Cash flow/Equity = $80,000/$1,000,000 = 8%. Keep in mind that this is not an IRR that would be earned over a holding period until the property is sold. The equity investor does not share any of the price appreciation in the value of the property with the lender.

For loans called "participation" loans, the lender might receive some of the price appreciation, but it would be in exchange for a lower interest rate on the loan.

Example 32

Leveraged IRR

Refer to the previous examples 30 and 31. Suppose the property is sold for $6 million after five years. What IRR will the equity investor receive on his or her investment?

Solution:

The cash flow received by the equity investor from the sale will be the sale price less the mortgage balance, or $6 million – $4 million = $2 million. Using a financial calculator,

PV = –$1,000,000 (using a calculator, this is input as a negative to indicate the negative cash flow at the beginning of the investment)

PMT = $80,000

$n = 5$

FV = $2,000,000

Solve for i = 21.14%

This is an IRR based on the equity invested in the property.

Example 33

Unleveraged IRR

Refer to the previous examples 30, 31, and 32. What would the IRR be if the property were purchased on an all-cash basis (no loan)?

Solution:

Now the equity investor will receive all the cash flow from sale ($6 million) and the NOI ($400,000). The initial investment will be $5 million. Using a financial calculator,

PV = –$5,000,000

PMT = $400,000

$n = 5$

FV = $6,000,000

Solve for i = 11.20%

This is an IRR based on an unleveraged (all-cash) investment in the property. The difference between this IRR (11.20 percent) and the IRR the equity investor receives with a loan calculated in Example 32 of 21.14 percent reflects positive financial leverage. The property earns 11.20 percent before adding a loan, and the loan is at 8 percent, so the investor is benefiting from the spread between 11.20 percent and 8 percent.

SUMMARY

Real estate property is an asset class that plays a significant role in many investment portfolios. Because of the unique characteristics of real estate property, it tends to behave differently from other asset classes, such as stocks, bonds, and commodities, and thus has different risks and diversification benefits. Private real estate investments are especially unique because the investments are not publicly traded and require different analytic techniques from publicly traded assets. Because of the lack of transactions, the appraisal process is required to value real estate property. Many of the indices and benchmarks used for private real estate also rely on appraisals, and because of this characteristic, they behave differently from indices for publicly traded assets, such as the S&P 500.

The factors that affect the performance of private real estate investments tend to be similar across countries, and the methods for valuing real estate property tend to be similar. Cross-border investment is facilitated by the development of standardized ways of analyzing real estate and by responses to the demand for transparency and sufficient data to do the necessary due diligence. As the availability of real estate data improves along with the technology to analyze the data, real estate markets are likely to become more efficient.

Key points of the reading include the following:

- Real estate investments make up a significant portion of the portfolios of many investors.

- Real estate investments can occur in four basic forms: private equity (direct ownership), publicly traded equity (indirect ownership claim), private debt (direct mortgage lending), and publicly traded debt (securitized mortgages).

- Each of the basic forms of real estate investment has its own risks, expected returns, regulations, legal structures, and market structures.

- There are many motivations for investing in real estate income property. The key ones are current income, price appreciation, inflation hedge, diversification, and tax benefits.

- Equity investors generally expect a higher rate of return than lenders (debt investors) because they take on more risk. The returns to equity real estate investors have two components: an income stream and a capital appreciation. Adding equity real estate investments to a traditional portfolio will potentially have diversification benefits because of the less-than-perfect correlation of equity real estate returns with returns to stocks and bonds. If the income stream can be adjusted for inflation and real estate prices increase with inflation, then equity real estate investments may provide an inflation hedge.

- Debt investors in real estate expect to receive their return from promised cash flows and typically do not participate in any appreciation in value of the underlying real estate. Thus, debt investments in real estate are similar to other fixed-income investments, such as bonds.

- Regardless of the form of real estate investment, the value of the underlying real estate property can affect the performance of the investment. Location is a critical factor in determining the value of a real estate property.

- Real estate property has some unique characteristics compared with other investment asset classes. These characteristics include heterogeneity and fixed location, high unit value, management intensiveness, high transaction costs, depreciation, sensitivity to the credit market, illiquidity, and difficulty of value and price determination.

- There are many different types of real estate properties in which to invest. The main commercial (income-producing) real estate property types are office, industrial and warehouse, retail, and multi-family. There are other types of commercial properties, which are typically classified by their specific use.

- There are risk factors common to commercial property, but each property type is likely to have a different susceptibility to these factors. The key risk factors that can affect commercial real estate include business conditions, lead time for new development, cost and availability of capital, unexpected inflation, demographics, lack of liquidity, environmental issues, availability of information, management expertise, and leverage.

- Location, lease structures, and economic factors, such as employment growth, economic growth, consumer spending, and population growth, affect the value of each property type.

- An understanding of the lease structure is important when analyzing a real estate investment.

- Appraisals estimate the value of real estate income property. Definitions of value include market value, investment value, value in use, and mortgage lending value.

- Generally, three different approaches are used by appraisers to estimate value: income, cost, and sales comparison.

- The income approach includes direct capitalization and discounted cash flow methods. Both methods focus on net operating income as an input to the value of a property.

- The cost approach estimates the value of a property based on adjusted replacement cost. This approach is typically used for unusual properties for which market comparables are difficult to obtain.

- The sales comparison approach estimates the value of a property based on what comparable properties are selling for in the current market.

- Due diligence investigates factors that might affect the value of a property. These factors include leases and lease history; operating expenses; environmental issues; structural integrity; lien, ownership, and property tax history; and compliance with relevant laws and regulations.

- Appraisal-based and transaction-based indices are used to track the performance of private real estate. Appraisal-based indices tend to lag transaction-based indices and appear to have lower volatility and lower correlation with other asset classes than transaction-based indices.

- When debt financing is used to purchase a property, additional ratios and returns calculated and interpreted by debt and/or equity investors include the loan-to-value ratio, the debt service coverage ratio, the equity dividend rate (cash-on-cash return), and leveraged and unleveraged internal rates of return.

PRACTICE PROBLEMS FOR READING 38

The following information relates to Questions 1 - 12[1]

Amanda Rodriguez is an alternative investments analyst for a U.S. investment management firm, Delphinus Brothers. Delphinus' Chief Investment Officer, Michael Tang, has informed Rodriguez that he wants to reduce the amount invested in traditional asset classes and gain exposure to the real estate sector by acquiring commercial property in the United States. Rodriguez is to analyze potential commercial real estate investments for Delphinus Brothers. Selected data on three commercial real estate properties is presented in Exhibit 1.

Exhibit 1	**Selected Property Data**		
	Property #1	**Property #2**	**Property #3**
Property Type	**Downtown Office Building**	**Grocery-Anchored Retail Center**	**Multi-Family Building**
Location	New York, NY	Miami, FL	Boston, MA
Occupancy	90.00%	93.00%	95.00%
Square Feet or Number of Units	100,000 sf	205,000 sf	300 units
Gross Potential Rent	$4,250,000	$1,800,000	$3,100,000
Expense Reimbursement Revenue	$330,000	$426,248	$0
Other Income (includes % Rent)	$550,000	$15,000	$45,000
Potential Gross Income	$5,130,000	$2,241,248	$3,145,000
Vacancy Loss	($513,000)	($156,887)	($157,250)
Effective Gross Income	$5,079,000	$2,084,361	$2,987,750
Property Management Fees	($203,160)	($83,374)	($119,510)
Other Operating Expenses	($2,100,000)	($342,874)	($1,175,000)
Net Operating Income (NOI)	$2,775,840	$1,658,113	$1,693,240

Rodriguez reviews the three properties with Tang, who indicates that he would like her to focus on Property #1 because of his prediction of robust job growth in New York City over the next ten years. To complete her analysis, Rodriquez assembles additional data on Property #1, which is presented in Exhibits 2, 3 and 4.

As part of the review, Tang asks Rodriguez to evaluate financing alternatives to determine if it would be better to use debt financing or to make an all cash purchase. Tang directs Rodriguez to inquire about terms with Richmond Life Insurance Company, a publicly traded company, which is an active lender on commercial real estate property. Rodriquez obtains the following information from Richmond Life for a loan on Property #1: loan term of 5 years, interest rate of 5.75% interest-only, maximum loan to value of 75%, and minimum debt service coverage ratio of 1.5x.

---

[1] This item set was developed by Mark Bhasin, CFA (New York, USA).

Exhibit 2	6-Year Net Operating Income (NOI) and DCF Assumptions for Property #1

	Year 1	Year 2	Year 3	Year 4	Year 5	Year 6
NOI	$2,775,840	$2,859,115	$2,944,889	$3,033,235	$3,124,232	$3,217,959

DCF Assumptions	
Investment Hold Period	5 years
Going-In Cap Rate	5.25%
Terminal Cap Rate	6.00%
Discount Rate	7.25%
Income/Value Growth Rate	Constant

Exhibit 3	Sales Comparison Data for Property #1

Variable	Property 1	Sales Comp A	Sales Comp B	Sales Comp C
Age (years)	10	5	12	25
Condition	Good	Excellent	Good	Average
Location	Prime	Secondary	Secondary	Prime
Sale price psf		$415 psf	$395 psf	$400 psf
Adjustments				
Age (years)		-10%	2%	10%
Condition		-10%	0%	10%
Location		15%	15%	0%
Total Adjustments		**-5%**	**17%**	**20%**

Exhibit 4	Other Selected Data for Property #1
Land Value	$7,000,000
Replacement Cost	$59,000,000
Total Depreciation	$5,000,000

After reviewing her research materials, Rodriguez formulates the following two conclusions:

Conclusion 1   Benefits of private equity real estate investments include owners' ability to attain diversification benefits, to earn current income, and to achieve tax benefits.

Conclusion 2   Risk factors of private equity real estate investments include business conditions, demographics, the cost of debt and equity capital, and financial leverage.

1. Which of the following is *least likely* accurate regarding Property #2 described in Exhibit 1?

    A. Operating expense risk is borne by the owner.

    B. The lease term for the largest tenant is three years.

    C. There is a significant amount of percentage rent linked to sales levels.

2. Based upon Exhibits 2, 3 and 4, which of the following statements is *most* accurate regarding the valuation of Property #1?

    A. The cost approach valuation is $71,000,000.

    B. The adjusted price psf for Sales Comp B is $423 psf.

    C. The terminal value at the end of year 5 in the income approach is $53,632,650.

3. Based on Exhibit 2, the growth rate of Property #1 is *closest* to:

    A. 0.75%

    B. 1.25%.

    C. 2.00%.

4. Based on Exhibit 2, the value of Property #1 utilizing the discounted cash flow method is *closest* to:

    A. $48,650,100.

    B. $49,750,900.

    C. $55,150,300.

5. Based on Exhibit 2, relative to the estimated value of Property #1 under the discounted cash flow method, the estimated value of Property #1 using the direct capitalization method is:

    A. equal.

    B. lower.

    C. higher.

6. Based upon Exhibits 1 and 3, the estimated value of Property #1 using the sales comparison approach (assigning equal weight to each comparable) is *closest* to:

    A. 40,050,000.

    B. 40,300,000.

    C. 44,500,000.

7. In the event that Delphinus purchases Property #2, the due diligence process would *most likely* require a review of:

    A. all tenant leases.

    B. tenant sales data.

    C. the grocery anchor lease.

8. Compared to an all-cash purchase, a mortgage on Property #1 through Richmond Life would *most likely* result in Delphinus earning:

    A. a lower return on equity.

    B. a higher return on equity.

    C. the same return on equity.

9. Assuming an appraised value of $48,000,000, Richmond Life Insurance Company's maximum loan amount on Property #1 would be *closest* to:

    A. $32,000,000.

    B. $36,000,000.

    C. $45,000,000.

10. Rodriguez's Conclusion 1 is:

   A. correct.

   B. incorrect, because tax benefits do not apply to tax-exempt entities.

   C. incorrect, because private real estate is highly correlated to stocks.

11. Rodriguez's Conclusion 2 is:

   A. correct.

   B. incorrect, because inflation is not a risk factor.

   C. incorrect, because the cost of equity capital is not a risk factor.

12. Richmond Life Insurance Company's potential investment would be *most likely* described as:

   A. private real estate debt.

   B. private real estate equity.

   C. publicly traded real estate debt.

The following information relates to Questions 13 - 28[2]

First Life Insurance Company, Ltd., a life insurance company located in the United Kingdom, maintains a stock and bond portfolio and also invests in all four quadrants of the real estate market; private equity, public equity, private debt, and public debt. Each of the four real estate quadrants has a manager assigned to it. First Life intends to increase its allocation to real estate. The Chief Investment Officer (CIO) has scheduled a meeting with the four real estate managers to discuss the allocation to real estate and to each real estate quadrant. Leslie Green, who manages the private equity quadrant, believes her quadrant offers the greatest potential and has identified three investment properties to consider for acquisition. Selected information for the three properties is presented in Exhibit 1.

Exhibit 1	Selected Information on Potential Private Equity Real Estate Investments		
	Property		
	A	**B**	**C**
Property description	**Single Tenant Office**	**Shopping Center**	**Warehouse**
Size (square meters)	3,000	5,000	9,000
Lease type	Net	Gross	Net
Expected loan to value ratio	70%	75%	80%
Total economic life	50 years	30 years	50 years
Remaining economic life	30 years	23 years	20 years
Rental income (at full occupancy)	£575,000	£610,000	£590,000
Other income	£27,000	£183,000	£29,500
Vacancy and collection loss	£0	£61,000	£59,000
Property management fee	£21,500	£35,000	£22,000
Other operating expenses	£0	£234,000	£0

---

2 This item set was developed by Karen O'Connor Rubsam, CFA (Phoenix, AZ USA).

Exhibit 1	**Continued**		

	Property		
	A	**B**	**C**
Property description	**Single Tenant Office**	**Shopping Center**	**Warehouse**
Discount rate	11.5%	9.25%	11.25%
Growth rate	2.0%	See Assumption 2	3.0%
Terminal cap rate		11.00%	
Market value of land	£1,500,000	£1,750,000	£4,000,000
Replacement costs			
■ Building costs	£8,725,000	£4,500,000	£12,500,000
■ Developer's profit	£410,000	£210,000	£585,000
Deterioration – curable and incurable	£4,104,000	£1,329,000	£8.021,000
Obsolescence			
■ Functional	£250,000	£50,000	£750,000
■ Locational	£500,000	£200,000	£1,000,000
■ Economic	£500,000	£100,000	£1,000,000
Comparable adjust price per square meter			
■ Comparable Property 1	£1,750	£950	£730
■ Comparable Property 2	£1,825	£1,090	£680
■ Comparable Property 3	£1,675	£875	£725

To prepare for the upcoming meeting, Green has asked her research analyst, Ian Cook, for a valuation of each of these properties under the income, cost and sales comparison approaches using the information provided in Exhibit 1, and the following two assumptions:

Assumption 1   The holding period for each property is expected to be five years.

Assumption 2   Property B is expected to have the same net operating income for the holding period due to existing leases, and a one-time 20% increase in year 6 due to lease rollovers. No further growth is assumed thereafter.

In reviewing Exhibit 1, Green notes the disproportionate estimated obsolescence charges for Property C relative to the other properties and asks Cook to verify the reasonableness of these estimates. Green also reminds Cook that they will need to conduct proper due diligence. In that regard, Green indicates that she is concerned whether a covered parking lot that was added to Property A encroaches (is partially located) on adjoining properties. Green would like for Cook to identify an expert and present documentation to address her concerns regarding the parking lot.

In addition to discussing the new allocation, the CIO informs Green that she wants to discuss the appropriate real estate index for the private equity real estate quadrant at the upcoming meeting. The CIO believes that the current index may result in over-allocating resources to the private equity real estate quadrant.

13. The *most* effective justification that Green could present for directing the increased allocation to her quadrant would be that, relative to the other quadrants, her quadrant of real estate investments:

   A. provides greater liquidity.

   B. requires less professional management.

   C. enables greater decision-making control.

14. Relative to the expected correlation between First Life's portfolio of public REIT holdings and its stock and bond portfolio, the expected correlation between First Life's private equity real estate portfolio and its stock and bond portfolio is *most likely* to be:

   A. lower.

   B. higher.

   C. the same.

15. Which of the properties in Exhibit 1 exposes the owner to the greatest risk related to operating expenses?

   A. Property A

   B. Property B

   C. Property C

16. Which property in Exhibit 1 is *most likely* to be affected by import and export activity?

   A. Property A

   B. Property B

   C. Property C

17. Which property in Exhibit 1 would *most likely* require the greatest amount of active management?

   A. Property A

   B. Property B

   C. Property C

18. Which property in Exhibit 1 is *most likely* to have a percentage lease?

   A. Property A

   B. Property B

   C. Property C

19. The disproportionate charges for Property C noted by Green are *least likely* to explicitly factor into the estimate of property value using the:

   A. cost approach.

   B. income approach.

   C. sales comparison approach.

20. Based upon Exhibit 1, which of the following statements regarding Property A is *most* accurate?

   A. The going-in capitalization rate is 13.5%.

   B. It appears the riskiest of the three properties.

   C. The net operating income in the first year is £298,000.

21. Based upon Exhibit 1, the value of Property C using the direct capitalization method is *closest* to:

   A. £3,778,900.

    B. £4,786,700.

    C. £6,527,300.

22. Based upon Exhibit 1 and Assumptions 1 and 2, the value of Property B using the discounted cash flow method, assuming a five-year holding period, is *closest* to:

    A. £4,708,700.

    B. £5,035,600.

    C. £5,050,900.

23. Which method under the income approach is *least likely* to provide a realistic valuation for Property B?

    A. Layer method

    B. Direct capitalization method

    C. Discounted cash flow method

24. Based upon Exhibit 1, the value of Property A using the cost approach is *closest* to:

    A. £5,281,000.

    B. £6,531,000.

    C. £9,385,000.

25. Based upon Exhibit 1, the value of Property B using the sales comparison approach is *closest* to:

    A. £4,781,000.

    B. £4,858,000.

    C. £6,110,000.

26. Which due diligence item would be *most* useful in addressing Green's concerns regarding Property A?

    A. Property survey

    B. Engineering inspection

    C. Environmental inspection

27. The real estate index currently being used by First Life to evaluate private equity real estate investments is *most likely:*

    A. an appraisal-based index.

    B. a transaction-based index.

    C. the NCREIF property index.

28. Based upon Exhibit 1, the property expected to be most highly leveraged is:

    A. Property A

    B. Property B

    C. Property C

SOLUTIONS FOR READING 38

1. B is correct. The lease term for the anchor tenant is typically longer than the usual 3 to 5 year term for smaller tenants. The data in Exhibit 1 suggest that the operating expenses are passed on to the tenant; the sum of Property Management Fees and Other Operating Expenses equal the Expense Reimbursement Revenue. Also, Other Income is only $15,000 suggesting that there is a minimal amount of percentage rent linked to sales thresholds.

2. C is correct. The terminal value using the income approach is $53,632,650 (= Year 6 NOI / terminal cap rate = $3,217,959 / 0.06). The value of the property using the cost approach is $61,000,000 (= Land Value + Building Replacement Cost – Total Depreciation = $7,000,000 + $59,000,000 – $5,000,000). The adjusted sales price per square foot for Sales Comp B is $462 psf (= $395 x 1.17).

3. C is correct. There is a constant growth rate in income and value; growth rate = discount rate (7.25%) – going-in cap rate (5.25%) = 2.00%.

4. B is correct. The value of Property 1 using the discounted cash flow method is $49,750,931, or $49,750,900 rounded, calculated as follows:

		Discount period	Discounted value*
Year 1 NOI	$2,775,840	1	$2,588,196
Year 2 NOI	$2,859,119	2	$2,485,637
Year 3 NOI	$2,944,889	3	$2,387,135
Year 4 NOI	$3,033,235	4	$2,292,540
Year 5 NOI	$3,124,232	5	$2,201,693
Terminal Value**	$53,632,650	5	$37,795,731
Property #1 DCF value			$49,750,932

* Discount rate = 7.25%
** The terminal value = Year 6 NOI/terminal cap rate = $3,217,959 / 0.06 = $53,632,650

5. C is correct. The direct capitalization method estimate of value for Property #1 is $52,873,143 (= Year 1 NOI / Going-in Cap Rate = $2,775,840 / 0.0525), which is greater than the estimated DCF value of $49,750,932.

Value of Property #1 under the discounted cash flow method:

		Discount period	Discounted value*
Year 1 NOI	$2,775,840	1	$2,588,196
Year 2 NOI	$2,859,119	2	$2,485,637
Year 3 NOI	$2,944,889	3	$2,387,135
Year 4 NOI	$3,033,235	4	$2,292,540
Year 5 NOI	$3,124,232	5	$2,201,693
Terminal Value**	$53,632,650	5	$37,795,731
Property #1 DCF value			$49,750,932

* Discount rate = 7.25%
** The terminal value = Year 6 NOI/terminal cap rate = $3,217,959 / 0.06 = $53,632,650

6. C is correct. The estimate of the value of Property #1 using the sales comparison approach is:

	Unadjusted psf	**Adjusted psf**
Sales Comp 1	$415	$394 (= $415 x 0.95)
Sales Comp 2	$395	$462 (= $395 x 1.17)
Sales Comp 3	$400	$480 (= $400 x 1.20)
Average	$403	$445

Estimated Value of Property #1 = $44,500,000 (= $445 psf x 100,000 sf)

7. C is correct. The due diligence process includes a review of leases for major tenants which would include the grocery anchor tenant. Typically, only major tenant leases will be reviewed in the due diligence process, and smaller tenant leases will likely not be reviewed. Also, the fact that Other Income is only $15,000 suggests that percentage rent linked to sales levels is minimal and has not been underwritten in the valuation and acquisition process.

8. B is correct. Delphinus will expect to earn a higher return on equity with the use of a mortgage to finance a portion of the purchase. The quoted mortgage interest rate of 5.75% is less than the discount rate of 7.25%.

9. A is correct. The maximum amount of debt that an investor can obtain on commercial real estate is usually limited by either the ratio of the loan to the appraised value of the property (loan to value or LTV) or the debt service coverage ratio (DSCR) depending on which measure results in the lowest loan amount. The maximum LTV is 75% of the appraised value of $48,000,000 or $36,000,000. The loan amount based on the minimum DSCR would be $32,183,652 determined as follows:

Maximum debt service = Year 1 NOI / DSCR = $2,775,840 / 1.5 = $1,850,560

Loan amount (interest only loan) = maximum debt service / mortgage rate = $1,850,560 / 0.0575 = $32,183,652 (rounded to $32,000,000).

10. A is correct. Benefits of private equity real estate investments include owners' ability to attain diversification benefits, to earn current income, and to achieve tax benefits.

11. A is correct. Business conditions, demographics, the cost of debt and equity capital, and financial leverage are characteristic sources of risk for real estate investments.

12. A is correct. Richmond Life's investment would be a mortgage which falls under private debt on the four quadrants.

13. C is correct. Private equity investments in real estate enable greater decision-making control relative to real estate investments in the other three quadrants. A private real estate equity investor or direct owner of real estate has responsibility for management of the real estate, including maintaining the properties, negotiating leases and collecting rents. These responsibilities increase the investor's control in the decision-making process. Investors in publicly traded REITs or real estate debt instruments would not typically have significant influence over these decisions.

14. A is correct. Evidence suggests that private equity real estate investments have a lower correlation with stocks and bonds than publicly traded REITs. When real estate is publicly traded it tends to behave more like the rest of the stock market than the real estate market.

15. B is correct. Property B is a gross lease, which requires the owner to pay the operating expenses. Accordingly, the owner, First Life, incurs the risk of Property B's operating expenses, such as utilities, increasing in the future.

16. C is correct. Property C is a warehouse, and is most likely affected by import and export activity in the economy. Property A (office) and Property B (retail) would typically be less dependent on import and export activity when compared to a warehouse property.

17. B is correct. Property B is a shopping center and would most likely require more active management than a single tenant office (Property A) or a warehouse (Property C); the owner would need to maintain the right tenant mix and promote the facility.

18. B is correct. Property B is a shopping center, a type of retail property. A percentage lease is a unique aspect of many retail leases, which requires the tenant to pay additional rent once their sales reach a certain level. The lease will typically specify a "minimum rent" that must be paid regardless of the tenant's sales. Percentage rent may be paid by the tenant once the tenant's sales reach a certain level or breakpoint.

19. B is correct. Obsolescence charges reduce the value of a property using the cost approach and are factored into the sales comparison approach by adjustments, including condition and location, to the price per square foot. The cash flows to the property should reflect obsolescence; less rent is received if the property is not of an appropriate design for the intended use, is in a poor location, or if economic conditions are poor. Therefore, obsolescence is implicitly, not explicitly, factored into the estimate of property value using the income approach.

20. B is correct. Property A has been assigned the highest discount rate (11.5%) and thus is considered to be the riskiest investment of the three alternatives. This may be because of the reliance on a single tenant. The going-in capitalization rate is 9.5% (cap rate = discount rate – growth rate). The net operating income (noi) is £580,500 (= rental income + other income – property management fee = £575,000 + £27,000 – £21,500).

21. C is correct. Under the direct capitalization method, the value of the property = NOI / (r – g).

Calculate net operating income (NOI):

> NOI = rental income + other income – vacancy and collection loss – property management costs

> NOI = £590,000 + £29,500 – £59,000 – £22,000 = £538,500

Then, value the property using the cap rate:

> Value of property = £538,500 / (11.25% – 3.0%) = £6,527,273, rounded to £6,527,300.

22. B is correct. The value of Property B using the discounted cash flow method is £5,035,600.

The value using the discounted cash flow method is based on the present value of the net operating income (NOI) and the estimated property resale price.

Calculate NOI (constant during five-year holding period from Assumption 2)

> NOI = rental income (at full occupancy) + other income – vacancy and collection loss – property management fee – other operating expenses

> NOI = £610,000 + £183,000 – £61,000 – £35,000 – £234,000 = £463,000

Estimate property value at end of five years:

> NOI starting in year 6 is 20% higher due to lease rollovers (from Assumption 2)

> NOI starting in year 6 = £463,000 x 1.20 = £555,600

Terminal cap rate (given) = 11%

> Applying the terminal cap rate yields a property value of £5,050,909 (= £555,600 / 0.11)

Find the present value of the expected annual NOI and the estimated property resale value using the given discount rate of 9.25%:

> N = 5

> FV = £5,050,909

> PMT = £463,000

> I = 9.25

Solving for PV, the current value of the property is estimated to be £5,034,643, or £5,034,600 rounded.

23. B is correct. The net operating income for Property B is expected to be level for the next 5 years, due to existing leases, and grow 20% in year 6. A direct capitalization method would not be appropriate due to the multiple growth rates. A discounted cash flow method that assigns a terminal value, or a layer method, should be used.

24. A is correct. The value of Property A using the cost method is equal to the replacement cost, adjusted for the different types of depreciation (loss in value):

> Value of Property A = land value + (replacement building cost + developer's profit) – deterioration – functional obsolescence – locational obsolescence – economic obsolescence = £1,500,000 + (£8,725,000 + £410,000) – £4,104,000 – £250,000 – £500,000 – £500,000 = £5,281,000

25. B is correct. The value of a property using the sales comparison approach equals the adjusted price per square meter using comparable properties times property size. The value of Property B using the sales comparison approach is:

> Average adjusted price per square meter of comparable properties 1, 2 and 3 for Property B = (£950 + £1,090 + £875) / 3 = £971.67

> Applying the £971.67 average adjusted price per square meter to Property B gives a value of £4,858,300 (= £971.67 x 5,000 square meters = £4,858,350, or £4,858,000 rounded).

26. A is correct. A property survey can determine whether the physical improvements, such as the covered parking lot, are in the boundary lines of the site and if there are any easements that would affect the value of the property.

27. A is correct. An appraisal-based index is most likely to result in the over-allocation mentioned by the CIO due to the appraisal lag. The appraisal lag tends to "smooth" the index meaning that it has less volatility. It behaves somewhat like a moving average of what an index would look like if based on values obtained from transactions rather than appraisals. Thus, appraisal-based indices may underestimate the volatility of real estate returns. Because of the lag in the index, appraisal-based real estate indices will also tend to have a

lower correlation with other asset classes. This is problematic if the index is used in asset allocation models; the amount allocated to the asset class that appears to have lower correlation with other asset classes and less volatility will be greater than it should be.

28. C is correct. Property C has an expected loan to value ratio of 80%, which is higher than the loan to value ratio for Property A (70%) or Property B (75%).

Publicly Traded Real Estate Securities

by Anthony Paolone, CFA, Ian Rossa O'Reilly, CFA, and David Kruth, CFA

LEARNING OUTCOMES

Mastery	The candidate should be able to:
☐	**a** describe types of publicly traded real estate securities;
☐	**b** explain advantages and disadvantages of investing in real estate through publicly traded securities;
☐	**c** explain economic value determinants, investment characteristics, principal risks, and due diligence considerations for real estate investment trust (REIT) shares;
☐	**d** describe types of REITs;
☐	**e** justify the use of net asset value per share (NAVPS) in REIT valuation and estimate NAVPS based on forecasted cash net operating income;
☐	**f** describe the use of funds from operations (FFO) and adjusted funds from operations (AFFO) in REIT valuation;
☐	**g** compare the net asset value, relative value (price-to-FFO and price-to-AFFO), and discounted cash flow approaches to REIT valuation;
☐	**h** calculate the value of a REIT share using net asset value, price-to-FFO and price-to-AFFO, and discounted cash flow approaches.

INTRODUCTION   1

This reading provides an overview of the publicly traded real estate securities, focusing on equity real estate investment trusts (REITs) and their valuation.

Real estate investments may play several roles in a portfolio. Investment in commercial real estate property—also called income-producing, rental, or investment property—may be either in the form of direct ownership investment or indirect investment by means of equity securities. They can provide an above-average current yield compared with other equity investments and may provide a degree of protection against inflation, especially when rental rates are inflation-indexed, rise periodically by pre-determined amounts, or are easily adjusted. Real estate investment can be an effective means of diversification in many investment portfolios.

REITs are the most widely held type of real estate equity security. The valuation of REITs is similar in some respects to the valuation of other kinds of equity securities, but also takes into account unique aspects of real estate and sometimes uses specialized measures. This reading introduces and describes REIT valuation.

The reading is organized as follows: Section 2 provides an overview of publicly traded real estate securities. Section 3 describes publicly traded equity REITs in detail, including their structure, investment characteristics, and analysis and due diligence considerations. Section 4 presents real estate operating companies (REOCs). Sections 5, 6, and 7 present net asset value, relative valuation, and discounted cash flow valuation for REIT shares, respectively. After a mini case study in Section 8, Section 9 summarizes the reading.

2 TYPES OF PUBLICLY TRADED REAL ESTATE SECURITIES

Publicly traded real estate securities fall into two principal categories: equity (i.e., ownership) investments in properties and debt investments (i.e., primarily mortgages secured by properties). Globally, the principal types of publicly traded real estate securities are real estate investment trusts, real estate operating companies, and mortgage-backed securities.

- **Real estate investment trusts** (REITs) are tax-advantaged entities (companies or trusts) that typically own, operate, and—to a limited extent—develop income-producing real estate property (hereafter, "real estate property" may simply be referred to as "real estate"). Such REITs are called equity REITs. Mortgage REITs make loans secured by real estate. REITs' tax-advantage is a result of being allowed to deduct dividends paid; this deduction effectively makes REITs exempt from corporate income tax.

- **Real estate operating companies** (REOCs) are ordinary taxable real estate ownership companies. Businesses are organized as REOCs, as opposed to REITs, when they are located in countries that do not have a tax-advantaged REIT regime in place or when they engage to a large extent in the development of real estate properties, often with the intent to sell. The primary cash inflows are from sales of developed or improved properties rather than from recurring lease or rental income.

- **Mortgage-backed securities** (MBS) are asset-backed securitized debt obligations that represent rights to receive cash flows from portfolios of mortgage loans—mortgage loans on commercial properties in the case of commercial mortgage-backed securities (CMBS) and mortgage loans on residential properties in the case of residential mortgage-backed securities (RMBS). The market capitalization of publicly traded real estate equity securities is greatly exceeded by the market value of real estate debt securities, in particular mortgage-backed securities. Real estate debt securities are discussed further in fixed-income readings in the CFA program curriculum.

In addition to publicly traded real estate securities, there are privately held real estate securities that include private REITs and REOCs, privately held mortgages, private debt issues, and bank debt. Exhibit 1 shows how real estate securities may be classified in four quadrants.

Exhibit 1	Types of Real Estate Securities	
	Public	**Private**
Equity	Equity REITs, REOCs	Private REITs, Private REOCs
Debt	Mortgage REITs, CMBS, RMBS	Mortgages, Private debt, Bank debt

As of the end of September 2011, the market value of publicly traded real estate investment trusts and real estate operating companies globally was approximately US$800 billion, whereas the total face value of residential and commercial mortgage-related securities was approximately US$9 trillion. Details about relative sizes by geographic areas and/or security types are shown in Exhibit 2.

Exhibit 2	Relative Size and Composition of Publicly Traded Real Estate Equity Securities Markets As of 30 September 2011

Panel A: Percentage of market value of publicly traded real estate equity securities (REITs and REOCs) in developed markets

By Region		By Country	
North America	50	United States	44.4
Asia	35	Hong Kong	11.7
Europe	15	Japan	10.2
		Australia	8.4
		United Kingdom	5.5
		Canada	5.3
		Singapore	4.2
		France	3.9
		Switzerland	1.4
		Netherlands	1.3
		Sweden	1.1
		Others	2.6

Panel B: Percentage of market value of publicly traded equity real estate equity securities in developed markets by type of structure

	Global	North America	Europe	Asia
REITs	74	97	68	43
Non-REITs, REOCs	26	3	32	57

Source: Based on data from FTSE EPRA/NAREIT

Publicly traded real estate securities typically retain some of the characteristics of direct ownership of income-producing real estate. Income-producing real estate usually provides relatively predictable, recurring, contractual rental income under the terms of lease agreements. It also tends to generate capital appreciation over the long term (provided there are no major distortions to rental markets from over-building) because the replacement cost of buildings and prices for land tend to increase. Capital appreciation can result from general price inflation, the scarcity of well-located property, local population increases, and/or growth in economic activity. It should be noted, however, that changes in discount rates (the required rate of return of property investors) can also have significant effects on the value of income-producing real estate.

As an investment asset class, income-producing real estate offers the advantages of stability of income based on its contractual revenue from leases and a measure of long-term inflation protection because, over the long term, rents tend to rise with inflation. In the United States over the past 30 years (1980–2010), the FTSE NAREIT All Equity REITs Index achieved a compounded annual total return of 11.9 percent compared with 10.7 percent for the S&P 500 Index and 8.9 percent for the Barclays Capital Aggregate Bond Index. The U.S. Consumer Price Index increased an average of 3.2 percent annually over the period.

The relative stability of income from income-producing real estate also permits substantial financial leverage to be used, typically in the form of mortgage debt (i.e., debt secured by a lien on real property as collateral). Use of financial leverage can enhance rates of return on equity capital when, on an after-tax basis, the rate of return on assets exceeds the interest rate on the mortgage. The ability, however, to use above-average financial leverage brings greater risk.

3   PUBLICLY TRADED EQUITY REITS

Most REITs are **equity REITs** that invest in ownership positions in income-producing real estate. Equity REITs seek to grow cash flows from their owned real estate, to expand ownership through investing in additional properties, and to selectively develop, improve, or redevelop properties.

Publicly traded equity REITs are the focus of this reading.[1] Other REIT types include mortgage REITs and hybrid REITs. **Mortgage REITs** are REITs that invest the bulk (typically 75 percent or more) of their assets in interest-bearing mortgages, mortgage securities, or short-term loans secured by real estate. The total market value of mortgage REITs is relatively small in comparison with equity REITs. **Hybrid REITs** are REITs that own and operate income-producing real estate, as do equity REITs, but invest in mortgages as well. There are relatively few hybrid REITs.

3.1 Market Background

For many decades, real estate equities have represented significant parts of European (notably the United Kingdom) stock markets, whereas real estate development and ownership has featured prominently in the diversified activities of a large number of Asian companies, notably in Hong Kong and Singapore. Real estate equities, although introduced earlier in the U.S. market, did not gain a large representation in U.S. equity markets until after the severe commercial property collapse of the early 1990s. That collapse left many properties either in financially troubled developer/investor hands or in foreclosure. Many such properties were securitized successfully as REITs, exploiting the conservative operating policies mandated by the REIT structure (especially the reliance on contractual rental income) and the conservative financial policies demanded by REIT investors, as discussed in Section 3.3.

---

1 Besides publicly traded REITs, private REITs exist. **Private REITs** are similar to equity REITs in their business model but do not trade on active exchanges. Private REITs are generally sponsored by real estate organizations and have limited liquidity. They are bought by institutional investors or are marketed to small investors by financial planners.

HISTORICAL DEVELOPMENT OF REITS

U.S. REITs, which have provided a model for REIT legislation worldwide, can trace their origins to business trusts formed in Boston, Massachusetts, in the mid-nineteenth century, when the wealth created by the industrial revolution led to increasing demand for real estate investments. State laws at the time prevented a corporation from owning real estate other than that required for its business. The so-called "Massachusetts trust" was the first U.S. legal entity created to specifically permit investment in real estate. It provided for the transfer of shares, limited liability for passive investors, elimination of federal taxation at the trust level, and the retention of specialized management. The structure became less desirable because of changes in tax laws in the first half of the twentieth century, but was revived by the U.S. Congress in 1960. By the early 1970s, a substantial portion of U.S. REITs' assets was concentrated in high risk construction and development loans. Banks, thrifts, and insurance companies could not directly engage in such high-yield lending because of regulations and statutory restrictions, but they did so indirectly by sponsoring publicly funded REITs that bore their names. But poor lending practices, high leverage, and conflicts of interest between banks and their REIT subsidiaries, as well as the effects of an economic recession, a real estate downturn, and changes in tax laws combined to generate numerous developer bankruptcies and a major decline in the number of REITs and their assets. Record high interest rates caused a severe contraction in the real estate industry in the early 1980s. It was not until the early 1990s, after another even more severe commercial property collapse, that REITs became the securitization vehicle of choice in moving property ownership from distressed owners into the better capitalized hands of long-term, income-oriented investors.

From 1990 to 1995, the equity market capitalization of U.S. REITs rose from US$8.5 billion to US$56 billion and the number of REITs almost doubled to 223. As of early 2011, the U.S. REIT industry consists of about 150 REITs with an equity capitalization of approximately US$350 billion.

REITs are important in a number of markets outside the United States. Beginning in the early 1990s, Canada had a significant increase in equity REITs. As of 2011, there are approximately 30 REITs in Canada with a market capitalization of C$38 billion. The REIT structure was introduced in Australia in 1971; as of 2011, there are 70 A-REITs with a market capitalization of over A$100 billion. REITs have been introduced in Japan (J-REITs in 2001), Singapore (S-REITs in 2002), Hong Kong (2005), the United Kingdom (2006), and Germany (G-REITs in 2007). In Brazil, REITs (called Fundos de Investimento Imobiliaro, or FIIs) have existed since 1993 but were first accorded exemption from income taxation in 2006 if owned by individual investors and listed on the stock exchange. The first REIT in the United Arab Emirates was formed in Dubai in 2010. As of early 2011, there are about 30 countries with legislation authorizing REITs.

REIT-type legislation is currently being studied in China, India, and Pakistan. In China, the planned large-scale introduction of REITs has been delayed by the financial crisis of 2007–2009 and government controls on the real estate industry. As a result of their strong growth since the early 1990s, REITs now represent the majority of the available publicly traded real estate equity securities in the world by number and market value.

As shown in Exhibit 3, REIT ownership in the United States—the largest market for REITs in the world—is widely diversified by type of investor.

Exhibit 3	Estimated Ownership of U.S. REITs by Type of Investor
Type of Investor	**Percent**
Index funds	25
Individual investors	15

(continued)

| Exhibit 3 | Continued |

Type of Investor	Percent
REIT sector dedicated funds	15
Pension funds	10
Insiders (managements, boards)	5
Other institutional investors (e.g., stock funds, income funds, hedge funds)	30

Source: J.P. Morgan estimates.

3.2 REIT Structure

REITs can have simple structures in which they hold and operate their properties directly; however, REITs are generally structured to facilitate the tax-efficient acquisition of properties. Umbrella partnership REITs (UPREITs) and DOWNREITs are examples of structures in which partnerships hold REIT properties; the structures have the purpose of avoiding recognition of taxable income if appreciated property is transferred to the REIT. In the United States, most REITs are structured as **UPREITs**, under which the REIT has a controlling interest in and serves as the general partner (with responsibility for operations) of a partnership that owns and operates all or most of the properties.[2] A **DOWNREIT** structure is a variation of the UPREIT under which the REIT owns more than one partnership and may own properties at both the REIT level and the partnership level. A DOWNREIT can form partnerships for each property acquisition it undertakes.

REITs are subject to the same regulatory, financial reporting, disclosure, and governance requirements as other public companies.

3.3 Investment Characteristics

REITs are typically exempt from income taxation at the corporate (or trust) level if a specified majority of their income and assets relate to income-producing property (75 percent or more, depending on the country) and all or virtually all their potentially taxable income is distributed to shareholders (or unit holders). REITs are a tax-efficient conduit for cash flows from rental income. In the United States, REIT distributions to shareholders are classified for tax purposes into ordinary income (taxed at investors' top marginal tax rates); return of capital (the portion of distributions in excess of a REIT's earnings, treated as a return of capital and deducted from the investor's share cost basis for tax purposes); and capital gains (qualifying for lower capital gains tax rates).

The investment characteristics of both public and private REITs generally include the following:

■ Exemption from income taxes at the corporate/trust level: REITs are typically required to distribute most of their potentially taxable income to gain exemption from corporate taxation.

■ High income distributions: As a result of the distribution requirement, dividend yields are typically significantly higher than the yields on most other publicly traded equities. Exhibit 4 shows representative historic yields for REITs, stocks, and bonds in the United States.

---

2 An UPREIT offers partnership-limited units (convertible into REIT units) to property sellers who do not pay capital gains taxes on their sale of property until they convert their limited-partnership units into REIT shares. Advantages to a property seller, in addition to tax deferral, include diversification, greater liquidity, and professional management.

| Exhibit 4 | Historic Yields on S&P U.S. REIT Index, S&P 500 Index, and 10-year U.S. Treasury Bonds |

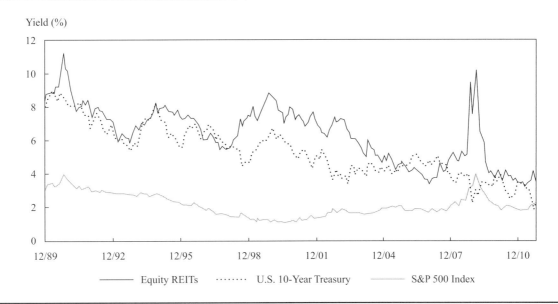

- Relatively low volatility of reported income: As a result of REIT regulations that require income to be predominantly from rents and interest, REITs typically use conservative, rental-property-focused business models. The contractual nature of rental income (with the exception of hotel REITs) results in relatively stable revenue streams.

- More frequent secondary equity offerings compared with industrial companies: As a result of the distribution requirement, REITs may not be able to retain earnings to finance growth and may need to issue equity to finance property acquisitions. REIT investors should be ready to evaluate the merits of these acquisitions and related financings.

As a result of these features, REITs are relatively stable savings, retirement, and income-producing investments. Compared with direct investments in income-producing property, REITs offer much greater ease of ownership in both small and large amounts, greater liquidity, and opportunities for broader diversification.

3.3.1 Advantages of Publicly Traded Equity Real Estate Securities

Compared with owning private real estate assets, publicly traded equity real estate securities, whether equity REITs or REOCs, offer the following advantages:

- *Greater liquidity*: The ability to trade shares on stock exchanges provides greater liquidity than is available in buying and selling real estate in property markets. Thus, such securities permit greater flexibility in timing the realization of cash values and gains/losses. By comparison, direct investments in real estate and in real estate partnerships are generally less immediately liquid and have greater transaction costs even where property markets are quite active and highly sophisticated. These contrasts result from the fact that property transactions are large in relation to average stock market transactions, involve unique properties, and require considerably more time to complete because of the need to negotiate the terms of the transaction and to conduct due diligence (which may include financial, legal, and environmental considerations).

- *Lower investment requirements*: Shares that represent fractional interests in REITs or REOCs can be bought with a much lower investment than a single commercial property.

- *Limited liability*: Similar to shareholders of other public companies, REIT investors have no liability for the debts and obligations of the REITs in which they invest beyond their original capital investment. Other types of real estate investments, such as limited partnership interests, also can offer limited liability; however, some types of real estate investment (e.g., general partnership interests) can expose the investor to potential liability exceeding his or her original investment.

- *Access to superior quality and range of properties*: Certain institutional-quality properties are difficult to acquire because most owners (pension funds, private corporations, and REITs) hold them for the long term. Such properties include super-regional shopping malls, large, prominent ("trophy") office buildings, and to a limited extent, landmark luxury hotels. These properties can command superior demand and pricing compared with other properties, given their extremely attractive location, architecture, and/or quality of construction. Investors can gain access to such properties by purchasing the shares of REITs that own them.

- *Active professional management*: Direct real estate ownership demands real estate expertise or asset/property management skills. Investors in publicly traded real estate equity securities do not require such expertise or skills; investors in REITs and REOCs benefit from having their property interests actively managed on their behalf by professional managers and from having their business interests overseen and guided by boards of directors. The REITs' standards of operating and financial efficiency benefit from the scrutiny and influence of public investors, which encourages best practices on the part of management and boards. Despite the constraint of low-income retention rates, capable managements can still add value by careful specialization by property type and region; by efficient operations focusing on maximizing rental rates and occupancies and minimizing operating costs; by property enhancements, refinancing, sales, and reinvestments; and/or by selected new development activity and property acquisitions financed on attractive terms with debt and/or equity.

- *Diversification*: By investing in REITs, investors can diversify their real estate portfolios by geography and property type. Such diversification is hard to achieve in direct property investing because of the typically large size and value of each property.

In addition, REITs tend to offer additional advantages compared with publicly traded REOCs:

- *Taxation*: REITs are typically exempt from the double taxation of income that comes from taxes being due at the corporate level and again when dividends or distributions are made to shareholders, as is the case in some jurisdictions such as the United States. In most jurisdictions, there are no taxes payable by a REIT if it: (1) meets certain requirements for types of assets held, typically rental property (75 percent of total assets in real estate for U.S. REITs), (2) derives the bulk of its income from rents or mortgage interest on real estate (75 percent for U.S. REITs), (3) has limited non-rental property assets, and (4) pays out in dividends/distributions nearly all of its taxable income (at least 90 percent in the United States). The dividends/distributions that REIT shareholders receive are typically divided into ordinary taxable income, capital gains, and return of capital, and are taxed at their respective rates in the first two cases. REIT shareholders do not have to pay current income tax on the portion of distributions that exceeds the REIT's taxable income (calculated after depreciation charges) because that portion of distributions is treated as a return of capital, which is deducted from the shareholders' cost basis for his/her shares. When the shares are eventually sold, the excess of the amount received over the cost basis of the shares is taxed as capital gains. This treatment of portions of their distributions as return of capital is generally favorable for investors from a tax perspective.

- *Earnings predictability*: The contractual nature of REITs' rental income tends to give them a greater degree of earnings predictability than that of most industrial and natural resource companies.

- *High income payout ratios and yields*: The typically high income payout ratios of REITs make them among the most stable and highest yielding of publicly traded equities.

REOCs have the following advantage compared with REITs:

- *Operating flexibility*: REOCs are free to invest in any kind of real estate or related activity subject only to the limitations that may be imposed by their articles of incorporation and/or the market. This flexibility gives management the opportunity to allocate more resources to development activity, which has the potential of delivering high returns. Compared with REITs, REOCs can retain more of their income for re-investment when they believe attractive opportunities exist to create value for investors. REOCs are free to use a wider range of capital structures and degrees of financial leverage in their activities.

In contrast with REOCs, REITs are constrained in their investments, operations, and distributions; these constraints may prevent REITs from maximizing their returns.

Example 1

Advantages of Publicly Traded Real Estate Investments

1. Which of the following assets requires the *most* expertise in real estate on the part of the investor?

    A. A REOC share

    B. An equity REIT share

    C. A direct investment in a single property

2. Which of the following has the *most* operating and financial flexibility?

    A. A REOC

    B. An equity REIT

    C. A direct investment in a single property

Solution to 1:

C is correct. Direct investment in a single property requires a high level of real estate expertise. Investment in publicly traded equity investments (in REITs or REOCs) requires much less expertise because investors benefit from having their property interests actively managed on their behalf by professional managers and from having their business interests overseen and guided by boards of directors, as in the case of all public corporations.

> ### Solution to 2:
>
> A is correct. REOCs are free to invest in any kind of real estate or related activity without limitation. This freedom gives management the opportunity to create more value in development activity and in trading real estate and to retain as much of their income as they believe is appropriate. A wider range of capital structures and degrees of financial leverage may be used in the process. In contrast with REOCs, REITs face restrictions on the amount of income and assets accounted for by activities other than collecting rent and interest payments. Direct investment is less liquid and divisible than REOC and REIT shares, which limits the operational flexibility of such investment.

3.3.2 Disadvantages of Publicly Traded Equity Real Estate Securities

Potential disadvantages of publicly traded real estate securities include those related to the following:

- *Taxation*: Although REITs are typically tax-advantaged compared with generic common share investment, direct property investment has tax advantages compared with both REIT and REOC investing. Unlike direct property ownership and partnership investments in some countries, REITs and REOCs generally cannot pass on tax losses to their investors as deductions from their taxable income. Also, in jurisdictions permitting deferral of tax when a property investment is exchanged or sold and replaced by similar property within a short period of time (e.g., the 180-day "Section 1031 Like-Kind Exchange" rule in the United States), REIT shares do not qualify for such tax-deferred exchanges.

- *Control*: Minority shareholders in a publicly traded REIT have less control over property-level investment decisions than do direct property owners.

- *Costs*: The maintenance of a publicly traded REIT structure is costly and may not be recouped by offsetting benefits if the REIT lacks sufficient economies of scale or the value added by management is small.

- *Stock market determined pricing and returns*: The stock market value of a REIT is more volatile than the appraised **net asset value** of a REIT, suggesting risk is lower for direct property investors. But net asset values based on appraised values rather than actual transaction prices tend to underestimate volatility.[3] Appraised values tend to be backward-looking by nature (because of typically being based on the sales price of comparable property transactions that have already closed) and may not react to changes in market trends. Additionally, there is a psychological tendency to smooth valuations by ignoring outlier transactions.

- *Structural conflicts and related costs*: The use of UPREIT and DOWNREIT structures can create conflicts of interest between the partnership and REIT shareholders when it comes to making decisions on the disposition of properties or increasing company debt levels and may involve additional

---

3 Appraised values are based on a range of considerations including recent market prices for comparable property sales (assuming willing buyers and willing sellers were involved), discounted cash flow analysis, and **depreciated replacement cost**. Property appraisal is discussed in the reading on private real estate investment.

administrative costs. For example, the disposition of a particular property or the use of more mortgage debt financing might have tax implications for the limited partners who sold the property to the operating partnership and tax considerations could cause their interests to vary from the best interests of the REIT as a whole.

- *Relatively moderate income growth potential*: The relatively low rate of income retention by REITs implies a low rate of reinvestment for future growth. This low rate of reinvestment tends to reduce income growth potential. Relatedly, the stock market's tendency to focus on earnings growth can cause REIT shares to underperform in periods during which the market highly values fast-growing companies; such periods tend to coincide with time of high consumer, business, and investor confidence.

- *Potential for forced equity issuance at disadvantageous prices*: REITs typically use financial leverage and are regularly in the debt markets to refinance their maturing debt. If a REIT's management of its overall financial leverage and the timing and type of its debt maturities is flawed, these issues can combine with a lack of substantial retained cash flow to force equity issuance at dilutive prices, especially during periods of weak credit availability (e.g., 2008–2009). Note that timely debt and equity financing and share repurchase activity if market prices fall below intrinsic values, using the retained portion of operating cash flows or the proceeds of debt issuance or property sales, can yield benefits to remaining REIT shareholders.

Example 2

Publicly Traded Real Estate Investments

1. Which of the following types of real estate investment is *most* appropriate for an investor seeking to maximize control?

   A. REIT

   B. REOC

   C. Direct investment in income-producing property

2. Which of the following best represents an advantage of REITs over a direct investment in an income-producing property?

   A. Diversification

   B. Operating flexibility

   C. Income growth potential

Solution to 1:

C is correct. Control is most characteristic of a direct investment in and ownership of income-producing property.

Solution to 2:

A is correct. REITs provide diversification of property holdings. B is incorrect because REITs do face restrictions on the amount of income and assets accounted for by activities other than collecting rent and interest payments; these restrictions can prevent a REIT from maximizing its returns. C is incorrect because the relatively low rates of income retention that are required to maintain a REIT's tax-free status can detract from income growth potential.

Example 3

Investment Objectives

Two real estate investors are each choosing from among the following investment types: REOC, equity REIT, or a direct investment in an income-producing property. Investor A's primary objective is liquidity, and Investor B's primary objective is maximum growth/capital gain potential. State and explain which real estate investment type best suits:

1. Investor A.

2. Investor B.

Solution to 1:

For Investor A, with a liquidity objective, REOC and REIT investments are most appropriate because REOCs and REITs are traded on stock exchanges and are more liquid. Direct investments in income-producing property are generally less liquid.

Solution to 2:

For Investor B, with a maximum growth objective, REOCs and direct property investment are most appropriate because REOCs and direct investors are free to invest in any kind of real estate or related activity without limitation and to reinvest as much of their income as they believe is appropriate for their objectives. This freedom gives them the opportunity to create more value in development activity and in trading real estate. REITs' constraints prevent them from retaining earnings to reinvest, so their growth opportunities are more limited.

3.4 Considerations in Analysis and Due Diligence

For equity REITs as a group, key specific investment characteristics, opportunities, and risks should be assessed when conducting due diligence of their shares for investment purposes.

- *Remaining lease terms.* Short remaining lease terms provide mark-to-market opportunities on rents. They are a positive consideration in an expansionary economy and/or rental rate environment and a negative one in a declining economy and/or rental market. Hotels and multi-family residential properties have the shortest lease terms, whereas shopping centers, offices, and industrial buildings typically have the longest lease terms.

- *Inflation protection.* Leases that have pre-set periodic increases in rent throughout the lease term (or that have minimum or base rents linked to the local inflation rate) provide a degree of inflation protection for investors.

- *Market rent analysis.* Current market rents should be compared with rents paid by existing tenants. Low in-place rents provide upside potential to cash flows upon lease re-negotiation and high in-place rents represent additional risk to maintaining current cash flows.

- *Costs of re-leasing space.* Costs to lease space when a lease matures typically include brokerage commissions, allowances for tenants' improvements to their space, free rent, and downtime between leases. Such costs can be burdensome for landlords.

- *Tenant concentration.* Tenants that rent significant amounts of space and the percentage of rents paid by these significant tenants should be noted. Assessing the financial strength of significant tenants and the risk they pose to the REIT are important parts of necessary due diligence.

- *Availability of new competitive supply.* The potential for new competitive supply to the REIT's existing properties should be analyzed by examining new buildings under construction or planned by other developers and by assessing the likelihood of more projects gaining approval.

- *Balance sheet/leverage analysis.* A detailed review of the REIT's balance sheet, including leverage levels, cost of debt, and debt maturity profile should be completed.

- *Management.* Due diligence should include a review of senior management's background, skill sets, track records, years of experience, and length of time with the REIT.

The next section describes subtypes of equity REITs and any due diligence considerations that apply specifically to the subtypes.

3.5 Equity REITs: Property Subtypes

Equity REITs, the predominant form of REITs, are actively managed enterprises seeking to maximize the returns from their property portfolios by applying management skills in operations and finance. For this reason, most REITs focus on a particular property type, striving to excel in operating efficiency and growth while still being mindful of risk-reducing strategies, including diversification by geography and by the number and quality of properties and tenants. The analysis of equity REITs is conducted along the same lines as that of publicly traded equities in general: commencing with industry analysis, followed by company analysis, and then equity valuation. Certain specific economic value determinants, investment characteristics, risks, and areas for analysis and due diligence, apply to each property subtype of REITs shown in Exhibit 5.

Exhibit 5	**Global REITs by Property Type Held**
Property Type	**Percentage of Total**
Shopping center/Retail	23.3
Office	14.5
Residential	11.3
Healthcare	6.8
Hotel/Resort	2.7
Industrial	4.2
Industrial/Office	1.0
Self-storage	2.6
Diversified	33.6

The following sections discuss these property types in more detail.

3.5.1 *Shopping Center/Retail REITs*

Shopping center or **retail REITs** invest in such retail properties as regional shopping malls, community/neighborhood shopping centers, and to a lesser degree, premium retail space in leading cities.

Regional shopping malls are large spaces, often enclosed, in which retailing tends to be in higher-priced discretionary goods (e.g., fashionable clothing). Tenants' leases in regional malls usually have terms of 3–10 years and typically require tenants—except for the largest "anchor" retailers—to pay the greater of a fixed-minimum rental rate and a percentage of their sales. "Anchor" retailers, however, have very long-term, fixed-rent leases or own their premises. As part of their total rent under typical **net leases**, tenants pay a **net rent**, all of which goes to the landlord, plus a share of the common area costs of the mall based on their proportionate share of the space leased. Despite the link between tenants' sales and rent, revenue streams are relatively stable because of high levels of minimum rent that often represent well over 90 percent of revenue.

Community shopping centers—consisting of stores linked by open-air walkways or, in the case of so-called "power centers" or "big-box centers," linked by parking lots—generally provide such basic necessity goods and services as food and groceries, home furnishings, hardware, discount merchandise, fast food, and banking, with similar lease maturities but non-participatory rents that are usually subject to periodic increases.

For shopping center REITs, analysts often analyze such factors as rental rates and sales per square foot/meter for the rental property portfolio, dividing them into same portfolio and new space addition components.

3.5.2 *Office REITs*

Office REITs invest in and manage multi-tenanted office properties in central business districts of cities and suburban markets. Lease terms are typically long (5–25 years) with contractual base rents that are fixed and adjust upward (typically every 5–10 years). In addition to base rents, tenants pay their proportionate share of operating expenses, common area costs, and property taxes. Rental income tends to be stable year-to-year, but over the longer term (5–10 years) it can be affected by changes in office market vacancy and rental rates that characterize the office industry cycle. This cycle arises because of long office tower construction and interior finishing periods (three or more years) and the willingness of developers to build large buildings in which only a portion of the space has been preleased. These factors result in the commencement of construction of new space during periods of strong economic growth and the completion of new space potentially during economic downturns when tenant demand is low.

Analysts of office REITs pay particular attention to new space under construction in a REIT's local market, to site locations and access to public transportation and highways, and to business conditions for a REIT's principal tenants. Analysts also focus on the quality of a REIT's office space, focusing on such factor as location, convenience, utilitarian and architectural appeal, and the age and durability of the building.

3.5.3 *Industrial REITs*

Industrial REITs hold portfolios of single-tenant or multi-tenant industrial properties that are used as warehouses, distribution centers, light manufacturing facilities, and small office or "flex" space for sales, administrative, or related functions.

Industrial property and industrial REITs are less cyclical than some other property/REIT types including hotel, health care, and storage. The long-term net leases (5–25 years) that pertain to industrial space, the short time required to build industrial buildings (usually well under a year), and the tendency to build and prelease and/or build space to suit particular tenants dampen any rapid change of rental income and values.

Analysts pay particular attention to trends in tenants' requirements and the impact these can have on the obsolescence of existing space and the need for new types of space. Strategic property locations—such as near a port, airport, or highway—are important positive considerations. Shifts in the composition of national and local industrial bases and trade play important roles in this regard and can sometimes be difficult to detect and forecast. Trends in new supply and demand in the local market are closely scrutinized.

3.5.4 *Multi-family/Residential REITs*

Multi-family/residential REITs invest in and manage rental apartments for lease to individual tenants, typically using one-year leases. Rental apartment demand tends to be relatively stable, but fluctuations in rental income can occur as a result of competition from condominium construction, tenant (move-in) inducements, regional economic strengths and weaknesses, the effects of inflation on such operating costs as energy and other utility costs, and taxes and maintenance costs (because apartment leases often tend to be **gross leases** under which many or all of such costs are paid for by the landlord).

Analysts pay particular attention to local demographics and income trends, age and competitive appeal, cost and availability of homeownership in local markets, and the degree of government control of local residential rents. Fuel and energy costs receive particular attention because properties are usually leased under gross leases that require landlords to pay for part or all of the building operating costs.

3.5.5 Storage REITs

Storage REITs own and operate self-storage properties, sometimes referred to as mini-warehouse facilities. Space in these facilities is rented under gross leases (i.e., no additional payments are due for operating costs or property taxes), usually on a monthly basis by individuals for storing personal items and by small businesses. Ease of entry into this growing field has led to periods of overbuilding.

Analysts pay special attention to the rate of construction of new competitive facilities, trends in housing sales activity that can affect the demand for temporary storage, local demographic trends, new business start-up activity, and seasonal trends in demand for storage facilities that can be significant in some markets.

3.5.6 Health Care REITs

Health care REITs invest in skilled nursing facilities (nursing homes), assisted living and independent residential facilities for retired persons, hospitals, medical office buildings, and rehabilitation centers. In many countries, REITs are not permitted to operate these facilities themselves if they wish to maintain their REIT status and must lease them to health care providers; these leases are usually net leases. REITs may jeopardize their tax status (no tax at trust level) if they are found to be operating a business in violation of their passive investment restriction. Although largely resistant to the effects of economic recessions, health care REITs are exposed to the effects of population demographics, government funding programs for health care, construction cycles, the financial condition of health care facilities operators/lessees, and any costs arising from litigation by residents.

Analysts scrutinize operating trends in facilities, in government funding, in litigation settlements, and insurance costs. Amounts of competitors' new facilities under construction in relation to prospective demand and prospects for acquisitions are also key points of focus.

3.5.7 Hotel REITs

Hotel REITs own hotel properties but, similar to health care REITs, in many countries they must refrain from operating their properties themselves to maintain their tax-advantaged REIT status. Hotel REITs typically lease all their properties to taxable REIT subsidiaries (or to third-party lessees) who operate them ensuring the hotel REIT parent receives passive rental income. This rental income typically accounts for the major portion of a hotel's net operating cash flow. Management of the hotel is usually turned over to hotel management companies, many of which own widely recognized hotel brands. The net effect of this structure is that although the hotel REIT is tax exempt to the extent that it meets its income distribution and other REIT requirements, a minor portion of net operating cash flow from hotel properties may be subject to income taxation. The hotel sector is cyclical because it is not protected by long-term leases and is thus exposed to business-cycle driven short-term changes in regional, national, and international business and leisure travel. Exposure to travel disruptions also increases revenue volatility.

Analysts examine trends in occupancies, average room rates, and operating profit margins by hotel type and geographic location; statistics are compared with industry averages published by government and private-sector hotel industry statistics providers. Revenue per available room (RevPAR), the product of average room rate by average occupancy, is a widely monitored barometer of the hotel business. Attention is also paid to trends in hotel room forward bookings by category (individual, corporate, group, and convention), in food and beverage and banqueting sales, and in margins. Expenditures on maintaining and improving property, plant, and equipment are scrutinized, and the rates of new room construction and completion in local markets are watched very closely in view of the cyclicality of demand and the long duration of hotel construction (typically 1.5 to 3 years). Because income is so variable in this sector, analysts need to be wary of hotel REITs that use high financial leverage.

3.5.8 Diversified REITs

Diversified REITs own and operate in more than one type of property and are more common in Europe and Asia than in the United States. Some investors favor the reduced risk and wider opportunities that come from diversification. An analysis of management's experience with each property type and degree of local market presence are obviously important in reviewing diversified REITs.

3.6 Economic Drivers

Exhibit 6 shows major economic factors affecting REITs and their relative importance for different types of equity REITs. The measures of relative importance should be viewed as an approximate guide only because the relative importance can vary especially for extreme changes in the economic factors. Over the course of a full business cycle, however, the measures of relative importance shown tend to apply.

Risks tend to be greatest for those REITs in property-type sectors where tenant/occupant demand for space can fluctuate most widely in the short-term (notably hotels) and in which dislocations between supply and demand are most likely to occur (notably office, hotel, and health care). However, the quality and locations of properties held by a REIT, their leasing, and financing status are also extremely important factors in determining a REIT's risk profile.

Exhibit 6	Importance of Factors Affecting Economic Value for Various Property Types				
	National GDP Growth	Job Creation	Retail Sales Growth	Population Growth	New Space Supply vs. Demand
Retail	1	3	2	4	4
Office	1	2	5	4	3
Industrial	1	5	2	3	4
Multi-family	1	2	5	2	4
Storage	1	3	5	2	4
Health care	1	4	5	2	3
Hotels	1	2	5	4	3

Note: 1 = most important, 5 = least important
Source: Based on data from the authors' research

Growth in the economy or national GDP is generally the most important single economic factor affecting the outlook for all types of property and REITs. Retail sales growth is reflected in the sales growth of shopping center tenants and influences directly (through rental rates based on a percentage of sales) and indirectly (through tenants' ability to pay more rent and landlords' efforts to take advantage of this increase) the rental rates and occupancies in shopping centers.

Job creation tends to be reflected in increased demand for office space to accommodate white collar workers and in requirements for more retail space to cater to related increases in spending. Job creation also tends to be reflected in (1) increased demand for multi-family accommodation as newly employed people gain the financial means to rent their own accommodation, (2) greater hotel room demand as leisure and business travel increase in response to an expanded workforce, and (3) increased use of storage space as personal and small business needs for space rise.

Office, hotel, and health care properties and the REITs that invest in those property types are more prone to supply–demand dislocations because of (1) the long time taken to construct new space (space on which construction commences in a booming economy may be completed two or three years later, potentially during a recession) and (2) the large size of many facilities, which can contribute to excess supply on completion. Population growth tends to be reflected in increased demand for multi-family accommodations, storage, and health care facilities.

Example 4

REITs and Due Diligence

1. Which of the following statistics is similarly relevant for a shopping center, office, or hotel REIT?

   A. Occupancy

   B. Forward bookings

   C. Sales per square foot

2. Which of the following types of REITs is *least* directly sensitive to population growth?

   A. Office

   B. Health care

   C. Multi-family residential

3. In addition to the analysis of occupancy, rental rate, lease expiry, and financing statistics, analysts of office REITs are *most likely* to pay particular attention to trends in:

   A. job creation.

   B. population growth.

   C. retail sales growth.

4. Which of the following types of REITs would be expected to experience the *greatest* cash flow volatility?

   A. Hotel

   B. Industrial

   C. Shopping center

Solution to 1:

A is correct. Occupancy is a critical variable for all three types of REITs. Forward bookings would be relevant for only hotel REITs; sales per square foot for shopping center REITs.

Solution to 2:

A is correct. Population growth ranks as a less significant factor for office REITs and a more significant factor for health care and multi-family residential REITs. Different economic factors affect different property types to a varying degree, given their lease structures and competitive environment.

Solution to 3:

A is correct. Job creation is most significant for office REITs. Population growth is more significant for multi-family, storage, and health care REITs than for office REITs, as shown in Exhibit 6, whereas retail sales growth is more significant for shopping center/retail and industrial REITs than for office REITs.

Solution to 4:

A is correct. Hotel room demand fluctuates with economic activity; there are no long-term leases on hotel rooms to protect hotel REITs' revenue streams from changes in demand. Industrial and shopping center REITs benefit from long-term leases on their properties and from the relatively mild dislocations between supply and demand caused by the construction of new space in these sub-sectors.

4   REAL ESTATE OPERATING COMPANIES

Publicly traded real estate equities exist in forms other than REITs. **Real estate operating companies** (REOCs) are ordinary taxable corporations that operate in the real estate industry in countries that do not have a tax-advantaged REIT regime in place or are engaged in real estate activities of a kind and to an extent that do not fit within their country's REIT framework. Such ineligible activity generally takes the form of development or land investment in which the cash flows are not recurring income from lease revenues. Examples of such REOCs are

- Hongkong Land, a leading office investor and residential developer listed in Singapore (registered in Bermuda, part of Singapore Straits Times Index; this company left Hong Kong prior to the 1997 transfer to China),
- Brookfield Office Properties, an international office investor and property manager listed in Toronto and New York with a low income payout ratio, and
- China Vanke, China's largest residential property developer.

REOCs offer essentially the same advantages and disadvantages as REITs with respect to investing in real estate directly, but with some differences.

REITs and REOCs face similar operating and financial risks as private real estate investments, including leasing, operating, financing, and market risks as well as exposure to general economic risk. Despite certain advantages of REOCs, such as operating flexibility, the equity markets of most countries show a preference for the tax advantages, high-income distributions, and rigorous operating and financial mandates that come with REIT status. Consequently, in many markets there is a tendency for REOCs to experience less access to equity capital and lower market valuations (and higher cost of equity) than REITs. REOCs are usually able to elect to convert to REIT status if they meet the general requirements of REITs but, depending on their countries of domicile, must consider potential local tax consequences for themselves and their shareholders that may be triggered by the change.[4]

Example 5

REOCs

1. Which of the following statements is *most* accurate?

    A. REOCs are subject to the same tax rules as trusts.

    B. REOCs are subject to the same tax rules as ordinary corporations.

    C. REITs usually cannot elect to convert to REOCs without changing their income payout rates and sources of income.

2. Which of the following statements is *most* accurate? REOCs:

    A. can invest in any type of real estate without losing their tax status.

    B. are a more prevalent and popular investment asset class than REITs globally.

    C. do not pay any income taxes if they pay out all their taxable income to their shareholders.

Solution to 1:

B is correct. REOCs are taxed in the same way as ordinary corporations. A is not correct because REOCs are taxed as corporations; C is not correct because REITs do not need to change their income payout rates or sources of income to become REOCs.

Solution to 2:

A is correct. REOCs, unlike REITs, can generally invest in any type of real estate without losing their tax status. C is incorrect because REOCs do not enjoy such a tax advantage. B is incorrect because, as shown in Exhibit 2, REOCs globally represent less invested capital than REITs.

VALUATION: NET ASSET VALUE APPROACH 　5

Approaches analysts take to valuing equity include those based on asset value estimates, price multiple comparisons, and discounted cash flow. These general approaches are used to value shares of REITs and REOCs and will be addressed in Sections 5, 6, and 7, respectively.

Two possible measures of value that analysts might use are book value per share (BVPS) and net asset value per share (NAVPS) based on reported accounting values and market values for assets, respectively. NAVPS is the relevant valuation measure for valuing REITs and REOCs.

NAVPS is often used as a fundamental benchmark for the value of a REIT or REOC. Discounts in the REIT share price from NAVPS are interpreted as indications

---

4 Because their leverage is high and they can use accelerated depreciation, REOCs' cash tax liabilities are frequently relatively low.

of potential undervaluation, and premiums in the REIT share price to NAVPS, in the absence of indications of positive future events, such as a successful property development completion or expected high value creation by a management team, suggest potential overvaluation. By way of qualification, however, these assessments must be made in the context of the stock market's tendency to be forward looking in its valuations and at times to have different investment criteria from property markets.

The net asset value may be viewed as the largest component of the intrinsic value of a REIT or REOC, the balance being investors' assessments of the value of any non-asset-based income streams (e.g., fee or management income), the value added by management of the REIT or REOC, and the value of any contingent liabilities.[5]

Section 5.1 explains why BVPS can diverge from NAVPS; analysts need to understand in detail the accounting for REITs' investment properties in order to evaluate the relevance of accounting information. Section 5.2 then illustrates the estimation of NAVPS.

5.1 Accounting for Investment Properties

The value of the investment property portfolio of a REIT or REOC is a very important element in the valuation of its shares. Analysts should take care to understand the basis on which a REIT's investment properties are valued. If accounting is on a fair value basis, accounting values may be relevant for asset-based valuation. If historical cost values are used, however, accounting values are generally not relevant.

Investment property is defined under International Financial Reporting Standards (IFRS) as property that is owned (or, in some cases, leased under a finance lease) for the purpose of earning rentals or capital appreciation or both. Buildings owned by a company and leased to tenants are investment properties. In contrast, other long-lived tangible assets (i.e., property considered to be property, plant, and equipment) are owner-occupied properties used for producing the company's goods and services or for housing the company's administrative activities. Investment properties do not include long-lived tangible assets held for sale in the ordinary course of business. For example, the houses and property owned by a housing construction company are considered to be its inventory.

Under IFRS, companies are allowed to value investment properties using either a cost model or a fair value model. The cost model is identical to the cost model used for property, plant, and equipment. Under the fair value model, all changes in the fair value of the asset affect net income. To use the fair value model, a company must be able to reliably determine the property's fair value on a continuing basis. In general, a company must apply its chosen model (cost or fair value) to all of its investment property. If a company chooses the fair value model for its investment property, it must continue to use the fair value model until it disposes of the property or changes its use such that it is no longer considered investment property (e.g., it becomes owner-occupied property or part of inventory). The company must continue to use the fair value model for that property even if transactions on comparable properties, used to estimate fair value, become less frequent.

Investment property appears as a separate line item on the balance sheet. Companies are required to disclose whether they use the fair value model or the cost model for their investment property. If the company uses the fair value model, it must make additional disclosures about how it determines fair value and must provide reconciliation between the beginning and ending carrying amounts of investment property. If the company uses the cost model, it must make additional disclosures—for example,

---

5 The intrinsic value of an investment, as discussed in other parts of the CFA curriculum, is the value ascribed to an investment on the basis of a hypothetically complete understanding of its characteristics. It is generally estimated on a going-concern basis.

the depreciation method and useful lives must be disclosed. In addition, if the company uses the cost model, it must also disclose the fair value of investment property.

In contrast to IFRS, under U.S. generally accepted accounting principles (U.S. GAAP), there is no specific definition of investment property. Most operating companies and real estate companies in the United States that hold investment-type property use the historical cost accounting model. This model does not accurately represent the economic values of assets and liabilities or the current economic return or income to a business in environments of significant price and cost changes. This issue is especially evident in companies whose businesses involve the purchase and long-term retention of assets, notably real estate, because under historical cost accounting, assets including buildings are generally carried at depreciated historical cost. These figures can be written down when they undergo a permanent impairment in economic value, but they can only be written up under exceptional circumstances, such as mergers, acquisitions, or reorganizations. The historical cost accounting practices that prevail in regard to investment property assets in the United States, the largest market for REITs in the world, tend to distort the measure of economic income and asset value by understating carrying values on long-held property assets and overstating depreciation on assets that are often appreciating in value because of general price inflation or other property-specific reasons.

5.2 Net Asset Value Per Share: Calculation

As a result of shortcomings in accounting reported values, investment analysts and investors use estimates of **net asset value per share**. NAVPS is the difference between a real estate company's assets and its liabilities, *all taken at current market values instead of accounting book values*, divided by the number of shares outstanding. NAVPS is a superior measure of the net worth of a company compared with book value per share.

In valuing a REIT's or REOC's real estate portfolio, analysts will look for the results of existing appraisals if they are available (such as those provided by companies reporting under IFRS). If they are not available or if they disagree with the assumptions or methodology of the appraisals, analysts will often capitalize the rental streams—represented by net operating income (NOI)—produced by a REIT's or REOC's properties, using a market required rate of return. The market required rate of return, usually referred to as the **capitalization rate** or "**cap rate**," is the rate used in the marketplace in recent transactions to capitalize similar-risk future income streams into a present value. It is calculated as the NOI of a comparable property or portfolio of comparable properties divided by the total value of the comparable(s) as represented by transaction prices. Analysts will often seek to corroborate the property valuations obtained with price per square foot information on transactions involving similar types of properties, as well as replacement cost information (adjusted for depreciation and the age and condition of the buildings). These estimated asset values will be substituted for the book values of the properties on the balance sheet and adjustments made to any related accounting assets, such as capitalized leases, to avoid double counting.

Generally, goodwill, deferred financing expenses, and deferred tax assets will be excluded to arrive at a "hard" economic value for total assets. Liabilities will be similarly adjusted to replace the face value of debt with market values if these are significantly different (e.g., as a result of changes in interest rates) and any such "soft" liabilities as deferred tax liabilities will be removed. The revised net worth of the company divided by the number of shares outstanding is the NAV. Although this figure is calculated before provision for any income or capital gains taxes that might be payable on liquidation, the inability to predict how the company or its assets might be sold and the prospect that it might be kept intact in an acquisition cause investors to look to the pre-tax asset value as their primary net worth benchmark. If a company has held its assets for many years and has a very low remaining depreciable value for its assets for tax purposes, this can color investors' perspectives on valuation. Quantifying the effects of a low adjusted cost base, however, is impeded by lack of knowledge of the tax circumstances and strategies of a would-be acquirer.

Exhibit 7 provides an example of the calculations involved in estimating NAV based on capitalizing rental streams. Because the book values of assets are based on historical costs, the analyst estimates NAVPS. First, by capitalizing NOI with certain adjustments, the analyst obtains an estimate of the value of rental properties, then the value of other tangible assets is added and the total netted of liabilities. This net amount, NAV, is then divided by the number of shares outstanding to obtain NAVPS.

The second line in Exhibit 7 shows the adjustment to remove **non-cash rents**; these are the result of the accounting practice of "straight lining" the rental revenue from long-term leases. (The amount of this deduction is the difference between the average contractual rent over the leases' terms and the cash rent actually paid.) NOI is also increased to reflect a full year's rent for properties acquired during the course of the year, resulting in pro forma "cash NOI" for the previous 12 months of $267,299,000. This figure is then increased to include expected growth for the next 12 months at 1.5 percent, resulting in expected next 12-months cash NOI of $271,308,000.

An appropriate capitalization rate is then estimated based on recent transactions for comparable properties in the property market. An estimated value for the REIT's operating real estate is obtained by dividing expected next 12-months cash NOI by the decimalized capitalization rate (in this case, 0.07). The book values of the REIT's other tangible assets including cash, accounts receivable, land for future development, and prepaid expenses are added to obtain estimated gross asset value. (Land is sometimes taken at market value if this can be determined reliably; but because land is often difficult to value and of low liquidity, analysts tend to use book values.) From this figure, debt and other liabilities (but not deferred taxes because this item is an accounting provision rather than an economic liability) are subtracted to obtain net asset value. Division by the number of shares outstanding produces NAVPS.

Exhibit 7	Analyst Adjustments to REIT financials to obtain NAVPS

Office Equity REIT Inc.
Net Asset Value Per Share Estimate
(In Thousands, Except Per Share Data)

Last 12-months real estate NOI	$270,432
Less: Non-cash rents	7,667
Plus: Adjustment for full impact of acquisitions (1)	4,534
Pro forma cash NOI for last 12 months	$267,299
Plus: Next 12 months growth in NOI (2)	$4,009
Estimated next 12 months cash NOI	$271,308
Assumed cap rate (3)	7.00%
Estimated value of operating real estate	$3,875,829
Plus: Cash and equivalents	$65,554
Plus: Land held for future development	34,566
Plus: Accounts receivable	45,667
Plus: Prepaid/Other assets (4)	23,456
Estimated gross asset value	$4,045,072
Less: Total debt	$1,010,988

Exhibit 7	Continued	

Office Equity REIT Inc.
Net Asset Value Per Share Estimate
(In Thousands, Except Per Share Data)

Less: Other liabilities	119,886
Net asset value	$2,914,198
Shares outstanding	55,689

(1) 50 percent of the expected return on acquisitions was made in the middle of 2010.
(2) Growth is estimated at 1.5 percent.
(3) Cap rate is based on recent comparable transactions in the property market.
(4) This figure does not include intangible assets.

NAVPS is calculated to be $2,914,198 divided by 55,689 shares, which equals $52.33 per share.

5.3 Net Asset Value Per Share: Application

REITs have a relatively active private investment market for their business assets; namely, the direct investment property market. This market facilitates the estimation of a REIT's or REOC's net asset value: an estimate of the value of their underlying real estate if it were sold in the private market, debt obligations were satisfied, and the remaining capital—the net asset value—was distributed to shareholders. This approach is unique to REITs and REOCs because commercial real estate assets transact relatively frequently in the private market, and as a result an investor can make observations about how such properties trade on the basis of the capitalization rate (the rate obtained by dividing net operating income by total value) or on the basis of price per square foot, and apply these valuations to the assets of a public company. In fact, in the United States, it is estimated that only 10–15 percent of commercial real estate is held by publicly traded REITs, thus making the private market far larger than the public market, although less active. To draw a parallel, using a NAV approach to value REITs is much like using the sum-of-the-parts approach to valuing a company with multiple business lines.

The NAV approach to valuation is most often used by sector-focused real estate investors that view REITs and REOCs primarily as liquid forms of commercial real estate ownership. Value-oriented investors also tend to focus on NAV when stocks are trading at significant discounts to the underlying value of the assets. In addition, NAV analysis becomes particularly important when there is significant leveraged buyout (LBO) activity in the broader market. At such times, LBO sponsors attempt to buy REITs trading at large discounts to NAV to realize their underlying real estate value. Conversely, when REIT stocks trade at large premiums to NAV, IPO activity and stock issuance activity increases because the public markets are essentially ascribing more value to the real estate than the private markets are. Over time, REITs and REOCs in the United States and globally have at times traded at premiums-to-NAV of more than 25 percent and at other times at discounts from NAV exceeding 25 percent. Thus, if the NAV of a REIT were $20/share, the stock might trade as low as $15/share or as high as $25/share, depending on a range of factors.

5.3.1 Important Considerations in a NAV-Based Approach to Valuing REITs

Although NAV estimates provide investors with a specific value, there are a number of important considerations that should be taken into account when using this approach to value REITs and REOCs. First, investors must understand the implications of using a private market valuation tool on a publicly traded security. In this context, it is useful to examine how NAVs are calculated.

The methods most commonly used to calculate NAV are (1) using a capitalization rate or "cap rate" approach to valuing the NOI of a property or portfolio of properties; (2) applying value per square foot (or unit) to a property or portfolio of properties; and/or (3) using appraised values disclosed in the company's financial statements (permitted under IFRS but not hitherto or currently under U.S. GAAP).[6] An analyst may adjust these appraised values reported by the company if he or she does not agree with the underlying assumptions and if there is sufficient information to do so. In the first two instances, the cap rates and values per square foot are derived from observing transactions that have occurred in the marketplace. In contrast, most sophisticated direct purchasers of commercial real estate arrive at a purchase price after doing detailed forecasting of the cash flows they expect to achieve from owning and operating a specific property over their investment time horizon. These cash flows are then discounted to a present value or purchase price. Whatever that present value or purchase price is, an analyst can estimate value by dividing an estimate of NOI by the cap rate, essentially the required rate of current return for income streams of that risk. In addition, an analyst can take the present value or purchase price and divide by the property's rentable area for a value per square foot. The point is that cap rates and values per square foot result from a more detailed analysis and discounted cash flow process. The discount rate used by a private owner/operator of commercial real estate could be different from the discount rate used by investors purchasing shares of REITs.

NAV reflects the value of a REIT's assets to a private market buyer, which may or may not be the same as the value that public equity investors ascribe to the business. This fact is one of the reasons for the wide historical premium/discount range stocks trade at relative to NAV estimates. Another reason is that the stock market tends to focus more on the outlook for short-term future changes in income and asset value than the property market, which is more focused on long term valuation. As alluded to earlier, it is possible that REITs and REOCs can trade at some premium or discount to NAV until the premium/discount becomes wide enough for market forces to close the arbitrage gap.

Another factor to consider when using a NAV approach to REIT/REOC valuation is that NAV implicitly treats a company as an individual asset or static pool of assets. In reality, such treatment is not consistent with a going concern assumption. Management teams have different track records and abilities to produce value over time, assets can be purchased and sold, and capital market decisions can add or subtract value. An investor must thus consider how much value a management team can add to (or subtract from) current NAV. For instance, an investor may be willing to purchase REIT A trading at a 10 percent premium to NAV versus REIT B trading at a small discount to NAV because the management team of REIT A has a stronger track record and better opportunities to grow the NAV compared with REIT B, therefore justifying the premium at which REIT A trades relative to REIT B.

NAV estimates can also become quite subjective when property markets become illiquid and few transactions are observable, or when REITs and REOCs own hundreds of properties, making it difficult for an investor to estimate exactly how much the portfolio would be worth if the assets were sold individually. There may also be a large-portfolio premium in good economic environments when prospective strategic purchasers may be willing to pay a premium to acquire a large amount of desired property at once, or a large-portfolio discount when there are few buyers for the kind of property in question. In addition, such assets as undeveloped land, very large

---

6 At the time of this writing, U.S. GAAP requires property assets to be carried in financial statements at depreciated cost.

properties with few comparable assets, properties with specific uses, service businesses, and joint ventures complicate the process of estimating NAV with accuracy and confidence.

5.3.2 Further Observations on NAV

Among institutional investors, the most common view is that if REIT management is performing well in the sense of creating value, REITs and REOCs should trade at premiums to underlying NAVPS. The rationale is based on the following:

1. Investors in the stocks have liquidity on a day-to-day basis, whereas a private investor in real estate does not, thus warranting a lower required return rate (higher value) in the public market than the private market for the same assets.

2. The competitive nature of the public markets and size of the organizations should attract above-average management teams, which should produce better real estate operating performance and lead to better investment decisions than the average private real estate concern.

In conclusion, although NAV is by its nature an absolute valuation metric, in practice it is often more useful as a relative valuation tool. If all REITs are trading above NAV or below NAV, selecting individual REITs could become a relative exercise—that is, purchasing the REIT stock trading at the smallest premium to NAV when REITs are trading above NAV, or selling the REIT trading at the smallest discount to NAV when REITs are all trading at a discount to NAV. In practice, NAV is also used as a relative metric by investors looking at implied cap rates. To calculate the implied cap rate of a REIT or REOC, the current price is used in an NAV model to work backward and solve for the cap rate. By doing so, an investor looking at two similar portfolios of real estate could ascertain if the market is valuing these portfolios differently based on the implied cap rates.

VALUATION: RELATIVE VALUE (PRICE MULTIPLE) APPROACH

6

Conventional equity valuation approaches, including "market-based" or relative value approaches, are used with some adaptations to value REITs and REOCs. Such multiples as price-to-funds from operations (P/FFO), price-to-adjusted funds from operations (P/AFFO), and enterprise value-to-earnings before interest, taxes, depreciation, and amortization (EV/EBITDA) are used for valuing shares of REITs and REOCs in much the same way as for valuing shares in other industries. Funds from operations and adjusted funds from operations are defined and discussed in detail in Section 6.2.

6.1 Relative Value Approach to Valuing REIT Stocks

The relative value measures most frequently used in valuing REIT shares are P/FFO and P/AFFO. The ratio EV/EBITDA is used to a lesser extent. Like the P/E and P/CF multiples used for valuing equities in industrial sectors, P/FFO and P/AFFO multiples allow investors to quickly ascertain the value of a given REIT's shares compared with other REIT shares, or to compare the current valuation level of a REIT's shares with historical levels.[7] Within the REIT sector, P/FFO and P/AFFO multiples are also often compared with the average multiple of companies owning similar properties; for

---

7 Comparisons with the overall market are not generally made.

example, comparing the P/FFO multiple of a REIT that owns office properties with the average P/FFO multiple for all REITs owning office properties. These multiples are typically calculated using current stock prices and year-ahead estimated FFO or AFFO.

There are three main drivers behind the P/FFO, P/AFFO, and EV/EBITDA multiples of most REITs and REOCs:

1. *Expectation for growth in FFO/AFFO*: The higher the expected growth, the higher the multiple or relative valuation. Growth can be driven by business model (e.g., REITs and REOCs successful in real estate development often generate above-average FFO/AFFO growth over time), geography (e.g., having a concentration of properties in primary, supply-constrained markets, such as New York City or London, can give landlords more pricing power and higher cash flow growth than can be obtained in secondary markets), and other factors (e.g., management skill or lease structure).

2. *Risk associated with the underlying real estate*: For example, owning apartments is viewed as having less cash flow variability than owning hotels. As such, apartment-focused REITs have tended to trade at relatively high multiples compared with hotel REITs.

3. *Risks associated with company's capital structures and access to capital*: As financial leverage increases, equities' FFO and AFFO multiples decrease because required return increases as risk increases.

Financial disclosure and transparency can also have material effects on multiples. As discussed in Section 6.2, FFO has some shortcomings; but because it is the most standardized measure of a REIT or REOC's earning power, P/FFO is the most frequently used multiple in analyzing the sector. It is, in essence, the REIT sector equivalent of P/E. Investors can derive a quick "cash flow" multiple by looking at P/AFFO because AFFO makes a variety of adjustments to FFO that result in an approximation of cash earnings.

6.2 Funds from Operations and Adjusted Funds from Operations

REIT analysts and investors make extensive use of two cash flow measures that are particularly relevant to real estate.[8] The objective of both is to improve on net earnings as a measure of profit. **Funds from operations** (FFO) is a widely accepted and reported supplemental measure of the operating income of a REIT or real estate operating company. FFO is defined as accounting net earnings excluding (1) depreciation charges (depreciation expense) on real estate, (2) deferred tax charges (the deferred portion of tax expenses), and (3) gains or losses from sales of property and debt restructuring.

Why is depreciation excluded? Investors believe that real estate maintains its value to a greater extent than other business assets, often appreciating in value over the long-term, and that depreciation deductions under IFRS and U.S. GAAP do not represent economic reality. A taxable REOC that uses a moderate degree of leverage and regularly chooses to reinvest most of its income in its business usually will be able to defer a large part of its annual tax liability; that is, its cash income taxes will be low as a result of the accelerated depreciation rates for tax purposes permitted in most countries. Analysts tend to exclude the deferred tax liability and the related periodic deferred tax charges because they regard them as economically questionable.

---

8 Note that "cash flow" is used in an approximate sense. FFO is closer to a cash number than net earnings, but it is not exactly a cash number.

The deferred tax liability may not be paid for many years, if at all, or may change in amount depending on future tax rates, laws, and corporate tax planning. Gains and losses from sales of property and debt restructuring are excluded on the grounds that they do not represent sustainable, normal income. Accordingly, depreciation and deferred tax charges are added back to net earnings, and gains and losses from sales of property and debt restructuring are excluded in computing FFO.

Adjusted funds from operations (AFFO), also known as **funds available for distribution** (FAD) or **cash available for distribution** (CAD), is a refinement of FFO that is designed to be a more accurate measure of current economic income. AFFO is most often defined as FFO adjusted to remove any non-cash rent and to subtract maintenance-type capital expenditures and leasing costs (including leasing agents' commissions and tenants' improvement allowances). So-called **straight-line rent** is the average contractual rent over a lease term and this figure is recognized as revenue under IFRS and U.S. GAAP. The difference between this figure and the cash rent paid during the period is the amount of the non-cash rent or **straight-line rent adjustment**. Because most long-term leases contain escalating rental rates, this difference in rental revenue recognition can be significant. Also, deductions from FFO for capital expenditures related to maintenance and for leasing the space in properties reflect costs that need to be incurred to maintain the value of properties. The purpose of the adjustments to net earnings made in computing FFO and AFFO is to obtain a more tangible, cash-focused measure of sustainable economic income that reduces reliance on non-cash accounting estimates and excludes non-economic, non-cash charges.

AFFO is superior to FFO as a measure of economic income because it takes into account the capital expenditures necessary to maintain the economic income of a property portfolio. It is open, however, to more variation and error in estimation than FFO. The precise annual provision required to maintain and lease the space in a property is difficult to predict, and the actual expense in any single year may be significantly more or less than the norm because of the timing of capital expenditure programs and the uneven expiration schedule of leases. Consequently, estimates of FFO are more frequently cited measures, although analysts and investors will tend to base their investment judgments to a significant degree on their AFFO estimates. Although many REITs and REOCs compute and refer to AFFO in their disclosures, their methods of computation and their assumptions vary. Firms that compile statistics and estimates of publicly traded enterprises for publications, such as Bloomberg and Thomson Reuters, tend not to gather AFFO estimates because of the absence of a universally accepted methodology for computing AFFO and inconsistent corporate reporting of actual AFFO figures, which hinders corroboration of analysts' estimates.

Net operating income was previously mentioned in relation to checking NAV estimates. It is an important income measure that analysts use as a starting point in making their adjustments to income and book value of assets. **Net operating income** (NOI) is defined as gross rental revenue minus operating costs (which include estimated vacancy and collection losses, insurance costs, taxes, utilities, and repairs and maintenance expenses) but before deducting depreciation, corporate overhead, and interest expense. After deduction from NOI of general and administrative (G&A) expenses, the figure obtained is earnings before interest, depreciation, and amortization (EBITDA). Subtracting interest expense from EBITDA results in FFO, and the further deduction of non-cash rent, maintenance type capital expenditures, and leasing commissions gives AFFO. Exhibit 8 illustrates the most straightforward, convenient way of calculating FFO and AFFO for hypothetical Office Equity REIT Inc.

Exhibit 8	Calculation of FFO and AFFO Office Equity REIT Inc (in thousands, except per share data)

Panel A: Calculation of funds from operations

Net income available to common	$160,638
Add: Depreciation and amortization	$101,100
Funds from operations	$261,738
FFO per share (55,689 shares outstanding)	**$4.70**

Panel B: Calculation of adjusted funds from operations

Funds from operations	$261,738
Less: Non-cash (straight-line) rent adjustment	$21,103
Less: Recurring maintenance-type capital expenditures and leasing commissions	$55,765
Adjusted funds from operations	$184,870
AFFO per share (55,689 shares outstanding)	**$3.32**

Example 6

Analyst Adjustments (I)

1. Which of the following is the *best* measure of a REIT's current economic return to shareholders?

    A. NOI

    B. FFO

    C. AFFO

2. An analyst gathers the following information for a REIT:

NOI	$115 million
Book value of properties	$1,005 million
Market value of debt outstanding	$505 million
Market cap rate	7%
Shares outstanding	100 million
Book value per share	$5.00

   The REITs NAV per share is *closest* to:

    A. $10.05.

    B. $11.38.

    C. $16.42.

3. All else equal, estimated NAV per share will decrease with an increase in/to the:

    A. capitalization rate.

    B. estimated growth rate.

    C. deferred tax liabilities.

Solution to 1:

C is correct. AFFO is calculated from FFO by deducting non-cash rent, capital expenditures for maintenance, and leasing costs.

B is incorrect because it does not account for non-cash rent, capital expenditures for maintenance, and leasing costs. A is incorrect because it does not account for interest expense, general and administrative expense, non-cash rent, capital expenditures for maintenance, and leasing costs, which are appropriate deductions in calculating current economic return.

Solution to 2:

B is correct. The NAVPS estimates real estate values by capitalizing NOI. Valuing $115 million of NOI with a capitalization rate of 7 percent yields a value for the properties of $1,642,857,000. After deducting $505 million of debt at market value, NAV is $1,137,857,000; NAVPS equals NAV divided by 100 million shares outstanding, or $11.38.

A is incorrect because it is the book value of the assets (not the net assets) per share: $1,005 million divided by 100 million shares = $10.05 per share. It does not take into account the market value of the assets and does not deduct debt. C is incorrect because it is the market value of the real estate; that is, NOI capitalized at 7 percent, divided by 100 million shares: $1,642,857,000/100,000,000 = $16.42. This calculation excludes other assets and liabilities of the entity.

Solution to 3:

A is correct. The capitalization rate is used to calculate the estimated value of operating real estate because it is the NOI as a percentage of the value of operating real estate: NOI/Capitalization rate = Estimated value. As the capitalization rate increases, the estimated value of operating real estate and thus the NAV will decrease.

B is incorrect because an increase in the estimated growth rate would increase the estimated NOI, and the estimated value of operating income. C is incorrect because deferred liabilities are not counted as "hard" liabilities and subtracted from the NAV.

Example 7

Analyst Adjustments (II)

1. An increase in the capitalization rate will *most likely* decrease a REIT's:

    A. cost of debt.

    B. estimated NOI.

    C. estimated NAV.

2. An analyst gathers the following information for a REIT:

Non-cash (straight-line) rent	£207,430
Depreciation	£611,900
Recurring maintenance-type capital expenditures and leasing commissions	£550,750
Adjusted funds from operations	£3,320,000
AFFO per share	£3.32

The REIT's funds from operations (FFO) per share is *closest* to:

A. £3.93.

B. £4.08.

C. £4.48.

3. Which of the following estimates is *least likely* to be compiled by firms that publish REIT analysts' estimates?

A. FFO

B. AFFO

C. Revenues

Solution to 1:

C is correct. The capitalization rate is used to estimate the market value of real estate, which is then used to calculate NAV.

A is incorrect because a higher capitalization rate does not decrease the REIT's cost of debt. B is incorrect because the estimated NOI is based on income growth, not the capitalization rate.

Solution to 2:

B is correct. FFO = AFFO + Non-cash (straight-line) rent + Recurring maintenance-type capital expenditures and leasing commissions = 3,320,000 + 550,750 + 207,430 = £4,078,180. The number of shares outstanding = 3,320,000/3.32 = 1,000,000. FFO/share = 4,078,180/1,000,000 ≈ £4.08.

A is incorrect because it adds depreciation to AFFO (3,320,000 + 611,900 = £3,931,900. 3,931,900/1,000,000 ≈ £3.93 per share.) Depreciation is added to NOI (not AFFO) to find FFO. C is incorrect because it also adds depreciation to AFFO + Non-cash (straight-line) rent + Recurring maintenance-type capital expenditures and leasing commissions. That is incorrect because depreciation is not part of the difference between FFO and AFFO.

Solution to 3:

B is correct. Firms that compile statistics and estimates of REITs tend not to gather AFFO estimates because of the absence of a universally accepted methodology for computing AFFO and inconsistent corporate reporting of actual AFFO figures.

6.3 P/FFO and P/AFFO Multiples: Advantages and Drawbacks

The U.S. REIT industry began to expand rapidly in the 1990s. Exhibit 9 presents some evidence on the U.S. REIT market for 1995–2011 (essentially, two complete commercial real estate cycles). REITs' trading multiples were lowest in late 1999 and early 2000, at about 7 to 8 times (denoted 8x) for P/FFO and about 9 to 10x for P/AFFO. Multiples for REITs and REOCs were at their highest in early 2007, when P/FFO multiples approached 20x and P/AFFO multiples were about 24x.

Exhibit 9	Historic P/FFO and P/AFFO Multiples for U.S. REITs

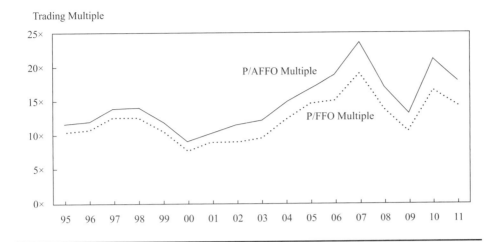

The key benefits of using P/FFO and P/AFFO multiples in the valuation of REITs and REOCs are as follows:

1. Multiples of earnings measures of this kind are widely accepted in evaluating shares across global stock markets and industries.

2. In light of this acceptance, portfolio managers can put the valuation of REITs and REOCs into context with other investment alternatives.

3. FFO estimates are readily available through market data providers, such as Bloomberg and Thomson Reuters, which facilitates calculating P/FFO multiples.

4. Multiples can be used in conjunction with such items as expected growth and leverage levels to deepen the relative analysis among REITs and REOCs.[9]

There are also drawbacks. Multiples are not a perfect basis for valuation because of the following:

1. Applying a multiple to FFO or AFFO may not capture the intrinsic value of all real estate assets held by the REIT or REOC; for example, land parcels and empty buildings may not currently produce income and hence do not contribute to FFO but have value.

2. P/FFO does not adjust for the impact of recurring capital expenditures needed to keep properties operating smoothly; and although P/AFFO should do so, wide variations in estimates and assumptions are incorporated into the calculation of AFFO.

3. In recent years, an increased level of such one-time items as gains and accounting charges, as well as new revenue recognition rules, have affected the income statement, thus making P/FFO and P/AFFO more difficult to compute and complicating comparisons between companies.

---

9 Neither FFO nor AFFO take into account differences in leverage; leverage ratios can be used to adjust for differences in leverage among REITs when comparing valuations based on FFO and AFFO multiples.

7   VALUATION: DISCOUNTED CASH FLOW APPROACH

REITs and REOCs generally return a significant portion of their income to their investors and tend to be high-dividend paying shares. Thus, dividend discount models for valuation are applicable. Discounted cash flow approaches are applied in the same manner as they are for companies in other industries. Most typically, investors use two- or three-step dividend discount models with near-term, intermediate-term, and/or long-term growth assumptions. In discounted cash flow models, investors will often use intermediate-term cash flow projections and a terminal value based on historical cash flow multiples.

7.1 Considerations in Forecasting Longer-Term Growth Rates

In looking at the specific drivers of growth for REITs and REOCs, four key considerations are generally taken into account when forecasting longer-term growth rates in these models.

1. *Internal growth potential* that stem from rent increases over time. In general, companies with portfolios of real estate located in supply-constrained markets with robust demand have a better ability to raise rents and increase cash flow. The opposite is true for portfolios in more supply-saturated markets or markets with tepid tenant demand conditions and prospects. Over the long term, well-managed property portfolios in good markets tend to generate cash flow growth at a level slightly above inflation.

2. *Investment activities*, such as acquisitions, new development, re-development, or dispositions of assets, have an impact on long-term growth. Successful development-oriented companies have shown better growth over time because returns on invested capital are generally higher on development than on acquisitions. Somewhat counter-intuitively, dispositions of weaker assets with below-average growth prospects are often dilutive to earnings because the cap rates at which such properties are sold are higher than the yields at which proceeds are re-invested, which reflects lower risk premiums. Thus, a REIT or REOC that undergoes a repositioning of a material portion of its portfolio into higher-quality properties could face cash flow growth pressure in the near term.

3. *Capital structure* can have an impact on growth, particularly in the short term as companies raise or lower their leverage. This is because of the positive leverage spread enjoyed by most REITs and REOCs; that is, going-in cap rates on property investments exceed the cost of debt. These benefits, however, can be reversed by adverse changes in the capital markets or missteps by management on acquisitions or operations. In general, REIT investors tend to be conservative and oriented toward stable, recurring income and to be averse to high leverage in REITs.

4. *Retaining and reinvesting a portion of free cash flow* can make a contribution to the growth rate. Although REITs often pay out the majority of cash flow to investors in the form of dividends, the high rates of depreciation allowed under most countries' tax laws allow companies, including REITs, to retain enough cash flow without incurring current income taxes to add 1 to 3 percentage points to annual growth.

7.2 Some Perspective on Long-Term Growth Rates

If the previously mentioned components of growth are added together, an analyst can derive a long-run growth rate. For successfully managed REITs and REOCs with good portfolios, the resulting growth rate should be in the high-single-digit percentage range. Given core cash flow growth of about 3–4 percent, 1–2 percent growth from investment activity over time, 2–3 percent growth from the financial leverage that magnifies the two growth drivers, and another 0–1 percent from reinvesting free cash flow, the long-run growth rate estimate ranges from 6 to 10 percent and the averages of the components would add up to an 8 percent long-run growth rate. The long-run growth for the average U.S. REIT from the mid-1990s through 2010, however, was barely more than 0 percent per year, with only the top companies achieving 4–7 percent average annual cash flow growth. So, although in theory REITs and REOCs should show higher growth rates, in reality the impact of the business cycle, operational and investment missteps, and a highly dilutive process of balance sheet strengthening through equity issuance after the credit crisis of 2008 and 2009 all have had a negative effect on growth.

The other key component in discounted cash flow models and dividend discount models is required returns. Although a detailed discussion about deriving required returns is beyond the scope of this reading, most rates used in practice have ranged widely from 7 percent to 13 percent. The conventional argument is that the risk premium—and thus the discount rate—associated with REITs and REOCs should be lower than the average stock in the broader market because the underlying business of owning income-producing real estate should be less volatile because of contractual revenue streams from leases. A long-term look at the betas of REIT shares suggests values tend to be less than 1.0, which supports this view.

Considering the points just outlined, the key drawback to using dividend discount models and discounted cash flow models for valuing REITs and REOCs is the high sensitivity of these valuation models to the key inputs of growth and discount rates.

Example 8

Valuation (I)

1. When using a relative P/AFFO or P/FFO multiple approach in the valuation of a REIT or REOC, which of the following considerations is the *most* important to take into account?

   A. The discount rate

   B. The NOI capitalization rate

   C. Relative AFFO or FFO growth rates and different leverage levels

2. Which of the following is the *most* significant contributor to P/FFO and P/AFFO valuation multiples for REITs and REOCs?

   A. The average age of the management team

   B. The exchange on which the REIT stock is listed

   C. The geographic location of properties in a REIT's portfolio

3. Which of the following is *not* a challenge in accurately estimating net asset value (NAV)?

   A. Estimating the value of goodwill and intangible assets

   B. Identifying the capitalization rates on comparable properties trading in the property market

   C. Ascribing an accurate value to a REIT's land holdings, projects under development, and joint ventures

4. Which of the following is *least likely* to cause persistent differences between estimated NAVs and stock prices?

   A. A surplus of takeover arbitrage capital in the markets

  B. Different discount rates being applied to privately held assets versus a liquid security

  C. A strong history of growth that prompts stock investors to pay a premium to the real estate value for a good management team

5. Which of the following are important in using a discounted cash flow model to value REITs?

  A. The capitalization rate

  B. The net asset value discount

  C. The payout ratio and the amount of financial leverage used by the REIT

Solution to 1:

C is correct. The main drivers of a relative multiple approach to valuation are risks associated with capital structure (leverage) and underlying real estate as well as expectations for growth (relative AFFO or FFO growth rates), so both should be considered.

A and B are incorrect because they relate to the dividend discount model and NAV approaches to valuation, respectively.

Solution to 2:

C is correct. Geography determines expectations for growth and risks, two main drivers of a relative multiple approach to valuation.

A is incorrect because although management skill may contribute to expected growth, management age does not. B is incorrect because the REIT's listing exchange is largely irrelevant to its investment value.

Solution to 3:

A is correct. These "soft" assets are ascribed no value by analysts in a net asset value calculation.

B is incorrect because estimating cap rates is a challenge in that they can be somewhat subjective when the properties sold differ significantly and/or few transactions are observable. C is incorrect because such assets as undeveloped land, buildings under construction, large properties with few comparable assets, service businesses, and joint ventures complicate the process of estimating NAV with accuracy and confidence.

Solution to 4:

A is correct. A surplus of takeover arbitrage capital in the markets is likely to close the gap between share prices and net asset values by generating takeovers.

B is incorrect because different discount rates may be used to reflect differences in liquidity, which persist until both securities are either publicly or privately traded. C is incorrect because the management's reputation and its effect on security value persist as long as the management remains.

Solution to 5:

C is correct. The payout ratio or level of retained cash flow affects long-term growth rates and the REIT's financial leverage is a determinant of its overall risk exposure and thus discount rate. Both growth and discount rates are key components of the discounted cash flow model.

A and B are incorrect because they both relate to the net asset value approach to REIT valuation.

REIT VALUATION: MINI CASE STUDY

8

In this section, we undertake the valuation of a REIT by using the previously outlined approaches for valuation. The REIT in our example is Capitol Shopping Center REIT Inc (CRE), a fictitious company that owns and operates retail shopping centers primarily in the Washington DC metropolitan area. The following are CRE's income statements, balance sheets, and cash flow statements for 2009 and 2010.

Exhibit 10	Capitol Shopping Center REIT Inc. (in thousands, except per share data)

Panel A: Income statements

	Three Months Ending 31 December		Year Ending 31 December	
	2010	**2009**	**2010**	**2009**
Rental revenue	$133,700	$130,300	$517,546	$501,600
Other property income	3,600	2,100	14,850	13,450
Total property revenue	$137,300	$132,400	$532,396	$515,050
Rental expenses	$29,813	$28,725	$112,571	$109,775
Property taxes	15,050	14,850	57,418	55,375
Total property expenses	$44,863	$43,575	$169,989	$165,150
Property net operating income	$92,437	$88,825	$362,407	$349,900
Other income	$450	$385	$1,840	$1,675
General & Administrative expenses	$6,150	$7,280	$23,860	$26,415
EBITDA	$86,737	$81,930	$340,387	$325,160
Depreciation & amortization	$28,460	$27,316	$115,110	$111,020
Net interest expense	$25,867	$25,015	$100,823	$99,173
Net income available to common	$32,410	$29,599	$124,454	$114,967
Weighted average common shares	61,100	60,100	60,600	60,100
Earnings per share	$0.53	$0.49	$2.05	$1.91

Panel B: Balance sheets

	Year Ending 31 December	
	2010	**2009**
Assets		
Real estate, at cost		
Operating real estate	$3,627,576	$3,496,370
Land held for future development	$133,785	$133,785
	$3,761,361	$3,630,155
Less accumulated depreciation	($938,097)	($822,987)
Net real estate	$2,823,264	$2,807,168
Cash and equivalents	$85,736	$23,856
Accounts receivable, net	$72,191	$73,699
Deferred rent receivable, net	$38,165	$33,053

(continued)

| Exhibit 10 | Continued |

Panel B: Balance sheets

	Year Ending 31 December	
	2010	2009
Prepaid expenses and other assets	$106,913	$101,604
Total Assets	$3,126,269	$3,039,380
Liabilities and Shareholders' Equity		
Liabilities		
Mortgages payable	$701,884	$647,253
Notes payable	$1,090,745	$1,090,745
Accounts payable and other liabilities	$219,498	$200,439
Total liabilities	$2,012,127	$1,938,437
Common shares and equity	$1,114,142	$1,100,943
Total Liabilities and Shareholders' Equity	$3,126,269	$3,039,380

Panel C: Cash Flow Statements

	Year Ending 31 December	
	2010	2009
Operating Activities		
Net income	$124,454	$114,967
Depreciation and amortization	$115,110	$111,020
Change in accounts receivable	$1,508	$452
Change in deferred rents	($5,112)	($4,981)
Change in prepaid expenses and other assets	($5,309)	$1,237
Change in accounts payable and other liabilities	$19,059	($11,584)
Net cash provided by operating activities	$249,710	$211,111
Investing Activities		
Acquisition of real estate	($111,200)	($22,846)
Capital expenditures on operating real estate	($20,006)	($18,965)
Net cash used in investing activities	($131,206)	($41,811)
Financing Activities		
Issuance of mortgages	$54,631	$14,213
Issuance of common shares	$58,425	$0
Dividends paid to common shareholders	($169,680)	($165,275)
Net cash used in financing activities	($56,624)	($151,062)
Increase (decrease) in cash and equivalents	$61,880	$18,238
Cash and cash equivalents, beginning of year	$23,856	$5,618
Cash and cash equivalents, end of year	$85,736	$23,856

CRE also publishes a supplemental investor packet that provides further disclosures used by the investment community to analyze the company. The following shows its adjustments to arrive at FFO and AFFO, and its calculation of dividend payouts based on dividends paid.

Exhibit 11 Capitol Shopping Center REIT Inc. FFO, AFFO, and Dividend Payouts (in thousands, except per share data)

	Three Months Ending 31 December		Year Ending 31 December	
	2010	2009	2010	2009
Funds from operations				
Net income available to common	$32,410	$29,599	$124,454	$114,967
Depreciation & amortization	$28,460	$27,316	$115,110	$111,020
Funds from operations	$60,870	$56,915	$239,564	$225,987
FFO/Share	$1.00	$0.95	$3.95	$3.76
Adjusted funds from operations				
Funds from operations	$60,870	$56,915	$239,564	$225,987
Less Non-cash rents (1)	($1,469)	($1,325)	($5,112)	($4,981)
Less Recurring capital expenditures (2)	($5,638)	($5,101)	($20,006)	($18,965)
Adjusted funds from operations	$53,763	$50,489	$214,446	$202,041
AFFO/Share	$0.88	$0.84	$3.54	$3.36
Dividends/Share	$0.70	$0.69	$2.80	$2.75
Dividend Payout Ratios				
On FFO	70.0%	72.6%	70.9%	73.1%
On AFFO	79.6%	82.1%	79.1%	81.8%
Weighted average common shares	61,100	60,100	60,600	60,100

(1) Non-cash rents include the impact of straight-lining contractual rent increases in leases, per accounting rules. The change in deferred rents can often provide the impact of this accounting on rental revenues.
(2) Recurring capital expenditures include those costs needed to maintain the revenue-producing ability of existing assets, such as leasing commissions to keep or attract new tenants, maintenance items such as roofs and parking lot repairs, and basic build-outs of space as an inducement to attract tenants.

The historical stock price and company's financial statements, including disclosures, are used to complete a simple analysis of the balance sheet, as follows.

Exhibit 12 Capitol Shopping Center REIT Inc. Balance Sheet Analysis (in thousands, except per-share data)

	Year Ending 31 December	
	2010	2009
Ending debt	$1,792,629	$1,737,998
Ending stock price	$72.36	$61.50
Ending shares	61,100	60,100
Ending market capitalization	$4,421,196	$3,696,150
Debt/Total market capitalization	*40.5%*	*47.0%*
Peer group debt/Total market capitalization	47.1%	56.7%

(continued)

Exhibit 1	Continued	

	Year Ending 31 December	
	2010	**2009**
All REITs debt/Total market capitalization	42.8%	49.6%
EBITDA	$340,387	$325,160
Interest expense	$100,823	$99,173
Interest coverage	*3.38x*	*3.28x*
Peer group interest coverage	2.35x	2.16x
All REITs interest coverage	2.58x	2.27x
Ending net debt	$1,706,893	$1,714,142
EBITDA	$340,387	$325,160
Net debt-to-EBITDA	*5.01x*	*5.27x*
Peer group net debt-to-EBITDA	7.10x	8.60x
All REITs net debt-to-EBITDA	6.70x	7.80x
Ending net debt	$1,706,893	$1,714,142
Ending gross real estate	$3,761,361	$3,630,155
Net debt/Gross real estate (Book)	*45.4%*	*47.2%*
Peer group net debt/Gross real estate (Book)	52.8%	55.1%
All REITs net debt/Gross real estate (Book)	49.6%	52.6%

The exhibits provide a recent historical picture of CRE's financial performance and balance sheet. Some key points about the company's properties operations, dividend policy, recent business activity, and historical trading attributes follow.

■ CRE owns properties that are generally considered defensive in the commercial real estate sector. This is because many of its properties are tenanted by basic necessity goods retailers such as grocery stores, drug stores, dry cleaners, etc.

■ CRE's location in the Washington, DC metropolitan area is generally viewed as favorable for two key reasons: (1) Washington, DC is the capital of the United States, and the government is the largest driver of employment, which has historically provided more stability compared with the private sector; and (2) the city is a fairly dense area with strict zoning restrictions and new construction of shopping centers is difficult, which limits competing new supply.

■ CRE has been able to increase its rents and net operating income by 2–3 percent each year, on average, in the past decade.

■ The past two reported years (2009 and 2010) were difficult for the broader commercial real estate markets. CRE was able to achieve positive growth while many of its REIT peers saw FFO and AFFO decline. As forecasts call for improving fundamental property-level conditions, CRE's portfolio may not have as much "upside" because it did not experience the decline in occupancy and rents that other REITs did.

■ In the middle of 2010, the company purchased a portfolio of three shopping centers from a local developer for a total price of $111.2 million. The return on these assets in the first year is an estimated 6.75 percent. The company was able to achieve a better going-in cap rate on this acquisition than the market averages of 6.0–6.25 percent because of its strong relationships and reputation with tenants, commercial property brokers, and competitors as well as its ability to act quickly because of its strong balance sheet. In addition, the property is not fully leased, leaving potential to increase net operating income if CRE can attract additional tenants. CRE funded the purchase with a $54.6 million mortgage at a 6 percent interest rate and cash from a common stock offering of 1 million shares and from cash on hand.

■ The company intends to make additional acquisitions in the future as part of its growth plan. It intends to use a combination of debt, common equity, and internally generated cash to make these purchases. It typically requires the properties it acquires to generate an unleveraged internal rate of return of 9.5 percent in the form of current yield and capital appreciation over time.

■ CRE's balance sheet strategy is to operate at less than 50 percent debt/market capitalization, with a preference for leverage to be closer to 40 percent. At year-end 2010, CRE's debt/market capitalization was 40.5 percent and its interest coverage was 3.38x. The company's current in-place average debt cost is 5.7 percent. By comparison, CRE's peers operate at an average leverage level of 47.1 percent and have an interest coverage ratio of 2.35x.

■ CRE's board has chosen a dividend policy that provides an approximate 80 percent payout of cash flow, or AFFO. This level allows the company to pay an attractive dividend to shareholders, retain some cash flow, provide a cushion in the event of a downturn, and remain in compliance with REIT payout requirements in the United States. It is easily able to meet these REIT payout requirements because the requirements are based on taxable net income, which is calculated after deducting depreciation. In fact, CRE's dividend level has run well in excess of taxable net income, according to comments made by its management.

■ Over the last decade, CRE has traded between 9 and19x FFO, while its peers have traded between 8 and 18x, and all REITs have traded between 7 and 20x. On an AFFO basis, CRE's historical multiple has been 10–21x, with its peers trading between 9–19x, and all REITs being in the 9–24x range.

■ Currently, shopping center REITs are estimated to be trading at 7.6 percent above analyst estimates of net asset value (NAV). The overall REIT sector is estimated to be trading at a 14.8 percent premium to estimate NAV.

■ CRE's historical beta to the broader equity market is 0.80. The current risk-free rate of return is 4.0 percent, and the market risk premium is estimated at 5.0 percent.

Investors and analysts that cover CRE have published estimates for its FFO/share, AFFO/share, and dividends/share for the next three years. Putting the average, or "consensus," of these estimates together with the company's reported results reveals the following FFO/AFFO and dividend snapshot.

Exhibit 13	Capitol Shopping Center REIT Inc. Historical and Forecast Earnings and Dividends (all amounts are per-share)

	Year Ending 31 December				
	2009A	2010A	2011E	2012E	2013E
CRE's FFO/Share	$3.76	$3.95	$4.23	$4.59	$4.80
Growth	—	5.1%	7.1%	8.5%	4.6%

(continued)

Exhibit 13	Continued				
		Year Ending 31 December			
	2009A	**2010A**	**2011E**	**2012E**	**2013E**
Peer group FFO/Share growth	—	3.4%	6.8%	8.2%	4.2%
All REITs FFO/Share growth	—	1.2%	7.9%	9.8%	10.2%
CRE's AFFO/Share	$3.36	$3.54	$3.76	$4.09	$4.31
Growth	—	5.4%	6.2%	8.8%	5.4%
Peer group AFFO/Share growth	—	−1.0%	6.2%	9.1%	4.8%
All REITs AFFO/Share growth	—	−3.0%	8.1%	9.7%	10.8%
CRE's dividends/Share	$2.75	$2.80	$2.98	$3.25	$3.40
Growth	—	1.8%	6.4%	9.1%	4.6%
Peer group dividends/Share growth	—	−2.0%	5.6%	7.9%	5.1%
All REITs dividends/Share growth	—	−5.0%	7.8%	8.9%	6.0%
CRE's dividend payout on AFFO	81.8%	79.1%	79.3%	79.5%	78.9%

Taking the recent stock price of $69.85/share and focusing on the next two years (as most analysts looking at multiples do), comparative FFO/AFFO multiples for CRE can be determined. A look at the multiples of its direct peers and the entire REIT industry trade is also included.

Exhibit 14	Comparative Multiple Analysis				
		P/FFO		**P/AFFO**	
	2011E	**2012E**	**2011E**	**2012E**
Capitol Shopping Center REIT, Inc (CRE) (1)	16.5x	15.2x	18.6x	17.1x
Shopping center oriented REITs	14.5x	13.3x	16.1x	14.5x
All REITs	14.2x	12.8x	16.5x	14.6x
CRE's Premium/(Discount) To...				
Shopping center REITs	13.8%	14.3%	15.5%	17.9%
All REITs	16.2%	18.8%	12.7%	17.1%

(1) Based on a current stock price of $69.85.

8.1 Checking the Valuation: Analysis Based on Relative Valuation

In analyzing CRE's FFO/AFFO multiples, we find that at the current stock price of $69.85, CRE trades at a premium valuation level compared with its direct peers (other shopping center REITs) as well as the overall REIT industry. When considering whether this level is warranted or not, the following items should be considered:

1. Is CRE's expected FFO and AFFO growth likely to be better or worse than those of its peers and the overall REIT industry in the next two years?

2. What is the historical FFO/AFFO multiple range for CRE, shopping center REITs, and the overall REIT industry?

3. Are there any company-specific considerations that justify a higher or lower relative multiple?

For the first consideration, we estimate that CRE's FFO and AFFO growth in 2011 should be approximately 6–7 percent and move up to 8–9 percent in 2012. As shown in Exhibit 13, this estimate is roughly in-line with that of its shopping center–focused peers but is lower than the growth expected from all REITs, which should average about 8 percent in 2011 and move up to nearly 10 percent in 2012. On its own, this estimate would suggest that CRE is expensive relative to its peers because its FFO and AFFO multiples are at premiums but its growth is largely in-line with its peers. CRE also appears expensive relative to all REITs because expected FFO and AFFO growth is lower than what is expected from REITs as a whole, yet CRE's multiples are higher than the REIT group average.

Regarding the second consideration, the company's FFO multiple has ranged from 9–19x over the last 10 years, compared with 8–18x for its peers and 7–20x for the overall REIT industry. Regarding historical AFFO trading multiples, CRE's range in the last 10 years has been 10–21x, with its shopping center REIT peers in the 9–19x range and the overall REIT industry in the 9–24x range. Based on these figures, it appears CRE has historically traded at some premium to its peers, but the current premium is larger than usual. Similarly, CRE appears to be trading at a larger premium to the overall REIT group than it has historically. In addition, it is noteworthy that for CRE's stock and the REIT sector, P/FFO and P/AFFO valuations are at the upper end of the historical range, suggesting that REITs in general are not cheap based on historical multiples.

Addressing the third consideration, it is notable that the company's geographic exposure is considered lower risk. In addition, the company has demonstrated positive AFFO growth during times when its peers saw declining AFFO, such as in 2010. It was also able to increase its dividend when other REITs made dividend cuts. An analyst might also note that CRE's leverage of 40.5 percent on the basis of debt to total market cap and interest coverage level of 3.38x is more conservative than its peers, as are virtually all of its other balance sheet leverage metrics. These points suggest that some premium valuation is warranted because of lower financial risk.

In total, the above analysis points to CRE being overvalued when using a relative multiple approach to valuation, or P/FFO and P/AFFO multiples. To derive a specific current value estimate for CRE, an investor might ascribe overall REIT group P/FFO and P/AFFO multiples to CRE in the near-term because of the company's expected growth being lower than the average REIT, offset by the company's historical premium for its geography and track record. In doing so, an investor would arrive at a share value of $60.07 using P/FFO of 14.2x for 2011 for the overall REIT group multiplied by CRE's expected FFO in 2011 of $4.23/share. Using the same methodology for AFFO equates to a $62.04 share value. These values imply that the share would need to decline by 11–14 percent to become more attractive to an investor using P/FFO and P/AFFO multiples.

8.2 Further Analysis Based on Net Asset Value Per Share

We now use NAVPS to value the shares of Capitol Shopping Center REIT Inc. To find the value, we use the previously detailed financial statements and commentary about where assets trade that are similar to those owned by CRE. By finding this information, we can estimate a value for the company if its properties were sold, debt was paid off, and capital was returned to shareholders. Our calculation to arrive at NAVPS is shown in Exhibit 15.

Exhibit 15	Capitol Shopping Center REIT Inc. Net Asset Value (NAV) Estimate (in thousands, except per-share data)
Last 12-Months real estate NOI	$362,407
Less: Non-cash rents	(5,112)
Plus: Adjustment for full impact of acquisitions (1)	3,753
Pro forma cash NOI for last 12 months	$361,048
Plus: Next 12-months growth (2)	$9,026
Estimated next 12-months cash NOI	$370,074
Assumed cap rate (3)	6.125%
Estimated value of operating real estate	$6,042,024
Plus: Cash and equivalents	$85,736
Plus: Land held for future development	133,785
Plus: Accounts receivable	72,191
Plus: Prepaid/Other assets (4)	53,457
Estimated gross asset value	$6,387,193
Less: Total debt	$1,792,629
Less: Other liabilities	219,498
Net asset value	$4,375,066
Shares outstanding	61,100
NAV/Share	**$71.61**

(1) Calculated as half of the 6.75% return on the company's $111.2 million investment made in the middle of 2010.
(2) Assuming the 2.5% midpoint of the company's historical 2-3% growth.
(3) At the midpoint of recent transactions in the market of 6-6.25%.
(4) We cut this to half of book to account for any non-tangible assets that could be included in the accounting figure.
Note: Due to rounding to nearest thousand, figures may not sum precisely.

As shown in Exhibit 15, CRE's NAV is estimated at $71.61/share. This NAV is higher than the current stock price of $69.85, implying that CRE is trading at a 2.5 percent *discount* to NAV. Although this value alone does not show that the shares are significantly undervalued compared with its real estate, an investor should also consider that (1) CRE's direct peers are trading at NAV *premiums* of 7–8 percent, (2) the overall REIT industry is trading at an average NAV premium of almost 15 percent, and (3) Capitol Shopping Center REIT's management team has been able to earn more from its properties and grow its cash flow faster than its competitors in the marketplace. Considering these factors, an investor could conclude that CRE should at least trade at a NAV premium in line with its direct peers, implying a value of about $77 for the shares. If it trades at a NAV premium in line with the overall REIT group, the share value is $82.

Whether the analyst takes a pure NAV valuation approach to valuing shares of CRE or uses NAV as a relative metric, the conclusion is that the shares of Capitol Shopping Center REIT are undervalued using this valuation method.

8.3 Further Analysis Based on a Dividend Discount Model Approach to Valuation

The final approach we take to valuing shares of Capitol Shopping Center REIT is to use a two-step dividend discount model (DDM). In the first step, we use the published estimates for the company's dividend in 2011, 2012, and 2013. In the second step, we assume a long-run dividend growth rate of 5 percent, essentially using Gordon's constant growth model. We arrive at this growth rate after considering the company's historical NOI growth of 2–3 percent, roughly 40–50 percent financial leverage, and future acquisitions that help drive growth. In addition, we assume CRE's board maintains an 80 percent dividend payout ratio. To arrive at a discount rate, we observe that CRE's historical beta to the broader equity market is 0.80, the assumed risk-free rate is 4 percent, and the assumed equity risk premium is 5 percent. Using the capital asset pricing model (CAPM), we calculate a cost of equity capital of 4% + 0.8(5%) = 8 percent for the stock. The next table combines our assumptions to derive a net present value of the projected dividends.

Exhibits 16 and 17 provide a summary of the dividends we use for steps one and two in the model.

Exhibit 16   **Capitol Shopping Center REIT Inc. Dividends for Use in a Two-Step DDM (all amounts are per-share)**

| | Year Ending 31 December | | | |
| | Step One | | Step Two | |
	2011E	2012E	2013E	In Perpetuity
AFFO/Share	$3.76	$4.09	$4.31	...
Growth	—	*8.8%*	*5.4%*	*5.0%*
Dividends/Share	$2.98	$3.25	$3.40	...
Growth	—	*9.1%*	*4.6%*	*5.0%*
Dividend payout on AFFO	79.3%	79.5%	78.9%	80.0%

Exhibit 17   **Capitol Shopping Center REIT Inc. Valuation Using Two-Step DDM (all amounts are per-share)**

| | | Year Ending 31 December | | | |
| | | Step One | | | Step Two |
		2011E	2012E	2013E	2014E
Dividends/Share		$2.98	$3.25	$3.40	$3.57
Value of stock at end of 2013 (1)		—	—	$119.00	
Cash flow to investors		$2.98	$3.25	$122.40	
Net Present Value Of Cash Flow (Dividends)	**$102.71**				

(1) Calculated as $3.57/(0.08 − 0.05).

Using a two-step dividend discount model approach to valuation, we calculate a share value of $102.71 for Capitol Shopping Center REIT Inc. This value is about 47 percent higher than the current price of $69.85 and suggests that the shares are currently undervalued. Compared with the relative valuation approaches, this approach indicates that CRE is undervalued, not overvalued. This result is consistent with the NAV approach, which also indicated that CRE is undervalued. The discrepancy between estimated value and price is largest using the dividend discount model. This result is not particularly surprising in light of the sensitivity of results when using this valuation approach to small differences in valuation assumptions that we referred to earlier.

8.4 Selection of Valuation Methods

As this discussion demonstrates, different valuation methods can yield different results. Under such circumstances, an analyst should re-examine the assumptions made to investigate why the approaches are generating such different results. The method(s) selected by an analyst may depend on which one(s) the analyst believes use(s) the most reliable assumptions, which one(s) the analyst believes will be used by other investors, or which one(s) best reflect the analyst's own investment philosophy or view of value. The analyst may choose to take a single valuation approach, a mid-point in the range of values obtained by using several approaches, or elect to use a weighted average of the values obtained based on the analyst's view of the relative reliability of the models used to arrive at the values.

Example 9

Valuation (II)

1. If the outlook for economic growth turns negative and property market transaction volumes decline, it is *least likely* that CRE's:

    A. P/FFO and P/AFFO would be lower.

    B. relative P/FFO and P/ AFFO multiples would be higher.

    C. NAV becomes the most useful valuation method.

2. If other REITs have no land on their balance sheets, how is CRE's "Land held for future development" *best* factored into a relative P/FFO or P/AFFO multiple valuation?

    A. There should be no impact on multiples as a result of land value.

    B. CRE would warrant lower multiples to account for land value.

    C. CRE would warrant higher multiples to account for land value.

3. An analyst speaks with private market real estate investors and learns that because interest rates have just increased 200 bps, buyers will require future property acquisitions to have going-in cap rates that are 100–200 bps higher than those on recent property market transactions. The analyst's estimate of NAV for CRE *most likely*:

    A. increases as cap rates are higher.

    B. decreases as cap rates are higher.

    C. remain the same unless CRE has debt maturing in the near term.

4. An analyst determines that CRE purchased its "Land held for future development" 15 years ago, and that on average land values at that time were one-third of what they are today. Which of the following *best* adjusts NAV to reflect this consideration?

    A. The cap rate on operating assets should be changed.

    B. Land value, and thus NAV, should be adjusted higher to reflect today's valuations.

    C. NAV is still mainly a representation of book values, thus there should be no adjustments.

5. Zoning in CRE's real estate markets is changed to allow more new space in the future, dampening CRE's long-term FFO growth by about 0.5 percent. The effect on CRE's valuation using a dividend discount model is *most likely* that the present value of the dividend stream:

   A. decreases because of lower growth.

   B. remains the same.

   C. increases because of the new supply.

Solution to 1:

C is correct. NAV becomes more subjective in a negative and less liquid market with fewer observable transactions, and thus this basis of valuation becomes less useful and reliable.

A and B are incorrect because P/FFO and P/AFFO are likely to fall in a negative economic environment, but investors may be willing to pay a relative premium for CRE's stock based on its superior stability in economically challenging times.

Solution to 2:

C is correct. Although it may not produce income that contributes to FFO or AFFO, the land has value and represents a source of greater internal growth potential. For that reason, A and B are incorrect.

Solution to 3:

B is correct. Estimated real estate value decreases as the cap rate increases. Because NAV is derived directly from estimated real estate value, it also decreases. For this reason, A is incorrect. C is incorrect because an increase in cap rates decreases asset values. The fact that CRE has debt maturing in the near term is not a key factor influencing NAV.

Solution to 4:

B is correct. An analyst tries to attribute market values to real property owned.

A is incorrect because the cap rate used by analysts in calculating NAVs represents the return on only the income-producing asset portfolio and does not relate to land holdings that are not currently producing any income. C is incorrect because NAV is not a representation of book values, which rely on accounting methodology rather than market values.

Solution to 5:

A is correct. Lower growth affects the projected dividend stream, decreasing its present value. For that reason, B and C are incorrect.

Example 10

Valuation (III)

1. An analyst gathers the following information for two REITs:

	Price/NAV	Capitalization rate used in NAV
REIT A	100%	6%
REIT B	99%	8%

If the REITs have similar property portfolio values, interest expense, and corporate overhead, which REIT *most likely* has the higher Price/FFO?

A. REIT A

B. REIT B

C. They will have similar P/FFOs because their ratios of price to NAV are almost identical.

2. An analyst gathers the following information for two REITs:

	P/NAV	P/AFFO	AFFO Payout Ratio	Est. annual AFFO growth
REIT A	98%	12.8 X	50%	4.0%
REIT B	101%	13.0 X	90%	3.5%

All else being equal, if both REITs have a 10 percent rate of return on retained and reinvested cash flows, which of the REITs is *most* attractively priced?

A. REIT A

B. REIT B

C. Neither REIT is more attractively priced than the other

Solution to 1:

A is correct. A lower capitalization rate (i.e., a lower NOI with such other parameters as interest costs and corporate expenses being the same) implies a lower FFO and hence a higher P/FFO ratio if P/NAV ratios are similar, as is the case here.

B is incorrect because A has a lower capitalization rate, implying a lower FFO and hence a higher P/FFO ratio if P/NAV ratios are similar, as is the case here. C is incorrect because it neglects the effect of the lower capitalization rate of REIT A.

Solution to 2:

B is correct. REIT B is cheaper because it is able to generate almost the same growth in AFFO as REIT A while retaining only 10 percent of AFFO compared with a 50 percent retention rate in the case of REIT A. Because both REITS are achieving a 10 percent return on retained AFFO, it suggests that REIT B has much more growth in returns coming from its existing portfolio of properties. Given very similar P/AFFO multiples for the two REITs, REIT B is more attractively priced. Also for these reasons, A and C are incorrect.

SUMMARY

This reading has presented publicly traded real estate securities, including their structure, economic drivers, investment characteristics, and valuation. Among the important points made by the reading are the following:

■ The principal types of publicly traded real estate securities available globally are real estate investment trusts, real estate operating companies, and residential and commercial mortgage-backed securities.

- Publicly traded equity real estate securities offer investors participation in the returns from investment real estate with the advantages of superior liquidity in small and large amounts; greater potential for diversification by property, geography, and property type; access to a superior quality and range of properties; the benefit of management services; limited liability; the ability to use shares as tax-advantaged currency in making acquisitions; protection accorded by corporate governance, disclosure, and other securities regulations; and, in the case of REITs, exemption from income taxation within the REIT if prescribed requirements are met.

- Disadvantages include the costs of maintaining a publicly traded corporate structure, pricing determined by the stock market and returns that can be volatile, potential for structural conflicts of interest, and tax differences compared with direct ownership of property that can be disadvantageous under some circumstances.

- Compared with other publicly traded shares, REITs offer higher than average yields and greater stability of income and returns. They are amenable to a net asset value approach to valuation because of the existence of active private markets for their real estate assets. Compared with REOCs, REITs offer higher yields and income tax exemption but have less operating flexibility to invest in a broad range of real estate activities as well as less potential for growth from reinvesting their operating cash flows because of their high income-to-payout ratios.

- In assessing the investment merits of REITs, investors analyze the effects of trends in general economic activity, retail sales, job creation, population growth, and new supply and demand for specific types of space. They also pay particular attention to occupancies, leasing activity, rental rates, remaining lease terms, in-place rents compared with market rents, costs to maintain space and re-lease space, tenants' financial health and tenant concentration in the portfolio, financial leverage, debt maturities and costs, and the quality of management.

- Analysts make adjustments to the historic cost-based financial statements of REITs and REOCs to obtain better measures of current income and net worth. The three principal figures they calculate and use are (1) funds from operations or accounting net earnings excluding depreciation, deferred tax charges, and gains or losses on sales of property and debt restructuring; (2) adjusted funds from operations, or funds from operations adjusted to remove straight-line rent and to provide for maintenance-type capital expenditures and leasing costs, including leasing agents' commissions and tenants' improvement allowances; and (3) net asset value or the difference between a real estate companies' assets and liabilities ranking prior to shareholders' equity, all valued at market values instead of accounting book values.

- REITs and REOCs are valued using a net asset value per share, price-to-FFO, price-to-AFFO, price-to-NAV, or a discounted cash flow approach, or combinations of these approaches. Three important factors influencing the P/FFO and P/AFFO of REITs and REOCs are expectations for growth in FFO/AFFO, risks associated with the underlying real estate, and risks associated with companies' capital structure and access to capital. The P/NAV approach to valuation can be used as either an absolute basis of valuation or a relative valuation approach. NAV reflects, however, the estimated value of a REIT's assets to a private market buyer, which may or may not be the same as the value that public equity investors ascribe to the business; this fact is one of the reasons for the wide historical premium/discount range at which REITs trade relative to NAV estimates.

- REITs and REOCs generally return a significant portion of their income to their investors and as a result tend to pay high dividends. Thus, dividend discount or discounted cash flow models for valuation are also applicable. These valuation approaches are applied in the same manner as they are for shares in other industries. Most typically, investors utilize two- or three-step dividend discount models with near-term, intermediate-term, and/or long-term growth assumptions. In discounted cash flow models, investors will often use intermediate-term cash flow projections and a terminal value based on historical cash flow multiples.

PRACTICE PROBLEMS FOR READING 39

The following information relates to Questions 1 -6[1]

Hui Lin, CFA is an investment manager looking to diversify his portfolio by adding equity real estate investments. Lin and his investment analyst, Maria Nowak, are discussing whether they should invest in publicly traded real estate investment trusts (REITs) or public real estate operating companies (REOCs). Nowak expresses a strong preference for investing in public REITs in taxable accounts.

Lin schedules a meeting to discuss this matter, and for the meeting, Lin asks Nowak to gather data on three specific REITs and come prepared to explain her preference for public REITs over public REOCs. At the meeting, Lin asks Nowak:

"Why do you prefer to invest in public REITs over pubic REOCs for taxable accounts?"

Nowak provides Lin with an explanation for her preference of public REITs and provides Lin with data on the three REITs shown in Exhibits 1 and 2.

The meeting concludes with Lin directing Nowak to identify the key investment characteristics along with the principal risks of each REIT and to investigate the valuation of the three REITs. Specifically, Lin asks Nowak to value each REIT using four different methodologies:

Method 1: Net asset value

Method 2: Discounted cash flow valuation using a two-step dividend model

Method 3: Relative valuation using property subsector average P/FFO multiple

Method 4: Relative valuation using property subsector average P/AFFO multiple

Exhibit 1	Select REIT Financial Information		
	REIT A	**REIT B**	**REIT C**
Property subsector	Office	Storage	Health Care
Estimated 12 months cash net operating income (NOI)	$350,000	$267,000	$425,000
Funds from operations (FFO)	$316,965	$290,612	$368,007
Cash and equivalents	$308,700	$230,850	$341,000
Accounts receivable	$205,800	$282,150	$279,000
Debt and other liabilities	$2,014,000	$2,013,500	$2,010,000
Non-cash rents	$25,991	$24,702	$29,808
Recurring maintenance-type capital expenditures	$63,769	$60,852	$80,961
Shares outstanding	56,100	67,900	72,300

---

1 This item set was developed by Karen O'Connor Rubsam, CFA (Phoenix, USA).

Exhibit 2	REIT Dividend Forecasts and Average Price Multiples		
	REIT A	**REIT B**	**REIT C**
Expected annual dividend next year	$3.80	$2.25	$4.00
Dividend growth rate in years 2 and 3	4.0%	5.0%	4.5%
Dividend growth rate (after year 3 into perpetuity)	3.5%	4.5%	4.0%
Assumed cap rate	7.0%	6.25%	6.5%
Property subsector average P/FFO multiple	14.4x	13.5x	15.1x
Property subsector average P/AFFO multiple	18.3x	17.1x	18.9x

Note: Nowak estimates an 8% cost of equity capital for all REITs and a risk-free rate of 4.0%.

1. Nowak's *most likely* response to Lin's question is that the type of real estate security she prefers:
    A. offers a high degree of operating flexibility.
    B. provides dividend income that is exempt from double taxation.
    C. has below-average correlations with overall stock market returns.

2. Based upon Exhibit 1, the value per share for REIT A using valuation Method 1 is *closest* to:
    A. $51.26.
    B. $62.40.
    C. $98.30.

3. Based upon Exhibits 1 and 2, the value per share of REIT B using valuation Method 3 is *closest* to:
    A. $40.77.
    B. $57.78.
    C. $73.19.

4. Based on Exhibit 2, the value per share of REIT C using valuation Method 2 is *closest* to:
    A. $55.83.
    B. $97.57.
    C. $100.91.

5. Based upon Exhibits 1 and 2, the value per share of REIT A using valuation Method 4 is *closest* to:
    A. $58.32.
    B. $74.12.
    C. $103.40.

6. The risk factor *most likely* to adversely impact an investment in REIT B is:
    A. new competitive facilities.
    B. tenants' sales per square foot.
    C. obsolescence of existing space.

The following information relates to Questions 7 – 12[2]

Tim Wang is a financial advisor specializing in commercial real estate investing. He is meeting with Mark Caudill, a new client who is looking to diversify his investment portfolio by adding real estate investments. Caudill has heard about various investment vehicles related to real estate from his friends and is seeking a more in-depth understanding of these investments from Wang.

Wang begins the meeting by advising Caudill of the many options that are available when investing in real estate, including:

Option 1   Direct ownership in real estate

Option 2   Publicly traded real estate investment trusts (REITs)

Option 3   Publicly traded real estate operating companies (REOCs)

Option 4   Publicly-traded residential mortgage-backed securities (RMBSs)

Wang next asks Caudill about his investment preferences. Caudill responds by telling Wang that he prefers to invest in equity securities that are highly liquid, provide high income, and are not subject to double taxation.

Caudill asks Wang how the economic performance of REITs and REOCs is evaluated, and how their shares are valued. Wang advises Caudill there are multiple measures of economic performance for REITs and REOCs, including:

Measure 1   Net operating income (NOI)

Measure 2   Funds from operations (FFO)

Measure 3   Adjusted funds from operations (AFFO)

In response, Caudill asks Wang:

"Which of the three measures is the best measure of a REIT's current economic return to shareholders?"

To help Caudill's understanding of valuation, Wang presents Caudill with data on Baldwin, a health care REIT that primarily invests in independent and assisted senior housing communities in large cities across the United States. Select financial data on Baldwin for the past two years are provided in Exhibit 1.

Before the meeting, Wang had put together some valuation assumptions for Baldwin in anticipation of discussing valuation with Caudill. Wang explains the process of valuing a REIT share using discounted cash flow analysis, and proceeds to estimate the value of Baldwin on a per share basis using a two-step dividend discount model using the data provided in Exhibit 2.

Exhibit 1	Baldwin REIT Summarized Income Statement (in thousands of dollars, except per share data)	
	Year Ending December 31	
	2011	**2010**
Rental income	339,009	296,777
Other property income	6,112	4,033
Total income	345,121	300,810

(continued)

---

2 This item set was developed by Bin Wang, CFA (Austin, TX, USA).

Exhibit 1	continued	

	Year Ending December 31	
	2011	**2010**
Rental expenses		
Property operating expenses	19,195	14,273
Property taxes	3,610	3,327
Total property expenses	22,805	17,600
Net operating income	322,316	283,210
Other income (gains on sale of properties)	2,162	1,003
General and administrative expenses	21,865	19,899
Depreciation and amortization	90,409	78,583
Net interest expenses	70,017	56,404
Net income	142,187	129,327
Weighted average shares outstanding	121,944	121,863
Earnings per share	1.17	1.06
Dividend per share	0.93	0.85
Price/FFO, based upon year-end stock price	11.5x	12.7x

Exhibit 2	Baldwin Valuation Projections and Assumptions

Current risk-free rate	4.0%
Baldwin beta	0.90
Market risk premium	5.0%
Appropriate discount rate (CAPM)	8.5%
Expected dividend per share, 1 year from today	$1.00
Expected dividend per share, 2 years from today	$1.06
Long-term growth rate in dividends, starting in year 3	5.0%

7. Based on Caudill's investment preferences, the type of real estate investment Wang is *most likely* to recommend to Caudill is:

   A. Option 2.

   B. Option 3.

   C. Option 4.

8. Relative to Option 2 and Option 3, an advantage of investing in Option 1 is:

   A. greater liquidity.

   B. lower investment requirements.

   C. greater control over property level investment decisions.

9. The Baldwin REIT is *least likely* to experience long-run negative effects from a/an:

   A. economic recession.

   B. unfavorable change in population demographics.

   C. major reduction in government funding of health care.

10. The *most appropriate* response to Caudill's question is:

    A. Measure 1

    B. Measure 2

    C. Measure 3

11. Based on Exhibit 1, the 2011 year-end share price of Baldwin was *closest* to:

    A. $13.23.

    B. $21.73.

    C. $30.36.

12. Based upon Exhibit 2, the intrinsic value of the Baldwin REIT on a per share basis using the two-step dividend discount model is *closest* to:

    A. $26.72.

    B. $27.59.

    C. $28.83.

SOLUTIONS FOR READING 39

1. B is correct. REITs are tax-advantaged entities whereas REOC securities are
    not typically tax-advantaged entities. More specifically, REITs are typically
    exempted from the double taxation of income that comes from taxes being due
    at the corporate level and again when dividends or distributions are made to
    shareholders in some jurisdictions such at the United States.

2. B is correct. The NAV is $62.40.

Estimated Cash NOI	350,000
Assumed cap rate	0.07
Estimated value of operating real estate (350,000/.07)	5,000,000
Plus: cash + accounts receivable	514,500
Less: Debt and other liabilities	2,014,000
Net Asset Value	3,500,500
Shares outstanding	56,100
NAV/share	**$62.40**

3. B is correct. The value per share is $57.78, calculated as:

    Funds from operations (FFO) = $290,612

    Shares outstanding = 67,900 shares

    FFO/share = $290,612/67,900 shares = $4.28

    Applying the property subsector average P/FFO multiple of 13.5x yields a
    value per share of:

    $4.28 x 13.5 = $57.78.

4. C is correct. The value per share for REIT C is $100.91.

		Step One			Step Two
		Year 1	Year 2	Year 3	Year 4
Dividends per share:		$4.00	$4.18	$4.37	$4.54
Value of stock at end of 2013[1]:				$113.57	
				$117.94	
Discount rate:	8.00%				
Net present value of all dividends[2]:	$100.91				

[1] Calculated as $4.54 / (0.08 − 0.04) = $113.57
[2] Calculated as: $4.00 / (1.08) + $4.18 / (1.08)^2 + $117.94 / (1.08)^3 = $100.91

5. B is correct. The value per share is $74.11, calculated as:

    Funds from operations (FFO) = $316,965

    Less: Non-cash rents: $25,991

    Less: Recurring maintenance-type capital expenditures: $63,769

Equals: AFFO: $227,205

Shares outstanding = 56,100 shares

AFFO/share = $227,205/56,100 shares = $4.05.

Applying the property subsector average P/AFFO multiple of 18.3x yields a value per share of:

$4.05 x 18.3 = $74.12.

6. A is correct. As a storage REIT, this investment faces competitive pressures because of the ease of entry into the field of self-storage properties can lead to periods of overbuilding.

7. A is correct. Option 2, publicly traded REITs, best satisfy Caudill's investment preferences. REITs are equity investments that, in general, are income tax exempt at the corporate/trust level, so there is no double income taxation. To qualify for the income tax exemption, REITs are legally obligated to pay out a high percentage of income to their shareholders, and this typically results in relatively high income for investors. Lastly, public REITs are generally liquid as they are traded in stock exchanges.

8. C is correct. Direct property ownership offers greater control over property level investment decisions in comparison to the level of control exhibited by shareholders in REITs and REOCs.

9. A is correct. Baldwin, a health care REIT, is largely resistant to economic recessions but is exposed to changes in population demographics and changes in government funding for health care.

10. C is correct. Measure 3, adjusted funds from operations (AFFO), is a refinement of FFO that is designed to be a more accurate measure of current economic income. In essence, FFO is adjusted to remove any non-cash rent and to include a provision for maintenance-type capital expenditures and leasing costs. Maintenance expenses are required for a business to continue as a going concern.

11. B is correct. Baldwin's FFO per share in 2011 was $1.89, and the resulting share price was $21.73. First, calculate FFO per share in 2011, and then apply the year-end P/FFO multiple of 11.5x.

FFO = accounting net earnings, excluding: (a) depreciation charges on real estate, (b) deferred tax charges, and (c) gains or losses from sales of property and debt restructuring.

2011 accounting net income: $142,187

2011 depreciation charges: $90,409

2011 deferred tax charges: N/A

2011 gains on sale of properties (other income): $2,162

2011 shares outstanding = 121,944

2011 year-end price/FFO = 11.5x

2011 Baldwin's FFO per share = ($142,187 + $90,409 – $2,162) / 121,944 shares = $1.89. At the given 2011 year-end price/FFO multiple of 11.5x, this results in a share price for Baldwin of $1.89 x 11.5 = $21.73.

12. C is correct. The estimated value per share for the Baldwin REIT using a two-step dividend discount model is $28.83, calculated as:

	Step One		Step Two
	Year 1	Year 2	Year 3
Dividends per share:	$1.00	$1.06	$1.11
Value of stock at end of Year 2[1]:		$31.80	
		$32.86	
Discount rate:	8.50%		
Net present value of all dividends[2]:	$28.83		

[1] Calculated as $1.11 / (0.085 − 0.05) = $31.80

[2] Calculated as: $1.00 / (1.085) + $32.86 / (1.085)^2 = $28.83

40

Private Equity Valuation

by Yves Courtois, CFA and Tim Jenkinson

LEARNING OUTCOMES

Mastery	The candidate should be able to:
☐	**a** explain sources of value creation in private equity;
☐	**b** explain how private equity firms align their interests with those of the managers of portfolio companies;
☐	**c** distinguish between the characteristics of buyout and venture capital investments;
☐	**d** describe valuation issues in buyout and venture capital transactions;
☐	**e** explain alternative exit routes in private equity and their impact on value;
☐	**f** explain private equity fund structures, terms, valuation, and due diligence in the context of an analysis of private equity fund returns;
☐	**g** explain risks and costs of investing in private equity;
☐	**h** interpret and compare financial performance of private equity funds from the perspective of an investor;
☐	**i** calculate management fees, carried interest, net asset value, distributed to paid in (DPI), residual value to paid in (RVPI), and total value to paid in (TVPI) of a private equity fund;
	A Note on Valuation of Venture Capital Deals: (Appendix 40)
☐	**j** calculate pre-money valuation, post-money valuation, ownership fraction, and price per share applying the venture capital method 1) with single and multiple financing rounds and 2) in terms of IRR;
☐	**k** demonstrate alternative methods to account for risk in venture capital.

INTRODUCTION

1

Private equity is playing an increasing role in the global economy. In the last decade, private equity has grown from a small, niche activity to a critical component of the financial system. One manifestation of this has been the huge amount of money that investors have committed to private equity, estimated at around $1.5 trillion globally between 1998 and 2006. And this is just the equity portion of total financing. As will be explained later, many private equity deals employ significant amounts of debt, and so the value of the transactions involving private equity funds is often 2 or 3 times the actual equity raised. Until recently, few people even knew the names of the main private equity players. But now such organizations as Blackstone, Carlyle, KKR, Texas Pacific Group, and Permira are recognized as major forces in the global financial system. Fund sizes have grown—to over $20 billion at their largest—as have the size and complexity of the transactions that private equity funds are able to undertake, such as the $45 billion acquisition of the U.S. energy company TXU. In 2006, it was estimated that private equity funds were involved in approximately one-quarter of all merger and acquisition activities.

There can be two perspectives on private equity valuation. In Section 2, we primarily take the perspective of the private equity firm that is evaluating potential investments. When a private equity firm is performing valuations of potential acquisitions, this effort is particularly complex because in most cases, except for public-to-private transactions, there will be no market prices to refer to. Private equity firms can face considerable challenges in valuing these companies, and this reading discusses the main ways in which valuation is approached. In Section 3, we take the perspective of an outside investor who is looking at the costs and risks of investing in a fund sponsored by the private equity firm.

Definitions of private equity differ, but in this reading we include the entire asset class of equity investments that are not quoted on stock markets. The private equity class stretches from venture capital (VC)—working with early stage companies that in many cases have no revenues but have potentially good ideas or technology—all the way through to large buyouts (leveraged buyout, or LBO) in which the private equity firm buys the entire company. In some cases, these companies might themselves be quoted on the stock market, and the private equity fund performs a public-to-private transaction thereby removing the entire company from the stock market. But in the majority of cases, buyout transactions will involve privately owned companies and, very often, a particular division of an existing company. There are many other forms of later-stage financing, such as providing capital to back the expansion of existing businesses, but for this reading we will refer simply to *venture capital* and *buyouts* as the two main forms of private equity.

Many classifications of private equity are available. Exhibit 1 provides a set of classifications proposed by the European Venture Capital Association (EVCA).

Exhibit 1	Classification of Private Equity in Terms of Stage and Type of Financing of Portfolio Companies

Broad Category	Subcategory	Brief Description
Venture capital	Seed stage	Financing provided to research business ideas, develop prototype products, or conduct market research.
	Start-up stage	Financing to recently created companies with well articulated business and marketing plans.
	Expansion stage	Financing to companies that have started their selling effort and may be already breaking even. Financing may serve to expand production capacity, product development, or provide working capital.
	Replacement capital	Financing provided to purchase shares from other existing venture capital investors or to reduce financial leverage.

Exhibit 1 *Continued*

Broad Category	Subcategory	Brief Description
Buyout	Acquisition capital	Financing in the form of debt, equity, or quasi-equity provided to a company to acquire another company.
	Leverage buyout	Financing provided by a LBO firm to acquire a company.
	Management buyout	Financing provided to the management to acquire a company, specific product line, or division (carve-out).
Special situations	Mezzanine finance	Financing generally provided in the form of subordinated debt and an equity kicker (warrants, equity, etc.) frequently in the context of LBO transactions.
	Distressed securities	Financing of companies in need of restructuring or facing financial distress.
	One-time opportunities	Financing in relation to changing industry trends and new government regulations.
	Others	Other forms of private equity financing are also possible (i.e., activist investing, etc.).

Source: www.evca.com.

These classifications are not exhaustive. Private equity funds may also be classified depending on their geographical (national, regional, or global) and/or sector focus (e.g., diversified industrials, telecommunications, biotechnologies, healthcare, industrials, etc.).

How is the invested money split between venture capital and buyout deals? In broad terms, around four-fifths of the money has been flowing into buyouts in recent years in both the United States and Europe. In part this is because of the sheer scale of buyouts in which an individual deal can absorb several billion dollars of capital. In contrast, venture capital deals tend to drip feed money into companies as they develop. But investors also have been increasingly focusing on buyout funds, in which, in recent years at least, the average returns earned have tended to be higher.

Where does the money come from and how are the private equity funds organized? Most of the money comes from institutional investors, such as pension funds, endowments, and insurance companies, although many high-net-worth individuals also invest directly or through fund-of-funds intermediaries who provide their investors with a more diversified portfolio of investments. At present, the proportion of assets allocated by investors to private equity is considerably higher in the United States than in Europe, although surveys of European investors find that the fund managers plan to increase their allocation to private equity. So the flow of money into private equity is likely to continue and indeed grow, depending, of course, on market conditions.

One distinctive characteristic of private equity investment is a buy-to-sell orientation. Private equity fund investors typically expect their money returned, with a handsome profit, within 10 years of committing their funds. The economic incentives of the funds are aligned with this goal, as is explained later. In the next section we discuss this buy-to-sell approach and how funds are typically organized.

2 INTRODUCTION TO VALUATION TECHNIQUES IN PRIVATE EQUITY TRANSACTIONS

This reading is not intended to be a comprehensive review of valuation techniques applicable to private equity transactions. Instead, we highlight some essential considerations specific to private equity. As you might expect, private equity firms are a rich laboratory for applying the principles of asset and equity valuation. The case study on venture capital valuation that follows this reading demonstrates how a specific valuation technique can be applied.

First and foremost, we must distinguish between the price paid for a private equity stake and the valuation of such private equity stake. The price paid for a private equity stake is the outcome of a negotiation process between two or more parties with each possibly assigning a different value to that same private equity stake. Unlike shares of public companies that are traded regularly on a regulated market, buyers and sellers of private equity interests generally employ more efforts to uncover their value. Private equity valuation is thus time bound and dependent on the respective motives and interests of buyers and sellers.

The selection of the appropriate valuation methodologies depends largely on the stage of development of a private equity portfolio company. Exhibit 2 provides an overview of some of the main methodologies employed in private equity valuation and an indication of the stage of company development for which they may apply.

Exhibit 2	Overview of Selected Valuation Methodologies and Their Possible Application in Private Equity	
Valuation Technique	**Brief Description**	**Application**
Income approach: Discounted cash flows (DCF)	Value is obtained by discounting expected future cash flows at an appropriate cost of capital.	Generally applies across the broad spectrum of company stages. Given the emphasis on expected cash flows, this methodology provides the most relevant results when applied to companies with a sufficient operating history. Therefore, most applicable to companies operating from the expansion up to the maturity phase.
Relative value: Earnings multiples	Application of an earnings multiple to the earnings of a portfolio company. The earnings multiple is frequently obtained from the average of a group of public companies operating in a similar business and of comparable size. Commonly used multiples include: Price/Earnings (P/E), Enterprise Value/EBITDA, Enterprise Value/Sales.	Generally applies to companies with a significant operating history and predictable stream of cash flows. May also apply with caution to companies operating at the expansion stage. Rarely applies to early stage or start-up companies.
Real option	The right to undertake a business decision (call or put option). Requires judgmental assumptions about key option parameters.	Generally applies to situations in which the management or shareholders have significant flexibility in making radically different strategic decisions (i.e., option to undertake or abandon a high risk, high return project). Therefore, generally applies to some companies operating at the seed or start-up phase.

	Exhibit 2	*Continued*

Valuation Technique	Brief Description	Application
Replacement cost	Estimated cost to recreate the business as it stands as of the valuation date.	Generally applies to early (seed and start-up) stage companies or companies operating at the development stage and generating negative cash flows. Rarely applies to mature companies as it is difficult to estimate the cost to recreate a company with a long operating history. For example, it would be difficult to estimate the cost to recreate a long established brand like Coca-Cola, whereas the replacement cost methodology may be used to estimate the brand value for a recently launched beverage (R&D expenses, marketing costs, etc.).

One other methodology, the venture capital method, is discussed more fully as part of the case study that follows this reading.

Note that in a vibrant and booming private equity market, there is a natural tendency among participants to focus primarily on the earnings approach to determine value. This approach is perceived as providing a benchmark value corresponding best to the state of the current private equity market. Because of the lack of liquidity of private equity investments, the concurrent use of other valuation metrics is strongly recommended.

Thus, valuation does not involve simply performing a net present value calculation on a static set of future profit projections. The forecasts of the existing management or vendors are, of course, a natural place to start, but one of the key ways private equity firms add value is by challenging the way businesses are run. The business would have additional value if the private equity firm improves the business's financing, operations, management, and marketing.

In most transactions, private equity investors are faced with a set of investment decisions that are based on an assessment of prospective returns and associated probabilities. Private equity firms are confronted generally with a large flow of information arising from detailed due diligence investigations and from complex financial models. It is essential to understand the extent of the upside and downside potential of internal and external factors affecting the business and their resulting effect on net income and free cash flows. Any possible scenario must pass the judgmental test of how realistic it is. The defined scenarios should be based not only on the analysis of past events, but on what future events may realistically happen, given knowledge of the present. The interplay between exogenous factors (such as favorable and unfavorable macroeconomic conditions, interest rates, and exchange rates) and value drivers for the business (such as sales margins and required investments) should also be considered carefully. For example, what will be the sales growth if competition increases or if competing new technologies are introduced?

When building the financial forecasts, all variables in the financial projections should be linked to key fundamental factors influencing the business with assigned subjective probabilities. The use of Monte Carlo simulation, often using a spreadsheet add-in such as Crystal Ball™ or @RISK, further enhances the quality of the analysis and may be instrumental in identifying significant financial upsides and downsides to the business. In a Monte Carlo simulation, the analyst must model the fundamental value drivers of the portfolio company, which are in turn linked to a valuation model. Base case, worst case, and best case scenarios (sometimes called a triangular approach) and associated probabilities should be discussed with line managers for each value driver with the objective being to ensure that the simulation is as close as possible to the realities of the business and encompasses the range of possible outcomes.

Other key considerations when evaluating a private equity transaction include the value of control, the impact of illiquidity, and the extent of any country risk. Estimating the discount for illiquidity and marketability and a premium for control are among the most subjective decisions in private equity valuation. The control premium is an incremental value associated with a bloc of shares that will be instrumental in gaining control of a company. In most buyouts, the entire equity capital is acquired by the private equity purchasers. But in venture capital deals, investors often acquire minority positions. In this case the control premium (if any) largely depends on the relative strength and alignment of interest of shareholders willing to gain control. For example, in a situation with only a limited number of investors able to acquire control, the control premium is likely to be much more significant relative to a situation with a dominant controlling shareholder invested along with a large number of much smaller shareholders.

The distinction between marketability and liquidity is more subtle. The cost of illiquidity may be defined as the cost of finding prospective buyers and represents the speed of conversion of the assets to cash, whereas the cost of marketability is closely related to the right to sell the assets. In practice, the marketability and liquidity discounts are frequently lumped together.

The cost for illiquidity and premium for control may be closely related because illiquidity may be more acute when there is a fierce battle for control. But there are many dimensions to illiquidity. The size of the illiquidity discount may be influenced by such factors as the shareholding structure, the level of profitability and its expected sustainability, the possibility of an initial public offering (IPO) in the near future, and the size of the private company. Because determining the relative importance of each factor may be difficult, the illiquidity discount is frequently assessed overall on a judgmental basis. In practice, the discount for illiquidity and premium for control are both adjustments to the preliminary value estimate instead of being factored into the cost of capital.

When valuing private equity portfolio companies in emerging markets, country risk may also represent a significant additional source of risk frequently added to a modified version of the standard CAPM. Estimating the appropriate country risk premium represents another significant challenge in emerging markets private equity valuation. These technical hurdles relate not only to private equity investments in emerging markets but also increasingly to global private equity transactions conducted "en-bloc" in multiple countries. More than 15 approaches exist for the estimation of the country risk premium.[1]

Valuation in private equity transactions is, therefore, very challenging. Whereas traditional valuation methodologies, such as discounted cash flow analysis, adjusted present value, and techniques based on comparisons from the public market of precedent transactions, are used frequently by investment and valuation professionals, they are applied to private equity situations with care, taking into consideration stress tests and a range of possible future scenarios for the business. Given the challenges of private equity valuation, value estimates based on a combination of several valuation methodologies will provide the strongest support for the estimated value. Private equity valuation is a process that starts as a support for decision making at the transaction phase but should also serve as a monitoring tool to capture new opportunities, or

---

1 The modified country spread model, also called the modified Goldman model, is frequently used in practice. The Erb, Harvey, and Viskanta model, also called the country risk rating model, is gaining increasing popularity among valuation practitioners, partly because of its ease of use and theoretical appeal. For a comprehensive analysis of this topic, see *Estimating Cost of Capital in Emerging Markets*, Yves Courtois, CFA Institute webcasts, www.cfawebcasts.org.

protect from losses, with the objective to continuously create value until the investment is exited. It also serves as a performance reporting tool to investors while the company remains in the fund portfolio. These ongoing valuation and reporting issues are discussed in Section 3.

2.1 How Is Value Created in Private Equity?

The question of how private equity funds actually create value has been much debated inside and outside the private equity industry. The survival of the private equity governance model depends on some economic advantages it may have over the public equity governance model. These potential advantages, described more fully below, include 1) the ability to re-engineer the private firm to generate superior returns, 2) the ability to access credit markets on favorable terms, and 3) a better alignment of interests between private equity firm owners and the managers of the firms they control.

Do private equity houses have superior ability to re-engineer companies and, therefore, generate superior returns? Some of the largest private equity organizations, such as Kohlberg Kravis Roberts (KKR), The Carlyle Group, Texas Pacific Group (TPG), or Blackstone Group, have developed in-house high-end consulting capabilities supported frequently by seasoned industry veterans (former CEOs, CFOs, senior advisers), and have a proven ability to execute deals on a global basis. Irrespective of their size, some of the very best private equity firms have developed effective re-engineering capabilities to add value to their investments. But it is hard to believe that this factor, all else being equal, is the main driver of value added in private equity. Assuming that private equity houses have a superior ability to re-engineer companies, this would mean that public companies have inherently less ability to conduct re-engineering or organizational changes relative to corporations held by private equity organizations. Many public companies, like General Electric or Toyota, have established a long track record of creating value. Thus, only a part of value added created by private equity houses may be explained by superior reorganization and re-engineering capabilities. The answer must also come from other factors.

Is financial leverage the main driver of private equity returns in buyouts? Ample availability of credit at favorable terms (such as low credit spreads and few covenants) led in 2006 and the first half of 2007 to a significant increase in leverage available to buyout transactions. Borrowing 6 to 8 times EBITDA (earnings before interest, taxes, depreciation, and amortization) has been frequent for large transactions conducted during this period. Note that in private equity, leverage is typically measured as a multiple of EBITDA instead of equity. Relative to comparable publicly quoted companies, there is a much greater use of debt in a typical buyout transaction.

When considering the impact of leverage on value, we should naturally turn to one of the foundations of modern finance: the Modigliani–Miller theorem.[2] This theorem, in its basic form, states that, in the absence of taxes, asymmetric information, bankruptcy costs, and assuming efficient markets, the value of a firm is not affected by how the firm is financed. In other words, it should not matter if the firm is financed by equity or debt. The relaxing of the "no taxes assumption" raises interesting questions in leveraged buyouts as the tax shield on the acquisition debt creates value as a result of tax deductibility of interest. One would also expect that the financial leverage of a firm would be set at a level where bankruptcy costs do not outweigh these tax benefits. Unlike public companies, private equity firms may have a better ability to raise higher levels of debt as a result of a better control over management but also as a result of their reputation for having raised, and repaid, such high levels of debt in previous transactions.

---

2 F. Modigliani and M. Miller, "The Cost of Capital, Corporation Finance and the Theory of Investment." *American Economic Review* (June 1958).

Such debt financing is raised initially from the syndicated loan market, but then is frequently repackaged via sophisticated structured products, such as collateralized loan obligations (CLOs), which consist of a portfolio of leveraged loans. In some cases the private equity funds issue high-yield bonds as a way of financing the portfolio company, and these often are sold to funds that create collateralized debt obligations (CDOs). This raises the question of whether a massive transfer of risks to the credit markets is taking place in private equity. If the answer to this last question is positive, then one would expect that it will self-correct during the next economic downturn. Note that at the time of this writing (early 2008), the CDO and CLO markets were undergoing a significant slowdown as a result of the credit market turmoil that started in the summer of 2007, triggered by the subprime mortgage crisis. The CDO and CLO markets are (at this time) inactive. As a result, the LBO market for very large transactions ("mega buyouts") was affected by a lack of financing. Additional leverage is also gained by means of equity-like instruments at the acquisition vehicle level, which are frequently located in a favorable jurisdiction such as Luxembourg, the Channel Islands, Cayman Islands, or the British Virgin Islands. Note that acquisitions by large buyout private equity firms are generally held by a top holding company in a favorable tax jurisdiction. The top holding company's share capital and equity-like instruments are held in turn by investment funds run by a general partner who is controlled by the private equity buyout firm. These instruments are treated as debt for tax purposes within the limits of thin capitalization rules in certain jurisdictions. In Luxembourg, such equity-like instruments are called convertible preferred equity certificates, or CPECs.

The effect of leverage may also be analyzed through Jensen's free cash flow hypothesis.[3] According to Jensen, low growth companies generating high free cash flows tend to invest in projects destroying value (i.e., with a negative net present value) instead of distributing excess cash to shareholders. This argument is a possible explanation[4] as to why a LBO transaction may generate value as excess cash is used to repay the senior debt tranche, effectively removing the management's discretionary use of cash. Part of the value added in private equity may thus be explained by the level of financial leverage.

What other factors may then significantly explain the returns earned by private equity funds? One important factor is the alignment of economic interests between private equity owners and the managers of the companies they control, which can crystallize management efforts to achieve ambitious milestones set by the private equity owners. Results-driven management pay packages, along with various contractual clauses, ensure that managers receive proper incentives to reach their targets, and that they will not be left behind after the private equity house exits their investment. Examples of such contract terms include tag-along, drag-along rights, which are contractual provisions in share purchase agreements that ensure any potential future acquirer of the company may not acquire control without extending an acquisition offer to all shareholders, including the management of the company.

Empirical evidence also shows that managers from public companies subsequently acquired by private equity groups tend to acknowledge an increased level of directness and intensity of input enabling them to conduct higher value-added projects over a longer time frame after the buyout, as opposed to the "short-termism" prevailing during their public market period. This short-termism is mostly driven by shareholders' expectations, the analyst community, and the broad market participants who place a significant emphasis on management to meet quarterly earnings targets. As private equity firms have a longer time horizon in managing their equity investments, they

3 Jensen, M., "Agency Costs of Free Cash Flow, Corporate Finance and Takeovers," *American Economic Review*, vol. 76 no. 2 (1986).
4 Jensen, M., "Eclipse of the Public Corporation," *Harvard Business Review*, 67 (1989).

are able to attract talented managers having the ability to implement sometimes profound restructuring plans in isolation of short-term market consequences. Note however, that private equity firms are not the sole catalysts of change at large companies. Some large organizations, for example General Electric, have a proven ability to stir entrepreneurship at all levels within the company and generate substantial value over a long time horizon.

Effective structuring of investments terms (called the "term sheet") results in a balance of rights and obligations between the private equity firm and the management team. In addition to the clauses discussed above, the following contractual clauses are important illustrations of how private equity firms ensure that the management team is focused on achieving the business plan and that if the objectives are not met, the control and equity allocation held by the private equity firm will increase:

- *Corporate board seats*: ensures private equity control in case of major corporate events such as company sale, takeover, restructuring, IPO, bankruptcy, or liquidation.

- *Noncompete clause*: generally imposed on founders and prevents them from restarting the same activity during a predefined period of time.

- *Preferred dividends and liquidation preference*: private equity firms generally come first when distributions take place, and may be guaranteed a minimum multiple of their original investment before other shareholders receive their returns.

- *Reserved matters*: some domains of strategic importance (such as changes in the business plan, acquisitions, or divestitures) are subject to approval or veto by the private equity firm.

- *Earn-outs (mostly in venture capital)*: mechanism linking the acquisition price paid by the private equity firm to the company's future financial performance over a predetermined time horizon, generally not exceeding 2 to 3 years.

Effective contractual structuring of the investment can thus be a significant source of return to private equity firms. In particular, it may allow venture capital firms, which invest in companies with considerable uncertainties over their future, to significantly increase their level of control over time and even seize control in case the company fails to achieve the agreed goals.

2.2 Using Market Data in Valuation

In most private equity transactions—with the exception of public-to-privates— there is no direct market evidence on the valuation of the company being acquired. But virtually all valuation techniques employ evidence from the market at differing stages in the calculation, rather than relying entirely on accounting data and management forecasts.

The two most important ways in which market data are used to infer the value of the entity being acquired are by analyzing comparison companies that are quoted on public markets and valuations implied by recent transactions involving similar entities. Typically, these techniques focus on the trading or acquisition multiples that exist in the public markets or in recent transactions. For instance, suppose a valuation is sought in the food sector for a retail chain, which is currently a privately owned company. The comparison company approach would look at the trading multiples—such as enterprise value to EBITDA—of comparable public companies, and use this multiple to value the target. Similarly, if there are recent M&A transactions in the food retail sector, the transactions multiples paid could be used to inform the current market value of the target. Of course, it is very important to make sure that the comparisons are appropriate, and this is not always possible, especially for certain businesses that operate in niche sectors or that are pioneering in terms of their products or services.

The use of market data is also important in the DCF approaches, in particular in estimating an appropriate discount rate. Cost of capital for private companies is estimated generally using the same weighted average cost of capital (WACC) formula[5] used for public companies. A serious challenge, however, in assessing the cost of equity in private equity settings is the lack of public historical data on share prices and returns. Therefore, beta (β), which represents the relative exposure of company shares to the market, must be estimated by means of a proxy. This is performed typically by estimating the beta for comparable companies, and then adjusting for financial and operating leverage. When conducting this benchmark exercise, several issues that may depend on analyst judgment should be considered: To what extent are the selected comparable public firms genuinely comparable to the target firm? Should outlying companies be excluded? What is the target debt-to-equity ratio of the target firm vs. industry average? What group of comparable public companies should be selected if the target firm operates in several business segments?

Finally, in DCF valuation techniques, forecasts of future financial performance usually are only available for a few years ahead. Therefore, it is almost always necessary to estimate the terminal value of the company beyond this forecasting horizon. In order to do this, it is possible to apply a perpetual growth rate assumption, although small changes in the assumed growth rate, which are very difficult to predict, can have a significant impact on the resulting valuation. An alternative is to use an assumption about the trading multiple that exists (or is predicted to exist) in public markets, and apply this to the last years' forecast values. For instance, if over the economic cycle the average enterprise value to EBITDA ratio for the publicly quoted companies in an industry is 10, then this might be applied to the final forecast value for EBITDA for the private target as a way of estimating the terminal value.

2.3 Contrasting Valuation in Venture Capital and Buyout Settings

Buyout and venture capital funds are the two main categories of private equity investments both in terms of number of funds and invested amounts. Whereas a venture capital firm may have a specialized industry focus—looking for the next rising star in technology, in life sciences, or another industry—LBO firms generally invest in a portfolio of firms with more predictable cash flow patterns. Venture capital firms (investing in new firms and new technologies) seek revenue growth, whereas buyout firms (investing in larger, established firms) focus more on EBIT or EBITDA growth. The approach to company valuation is thus fundamentally different, and Exhibit 3 presents some of the key distinctions.

Exhibit 3	Characteristics of Buyout and Venture Capital Investments

Buyout Investments:	**Venture Capital Investments:**
▪ Steady and predictable cash flows	▪ Low cash flow predictability, cash flow projections may not be realistic
▪ Excellent market position (can be a niche player)	▪ Lack of market history, new market and possibly unproven future market (early stage venture)
▪ Significant asset base (may serve as basis for collateral lending)	▪ Weak asset base

---

5 WACC = $[E/(E + D)] \times$ (Cost of equity) $+ [D/(E + D)] \times$ (Cost of debt) $(1 - \text{Tax rate})$, where E is the market value of equity and D is the market value of debt.

| Exhibit 3 | Continued |

Buyout Investments:

- Strong and experienced management team

- Extensive use of leverage consisting of a large proportion of senior debt and significant layer of junior and/or mezzanine debt

- Risk is measurable (mature businesses, long operating history)

- Predictable exit (secondary buyout, sale to a strategic buyer, IPO)

- Established products

- Potential for restructuring and cost reduction

- Low working capital requirement

- Buyout firm typically conducts full blown due diligence approach before investing in the target firm (financial, strategic, commercial, legal, tax, environmental)

- Buyout firm monitors cash flow management, strategic, and business planning

- Returns of investment portfolios are generally characterized by lower variance across returns from underlying investments; bankruptcies are rare events

- Large buyout firms are generally significant players in capital markets

- Most transactions are auctions, involving multiple potential acquirers

- Strong performing buyout firms tend to have a better ability to raise larger funds after they have successfully raised their first funds[a]

- Variable revenue to the general partner (GP) at buyout firms generally comprise the following three sources: carried interest, transaction fees, and monitoring fees[c]

Venture Capital Investments:

- Newly formed management team with strong individual track record as entrepreneurs

- Primarily equity funded. Use of leverage is rare and very limited

- Assessment of risk is difficult because of new technologies, new markets, lack of operating history

- Exit difficult to anticipate (IPO, trade sale, secondary venture sale)

- Technological breakthrough but route to market yet to be proven

- Significant cash burn rate required to ensure company development and commercial viability

- Expanding capital requirement if in the growth phase

- Venture capital firm tends to conduct primarily a technology and commercial due diligence before investing; financial due diligence is limited as portfolio companies have no or very little operating history

- Venture capital firm monitors achievement of milestones defined in business plan and growth management

- Returns of investment portfolios are generally characterized by very high returns from a limited number of highly successful investments and a significant number of write-offs from low performing investments or failures

- Venture capital firms tend to be much less active in capital markets

- Many transactions are "proprietary," being the result of relationships between venture capitalists and entrepreneurs

- Venture capital firms tend to be less scalable relative to buyout firms; the increase in size of subsequent funds tend to be less significant[b]

- Carried interest (participation in profits) is generally the main source of variable revenue to the general partner at venture capital firms; transaction and monitoring fees are rare in practice[d]

[a] Andrew Metrick and Ayako Yasuda, "The Economics of Private Equity Funds." University of Pennsylvania, The Wharton School (September 9, 2007).
[b] Ibid.
[c] Ibid.
[d] Ibid.

2.4 Valuation Issues in Buyout Transactions

A buyout is a form of private equity transaction in which the buyer acquires from the seller a controlling stake in the equity capital of a target company. The generic term "buyout" thus refers explicitly to the notion of acquiring control. It comprises a wide range of techniques, including but not limited to, management buyouts (MBOs), leveraged buyouts (LBOs), or takeovers. Our focus in this reading will be on LBOs, which consist in the acquisition of a company using borrowed money to finance a significant portion of the acquisition price.

Typically, the structuring of LBO transactions involves a negotiation between the providers of equity capital, senior debt, high yield bonds, and mezzanine finance. Mezzanine finance[6] is a hybrid form of financing that may be perceived as a bridge between equity and debt. It is generally structured flexibly and tailored to fit the specific requirements of every transaction.

2.4.1 *The LBO Model*

The LBO model is not a separate valuation technique, but rather a way of determining the impact of the capital structure, purchase price, and various other parameters on the returns expected by the private equity fund from the deal.

The LBO model has three main input parameters: the cash flow forecasts of the target company, the expected return from the providers of financing (equity, senior debt, high yield bonds, mezzanine), and the amount of financing available for the transaction. The free cash flow forecasts of the target company are generally prepared by the management of the target company and are subject to an extensive due diligence process (strategic, commercial, financial, legal, and environmental) to determine the reliability of such forecasts. These forecasts are prepared on the basis of an explicit forecast horizon that generally corresponds to the expected holding horizon of the private equity firm in the equity capital of the target company.

The exit year is typically considered as a variable with the objective to determine the expected IRR sensitivity on the equity capital around the anticipated exit date. The exit value is determined most frequently by reference to an expected range of exit multiples determined on the basis of a peer group of comparable companies (Enterprise Value-to-EBITDA).

On the basis of the input parameters, the LBO model provides the maximum price that can be paid to the seller while satisfying the target returns for the providers of financing. This is why the LBO model is not a valuation methodology per se. It is a negotiation tool that helps develop a range of acceptable prices to conclude the transaction.

Exhibit 4 is a "value creation chart," summarizing the sources of the additional value between the exit value and the original cost. Value creation comes from a combination of factors: earnings growth arising from operational improvements and enhanced corporate governance; multiple expansion depending on pre-identified potential exits; and optimal financial leverage and repayment of part of the debt with operational cash flows before the exit. Each component of the value creation chart should be carefully considered and backed by supporting analyses, frequently coming from the lengthy due diligence process (especially commercial, tax, and financial) and also from a strategic review with the objective to quantify the range of plausible value creation.

---

[6] For a more comprehensive discussion of mezzanine finance, refer to "Mezzanine Finance—A Hybrid Instrument with a Future," *Economic Briefing No 42*, Credit Suisse (2006).

	Typical Leveraged Buyout Value Creation Chart
Exhibit 4	

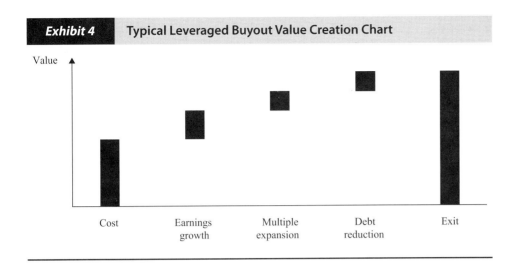

Exhibit 5 provides an example of a €5,000 (amounts in millions) investment in a private equity transaction. The transaction is financed with 50 percent debt and 50 percent equity. The €2,500 equity investment is further broken into €2,400 of preference shares owned by the private equity fund, €95 of equity owned by the private equity fund, and €5 of management equity. The preference shares are promised a 12 percent annual return (paid at exit). The private equity firm equity is promised 95 percent of the residual value of the firm after creditors and preference shares are paid, and management equity holders are promised the remaining 5 percent.

	Stakeholder Payoffs
Exhibit 5	

	Invested	Proceeds	Multiple	IRR
Management	€5m	€109m	21.8x	85%
PE fund	€2,495m	€6,291m	2.5x	20%

€5,000m enterprise value
12% rolled up dividend to preference shares
Management contribute €5m of equity
PE fund €95m equity and all the preference shares
Lenders fund the debt

€5,000m

€8,000m

2008	2013
Management Equity 5	Management 109
PE Equity 95	PE Fund's Equity 2,061
Preference Shares 2,400	Preference Shares 4,230
Debt 2,500	Debt 1,600

Assume that the exit value, five years after investment, is 1.6 times the original cost. The initial investment of €5,000 has an exit value of €8,000. The specific payoffs for the four claimants are as follows:

■ Senior debt has been partially retired with operational cash flows, reducing debt from €2,500 to €1,600. So debtholders get €1,600.

- Preference shares are paid a 12 percent return for 5 years, so they receive €2,400(1.12)^5 = €4,230.

- PE Fund equity receives 95 percent of the terminal equity value, or 0.95[8000 − (4230 + 1600)] = €2,061.

- Management equity receives 5 percent of the terminal equity value, or 0.05[8000 − (4230 + 1600)] = €109.

As you can see, preference shares increase in value over time as a result of their preferred dividend being capitalized, and the equity held by the PE fund and by the management is expected to increase significantly depending on the total enterprise value upon exit. Both the equity sold to managers, frequently known as the management equity program (MEP), and the equity held by the private equity firm are most sensitive to the level of the exit. The larger the exit multiple, the larger the upside potential for both the MEP and the equity held by the private equity firm. In the example, assuming that an exit of 1.6 times cash may be achieved at the anticipated exit date (2013), the management would realize an IRR of 85 percent per annum on its investment and the private equity fund equity holders an IRR of 20 percent per annum. The private equity firm also earns 12 percent per annum on its preference shares.

This chart also demonstrates the critical importance of leverage in buyout transactions. A reduction in financial leverage over time is instrumental in magnifying returns available to shareholders. Note that the bulk of financial leverage in LBOs consists of senior debt, much of which will be amortizing. Therefore, the reduction in financial leverage gradually increases over time as a proportion of principal is paid back to senior lenders on an annual or semi-annual basis depending on the terms of senior debt. As a result of senior debt gradual repayment over time, a larger proportion of operating cash flows becomes available to equity holders. Of course, this mechanism works well as long as no significant adverse economic factors negatively impact the business of the target LBO company and also provided that a successful exit can be handled in the foreseeable future. It should be remembered, however, that these high levels of debt increase significantly the risks borne by the equity investors, and such increased risk should be taken into account when comparing the realized returns with alternative investment classes (such as investments in the stock market).

Typically, a series of scenarios with varying levels of cash exits, growth assumptions, and debt levels are engineered with the use of an LBO model, using as inputs the required rate of return from each stakeholder (equity, mezzanine, senior debt holders), to gain a sound understanding of the buyout firm's flexibility in conducting the deal.

2.5 Valuation Issues in Venture Capital Transactions

In venture capital, pre-money valuation and post-money valuation are two fundamental concepts. Pre-money valuation (PRE) refers to the agreed value of a company prior to a round of financing or investment (I). Post-money valuation (POST) is the value of a company after the financing or investing round. Therefore:

POST = PRE + I

The proportionate ownership of the venture capital investor is determined by I/POST.

Example 1

Investment and Ownership Interest of a VC Firm

A venture capital firm invests £1 million on a £1.5 million pre-money valuation and the VC firm obtains 40 percent of shares. In this case, PRE is £1.5 million, POST is £2.5 million, and the proportion financed by venture capital is £1 million/£2.5 million. The parties agreed that the VC firm would retain 40 percent of the shares and have that proportion of the rights of shareholders should dividends be paid or the firm sold.

Typically, both pre-money valuation and the level of the venture capital investment are subject to intense negotiations between the founders and the venture capital firm, bearing in mind the fundamental issue of dilution of ownership. Dilution of ownership is the reduction in the proportional ownership of a shareholder in the capital of a company resulting from the issuance of additional shares and/or of securities convertible into shares at some stage in the future. Additional financing rounds and the issuance of stock options to the management of a company are examples of dilution of ownership.

In VC transactions, there is typically significant uncertainty surrounding the projected future cash flows. Consequently, the discounted cash flow methodology is rarely used as the first method to determine value. Similarly, there are challenges applying the comparable companies approach as start-ups generally have unique features and it may be extremely difficult to find comparable quoted companies operating in the same field. Alternative valuation methodologies including the venture capital approach[7] or the real option methodology are also used to determine value. Traditional valuation methodologies typically comprise the income approach (discounted cash flow valuation), the relative value or market approach (information relative to a group of comparable companies is gathered and normalized relative to the EBITDA, EBIT, and revenue of the company being valued), and the cost approach (cost to recreate or replace the asset or company). Generally speaking, the appraisal of intangible assets, comprising the founder's know-how, experience, licenses, patents, and in progress research and development (IPRD), along with an assessment of the expected market potential of the company's product or products in development form the basis for assessing a pre-money valuation. Because of the significant level of uncertainty surrounding the business, it is not infrequent to observe a cap on the pre-money valuation (i.e., €3 million, €5 million, etc.).

In buyouts, given the significant predictability of cash flows, the income-based approach (discounted cash flows, adjusted present value, LBO model, target IRR) is frequently used as a primary method to determine the value of equity, considering the expected change in leverage until the time of exit of the investment. The initial high and declining financial leverage is the main technical valuation issue that needs to be adequately factored into the income approach when applied to a buyout valuation. The value is also frequently corroborated by an analysis of the peer group of comparable publicly traded companies.

2.6 Exit Routes: Returning Cash to Investors

The exit is among the most critical mechanisms to unlock value in private equity. Most private equity firms consider their exit options prior to investing and factor their assessment of the exit outcome into their analysis of target and expected internal rate of return.

Private equity investors generally have access to the following four exit routes for their investments:

- *Initial Public Offering (IPO)*: going public offers significant advantages including higher valuation multiples as a result of an enhanced liquidity,

---

7 Discussed in "A Note on Valuation of Venture Capital Deals."

access to large amounts of capital, and the possibility to attract higher caliber managers. But an IPO comes at the expense of a cumbersome process, less flexibility, and significant costs. Therefore, an IPO is an appropriate exit route for private companies with an established operating history, excellent growth prospects, and having a sufficient size. Timing of the IPO is also an important consideration. After the internet bubble collapse in March 2000, the number of successful IPOs plummeted in the subsequent years, forcing venture capital firms to change their exit plans for many of their investments.

■ *Secondary Market*: sale of stake held by a financial investor to other financial investors or to strategic investors (companies operating or willing to establish in the same sector or market of the portfolio company). With the increased segmentation of private equity, secondary market transactions tend to occur within each segment, i.e., buyout firms tend to sell to other buyout firms (secondary buyouts) and venture firms to other venture firms (secondary venture capital transactions). These secondary market transactions are very common in practice and currently account for a significant proportion of exits, especially in the buyout segment. Venture capital exits by means of a buyout are also possible but rare in practice as buyout firms are reluctant to finance development stage companies with a significant amount of leverage. The two main advantages of secondary market transactions are 1) the possibility to achieve the highest valuation multiples in the absence of an IPO, and 2) with the segmentation of private equity firms, specialized firms have the skill to bring their portfolio companies to the next level (restructuring, merger, new market) and sell either to a strategic investor seeking to exploit synergies or to another private equity firm having another set of skills and the ability to further add value to the portfolio company.

■ *Management Buyout (MBO)*: takeover by the management group using significant amounts of leverage to finance the acquisition of the company. Alignment of interest is optimal under this exit scenario but may come at the expense of an excessive leverage that may significantly reduce the company's flexibility.

■ *Liquidation*: controlling shareholders have the power to liquidate the company if the company is no longer viable. This exit mechanism generally results in a floor value for the portfolio company but may come at a cost of very negative publicity for the private equity firm if the portfolio company is large and the employee count is significant.

Timing the exit and determining the optimal exit route are important investment management decisions to be made by private equity firms. Although the exit may be carefully planned, the unexpected can cause changes to the exit plan. This may mean that the exit could be delayed or accelerated depending on the market or purely opportunistic circumstances. Suppose, for example, that an LBO firm is planning an exit of one of its portfolio companies but the public market and economic conditions have collapsed, rendering any exit via a trade sale or an IPO unprofitable. The LBO firm may instead conduct another acquisition at depressed prices, merge this acquisition with the portfolio company with the objective to strengthen its market position or product range, and wait for better market conditions before conducting the sale. Flexibility is thus critical in private equity during harder times and underlines the importance for a private equity firm to have sufficient financial strength.

There seems to be no boundaries to the size of the largest buyout transactions as expectations have been consistently exceeded over the past few years and the $50 billion threshold appears now to be in sight for the largest buyout firms. The three largest buyout transactions in history, HCA Inc., Equity Office, and TXU Corporation, were all undertaken over the eighteen months before this reading was written. Private equity firms appear to be moving into uncharted territory in regards to managing exits at that level. The central question about these mega buyout transactions is how the exit will take place given that the extent of the exit possibilities is much more limited relative to smaller deals. IPOs, for example, raise significantly more challenges, such as the need for a gradual exit over time because only a single block of shares can be sold initially, and may prove excessively risky if market conditions are suboptimal. Some large companies may be viewed as holding companies of a portfolio of real assets. Such companies may be sold in tranches to prospective buyers. The real challenge will be for unified companies for which an exit will need to take place for the entire entity.

Understanding the anticipated exit provides clues as to what valuation methodologies or IRR models to employ. Timing of the exit will influence the way stress testing is conducted on the expected exit multiple. When the exit is anticipated in the near future (one to two years), the prevailing valuation multiples extracted from comparable quoted firms provide good guidance on the expected exit multiple. Stress tests on that value may be conducted for small incremental changes and on the basis of market knowledge. If the exit is anticipated in a much longer time horizon, the current valuation multiples are less relevant and stress tests may need to be conducted on a wider range of values to determine the anticipated exit multiple. Stress testing in this context consists of simulating incremental changes in the input variables of the valuation model (such as components of the discount factor, terminal growth rates, etc.) and to financial forecasts (sales growth, assumed future operating margins, etc.) in order to determine the range of value outcomes and to assess the stability of the valuation methodology.

2.7 Summary

Valuation is the most critical aspect of private equity transactions. The investment decision-making process typically flows from the screening of investment opportunities to preparing a proposal, appraising the investment, structuring the deal, and finally to the negotiating phase. Because of the difficulties in valuing private companies, a variety of alternative valuation methods are typically used to provide guidance on the appropriate range. Along with the various due diligence investigations (commercial or strategic, financial, legal, tax, environmental) generally conducted on private equity investment opportunities, valuation serves a dual purpose: assessing a company's ability to generate superior cash flows from a distinctive competitive advantage and serving as a benchmark for negotiations with the seller. After all, although seeing opportunities for adding value is important, it is also essential—for the investors in the private equity fund—that the seller does not appropriate all the potential gains by extracting a high price during the transaction.

Post-investment, valuation of private equity investments is also very important, as investors expect to be fully informed about the performance of the portfolio companies. This raises a separate set of issues, which are considered in the next section.

PRIVATE EQUITY FUND STRUCTURES AND VALUATION

3

When analyzing and evaluating financial performance of a private equity fund from the perspective of an investor, a solid grasp of private equity fund structures, terms of investment, private equity fund valuation, and due diligence are an absolute prerequisite. The distinctive characteristics of private equity relative to public equities raise many more challenges when interpreting financial performance. Two of the main differentiating characteristics of private equity, in addition to the structure and terms, relate to the nature of subscriptions made by investors in private equity structures and to the "J" curve effect. Investors commit initially a certain amount to the private equity fund that is subsequently drawn by the fund as the fund's capital is deployed in target portfolio companies. This contrasts with public market investing in which investment orders typically are disbursed fully at the time the orders are settled on the markets. The "J-curve" effect refers to the typical time profile of reported returns by private equity funds, whereby low or negative returns are reported in the early years of a private equity fund (in large part as a result of the fees' impact on net returns), followed by increased returns thereafter as the private equity firm manages portfolio companies toward the exit.

3.1 Understanding Private Equity Fund Structures

The limited partnership has emerged as the dominant form for private equity structures in most jurisdictions. Funds that are structured as limited partnerships are governed by a limited partnership agreement between the fund manager, called the general partner (GP), and the fund's investors, called limited partners (LPs). Whereas the GP has management control over the fund and is jointly liable for all debts, LPs have limited liability, i.e., they do not risk more than the amount of their investment in the fund. The other main alternative to the limited partnership is a corporate structure, called company limited by shares, which mirrors in its functioning the limited partnership but offers a better legal protection to the GP and to some extent the LPs, depending on the jurisdictions. Some fund structures, especially the Luxembourg-based private equity fund vehicle SICAR (société d'investissement en capital à risque), are subject to a light regulatory oversight offering enhanced protection to LPs. The vast majority of these private equity fund structures are "closed end," which restricts existing investors from redeeming their shares over the lifetime of the fund and limiting new investors to entering the fund only at predefined time periods, at the discretion of the GP.

Private equity firms operate effectively in two businesses: the business of managing private equity investments and the business of raising funds. Therefore, private equity firms tend to plan their marketing efforts well in advance of the launch of their funds to ensure that the announced target fund size will be met successfully once the fund is effectively started. The premarketing phase of a private equity fund, depending on whether it is a first fund or a following fund, may take between one to two years. Once investors effectively commit their investments in the fund, private equity managers draw on investors' commitments as the fund is being deployed and invested in portfolio companies. Private equity funds tend to have a duration of 10–12 years, generally extendable to an additional 2–3 years. Exhibit 6 illustrates the funding stages for a private equity fund.

Exhibit 6	Funding Stages for a Private Equity Fund

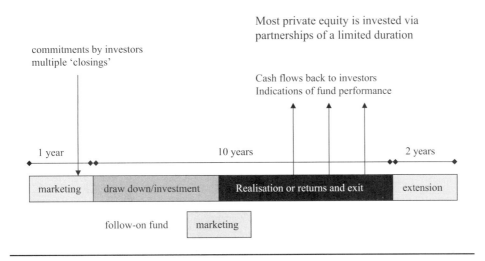

How are private equity funds structured?

Fund terms are contractually defined in a fund prospectus or limited partnership agreement available to qualified prospective investors. The definition of qualified investors depends on the jurisdiction. Typically, wealth criteria (exceeding US$1 million, for example) and/or a minimum subscription threshold (minimum €125,000, for example) apply. The nature of the terms are frequently the result of the balance of negotiation power between GPs and LPs. Although the balance of negotiation power used to be in favor of LPs, it has now turned in favor of GPs, at least among the over-subscribed funds. Any significant downturn in private equity may change the balance of power in favor of LPs. Negotiation of terms has the objective to ensure alignment of interests between the GP and LPs and defining the GP's incentives (transaction fees, profit shares, etc.) The most significant terms may be categorized into economic and corporate governance terms.

Economic Terms

- *Management fees* represent a percentage of committed capital paid annually to the GP during the lifetime of the fund. Fees in the region of 1.5 percent to 2.5 percent are fairly common. Although less frequent, management fees may also be calculated on the basis of the net asset value or on invested capital.

- *Transaction fees* are fees paid to GPs in their advisory capacity when they provide investment banking services for a transaction (mergers and acquisitions, IPOs) benefiting the fund. These fees may be subject to sharing agreements with LPs, typically according to a 50/50 split between the GP and LPs. When such fee-sharing agreements apply, they generally come as a deduction to the management fees.

- *Carried interest* represents the general partner's share of profits generated by a private equity fund. Carried interest is frequently in the region of 20 percent of the fund's profits (after management fees).

- *Ratchet* is a mechanism that determines the allocation of equity between shareholders and the management team of the private equity controlled company. A ratchet enables the management team to increase its equity allocation depending on the company's actual performance and the return achieved by the private equity firm.

■ *Hurdle rate* is the internal rate of return that a private equity fund must achieve before the GP receives any carried interest. The hurdle rate is typically in the range of 7 percent to 10 percent. The objective is to align the interests of the GP with those of LPs by giving additional incentives to the GP to outperform traditional investment benchmarks.

Example 2

Calculation of Carried Interest

Suppose that a LBO fund has committed capital of US$100 million, carried interest of 20 percent, and a hurdle rate of 8 percent. The fund called 75 percent of its commitments from investors at the beginning of year 1, which was invested at the beginning of year 1 in target company A for $40 million and target company B for $35 million. Suppose that at the end of year 2, a profit of $5 million has been realized by the GP upon exit of the investment in company A, and the value of the investment in company B has remained unchanged. Suppose also that the GP is entitled to carried interest on a deal-by-deal basis, i.e., the IRR used to calculate carried interest is calculated for each investment upon exit. A theoretical carried interest of $1 million (20 percent of $5 million) could be granted to the GP, but the IRR upon exit of investment in company A is only 6.1 percent. Until the IRR exceeds the hurdle rate, no carried interest may be paid to the GP.

■ *Target fund size* is expressed as an absolute amount in the fund prospectus or information memorandum. This information is critical as it provides a signal both about the GP's capacity to manage a portfolio of a predefined size and also in terms of fund raising. A fund that closed with a significantly lower size relative to the target size would raise questions about the GP's ability to raise funds on the market and would be perceived as a negative signal.

■ *Vintage year* is the year the private equity fund was launched. Reference to vintage year allows performance comparison of funds of the same stage and industry focus.

■ *Term of the fund* is typically 10 years, extendable for additional shorter periods (by agreement with the investors). Although infrequently observed, funds can also be of unlimited duration, and in this case are often quoted on stock markets (such as investment trusts).

Corporate Governance Terms

■ *Key man clause.* Under the key man clause, a certain number of key named executives are expected to play an active role in the management of the fund. In case of the departure of such a key executive or insufficient time spent in the management of the fund, the "key man" clause provides that the GP may be prohibited from making any new investments until a new key executive is appointed.

■ *Disclosure and confidentiality.* Private equity firms have no obligations to disclose publicly their financial performance. A court ruling[8] requiring California Public Employees Retirement System (CalPERS) to report publicly its returns on private equity investments, the Freedom of Information Act

---

8 S. Chaplinsky and S. Perry, "CalPERS vs. Mercury News: Disclosure comes to private equity," Darden Business Publishing.

(FOIA) in the United States, and similar legislation in other European countries have led public pension funds to report information about their private equity investments. Disclosable information relates to financial performance of the underlying funds but does not extend to information on the companies in which the funds invest. This latter information is not typically disclosed. The reporting by CalPERS is a prominent example of the application of this clause.[9] Some private equity fund terms may be more restrictive on confidentiality and information disclosure and effectively limit information available to investors subject to FOIA.

■ *Clawback provision.* A clawback provision requires the GP to return capital to LPs in excess of the agreed profit split between the GP and LPs. This provision ensures that, when a private equity firm exits from a highly profitable investment early in the fund's life but subsequent exits are less profitable, the GP pays back capital contributions, fees, and expenses to LPs to ensure that the profit split is in line with the fund's prospectus. The clawback is normally due on termination of the fund but may be subject to an annual reconciliation (or "true-up").

■ *Distribution waterfall.* A distribution waterfall is a mechanism providing an order of distributions to LPs first before the GP receives carried interest. Two distinct distribution mechanisms are predominant: deal-by-deal waterfalls allowing earlier distribution of carried interest to the GP after each individual deal (mostly employed in the United States) and total return waterfalls resulting in earlier distributions to LPs as carried interest is calculated on the profits of the entire portfolio (mostly employed in Europe and for funds-of-funds). Under the total return method, two alternatives are possible to calculate carried interest. In the first alternative, the GP receives carried interest only after the fund has returned the entire committed capital to LPs. In the second alternative, the GP receives carried interest on any distribution as long as the value of the investment portfolio exceeds a certain threshold (usually 20 percent) above invested capital.

Example 3

Distribution Waterfalls

Suppose a private equity fund has a committed capital totaling £300 million and a carried interest of 20 percent. After a first investment of £30 million, the fund exits the investment 9 months later with a £15 million profit. Under the deal-by-deal method, the GP would be entitled to 20 percent of the deal profit, i.e., £3 million. In the first alternative of the total return method, the entire proceeds of the sale, i.e., £45 million, are entitled to the LPs and nothing (yet) to the GP. In the second alternative, the exit value of £45 million exceeds by more than 20 percent the invested value of £30 million. The GP would thus be entitled to £3 million.

Continuing the above example with a clawback provision with an annual true-up, suppose that the deal-by-deal method applies and that a second investment of £25 million is concluded with a loss of £5 million 1 year later. Therefore, at the annual true-up, the GP would have to pay back £1 million to LPs. In practice, an escrow account is used to regulate these fluctuations until termination of the fund.

---

9 Information about CalPERS' private equity holdings is available from the company's website, www.calpers.gov.

■ *Tag-along, drag along rights* are contractual provisions in share purchase agreements that ensure any potential future acquirer of the company may not acquire control without extending an acquisition offer to all shareholders, including the management of the company.

■ *No-fault divorce.* A GP may be removed without cause, provided that a super majority (generally above 75 percent) of LPs approve that removal.

■ *Removal for "cause"* is a clause that allows either a removal of the GP or an earlier termination of the fund for "cause." Such "cause" may include gross negligence of the GP, a "key person" event, a felony conviction of a key management person, bankruptcy of the GP, or a material breach of the fund prospectus.

■ *Investment restrictions* generally impose a minimum level of diversification of the fund's investments, a geographic and/or sector focus, or limits on borrowing.

■ *Co-investment.* LPs generally have a first right of co-investing along with the GP. This can be advantageous for the LPs as fees and profit share are likely to be lower (or zero) on co-invested capital. The GP and affiliated parties are also typically restricted in their co-investments to prevent conflicts of interest with their LPs. Crossover co-investments are a classic example of a conflict of interest. A crossover co-investment occurs when a subsequent fund launched by the same GP invests in a portfolio company that has received funding from a previous fund.

3.2 What Are the Risks and Costs of Investing in Private Equity?

Private equity investing is typically restricted by laws and regulations in most jurisdictions to "qualified investors" comprising institutions and high-net-worth individuals meeting certain wealth criteria. These restrictions are motivated by the high levels of risks incurred in private equity investing, and are generally subject to disclosure in the private equity fund prospectus. Such risks may be categorized as general private equity risk factors, investment strategy specific risk factors (buyout, venture capital, mezzanine), industry specific risk factors, risk factors specific to the investment vehicle, and sometimes regional or emerging market risks when applicable.

Following are some general private equity risk factors:

■ *Illiquidity of investments*: Because private equity investments are generally not traded on any securities market, the exit of investments may not be conducted on a timely basis.

■ *Unquoted investments*: Investing in unquoted securities may be risky relative to investing in securities quoted on a regulated securities exchange.

■ *Competition for attractive investment opportunities*: Competition for finding investment opportunities on attractive terms may be high.

■ *Reliance on the management of investee companies (agency risk)*: There is no assurance that the management of the investee companies will run the company in the best interests of the private equity firm, particularly in earlier stage deals in which the management may retain a controlling stake in the company and enjoy certain private benefits of control.

■ *Loss of capital*: High business and financial risks may result in substantial loss of capital.

■ *Government regulations*: Investee companies' product and services may be subject to changes in government regulations that adversely impact their business model.

- *Taxation risk*: Tax treatment of capital gains, dividends, or limited partnerships may change over time.

- *Valuation of investments*: Valuation of private equity investments is subject to significant judgment. When valuations are not conducted by an independent party, they may be subject to biases.

- *Lack of investment capital*: Investee companies may require additional future financing that may not be available.

- *Lack of diversification*: Investment portfolios may be highly concentrated and may, therefore, be exposed to significant losses. Investors generally want to invest in a mix of private equity funds of different vintages, different stages of developments for underlying investments in portfolio companies, and achieve a certain level of diversification across various private equity strategies (large and mid-market buyout, venture capital, mezzanine, restructuring).

- *Market risk*: Changes in general market conditions (interest rates, currency exchange rates) may adversely affect private equity investments. The impact of market risk is, however, long term in nature given the long-term horizon of private equity firms. Temporary short-term market fluctuations are generally irrelevant.

Costs associated with private equity investing are substantially more significant relative to public market investing. These costs may be broken down as follows:

- *Transaction fees*: Corresponding to due diligence, bank financing costs, legal fees for arranging acquisition, and sale transactions in investee companies.

- *Investment vehicle fund setup costs*: Comprises mainly legal costs for the setup of the investment vehicle. Such costs are typically amortized over the life of the investment vehicle.

- *Administrative costs*: Custodian, transfer agent, and accounting costs generally charged yearly as a fraction of the investment vehicle's net asset value.

- *Audit costs*: A fixed annual fee.

- *Management and performance fees*: These are generally more significant relative to plain investment funds. A 2 percent management fee and a 20 percent performance fee are common in the private equity industry.

- *Dilution*: A more subtle source of cost, dilution may come from stock option plans granted to the management and to the private equity firm and from additional rounds of financing.

- *Placement fees*: Fundraising fees may be charged up front or by means of a trailer fee by the fund raiser. A trailer fee is generally charged annually, corresponding to a fraction of the amount invested by limited partners as long as these amounts remain invested in the investment vehicle. An up front placement fee of 2 percent is not uncommon in private equity.

3.3 Due Diligence Investigations by Potential Investors

Prior to investing in a private equity fund, prospective investors generally conduct a thorough due diligence on the fund. Several fundamental characteristics of private equity funds underline the importance of the due diligence process.

- Private equity funds tend to exhibit a strong persistence of returns over time. This means that top performing funds tend to continue to outperform and poor performing funds also tend to continue to perform poorly or disappear.

- The performance range between funds is extremely large. For example, the difference between top quartile and third quartile fund IRRs can be about 20 percentage points.

- Liquidity in private equity is typically very limited and thus LPs are locked for the long term. On the other hand, when private equity funds exit an investment, they return the cash to the investors immediately. Therefore, the "duration" of an investment in private equity is typically shorter than the maximum life of the fund.

The European Venture Capital association (EVCA) has issued an "Illustrative due diligence questionnaire—Venture capital funds," that may serve as a guide, but not as a substitute, for the due diligence process conducted by LPs before investing in a venture capital or private equity fund.

3.4 Private Equity Fund Valuation

The description of private equity valuation[10] in a fund prospectus is generally associated with the fund's calculation of net asset value (NAV). The NAV is generally defined as the value of the fund assets less liabilities corresponding to the accrued fund expenses. The fund's assets are frequently valued by GPs, depending on their valuation policies, in the following ways:[11]

1. at cost with significant adjustments for subsequent financing events or deterioration

2. at lower of cost or market value

3. by a revaluation of a portfolio company whenever a new financing round involving new investors takes place

4. at cost with no interim adjustment until the exit

5. with a discount for restricted securities[12]

6. more rarely, marked to market by reference to a peer group of public comparables and applying illiquidity discounts.

Private equity industry valuation standards, such as those originally produced by the British, French, and European industry associations (latest revisions can be found at www.privateequityvaluation.com), have increasingly been adopted by funds operating in many jurisdictions.

Industry practices suggest that because a valuation is adjusted with a new round of financing, the NAV may be more stale in down markets when there is a long gap between funding rounds. This mechanism is similar to the valuation of investment funds of publicly quoted securities. There is thus a fundamental implicit break-up assumption whereby the fund may be broken up at any time, the funds underlying investments may be liquidated individually and immediately, and the proceeds returned to LPs. Whereas this fundamental break-up assumption may hold for publicly traded securities, which are marked to market, this assumption may be more questionable for private equity investment portfolios typically held over a long period of time. The fundamental question facing investors is: At what value should investments in portfolio companies be reported, prior to the private equity fund exiting the investment and returning the proceeds to the LPs? There is no straight answer to that question as there is no market for securities issued by private equity companies.

---

10 For a comprehensive discussion of this topic, refer to Thomas Meyer and Pierre-Yves Mathonet, *Beyond the J Curve: Managing a Portfolio of Venture Capital and Private Equity Funds*, Wiley, (2004).
11 Foster Center for Entrepreneurship and Private Equity, Dartmouth College.
12 Example: Reg. 144 securities.

Undrawn LP commitments raise additional challenges for private equity fund valuation. Although undrawn commitments represent a LP's legal obligations to meet capital calls in the future, they are not accounted for in the NAV calculation. The value of such undrawn commitments largely depends on the expected cash flows that will be generated by future investments made by the GP. Although undrawn commitments are not part of the NAV, they should be viewed as unfunded liabilities. McGrady[13] suggested to "gauge the reaction to the unfunded portion, a seller may consider the ease with which a general partnership could raise another fund in the current market."

Comparisons between private equity funds following different investment strategies require a careful analysis of their respective valuation policies in order to avoid biases. Whereas, for example, an early stage venture capital fund may keep its investments at cost, a late stage development capital fund may mark its portfolio companies by reference to public market comparables. At times when a market bubble is forming in certain sectors, such as the technology bubble in 2000, such reference to public market comparables may distort the valuation of portfolio companies and thus reported fund returns.

Another important aspect of private equity valuations is that they are mostly performed by GPs. Under the pressure from LPs, an increasing number of annual or semi-annual valuations are performed by independent valuers that are mandated by GPs.

The above discussion on private equity valuation emphasizes both the qualitative and quantitative issues that need to be taken into consideration.

3.5 Evaluating Fund Performance

Because each private equity fund is unique, the assessment of financial performance needs to be made with a good knowledge of the specific fund structure, terms, valuation policies, and the outcome of the due diligence. Typically, an analysis of a private equity fund's financial performance includes the following.

3.5.1 Analysis of IRR and Multiples Gross and Net of Fees since Inception

Here, net of fees means net of management fees, carried interest, or of any other financial arrangements that accrue to the GP. The IRR, a cash-flow-weighted rate of return, is deemed the most appropriate measure of private equity performance by the Global Investment Performance Standards (GIPS), Venture Capital and Private Equity Valuation Principles, and by other venture capital and private equity standards. The interpretation of IRR in private equity should, however, be subject to caution because an implicit assumption behind the IRR calculation is that the fund is fully liquid, whereas a significant portion of the NAV is illiquid during a substantial part of a private equity fund's life. Therefore, valuation of portfolio companies according to industry standards is important to ensure the quality of the IRR figures.

The distinction between gross and net IRR is also important. Gross IRR relates cash flows between the private equity fund and its portfolio companies and is often considered a good measure of the investment management team's track record in creating value. Net IRR relates cash flows between the private equity fund and LPs, and so captures the returns enjoyed by investors. Fees and profit shares create significant deviations between gross and net IRRs. IRR analysis is often combined with a benchmark IRR analysis, i.e., the median IRR for the relevant peer group of comparable private equity funds operating with a similar investment strategy and vintage year. This is particularly important because there are clear trends over time in private equity returns, with some vintage years producing much higher returns than others.

In addition to IRR, multiples are used frequently as a measure of performance. Multiples simply measure the total return to investors relative to the total sum invested. Although multiples ignore the time value of money, their ease of calculation and

---

13 C. McGrady, Pricing private equity secondary transactions, Dallas, TX, Cogent Partners (2002).

their ability to differentiate between "realized" actual proceeds from divestments and "unrealized" portfolio subject to GP valuation make these ratios very popular among LPs. The multiples used most frequently by LPs and also defined by GIPS that provide additional information about private equity funds performance are as follows:

- PIC (paid in capital): the ratio of paid in capital to date divided by committed capital. This ratio provides information about the proportion of capital called by a GP.

- DPI (distributed to paid in): cumulative distributions paid out to LPs as a proportion of the cumulative invested capital. This ratio is often called "cash-on-cash return." It provides an indication of the private equity fund's realized return on investment. DPI is presented net of management fees and carried interest.

- RVPI (residual value to paid in): value of LPs' shareholding held with the private equity fund as a proportion of the cumulative invested capital. The numerator is measured as the remaining portfolio companies as valued by the GP. This ratio is a measure of the private equity fund's unrealized return on investment. RVPI is presented net of management fees and carried interest.

- TVPI (total value to paid in): the portfolio companies' distributed and undistributed value as a proportion of the cumulative invested capital. TVPI is the sum of DPI and RVPI. TVPI is presented net of management fees and carried interest.

In addition to quantitative measures of return, an analysis of a private equity fund financial performance also includes:

- an analysis of realized investments since inception, commenting on all successes and failures;

- an analysis of unrealized investments, highlighting all red flags in the portfolio and the expected time to exit per portfolio company;

- a cash flow forecast at the portfolio company level and for the aggregate portfolio; and

- an analysis of portfolio valuation, audited financial statements, and the NAV.

Example 4

Calculating and Interpreting a Private Equity Fund Performance

Suppose that a private equity fund has a DPI of 0.07 and a RVPI of 0.62 after 5 years. IRR is −17 percent. The fund follows a venture capital strategy in high technology, has a vintage year of 1999, and a term of 10 years. A DPI of 7 percent indicates that few successful exits were made. A RVPI of 62 percent points to an extended J-curve effect for the fund as TVPI amounts to 69 percent at the midlife of the fund. A vintage year of 1999 provides hints that the fund was actually started before the technology market crash of 2000 and that the routes to exit for portfolio companies have been dramatically changed. During the technology market crash, the investment portfolio probably suffered a number of complete write-offs. In this situation, an LP should thus consider the state of the existing portfolio to examine the number of write-offs and other signals of ailing companies in the fund portfolio. The risk of not recovering the invested amount at termination of the fund is significant. Compliance with valuation policies by the GP should also be closely monitored by LPs to ensure that the GP's expectations are not excessive given the current state of the portfolio.

Note that with the increased allocations to private equity, performance comparisons across asset classes are often misinterpreted. IRR, the standard measure of private equity returns, is cash-flow-weighted, whereas performance of most other asset classes is measured in terms of time-weighted rate of return. In an attempt to solve these performance comparison issues, new performance measurement techniques have been developed. One of them, called the Public Market Equivalent (PME), was proposed by Austin Long and Craig Nickles in the mid-1990s. It provides a solution to this benchmarking issue, but its reliability poses, at times, serious problems.[14] Put simply, PME is the cash-flow-weighted rate of return of an index (S&P 500 or any other index) assuming the same cash flow pattern as a private equity fund. It is thus an index return measure.

CONCEPT IN ACTION: EVALUATING A PRIVATE EQUITY FUND

4

This section illustrates the use of many of the concepts above to evaluate the performance of a private equity fund.

Michael Hornsby, CFA, is a Senior Investment Officer at Icarus, a U.K.-based institutional investor in private equity. He is contemplating an investment in Europa Venture Partners III, a new late stage technology venture capital fund, after a thorough due diligence performed on the fund and an updated due diligence on the GP. Icarus has been an investor in Europa Venture Partners' (EVP) previous two funds, EVP I and EVP II. Icarus has been satisfied with the performance of EVP so far and is seeking to further expand its relationship with this GP because Icarus considers it a niche venture capital firm operating in a less crowded segment of the pan-European technology markets. As a result of its success, EVP decided to increase its carried interest for the third fund to 25 percent from 20 percent for the previous two funds. Hornsby has received the information about the fund's financial performance and is seeking assistance in calculating and interpreting financial performance for a number of specific queries as outlined below.

Europa Venture Partners (EVP)

General Partner — Europa Venture Partners (EVP) was established to provide equity financing to later stage technology companies in need of development capital across Europe. The GP seeks to provide strategic support to seasoned entrepreneurial teams and bring proven new technologies to the market. The GP targets investment in portfolio companies between €2 million and €10 million.

		Established in 1999		Type: Development Capital				
Fund	Vintage	Actual Fund Size (€ Millions)	Capital Called (%)	Mgmt Fees (%)	Carried Interest (%)	Hurdle Rate (%)	Term	Report Date
EVP I	2001	125	92	2	20	8	2009	31 Dec 2006
EVP II	2003	360	48	2	20	8	2012	31 Dec 2006

Financial performance for investments by Icarus in EVP funds

(continued)

---

14 Christophe Rouvinez, "Private Equity Benchmarking with PME +," *Venture Capital Journal* (August 2003).

Fund	**Committed Capital (€ Millions)**	**Capital Called Down**	**Gross IRR (%)**	**Net IRR (%)**	**DPI (X)**	**RVPI (X)**	**TVPI (X)**	**Quartile**
EVP I	10	9.2	16.1	11.3	1.26	1.29	2.55	1
EVP II	25	12.0	1.6	(0.4)	0.35	1.13	1.48	2

Hornsby also is interested in verifying management fees, carried interest, and the NAV of EVP I. He has the following information about yearly capital calls, operating results, and distributions.

Calls, Operating Results, and Distributions (€ Million)

	2001	2002	2003	2004	2005	2006
Called-down	50	15	10	25	10	5
Realized results	0	0	10	35	40	80
Unrealized results	−5	−15	15	10	15	25
Distributions	—	—	—	25	45	75

Operating results correspond to the sum of realized results from exits of portfolio companies and of unrealized results from the revaluation of investments held in portfolio companies. In addition to the information available on EVP I, Hornsby also knows from the fund prospectus that the distribution waterfall is calculated according to the total return method following the first alternative, i.e., the GP receives carried interest only after the fund has returned the entire committed capital to LPs. Management fees are calculated on the basis of the paid-in capital. Hornsby also wants to calculate DPI, RVPI, and TVPI of EVP I for 2006 and is interested in understanding how to calculate gross and net IRRs.

1. Interpret and compare the financial performance of EVP I and EVP II.

2. Based on the information given, calculate the management fees, carried interest, and the NAV of EVP I. Also calculate DPI, RVPI, and TVPI of EVP I for 2006. Explain on the basis of EVP I how gross and net IRRs are calculated, and calculate the gross and net IRRs.

Solution to 1:   In the table above, the first venture capital fund (EVP I) made its first capital call in 2001 and returned €1.26 (all amounts in millions) for every €1 that had been drawn down to LPs two years ahead of the termination of the fund. EVP I residual value remains high at 1.29 times capital drawn down, which is a good signal about the profitability of the fund at termination. The fund ranks in the first quartile, which means that it belongs to the best performing funds of that category and vintage year. Gross IRR of 16.1 percent after 6 years of operations, and 11.3 percent net of fees represents a good performance.

The second fund exhibits, to date, very modest performance in terms of gross and net IRR, which indicates that the fund is still experiencing the J-curve effect. EVP II has returned 35 percent of capital drawn down to LPs and a residual value of 113 percent of capital drawn down, which indicates that despite the fund being in its early years, the GP has already managed a number of profitable exits and increased the value of the investment portfolio halfway through the termination of the fund.

Actual fund size significantly exceeds previous fund size and is an indication that the GP is gaining momentum in terms of fund raising, probably partly attributable to the strong performance of the first fund.

Solution to 2:

					Cash Flows and Distributions (€ Million)			
Year	Called-down (1)	Paid-in Capital (2)	Mgmt Fees (3)	Operating Results (4)	NAV before Distributions (5)	Carried Interest (6)	Distributions (7)	NAV after Distributions (8)
2001	50	50	1.0	−5	44.0			44.0
2002	15	65	1.3	−15	42.7			42.7
2003	10	75	1.5	25	76.2			76.2
2004	25	100	2.0	45	144.2	3.8	25	115.4
2005	10	110	2.2	55	178.2	6.8	45	126.4
2006	5	115	2.3	105	234.1	11.2	75	147.9

Based on this table, the calculations of DPI, RVPI, and TVPI can be derived as follows:

- Paid-in capital = Cumulative capital called-down (shown in Column 2)

- Management fees = (2 Percent) × (Column 2)

- Carried interest: The first year that NAV is higher than committed capital (€125m), carried interest is 20 percent of the excess, or (20 Percent) ([NAV in Column 5] – €125m). Thereafter, provided that NAV before distribution exceeds committed capital, carried interest is (20 Percent)(increase in NAV before distributions). For example, carried interest in 2006 is calculated as follows: (20 Percent)(234.1 – 178.2)

- NAV before distributions = NAV after distributions$_{t-1}$ + (Column 1) – (Column 3) + (Column 4)

- NAV after distributions = (Column 5) – (Column 6) – (Column 7)

- DPI = (25 + 45 + 75)/115 or 1.26x

- RVPI = 147.9/115 or 1.29x

- TVPI = 1.26 + 1.29 = 2.55x

The IRRs may be developed as follows:

- Gross IRRs are estimated by calculating the internal rate of return between the following cash flows: called down capital at the beginning of period (Column 1) and operating results (Column 4).

- Net IRRs are estimated by calculating the internal rate of return between the following cash flows: called down capital at the beginning of period (Column 1) and operating results (Column 4) net of management fees (Column 3) and carried interest (Column 6). The calculated IRRs are in the bottom row of the following table.

Year End	Cash Flows for Gross IRR	Cash Flows for Net IRR
2000	−50	−50.0
2001	−20	−21.0

(continued)

Year End	Cash Flows for Gross IRR	Cash Flows for Net IRR
2002	−25	−26.3
2003	0	−1.5
2004	35	29.2
2005	50	41.0
2006	105	91.5
IRR	16.1%	11.3%

5   PREFATORY COMMENTS ON THE CASE STUDY

The case study that follows is a complement to this private equity valuation reading and is included to show the reader how to apply in context valuation methodologies in a private equity setting.

A Note on Valuation of Venture Capital Deals

This technical note on the valuation of venture capital deals is meant to explain the foundations of the venture capital method for valuing venture capital investments, the specific issues and diligences that must be addressed, and illustrate the concept in action with a case study.

SUMMARY

This reading focuses on valuation issues confronting investors in a private equity fund and the methods that the funds use to make investment decisions.

- Private equity funds seek to add value by various means, including optimizing financial structures, incentivizing management, and creating operational improvements.

- Private equity can be thought of as an alternative system of governance for corporations: rather than ownership and control being separated as in most publicly quoted companies, private equity concentrates ownership and control. Many view this governance arbitrage as a fundamental source of the returns earned by the best private equity funds.

- A critical role for the GP is valuation of potential investments. But because these investments are usually privately owned, valuation encounters a myriad of challenges, some of which have been discussed in this reading.

- Valuation techniques differ according to the nature of the investment. Early stage ventures require very different techniques than leveraged buyouts. Private equity professionals tend to use multiple techniques when performing a valuation, and they explore many different scenarios for the future development of the business.

- In buyouts the availability of debt financing can have a big impact on the scale of private equity activity and also seems to impact the valuations observed in the market.

- Because private equity funds have incentives to acquire, add value, and then exit within the lifetime of the fund, they are considered buy-to-sell investors.

Planning the exit route for the investment is a critical role for the GP, and a well-timed and executed investment can be a significant source of realized value.

- In addition to the problems encountered by the private equity funds in valuing potential portfolio investments, many challenges exist in valuing the investment portfolio on an ongoing basis. This is because the investments have no easily observed market value, and there is a high element of judgment involved in valuing each of the portfolio companies prior to their sale by the fund.

- The two main metrics for measuring the ongoing and ultimate performance of private equity funds are IRR and multiples. Comparisons of the observed returns from private equity across funds and with other assets are demanding because it is important to control for the timing of cash flows, differences in risk, portfolio composition, and vintage year effects.

APPENDIX: A NOTE ON VALUATION OF VENTURE CAPITAL DEALS[15]

When times are mysterious serious numbers are eager to please.

—Musician, Paul Simon, in the lyrics to his song *When Numbers Get Serious*

In this note, I discuss some of the fundamental issues of valuation in venture capital deals. The topics discussed are not necessarily limited to venture capital-backed companies, but they frequently surface in entrepreneurial companies that are financed either by venture capitalists or other private equity investors.

In Section 1, I introduce the so-called venture capital method. This is really a simple net present value (NPV) method that takes the perspective of the investor instead of the firm. This method has the advantage of extreme simplicity, but it makes many strong assumptions that limit its usefulness. I focus on three main issues in the remaining sections. In Section 2, I examine the problem of determining the terminal value. In Section 3, I examine the treatment of risk. In Section 4, I examine how to determine the funding requirements and I examine a number of ways of dealing with multiple financing rounds. In Section 5, I briefly cover the use of these methods in actual negotiations.

1   The Basic Venture Capital Method

1.1   An Example

There exists a simple approach to valuation that is sometimes refereed to as the venture capital method. The method is sometimes explained in the language of internal rates of return (IRR) and sometimes in terms of NPV. Since most of you have been more exposed to the NPV framework, I will use that language. I will then show that it is in fact *identical* to the IRR framework.

To illustrate my method I will use a fictional start-up company called "Spiffy-Calc," which is seeking financing from a venture capital fund by the name of "Vulture Ventures." Studying their crystal ball, the founders of SpiffyCale expect to be able to sell the company for $25 million in four years.[16] At this point they need to raise

---

15 This note was prepared by Thomas Hellmann, Assistant Professor of Strategic Management, Stanford University, as the basis for class discussion rather than to illustrate either effective or ineffective handling of an admistrative situation.

16 In Section 2, I discuss how one might replace the crystal ball by a liquid crystal display screen, as a slight improvement in the art of future telling.

$3 million. Vulture Ventures considers this a risky business and wants to apply a discount rate of 50 percent to be adequately compensated for the risk they will bear.[17] The entrepreneurs also decided that whatever valuation they would get, they wanted to own 1 million shares, which they thought would be a cool number to brag about.

It is useful to define variables for the key assumptions we have made.

V = terminal value (at time of exit) = $25 million (in four years)
t = time to exit event = 4 years
I = amount of investment = $3 million
r = discount return used by investors = 50 percent
x = number of existing shares (owned by the entrepreneurs) = 1 million

Step 1: Determine the Post-Money Valuation

The only positive cash flow in this model occurs at the time of exit (typically an IPO or an acquisition), where we measure the terminal value of the company, denoted by V = $25 million. This means that after receiving the required $3 million, the initial value of the company is simply the discounted terminal value in 4 years' time. If Vulture Ventures is using a discount rate of 50 percent, the NPV of the terminal value in four years is $V/(1 + r)^t$ = $25 million/$(1.5)^4$ = $4,938,272 = POST. This is called the post-money valuation, i.e., the value of the company once the initial investment has been made. Intuitively, this is the value that is being placed on the entire company. This value is obviously not realized at the time of financing, as it depends on the belief that there will be great financial returns in the future.

Step 2: Determine the Pre-Money Valuation

Subtracting the cost of the investment of $3 million from the post-money valuation yields PRE = $1,938,272. This is called the pre-money valuation.

Step 3: Determine the Ownership Fraction

Vulture Ventures is investing $3 million in a venture valued at $4,938,272. In order to get back its money it therefore needs to own a sufficient fraction of the company. If they own a fraction F = $3 million/$4,938,272 = 60.75 percent, they get their required rate of return on their investment.

Step 4: Obtain the Number of Shares

The founders want to hold 1 million shares. When Vulture Ventures makes its investment it needs to calculate the number of shares required to achieve its desired ownership fraction. In order to obtain a 60.75 percent ownership share, Vulture Venture makes the following calculation: let x be the number of shares owned by the founders (x = 1 million) and y be the number of shares that Vulture Ventures requires, then $y/(1,000,000 + y) = F$ = 60.75 percent. After some algebraic transformation we get y = 1,000,000 [0.6075/(1−0.6075)] = 1,547,771. Vulture Ventures thus needs 1,547,771 shares to obtain their desired 60.75 percent of the company.

Step 5: Obtain the Price of Shares

The price of shares is thus given by $3 million/1,547,771 = $1.94.

1.2 The General Case

We can calculate all important variables of a deal in a simple five step procedure:

Step 1   POST = $V/(1 + r)^t$

POST is the post-money valuation.

Step 2   PRE = POST − I

PRE is the pre-money valuation.

---

17 In Section 3, I discuss discount rates in more detail.

Step 3 $F = I/POST$

F is the required ownership fraction for the investor.

Step 4 $y = x\,[F/(1 - F)]$

y is the number of shares the investors require to achieve their desired ownership fraction.

Step 5 $p_1 = I/y$

p_1 is the price per share.

1.3   Sensitivity Analysis with the Basic Venture Capital Method

It is interesting to do some sensitivity analysis. How will the value of the company change if we change our assumptions? We will examine the effect of changing the following assumptions:

Variation 1   reduce the terminal value by 10 percent

Variation 2   increase the discount rate by an absolute 10 percent

Variation 3   increase investment by 10 percent

Variation 4   increase time to exit by 10 percent

Variation 5   increase the number of exiting shares: this has no effect on any real values!

Single Period NPV Method		Base Model	Variation 1	Variation 2
Exit Value	V	$25,000,000	**$22,500,000**	$25,000,000
Time to exit	t	4	4	4
Discount rate	r	50.00%	50.00%	**60.00%**
Investment amount	I	$3,000,000	$3,000,000	$3,000,000
Number of existing shares	x	1,000,000	1,000,000	1,000,000
Post-Money	POST	$4,938,272	$4,444,444	$3,814,697
Pre-Money	PRE	$1,938,272	$1,444,444	$814,697
Ownership fraction of investors	F	60.75%	67.50%	78.64%
Ownership fraction of entrepreneurs	1 – F	39.25%	32.50%	21.36%
Number of new shares	y	1,547,771	2,076,923	3,682,349
Price per share	p	$1.94	$1.44	$0.81
Final wealth of investors		$15,187,500	$15,187,500	$19,660,800
Final wealth of entrepreneurs		$9,812,500	$7,312,500	$5,339,200
NPV of investors' wealth		$3,000,000	$3,000,000	$3,000,000
NPV of entrepreneurs' wealth		$1,938,272	$1,444,444	$814,697

Single Period NPV Method		Variation 3	Variation 4	Variation 5
Exit Value	V	$25,000,000	$25,000,000	$25,000,000
Time to exit	t	4	**4.4**	4
Discount rate	r	50.00%	50.00%	50.00%
Investment amount	I	**$3,300,000**	$3,000,000	$3,000,000
Number of existing shares	x	1,000,000	1,000,000	**2,000,000**
Post-Money	POST	$4,938,272	$4,198,928	$4,938,272
Pre-Money	PRE	$1,638,272	$1,198,928	$1,938,272

(continued)

Single Period NPV Method		Variation 3	Variation 4	Variation 5
Ownership fraction of investors	F	66.83%	71.45%	60.75%
Ownership fraction of entrepreneurs	$1 - F$	33.18%	28.55%	39.25%
Number of new shares	y	2,014,318	2,502,235	3,095,541
Price per share	p	$1.64	$1.20	$0.97
Final wealth of investors		$16,706,250	$17,861,700	$15,187,500
Final wealth of entrepreneurs		$8,293,750	$7,138,300	$9,812,500
NPV of investors' wealth		$3,300,000	$3,000,000	$3,000,000
NPV of entrepreneurs' wealth		$1,638,272	$1,198,928	$1,938,272

1.4   The Treatment of Option Pools

One subtle point in this calculation is the treatment of an employee option pool. Most venture capital deals include a nontrivial amount of shares for the option pool. This option pool will be depleted over time as the company hires executives and other employees. How do we account for the option pool in these calculations? The norm is that the entrepreneurs' shares and the option pool are lumped into one. Consider an example where the entrepreneurs receive 2 million shares, the investors receive 2 million shares, and there is an option pool of 1 million shares. Investors are investing $2 million at $1 per share. We then say that the post-money valuation is $5 million and the pre-money valuation is $3 million. Note, however, that from the entrepreneurs' perspective they are getting only $2 million of the pre-money valuation. The other $1 million is reserved for the option pool.

1.5   An Alternative Phrasing of the Venture Capital Method in Terms of IRR

The so-called venture capital method is often explained in the language of IRRs. While the IRR is often a problematic method in finance, our venture capital method is sufficiently simple that the IRR and the NPV method give *exactly the same answer*. Below I use the above example to walk you through the logic of the IRR calculation in the way it is sometimes presented as the venture capital method.

Step 1: Determine the future wealth that Vulture Ventures needs to obtain in order to achieve their desired IRR.

When Vulture Ventures decides to invest in a company, it formulates a "desired rate of return." Suppose that Vulture Ventures is asking for 50 percent IRR. Also, SpiffyCalc needs an investment of $3 million. We can then determine how much money Vulture Ventures needs to accumulate in order to achieve its desired return. Vulture Ventures would want to make $3 million × $(1.5)^4$ = $15,187,500 in four years.

Step 2: Determine the fraction of shares that Vulture Ventures needs to hold in order to achieve the desired IRR.

To find out the required percentage of shares that Vulture Ventures needs to achieve a 50 percent IRR, we simply divide its required wealth by the estimated value of the company, i.e., $15,187,500/$25 million = 0.6075. Vulture Ventures would thus need 60.75 percent of the shares.

Step 3: Determine the number of shares.

When Vulture Ventures makes its investment it needs to calculate the number of shares required to achieve its desired ownership fraction. We assume that the founders of SpiffyCalc issued themselves 1,000,000 shares, and nobody else owns any other shares. We then calculate how many shares Vulture Ventures needs to obtain a 60.75 percent ownership share in the company. Using the same reasoning as before let x be the number of shares owned by the founders (x = 1,000,000) and y be the number of shares that Vulture Ventures requires, then $y/(1,000,000 + y) = 0.6075$. After some algebraic transformation we have $y = 1,000,000 \, [0.6075/(1 - 0.6075)] = 1,547,771$. Vulture Ventures thus needs 1,547,771 shares to obtain their desired 60.75 percent of the company.

Step 4: Determine the price of shares.

Given that Vulture Ventures is investing $3 million, the price of a share is $3 million/1,547,771 = $1.94.

Step 5: Determine post-money valuation.

The post-money valuation can actually be calculated in a number of ways. First, if an investment of $3 million buys 60.75 percent of the company, then it must be that 60.75 percent × post-money valuation = $3 million. It follows that the post-money valuation is given by $3 million/0.6075 = $4,938,272. Another way to obtain the post-money valuation is to note that there are 2,547,771 shares in the company that are valued at $1.94, so the post-money valuation is $2,547,771 × \$1.94 \approx \$4.94$ million (allowing for rounding error).

Step 6: Determine pre-money valuation.

To calculate the pre-money valuation we simply subtract the value of the VC's investment from the post-money valuation. This is $4,938,272 – $3 million = $1,938,272. Another way of calculating the pre-money valuation is to evaluate the existing shares at the new price, i.e., $1,000,000 × \$1.94 \approx \$1.94$ million (again allowing for rounding error).

We note that all the values are exactly the same as for the NPV method. The only difference is that one additional step was needed in the IRR method, namely to calculate the required wealth of the investors at a future point in time.[18]

Again, we can write down the general case:

Step 1 $W = I \, (1 + r)^t$

W is the amount of wealth investors expect to accumulate.

Step 2 $F = W/V$

F is the fraction of share ownership required by investors.

Step 3 $y = x \, [F/(1 - F)]$

y is the number of shares the investors require to achieve their desired ownership fraction.

Step 4 $p_1 = I/y$

p_1 is the price per share.

Step 5 $POST = I/F$ or $POST = p_1 \times (x + y)$

POST is the post-money valuation.

Step 6 $PRE = POST - I$ or $PRE = p_1 \times x$

PRE is the pre-money valuation.

2   Estimating the Terminal Value

Conceptually the terminal value represents the value of the company at the time of an exit event, be it an IPO or an acquisition.[19] Probably the most frequently used method to determine the terminal value is to take a multiple of earnings at the time of exit. Typically an estimate is taken of what the earnings are before tax, and then an industry multiple is taken. The difficulty is obviously to come up with a good estimate of the earnings and to find an appropriate industry multiple. This is particularly difficult for highly innovative ventures that operate in new or emerging industries.

---

18 In the spreadsheet that accompanies the case, future wealth is also discounted back into the present to obtain the NPV of the stakes for the entrepreneurs and investors.

19 To be precise, the relevant value is the pre-money valuation at the exit event.

Instead of taking a multiple of earnings, one might also consider taking multiples of sales or assets, or indeed of whatever other accounting measure is meaningful in that specific industry. The common methodology of all these multiples calculations is to look at comparable firms in the industry. One problem is that it is often difficult to find truly comparable companies. Another problem is that one typically looks at recent comparable deals. If a company is financed at a time when the stock market peaks and it uses recent IPOs as a basis of comparison, it will obtain large multiples. But these multiples may not reflect the multiples that it will be able to obtain when it plans to go public several years later.[20]

In principle, better methods of estimating terminal value would be to use NPV, CAPM, APT, or whatever equilibrium valuation model we think fits the data best. The problem, however, is that it is exceedingly difficult to come up with reasonable cash flow projections. And indeed, again one would look at comparable firms in the industry to come up with these estimates. These calculations may therefore not be much more accurate than the rough estimates using the multiples method.

Note that the implicit assumption for these estimates of the terminal value is typically that they measure the value of the company in case of success. This leads us to examine the issue of risk more carefully.

3   Accounting for Risk

In the venture capital method of valuation, the estimate of the terminal value is typically based on some kind of success scenario. Because there is considerable risk involved in a typical venture capital deal, venture capitalists usually apply a very high discount risk "to compensate for the risk." It is not hard to see why they use this method. Venture capitalists are negotiating with entrepreneurs who are often overconfident and have a strong tendency to overstate the prospects of their new ventures. Venture capitalists can argue with them for some time, but rather than having a long and aggravating debate about these estimates, the VCs can simply deflate them by applying a higher discount rate. I therefore suspect that the venture capital method is simply a victim of bargaining dynamics. The method, however, is rather confusing, as it combines two distinct reasons for discounting. One of the reasons is that VCs need to be compensated for holding significant (and typically nondiversifiable) risk. The second is that VCs do not believe that the venture will necessarily succeed. The problem here is that the earnings estimate does not represent the *expected* earnings, but the earnings in case of success.[21] There are two closely related ways of dealing with this.

The first method is to simply recognize the fact that the discount rate incorporates a "risk of failure" component, as well as a true risk–diversification component. Since venture capitalists are not diversified, they may use a high discount rate to account for the variability of returns around their expected value.[22] Suppose, for example, that the risk–aversion of the VC fund implies an approximate risk-adjusted discount rate of 20 percent. If it was certain that this company would succeed, then the post-money valuation would simply be given by $25 million/ $(1.2)^4$ = $12,056,327. But suppose now that the investors actually believe that the company might simply falter (with no value left) and that the probability of that event happening is 20 percent each year. The probability of getting the terminal valuation is only (80 percent)^4 = 40.96 percent, so that that the expected postmoney valuation is only 0.4096 × $12,056,327

---

20 While one would think that venture capitalists take this effect into account (and indeed they typically use that argument to talk multiples down) it is still true that venture capital valuations appreciate in times of rising stock markets.
21 Technically speaking, the first aspect is true risk as measured in terms of the variance (or covariance) of returns. The second aspect does not concern the variance, but the overestimation of the mean.
22 The limited partners of the VC funds, however, tend to be very diversified. This can lead to some conflicts of interest, which we will not dwell on here.

= \$4,938,272. We chose those numbers such that we get the same post-money valuation as before. This can be seen from the following: Let π be the probability of failure in any one year, then

$$\text{POST} = \frac{(1-\pi)^t X}{(1+r)^t} = \left(\frac{1-\pi}{1+r}\right)^t X = \frac{X}{(1+\tilde{r})^t} \text{ where } \tilde{r} = \frac{1+r}{1-\pi} - 1$$

$$= \frac{r+\pi}{1-\pi}$$

In our case $\tilde{r} = \dfrac{1+0.2}{1-0.2} - 1 = 0.5$: a 20 percent failure rate, combined with a 20 percent discount rate, have the combined effect of a 50 percent discount rate. Note that these numbers do not simply add up, so we need to go through the above formulas.

The second method is to allow for a variety of scenarios to generate a less biased estimate of expected returns. Typically we would try to adjust the terminal value to better reflect our true expectations. For example, SpiffyCalc's estimate of \$25 million may have been based on an estimated earnings of \$2.5 million and a multiple of 10. Suppose now that \$2.5 million earnings is in fact an optimistic estimate. Suppose that there is a possibility that SpiffyCalc's product won't work, in which case the company will have no earnings. Or it may work, but the opportunity is smaller than originally hoped for, so that earnings in year 3 are only \$1 million and the multiple is only 5, reflecting a lower growth potential. Suppose now that each of these three scenarios are equally likely. The expected terminal value is not \$25 million but only $1/3 \times \$0 + 1/3 \times 5 \times \$1$ million $+ 1/3 \times 10 \times \$2.5$ million = \$10 million.

When valuing the company, the VC may now use a lower discount rate that reflects only the true amount of risk in the venture. Using the corrected estimate of \$10 million and applying a 20 percent discount rate as before leads to a post-money valuation of \$4,822,531. The VC would need to own 62.21 percent of the company.

4 Investment Amounts and Multiple Rounds Of Finance

How do we determine the amount of money that needs to be raised? Again, there are a variety of methods. A simple and powerful method is to go to the entrepreneurs' financial projections and look at their cash flow statement, which tracks the expected cash balances of the company over time. An important insight that comes out of this method is that it is often better to raise money in several rounds. We illustrate this with our hypothetical example of SpiffyCalc.

4.1 An Example

Starting with a cash balance of \$0, the company projects the following cash balances:

End of Year 1	End of Year 2	End of Year 3	End of Year 4	End of Year 5
\$(1,600,000)	\$(2,700,000)	\$(4,600,000)	\$(2,600,000)	\$1,200,000

Looking at these numbers, SpiffyCalc realized that raising \$3 million would get the company through its first two years. But after two years the company would need some additional money to survive. Indeed, SpiffyCalc estimated that the lowest cash balance would occur at the end of year 3, and that it would generate positive cash flows thereafter. The company therefore recognized that it needed to raise a total of \$4.6 million. It also thought that it was more prudent to leave itself with some safety cushion, so it decided to raise a total of \$5 million dollars. When it put those numbers into its spreadsheet, however, the numbers demonstrated that investors needed to receive 101.25 percent of the company and that its pre-money valuation was –$61,728. This obviously means that at $5 million, the project was a negative NPV project.

But SpiffyCalc also noticed that it didn't need to raise the entire $5 million right from the start. For example, it could initially raise $3 million, and then raise the remaining $2 million after two years. In this case, the valuation method needs to take into account that the equity that first-round investors put into the business will be diluted in future rounds. This is a difficult problem, as it requires that we make assumptions about the terms of financing of these future rounds. While these assumptions may be difficult to get by, ignoring them will almost certainly lead to an inaccurate valuation. Indeed, ignoring future dilution will lead the venture capitalist to pay too much. The NPV framework is the most flexible and powerful method to account for future dilution.[23]

Suppose now that SpiffyCalc has already identified "Slowtrain Investors" as a potential investor for that second round. Suppose also that all investors apply a 50 percent discount rate through the four years before SpiffyCalc expects to be acquired. At the end of the second year, when "Slowtrain Investors" makes the second round investment, it would be doing the same calculation as we did above. It would use $POST_2 = \$25$ million$/(1.5)^2 = \$11,111,111$ as the postmoney valuation. It would ask for a $2,000,000/11,111,111 = 18.00$ percent ownership stake. This means that the existing owners of the firm (the founders) and the first round investors (Vulture Ventures) would jointly only retain 82 percent of the company, or $0.82 \times \$11,111,111 = \$9,111,111$. This is also the pre-money valuation at the time of this second round of financing, and no coincidence, since the pre-money valuation measures precisely the value for the existing owners of the firm.

For the first round investment, Vulture Ventures can then expect the company to be worth $9,111,111 at the time of the second round, i.e., in two years' time. It then uses the same method as above to calculate the post-money valuation at the time of the first round, i.e., $POST_1 = \$9,111,111/(1.5)^2 = \$4,049,383$. This implies that it will ask for $3,000,000/\$4,049,383 = 74.09$ percent of the shares of the company. Note, however, that Vulture Ventures will not own 74.09 percent after four years. Instead, it expects a future dilution that will bring its ownership down to $f_1 = 0.82 \times 0.7409 = 60.75$ percent (the lower case notation indicates final ownership, after dilution). This is obviously a familiar number, as we have seen before that Vulture Ventures needs exactly 60.75 percent to get their required return on their investment of $3 million.

So far we haven't said anything about the number of shares and the price of shares for either the first or second round. In fact, we cannot calculate the price and number of shares for the second round before we calculate the price and number of shares for the first round. For this first round, we use the usual method, i.e., $y_1 = x_1 F_1/(1 - F_1) = 1,000,000 \times 0.7409/(1 - 0.7409) = 2,858,824$ and thus $p_1 = 3,000,000/2,858,824 = \$1.05$. For the second round we repeat the exercise. The important step, however, is to use the correct number of shares, namely the total number of existing shares (irrespective of whether they are owned by the entrepreneur or the investor). We have $x_2 = (x_1 + y_1) = 1,000,000 + 2,858,824 = 3,858,824$ as the number of existing shares at the time of the second round. The new number of shares required is thus $y_2 = x_2 F_2/(1 - F_2) = 3,858,824(0.18)/(1 - 0.18) = 847,059$. The price of the second round shares is then given by $\$2,000,000/847,059 = \$2.36$.

---

23 It is sometimes argued that future dilution does not matter in efficient markets, but we have to be careful with this argument. In a typical venture capital situation the company can only meet its financial projections if it manages to raise additional capital. In that sense the future dilution applies not to new investment opportunities of the company, but to the realization of the current investment opportunity. As an early round investor we therefore want to take account of the future dilution. This is different from the scenario in which future dilution relates to raising money for future investment opportunities that are additively separable from the current investment.

The following table summarizes these assumptions and results.

NPV Method with Two Rounds of Financing	Time of Exit	Second Round	First Round
Exit Value	$25,000,000		
Compound discount rate		2.25	2.25
Investment amount		2,000,000	3,000,000
Number of existing shares		3,858,824	1,000,000
Post-Money		$11,111,111	$4,049,383
Pre-Money		$9,111,111	$1,049,383
Ownership Fraction		18.00%	74.09%
Number of new shares		847,059	2,858,824
Price per share		$2.36	$1.05
Ownership shares of entrepreneurs	21.25%		
Wealth of entrepreneurs	$5,312,500	$2,361,111	$1,049,383
Ownership shares of first round investors	60.75%		
Wealth of first round investors	$15,187,500	$6,750,000	$3,000,000
Ownership shares of second round investors	18.00%		
Wealth of second round investors	$4,500,000	$2,000,000	

4.2   The General Case with Multiple Rounds of Financing

We are now in a position to examine the general case. We show the formulas for the case where there are two rounds of financing. All variables pertaining to round 1 (2) will have the subscript $_{1\,(2)}$. The case with an arbitrary number of rounds is a straight-forward extension discussed at the end of the section.

Step 1   *Define appropriate compound interest rates.*

Suppose that the terminal value is expected to occur at some date T_3, the second round at some date T_2, and the first round is happening at date T_1. Define $(1 + R_2)$ as the compound discount rate between time T_2 and T_3. If, for example, there are three years between the second round and the exit time, and if the discount rate for these three years is 40 percent, 35 percent, and 30 percent, respectively, then $(1 + R_2) = 1.4 \times 1.35 \times 1.3$. The compound discount rate $(1 + R_1)$ is defined similarly for the time between dates T_1 and T_2 (not T_3!!!).

Step 2 $POST_2 = V/(1 + R_2)$

Where $POST_2$ is the post-money valuation at the time of the second round, V is the terminal value and R_2 is the compound discount rate between the time of the second round and the time of exit.

Step 3 $PRE_2 = POST_2 - I_2$

PRE_2 is the pre-money valuation at the time of the second round of financing and I_2 is the amount raised in the second round.

Step 4 $POST_1 = PRE_2/(1 + R_1)$

Where $POST_1$ is the post-money valuation at the time of the first round and R_1 is the compound discount rate between the time of the first and second rounds.

Step 5 $PRE_1 = POST_1 - I_1$

PRE_1 is the pre-money valuation at the time of the first round of financing, and I_1 is the amount raised in the first round.

Step 6 $F_2 = I_2/POST_2$

F_2 is the required ownership fraction for the investors in the second round.

Step 7 $F_1 = I_1/POST_1$

F_1 is the required ownership fraction for the investors in the first round (this is not their final ownership share, as they will get diluted by a factor of $(1 - F_2)$ in the second round).

Step 8 $y_1 = x_1 [F_1/(1 - F_1)]$

y_1 is the number of new shares that the investors in the first round require to achieve their desired ownership fraction, and x_1 is the number of existing shares.[24]

Step 9 $p_1 = I_1/y_1$

p_1 is the price per share in the first round.

Step 10 $x_2 = x_1 + y_1$

x_2 is the number of existing shares at the time of the second round.

Step 11 $y_2 = x_2 [F_2/(1 - F_2)]$

y_2 is the number of new shares that the investors in the second round require to achieve their desired ownership fraction.

Step 12 $p_2 = I_2/y_2$

p_2 is the price per share in the second round.

The general case is a straightforward extension of the case with two rounds. First we need to define the compound discount rates between all the rounds. Then we find the post- and pre-money valuations working backwards from the terminal value to each round of financing, all the way back to the first round of financing. For each round we discount the pre-money valuation of the subsequent round to get the post-money valuation of the round. Once we have the post-money valuations for all rounds we can calculate all the required ownership shares. To get the number and prices of shares we begin with the usual formula for the first round and then count up for each round.

4.3   Some Further Examples

Consider a first variation of the model. Suppose that the discount rate is highest in the early years and becomes lower after a while. For example, assume that the discount rate is 60 percent in the first year, stays at 50 percent in years two and three, and falls to 40 percent in the fourth year. This changes our compound discount rates: we have $(1 + R_2) = 1.5 \times 1.4 = 2.1$ and $(1 + R_1) = 1.6 \times 1.5 = 2.4$.

Variation 1	Time of Exit	Second Round	First Round
Exit Value	$25,000,000		
Compound discount rate		2.1	2.4
Investment amount		2,000,000	3,000,000
Number of existing shares		3,661,972	1,000,000
Post-Money		$11,904,762	$4,126,984
Pre-Money		$9,904,762	$1,126,984
Ownership Fraction		16.80%	72.69%
Number of new shares		739,437	2,661,972
Price per share		$2.70	$1.13
Ownership shares of entrepreneurs	22.72%		

[24] If there are no pre-existing shares, one may also fix a total number of shares and then simply allocate them according to the fractions F_1 and $(1 - F_1)$.

Variation 1	Time of Exit	Second Round	First Round
Wealth of entrepreneurs	$5,680,000	$2,704,762	$1,126,984
Ownership shares of first round investors	60.48%		
Wealth of first round investors	$15,120,000	$7,200,000	$3,000,000
Ownership shares of second round investors	16.80%		
Wealth of second round investors	$4,200,000	$2,000,000	

There are many other variations that we can examine in this model. A second variation of particular interest is to examine the role of the timing of the second round. Suppose, for example, that SpiffyCalc might be able to delay the timing of the second round by one year. In this case the compound discount rates are given by $(1 + R_2) = 1.4$ and $(1 + R_1) = 1.6 \times 1.5 \times 1.5 = 3.6$. Delaying the second round of financing would improve the valuation of the company.

Variation 2	Time of Exit	Second Round	First Round
Exit Value	$25,000,000		
Compound discount rate		1.4	3.6
Investment amount		2,000,000	3,000,000
Number of existing shares		3,135,593	1,000,000
Post-Money		$17,857,143	$4,404,762
Pre-Money		$15,857,143	$1,404,762
Ownership Fraction		11.20%	68.11%
Number of new shares		395,480	2,135,593
Price per share		$5.06	$1.40
Ownership shares of entrepreneurs	28.32%		
Wealth of entrepreneurs	$7,080,000	$5,057,143	$1,404,762
Ownership shares of first round investors	60.48%		
Wealth of first round investors	$15,120,000	$10,800,000	$3,000,000
Ownership shares of second round investors	11.20%		
Wealth of second round investors	$2,800,000	$2,000,000	

5   The Determinants of Valuation: Looking beyond the Numbers

To put things in perspective, it should be said that any method of valuation depends critically on the assumptions we make. Indeed, any valuation number can be justified by an appropriate choice of the discount rates and the terminal value. There is a more fundamental point here. A valuation method is a sophisticated tool for determining how entrepreneurs and venture capitalists should split the returns of the new venture. But the actual split, i.e., the actual deal, is not really driven by the valuation method, but rather by the outcome of the bargaining between the entrepreneurs and the venture capitalists. The relative bargaining power is thus the true economic determinant of the valuation that entrepreneurs will obtain for their companies. The valuation method, however, is an important tool to master for all parties involved, as it often provides the quantitative basis for the negotiation.

PRACTICE PROBLEMS FOR READING 40

1. Jo Ann Ng is a senior analyst at SING INVEST, a large regional mid-market buyout manager in Singapore. She is considering the exit possibilities for an existing investment in a mature automotive parts manufacturer that was acquired 3 years ago at a multiple of 7.5 times EBITDA. SING INVEST originally anticipated exiting its investment in China Auto Parts, Inc. within 3 to 6 years. Ng noted that current market conditions have deteriorated and that companies operating in a similar business trade at an average multiple of 5.5 times EBITDA. She deemed, however, based on analyst reports and industry knowledge that the market is expected to recover strongly within the next two years because of the fast increasing demand for cars in emerging markets. Upon review of market opportunities, Ng also noted that China Gear Box, Inc., a smaller Chinese auto parts manufacturer presenting potential strong synergies with China Auto Parts, Inc., is available for sale at an EBITDA multiple of 4.5. Exits by means of an IPO or a trade sale to a financial or strategic (company) buyer are possible in China. How would you advise Ng to enhance value upon exit of China Auto Parts?

2. Wenda Lee, CFA, is a portfolio manager at a U.K.-based private equity institutional investor. She is considering an investment in a mid-market European buyout fund to achieve a better diversification of her firm's existing private equity portfolio. She short listed two funds that she deemed to have a similar risk return profile. Before deciding which one to invest in, she is carefully reviewing and comparing the terms of each fund.

	Mid-Market Fund A	Mid-Market Fund B
Management fees	2.5%	1.5%
Transaction fees	100% to the GP	50–50% split
Carried interest	15%	20%
Hurdle rate	6%	9%
Clawback provision	No	Yes
Distribution waterfall	Deal-by-deal	Total return

Based on the analysis of terms, which fund would you recommend to Lee?

3. Jean Pierre Dupont is the CIO of a French pension fund allocating a substantial portion of its assets to private equity. The existing private equity portfolio comprises mainly large buyout funds, mezzanine funds, and a limited allocation to a special situations fund. The pension fund decided to further increase its allocation to European venture capital. The investment committee of the pension fund requested Dupont present an analysis of five key investment characteristics specific to venture capital relative to buyout investing. Can you assist Dupont in this request?

4. Discuss the ways that private equity funds can create value.

5. What problems are encountered when using comparable publicly traded companies to value private acquisition targets?

6. What are the main ways in which the performance of private equity limited partnerships can be measured A) during the life of the fund, and B) once all investments have been exited?

The following information relates to Questions 7–12

Martha Brady is the chief investment officer (CIO) of the Upper Darby County (UDC) public employees' pension system. Brady is considering an allocation of a portion of the pension system's assets to private equity. She has asked two of her analysts, Jennifer Chau, CFA, and Matthew Hermansky, to provide more information about the workings of the private equity market.

Brady recognizes that the private equity asset class covers a broad spectrum of equity investments that are not traded in public markets. She asks Chau to describe the major differences between assets that constitute this asset class. Chau notes that the private equity class ranges from venture capital financing of early stage companies to complete buyouts of large publicly traded or even privately held companies. Chau describes some of the characteristics of venture capital and buyout investments.

Chau mentions that private equity firms take care to align the economic interests of the managers of the investments they control with the interests of the private equity firms. Various contractual clauses are inserted in the compensation contracts of the management team in order to reward or punish managers who do not meet agreed on target objectives.

One concern is the illiquidity of private equity investments over time. But some funds are returned to investors over the life of the fund because a number of investment opportunities are exited early. A number of provisions describe the distribution of returns to investors, some of which favor the limited partners. One such provision is the distribution waterfall mechanism that provides distributions to limited partners (LP) before the general partner (GP) receives the carried interest. This distribution mechanism is called the total return waterfall.

Chau prepares the following data to illustrate the distribution waterfall mechanism and the funds provided to limited partners when a private equity fund with a zero hurdle rate exits from its first three projects during a three-year period.

Exhibit 1	Investment Returns and Distribution Waterfalls
Private equity committed capital	$400 million
Carried interest	20%
First project investment capital	$20 million
Second project investment capital	$45 million
Third project investment capital	$50 million
Proceeds from first project	$25 million
Proceeds from second project	$35 million
Proceeds from third project	$65 million

Chau cautions that investors must understand the terminology used to describe the performance of private equity funds. Interpretation of performance numbers should be made with the awareness that much of the fund assets are illiquid during a substantial part of the fund's life. She provides the latest data in Exhibit 2 for Alpha, Beta, and Gamma Funds—diversified high-technology venture capital funds formed five years ago and each with five years remaining to termination.

Chau studies the data and comments: "Of the three funds, the Alpha Fund has the best chance to outperform over the remaining life. First, because the management has earned such a relatively high residual value on capital and will be able to earn a high return on the remaining funds called down. At termination, the RVPI will earn double the '0.65' value when the rest of the funds are called down. Second, its 'cash on cash' return as measured by DPI is already as high as that of the Beta Fund. PIC, or paid-in capital, provides information about the proportion of capital called by the GP. The PIC of Alpha is relatively low relative to Beta and Gamma."

Exhibit 2	Financial Performance of Alpha, Beta, and Gamma Funds		
Fund	PIC	DPI	RVPI
Alpha	0.30	0.10	0.65
Beta	0.85	0.10	1.25
Gamma	0.85	1.25	0.75

Hermansky notes that a private equity fund's ability to properly plan and execute its exit from an investment is vital for the fund's success. Venture funds such as Alpha, Beta, and Gamma take special care to plan for exiting from investments. Venture funds tend to focus on certain types of exits, especially when equity markets are strong.

Brady then asks the analysts what procedures private equity firms would use to value investments in their portfolios as well as any other investments that might be added to the portfolio. She is concerned about buying into a fund with existing assets that do not have public market prices to ascertain value. In such cases, the GP may overvalue the assets and new investors in the fund will pay a higher NAV for the fund assets than they are worth.

Hermansky makes three statements regarding the valuation methods used in private equity transactions during the early stages of selling a fund to investors.

Statement 1   For venture capital investment in the early stages of analysis, emphasis is placed on the discounted cash flow approach to valuation.

Statement 2   For buyout investments, income-based approaches are used frequently as a primary method of valuation.

Statement 3   If a comparable group of companies exist, multiples of revenues or earnings are used frequently to derive a value for venture capital investments.

7. The characteristic that is *most likely* common to both the venture capital and buyout private equity investment is:

    A. measurable and assessable risk.

    B. the extensive use of financial leverage.

    C. the strength of the individual track record and ability of members of management.

8. The contractual term enabling management of the private equity controlled company to be rewarded with increased equity ownership as a result of meeting performance targets is called:

    A. a ratchet.

    B. the tag-along right.

    C. the clawback provision.

9. For the projects described in Exhibit 1, under a deal-by-deal method with a clawback provision and true-up every three years, the cumulative dollar amount the GP receives by the end of the three years is equal to:

    A. one million.

    B. two million.

    C. three million.

10. Are Chau's two reasons for interpreting Alpha Fund as the best performing fund over the remaining life correct?

    A. No.

    B. Yes.

    C. The first reason is correct, but the second reason is incorrect.

11. The exit route for a venture capital investment is *least likely* to be in the form of a(n):

    A. initial public offering (IPO).

    B. sale to other venture funds targeting the same sector.

    C. buyout by the management of the venture investment.

12. Which statement by Hermansky is the *least* valid?

    A. Statement 1.

    B. Statement 2.

    C. Statement 3.

SOLUTIONS FOR READING 40

1. The exit strategies available to SING INVEST to divest their holding in China Auto Parts, Inc. will largely depend on the following two factors:
   - Time remaining until the fund's term expires. If the time remaining is sufficiently long, the fund's manager has more flexibility to work out an exit at more favorable market circumstances and terms.
   - Amount of undrawn commitments from LPs in the fund. If sufficient LP commitments can be drawn, the fund manager may take advantage of current market investment opportunities at depressed market prices with the objective to enhance returns upon exit in an expected more favorable market environment.

   In the case of China Auto Parts Inc., depending on an analysis of the above, Ng could advise the acquisition of China Gear Box, Inc. subject to an indepth analysis of potential synergies with China Auto Parts, Inc. The objective here may thus be twofold: benefit from short-term market conditions and enhance the value of existing investments by reinforcing their market potential with a strategic merger.

2. Assuming that both funds have similar risk return characteristics, a closer analysis of economic and corporate governance terms should be instrumental in determining which fund to select.

   In economic terms, Mid-Market Fund B has a higher carried interest relative to Mid-Market Fund A, but Mid-Market Fund B has a fee structure that is better aligned with the interests of LPs. A larger proportion of Mid-Market Fund B's fees will be on achieving successful exits (through the carried interest), whereas Mid-Market Fund A will earn relatively larger fees on running the fund (management fees and transaction fees) without necessarily achieving high performance. In addition, the 9 percent hurdle rate of Mid-Market Fund B is indicative of a stronger confidence of the fund manager to achieve a minimum compounded 9 percent return to LPs under which no carried interest will be paid.

   In corporate governance terms, Mid-Market Fund B is far better aligned with the interests of LPs as a result of a clawback provision and a more favorable distribution waterfall to LPs that will allow payment of carried interest on a total return basis instead of deal-by-deal.

   The conclusion is that Mid-Market Fund B appears better aligned with the interests of LPs.

3.

Venture Capital	Buyout
Primarily equity funded. Use of leverage is rare and very limited.	Extensive use of leverage consisting of a large proportion of senior debt and a significant layer of junior and/or mezzanine debt.
Returns of investment portfolios are generally characterized by very high returns from a limited number of highly successful investments and a significant number of write-offs from low performing investments or failures.	Returns of investment portfolios are generally characterized by lower variance across returns from underlying investments. Bankruptcies are rare events.

Venture Capital	Buyout
Venture capital firm monitors achievement of milestones defined in business plan and growth management.	Buyout firm monitors cash flow management and strategic and business planning.
Expanding capital requirement if in the growth phase.	Low working capital requirement.
Assessment of risk is difficult because of new technologies, new markets, and lack of operating history.	Risk is measurable (e.g., mature businesses, long operating history, etc.).

4. The main ways that private equity funds can create value include the following:

   - Operational improvements and clearly defined strategies. In the case of later stage companies and buyouts, private equity owners can often create value by focusing the business on its most profitable opportunities and providing new strategic direction for the business. In the case of venture capital deals, the private equity funds can provide valuable business experience, mentor management, and offer access to their network of contacts and other portfolio companies.

   - Creating incentives for managers and aligning their goals with the investors. This is often achieved by providing significant monetary rewards to management if the private equity fund secures a profitable exit. In the case of buyouts, the free cash flow available to management is minimized by taking on significant amounts of debt financing.

   - Optimizing the financial structure of the company. In the case of buyouts, the use of debt can reduce the tax payments made by the company and reduce the cost of capital. There may also be opportunities in certain market conditions to take advantage of any mispricing of risk by lenders, which can allow the private equity funds to take advantage of interest rates that do not fully reflect the risks being carried by the lenders. Many would point to the period from mid-2006 to mid-2007 as a period when such conditions prevailed.

5. There are many complexities in using comparable companies to value private targets, including the following:

   - The lack of public comparison companies operating in the same business, facing the same risks, and at the same stage of development. It is often possible to identify "approximate" comparisons but very rare to find an exact match. It is essential, therefore, to use judgment when using comparison company information, rather than just taking the average multiples derived from a sample of disparate companies.

   - Comparison companies may have different capital structures, so estimated beta coefficients and some financial ratios should be adjusted accordingly.

   - Reported accounting numbers for earnings must be chosen carefully and adjusted for any exceptional items, atypical revenues, and costs in the reference year. Care must also be taken to decide which earnings figures to compare—the main choices are trailing earnings (the last 12 months), earnings from the last audited accounts, or prospective year-ahead earnings.

6. In the early years of a fund, all measures of returns are of little relevance because fees drag down the reported returns and investments are initially valued at cost. This produces the J-curve effect. After a few years (longer in the case of venture capital investments), performance measures become

more meaningful and the two main measures used by investors are IRR and return multiples (of the initial sum invested). During the life of the fund it is necessary to value the non-exited investments and add them to the realized returns. The former inevitably involves an element of judgment on the part of the General Partner, especially when it is difficult to estimate the likely market value of the investment. Once all the investments have been exited, the multiples and IRR can be estimated easily, taking account of the exact timing of the cash flows into and out of the fund. The most relevant measures for investors are computed net of management fees and any carried interest earned by the General Partner.

7. C is correct. Members of both the firm being bought out and the venture capital investment usually have strong individual management track records. Extensive financial leverage is common in buyouts but not venture capital investments, whereas measurable risk is more common in buyouts than in venture capital situations.

8. A is correct.

9. B is correct. On a cumulative basis for three years, the fund earns $10 million, of which $2 million goes to the GP. The $2 million earned by the GP corresponds to 20 percent of the difference between total three-year proceeds and three-year invested capital, or $0.2[(25 + 35 + 65) - (20 + 45 + 50)]$.

10. A is correct. Chau misinterprets DPI, RVPI, and PIC. The returns earned to date are for each dollar of invested capital, that which has been drawn down, not total returns. Chau mistakenly believes (assuming the same management skill) the result for Alpha Fund at termination will be on the order of $3 \times 0.65 = 1.95$ instead of 0.65. In both cases, Alpha Fund has underperformed relative to the other two funds.

11. C is correct. Leverage needed to finance a management buyout is not readily available to firms with limited history.

12. A is correct. Statement 1 is the least likely to be valid.

41

Investing in Hedge Funds: A Survey

by Keith H. Black, CFA

LEARNING OUTCOMES

Mastery	The candidate should be able to:
☐	**a** distinguish between hedge funds and mutual funds in terms of leverage, use of derivatives, disclosure requirements and practices, lockup periods, and fee structures;
☐	**b** describe hedge fund strategies;
☐	**c** explain possible biases in reported hedge fund performance;
☐	**d** describe factor models for hedge fund returns;
☐	**e** describe sources of non-normality in hedge fund returns and implications for performance appraisal;
☐	**f** describe motivations for hedge fund replication strategies;
☐	**g** explain difficulties in applying traditional portfolio analysis to hedge funds;
☐	**h** compare funds of funds to single manager hedge funds.

Although the media and many investors perceive hedge funds to be uniformly risky, the facts are that little about the hedge fund universe is homogenous. Some hedge funds hedge, whereas others take directional market risks. As a result of the private and opaque nature of hedge fund investing, a multitude of data challenges exist because hedge funds are not required to report their returns to regulators or any single database. Much of the literature describes adjustments and caveats to working with as-reported hedge fund returns and risk data.

"Hedge fund" is a term used to describe a wide variety of investment strategies. As a general rule, these strategies are less regulated and more opaque than long-only funds offered by traditional investment managers. Rather than taking a long-only exposure to a single asset class, many hedge fund strategies involve the use of leverage, derivative products, multiple asset classes, and short selling. The net market exposure of hedge funds can vary over time, which makes it more difficult to analyze performance, manage risk, and decide on the proper allocation of hedge funds in investor portfolios.

Stulz (2007) draws several contrasts between mutual funds and hedge funds. Hedge fund assets have grown explosively to more than $1 trillion, which is now more than 10 percent of the size of the mutual fund industry.

In the United States, mutual funds are required to report to the U.S. Securities and Exchange Commission (SEC). This requirement includes filing a prospectus, full disclosure of portfolio holdings on a semiannual basis, and the daily dissemination of a net asset value (NAV). Mutual funds are also subject to limits on leverage. In exchange for this regulation, mutual fund providers are allowed to market their products to a wide variety of investors, ask for low minimum investments, and offer universal availability to investors.

Hedge funds may earn exemptions from many of these regulatory requirements. By choosing to not market their investments to the public and restricting fund investments to certain types of high-net-worth investors, hedge funds are exempt from disclosure requirements. The unregulated nature of hedge funds, then, simply refers to the ability to provide less disclosure to investors and little or no disclosure to noninvestors. The opaque nature of hedge funds makes it difficult to calculate exact statistics on the size and performance of hedge funds because even their existence may not be disclosed.

Although exempt from disclosure requirements, hedge funds are not entirely unregulated. Hedge fund managers must still follow other laws determined by securities regulators. Hedge funds may not misrepresent performance, steal client funds, or engage in insider trading, manipulative trading, or front running.

In contrast to the low minimum investment and daily liquidity of mutual fund shares, investments in hedge funds are much less liquid. Most hedge funds report a NAV at the end of each month or calendar quarter. Many hedge funds also have lockup periods that restrict withdrawals from the hedge fund for some period of time. Popular lockups at hedge funds are one and two years, and three-year lockups are becoming more common. A "hard lockup" states that no provisions exist for the redemption of hedge fund investments for the stated period of time. A "soft lockup" period suggests a minimum investment period, but investors have the ability to sell their shares before the expiration of the lockup period by paying a redemption fee, which is often in the range of 1–3 percent. As a result of regulatory requirements that limit the number of investors in each fund, hedge funds typically have high minimum investment requirements, generally ranging from $500,000 to $10 million per investor.

1   FEE STRUCTURES

Much has been written about hedge fund fee structures. Hedge fund performance is typically reported net of all fees. Stulz (2007) explains that hedge funds can earn both management fees and incentive fees. A typical management fee is 1–2 percent annually based on the assets under management. Incentive fees, also called performance fees, are calculated as a set percentage of the profits on the underlying pool of assets. A hedge fund manager might earn 15–25 percent of profits in addition to the management fee. Few mutual funds charge performance fees because U.S. regulations require the fees to be symmetrical, meaning the investment manager must share equally in both gains and losses.

Hedge fund incentive fees are paid on a quarterly or annual basis and are often subject to a high-water mark provision. These fees are earned by a manager only during time periods of positive investment performance. The high-water mark provision ensures that incentive fees are earned only once for a given dollar of investment return. For example, a hedge fund earns a 10 percent gain, net of fees, in a calendar year for which incentive fees are paid. If the fund posts a return of –9 percent the following year, no incentive fees are paid because performance was negative. In the next year, the hedge fund returns 15 percent. The incentive fees in that year are paid only on the gains in excess of the high-water mark, which is the 5 percent of gains in excess of the NAV of the fund at the end of the first year. Anson (2001) has described hedge fund incentive fees as a free call option because the manager earns high fees for large investment gains but does not share in any investor losses. This lack of sharing in losses could provide an incentive for the manager to take risks larger than the investor would choose. An offsetting factor to this asymmetrical fee structure is when the investment manager has invested a substantial portion of his or her net worth in the fund, which would cause the manager and the investor to simultaneously experience trading losses.

Although a large percentage of hedge funds use a high-water mark in their fee calculations, a small minority also use hurdle rates. Hedge funds with hurdle rates do not earn any incentive fee until a minimum return threshold has been reached. Typical hurdle rates may be a stated short-term interest rate or a fixed annual rate, such as 5 percent.

Some investors have chosen not to allocate assets to hedge funds because of the size of fees paid to hedge fund managers. Asness (2006) suggests several modifications to hedge fund fee structures. Higher hedge fund fees should be paid to managers that have demonstrated skill by earning alpha, which is a high return after adjusting for all applicable risks. Leveraged hedge funds may also justify higher fees because these strategies earn a greater benefit from the manager's insight for each dollar of invested capital. Hedge fund investors are starting to separate alpha from beta in their performance calculation, leading them to ask hedge funds to charge lower fees for beta exposures to traditional market factors. By replacing high beta hedge funds with index funds or hedge fund beta replications (see the section "Hedge Fund Replication"), investors can substantially reduce the fees they pay. As the hedge fund industry comes to rely more on institutional investors, such as pension plans, and less on high-net-worth individuals, hedge fund fees for larger investments are likely to decline.

A WIDE VARIETY OF HEDGE FUND STRATEGIES 2

Black (2004) provides a comprehensive overview of hedge fund strategies and follows the fund style classification methodology of the Credit Suisse/Tremont Hedge Fund Index (www.hedgeindex.com).

Arbitrage-based funds typically have a lower standard deviation of returns because they are the hedge funds that explicitly hedge. By design, the risk and size of the long positions are highly correlated with the risk and size of the short positions. In many cases, these funds have short volatility exposures that lead to gains in quiet markets and losses in turbulent markets. These strategies typically have annualized standard deviations of 5–7 percent, which result in the highest Sharpe ratios of all hedge fund strategies. Many of these strategies, however, make money slowly and lose money quickly, which leads to unattractive negative skewness and fat tail risk (i.e., large excess kurtosis).

Convertible bond arbitrage strategies purchase a portfolio of convertible bonds and take short positions in the related equity security. A convertible bond is typically a corporate debt issue that includes a call option on the stock price of the issuer. Investors accept a lower yield on convertible bonds compared with option-free debt of the same issuer because they are compensated for the lower yield through the call option. For example, a corporation that typically borrows at 7 percent in the bond market may issue a convertible bond with a 4 percent yield, which prices the call option at the present value of the foregone 3 percent interest. A convertible bond strategy is deemed to be market neutral when the price of the fund does not change with small changes in the underlying stock prices. Market neutrality is achieved when the size of the short-stock position matches the long-delta position of the embedded call options. Convertible bond arbitrage performs well in times of declining credit spreads and high stock price volatility. In times of rising credit spreads, convertible bond arbitrage funds can suffer steep losses because bond prices are falling quickly and liquidity of convertible bonds declines rapidly in a flight to quality market.

Equity market neutral funds seek to take, on average, a zero beta exposure to equity markets. Many funds aim for a zero exposure on average but may take temporary risks of up to a beta of ±0.20. Although beta risks are minimized in this strategy, fund managers may take substantial risks in other areas of the equity markets, such as market capitalization, value, growth, or industry. To reach beta neutrality, the size and beta of the long positions are closely matched through the size and beta of the short positions. Many market neutral funds are driven through a quantitative process. Quantitative funds with longer holding periods (months) may be based on factor models with such themes as value, growth, momentum, and earnings quality. Quantitative funds with shorter holding periods (minutes to days) may be called statistical arbitrage and are largely based on trading long–short pairs of stocks with a high long-term correlation with divergent short-term stock movements.

Event driven funds are focused on a single strategy, such as distressed investments or risk arbitrage. Multistrategy implementations of event driven investing can combine these two strategies with others, such as spinoffs, cross-ownership, or index reconstitution strategies. Distressed funds typically invest in debt securities of issuers currently in default or expected to default soon. Distressed funds have, perhaps, the most significant liquidity risk of any hedge fund strategy because many investors are not willing or able to buy the debt of firms currently in bankruptcy. Distressed investors can be passive, simply willing to earn the return on the bonds they purchase. Others, however, are very active investors who will become involved in the bankruptcy process. Capital structure arbitrage implementations of distressed investments include spreads between many parts of a given company's capital structure, perhaps by buying debt and selling short the stock or trading credit default swaps against stock options.

Risk arbitrage, or merger arbitrage, funds seek to predict the outcome of announced corporate merger transactions. The classic implementation is to purchase the stock of the target company and sell short the stock of the acquiring company in the ratio of the stock swap transaction. This strategy is the definition of event risk and higher moment risk because these funds make money slowly and lose money quickly. The target return of a successful investment may be only 5–10 percent, which is earned during the 3–18 months between the announcement and consummation of the deal. Risk arbitrage funds can experience substantial losses when a planned merger is cancelled because the stock of the target company can fall 30 percent or more in a single day. Risk arbitrage is considered a short volatility strategy because the hedge fund has sold insurance against a broken deal in consideration of the expected return of the completed deal.

Fixed-income arbitrage typically invests with a positive income orientation that benefits during times of declining credit spreads. Fixed-income arbitrage strategies purchase higher yielding bonds, which can be investment- or speculative-grade corporate bonds, mortgage-backed securities, or debt issued by emerging market governments. Higher quality debt is sold or leverage is acquired at lower rates. The strategy usually earns a positive income because the purchased bonds have a higher yield than the higher quality debt or the cost of the leverage. This strategy benefits when credit spreads are stable or tightening and markets are relatively liquid. Fixed-income arbitrage funds can suffer catastrophic losses during flight to quality markets because credit spreads widen quickly, leverage becomes more expensive, and markets for lower quality debt become much less liquid.

Medium volatility hedge fund strategies typically take both long and short positions, but these positions are not always designed as hedges. The long and short positions may differ dramatically in size and/or risk, often resulting in a net long position in an underlying stock, bond, commodity, or currency market. These strategies have an average volatility of 10–12 percent per year, which is slightly less than the volatility of the underlying markets.

Global macro funds typically focus on long and short investments in broad markets, such as equity indices, currencies, commodities, and interest rate markets. Rather than selecting specific securities, macro funds focus on the macroeconomic picture, selecting asset classes and countries that will benefit from the manager's market view. In many cases, these views will be driven by market changes related to governmental actions, such as the transition from fixed to floating rate currencies. Macro funds can take concentrated positions and be quite volatile. Because macro fund managers have the entire world of securities to choose from, they tend to be difficult to replicate and have a relatively low correlation with other managers trading the same strategy.

Long–short equity funds are the largest hedge fund strategy, earning nearly 40 percent of all investor dollars allocated to hedge funds. The implementation is very similar to that of equity market neutral hedge funds, except that long–short funds do not target a zero beta exposure to underlying equity markets. During long periods of time, these funds may average a net long beta of 0.3 to 0.6. When bear markets are expected, however, managers have the flexibility to take a neutral or short exposure to equity markets.

Managed futures funds, in which the managers are also called commodity trading advisers (CTAs), use a strategy dominated by systematic trend following that seeks to profit through the quantitative prediction of market trends. These funds will invest in currencies, commodities, equity indices, and interest rate futures. They seek to take long positions during times of rising prices and short positions during times of falling prices. Managed futures funds typically have no target for the mix of long and short positions but simply build a bottom-up portfolio of positions expected to benefit from the anticipated trends in market prices. Although the risk–return profile of the managed futures index does not seem to be attractive on a stand-alone basis, this strategy offers the best hedging and diversification characteristics of any hedge fund strategy. Valuation risk, liquidity risk, complexity risk, and counterparty risk are typically minimal in this sector.

Multistrategy funds are similar to funds of funds in that they diversify broadly among a variety of hedge fund strategies. A fund of funds invests with a number of underlying managers and charges a second layer of fees at the fund-of-funds level. Multistrategy funds charge only a single layer of fees but typically manage all of the assets with managers employed by a single hedge fund management company.

Directional hedge fund strategies are the most volatile of all because little to no hedging activity is used. As such, these strategies inherit the full volatility (15–17 percent or more) of the underlying markets in which the funds are invested.

Dedicated short bias funds typically invest exclusively in the short sale of equity securities. Although the funds often have a beta exposure close to –1.0, their returns can add significant value if the manager displays skill in predicting which stocks will underperform the market index.

Emerging market hedge funds are often long only because the ability to trade derivative securities or sell short is either not developed or is prohibitively expensive in these markets. Although some funds may focus on specific regions or trade exclusively fixed-income or equity market funds, others may invest globally and mix stocks and bonds in the same fund. When the debt of emerging market countries is rated below investment grade, these bonds may have risk and return characteristics similar to equity securities.

3   HEDGE FUND DATABASES AND PERFORMANCE BIASES

Hamza, Kooli, and Roberge (2006), Fung and Hsieh (2004), and Malkiel and Saha (2005) describe a number of features of hedge fund databases. A variety of databases exist, including Hedge Fund Research (HFR), Credit Suisse/Tremont, MSCI, Lipper TASS, EACM, Zurich, Eurekahedge, Tuna, and Center for International Securities and Derivatives Market (CISDM). Although each database contains hundreds, or thousands, of hedge funds and their associated returns, no database is complete. In fact, a surprisingly high number of hedge funds report only to a subset of available databases. Many academics and large hedge fund investors subscribe to multiple databases to get a more complete picture of the hedge fund universe.

Each hedge fund database provider has its own methodology for the inclusion of funds, style classification of funds, and the index weight. For example, HFR is equally weighted whereas Credit Suisse/Tremont is asset weighted. This difference in fund weighting methodology can lead to substantial differences in hedge fund index returns, risks, and correlations across databases. Although equally weighted databases are more representative of the "average" hedge fund, this methodology places a larger weight on funds with lower levels of assets under management (AUM). Equally weighted databases also require a rebalancing methodology, which may not be feasibly implemented in a world with large minimum investments and substantial lockup periods. An asset weighted database places a larger weight on hedge funds with larger AUM, which leads the index to be more representative of the hedge fund industry than of the average hedge fund.

As a result of the lack of disclosure requirements by hedge funds, reporting to databases is voluntary. Some analysts believe that managers with higher returns and lower risks are more likely to report returns to database providers, whereas managers of funds with less attractive track records are less likely to provide their track record to the database. This lack of reporting leads to selection bias or self-reporting bias, in which the risk–return trade-off of hedge funds represented by databases is more attractive than what is actually experienced by the full universe of hedge fund investors.

Selection bias is closely related to backfill bias, which is also termed instant history or incubation bias. When a manager decides to report to a database, he or she frequently does so after earning attractive returns for the first one to three years of managing the fund. Databases note the first month that the fund started to report returns but include the fund's entire track record as "backfilled" data. For example, a fund may choose to report to a database in December 2008 and send the fund's return history since its July 2007 inception. The first live month of performance would be December 2008, and the returns since July 2007 would be backfilled. Hamza, Kooli, and Roberge (2006) estimate that dropping the first two years of each fund's returns would reduce the returns to the average fund in the HFR database by 0.5 percent annually and by 1.4 percent per year in TASS. Malkiel and Saha (2005) estimate the size of the incubation bias to be 5.74 percent, where median backfilled returns exceed returns reported in real time. Many researchers are now using the database codes to analyze only returns reported live, discounting the performance during the backfilled period to get a more accurate estimate of hedge fund performance.

Survivor bias is a substantial topic of discussion in hedge fund literature as a result of the short average life time of hedge funds. Gregoriou, Hübner, Papageorgiou, and Rouah (2005) discuss the mortality of commodity trading advisers and report that the median fund survived only 4.4 years. Malkiel and Saha (2005) report that less than 25 percent of funds operating in 1996 were still reporting to databases in 2004. Because liquidated funds tend to have lower returns and higher risks than funds with continuing operations, a database in which the track records of nonsurviving funds are excluded will produce an analysis that suffers from survivor, or survivorship, bias. In the literature, authors report a wide range of estimates of survivor bias; the returns to live funds exceed the returns to the combination of live and defunct funds by between 0.6 percent and 3.6 percent per year. By not including failed funds in return calculations, hedge fund returns will be overstated by this amount.

Survivor bias is greatest in equally weighted indices and those without a listing of deceased, or graveyard, funds. This bias is substantially reduced when working with funds of funds, asset weighted indices, investible indices, and databases that continue to carry the returns of liquidated funds. Survivor bias and backfill bias are decreasing as the hedge fund industry matures, database methodologies are improved, and the AUM of hedge funds are increasingly concentrated among a smaller number of very large funds. Fung and Hsieh (2004) report that 25 percent of hedge funds manage more than 75 percent of the industry's AUM, and concentration has increased since their study. At the inception of a database, which is frequently between 1990 and 1994, backfill bias may be larger because all funds added at that time reported returns since the inception of each fund. Sharma (2004) reports that HFR and Credit Suisse/Tremont have minimal survivor bias because these databases retain the returns of liquidated funds in their index calculations.

Hedge fund style indices may not be appropriate benchmarks, even for managers that profess to trade in a specific style. Besides the biases already discussed, funds within a specific trading style generally do not have homogenous trading algorithms and do not disclose their market exposures. Some styles with a limited opportunity set (e.g., risk arbitrage) or static market exposures (e.g., equity market neutral) will have a higher correlation and a lower return dispersion across funds. Other styles that provide a greater breadth of asset classes, trading strategies, and market exposures, such as global macro and multistrategy, will have a greater dispersion of returns and a lower correlation of returns across funds.

FACTOR MODELS FOR HEDGE FUND RETURNS
4

Hedge fund investors must understand the risks they are taking and the fees they are paying. To evaluate the value added by a hedge fund, investors need to decompose returns into alpha (manager skill) and beta (market exposure). Ideally, hedge funds would earn returns uncorrelated with the investor's existing stock and bond portfolio (low beta), and the high fees paid to hedge funds would earn the investor returns composed entirely of alpha.

Hedge fund factor analysis is discussed by Kat (2004), Fung and Hsieh (2004), Beckers, Curds, and Weinberger (2007), and others. In a hedge fund factor model, a regression is performed to determine the portion of risk derived from the market and the value added by the hedge fund manager. The typical regression is

$$\text{Hedge fund return} = \text{Alpha} + \text{Risk free rate} + \sum_i \text{Beta}_i \times \text{Factor}_i$$

Notice that alpha in this model is the total return of the hedge fund in excess of the risk free rate and the included factor or market exposures. A misspecification of this model that omits relevant risk factors will overestimate alpha. For example, assume that the return to the S&P 500 Index is included in the model and the resulting alpha is 5 percent per year. This alpha calculation assumes that the hedge fund is only taking on the risk of the price of large-capitalization U.S.-based companies. If another significant risk factor is included, the alpha estimate will decline, so it is imperative to include all relevant risk factors.

Most models use a multitude of traditional market factors, such as local and global stock and bond indices, currency, and commodity market returns. Popular factors in the literature include the S&P 500 Index, Russell 1000 and 2000 indices, Europe/ Australasia/Far East Index, emerging market stock and bond indices, changes in high yield and investment grade credit spreads, and the slope of the U.S. Treasury yield curve. Notice that all of these traditional market factors are commonly included in investor portfolios and exposures can be achieved by using low-cost index funds. Traditional market risk factors explain 50–80 percent of the variation in hedge fund returns. Far from being pure alpha, market neutral, or absolute return investments, many hedge fund styles take significant risks in traditional market factors.

Some hedge fund strategies, especially those in the market neutral or arbitrage categories, typically take a lower exposure to traditional market factors, such as equity beta or bond market duration. Although a fund may take minimal factor exposure with traditional beta risks, many hedge fund styles focus on taking risks with exotic betas or hedge fund betas. These exotic beta exposures are typically not prevalent in most investor portfolios. Exotic betas could include equity market volatility, credit default swaps, spreads between large- and small-cap stock returns, and spreads between value and growth stocks. In the newest literature, authors are modeling hedge fund strategies as separate beta exposures and using a naive strategy to replicate returns to merger arbitrage or managed futures funds.

Dynamic betas can be replicated through the modeling of a trend following methodology, the purchase or sale of options on a variety of underlying markets, or the use of rolling window analysis. Fung and Hsieh (2004) found six significant factors in their analysis that explained 55 percent of the variation in the HFR fund-of-funds index from 1994 to 2002. The betas calculated from the factor analysis regression showed the hedge fund index's average exposure over time. Many hedge funds, however, do not have static beta exposures but vary their market exposures substantially over time. By splitting the sample into smaller time periods, such as January 1994 to September 1998 or April 2000 to December 2002, the R^2 of the regression climbed as high as 80 percent. Beckers et al. (2007) used a 36-month rolling window regression to explain the returns of funds of funds. Ideally, hedge funds will take greater exposure in rising markets and less exposure in declining markets. Unfortunately, these authors found evidence of negative market timing skill among fund-of-funds managers.

5   NON-NORMALITY OF HEDGE FUND RETURNS

Much of the traditional finance literature has made the implicit assumption that investment returns are normally distributed and linearly related to asset class returns. Sharpe ratios and Markowitz's efficient frontier analysis include return and standard deviation of return in their calculations of risk–return trade-offs. The calculation of beta, and the resulting Jensen's alpha, include the assumption that investment returns are earned from taking risk exposures to traditional market factors and that these exposures are relatively constant through time. Unfortunately, many of these assumptions are violated when investing in hedge funds. Because hedge fund returns are often not normally distributed or linearly related to traditional market exposures, Kat (2003) and Cremers, Kritzman, and Page (2005) show that applying many of the classical techniques and ratios to hedge fund returns without accounting for nonlinearities can cause investors to reach inappropriate conclusions about the attractiveness of hedge funds. As a result, some investors allocate too much of their portfolio to hedge funds and are disappointed when their assumptions are violated.

The Sharpe ratio and efficient frontier analysis assume that standard deviation is the only investment risk, but many hedge fund strategies have return profiles in which the skewness and kurtosis of returns do not closely match the assumptions of the normal distribution. Investors prefer a large mean and positive skewness of returns, while also preferring lower variance and smaller kurtosis. Hedge funds generally have higher moment risks, in which returns have negative skewness (i.e., the third moment of the return distribution) and large excess kurtosis (i.e., the fourth moment of the return distribution, also called fat tails). These return characteristics come from managers' spread trading strategies, which Kat (2004) deemed to be "pseudo" arbitrages and showed that these trades are far from risk free. Because these trades typically have a low volatility, leverage is frequently used.

Consider a merger arbitrage trade in which the fund manager purchases the target company and sells short the acquiring company with the intention of earning a 10 percent return during the next 12 months. When the deal is consummated at the time and terms as expected, it seems to be a low risk, low volatility strategy. In actuality, this trade is selling insurance. Investors sell the target company at a discount to its stated deal price to hedge the risk that the deal will fail. By offering the hedge fund the last 10 percent of return, the investor avoids the risk of a one week decline of 30 percent or more in the target stock should the merger not proceed as planned. Notice that this trade is negatively skewed and highly kurtotic because the potential loss is larger than the potential gain and the losses come much more quickly than the gains.

Similar return profiles can be found in fixed-income arbitrage, option selling strategies, and currency carry trades. Evaluating the returns to these funds during quiet and converging market conditions can underestimate the potential losses that these funds could experience during turbulent markets in which credit spreads widen and stock prices decline quickly. Black (2006), Weisman (2002), and Kat (2003) demonstrate that these trading styles are short volatility, meaning these strategies incur substantial losses at times when equity market volatility is rising. Adding long volatility strategies, such as managed futures or purchased options, to a hedge fund portfolio can cause portfolio returns to be closer to normally distributed. When balancing long volatility and short volatility in a hedge fund portfolio, reported volatility will increase and the Sharpe ratio will decline but the skewness and kurtosis exposures will be much more attractive to investors. Much of the nonlinearities in hedge fund returns can be traced back to extreme events, such as the demise of Long-Term Capital Management in 1998 (see Kazemi and Schneeweis 2004).

LIQUIDITY, COMPLEXITY, AND VALUATION RISKS

6

Hedge fund factor exposures vary in their ease of being added to a factor model compared with traditional market exposures, which are better understood and easy to add to a factor model. Hedge fund strategies and exotic betas are more difficult to derive, but once derived they are straightforward to add to the factor model. Some of the hedge fund returns attributed to alpha could simply be compensation for bearing liquidity and complexity risks. That is, some investments should offer higher returns simply because they are more difficult to understand or value.

Till (2004) discusses the costs of illiquidity in hedge funds. As mentioned earlier, investors should be compensated for longer lockup periods, and many hedge funds are now offering lower fees in exchange for investors agreeing to longer lockup periods. Investors should also be compensated for short volatility risk and event risk. Illiquid assets, such as emerging markets, over-the-counter derivatives, microcap stocks, and distressed fixed-income securities, are difficult to value and difficult to trade. Investors in these assets are taking the risk that the assets will be valued at a price far different from what would be realized when asking the market for liquidity. Should the hedge fund choose or be forced to sell during a liquidity crisis, prices will be even lower.

In these illiquid asset classes, many holdings are valued using a mark-to-model methodology. Because these assets do not have a liquid market, marking to market is not feasible. These assets also trade infrequently, so valuations change relatively slowly when compared with prices in more liquid markets. This tendency to change valuations slowly is termed stale pricing. When funds exhibit stale pricing, the risk of the fund's holdings will be understated because volatility and the correlation with freely traded assets are likely to be understated. Kat (2004) estimates that this artificial smoothing of net asset values can underestimate risk by as much as 40 percent. Although it seems logical to include illiquidity in a factor model, Kat (2004) states that no study has adequately modeled this common risk of hedge fund investing. The Sharpe ratio of funds with smoothed returns is dramatically overstated, as the standard deviation of reported returns is far below the true economic standard deviation.

Although it can be difficult to include illiquidity in a factor model, a number of authors have suggested adjustments to smoothed data to estimate the true, or unsmoothed, risk of these illiquid investments. Getmansky, Lo, and Makarov (2004) explain the procedures for adjusting for stale prices, which can be detected through the use of serial correlation. When analysis shows that autocorrelation is present in hedge fund returns, it is said that the returns have been smoothed and that prior month returns can be used to predict the current month returns. The factor analysis equation given earlier can be modified as follows:

$$\text{Hedge fund return } (t) = \text{Alpha} + \text{Risk free rate} + \text{Hedge fund return } (t-1)$$
$$+ \sum_i \text{Beta}_i \times \text{Factor}_i$$

By including the prior month's return, the analysis shows that this hedge fund trading strategy incurs illiquidity risks. When the prior month's return is statistically significant, a new explanatory factor is added to the analysis. The typical result is that the R^2 of the regression increases and the alpha of the hedge fund style declines. Some authors include lagged values of a hedge fund index or a traditional market beta source. When the current month and the prior month both have a statistically significant exposure to a given factor, Kazemi and Schneeweis (2004) show that the true risk to that factor is the sum of the current and prior month's factor betas. For example, rather than the fund beta being 0.3 from the S&P 500 Index return in the current month, the true beta would be 0.5 if the regression also showed a statistically significant beta of 0.2 from the prior month's return on the S&P 500 Index.

Getmansky, Lo, and Makarov (2004) show that stale pricing risks are most prominent in fixed-income and convertible bond strategies, as well as event driven and relative value strategies and emerging markets. These markets are known for their illiquidity and the need for mark-to-market valuation. Strategies that rely on trading in more liquid markets, such as large-cap stocks, currencies, and commodity futures, do not show evidence of stale pricing because fund managers can easily calculate NAV from each day's market settlement prices.

Beyond the effect of underestimated risks, stale pricing can have clear financial implications for investors. If the monthly NAV for a hedge fund is struck using stale prices, investors who sell hedge fund interests during a bull market may receive proceeds of less than the fair value for those assets. Conversely, investors who redeem hedge fund interests during a bear market will receive a higher than realistic price for their assets because future prices are likely to be lower when full markdowns of assets are taken.

ALPHA AND THE CAPACITY FOR HEDGE FUNDS TO INCREASE ASSETS   **7**

Géhin and Vaissié (2006) and Amenc and Martinelli (2002) discuss the proper calculation of the alpha earned by hedge funds. Alpha is the return to the hedge fund after accounting for the risks incurred by both traditional and alternative beta exposures. Amenc and Martinelli (2002) estimate the alpha of hedge funds to be 5.8 percent per year in excess of the exposure to traditional beta risks. After adding the exposure to alternative beta risks, the alpha declines to –1.0 percent. The implication of this analysis is that hedge funds, as a group, do not earn positive alpha but simply provide investors with the ability to access alternative beta exposures.

Of course, alpha varies over time and by strategy. Concerns exist that as the size of the hedge fund industry increases, the alpha earned by the average hedge fund will decline. More simply, Hsieh (2006) estimates that by exploiting market inefficiencies a static $30 billion in alpha is available to be earned by all hedge fund managers combined. This amount is based on 3 percent alpha from a hedge fund industry size of $1 trillion, but as hedge fund assets grow to $2 trillion, the percentage return to each fund in alpha terms would decline to 1.5 percent. This argument assumes that a finite capacity for AUM for hedge funds exists, both as an industry and in each strategy. As greater assets enter each strategy, the market inefficiencies disappear more quickly, making the future prognosis for hedge fund growth dim. Géhin and Vaissié (2006), however, find no clear evidence of a declining trend in alpha. The capacity for hedge fund managers to profitably invest is based on alpha and beta factors. If hedge funds derive most of their returns from beta factors, then the industry can continue to grow in terms of assets and managers. If hedge funds are dependent on alpha and disappearing market inefficiencies, then the capacity of AUM for the hedge fund industry is more limited.

Géhin and Vaissié (2006) believe that investors overstate the importance of alpha and understate the importance of beta when analyzing the returns to hedge funds. The three drivers of hedge fund returns are static beta exposures, dynamic beta exposures (market timing), and alpha (security selection skill). The authors estimate that approximately half of hedge fund variance comes from static betas, whereas the remaining variance is evenly split between dynamic betas and alpha. Nearly the entire return to hedge funds can be attributed to static betas, whereas dynamic betas incur losses over time and alpha adds value.

HEDGE FUND REPLICATION   **8**

Hedge fund replication is widely discussed in the literature, with Jaeger and Wagner (2005), Fung and Hsieh (2004), and Kat (2007) leading the discussion. The original discussion of hedge fund replication was based on the factor models mentioned earlier and the concept of alpha–beta separation. If traditional stock and bond market indices can explain the majority of hedge fund return variance, then investors may be able to replicate hedge fund returns by using index funds and swaps products. Replication strategies can be attractive when hedge fund managers are not earning a positive alpha, when investors are worried about the size of the fees paid to hedge fund managers, or because of the historical lack of liquidity and transparency of hedge fund investments. A common theme in the replication literature is that replication products are relatively simple to manage and can, therefore, be offered to investors at fees much lower than those charged by hedge fund managers.

The simplest form of replication uses static weights to invest in traditional market products. Jaeger and Wagner (2005) develop replicating factor strategies, which can replicate many hedge fund styles with just three or four traditional market exposures. Of 11 styles tested, 8 could be replicated with an R^2 above 49 percent. Long–short equity, emerging market, short selling, and distressed strategies can be most closely replicated, with an R^2 of between 68 percent and 88 percent. Less efficient replications can be developed for equity market neutral, risk arbitrage, fixed-income arbitrage, convertible-bond arbitrage, global macro, and managed futures strategies. For example, a simple replication of a fixed-income arbitrage fund would take a long position in a credit fund, such as corporate bonds, high yield bonds, or mortgage-backed securities, and a short position in a Treasury securities fund of a similar duration. The weights for each fund would be determined through a linear regression of long-term hedge fund returns on the traditional bond market sector funds. A slightly more complex form of replication uses dynamic weights with the same traditional market factors. Rather than having static weights, the beta exposure to each market sector is determined through the use of rolling regressions, with common look back periods of one to three years.

Fung and Hsieh (2004) add dynamic strategies to the factor mix, simulating the use of look back straddles on bond, currency, and commodity indices. These dynamic factors can simulate the use of trend following strategies, as well as short or long volatility exposures.

Berger, Crowell, and Kabiller (2008) seek to separate hedge fund beta from hedge fund replication. Hedge fund replication using factor models and liquid index products avoids many of the issues of liquidity and complex valuation faced by hedge funds that invest in specific securities. To capture the returns to event risk, illiquidity, and complex securities, the hedge fund beta strategy seeks to mechanically reproduce hedge fund strategies by investing in specific securities. A fund designed to provide merger arbitrage beta, for example, would purchase the target company and sell short the acquiring company in all announced merger transactions. Beta exposure to managed futures could be developed through a mechanical trend following system that seeks to buy futures in any market with a trend of rising prices and sell short futures in any market in which prices are expected to decline. A distressed or convertible arbitrage beta could be devised through the purchase of those specific fixed-income securities, perhaps by selling short the related equity security.

9   HEDGE FUND PORTFOLIO ANALYSIS

Hedge fund investors are interested in how an allocation to hedge funds would modify the risk and return of their entire portfolio, including exposures to traditional stock and bond markets. Fund-of-funds managers are concerned with building the most efficient portfolio of hedge funds. In each case, the goal is to minimize the risk for each level of expected return. Ideally, adding hedge funds to a traditional investment portfolio would reduce portfolio risk without reducing portfolio return.

Traditional portfolio theory says that the calculation of efficient portfolios requires estimates of return, correlation, and volatility for each asset class. The factor analysis techniques discussed earlier can give clues to future correlation and volatility. For example, long–short equity funds are highly correlated with stock market indices in which volatility is scaled by the average beta through time. Géhin and Vaissié (2006) state that managed futures, fixed-income and convertible bond arbitrage, and market neutral equity funds provide the best diversification properties when added to an equity portfolio. Similarly, event driven, long–short equity, emerging market, and convertible bond arbitrage funds add diversification to a fixed-income portfolio.

Allison and Lin (2004) show that a number of caveats exist when attempting to model the addition of hedge funds to traditional portfolios. Specifically, it is difficult to develop expected return assumptions for hedge funds given the survivor, selection, stale pricing, and backfill biases inherent in hedge fund databases. Correlation and volatility of historical hedge fund returns, however, can be appropriately used to develop estimates of future risks. After determining the beta of each hedge fund strategy in relation to the underlying traditional market factors, an expected return assumption for the hedge fund style can be derived by adding estimated alpha to the beta adjusted expected returns of the underlying asset classes.

Dopfel (2005) also uses the alpha and beta estimates of factor analysis to derive expected returns for hedge fund strategies. Investors need to be aware, however, that hedge fund performance can be quite dynamic, with correlation, volatility, and beta exposures that can change significantly over time. In addition, derivatives and short volatility trading strategies can add nonlinearities to the hedge fund return generation process. These properties can lead hedge funds to have asymmetrical beta exposures, in which the beta of the hedge fund differs according to the volatility and the direction of the underlying market. For example, managed futures and dedicated short bias funds have attractive asymmetrical exposures to equity index prices, with higher betas in rising markets and lower betas in falling markets. Multistrategy and market neutral equity funds have little exposure to asymmetrical beta. Unfortunately, all other hedge fund styles have negative asymmetrical beta exposures, and betas tend to rise in falling markets. Dopfel (2005) also discusses using factor analysis to target overall asset allocation. When the hedge fund portfolio has a persistent beta relative to equity markets, it is wise to reduce the portfolio's exposure to equity markets by a similar amount to ensure that equity market risk is consistent with the strategic asset allocation.

Kat (2004) warns about the use of mean–variance optimization and Sharpe ratios in building hedge fund portfolios because standard deviation is not a complete measure of risk for hedge funds. Some hedge fund styles are known to smooth returns, as well as experience negative skewness and excess kurtosis. In fact, the hedge fund styles with the lowest standard deviations and highest Sharpe ratios are often the ones with the most unattractive higher moment exposures. A high Sharpe ratio and high alpha are simply invitations to further research the hedge fund manager's trading strategy. Investors need to determine whether the trading strategy is a short volatility, convergence related, or event-risk-laden strategy in which future risks could potentially be larger than historical risk. The typical result of adding hedge funds to a portfolio of traditional investments is that standard deviation will decline and the Sharpe ratio will increase but at the cost of worsening higher moment exposures. This result is attributed to the variable correlation and asymmetrical beta exposures of hedge funds, in which losses to hedge fund portfolios tend to increase during times of extreme losses in stock and bond markets. Mean–variance optimization also assumes that assets have the same liquidity characteristics and return distributions. If mean–variance optimization is to be used to add hedge funds to traditional investment portfolios, constraints on the deterioration of skewness and kurtosis risks should be added to the optimization equation. Placing constraints on the nonlinearities of hedge funds will cause investors to choose lower allocations to hedge funds than when mean–variance optimization is used without considering higher moment risks.

Sharma (2004) states that higher moment risks are more prevalent in lower volatility strategies because 75 percent of nondirectional strategies have returns that are not normally distributed, whereas only 39 percent of directional strategies reject normality.

Kat (2004) discusses the differences in analyzing hedge fund index data and the returns to individual hedge funds. Individual hedge funds typically have a higher standard deviation than their style index because a less than perfect correlation exists between funds in the same style. When aggregating hedge funds into a style index, the standard deviation of the index is lower than the standard deviation of the average fund, but the index tends to have more negative skewness and a higher correlation with equity markets. Although each fund has its own specific risks and market timing, those exposures are averaged when funds are bundled into an index. Although it diversifies the specific risk of each fund, the indexing process reduces standard deviation but increases the exposures to common factor risks.

10   PERFORMANCE PERSISTENCE OF HEDGE FUNDS

Beckers et al. (2007) discuss the performance persistence of hedge funds and find that the persistence of alpha is higher than the persistence of total returns. The persistence of funds with high information ratios (i.e., alpha divided by the standard deviation of alpha) is greater than that of funds with high Sharpe ratios. Specifically, funds with top quartile rankings of information ratios during the trailing three years have a 51 percent chance of remaining in the top quartile of that same measure during the subsequent year. Persistence is also strong for lower quartile funds because a large percentage of funds repeat as below average performers. Funds of funds show much greater persistence than single strategy hedge funds. The common factor risks tend to dominate the performance of single strategy funds, which are often clustered around the average return for the strategy. Funds of funds diversify among hedge fund styles, which diversifies the risks of relying on returns from a specific market factor.

Naik and Agarwal (2000) analyzed the performance persistence of hedge funds by calculating the alpha of each fund relative to its style index using quarterly returns. Past performance was calculated by using a variety of methodologies, including regressions, contingency tables, and appraisal ratios, which explicitly consider volatility and leverage. The results indicated that persistence varies by hedge fund style because 6 to 8 of 13 strategies showed reasonable persistence using different methodologies. Losers tend to exhibit greater persistence than winners, which shows the importance of manager selection when building a portfolio of hedge funds.

11   FUNDS OF FUNDS

Funds of funds allow investors to one-stop shop for their hedge fund needs at a low minimum investment. Fothergill and Coke (2001) describe the advantages and disadvantages of investing in funds of funds. Funds of funds use investment managers that perform due diligence on single strategy hedge fund investments, with the goal of building a lower risk, well-diversified hedge fund portfolio. By investing in 15 to 20 single manager hedge funds across a variety of trading styles, funds of funds can reduce the standard deviation of a hedge fund portfolio. Smaller investors may be able to access a fund of funds portfolio with a minimum investment as low as $100,000, far lower than the $7 million to $20 million required to meet the minimum investment requirements of each of the underlying hedge fund managers. Funds of funds may offer preferential liquidity terms to investors, perhaps allowing monthly redemptions, which are preferable to the quarterly or annual redemptions of the underlying managers.

Smaller investors may appreciate the due diligence performed by funds-of-funds managers because this task can require significant investment skill, manager relationships, and research costs. Of course, the funds-of-funds manager gets paid for providing access, diversification, risk management, and due diligence benefits to investors. A common fee structure requires a 1 percent management fee and a 10 percent performance fee to be paid to the funds-of-funds manager, which is in addition to the 2 percent and 20 percent fees paid to the underlying hedge fund managers. Beckers et al. (2007) calculate that the average fund-of-funds fee is 1.3 percent plus 8.1 percent.

This double layer of fees presents a high hurdle for funds of funds to earn an alpha in excess of the required return for taking risks in the traditional and exotic beta exposures. The fund-of-funds business is becoming increasingly concentrated—the largest 25 percent of funds of funds manage more than 75 percent of all assets in this sector.

Funds of funds, as a result of their diversification among strategies and managers, tend to have average performance. Although single hedge fund managers and strategies will dominate the top and bottom of the performance charts, funds of funds tend to approximate hedge fund index performance before adding their second layer of fees. Beckers et al. (2007) show that the lowest quartile of funds of funds outperforms the lowest quartile of single manager funds (i.e., 6.3 percent versus 5.5 percent annually), whereas the top quartile of funds of funds offers lower returns than the top hedge funds (i.e., 15.1 percent versus 23.2 percent). Funds of funds also tend to have lower mortality, survivor bias, and backfill bias than single manager hedge funds. On average, funds of funds tend to add more value through risk reduction rather than return enhancement.

Funds of funds tend to take less factor risk than is found through the analysis of a broad hedge fund index. The typical hedge fund examined by Beckers et al. (2007) has an R^2 to traditional market factors of only 40 percent, but those common factor risks are rising over time. The authors find that even the lowest quartile of funds of funds earned alpha in excess of traditional market factor exposures, but exotic and hedge fund betas were not included in the analysis. Unfortunately, funds of funds have consistently taken common factor bets at the wrong time because beta exposures reduced returns in 8 of the 12 years of the study.

Hsieh (2006) explains that many funds of funds take substantial risk in traditional market factors. Investors in these beta funds may be paying high fees for risk exposures that can be sourced more cheaply outside of the hedge fund universe. Hsieh (2006) predicts that the limited number of funds of funds that provide true alpha with low beta risks will rapidly grow as a share of the industry's AUM, whereas funds of funds that provide beta exposures with minimal value added will struggle to retain market share.

Fung, Hsieh, Naik, and Ramadorai (2008) calculated the alpha earned by funds of funds in three different time periods. Factor risks have statistically significant variations in exposure across three periods, with structural breaks at the time of the Long-Term Capital Management crisis and the end of the internet stocks era. They found that funds of funds did not earn statistically significant alpha between January 1995 and September 1998 or from April 2000 to December 2004. Funds of funds, however, did earn alpha from October 1998 to March 2000. Although the universe of hedge funds may not always earn alpha, some funds of funds always can. On average, 22 percent of funds of funds provided alpha, whereas the rest were simply providing factor exposures without value added. Of course, the portion of "have alpha" funds of funds varies over time, peaking at 42 percent in 2000.

Funds of funds with proven alpha tend to have longer lives and larger asset inflows. Unfortunately, the larger the inflows become, the more difficult it is to continue to earn high levels of alpha. Capital flows to alpha funds, presumably from sophisticated institutional investors, are relatively constant. Capital flows to beta funds are cyclical, with large flows from individual investors after times of high returns.

RISK MANAGEMENT   **12**

Some funds of funds will closely manage their risks, especially to traditional beta exposures. Beta risks can be limited in the portfolio construction process by closely understanding the beta exposures of individual hedge fund managers and increasing the allocation to funds with lower market risks. Alternatively, the funds of funds will allocate to managers with the highest alpha and then hedge away the common factor risks at the fund-of-funds level. Hedging can be accomplished through the use of futures that linearly reduce market risks. Equity index options are also used, which reduce downside risks of the portfolio without capping the upside return potential.

Beyond market risks, hedge fund investors need to understand and manage a number of other risks. These include event risk, operational risk, leverage, and counterparty risks. In fact, many of these risks tend to magnify market risks, so a global view of risk is very important for hedge fund investors and fund-of-funds managers.

Event risks are commonly focused in event driven funds, such as those following mergers and distressed or special situation investments. Although event driven funds may offer a lower correlation with market indices, their returns can change dramatically at the emergence of event risk, such as when a merger deal is not completed or when a company defaults on debt that the manager assumed was issued by a going concern. Event risk can also be present in a number of other hedge fund styles, either from hedge fund managers explicitly including event driven investments in their fund or from the effect that specific events may have on broader market risks.

Operational risks can lead to a total loss of investments in a specific hedge fund. Kundro and Feffer (2003, 2004) estimate that 54 percent of hedge fund failures can be attributed, at least in part, to operational risks. Of the funds that failed as a result of operational failures, they estimate that 6 percent of occurrences were because of inadequate resources, 14 percent were the result of unauthorized trading and style drift, 30 percent were from the theft of investor assets, and 41 percent were from the misrepresentation of investments and performance. Further, they estimate that 38 percent of hedge fund failures had only investment risk, meaning that the operational controls were in place and effective. Surprisingly, 54 percent of hedge fund failures were the result of operational risk, whereas the final 8 percent of hedge fund debacles could be attributed to business risk or a combination of different risks.

In a series of case studies, Black (2007) shows that a key way to minimize operational risks is to ensure a strict delineation of duties within a hedge fund. This structure means the portfolio manager is separate from the risk manager, the pricing process, and the auditing function. A proper system of checks and balances ensures that the hedge fund manager stays within the risk limits stated in the hedge fund documentation. Ideally, a hedge fund should be diversified among securities and have leverage and market exposure limits consistent with a low probability of catastrophic losses. The valuation of securities should be handled outside of the portfolio management group to ensure accurate statements of risk and return. The auditing of returns should be handled by a reputable third party because the misstatement of hedge fund returns can prolong fraudulent behavior and allow a manager to continue to attract assets from new investors. Clearly, assets should be appropriately segregated—client funds should be kept safe and separate from the hedge fund's corporate and the manager's personal accounts. Many hedge fund investors insist on separate accounts or managed accounts in which the assets are held in custody with the investor's broker. The investor allows the manager to trade his or her account, but the complete transparency disallows excessive concentration or leverage risks that can cause catastrophic losses. A separate account format also prevents the misstatement of investment performance or the theft of client assets. Many investors perform a background check on hedge fund managers to ensure that the biography is correct and that the manager has not previously been disciplined by regulatory authorities or sued by prior investors.

Brown, Goetzmann, Liang, and Schwarz (2009) derive a quantitative operational risk score, ω, that can be calculated from information in hedge fund databases. This quantitative factor score can be used as a supplement for qualitative due diligence, which includes manager interviews, on-site visits, and background checks. The score is used to define "problem funds" that subsequently have lower mean returns, lower Sharpe ratios, lower incentive fees, and less frequent high-water mark provisions than nonproblem funds. Similar to Altman's (1968) z-score, which is used to predict corporate bankruptcies, the ω-score can be used to predict operational risks and the demise of hedge funds because the half-life of funds with an ω-score exceeding one is just 4.2 years. Funds with lower returns, higher standard deviations, and lower incentive fees have characteristics that correlate with operational issues, such as conflicts of interests, concentrated ownership of the management company, relationships with investment advisers or broker/dealers, and the ability of fund staff to trade the same securities as the fund.

Counterparty risk arises whenever a hedge fund deals with investors, prime brokers, and other market participants. In the over-the-counter market, counterparty risk arises when a hedge fund is owed money on a swaps or options contract but the seller of the contract fails to deliver the required investment gains. Counterparty risk to prime brokers or investors is less obvious to discern but just as important.

A special concern is leverage that can magnify market risk and counterparty risk. Leverage allows a hedge fund manager to take economic exposure in excess of the assets invested by clients. Leverage can be explicit debt, borrowed either in the repurchase market or from a prime broker. For example, a fund with $100 million in client assets may be allowed to borrow $900 million and invest the entire $1 billion fund value in fixed-income securities. When the return to the investment exceeds the borrowing costs, returns are increased through leverage. Of course, losses are also magnified. So, a 10 percent loss on the $1 billion investment will cause a 100 percent loss of the clients' $100 million investment. Leverage can also be gained through the use of derivative products, such as swaps, options, and futures, which can increase market exposure with initial capital requirements ranging from 0 to 20 percent of the notional value of the investment.

Sharma (2004) describes the dangers of leverage and the interaction between leverage, counterparty risk, and market risk. Leverage increases the probability of large investment losses because the increase in assets beyond investor capital magnifies the beta of the investment portfolio. Leverage also increases the vulnerability to margin calls and forced liquidations. Counterparty risk and leverage are a dangerous mix because the prime broker sets the credit limit for each hedge fund. For example, consider the fund mentioned earlier that invested $1 billion based on only $100 million in investor capital. If the prime broker reduces the credit limit from $900 million to $400 million, the fund manager is required to sell half of the fund's assets in just a few days' time. Credit limits are typically reduced during turbulent markets when it is difficult to sell assets for their fair value. This forced liquidation can be sufficient to cause catastrophic losses for the hedge fund because rapidly selling assets in a falling market can incur market impact sufficient to wipe out the investors' equity in the fund. Investor redemptions can also cause forced liquidations because managers are forced to sell assets in less than 30 to 60 days to return investor capital on a timely basis.

It is important for hedge fund managers to align the lockup policies of the fund with the liquidity of the underlying assets and the terms of financing used in the investment strategy. A fund of funds offering monthly liquidity to investors but investing in hedge funds with an average lockup period of two years is a recipe for a liquidity crisis that can cause dramatic losses to a fund.

SUMMARY

When allocating assets to hedge funds, investors need to clearly understand the characteristics of these investments. It is important to delineate the differences between fund strategies and to understand the level and volatility of the resulting alpha and beta exposures. This analysis can show the value added by the fund manager, as well as the fit between the hedge fund investments and the investor's traditional investments in equity and fixed-income securities. Beyond market risks, investors also need to investigate fee structures, operational risks, and the capacity of the market to absorb increased levels of hedge fund assets.

REFERENCES

Editor's Note: References mentioned in the text are marked with an asterisk.

Ackermann, Carl, Richard McEnally, and David Ravenscraft. 1999. "The Performance of Hedge Funds: Risk, Return, and Incentives." *Journal of Finance*, vol. 54, no. 3 (June):833–874. "Hedge funds display several interesting characteristics that may influence performance, including flexible investment strategies, strong managerial incentives, substantial managerial investment, sophisticated investors, and limited government oversight. Using a large sample of hedge fund data from 1988–1995, we find that hedge funds consistently outperform mutual funds, but not standard market indices. Hedge funds, however, are more volatile than both mutual funds and market indices. Incentive fees explain some of the higher performance, but not the increased total risk. The impact of six data-conditioning biases is explored. We find evidence that positive and negative survival-related biases offset each other." (p. 833)

Agarwal, Vikas, and Narayan Y. Naik. 2000. "Multi-Period Performance Persistence Analysis of Hedge Funds." *Journal of Financial and Quantitative Analysis*, vol. 35, no. 3 (September):327–342 . "Since hedge funds specify significant lockup periods, we investigate persistence in the performance of hedge funds using a multi-period framework in which the likelihood of observing persistence by chance is lower than that in the traditional two-period framework. Under the null hypothesis of no manager skill (no persistence), the theoretical distribution of observing wins or losses follows a binomial distribution. We test this hypothesis using the traditional two-period framework and compare the findings with the results obtained using our multi-period framework. We examine whether persistence is sensitive to the length of return measurement intervals by using quarterly, half-yearly and yearly returns. We find maximum persistence at the quarterly horizon indicating that persistence among hedge fund managers is short-term in nature. It decreases as one moves to yearly returns and this finding is not sensitive to whether returns are calculated on a pre- or post-fee basis suggesting that the intra-year persistence finding is not driven by the way performance fees are imputed. The level of persistence in the multi-period framework is considerably smaller than that in the two-period framework with virtually no evidence of persistence using yearly returns under the multi-period framework. Finally persistence, whenever present, seems to be unrelated to whether the fund took directional bets or not." (p. 327)

Agarwal, Vikas, and Narayan Y. Naik. 2004. "Risks and Portfolio Decisions Involving Hedge Funds." *Review of Financial Studies*, vol. 17, no. 1 (Spring):63–98 . "This article characterizes the systematic risk exposures of hedge funds using buy-and-hold and option-based strategies. Our results show that a large number of equity-oriented hedge fund strategies exhibit payoffs resembling a short position in a put option on the market index and, therefore, bear significant left-tail risk, risk that is ignored by the commonly used mean–variance framework. Using a mean–conditional value-at-risk framework, we demonstrate the extent to which the mean-variance framework underestimates the tail risk. Finally, working with the systematic risk exposures of hedge funds, we show that their recent performance appears significantly better than their long-run performance." (p. 63)

*   Allison, Douglas T., and Felix T. Lin. 2004. "Including Hedge Funds in Private Client Portfolios." *AIMR Conference Proceedings: Integrating Hedge Funds into a Private Wealth Strategy* (February):6–20. "Hedge funds can play a vital role in client portfolios, but clients need to be aware of all the issues involved—issues ranging from the impact of incorporating hedge funds into the portfolio mix to understanding the potential risks involved to the pros and cons of hedge fund investing. Once the decision has been made to include hedge funds in the portfolio mix, the allocation must be determined and should be based on future expectations for hedge fund performance. Finally, by using an optimizer, an ideal mix of hedge fund strategies can be established. The end result is a portfolio that meets client goals and objectives and has the potential to decrease risk and enhance return." (p. 6)

*   Altman, Edward I. 1968. "Financial Ratios, Discriminant Analysis and the Prediction of Corporate Bankruptcy." *Journal of Finance*, vol. 23, no. 4 (September):589–609. "Academicians seem to be moving toward the elimination of ratio analysis as an analytical technique in assessing the performance of the business enterprise. Theorists downgrade arbitrary rules of thumb, such as company ratio comparisons, widely used by practitioners. Since attacks on the relevance of ratio analysis emanate from many esteemed members of the scholarly world, does this mean that ratio analysis is limited to the world of 'nuts and bolts'? Or, has the significance of such an approach been unattractively garbed and therefore unfairly handicapped? Can we bridge the gap, rather than sever the link, between traditional ratio 'analysis' and the more rigorous statistical techniques which have become popular among academicians in recent years? The purpose of this paper is to attempt an assessment of this issue—the quality of ratio analysis as an analytical technique. The prediction of corporate bankruptcy is used as an illustrative case. Specifically, a set of financial and economic ratios will be investigated in a bankruptcy prediction context wherein a multiple discriminant statistical methodology is employed. The data used in the study are limited to manufacturing corporations." (p. 589)

* Amenc, N., and L. Martinelli. 2002. "Portfolio Optimization and Hedge Fund Style Allocation Decisions." *Journal of Alternative Investments*, vol. 5, no. 2 (Fall):7–20. "This paper attempts to evaluate the out-of-sample performance of an improved estimator of the covariance structure of hedge fund index returns, focusing on its use for optimal portfolio selection. Using data from CSFB/Tremont hedge fund indices, we find that ex-post volatility of minimum variance portfolios generated using implicit factor based estimation techniques is between 1.5 and 6 times lower than that of a value-weighted benchmark, such differences being both economically and statistically significant. This strongly indicates that optimal inclusion of hedge funds in an investor portfolio can potentially generate a dramatic decrease in the portfolio volatility on an out-of-sample basis. Differences in mean returns, on the other hand, are not statistically significant, suggesting that the improvement in terms of risk control does not necessarily come at the cost of lower expected returns." (p. 7)

Amin, Gaurav S., and Harry M. Kat. 2003. "Hedge Fund Performance 1990–2000: Do the 'Money Machines' Really Add Value?" *Journal of Financial and Quantitative Analysis*, vol. 38, no. 2 (June):251–274 . "In this paper we investigate the claim that hedge funds offer investors a superior risk–return trade-off. We do so using a continuous time version of Dybvig's (1988a,1988b) payoff distribution pricing model. The evaluation model, which does not require any assumptions with regard to the return distribution of the funds in question, is applied to the monthly returns of 77 hedge funds and 13 hedge fund indices over the period May 1990–April 2000. The results show that as a stand-alone investment hedge funds do not offer a superior risk-return profile. We find 12 indices and 72 individual funds to be inefficient, with the average efficiency loss amounting to 2.76% per annum for indices and 6.42% for individual funds. Part of the inefficiency cost of individual funds can be diversified away. Funds of funds, however, are not the preferred vehicle for this as their performance appears to suffer badly from their double fee structure. Looking at hedge funds in a portfolio context results in a marked improvement in the evaluation outcomes. Seven of the 12 hedge fund indices and 58 of the 72 individual funds classified as inefficient on a stand-alone basis are capable of producing an efficient payoff profile when mixed with the S&P 500. The best results are obtained when 10–20% of the portfolio value is invested in hedge funds." (p. 251)

* Anson, Mark J.P. 2001. "Hedge Fund Incentive Fees and the 'Free Option.'" *Journal of Alternative Investments*, vol. 4, no. 2 (Fall):43–48. "One of the ironies of hedge fund investing is that investors can provide conflicting incentives to the hedge fund manager. While hedge fund managers earn a management fee, which is a constant percentage applied to the amount of assets managed in the hedge fund, they receive an incentive fee, which is a form of profit sharing when a profitable return is earned for their investors. The standard Black–Scholes analysis is used to determine the value of the call option on hedge fund incentives. The article also discusses how this call option might provide an inconsistent incentive compared to the desires of investors in the hedge fund." (p. 43)

Asness, Clifford. 2004. "Sources of Change and Risk for Hedge Funds." *CFA Institute Conference Proceedings: Challenges and Innovation in Hedge Fund Management* (August):4–9. "A lot of change is on the horizon for hedge funds, particularly given institutional investors' growing use of alternative investments.

The changes will likely bring a greater focus on benchmarking, calls for increased transparency, a need for better articulation of investment strategies, rationalization of hedge fund fees, and the need for solid risk control mechanisms. The future also brings subtle shifts in hedge fund risk. And although the risk of blowups still exists, perhaps the larger future risk will relate to diminished returns." (p. 4)

* Asness, Clifford. 2006. "The Future Role of Hedge Funds." *CFA Institute Conference Proceedings Quarterly*, vol. 23, no. 2 (June):1–9 . "Hedge funds generate returns through managers' skill (measured by alpha) as well as managers' systematic risk taking (measured by hedge fund beta). Hedge funds combined with index funds are now poised to replace traditional active management. To position themselves for such a future role, hedge funds must correct some of the industry's negative characteristics, including high correlations with the market, the misuse of momentum strategies, and lags in marking to market. To appeal to institutional investors, hedge funds must also improve their professionalism by altering the way they make decisions, reducing their fees (or at least rationalizing them), and striving for increased transparency." (p. 1)

Asness, Clifford, Robert Krail, and John Liew. 2001. "Do Hedge Funds Hedge?" *Journal of Portfolio Management*, vol. 28, no. 1 (Fall):6–19. "Many hedge funds claim to provide significant diversification for traditional portfolios, besides attractive returns. The authors provide empirical evidence regarding the return and diversification benefits of hedge fund investing using the CSFB/Tremont hedge fund indexes over 1994–2000. Like many others, they find that simple regressions of monthly hedge fund excess returns on monthly S&P 500 excess returns seem to support the claims about the benefits of hedge funds. The regressions show only modest market exposure and positive added value. This type of analysis can produce misleading results, however. Many hedge funds hold, to various degrees and combinations, illiquid exchange-traded securities or difficult-to-price over-the-counter securities. For the purposes of monthly reporting, hedge funds often price these securities using either the last available traded prices or estimates of current market prices. These practices can lead to reported monthly hedge fund returns that are not perfectly synchronous with monthly S&P 500 returns. Non-synchronous return data can lead to understated estimates of actual market exposure. When the authors apply standard techniques that account for this problem, they find that hedge funds in the aggregate have significantly more market exposure than simple estimates indicate. Furthermore, after accounting for this increased market exposure, they find that taken as a whole the broad universe of hedge funds does not add value over this period." (p. 6)

* Beckers, Stan, Ross Curds, and Simon Weinberger. 2007. "Funds of Hedge Funds Take the Wrong Risks." *Journal of Portfolio Management*, vol. 33, no. 3 (Spring):108–121. "On average, the funds of hedge funds industry over the last 15 years has delivered alpha with a high information ratio. Unfortunately, these alphas come with significant common-factor exposures for which the typical fund was unrewarded. While funds of hedge funds can deliver a valuable product, sloppy manager selection and portfolio construction typically result in less-than-pure alpha generation. A naive selection of a fund of hedge funds may thus lead to assuming relatively expensive common-factor exposure without necessarily

accessing significant skill-based returns. A multifactor model-ing of fund of hedge fund returns can help to identify skillful value-added." (p. 108)

* Berger, A., B. Crowell, and D. Kabiller. 2008. "Is Alpha Just Beta Waiting to be Discovered? What the Rise of Hedge Fund Beta Means for Investors." AQR Capital Management, Working paper (July): www.aqrcapital.com/research_15.htm. "Alpha is shrinking, and it's good news for investors. This idea may seem paradoxical. But alpha is really just the portion of a portfolio's returns that cannot be explained by exposure to common risk factors (betas). With the emergence of new betas, the unex-plained portion (alpha) shrinks—alpha gets reclassified as beta. The rise of a group of risk factors we call hedge fund betas makes this transformation especially relevant today. Hedge fund betas are the common risk exposures shared by hedge fund manag-ers pursuing similar strategies. We believe these risk factors can capture not just the fundamental insights of hedge funds, but also a meaningful portion of their returns. Hedge fund betas are available for investment and can also be used to enhance portfolio construction and risk management. Ultimately, we believe the rise of hedge fund betas will lead not only to the reclassification of alpha, but also to better-diversified portfolios with greater transparency, improved risk control, and—perhaps most importantly—higher net returns." (p. 1)

* Black, K. 2004. *Managing a Hedge Fund: A Complete Guide to Trading, Business Strategies, Risk Management and Regulations.* New York: McGraw-Hill. This book covers an extensive array of topics concerning hedge funds, including a discussion of the impact of hedge funds on portfolios, mea-suring the performance of hedge funds, managing the risks of hedge funds, and appropriate hedge fund due diligence.

* Black, K. 2006. "Improving Hedge Fund Risk Exposures by Hedging Equity Market Volatility, or How the VIX Ate My Kurtosis." *Journal of Trading*, vol. 1, no. 2 (Spring):6–15. "In 2004 investors began trading futures on the volatility index (VIX). Investors can directly trade the volatility implied in stock index options. Because the VIX has a negative correla-tion to the S&P 500 Index and most hedge fund styles, we find that adding a small VIX position to an investment portfolio significantly reduced portfolio volatility. This strategy may be more effective at improving the robustness of Sharpe ratios than other methods explored in the literature. Even more important, VIX rises quickly during the most risky market conditions, which dramatically improves the skewness and kurtosis characteristics of many hedge fund strategies." (p. 6)

Black, K. 2007. "Preventing and Detecting Hedge Fund Failure Risk through Partial Transparency." *Derivatives Use, Trading Regulation*, vol. 12, no. 4 (February):330–341 . "Some hedge fund investors may pay close attention to market risk while not spending enough time considering operational risks. The examples of Bayou, Wood River, and Lancer are used to illus-trate the operational risks that are all too present in hedge funds. A proposal to gather and aggregate data directly from brokers and custodians could reveal a large portion of the data necessary to make well-informed risk management decisions. Investors do not really need to know the details of every posi-tion owned by a hedge fund. They only need to see the partial transparency of aggregated risk statistics. A risk management system that is less intrusive to managers and more useful to investors could be an invaluable tool to fight hedge fund fraud." (p. 330)

Brooks, Chris, and Harry M. Kat. 2002. "The Statistical Properties of Hedge Fund Index Returns and Their Implications for Investors." *Journal of Alternative Investments*, vol. 5, no. 2 (Fall):26–44. "The monthly return distributions of many hedge fund indices exhibit highly unusual skewness and kurtosis properties as well as first-order serial correlation. This has important consequences for investors. Although many hedge fund indices are highly attractive in mean–variance terms, this is much less the case when skewness, kurtosis and autocorre-lation are taken into account. Sharpe ratios will substantially overestimate the true risk–return performance of (portfolios containing) hedge funds. Similarly, mean–variance portfo-lio analysis will overestimate the benefits of including hedge funds in an investment portfolio and, therefore, overallocate to hedge funds. We also find substantial differences between indices that aim to cover the same type of strategy. Investors' perceptions of hedge fund performance and value added will, therefore, strongly depend on the indices used." (p. 26)

Brown, Stephen J., and William N. Goetzmann. 2003. "Hedge Funds with Style." *Journal of Portfolio Management*, vol. 29, no. 2 (Winter):101–112. "The popular perception is that hedge funds follow a reasonably well-defined market-neutral investment style. Investigation of the monthly return history of hedge funds over 1989–2000, however, finds there are in fact distinct styles of management that account for about 20% of the cross-sectional variability in performance. This result is consistent across the years in the sample and robust as to the way investment style is determined. Appropriate style analy-sis and style management are crucial to success for investors looking to invest in hedge funds." (p. 101)

Brown, Stephen J., William N. Goetzmann, and Roger G. Ibbotson. 1999. "Offshore Hedge Funds: Survival and Performance, 1989-95." *Journal of Business*, vol. 72, no. 1 (January):91–117 . "We examine the performance of the off-shore hedge fund industry over the period 1989 through 1995 using a database that includes both defunct and currently operating funds. The industry is characterized by high attri-tion rates of funds, low covariance with the U.S. stock mar-ket, evidence consistent with positive risk-adjusted returns over the time, and little evidence of differential manager skill." (p. 91)

Brown, Stephen J., William N. Goetzmann, and James Park. 2001. "Careers and Survival: Competition and Risk in the Hedge Fund and CTA Industry." *Journal of Finance*, vol. 56, no. 5 (October):1869–1886 . "Investors in hedge funds and commodity trading advisors (CTAs) are concerned with risk as well as return. We investigate the volatility of hedge funds and CTAs in light of managerial career concerns. We find an association between past performance and risk levels consistent with previous findings for mutual fund manag-ers. Variance shifts depend upon relative rather than abso-lute fund performance. The importance of relative rankings points to the importance of reputation costs in the invest-ment industry. Our analysis of factors contributing to fund disappearance shows that survival depends on absolute and relative performance, excess volatility, and on fund age." (p. 1869)

* Brown, Stephen J., William N. Goetzmann, Bing Liang, and Christopher Schwarz. 2009. "Estimating Operational Risk for Hedge Funds: The ω-Score." *Financial Analysts Journal*, vol. 65, no. 1 (January/February):43–53 . "Using a complete set

of U.S. SEC filing information on hedge funds (Form ADV) and data from the Lipper TASS Hedge Fund Database, the study reported here developed a quantitative model called the ω-score to measure hedge fund operational risk. The ω-score is related to conflict-of-interest issues, concentrated ownership, and reduced leverage in the Form ADV data. With a statistical methodology, the study further related the ω-score to such readily available information as fund performance, volatility, size, age, and fee structures. Finally, the study demonstrated that although operational risk is more significant than financial risk in explaining fund failure, a significant and positive interaction exists between operational risk and financial risk." (p. 43)

Brunnermeier, Markus K., and Stefan Nagel. 2004. "Hedge Funds and the Technology Bubble." *Journal of Finance*, vol. 59, no. 5 (October):2013–2040 . "This paper documents that hedge funds did not exert a correcting force on stock prices during the technology bubble. Instead, they were heavily invested in technology stocks. This does not seem to be the result of unawareness of the bubble: Hedge funds captured the upturn, but, by reducing their positions in stocks that were about to decline, avoided much of the downturn. Our findings question the efficient markets notion that rational speculators always stabilize prices. They are consistent with models in which rational investors may prefer to ride bubbles because of predictable investor sentiment and limits to arbitrage." (p. 2013)

* Cremers, Jan-Hein, Mark Kritzman, and Sebastien Page. 2005. "Optimal Hedge Fund Allocations." *Journal of Portfolio Management*, vol. 31, no. 3 (Spring):70–81. "Hedge funds have return peculiarities not commonly associated with traditional investment vehicles. They are more inclined to produce return distributions with significantly non-normal skewness and kurtosis. Investor preferences may be better represented by bilinear utility functions or S-shaped value functions than by neoclassical utility functions, and mean–variance optimization is thus not appropriate for forming portfolios that include hedge funds. Portfolios of hedge funds formed using both mean–variance and full-scale optimization, given a wide range of assumptions about investor preferences, reveal that higher moments of hedge funds do not meaningfully compromise the efficacy of mean–variance optimization if investors have power utility; mean–variance optimization is not particularly effective for identifying optimal hedge fund allocations if preferences are bilinear or S-shaped; and, contrary to conventional wisdom, investors with S-shaped preferences are attracted to kurtosis as well as negative skewness." (p. 70)

* Dopfel, Frederick E. 2005. "How Hedge Funds Fit." *Journal of Portfolio Management*, vol. 31, no. 4 (Summer):9–20. "Hedge funds fit in an institutional investor's portfolio only if one can evaluate how the inclusion of hedge fund strategies would improve the performance of the entire portfolio, after considering both beta and alpha characteristics. This is more challenging than it first appears because of the opaqueness and the complexity of most hedge fund strategies. The key is to identify institutional-quality hedge funds that permit a clear understanding of the normal portfolio and provide confidence in projecting a positive, pure alpha. If these conditions can be satisfied, there are two possible approaches to incorporating institutional-quality hedge funds: 1) hedge funds as an active overlay at the total portfolio level, or 2) hedge funds as portable alpha within a traditional asset class." (p. 9)

Edwards, Franklin R. 1999. "Hedge Funds and the Collapse of Long-Term Capital Management." *Journal of Economic Perspectives*, vol. 13, no. 2 (Spring):189–210. "The Fed-engineered rescue of Long-Term Capital Management (LTCM) in September 1998 set off alarms throughout financial markets about the activities of hedge funds and the stability of financial markets in general. With only $4.8 billion in equity, LTCM managed to leverage itself to the hilt by borrowing more than $125 billion from banks and securities firms and entering into derivatives contracts totaling more than $1 trillion (notional). When LTCM's speculations went sour in the summer of 1998, the impending liquidation of LTCM's portfolio threatened to destabilize financial markets throughout the world. Public policy response to LTCM should focus on risks of systemic fragility and ways in which bank regulation can be improved." (p. 189)

Edwards, Franklin R., and Mustafa Onur Caglayan. 2001. "Hedge Fund Performance and Manager Skill." *Journal of Futures Markets*, vol. 21, no. 11 (November):1003–1028 . "Using data on the monthly returns of hedge funds during the period January 1990 to August 1998, we estimate six-factor Jensen alphas for individual hedge funds, employing eight different investment styles. We find that about 25 percent of the hedge funds earn positive excess returns and that the frequency and magnitude of funds' excess returns differ markedly with investment style. Using six-factor alphas as a measure of performance, we also analyze performance persistence over 1-year and 2-year horizons and find evidence of significant persistence among both winners and losers. These findings, together with our finding that hedge funds that pay managers higher incentive fees also have higher excess returns, are consistent with the view that fund manager skill may be a partial explanation for the positive excess returns earned by hedge funds." (p. 1003)

Eichengreen, Barry, and Donald Mathieson.*eds.* 1998. *Hedge Funds and Financial Market Dynamics*. Washington, DC: International Monetary Fund. This book discusses many aspects of hedge funds, including their operations, the hedge fund industry, hedge fund market dynamics, regulation, and recent crises and hedge funds.

* Fothergill, Martin, and Carolyn Coke. 2001. "Funds of Hedge Funds: An Introduction to Multi-Manager Funds." *Journal of Alternative Investments*, vol. 4, no. 2 (Fall):7–16. "In addition to the enhanced risk–return profile of funds of hedge funds, there are numerous additional structural benefits to investment in multi-manager hedge funds. This article both reviews the characteristics of various hedge fund strategies and emphasizes the unique structural characteristics of multi-manager hedge funds." (p. 7)

Fung, William, and David A. Hsieh. 1997. "Empirical Characteristics of Dynamic Trading Strategies: The Case of Hedge Funds." *Review of Financial Studies*, vol. 10, no. 2 (Summer):275–302 . "This article presents some new results on an unexplored dataset on hedge fund performance. The results indicate that hedge funds follow strategies that are dramatically different from mutual funds, and support the claim that these strategies are highly dynamic. The article finds five dominant investment styles in hedge funds, which when added to Sharpe's (1992) asset class factor model can provide an integrated framework for style analysis of both buy-and-hold and dynamic trading strategies." (p. 275)

Fung, William, and David A. Hsieh. 1999. "A Primer on Hedge Funds." *Journal of Empirical Finance*, vol. 6, no. 3 (September):309–331 . "In this paper, we provide a rationale for how hedge funds are organized and some insight on how hedge fund performance differs from traditional mutual funds. Statistical differences among hedge fund styles are used to supplement qualitative differences in the way hedge fund strategies are described. Risk factors associated with different trading styles are discussed. We give examples where standard linear statistical techniques are unlikely to capture the risk of hedge fund investments where the returns are primarily driven by non-linear dynamic strategies." (p. 309)

Fung, William, and David A. Hsieh. 2000. "Performance Characteristics of Hedge Funds and Commodity Funds: Natural vs. Spurious Biases." *Journal of Financial and Quantitative Analysis*, vol. 35, no. 3 (September):291–307 . "It is well known that the pro forma performance of a sample of investment funds contains biases. These biases are documented in Brown, Goetzmann, Ibbotson, and Ross (1992) using mutual funds as subjects. The organization structure of hedge funds, as private and often offshore vehicles, makes data collection a much more onerous task, amplifying the impact of performance measurement biases. This paper reviews these biases in hedge funds. We also propose using funds of hedge funds to measure aggregate hedge fund performance, based on the idea that the investment experience of hedge fund investors can be used to estimate the performance of hedge funds." (p. 291)

Fung, William, and David A. Hsieh. 2001. "The Risk in Hedge Fund Strategies: Theory and Evidence from Trend Followers." *Review of Financial Studies*, vol. 14, no. 2 (Summer):313–341. "Hedge fund strategies typically generate option-like returns. Linear-factor models using benchmark asset indices have difficulty explaining them. Following the suggestions in Glosten and Jagannathan (1994), this article shows how to model hedge fund returns by focusing on the popular 'trend-following' strategy. We use lookback straddles to model trend-following strategies, and show that they can explain trend-following funds' returns better than standard asset indices. Though standard straddles lead to similar empirical results, lookback straddles are theoretically closer to the concept of trend following. Our model should be useful in the design of performance benchmarks for trend-following funds." (p. 313)

* Fung, William, and David A. Hsieh. 2004. "Hedge Fund Benchmarks: A Risk-Based Approach." *Financial Analysts Journal*, vol. 60, no. 5 (September/October):65–80 . "Following a review of the data and methodological difficulties in applying conventional models used for traditional asset class indices to hedge funds, this article argues against the conventional approach. Instead, in an extension of previous work on asset-based style (ABS) factors, the article proposes a model of hedge fund returns that is similar to models based on arbitrage pricing theory, with dynamic risk-factor coefficients. For diversified hedge fund portfolios (as proxied by indices of hedge funds and funds of hedge funds), the seven ABS factors can explain up to 80 percent of monthly return variations. Because ABS factors are directly observable from market prices, this model provides a standardized framework for identifying differences among major hedge fund indexes that is free of the biases inherent in hedge fund databases." (p. 65)

* Fung, William, David A. Hsieh, Narayan Y. Naik, and Tarun Ramadorai. 2008. "Hedge Funds: Performance, Risk, and Capital Formation." *Journal of Finance*, vol. 63, no. 4 (August):1777–1803 . "We use a comprehensive data set of funds of funds to investigate performance, risk, and capital formation in the hedge fund industry from 1995 to 2004. While the average fund of funds delivers alpha only in the period between October 1998 and March 2000, a subset of funds of funds consistently delivers alpha. The alpha-producing funds are not as likely to liquidate as those that do not deliver alpha and experience far greater and steadier capital inflows than their less fortunate counterparts. These capital inflows attenuate the ability of the alpha producers to continue to deliver alpha in the future." (p. 1777)

* Géhin, Walter, and Mathieu Vaissié. 2006. "The Right Place for Alternative Betas in Hedge Fund Performance: An Answer to the Capacity Effect Fantasy." *Journal of Alternative Investments*, vol. 9, no. 1 (Summer):9–18. "In recent months, concerns have been raised about the profitability prospects for hedge funds. This article argues that market participants' pessimistic view of the hedge fund industry's capacity to generate long-term returns is a direct result of their continued focus on alpha. It illustrates the importance of considering not only the exposure to the market (the traditional beta), but also other exposures (the alternative betas) to characterize alternative sources of hedge fund returns. It also revisits the capacity issue by distinguishing between market capacity and manager capacity. The results show that alternative betas are an important source of hedge fund returns that reduce the importance of alpha. The authors conclude that capacity issues do not significantly impact alpha by illustrating that alpha is generated by successful bets on numerous exposures rather than by exploiting market opportunities." (p. 9)

* Getmansky, Mila, Andrew W. Lo, and Igor Makarov. 2004. "An Econometric Model of Serial Correlation and Illiquidity in Hedge Fund Returns." *Journal of Financial Economics*, vol. 74, no. 3 (December):529–609 . "The returns to hedge funds and other alternative investments are often highly serially correlated. In this paper, we explore several sources of such serial correlation and show that the most likely explanation is illiquidity exposure and smoothed returns. We propose an econometric model of return smoothing and develop estimators for the smoothing profile as well as a smoothing-adjusted Sharpe ratio. For a sample of 908 hedge funds drawn from the TASS database, we show that our estimated smoothing coefficients vary considerably across hedge-fund style categories and may be a useful proxy for quantifying illiquidity exposure." (p. 529)

* Gregoriou, Greg N., Georges Hübner, Nicolas Papageorgiou, and Fabrice Rouah. 2005. "Survival of Commodity Trading Advisors: 1990-2003." *Journal of Futures Markets*, vol. 25, no. 8 (August):795–815 . "This article investigates the mortality of Commodity Trading Advisors (CTAs) over the 1990–2003 period, a longer horizon than any encompassed in the literature. A detailed survival analysis over the full range of CTA classifications is provided, and it is found that the median lifetime of CTAs in this sample is different than previously documented. Through the implementation of nonparametric, parametric, and semiparametric statistical techniques, it is emphasized that CTA survivorship is heavily contingent on the strategy followed by the fund. Furthermore, a significant

positive size effect on survival is shown, whereas poor returns, and to a lesser extent, high-risk exposure, appear to hasten mortality." (p. 795)

* Hamza, Olfa, Maher Kooli, and Mathieu Roberge. 2006. "Further Evidence on Hedge Fund Return Predictability." *Journal of Wealth Management*, vol. 9, no. 3 (Winter):68–79. "In this article, the authors provide new evidence of the out-of-sample predictability of hedge fund returns. They first adopt a rigorous model-construction process to find the best predictive variables for each hedge fund style. They then examine whether the perceived predictability could translate into profitable 'tactical style' allocation strategies. Nine out of ten hedge funds strategies outperform the passive benchmark. For robustness, they test the performance of optimized strategies and confirm the profitability of tactical style allocation based on the prediction of our multifactor models." (p. 68)

Henriksson, Roy D. 1984. "Market Timing and Mutual Fund Performance: An Empirical Investigation." *Journal of Business*, vol. 57, no. 1 (January):73–96 . "The evaluation of the performance of investment managers is a topic of considerable interest to practitioners and academics alike. Using both the parametric and non-parametric tests for the evaluation of forecasting ability presented by Henriksson and Merton, the market-timing ability of 116 open-end mutual funds is evaluated for the period 1968–80. The empirical results do not support the hypothesis that mutual fund managers are able to follow an investment strategy that successfully times the return on the market portfolio." (p. 73)

* Hsieh, David A. 2006. "The Search for Alpha—Sources of Future Hedge Fund Returns." *CFA Institute Conference Proceedings Quarterly*, vol. 23, no. 3 (September):79–89 . "Two types of hedge fund investors exist: alpha seekers and beta chasers. If alpha seekers dominate the market, the decline in alpha per dollar invested in the hedge fund industry is likely to continue as long as the supply of alpha is finite. If, however, beta chasers dominate, growth in the industry should be sustainable because beta return is easily replicated and, therefore, the supply of beta virtually unlimited." (p. 79)

* Jaeger, L., and C. Wagner. 2005. "Factor Modeling and Benchmarking of Hedge Funds: Can Passive Investments in Hedge Fund Strategies Deliver?" *Journal of Alternative Investments*, vol. 8, no. 3 (Winter):9–36. "The hedge fund industry is starting to recognize that the main component of its returns corresponds to risk premia rather than market inefficiencies, i.e. from 'beta' instead of 'alpha.' This has some implication for the industry and investors, among which is the endeavor to construct investable benchmarks for hedge funds on the basis of an analysis of the underlying systematic risk factors. This issue is closely linked to the rationale for constructing investable versions of hedge fund indices. An important question is whether investable benchmarks based on risk factor analysis offer a valid, more theoretically sound, and cheaper alternative to the hedge fund index products currently available? This article reflects on this most recent discussion within the global hedge fund industry about the 'beta versus alpha' controversy, investable hedge fund indices, and finally, capacity issues. It illustrates how the current research might turn the hedge fund industry upside down in coming years." (p. 9)

* Kat, Harry M. 2003. "Taking the Sting Out of Hedge Funds." *Journal of Wealth Management*, vol. 6, no. 3 (Winter):67–76.

"Although the inclusion of hedge funds in an investment portfolio can significantly improve that portfolio's mean–variance characteristics, it can also be expected to lead to significantly lower skewness and higher kurtosis. In this article, the author shows how this highly undesirable side effect can be neutralized by allocating a fraction of wealth to out-of-the-money put options on the relevant stock index. Roughly speaking, the costs of the proposed skewness reduction strategy will be higher 1) the higher the hedge fund allocation, 2) the lower the expected equity risk premium, and 3) the higher the bond allocation relative to the equity allocation. In the current low interest rate environment, for portfolios with a more or less equal allocation to stocks and bonds, the costs of skewness reduction are unlikely to be much higher than 1 percent per annum. For portfolios with relatively high bond allocations, however, the costs could amount to 3 percent or even more. This confirms that the benefits of hedge funds heavily depend on the portfolio they are added to and that the attractive mean-variance properties of (portfolios including) hedge funds may come at a significant price." (p. 67)

* Kat, Harry M. 2004. "Hedge Funds versus Common Sense: An Illustration of the Dangers of Mechanical Investment Decision Making." In *Intelligent Hedge Fund Investing*. Edited by Barry Schachter. London: Risk Books. "It has become clear that hedge funds are a lot more complicated than common stocks and investment grade bonds and may not be as phenomenally attractive as many hedge fund managers and marketers want investors to believe. Hedge fund investing requires a more elaborate approach to investment decision making than most investors are used to. Mechanically applying the same decision-making processes that are typically used for stock and bond investment may lead to some very nasty surprises." (p. 9)

Kat, Harry M. 2005. "Integrating Hedge Funds into the Traditional Portfolio." *Journal of Wealth Management*, vol. 7, no. 4 (Spring):51–57. "In this summary article, the author shows how investors can neutralize the unwanted skewness and kurtosis effects from investing in hedge funds by 1) purchasing out-of-the-money equity puts, 2) investing in managed futures, and/or by 3) overweighting equity market neutral and global macro and avoiding distressed securities and emerging market funds. The analysis suggests that all three alternatives are up to the job but also come with their own specific price tag." (p. 51)

* Kat, Harry M. 2007. "Alternative Routes to Hedge Fund Return Replication." *Journal of Wealth Management*, vol. 10, no. 3 (Winter):25–39. "The author starts with the observation that although institutions are still pouring more and more money into hedge funds, hedge fund performance is clearly deteriorating. In part, this reflects lower interest rates and a global decline in risk premiums. Part of hedge funds' disappointing performance, however, is also due to the huge inflow of institutional money itself. The author then notes that, driven by a desire to reduce costs and improve investor returns, the market has recently seen several attempts to 'replicate' hedge fund index returns. Stating that the driving force behind hedge fund replication is the realization that the majority of hedge fund managers do not have enough skill to make up for the fees they charge, the author argues that it may be worthwhile to replace the managers in question with a synthetic hedge fund. Synthetic hedge funds produce no pre-fee alpha, but they don't cost a fortune to run and may therefore very well

produce significant after-fee alpha. In addition, synthetic hedge funds come with great improvements in liquidity, transparency, capacity, etc. The article proceeds to discuss three different approaches to replications." (p. 25)

* Kazemi, Hossein B., and Thomas Schneeweis. 2004. "Hedge Funds: Stale Prices Revisited." Working paper, CISDM (April). "The growth in hedge fund has in part been due to their historical return to risk performance. Concern, however, has been expressed that one reason for the superior return to risk tradeoff for hedge funds, is that, unlike traditional mutual funds, hedge funds often trade in illiquid securities and may have the ability to smooth prices such that reported volatility and systematic risk are less than actual volatility and systematic risk. In this paper we show that previous research which has used the lagged values of S&P 500 returns to test the potential impact of stale prices may simply reflect a unique historical anomaly in the relationship between hedge fund returns and lagged returns on the S&P 500. While price smoothing may still exist in various hedge fund strategies, we show that the empirical results presented in previous papers have an alternative explanation that is unrelated to stale prices or data smoothing." (p. 1)

* Kundro, Christopher, and Stuart Feffer. 2003. "Understanding and Mitigating Operational Risk in Hedge Fund Investments." Capco white paper series (March): www.capco.com/content/knowledge-ideas?q=content/research. "As the hedge fund industry has grown explosively, so too has the list of fund failures and burned investors. To better understand the reason why hedge funds fail in ways that often result in substantial investor losses and how such failures could be prevented or at least avoided, Capco initiated a study. Our initial analysis shows that operational issues account for an alarmingly high proportion of hedge fund failures (50%) and that expanding due diligence and monitoring practices to understand 'back office' capabilities can make a big difference in preventing or avoiding these failures." (p. 3)

* Kundro, Christopher.and Stuart Feffer. 2004. "Valuation Issues and Operational Risk in Hedge Funds." Working paper, Capco (March). "In our recent study on the root causes of hedge fund failures, we identified a number of operational risk factors that together seem to account for approximately half of catastrophic cases. Issues related to valuation—the determination of fair-market value for all of the positions that make up a fund—underlie many of these operational risk factors. Recently, valuation problems have also been much in the news. These headlines suggest that the industry is not yet taking the steps needed to address problems in the valuation process. In fact, we believe that issues related to valuation of portfolios will likely become the next major 'black eye' for the hedge fund industry. Unless certain practices discussed in this paper become more widespread, we believe that hedge funds face a potential crisis of confidence with institutional and high net worth investors. Therefore, we are using this paper to consider the issues related to the valuation of hedge fund portfolios more closely, in particular as they pertain to the issue of managing operational risks associated with hedge fund investments." (p. 1)

Liang, Bing. 1999. "On the Performance of Hedge Funds." *Financial Analysts Journal*, vol. 55, no. 4 (July/August):72–85. "Empirical evidence indicates that hedge funds differ substantially from traditional investment vehicles, such as mutual funds. Unlike mutual funds, hedge funds follow dynamic trading strategies and have low systematic risk. Hedge funds' special fee structures apparently align managers' incentives with fund performance. Funds with 'high watermarks' (under which managers are required to make up previous losses before receiving any incentive fees) significantly outperform those without. Hedge funds provide higher Sharpe ratios than mutual funds, and their performance in the period of January 1992 through December 1996 reflects better manager skills, although hedge fund returns are more volatile. Average hedge fund returns are related positively to incentive fees, fund assets, and the lockup period." (p. 72)

Liang, Bing. 2000. "Hedge Funds: The Living and the Dead." *Journal of Financial and Quantitative Analysis*, vol. 35, no. 3 (September):309–326 . "In this paper, we examine survivorship bias in hedge fund returns by comparing two large databases. We find that the survivorship bias exceeds 2 percent per year. We reconcile the conflicting results about survivorship bias in previous studies by showing that the two major hedge fund databases contain different amounts of dissolved funds. Empirical results show that poor performance is the main reason for a fund's disappearance. Furthermore, we find that there are significant differences in fund returns, inception date, net assets value, incentive fee, management fee, and investment styles for the 465 common funds covered by both databases. One database has more return and NAV observations, longer fund return history, and more funds with fee information than the other database. There are at least 5 percent return numbers and 5 percent NAV numbers which differ dramatically across the two databases. Mismatching between reported returns and the percentage changes in NAVs can partially explain the difference. The two databases also have different style classifications. Results of survivorship bias by styles indicate that the biases are different across styles and significant for ten out of fifteen styles in one database but none is significant for the other one." (p. 309)

Lo, Andrew W. 2001. "Risk Management for Hedge Funds: Introduction and Overview." *Financial Analysts Journal*, vol. 57, no. 6 (November/December):16–33 . "Although risk management has been a well-plowed field in financial modeling for more than two decades, traditional risk management tools such as mean–variance analysis, beta, and value-at-risk do not capture many of the risk exposures of hedge-fund investments. In this article, I review several unique aspects of risk management for hedge funds—survivorship bias, dynamic risk analytics, liquidity, and nonlinearities—and provide examples that illustrate their potential importance to hedge-fund managers and investors. I propose a research agenda for developing a new set of risk analytics specifically designed for hedge-fund investments, with the ultimate goal of creating risk transparency without compromising the proprietary nature of hedge-fund investment strategies." (p. 16)

Lo, Andrew W. 2002. "The Statistics of Sharpe Ratios." *Financial Analysts Journal*, vol. 58, no. 4 (July/August):36–52 . "The building blocks of the Sharpe ratio—expected returns and volatilities—are unknown quantities that must be estimated statistically and are, therefore, subject to estimation error. This raises the natural question: How accurately are Sharpe ratios measured? To address this question, I derive explicit expressions for the statistical distribution of the Sharpe ratio using standard asymptotic theory under several sets of assumptions for the return-generating process—independently and identically distributed returns, stationary returns, and with time aggregation. I show that monthly Sharpe ratios cannot be annualized by multiplying by $\sqrt{12}$ except under very special circumstances, and I derive the correct method of conversion in the general case of stationary returns. In an illustrative empirical example of mutual funds and hedge funds, I find that the annual Sharpe ratio for a hedge fund can be overstated by as much as 65 percent because of the presence of serial correlation in monthly returns, and once this serial correlation is properly taken into account, the rankings of hedge funds based on Sharpe ratios can change dramatically." (p. 36)

Lowenstein, Roger. 2000. *When Genius Failed: The Rise and Fall of Long-Term Capital Management.* New York: Random House. This book tells the compelling story of Long-Term Capital Management. In 1993, the best and brightest bond arbitrageurs allied themselves with two future Nobel Prize winners to form a firm that was so sure of its models, it believed it could use leverage without limit to generate fabulous profits. But by 1997, when the Russia default touched off a scenario not anticipated by the models, the staggering amounts of leverage used by LTCM threatened to bring down the world's financial system.

* Malkiel, Burton G., and Atanu Saha. 2005. "Hedge Funds: Risk and Return." *Financial Analysts Journal*, vol. 61, no. 6 (November/December):80–88 . "From a database that is relatively free of bias, this article provides measures of the returns of hedge funds and of the distinctly non-normal characteristics of the data. The results include risk-adjusted measures of performance and tests of the degree to which hedge funds live up to their claim of market neutrality. The substantial attrition of hedge funds is examined, the determinants of hedge fund demise are analyzed, and results of tests of return persistence are presented. The conclusion is that hedge funds are riskier and provide lower returns than is commonly supposed." (p. 80)

* Naik, Narayan Y., and Vikas Agarwal. 2000. "On Taking the 'Alternative' Route: The Risks, Rewards, and Performance Persistence of Hedge Funds." *Journal of Alternative Investments*, vol. 2, no. 4 (Spring):6–23. "The risk–return characteristics, risk exposures, and performance persistence of various hedge fund strategies remains an area of interest to alternative asset investors. Using a database on hedge fund indices and individual hedge fund managers in a mean–variance framework, results show that a combination of alternative investments and passive indexing provides a significantly better risk–return trade-off than passively investing in the different asset classes. Moreover, using parametric and non-parametric methods, a reasonable degree of persistence is found for hedge fund managers. This seems to be attributable more to the losers continuing to be losers instead of winners continuing to be winners and highlights the importance of manager selection in case of hedge funds." (p. 6)

* Sharma, Milind. 2004. "A.I.R.A.P—Alternative Views on Alternative Investments." Working paper (January). "This paper investigates issues of risk-adjusted performance, value added and leverage for hedge funds. It applies AIRAP (Alternative Investments Risk Adjusted Performance), which is the power utility implied certain return that a risk-averse investor would trade off for holding risky assets, to hedge fund indices and individual hedge fund data. Inferences are made about the value added by hedge funds and the difference between directional and non-directional strategies. Evidence of non-normality, higher moment risks, and the trade-off between mean–variance profile vis-à-vis skewness and kurtosis is noted across style categories. Further, survivorship bias is estimated across style categories in the first four moments." (p. 1)

* Stulz, René. 2007. "Hedge Funds: Past, Present, and Future." *Journal of Economic Perspectives*, vol. 21, no. 2 (Spring):175–194 . "Assets managed by hedge funds have grown faster over the last 10 years than assets managed by mutual funds. Hedge funds and mutual funds perform the same economic function, but hedge funds are largely unregulated while mutual funds are tightly regulated. This paper compares the organization, performance, and risks of hedge funds and mutual funds. It then examines whether one can expect increasing convergence between these two investment vehicles and concludes that the performance gap between hedge funds and mutual funds will narrow, that regulatory developments will limit the flexibility of hedge funds, and that hedge funds will become more institutionalized." (p. 175)

* Till, Hilary. 2004. "Benefits and Costs of Illiquidity." In *Intelligent Hedge Fund Investing*. Edited by Barry Schachter. London: Risk Books. "Illiquidity affects the valuation of hedge fund investments in several ways. Despite the quantitative definition of illiquidity, some of those effects are behavioral. Further, and somewhat surprising, not all the effects might be considered as negative. We discuss what we know about the various impacts of illiquidity on the decision to invest in hedge funds, and, where appropriate, how an investor may take aspects of illiquidity into account to compare investments with dissimilar liquidity." (p. 75)

* Weisman, Andrew. 2002. "Informationless Investing and Hedge Fund Performance Measurement Bias." *Journal of Portfolio Management*, vol. 28, no. 4 (Summer):80–91. "Asset managers have the ability to engage in essentially 'informationless' investment strategies that can produce the appearance of return enhancement without necessarily providing any value to an investor. Statistical estimates of risk, return, and association therefore frequently mischaracterize investment returns. These mischaracterizations, the author argues, have significant negative implications for both the asset allocation process and the validity of related academic research. He presents three specific informationless investment strategies, which he believes are endemic to the hedge fund industry, and assesses their consequences with respect to performance measurement and asset allocation." (p. 80)

PRACTICE PROBLEMS FOR READING 41

The following information relates to Questions 1–6[1]

Ian Wang is an alternative investments analyst for the U.S. investment management firm Garnier Brothers. The firm has $500 million of assets under management and a 25-year track record. Garnier's current asset allocation consists of 55% domestic equities (equity mutual funds that invest in S&P 500 companies), 40% fixed-income (U.S. government and U.S. corporate bonds), and 5% direct equity investments in U.S. commercial real estate. Garnier's C.I.O, Michelle Perez, has informed Wang that over the next 1 to 2 months she wants to reduce the amount invested in traditional asset classes and to invest the proceeds in hedge funds. Wang's current assignment is to analyze the hedge fund industry including different investment strategies as potential investment opportunities for Garnier Brothers. As a basis for his analysis Wang will use the CISDM Hedge Fund Composite Index (HFCI) as a benchmark for the hedge fund universe. To complete his analysis he gathers the selected returns data in Exhibits 1 and 2.

Exhibit 1	HFCI and Garnier's S&P 500 Equity Holdings Selected Returns Data			
	1990–2007		**2000–2007**	
Measure	**HFCI**	**S&P 500**	**HFCI**	**S&P 500**
Average Monthly Return (Annualized)	13.5%	10.9%	6.8%	−2.3%
Monthly Standard Deviation (Annualized)	5.7%	14.7%	4.8%	16.4%
Sharpe ratio	1.61	0.45	0.86	−0.31

Exhibit 2	Hedge Fund Investment Strategies Selected Returns Data 1990–2007		
Strategy or Index	**Average Monthly Return (Annualized)**	**Monthly Standard Deviation (Annualized)**	**Sharpe Ratio**
HFCI	13.5%	5.7%	1.61
Event driven	13.5	5.6	1.64
Equity market neutral	9.2	2.5	1.96
Fixed-income arbitrage	7.6	3.6	0.92
Convertible arbitrage	10.2	4.0	1.48
Fund of Funds	7.0	2.0	1.35

After reviewing his research materials as well as Exhibits 1 and 2, Wang formulates the following conclusions:

> Conclusion 1   The primary reasons that the hedge fund universe (as proxied by the HFCI) outperformed Garnier's S&P 500 equity holdings during

the 2000–2007 period are the hedge funds' ability to short sell securities; to utilize financial leverage; and to employ derivatives.

Conclusion 2   The greater return exhibited by event driven funds relative to equity market neutral funds is due to event driven funds capturing a significant liquidity premium and equity market neutral funds minimizing risk exposures to market capitalization, value, growth, and industry.

Conclusion 3   Hedge fund managers implementing event driven strategies have historically outperformed the S&P 500 because of alpha creation.

Conclusion 4   The Sharpe ratio is not the optimal risk-adjusted return measure for hedge funds because of the negative skewness and negative excess kurtosis exhibited by hedge fund returns.

Wang notes that the relatively high fees charged by hedge funds make them an unattractive investment. His research indicates that replication strategies can be an attractive alternative to hedge funds when investors wish to avoid the large fees charged by hedge fund managers. Wang describes two such replication strategies in his report:

Replication Strategy 1   A long position in high yield corporate bonds and a short position in U.S. Treasury securities with a similar duration.

Replication Strategy 2   A long position in convertible bonds and a short position in the equity of the firm issuing the convertible bond.

After reading Wang's report on hedge funds, Perez concludes that the performance data is more reliable for fund-of-funds rather than the single-manager hedge fund, therefore implementing Garnier's hedge fund exposure should be accomplished through a fund-of-funds vehicle rather than a single-manager hedge fund.

1. Wang's Conclusion 1 is:

   A. correct.

   B. incorrect because short selling is not permitted.

   C. incorrect because the use of financial leverage is not permitted.

2. Wang's Conclusion 2 is:

   A. correct.

   B. incorrect because liquidity premiums are insignificant for event driven hedge funds.

   C. incorrect because equity market neutral funds do not minimize risk exposures to market capitalization, value, growth, and industry.

3. Wang's Conclusion 3 is:

   A. correct.

   B. incorrect because event driven hedge funds assume greater risk-adjusted returns through higher traditional betas.

   C. incorrect because event driven hedge funds earn excess returns from taking significant risks in untraditional market factors.

4. Wang's Conclusion 4 is:

   A. correct.

   B. incorrect because the Sharpe ratio is unaffected by higher moment exposures.

   C. incorrect because hedge fund returns exhibit negative skewness and positive excess kurtosis.

5. Which of the following hedge fund strategies can be replicated by Replication Strategy 1 and Replication Strategy 2?

   A. Fixed-income arbitrage for both strategies

   B. Fixed-income arbitrage for Replication Strategy 1 and convertible arbitrage for Replication Strategy 2

   C. Convertible arbitrage for Replication Strategy 1 and fixed-income arbitrage for Replication Strategy 2

6. Which of the following statements most likely supports Perez's conclusion relating to implementing Garnier's hedge fund exposure?

   A. Fund-of-fund returns are less risky than single manager returns.

   B. Fund-of-fund returns are prone to smaller backfill and selection bias.

   C. Fund-of-funds tend to exhibit more average performance than single manager hedge funds.

SOLUTIONS FOR READING 41

1. A is correct.

2. C is correct. Equity market neutral funds may take substantial risks in other areas of the equity markets, such as market capitalization, value, growth, or industry.

3. C is correct. Event driven hedge funds exhibit strong risk-adjusted returns by taking significant risks in untraditional market factors.

4. C is correct. Many hedge fund styles have higher moment risks in which returns have negative skewness and fat tails (i.e. large excess kurtosis).

5. B is correct. Fixed-income arbitrage replication would take a long position in a credit fund, such as high-yield bonds or mortgage-backed securities, and a short position in a Treasury securities fund of a similar duration. Convertible arbitrage replication would be achieved by purchasing convertible bonds and shorting the equity of the firm issuing the convertible bond.

6. B is correct. Fund of funds, as a result of their diversification among strategies and managers, tend to exhibit lower mortality, survivor bias, and backfill bias than single manager hedge funds.

Index			What Percentage change	
Japan (Nikkei)			Base Price day	2011
Seoul				
Johan. (Comp.)				
Mumbai				
Singapore	18			
Sydney				-4.5%
Shanghai B	297.0	7.1%		-4.7%
Hong Kong	4644.0	0.9%		-10.5%
Toronto	316.8	0.7%		-6.9%
Stockholm	22,700.9	0.5%		-4.2%
Mexico Ci	13,524.8	0.1%		4.1%

Fixed Income

TOPIC LEVEL LEARNING OUTCOME

The candidate should be able to estimate the risks and expected returns for fixed income instruments, analyze the term structure of interest rates and yield spreads, and evaluate fixed income instruments with embedded options and unique features.

Fixed Income:

Valuation Concepts

This study session covers essential knowledge and skills needed for the valuation of fixed income investments. It begins with a discussion of credit analysis and how credit standards affect liquidity. Interest rate volatility and term structure are presented next and are then followed by an introduction to embedded options in fixed income securities.

READING ASSIGNMENTS

Reading 42 *Fundamentals of Credit Analysis*

> By Christopher L. Gootkind, CFA

Reading 43 *Term Structure and Volatility of Interest Rates*

> *Fixed Income Analysis for the Chartered Financial Analyst®*
> *Program,* Second Edition, by Frank J. Fabozzi, CFA

Reading 44 *Valuing Bonds with Embedded Options*

> *Fixed Income Analysis for the Chartered Financial Analyst®*
> *Program,* Second Edition, by Frank J. Fabozzi, CFA

Index		Percentage change	
Tokyo (Nikkei)			
Seoul			
Jakarta (Comp.)			
Mumbai			
Singapore			
Sydney	2921.0	1.1%	-4.7%
Shanghai B	464.0	0.9%	-10.5%
Hong Kong	316.8	0.7%	-6.9%
Toronto	22,700.9	0.5%	-4.2%
Stockholm	13,524.8	0.1%	4.1%
Mexico City			

42

Fundamentals of Credit Analysis

by Christopher L. Gootkind, CFA

LEARNING OUTCOMES

Mastery	The candidate should be able to:
☐	**a** describe credit risk and credit-related risks affecting corporate bonds;
☐	**b** describe seniority rankings of corporate debt and explain the potential violation of the priority of claims in a bankruptcy proceeding;
☐	**c** distinguish between corporate issuer credit ratings and issue credit ratings and describe the rating agency practice of "notching";
☐	**d** explain risks in relying on ratings from credit rating agencies;
☐	**e** explain the components of traditional credit analysis;
☐	**f** calculate and interpret financial ratios used in credit analysis;
☐	**g** evaluate the credit quality of a corporate bond issuer and a bond of that issuer, given key financial ratios for the issuer and the industry;
☐	**h** describe factors that influence the level and volatility of yield spreads;
☐	**i** calculate the return impact of spread changes;
☐	**j** explain special considerations when evaluating the credit of high yield, sovereign, and municipal debt issuers and issues.

INTRODUCTION

1

With bonds outstanding worth many trillions of U.S. dollars, the debt markets play a critical role in the global economy. Companies and governments raise capital in the debt market to fund current operations; buy equipment; build factories, roads, bridges, airports, and hospitals; acquire assets, and so on. By channeling savings into productive investments, the debt markets facilitate economic growth. Credit analysis has a crucial function in the debt capital markets—efficiently allocating capital by properly assessing credit risk, pricing it accordingly, and repricing it as risks change. How do fixed-income investors determine the riskiness of that debt, and how do they decide what they need to earn as compensation for that risk?

The author would like to thank several of his Fixed Income Research colleagues at Loomis, Sayles & Company for their assistance with this reading: Paul Batterton, Diana Leader-Cramer, Diana Monteith, Shannon O'Mara, CFA, and Laura Sarlo, CFA.

This reading will cover the basic principles of credit analysis, which may be broadly defined as the process by which credit risk is evaluated. Readers will be introduced to such concepts as the definition of credit risk, credit ratings, components of traditional credit analysis, measures of cash flow, key financial metrics and ratios, bond issuer creditworthiness comparisons within a given industry as well as across industries, the pricing of credit risk in the bond market, and the effects of changes in prices on holding period return.

The reading focuses primarily on analysis of corporate debt; however, credit analysis of sovereign and sub-sovereign (municipal) government bonds will also be addressed. Structured finance, a segment of the debt markets that includes securities backed by pools of assets, such as residential and commercial mortgages as well as other consumer loans, will not be covered here.

The key components of credit risk—default probability and loss severity—are introduced in the next section along with such credit-related risks as spread risk, credit migration risk, and liquidity risk. Section 3 discusses the relationship between credit risk and the capital structure of the firm. Credit ratings and the role of credit rating agencies are addressed in Section 4. Section 5 focuses on the process of analyzing the credit risk of corporations, whereas Section 6 examines the impact of credit spreads on risk and return. Special considerations applicable to the analysis of (i) high-yield (low-quality) corporate bonds and (ii) government bonds are presented in Section 7. Section 8 gives a brief summary, and a set of review questions concludes the reading.

2   CREDIT RISK

Credit risk is the risk of loss resulting from the borrower (issuer of debt) failing to make full and timely payments of interest and/or principal. Credit risk has two components. The first is known as **default risk**, or **default probability**, which is the probability that a borrower defaults—that is, fails to meet its obligation to make full and timely payments of principal and interest, according to the terms of the debt security. The second component is **loss severity** (also known as "loss given default") in the event of default—that is, the portion of a bond's value (including unpaid interest) an investor loses. A default can lead to losses of various magnitudes. In most instances, in the event of default, bondholders will recover some value, so there will not be a total loss on the investment. Thus, credit risk is reflected in the distribution of potential losses that may arise if the investor is not paid in full and on time. Although it is sometimes important to consider the entire distribution of potential losses and their respective probabilities,[1] it is often convenient to summarize the risk with a single default probability and loss severity and to focus on the **expected loss**:

Expected loss = Default probability × Loss severity given default

The loss severity, and hence the expected loss, can be expressed as either a monetary amount (e.g., €450,000) or as a percentage of the principal amount (e.g., 45 percent). The latter form is generally more useful for analysis because it is independent of the amount of investment. Loss severity is often expressed as (1 − Recovery rate), where the recovery rate is the percentage of the principal amount recovered in the event of default.

---

[1] As an example, careful attention to the full distribution of potential losses is important in analyzing credit risk in structured finance products because the various tranches usually share unequally in the credit losses on the underlying loans or securities. A particular tranche typically bears none of the losses up to some level of underlying losses, then it bears all of the underlying losses until the tranche is wiped out. Losses on a "thin" tranche are very likely to be either 0 percent or 100 percent, with relatively small probabilities on intermediate loss severities. This situation is not well described by a single "average" loss severity.

Because default risk (default probability) is quite low for most good quality debt issuers, bond investors tend to focus primarily on assessing this likelihood and devote less effort to assessing the potential loss severity arising from default. However, as an issuer's default risk rises, investors will focus more on what the recovery rate might be in the event of default. This issue will be discussed in more detail later. Other important forms of credit-related risk include the following:

Spread risk. Corporate bonds and other "credit-risky" debt instruments typically trade at a yield premium, or spread, to bonds that have been considered "default-risk free," such as U.S. Treasury bonds or German government bonds. Yield spreads, expressed in basis points, widen based on two primary factors: (1) a decline in an issuer's creditworthiness, sometimes referred to as **credit migration** or **downgrade risk**, and (2) an increase in **market liquidity risk**. These two risks are separate but frequently related.

Credit migration (or downgrade) risk. This is the risk that a bond issuer's creditworthiness deteriorates, or migrates lower, leading investors to believe the risk of default is higher and thus causing the yield spreads on the issuer's bonds to widen and the price of its bonds to fall. The term "downgrade" refers to action by the major bond rating agencies, whose role will be covered in more detail in Section 4.

Market liquidity risk. This is the risk that the price at which investors can actually transact—buying or selling—may differ from the price indicated in the market. To compensate investors for the risk that there may not be sufficient market liquidity for them to buy or sell bonds in the quantity they desire, the spread or yield premium on corporate bonds includes a market liquidity component, in addition to a credit risk component. Unlike stocks, which trade on exchanges, most markets bonds trade primarily over the counter, through broker–dealers trading for their own accounts. Their ability and willingness to make markets, as reflected in the bid–ask spread, is an important determinant of market liquidity risk. The two main issuer-specific factors that affect market liquidity risk are (1) the size of the issuer (that is, the amount of publicly traded debt an issuer has outstanding) and (2) the credit quality of the issuer. In general, the less debt an issuer has outstanding, the less frequently its debt trades, and thus the higher the market liquidity risk. And the lower the quality of the issuer, the higher the market liquidity risk.

During times of financial stress or crisis, such as in late 2008, market liquidity can decline sharply, causing yield spreads on corporate bonds, and other credit-risky debt, to widen and their prices to drop. Some research has been done on trying to quantify market liquidity risk,[2] and more is likely to be done in the aftermath of the financial crisis.

Example 1

Defining Credit Risk

1. Which of the following *best* defines credit risk?

   A. The probability of default times the severity of loss given default

   B. The loss of principal and interest payments in the event of bankruptcy

   C. The risk of not receiving full interest and principal payments on a timely basis

2. Which of the following is the *best* measure of credit risk?

   A. The expected loss

---

2 For example, see Francis A. Longstaff, Sanjay Mithal, and Eric Neis, "Corporate Yield Spreads: Default Risk or Liquidity? New Evidence from the Credit-Default Swap Market," NBER Working Paper No. 10418 (April 2004).

      B. The severity of loss

      C. The probability of default

   3. Which of the following is NOT credit or credit-related risk?

      A. Default risk

      B. Interest rate risk

      C. Downgrade or credit migration risk

Solution to 1:

C is correct. Credit risk is the risk that the borrower will not make full and timely payments.

Solution to 2:

A is correct. The expected loss captures both of the key components of credit risk: (the product of) the likelihood of default and the loss severity in the event of default. Neither component alone fully reflects the risk.

Solution to 3:

B is correct. Bond price changes due to general interest rate movements are not considered credit risk.

3 CAPITAL STRUCTURE, SENIORITY RANKING, AND RECOVERY RATES

The various debt obligations of a given borrower will not necessarily all have the same **seniority ranking**, or priority of payment. In this section, we will introduce the topic of an issuer's capital structure and discuss the various types of debt claims that may arise from that structure, as well as their ranking and how those rankings can influence recovery rates in the event of default.

3.1 Capital Structure

The composition and distribution across operating units of a company's debt and equity—including bank debt, bonds of all seniority rankings, preferred stock, and common equity—is referred to as its **capital structure**. Some companies and industries have straightforward capital structures, with all the debt equally ranked and issued by one main operating entity. Other companies and industries, due to their frequent acquisitions and divestitures (e.g., media companies or conglomerates) or high levels of regulation (e.g., banks and utilities), tend to have more complicated capital structures. Companies in these industries often have many different subsidiaries, or operating companies, that have their own debt outstanding and parent holding companies that also issue debt, with different levels or rankings of seniority. Similarly, the cross-border operations of multi-national corporations tend to increase the complexity of their capital structures.

3.2 Seniority Ranking

Just as borrowers can issue debt with many different maturity dates and coupons, they can also have many different rankings in terms of seniority. The ranking refers to the priority of payment, with the most senior or highest-ranking debt having the first claim on the cash flows and assets of the issuer. This level of seniority can affect the value of an investor's claim in the event of default and restructuring. Broadly, there is **secured debt** and **unsecured debt**. Unsecured bonds are often referred to as debentures. Secured debt means the debtholder has a direct claim—a pledge from the issuer—on certain assets and their associated cash flows. Unsecured bondholders have only a general claim on an issuer's assets and cash flow. In the event of default, unsecured debtholders' claims rank below (i.e., get paid after) those of secured creditors[3] under what's known as the **priority of claims**.

Exhibit 1	Seniority Ranking

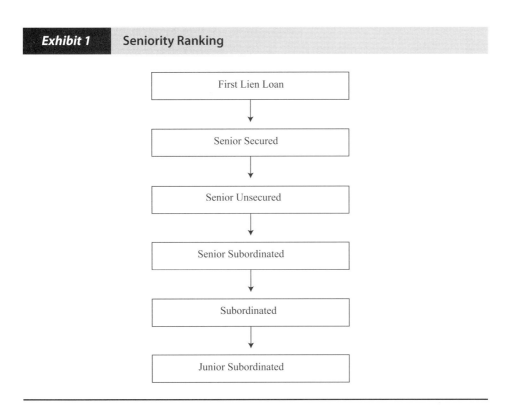

Within each category of debt, there are finer gradations of types and rankings. Within secured debt, there is first mortgage or first lien debt, which is the highest-ranked debt in terms of priority of repayment. **First mortgage debt** refers to the pledge of a specific property (e.g., a power plant for a utility or a specific casino for a gaming company). **First lien debt** refers to a pledge of certain assets that could include buildings but might also include property and equipment, licenses, patents, brands, and so on. There can also be **second lien**, or even third lien, secured debt, which, as the name implies, has a secured interest in the pledged assets but ranks below first lien debt in both collateral protection and priority of payment.

Within unsecured debt, there can also be finer gradations and seniority rankings. The highest-ranked unsecured debt is senior unsecured debt. It is the most common type of all corporate bonds outstanding. Other, lower-ranked debt includes **subordinated debt** and junior subordinated debt. Among the various creditor classes, these obligations have among the lowest priority of claims and frequently have little or no recovery in the event of default. That is, their loss severity can be as high as 100 percent. (See Exhibit 1 for seniority ranking.) For regulatory and capital purposes, banks

---

3 The term "creditors" is used throughout this reading to mean holders of debt instruments, such as bonds and bank loans. Unless specifically stated, it does not include such obligations as trade credit, tax liens, or employment-related obligations.

in Europe and the United States have issued debt and debt-like securities that rank even lower than subordinated debt[4] and are intended to provide a capital cushion in times of financial distress. Many of them did not work as intended during the financial crisis that began in 2008, and most were phased out, potentially to be replaced by more effective instruments that automatically convert to equity in certain circumstances.

There are many reasons why companies issue—and investors buy—debt with different seniority rankings. Issuers are interested in optimizing their cost of capital—finding the right mix of the various types of both debt and equity—for their industry and type of business. Issuers may offer secured debt because that is what the market (i.e., investors) may require, given a company's perceived riskiness, or because secured debt is generally lower cost due to the reduced credit risk inherent in its higher priority of claims. Or, issuers may offer subordinated debt because (1) they believe it is less expensive than issuing equity[5] (and doesn't dilute existing shareholders) and is typically less restrictive than issuing senior debt and (2) investors are willing to buy it because they believe the yield being offered is adequate compensation for the risk they perceive. Credit risk versus return will be discussed in more detail later in the reading.

Example 2

Seniority Ranking

The Acme Company has senior unsecured bonds as well as both first and second lien debt in its capital structure. Which ranks higher with respect to priority of claims: senior unsecured bonds or second lien debt?

Solution:

Second lien debt ranks higher, by virtue of its secured position.

3.3 Recovery Rates

All creditors at the same level of the capital structure are treated as one class; thus, a senior unsecured bondholder whose debt is due in 30 years has the same pro rata claim in bankruptcy as one whose debt matures in six months. This provision is referred to as bonds ranking **pari passu** ("on an equal footing") in right of payment.

Defaulted debt will often continue to be traded by investors and broker–dealers based on their assessment that either in liquidation of the bankrupt company's assets or in some form of reorganization, the bonds will have some recovery value. In the case of reorganization, or restructuring (whether through formal bankruptcy or on a voluntary basis), new debt, equity, cash, or some combination thereof could be issued in exchange for the original defaulted debt.

As discussed, recovery rates vary by seniority of ranking in a company's capital structure, under the priority of claims treatment in bankruptcy. Over many decades, there have been enough defaults to generate statistically meaningful historical data on recovery rates by seniority ranking. Exhibit 2 provides recovery rates by seniority ranking for North American non-financial companies.[6] For example, as shown in

---

4 These have various names such as hybrids, trust preferred, and upper and lower Tier 2 securities. In some cases, the non-payment or deferral of interest does not constitute an event of default, and in other cases, they might convert into perpetual securities—that is, securities with no maturity date.

5 Debtholders require a lower return than equity holders because they have prior claims to an issuer's cash flow and assets. That is, the cost of debt is lower than the cost of equity. In most countries, this cost differential is even greater due to the tax deductibility of interest payments.

6 The recovery rates shown for default years 2009 and 2010 should be viewed as preliminary because some of the numbers are based on the relatively small number of defaults for which final recovery had been determined at the time of the Moody's study. For example, the 2010 senior unsecured recovery rate reflects only two bonds.

Exhibit 2, investors on average recovered 51.6 percent of the value of senior unsecured debt that defaulted in 2009 but only 28.0 percent of the value of senior subordinated issues that defaulted that year.

Exhibit 2	Average Corporate Debt Recovery Rates Measured by Ultimate Recoveries					
	Emergence Year*			**Default Year**		
Seniority ranking	**2010**	**2009**	**1987–2010**	**2010**	**2009**	**1987–2010**
Senior secured	64.4%	59.0%	63.5%	56.3%	65.6%	63.5%
Senior unsecured	51.0%	48.3%	49.2%	26.5%	51.6%	49.2%
Senior subordinated	20.5%	26.2%	29.4%	21.7%	28.0%	29.4%
Subordinated	53.4%	34.3%	29.3%	0.0%	58.3%	29.3%
Junior subordinated	NA	0.5%	18.4%	NA	0.0%	18.4%

Notes: Emergence year is typically the year the defaulted company emerges from bankruptcy. Default year data refer to the recovery rate of debt that defaulted in that year (i.e., 2009 and 2010) or range of years (i.e., 1987–2010). Data are for North American nonfinancial companies. NA indicates not available.

Source: Based on data from Moody's Investors Service, Inc.'s Ultimate Recovery Database.

There are a few things worth noting:

1. **Recovery rates can vary widely by industry**. Companies that go bankrupt in industries that are in secular decline (e.g., newspaper publishing) will most likely have lower recovery rates than those that go bankrupt in industries merely suffering from a cyclical economic downturn.

2. **Recovery rates can also vary depending on when they occur in a credit cycle**.[7] As shown in Exhibit 3, at or near the bottom of a credit cycle—which is almost always closely linked with an economic cycle—recoveries will tend to be lower than at other times in the credit cycle. This is because there will be many companies closer to, or already in, bankruptcy, causing valuations to be depressed.

---

7 Credit cycles describe the changing availability—and pricing—of credit. When the economy is strong or improving, the willingness of lenders to extend credit, and on favorable terms, is high. Conversely, when the economy is weak or weakening, lenders pull back, or "tighten" credit, by making it less available and more expensive. This frequently contributes to asset values, such as real estate, declining, causing further economic weakness and higher defaults. Central banks frequently survey banks to assess how "tight" or "loose" their lending standards are. This information, as well as the level and direction of corporate bond default rates, helps provide a good sense of where one is in the credit cycle.

Exhibit 3	Global Recovery Rates by Seniority Ranking, 1990–2010

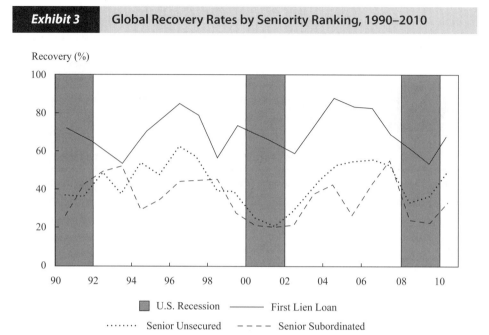

Source: Based on data from Moody's Investors Service, Inc.'s Ultimate Recovery Database.

3. **These recovery rates are averages**. In fact, there can be large variability, both across industries, as noted above, as well as across companies within a given industry. Factors might include composition and proportion of debt across an issuer's capital structure. An abundance of secured debt will lead to smaller recovery rates on lower-ranked debt.

Understanding recovery rates is important because they are a key component of credit analysis and risk. Recall that the best measure of credit risk is expected loss—that is, probability of default times loss severity given default. And loss severity equals (1 − Recovery rate). Having an idea how much one can lose in the event of default is a critical factor in valuing credit, particularly lower-quality credit, as the default risk rises.

Priority of claims: Not always absolute. The priority of claims in bankruptcy—the idea that the highest-ranked creditors get paid out first, followed by the next level, and on down, like a waterfall—is well established and is often described as "absolute." In principle, in the event of bankruptcy or liquidation:

■ Creditors with a secured claim have the right to the value of that specific property before any other claim. If the value of the pledged property is less than the amount of the claim, then the difference becomes a senior unsecured claim.

■ Unsecured creditors have a right to be paid in full before holders of equity interests (common and preferred shareholders) receive value on their interests.

■ Senior creditors take priority over junior (i.e., subordinated) creditors. A creditor is senior unless expressly subordinated.

In practice, however, more junior creditors and even shareholders may receive some consideration without more senior creditors being paid in full. Why might this be the case? In bankruptcy, there are different classes of claimants, and all classes that are impaired (that is, receive less than full claim) get to vote to confirm the plan of reorganization. This vote is subject to the absolute priority of claims. Either by consent of the various parties or by the judge's order, however, absolute priority may not be strictly enforced in the final plan. There may be disputes over the value of various assets in the bankruptcy estate (e.g., what is a plant, or a patent portfolio, worth?) or the present value or timing of payouts. For example, what is the value of the new debt I'm receiving for my old debt of a reorganized company before it emerges from bankruptcy?

Resolution of these disputes takes time, and cases can drag on for months and years. In the meantime, during bankruptcy, substantial expenses are being incurred for legal and accounting fees, and the value of the company may be declining as key employees leave, customers go elsewhere, and so on. Thus, to avoid the time, expense, and uncertainty over disputed issues, such as the value of property in the estate, the legality of certain claims, and so forth, the various claimants have a strong incentive to negotiate and compromise. This frequently leads to more junior creditors and other claimants (e.g., even shareholders) receiving more consideration than they are legally entitled to.

It's worth noting that in the United States, the bias is toward reorganization and recovery of companies in bankruptcy, whereas in other jurisdictions, such as the United Kingdom, the bias is toward liquidation of companies in bankruptcy and maximizing value to the banks and other senior creditors. It's also worth noting that bankruptcy and bankruptcy laws are very complex and can vary greatly by country, so it is difficult to generalize about how creditors will fare. As shown in the earlier chart, there is huge variability in recovery rates for defaulted debt. Every case is different.

Example 3

Priority of Claims

1. Under which circumstance is a subordinated bondholder *most likely* to recover some value in a bankruptcy without a senior creditor getting paid in full? When:

   A. absolute priority rules are enforced.

   B. the various classes of claimants agree to it.

   C. the company is liquidated rather than reorganized.

2. In the event of bankruptcy, claims at the same level of the capital structure are:

   A. on an equal footing, regardless of size, maturity, or time outstanding.

   B. paid in the order of maturity from shortest to longest, regardless of size or time outstanding.

   C. paid on a first-in, first-out (FIFO) basis so that the longest-standing claims are satisfied first, regardless of size or maturity.

Solution to 1:

B is correct. All impaired classes get to vote on the reorganization plan. Negotiation and compromise are often preferable to incurring huge legal and accounting fees in a protracted bankruptcy process that would otherwise reduce the value of the estate for all claimants. This process may allow junior creditors (e.g., subordinated bondholders) to recover some value even though more senior creditors do not get paid in full.

Solution to 2:

A is correct. All claims at the same level of the capital structure are pari passu (on an equal footing).

RATINGS AGENCIES, CREDIT RATINGS, AND THEIR ROLE IN THE DEBT MARKETS

The major credit ratings agencies—Moody's Investors Service ("Moody's"), Standard & Poor's ("S&P"), and to a somewhat lesser extent, Fitch Ratings ("Fitch")—play a central, if somewhat controversial, role in the credit markets. For the vast majority of outstanding bonds, at least two of the agencies provide ratings: a symbol-based measure of the potential risk of default of a particular bond or issuer of debt. In the public and quasi-public bond markets,[8] issuers won't offer, and investors won't buy, bonds that do not carry ratings from Moody's and/or S&P (and Fitch). This practice applies for all types of bonds—government or sovereign, government related,[9] supranational,[10] corporate, municipal, and mortgage- and asset-backed debt. How did the ratings agencies attain such a dominant position in the credit markets? What are credit ratings, and what do they mean? How does the market use credit ratings? What are the risks of relying solely or excessively on credit ratings?

The history of the major ratings agencies goes back more than 100 years. John Moody began publishing credit analysis and opinions on U.S. railroads in 1909. S&P published its first ratings in 1916. They have grown in size and prominence since then. Many bond investors like the fact that there are independent analysts who meet with the issuer and often have access to material, non-public information, such as financial projections that investors cannot receive, to aid in the analysis. What has also proven very attractive to investors is that credit ratings provide direct and easy comparability of the relative credit riskiness of all bond issuers, within and across industries and bond types, although there is some debate about ratings comparability across the types of bonds.[11]

Several factors have led to the near universal use of credit ratings in the bond markets and the dominant role of the major credit rating agencies. These factors include the following:

■ Independent assessment of credit risk

■ Ease of comparison across bond issuers, issues, and market segments

■ Regulatory and statutory reliance and usage[12]

■ Issuer payment for ratings[13]

■ Huge growth of debt markets

■ Development and expansion of bond portfolio management and the accompanying bond indices.

However, in the aftermath of the financial crisis of 2008–2009, when the rating agencies were blamed for at least contributing to the crisis with their overly optimistic

---

8 That is, underwritten by investment banks, as opposed to privately placed on a "best efforts" basis.

9 These are government agencies or instrumentalities that may have implicit or explicit guarantees from the government. Examples include Ginnie Mae in the United States and *Pfandbriefe* in Germany.

10 Supranationals are international financial institutions, such as the International Bank for Reconstruction and Development ("World Bank"), the Asian Development Bank, and the European Investment Bank, that are established by treaty and owned by several member governments.

11 Investigations conducted after the late 2008/early 2009 financial crisis suggested that, for a given rating category, municipal bonds have experienced a lower historical incidence of default than corporate debt.

12 It is common for regulations to make reference to ratings issued by recognized credit ratings agencies. In light of the role played by the agencies in the sub-prime mortgage crisis, however, some jurisdictions (e.g., the United States) are moving to remove such references. Nonetheless, the so-called Basel III global framework for bank supervision developed beginning in 2009 retains such references.

13 The "issuer pay" model allows the distribution of ratings to a broad universe of investors and undoubtedly facilitated widespread reliance on ratings. It is controversial, however, because some believe it creates a conflict of interest among the rating agency, the investor, and the issuer. Studies suggest, however, that ratings are not biased upward and alternate payment models, such as "investor pays," have their own shortcomings, including the "free rider" problem inherent in a business where informatins is widely available and freely shared. So, despite its potential problems, and some calls for a new payment model, the "issuer pay" model remains entrenched in the market.

ratings on securities backed by subprime mortgages, there were attempts to reduce the role and dominant positions of the major credit rating agencies. New rules, regulations, and legislation were passed to require the agencies to be more transparent, reduce conflicts of interest, and stimulate more competition. Challenging the hegemony of Moody's, S&P, and Fitch, additional credit rating agencies have emerged, while existing ones that have a strong presence in their home markets but are not so well known globally, such as Dominion Bond Rating Service (DBRS) in Canada and Mikuni & Co. in Japan, have tried to raise their profiles. The market dominance of the biggest credit rating agencies, however, remains largely intact.

4.1 Credit Ratings

The three major global credit rating agencies—Moody's, S&P, and Fitch—use similar, symbol-based ratings that are basically an assessment of a bond issue's risk of default. Exhibit 4 shows their long-term ratings ranked from highest to lowest.[14]

Exhibit 4	Long-Term Ratings Matrix: Investment Grade vs. Non-Investment Grade			
		Moody's	**S&P**	**Fitch**
Investment Grade	High-Quality Grade	Aaa	AAA	AAA
		Aa1	AA+	AA+
		Aa2	AA	AA
		Aa3	AA–	AA–
	Upper-Medium Grade	A1	A+	A+
		A2	A	A
		A3	A–	A–
	Low-Medium Grade	Baa1	BBB+	BBB+
		Baa2	BBB	BBB
		Baa3	BBB–	BBB–
Non-Investment Grade "Junk" or "High Yield"	Low Grade or Speculative Grade	Ba1	BB+	BB+
		Ba2	BB	BB
		Ba3	BB–	BB–
		B1	B+	B+
		B2	B	B
		B3	B–	B–
		Caa1	CCC+	CCC+
		Caa2	CCC	CCC
		Caa3	CCC–	CCC–
		Ca	CC	CC
		C	C	C
	Default	C	D	D

---

14 The rating agencies also provide ratings on short-term debt instruments, such as bank deposits and commercial paper. However, they use different scales: From the highest to lowest rating, Moody's uses P-1, P-2, P-3; S&P uses A-1+, A-1, A-2, A-3; Fitch uses F-1, F-2, F-3. Below that is not prime. Short-term ratings are typically used by money market funds, with the vast majority of the debt instruments they own rated in the highest (or in the case of S&P, the highest or second-highest) category. These top ratings basically map to a single-A or higher long-term rating.

Bonds rated triple-A (Aaa or AAA) are said to be "of the highest quality, with minimal credit risk"[15] and thus have extremely low probabilities of default. Double-A (Aa or AA) rated bonds are referred to as "high-quality grade" and are also regarded as having very low default risk. Bonds rated single-A are referred to as "upper-medium grade." Baa (Moody's) or BBB (S&P and Fitch) are called "low-medium grade." Bonds rated Baa3/BBB– or higher are called "investment grade." Bonds rated Ba1 or lower by Moody's and BB– or lower by S&P and Fitch, respectively, have speculative credit characteristics and increasingly higher default risk. As a group, these bonds are referred to in a variety of ways: "low grade," "speculative grade," "non-investment grade," "below investment grade," "high yield," and, in an attempt to reflect the extreme level of risk, some observers refer to these bonds as "junk bonds." The D rating is reserved for securities that are already in default in S&P's and Fitch's scales. For Moody's, bonds rated C are likely, but not necessarily, in default. Generally, issuers of bonds rated investment grade are more consistently able to access the debt markets and can borrow at lower interest rates than those rated below investment grade.

In addition, rating agencies will typically provide outlooks on their respective ratings—positive, stable, or negative—and may provide other indicators on the potential direction of their ratings under certain circumstances, such as "On Review for a Downgrade" or "On CreditWatch for an Upgrade."[16] It should also be noted that, in support of the ratings they publish, the rating agencies also provide extensive written commentary and financial analysis on the obligors they rate, as well as summary industry statistics.

4.2 Issuer vs. Issue Ratings

Rating agencies will typically provide both issuer and issue ratings, particularly as they relate to corporate debt. Terminology used to distinguish between issuer and issue ratings includes corporate family rating (CFR) and corporate credit rating (CCR) or issuer credit rating and issue credit rating. An issuer credit rating is meant to address an obligor's overall creditworthiness—its ability and willingness to make timely payments of interest and principal on its debt. The issuer credit rating usually applies to its senior unsecured debt.

Issue ratings refer to specific financial obligations of an issuer and take into consideration such factors as ranking in the capital structure (e.g., secured or subordinated). Although **cross-default provisions**, whereby events of default such as non-payment of interest[17] on one bond trigger default on all outstanding debt,[18] implies the same default probability for all issues, specific issues may be assigned different credit ratings—higher or lower—due to a ratings adjustment methodology known as **notching**.

Notching. For the rating agencies, likelihood of default is the primary factor in assigning their ratings. However, there are secondary factors as well. These factors include the priority of payment in the event of a default (e.g., secured versus senior unsecured versus subordinated) as well as potential loss severity in the event of default. Another rating factor is so-called **structural subordination**, which can arise when a corporation with a holding company structure has debt at both its parent

---

15 Moody's Investors Service, "Ratings Symbols and Definitions" (July 2011).

16 Additional detail on their respective ratings definitions, methodologies, and criteria can be found on each of the major rating agency's websites: www.moodys.com, www.standardandpoors.com, and www.fitch.com.

17 This issue will be covered in greater detail in the section on covenants.

18 Nearly all bonds have a cross-default provision. Rare exceptions to this cross-default provision include the deeply subordinated, debt-like securities referenced earlier in this reading.

holding company and operating subsidiaries. Debt at the operating subsidiaries will get serviced by the cash flow and assets of the subsidiaries before funds can be passed ("upstreamed") to the holding company to service debt at that level.

Recognizing these different payment priorities, and thus the potential for higher (or lower) loss severity in the event of default, the rating agencies have adopted a notching process whereby their credit ratings on issues can be moved up or down from the issuer rating (senior unsecured). As a general rule, the higher the senior unsecured rating, the smaller the notching adjustment will be. The reason behind this is that the higher the rating, the lower the perceived risk of default, so the need to "notch" the rating to capture the potential difference in loss severity is greatly reduced. For lower-rated credits, however, the risk of default is greater and thus the potential difference in loss from a lower (or higher) priority ranking is a bigger consideration in assessing an issue's credit riskiness. Thus, the rating agencies will typically apply larger rating adjustments. For example, S&P applies the following notching guidelines:

> As default risk increases, the concern over what can be recovered takes on greater relevance and, therefore, greater rating significance. Accordingly, the LGD [Loss Given Default] aspect of ratings is given more weight as one moves down the rating spectrum. For example, subordinated debt can be rated up to two notches below a noninvestment grade corporate credit rating, but one notch at most if the corporate credit rating is investment grade. (In the same vein, issues of companies with an 'AAA' rating need not be notched at all.)[19]

Exhibit 5 is an example of S&P's notching criteria, as applied to United Rentals, Inc. (URI). URI is a U.S.-based equipment rental company whose corporate credit—and senior unsecured—rating is single-B. Note how the company's subordinated debt is rated two notches lower, at CCC+.

Exhibit 5	URI's S&P Ratings Detail, 27 May 2011
Corporate credit rating	B/Stable/–
Preferred stock (1 issue)	CCC
Senior unsecured (2 issues)	B
Subordinated (4 issues)	CCC+

Source: Based on data from Standard & Poor's Financial Services, LLC.

4.3 Risks in Relying on Agency Ratings

The dominant position of the rating agencies in the global debt markets, and the near-universal use of their credit ratings on debt securities, suggests that investors believe they do a good job assessing credit risk. In fact, with a few exceptions (e.g., too high ratings on U.S. subprime mortgage-backed securities issued in the mid-2000s, which turned out to be much riskier than expected), their ratings have proved quite accurate as a relative measure of default risk. For example, Exhibit 6 shows historical S&P one-year global corporate default rates by rating category from 1991 to 2010.[20]

---

19 Standard & Poor's, "Rating Each Issue," in *Corporate Ratings Criteria 2008* (New York: Standard and Poor's, 2008):89.
20 S&P uses a static pool methodology here. It measures the percentage of issues that defaulted in a given calendar year based on how they were rated at the beginning of the year.

Exhibit 6	Global Corporate Annual Default Rates by Rating Category (%)						
	AAA	**AA**	**A**	**BBB**	**BB**	**B**	**CCC/C**
1991	0.00	0.00	0.00	0.55	1.68	13.84	33.87
1992	0.00	0.00	0.00	0.00	0.00	6.99	30.19
1993	0.00	0.00	0.00	0.00	0.70	2.62	13.33
1994	0.00	0.00	0.14	0.00	0.27	3.08	16.67
1995	0.00	0.00	0.00	0.17	0.98	4.59	28.00
1996	0.00	0.00	0.00	0.00	0.67	2.91	4.17
1997	0.00	0.00	0.00	0.25	0.19	3.49	12.00
1998	0.00	0.00	0.00	0.41	0.97	4.61	42.86
1999	0.00	0.17	0.18	0.19	0.95	7.28	32.35
2000	0.00	0.00	0.26	0.37	1.25	7.73	34.12
2001	0.00	0.00	0.35	0.33	3.13	11.24	44.55
2002	0.00	0.00	0.00	1.01	2.81	8.11	44.12
2003	0.00	0.00	0.00	0.23	0.56	4.01	32.93
2004	0.00	0.00	0.08	0.00	0.53	1.56	15.33
2005	0.00	0.00	0.00	0.07	0.20	1.73	8.94
2006	0.00	0.00	0.00	0.00	0.30	0.81	12.38
2007	0.00	0.00	0.00	0.00	0.19	0.25	15.09
2008	0.00	0.38	0.38	0.48	0.78	3.98	26.26
2009	0.00	0.00	0.22	0.54	0.72	10.38	48.68
2010	0.00	0.00	0.00	0.00	0.55	0.80	22.27
Mean	0.00	0.03	0.08	0.23	0.87	5.00	25.91
Max	0.00	0.38	0.38	1.01	3.13	13.84	48.68
Min	0.00	0.00	0.00	0.00	0.00	0.25	4.17

Source: Based on data from Standard & Poor's Financial Services, LLC.

As Exhibit 6 shows, the highest-rated bonds have extremely low default rates. With very few exceptions, the lower the rating, the higher the annual rate of default, with bonds rated CCC and lower experiencing the highest default rates by far. There are limitations and risks, however, to relying on credit rating agency ratings, including the following:

1. **Credit ratings can be very dynamic**. That is, over a long time period (e.g., many years), credit ratings can migrate—move up or down—significantly from the time of bond issuance. Using Standard & Poor's data, Exhibit 7 shows the average three-year migration (or "transition") by rating from 1981 to 2010. Note that the higher the credit rating, the greater the ratings stability. Even for AAA rated credits, however, only about 70 percent (70 percent in the United States and 68 percent globally) of the time did ratings remain in that rating category over a three-year period. (Of course, AAA rated credits can have their ratings move in only one direction—down.) A very small fraction of AAA rated credits became non-investment grade or defaulted within three years. For single-B rated credits, only about 40 percent (40 percent in the United States and

39 percent globally) of the time did ratings remain in that rating category over three-year periods. This observation about the dynamism of credit ratings isn't meant to be a criticism of the rating agencies. It is meant to demonstrate that creditworthiness can and does change—up or down—and that bond investors should not assume an issuer's credit rating will remain the same from time of purchase through the entire holding period.

| Exhibit 7 | Average Three-Year Corporate Transition Rates, 1981–2010 (%) |

From/To	AAA	AA	A	BBB	BB	B	CCC/C	D	NR*
United States									
AAA	69.75	16.60	2.47	0.38	0.21	0.13	0.13	0.17	10.15
AA	1.32	65.46	17.75	2.52	0.47	0.42	0.04	0.20	11.82
A	0.11	4.34	67.32	12.05	1.79	0.69	0.14	0.42	13.16
BBB	0.04	0.47	8.61	62.21	8.03	2.47	0.35	1.22	16.60
BB	0.02	0.10	0.78	10.95	43.95	13.59	1.40	5.60	23.61
B	0.01	0.06	0.42	1.08	10.06	40.27	4.94	15.79	27.37
CCC/C	0.00	0.00	0.38	0.98	1.97	12.19	13.47	43.98	27.02
Global									
AAA	68.09	18.85	2.46	0.34	0.14	0.08	0.11	0.14	9.78
AA	1.30	65.78	18.59	2.24	0.37	0.26	0.03	0.15	11.29
A	0.08	4.53	67.31	11.84	1.42	0.57	0.12	0.34	13.80
BBB	0.03	0.41	8.90	61.42	7.44	2.12	0.36	1.20	18.12
BB	0.01	0.07	0.67	11.31	43.97	12.06	1.37	5.17	25.37
B	0.01	0.05	0.34	1.08	10.90	38.93	4.61	15.25	28.84
CCC/C	0.00	0.00	0.29	0.91	2.05	16.04	12.39	40.47	27.85

*NR means not rated—that is, certain corporate issuers were no longer rated by S&P. This could occur for a variety of reasons, including issuers paying off their debt and no longer needing ratings.
Source: Based on data from Standard & Poor's Financial Services, LLC.

2. **Rating agencies are not infallible**. The mis-rating of billions of dollars of subprime-backed mortgage securities is one example. Other examples include the mis-ratings of U.S. companies Enron and WorldCom and European issuer Parmalat. Like many investors, the rating agencies did not see the accounting fraud being committed in those companies.

3. **Other types of so-called idiosyncratic or event risk are difficult to capture in ratings**. Examples of this include litigation risk, such as that which can affect tobacco companies, or environmental and business risks faced by chemical companies and utility power plants. This would also include such unpredictable events as the earthquake and tsunami that hit Japan in March 2011 and its credit impact on debt issuer Tokyo Electric Power Company (TEPCO). Leveraged transactions, such as debt-financed acquisitions and large stock buybacks, are often difficult to anticipate and thus to capture in credit ratings.

4. **Ratings tend to lag market pricing of credit**. Bond prices and credit spreads frequently move more quickly because of changes in perceived creditworthiness than rating agencies change their ratings (or even outlooks) up or down. Bond prices and relative valuations can move every day, whereas bond ratings, appropriately, don't change that often. Even over long time periods, however,

credit ratings can badly lag changes in bond prices. Exhibit 8 shows the price and Moody's rating of a bond from U.S. automaker Ford Motor Company before, during, and after the financial crisis in 2008. Note how the bond's price moved down sharply well before Moody's downgraded its credit rating—multiple times—and also how the bond's price began to recover—and kept recovering—well before Moody's upgraded its credit rating on Ford debt.

Exhibit 8	**Ford Motor Company Senior Unsecured Debt: Price vs. Moody's Rating Since 2005**

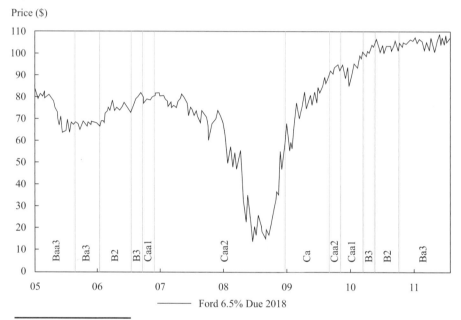

Sources: Data based on Bloomberg Finance L.P. and Moody's Investors Service.

Moreover, particularly for certain speculative-grade credits, two bonds with similar ratings may trade at very different valuations. This is partly a result of the fact that credit ratings primarily try to assess the risk of default, whereas for low-quality credits, the market begins focusing more on expected loss (default probability times loss severity). So, bonds from two separate issuers with comparable (high) risk of default but different recovery rates may have similar ratings but trade at significantly different dollar prices.[21]

Thus, bond investors who wait for rating agencies to change their ratings before making buy and sell decisions in their portfolios may be at risk of underperforming other investors who make portfolio decisions in advance of—or not solely based on—rating agency changes.

As described, there are risks in relying on credit rating agency ratings when investing in bonds. Thus, while the credit rating agencies will almost certainly continue to play a significant role in the bond markets, it's important for investors to perform their own credit analyses and draw their own conclusions regarding the credit risk of a given debt issue or issuer.

---

21 See Christopher L. Gootkind, "Improving Credit Risk Analysis," in *Fixed-Income Management for the 21st Century* (Charlottesville, VA: Association for Investment Management and Research, 2002).

Example 4

Credit Ratings

1. Using the S&P ratings scale, investment grade bonds carry which of the following ratings?

    A. AAA to EEE

    B. BBB– to CCC

    C. AAA to BBB–

2. Using both Moody's and S&P ratings, which of the following pairs of ratings is considered high yield, also known as "below investment grade," "speculative grade," or "junk"?

    A. Baa1/BBB–

    B. B3/CCC+

    C. Baa3/BB+

3. What is the difference between an issuer rating and an issue rating?

    A. The issuer rating applies to all of an issuer's bonds, whereas the issue rating considers a bond's seniority ranking.

    B. The issuer rating is an assessment of an issuer's overall creditworthiness, whereas the issue rating is always higher than the issuer rating.

    C. The issuer rating is an assessment of an issuer's overall creditworthiness, typically reflected as the senior unsecured rating, whereas the issue rating considers a bond's seniority ranking (e.g., secured or subordinated).

4. Based on the practice of notching by the rating agencies, a subordinated bond from a company with an issuer rating of BB would likely carry what rating?

    A. B+

    B. BB

    C. BBB–

5. The fixed-income portfolio manager you work with asked you why a bond from an issuer you cover didn't rise in price when it was upgraded by Fitch from B+ to BB. Which of the following is the *most likely* explanation?

    A. Bond prices never react to rating changes.

    B. The bond doesn't trade often so the price hasn't adjusted to the rating change yet.

    C. The market was expecting the rating change, and so it was already "priced in" to the bond.

6. Amalgamated Corp. and Widget Corp. each have bonds outstanding with similar coupons and maturity dates. Both bonds are rated B2, B–, and B by Moody's, S&P, and Fitch, respectively. The bonds, however, trade at very different prices—the Amalgamated bond trades at €89, whereas the Widget bond trades at €62. What is the *most likely* explanation of the price (and yield) difference?

    A. Widget's credit ratings are lagging the market's assessment of the company's credit deterioration.

    B. The bonds have similar risks of default (as reflected in the ratings), but the market believes the Amalgamated bond has a higher expected loss in the event of default.

C. The bonds have similar risks of default (as reflected in the ratings), but the market believes the Widget bond has a higher expected recovery rate in the event of default.

Solution to 1:

C is correct.

Solution to 2:

B is correct. Note that issuers with ratings such as Baa3/BB+ (answer C) are called "crossovers" because one rating is investment grade (the Moody's rating of Baa3) and the other is high yield (the S&P rating of BB+).

Solution to 3:

C is correct.

Solution to 4:

A is correct. The subordinated bond would have its rating notched lower than the company's BB rating, probably by two notches, reflecting the higher weight given to loss severity for below-investment-grade credits.

Solution to 5:

C is correct. The market was anticipating the rating upgrade and had already priced it in. Bond prices often do react to rating changes, particularly multi-notch ones. Even if bonds don't trade, their prices adjust based on dealer quotations given to bond pricing services.

Solution to 6:

A is correct. Widget's credit ratings are probably lagging behind the market's assessment of its deteriorating creditworthiness. Answers B and C both state the situation backwards. If the market believed that the Amalgamated bond had a higher expected loss given default, then that bond would be trading at a lower, not a higher, price. Similarly, if the market believed that the Widget bond had a higher expected recovery rate in the event of default, then that bond would be trading at a higher, not a lower, price.

5   TRADITIONAL CREDIT ANALYSIS: CORPORATE DEBT SECURITIES

The goal of credit analysis is to assess an issuer's ability to satisfy its debt obligations, including bonds and other indebtedness, such as bank loans. These debt obligations are contracts, the terms of which specify the interest rate to be paid, the frequency and timing of payments, the maturity date, and the covenants that describe the permissible and required actions of the borrower. Because corporate bonds are contracts, enforceable by law, credit analysts generally assume an issuer's willingness to pay and concentrate instead on assessing its ability to pay. Thus, the main focus in credit analysis is to understand a company's ability to generate cash flow over the term of its debt obligations. In so doing, analysts must assess both the credit quality of the company and the fundamentals of the industry in which the company operates. Traditional credit analysis considers the sources, predictability, and sustainability of cash generated by a company to service its debt obligations. This section will focus on corporate credit analysis; in particular, it will emphasize non-financial companies.

Financial institutions have very different business models and funding profiles from industrial and utility companies.

5.1 Credit Analysis vs. Equity Analysis: Similarities and Differences

The above description of credit analysis suggests credit and equity analyses should be very similar; in many ways, they are. There are motivational differences, however, between equity and fixed-income investors that are an important aspect of credit analysis. Strictly speaking, management works for the shareholders of a company. Its primary objective is to maximize the value of the company for its owners. In contrast, management's legal duty to its creditors—including bondholders—is to meet the terms of the governing contracts. Growth in the value of a corporation from rising profits and cash flow accrues to the shareholders, while the best outcome for bondholders is to receive full, timely payment of interest and repayment of principal when due. Conversely, shareholders are more exposed to the decline in value as a company's future earnings power and cash flow decline because bondholders have a priority claim on cash flow and assets. Should a company's earnings power and cash flow decline to the extent that it can no longer make its debt payments, however, then bondholders are at risk of loss as well.

In summary, in exchange for a priority claim on cash flow and assets, bondholders do not share in the growth in value of a company (except to the extent that its creditworthiness improves) but have downside risk in the event of default. In contrast, shareholders have theoretically unlimited upside opportunity, but in the event of default, their investment is typically wiped out before the bondholders suffer a loss. This is very similar to the type of payoff patterns seen in financial options. In fact, in recent years, a great deal of credit modeling has been predicated on a sophisticated application of financial option theory and mathematics. Although it is beyond the scope of this present introduction to the subject, it is an expanding area of interest to both institutional investors and rating agencies.

Thus, although the analysis is similar in many respects for both equity and credit, equity analysts are interested in the strategies and investments that will increase a company's value and grow earnings per share. They then compare that earnings power and growth potential with that of other companies in a given industry. Credit analysts will look more at the downside risk by measuring and assessing the sustainability of a company's cash flow relative to its debt levels and interest expense. Importantly for credit analysts, the balance sheet will show the composition of an issuer's debt—the overall amount, how much is coming due and when, and the distribution by seniority ranking. In general, equity analysts will focus more on income and cash flow statements, whereas credit analysts tend to focus more on the balance sheet and cash flow statements.

5.2 The Four Cs of Credit Analysis: A Useful Framework

Traditionally, it has been convenient to consider what is often called the "four Cs of credit analysis":[22]

- Capacity
- Collateral

---

[22] There is no unique list of Cs. In addition to those listed here, one may see "capital" and/or "conditions" on a particular author's list of four (or five) Cs. Conditions typically refers to overall economic conditions. Capital refers to the company's accumulated capital and its specific capital assets and is essentially subsumed within the categories of capacity and collateral. Keep in mind that the list of Cs is a convenient way to summarize the important aspects of the analysis, not a checklist to be applied mechanically.

- Covenants
- Character

Capacity refers to the ability of the borrower to make its debt payments on time; this is the focus of this section. **Collateral** refers to the quality and value of the assets supporting the issuer's indebtedness. **Covenants** are the terms and conditions of lending agreements that the issuer must comply with. **Character** refers to the quality of management. Each of these will now be covered in greater detail.

5.2.1 *Capacity*

Capacity is the ability of a borrower to service its debt. To determine that, credit analysis, in a process similar to equity analysis, starts with industry analysis and then turns to examination of the specific issuer (company analysis).

Industry structure. A useful framework for analyzing industry structure was developed by business school professor and consultant Michael Porter.[23] The framework looks at the five major forces of competition in an industry:

1. **Power of suppliers.** An industry that relies on just a few suppliers has greater credit risk than an industry that has multiple suppliers. Industries and companies with just a few suppliers have limited negotiating power to keep them from raising prices to their customers, whereas industries that have many suppliers can play them off against each other to keep prices in check.

2. **Power of buyers/customers.** Industries that rely heavily on just a few main customers have greater risk because the negotiating power lies with the buyers. For example, a toolmaker that sells 50 percent of its products to one large global retailer has limited negotiating power with its principal customer.

3. **Barriers to entry.** Industries with high entry barriers tend to have lower risk than industries with low entry barriers because competition may not be as fierce and pricing power is strong or at least sufficient. High entry barriers can take many forms, including high capital investment, such as in aerospace; large, established distribution systems, such as in auto dealerships; patent protection, such as in technology or pharmaceutical industries; or a high degree of regulation, such as in utilities.

4. **Substitution risk.** Industries (and companies) that offer products and services that provide great value to their customers, and for which there are not good or cost-competitive substitutes, typically have strong pricing power, generate substantial cash flows, and represent less credit risk than other industries or companies. Certain (patent-protected) drugs are an example, as are large jet airplanes. Over time, however, disruptive technologies and inventions can increase substitution risk. For example, years ago, airplanes began displacing many trains and steamships. Newspapers were considered to have a nearly unassailable market position until television and then the internet became substitutes for how people received news and information. Over time, recorded music has shifted from records to tapes, to compact discs, to mp3s and other forms of digital media.

5. **Level of competition.** Industries with heavy competition—characterized by a large number of participants, none of whom has significant market share—tend to have less cash flow predictability and, therefore, represent higher credit risk than industries with less competition. Regulation can play an important role in competition as well. For example, regulated utilities typically have a monopoly

---

23 Michael E. Porter, *Competitive Strategy: Techniques for Analyzing Industries and Competitors* (New York; The Free Press, 1980).

position in a given market, which results in relatively stable and predictable cash flows. (They often carry higher debt levels, however, as a result of that monopoly position and the more stable cash flows.)

It is also important to consider how companies in an industry generate revenues and earn profits. Is it an industry with high fixed costs and capital investment or one with modest fixed costs? These structures generate revenues and earn profits in very different ways. Two of the best examples of industries with high fixed costs, also referred to as "having high operating leverage," are airlines and hotels. Many of their costs are fixed—running a hotel, flying a plane—so they cannot easily cut costs. If an insufficient number of people stay at a company's hotel, or fly in its planes, then the company will have trouble covering its fixed costs and will be at risk of losing lots of money. With high occupancy, however, revenues are strong, fixed costs get more than covered, and the company can earn substantial profits.

Industry fundamentals. After understanding an industry's structure, the next step is to assess its fundamentals, including its sensitivity to macroeconomic factors, its growth prospects, its profitability, and its business need—or lack thereof—for strong credit quality. Judgments about these can be made by looking at the following:

- *Cyclical or non-cyclical.* This is a crucial assessment because industries that are cyclical—that is, have greater sensitivity to broader economic performance—have more volatile revenues, margins, and cash flows and thus are inherently riskier than non-cyclical industries. Consumer product and health care companies are typically considered non-cyclical, whereas auto and steel companies can be very cyclical. Companies in cyclical industries should carry lower levels of debt relative to their ability to generate cash flow over an economic cycle than companies in less-cyclical or non-cyclical industries.

- *Growth prospects.* Although growth is typically a greater focus for equity analysts than for credit analysts, bond investors have an interest in growth as well. Industries that have little or no growth tend to consolidate via mergers and acquisitions. Depending upon how these are financed (e.g., using stock or debt) and the economic benefits (or lack thereof) of the merger, they may or may not be favorable to corporate bond investors. Weaker competitors in slow-growth industries may begin to struggle financially, adversely affecting their creditworthiness.

- *Published industry statistics.* Analysts can get a strong sense of an industry's fundamentals and performance by researching statistics that are published by and available from a number of different sources, including the rating agencies, investment banks, industry publications, and frequently, government agencies.

Company fundamentals. Following analysis of an industry's structure and fundamentals, the next step is to assess the fundamentals of the company: the corporate borrower. Analysts should examine the following:

- Competitive position
- Track record/operating history
- Management's strategy and execution
- Ratios and ratio analysis

Competitive position. Based on their knowledge of the industry structure and fundamentals, analysts assess a company's competitive position within the industry. What is its market share? How has it changed over time: Is it increasing, decreasing, holding steady? Is it well above (or below) its peers? How does it compare with respect to cost structure? How might it change its competitive position? What sort of financing might that require?

Track record/Operating history. How has the company performed over time? It's useful to go back several years and analyze the company's financial performance, perhaps during times of both economic growth and contraction. What are the trends in revenues, profit margins, and cash flow? Capital expenditures represent what percent of revenues? What are the trends on the balance sheet—use of debt versus equity? Was this track record developed under the current management team? If not, when did the current management team take over?

Management's strategy and execution. What is management's strategy for the company: to compete and to grow? Does it make sense, and is it plausible? How risky is it, and how differentiated is it from its industry peers? Is it venturing into unrelated businesses? Does the analyst have confidence in management's ability to execute? What is management's track record, both at this company and at previous ones? Credit analysts also want to know and understand how management's strategy will affect its balance sheet. Does management plan to manage the balance sheet prudently, in a manner that doesn't adversely affect bondholders? Analysts can learn about management's strategy from reading comments, discussion, and analysis that are included with financial statements filed with appropriate regulators, listening to conference calls about earnings or other big announcements (e.g., acquisitions), going to company websites to find earnings releases and copies of slides of presentations at various industry conferences, visiting and speaking with the company, and so on.

Example 5

Industry and Company Analysis

1. Given a hotel company, a chemical company, and a consumer products company, which is *most likely* to be able to support a high debt load over an economic cycle?

   A. The hotel company, because people need a place to stay when they travel.

   B. The chemical company, because chemicals are a key input to many products.

   C. The consumer products company, because consumer products are typically resistant to recessions.

2. Why do heavily regulated monopoly companies, such as utilities, carry high debt loads?

   A. Regulators require them to carry high debt loads.

   B. They generate strong and stable cash flows, enabling them to support high levels of debt.

   C. They are not very profitable and need to borrow heavily to maintain their plant and equipment.

3. XYZ Corp. manufactures a commodity product in a highly competitive industry in which no company has significant market share and where there are low barriers to entry. Which of the following *best* describes XYZ's ability to take on substantial debt?

   A. Its ability is very limited because companies in industries with those characteristics generally cannot support high debt loads.

   B. Its ability is strong because companies in industries with those characteristics generally have high margins and cash flows that can support significant debt.

   C. We don't have enough information to answer the question.

Solution to 1:

C is correct. Consumer products companies are considered non-cyclical, whereas hotel and chemical companies are more cyclical and thus more vulnerable to economic downturns.

Solution to 2:

B is correct. Because such monopolies' financial returns are generally dictated by the regulators, they generate consistent cash flows and are, therefore, able to support high debt levels. In addition, significant barriers to entry arising from high capital investment requirements and the regulatory process can contribute to debt capacity.

Solution to 3:

A is correct. Companies in industries with those characteristics typically have low margins and limited cash flow and thus cannot support high debt levels.

Ratios and ratio analysis. To provide context and metrics to the analysis and understanding of a company's fundamentals—based on the industry in which it operates, its competitive position, its strategy and execution—a number of financial ratios derived from the company's principal financial statements are examined: the income statement, balance sheet, and cash flow statement. Credit analysts calculate a number of ratios to assess the financial health of a company, identify trends over time, and compare companies across an industry to get a sense of relative creditworthiness. Note that typical values of these ratios vary widely from one industry to another because of different industry characteristics previously identified: competitive structure, economic cyclicality, regulation, and so on.

We will categorize the key credit analysis ratios into three different groups:

- Profitability and cash flow

- Leverage

- Coverage

Profitability and cash flow measures. It is from profitability and cash flow generation that companies can service their debt. Credit analysts typically look at operating profit margins and operating income to get a sense of a company's underlying profitability and see how it varies over time. Operating income is defined as operating revenues minus operating expenses and is commonly referred to as "earnings before interest and taxes" (EBIT). Credit analysts focus on EBIT because it is useful to determine a company's performance prior to costs arising from its capital structure (i.e., how much debt it carries versus equity). And "before taxes" is used because interest expense is paid before income taxes are calculated.

There are several measures of cash flow used in credit analysis; some are more conservative than others because they make certain adjustments for cash that gets used in managing and maintaining the business or in making payments to shareholders.

- **Earnings before interest, taxes, depreciation, and amortization (EBITDA).** EBITDA is a commonly used measure of cash flow that takes operating income and adds back depreciation and amortization expense because those are non-cash items. This is a somewhat crude measure of cash flow because it excludes certain cash-related expenses of running a business, such as capital expenditures and changes in (non-cash) working capital. Thus, despite its popularity as a cash flow metric, analysts look at other measures in addition to EBITDA.

▪ **Funds from operations (FFO).** Standard & Poor's defines funds from operations as net income from continuing operations plus depreciation, amortization, deferred income taxes, and other non-cash items.[24]

▪ **Free cash flow before dividends.**[25] This measures excess cash flow generated by the company (excluding non-recurring items) before payments to shareholders or that could be used to pay down debt or pay dividends. It includes net income plus depreciation and amortization minus capital expenditures minus increase (plus decrease) in non-cash working capital, and excludes non-recurring items. Companies that have negative free cash flow before payments to shareholders will be consuming cash they have or will need to rely on additional financing—from banks, bond investors, or equity investors. This obviously represents higher credit risk.

▪ **Free cash flow after dividends.** This measure just takes the preceding calculation and subtracts dividend payments. If this number is positive, it represents cash that could be used to pay down debt or build up cash on the balance sheet. Either outcome is a form of deleveraging, which is favorable from a credit risk standpoint. Some credit analysts will calculate net debt by subtracting balance sheet cash from total debt, although they shouldn't assume the cash will be used to pay down debt. Actual debt paid down from free cash flow is a stronger form of deleveraging. Some analysts will also deduct stock buybacks to get the "truest" form of free cash flow that can be used to de-lever on either a gross or net debt basis; however, others view stock buybacks as more discretionary and as having less certain timing than dividends, and thus treat those two forms of shareholder payments differently when calculating free cash flow.

▪ **Leverage ratios.** There are a few measures of leverage used by credit analysts. The most common are the debt/capital, debt/EBITDA, and FFO/debt ratios. Note that many analysts adjust a company's reported debt levels for debt-like liabilities, such as underfunded pensions and other retiree benefits, as well as operating leases. When adjusting for leases, analysts will typically add back the imputed interest or rent expense to various cash flow measures.

▪ **Debt/capital.** Capital is calculated as total debt plus shareholders equity. This ratio shows the percent of a company's capital base that is financed with debt. A lower percentage of debt indicates lower credit risk. This traditional ratio is generally used for investment-grade corporate issuers. Where goodwill or other intangible assets are significant (and subject to obsolescence, depletion, or other forms of devaluation), it is often informative to also compute the debt to capital ratio after assuming a write-down of the after-tax value of such assets.

▪ **Debt/EBITDA.** This ratio is a common leverage measure. Analysts use it on a "snapshot" basis, as well as to look at trends over time and at projections and to compare companies in a given industry. Rating agencies often use it as a trigger for rating actions, and banks reference it in loan covenants. A higher ratio indicates more leverage and thus higher credit risk. Note that this ratio can

---

24 The funds from operations differs only slightly from the better known cash flow from operations in that it excludes working capital changes. The idea behind using FFO in credit analysis is to take out the near-term swings and seasonality in working capital that can potentially distort the amount of operating cash flow a business is generating. Over time, the working capital swings are expected to even out. Analysts tend to look at both FFO and cash flow from operations, particularly for businesses with large working capital swings (e.g., very cyclical manufacturing companies).
25 In other parts of the CFA curriculum, this is referred to as free cash flow to the firm (FCFF). These can be regarded as interchangeable.

be very volatile for companies with high cash flow variability, such as those in cyclical industries and with high operating leverage (fixed costs).

■ **FFO/debt.** Credit rating agencies like using this leverage ratio. They publish key median and average ratios, such as this one, by rating category so analysts can get a sense of why an issuer is assigned a certain credit rating, as well as where that rating may migrate based on changes to such key ratios as this one.

■ **Coverage ratios.** Coverage ratios measure an issuer's ability to meet—to "cover"—its interest payments. The two most common are the EBITDA/interest expense and EBIT/interest expense ratios.

■ **EBITDA/interest expense.** This measurement of interest coverage is a bit more liberal than the one that uses EBIT because it does not subtract out the impact of (non-cash) depreciation and amortization expense. A higher ratio indicates better credit quality.

■ **EBIT/interest expense.** Because EBIT does not include depreciation and amortization, it is considered a more conservative measure of interest coverage. This ratio is now used less frequently than EBITDA/interest expense.

Exhibit 9 is a good example of the key average credit ratios by rating category for industrial companies over a three-year period, as published by Standard & Poor's.

Exhibit 9	Industrial Comparative Ratio Analysis							
Credit Rating	EBITDA Margin (%)	Return on Capital (%)	EBIT Interest Coverage (x)	EBITDA Interest Coverage (x)	FFO/Debt (%)	Free Operations Cash Flow/ Debt (%)	Debt/ EBITDA (x)	Debt/Debt plus Equity (%)
AAA								
U.S.	29.6	36.8	60.2	68.0	251.1	197.0	0.4	15.7
EMEA	NA	NA	NA	NA	NA	NA	NA	NA
AA								
U.S.	24.6	24.5	16.8	20.5	69.9	52.3	1.2	36.0
EMEA	25.2	21.7	14.4	17.6	163.9	82.5	0.9	23.7
A								
U.S.	24.2	21.0	22.0	29.0	96.7	65.9	1.5	36.0
EMEA	21.5	17.1	9.0	12.3	92.8	60.1	1.6	34.5
BBB								
U.S.	21.8	16.1	8.8	12.2	54.0	32.8	2.7	46.3
EMEA	19.7	13.1	5.3	7.9	52.1	23.7	2.6	44.9
BB								
U.S.	23.4	11.8	4.1	6.2	35.7	13.6	3.3	54.9
EMEA	20.3	11.0	5.3	7.2	31.8	9.7	3.3	51.0
B								
U.S.	19.4	8.0	1.6	2.9	17.5	5.1	6.6	84.0
EMEA	20.5	6.8	1.7	3.4	19.1	2.2	7.0	78.4

Notes: Data are as of 24 August 2011. EMEA is Europe, Middle East, and Africa.
Source: Based on data from Standard & Poor's Financial Services, LLC.

Comments on issuer liquidity. An issuer's access to liquidity is also an important consideration in credit analysis. Companies with strong liquidity represent lower credit risk than those with weak liquidity, other factors being equal. The financial crisis of 2008–2009 showed companies and investors that access to liquidity via the debt and equity markets should not be taken for granted, particularly for those that do not have strong balance sheets or steady operating cash flow.

When assessing an issuer's liquidity, credit analysts tend to look at the following:

- **Cash on the balance sheet.** Cash holdings provide the greatest assurance of having sufficient liquidity to make promised payments.

- **Net working capital.** The big U.S. automakers used to have enormous negative working capital, despite having high levels of cash on the balance sheet. This proved disastrous when the financial crisis hit in 2008 and the economy contracted sharply. Auto sales—and thus revenues—fell, the auto companies cut production, and working capital consumed billions of dollars in cash as accounts payable came due when the companies most needed liquidity.

- **Operating cash flow.** Analysts will project this figure out a few years and consider the risk that it may be lower than expected.

- **Committed bank lines.** Committed but untapped lines of credit provide contingent liquidity in the event that the company is unable to tap other, potentially cheaper, financing in the public debt markets.

- **Debt coming due and committed capital expenditures in the next one to two years.** Analysts will compare the sources of liquidity with the amount of debt coming due as well as with committed capital expenditures to ensure that companies can repay their debt and still invest in the business if the capital markets are somehow not available.

As will be discussed in more detail in the section on special considerations for high-yield credits, issuer liquidity is a bigger consideration for high-yield companies than for investment grade companies.

Example 6

Watson Pharmaceuticals, Inc. is a U.S.-based specialty health care company. As a credit analyst, you have been asked to assess its creditworthiness—on its own, relative to another competitor and its overall industry, and compared with a similarly rated company in a different industry. Using the financial statements provided in Exhibits 10 through 13 for the three years ending 31 December 2008, 2009, and 2010, address the following:

1. Calculate Watson Pharmaceuticals' operating profit margin, EBITDA, and free cash flow. (*Note:* The company did not pay dividends in 2008–2010.)

2. Determine Watson's leverage ratios: debt/EBITDA, debt/capital, free cash flow/debt.

3. Calculate Watson's interest coverage using both EBIT and EBITDA.

4. Using the statistics provided on the pharmaceutical industry and on competitor Johnson & Johnson, compare the credit ratios of Watson and Johnson & Johnson and explain the relative creditworthiness and ratings of the two companies.

5. Contrast the credit ratios of Watson with Luxembourg-based ArcelorMittal, one of the world's largest global steelmakers. Comment on the volatility of the credit ratios of the two companies. Which company looks to be more cyclical? What industry factors might explain some of the differences? In comparing the creditworthiness of these two companies, what other factors might be considered to offset greater volatility of credit ratios?

| **Exhibit 10A** | Watson Pharmaceuticals' Financial Statements |

Consolidated Statements of Operations	Years Ended December 31		
(dollars in millions except per share amounts)	2008	2009	2010
Net revenues	2,535.5	2,793.0	3,566.9
Operating expenses:			
Cost of sales (excludes amortization)	1,502.8	1,596.8	1,998.5
Research and development	170.1	197.3	296.1
Selling and marketing	232.9	263.1	320.0
General and administrative	190.5	257.1	436.1
Amortization	80.7	92.6	180.0
Loss on asset sales and impairments	0.3	2.2	30.8
Total operating expenses	2,177.3	2,409.1	3,261.5
Operating income	358.2	383.9	305.4
Other (expense) income:			
Interest income	9.0	5.0	1.6
Interest expense	(28.2)	(34.2)	(84.1)
Other income	19.3	7.9	27.7
Total other (expense) income, net	0.1	(21.3)	(54.8)
Income before income taxes and noncontrolling interest	358.3	362.6	250.6
Provision for income taxes	119.9	140.6	67.3
Net income	238.4	222.0	183.3
Loss attributable to noncontrolling interest	—	—	1.1
Net income attributable to common shareholders	238.4	222.0	184.4

Source: Based on data from Watson Pharmaceuticals' Company Annual Report (2010).

| **Exhibit 10B** | Watson Pharmaceuticals' Financial Statements |

Consolidated Balance Sheets	Years Ended December 31		
(dollars in millions)	2008	2009	2010
ASSETS			
Current assets:			
Cash and cash equivalents	507.6	201.4	282.8

(continued)

Exhibit 10B	Continued

Consolidated Balance Sheets	Years Ended December 31		
(dollars in millions)	2008	2009	2010
Marketable securities	13.2	13.6	11.1
Accounts receivable	305.0	517.4	560.9
Inventories, net	473.1	692.3	631.0
Prepaid expenses and other current assets	48.5	213.9	134.2
Deferred tax assets	111.0	130.9	179.4
Total current assets	**1,458.4**	**1,769.5**	**1,799.4**
Property and equipment, net	658.5	694.2	642.3
Investments and other assets	80.6	114.5	84.5
Deferred tax assets	52.3	110.8	141.0
Product rights and other intangibles, net	560.0	1,713.5	1,632.0
Goodwill	868.1	1,501.0	1,528.1
Total assets	**3,677.9**	**5,903.5**	**5,827.3**
LIABILITIES AND EQUITY			
Current liabilities:			
Accounts payable and accrued expenses	381.3	614.3	741.1
Income taxes payable	15.5	78.4	39.9
Short-term debt and current portion of long-term debt	53.2	307.6	—
Deferred tax liabilities	15.9	31.3	20.8
Deferred revenue	16.1	16.3	18.9
Total current liabilities	**482.0**	**1,047.9**	**820.7**
Long-term debt	824.7	1,150.2	1,016.1
Deferred revenue	30.1	31.9	18.2
Other long-term liabilities	4.9	118.7	183.1
Other taxes payable	53.3	76.0	65.1
Deferred tax liabilities	174.3	455.7	441.5
Total liabilities	**1,569.3**	**2,880.4**	**2,544.7**
Equity:			
Preferred stock	—	—	—
Common stock	0.4	0.4	0.4
Additional paid-in capital	995.9	1,686.9	1,771.8
Retained earnings	1,418.1	1,640.1	1,824.5
Accumulated other comprehensive (loss) income	(3.2)	1.9	(2.5)
Treasury stock, at cost (9.7 and 9.6 shares held, respectively)	(302.6)	(306.2)	(312.5)
Total stockholders' equity	**2,108.6**	**3,023.1**	**3,281.7**
Noncontrolling interest	—	—	0.9

Exhibit 10B *Continued*

Consolidated Balance Sheets	Years Ended December 31		
(dollars in millions)	2008	2009	2010
Total equity	2,108.6	3,023.1	3,282.6
Total liabilities and equity	3,677.9	5,903.5	5,827.3

Source: Based on data from Watson Pharmaceuticals' Company Annual Report (2010).

Exhibit 10C Watson Pharmaceuticals' Financial Statements

Consolidated Statements of Cash Flow	Years Ended December 31		
(dollars in millions)	2008	2009	2010
Cash flows from operating activities:			
Net income	238.4	222.0	183.3
Reconciliation to net cash provided by operating activities:			
Depreciation	90.0	96.4	101.9
Amortization	80.7	92.6	180.0
Provision for inventory reserve	45.7	51.0	50.0
Share-based compensation	18.5	19.1	23.5
Deferred income tax (benefit) provision	3.5	(19.0)	(118.3)
(Gain) loss on sale of securities	(9.6)	1.1	(27.3)
Loss on asset sales and impairment	0.3	2.6	29.8
Increase in allowance for doubtful accounts	1.2	3.4	9.5
Accretion of preferred stock and contingent payment consideration	—	2.2	38.4
Other, net	(13.9)	(7.6)	11.3
Changes in working capital	(38.2)	(87.0)	88.9
Net cash provided by operating activities	416.6	376.8	571.0
Cash flows from investing activities:			
Additions to property and equipment	(63.5)	(55.4)	(56.6)
Additions to product rights and other intangibles	(37.0)	(16.5)	(10.9)
Additions to marketable securities	(8.2)	(8.0)	(5.5)
Additions to long-term investments	—	—	(43.7)
Proceeds from sale of property and equipment	—	3.0	2.7
Proceeds from sale of marketable securities	6.7	9.0	9.5
Proceeds from sale of investments	8.2	—	95.4
Acquisition of business, net of cash acquired	—	(968.2)	(67.5)
Other investing activities, net	0.4	—	2.5
Net cash used in investing activities	(93.4)	(1,036.1)	(74.1)

(continued)

Exhibit 10C   Continued

Consolidated Statements of Cash Flow	Years Ended December 31		
(dollars in millions)	2008	2009	2010
Cash flows from financing activities:			
Proceeds from issuance of long-term debt	—	1,109.9	—
Principal payments on debt	(95.6)	(786.6)	(459.7)
Proceeds from borrowings on short-term debt	67.9	—	—
Proceeds from stock plans	8.4	33.4	54.7
Repurchase of common stock	(0.9)	(3.6)	(6.3)
Net cash provided by (used in) financing activities	(20.2)	353.1	(411.3)
Effect of currency exchange rate changes	—	—	(4.2)
Net increase (decrease) in cash and cash equivalents	303.0	(306.2)	81.4
Cash and cash equivalents at beginning of period	204.6	507.6	201.4
Cash and cash equivalents at end of period	507.6	201.4	282.8

Source: Based on data from Watson Pharmaceuticals' Company Annual Report (2010).

Exhibit 11   Johnson & Johnson's Credit Ratios

	2008	2009	2010
Operating margin	25.1%	25.2%	26.8%
Debt/EBITDA	0.6x	0.8x	0.9x
EBITDA/Interest	43.3x	40.7x	42.8x
FCF/Debt	58.1%	61.1%	48.9%
Debt/Capital	21.8%	22.3%	22.9%

Source: Company Filings, Loomis, Sayles & Company.

Exhibit 12   Pharmaceuticals: U.S. Industry Credit Ratios (average of past three fiscal years as of 27 June 2011)

	Corp. Credit Rating (1)	Return on Capital (%)	EBIT Interest Coverage (x)	EBITDA Interest Coverage (x)	FFO/ Debt (%)	Free Operating Cash Flow/ Debt (%)	Debt/ EBITDA (x)	Debt/ Debt plus Equity (%)
Abbott Laboratories	AA/ Stable/ A-1+	23.7	12.4	15.7	65.4	48.4	1.3	36.3
Allergan, Inc.	A+/ Stable/ A-1	17.0	12.8	16.9	51.2	37.3	1.4	30.5

Exhibit 12	Continued							
	Corp. Credit Rating (1)	**Return on Capital (%)**	**EBIT Interest Coverage (x)**	**EBITDA Interest Coverage (x)**	**FFO/ Debt (%)**	**Free Operating Cash Flow/ Debt (%)**	**Debt/ EBITDA (x)**	**Debt/ Debt plus Equity (%)**
Axcan Intermediate Holdings Inc.	BB–/ Stable/–	14.0	2.2	3.1	20.2	18.6	2.7	55.2
Bristol-Myers Squibb	A+/ Stable/ A-1	31.7	14.3	15.0	105.3	82.8	0.7	23.0
Catalent	B+/ Stable/–	2.5	0.5	1.8	4.0	2.0	8.9	82.5
Eli Lilly and Company	AA/ Stable/ A-1+	39.6	18.6	22.7	116.6	101.9	0.7	33.1
Johnson & Johnson	AAA/ Stable/ A-1+	31.8	30.9	36.4	209.6	175.7	0.4	14.0
King Pharmaceuticals, Inc.	BB/ Stable/–	16.0	10.9	14.9	68.3	58.2	1.2	26.3
Merck & Co., Inc.	AA–/ Positive/ A-1+	28.2	22.3	20.2	150.8	114.1	0.6	12.1
Mylan Inc.	BB/ Stable/–	7.5	2.0	3.1	11.7	4.4	5.6	63.5
Pfizer Inc.	AA/ Stable/ A-1+	22.5	21.4	25.9	141.9	179.6	0.4	12.2
Valeant Pharmaceuticals International	BB–/ Stable/–	15.1	3.3	4.9	22.0	21.1	2.9	67.0
Watson Pharmaceuticals, Inc.	BBB–/ Stable/ –	11.5	9.5	14.2	39.4	29.4	2.0	33.6
Median		17.0	12.4	15.0	65.4	48.4	1.3	33.1

Source: Standard and Poor's Financial Services LLC (S&P). (1) As of June 27, 2010.

Exhibit 13	ArcelorMittal Credit Ratios		
	2008	**2009**	**2010**
Operating margin	10.2%	–2.4%	4.6%
Debt/EBITDA	2.0x	8.0x	3.3x
EBITDA/Interest	7.4x	1.1x	3.6x
FCF/Debt	20.0%	13.0%	–2.1%
Debt/Capital	36.5%	27.5%	28.2%

Source: Company Filings, Loomis, Sayles & Company.

Solutions:

1. Operating profit margin (%) = Operating income/Revenue

    2008: 358.2/2535.5 = 0.141 or 14.1 percent

    2009: 383.9/2793.0 = 0.137 or 13.7 percent

    2010: 305.4/3566.9 = 0.086 or 8.6 percent

    EBITDA = Operating income + Depreciation + Amortization

    2008: 358.2 + 90.0 + 80.7 = 528.9

    2009: 383.9 + 96.4 + 92.6 = 572.9

    2010: 305.4 + 101.9 + 180.0 = 587.3

    FCF = Cash flow from operations – Capital expenditures – Dividends

    2008: 416.6 – (63.5 + 37.0 – 0.0) – 0 = 316.1

    2009: 376.8 – (55.4 + 16.5 – 3.0) – 0 = 307.9

    2010: 571.0 – (56.6 + 10.9 – 2.7) – 0 = 506.2

    where

    Capital expenditures = Additions to property and equipment + Additions to product rights and intangibles – Proceeds of sale of property and equipment

    Note that "Additions to product rights and intangibles" is included in capital expenditures here because such activities are likely to be both material and recurring for a health care/drug company. For other types of businesses, the analyst might elect to exclude this item from capital expenditures when calculating FCF.

2. Debt/EBITDA

    Total debt = Short-term debt and Current portion of long-term debt + Long-term debt

    2008: Debt: 53.2 + 824.7 = 877.9

      Debt/EBITDA: 877.9/528.9 = 1.7x

    2009: Debt: 307.6 + 1150.2 = 1457.8

      Debt/EBITDA: 1457.8/572.9 = 2.5x

    2010: Debt: 0 + 1016.1 = 1016.1

      Debt/EBITDA: 1016.1/587.3 = 1.7x

    Debt/Capital (%)

    Capital = Debt + Equity

    2008: Capital: 877.9 + 2108.6 = 2986.5

      Debt/Capital: 877.9/2986.5 = 29.4 percent

    2009: Capital: 1457.8 + 3023.1 = 4480.9

      Debt/Capital: 1457.8/4480.9 = 32.5 percent

    2010: Capital: 1016.1 + 3282.6 = 4298.7

      Debt/Capital: 1016.1/4298.7 = 23.6 percent

    FCF/Debt (%)

    2008: 316.1/877.9 = 36.0 percent

    2009: 307.9/1457.8 = 21.1 percent

    2010: 506.2/1016.1 = 49.8 percent

3. EBIT/Interest expense

    2008: 358.2/28.2 = 12.7x

    2009: 383.9/34.2 = 11.2x

    2010: 305.4/84.1 = 3.6x

EBITDA/Interest expense

2008: 528.9/28.2 = 18.8x

2009: 572.9/34.2 = 16.8x

2010: 587.3/84.1 = 7.0x

4. Based just on these credit ratios, Johnson & Johnson (J&J) has a higher operating margin, better leverage ratios, a much better Debt/EBITDA, a better FCF/debt over the three years (though slightly lower in 2010), a lower debt/capital (although pretty close in 2010), and a much better interest coverage as measured by EBITDA/interest. Collectively, those ratios suggest J&J is a stronger credit than Watson.

Watson Pharmaceuticals' Credit Ratios	2008	2009	2010
Operating margin	14.1%	13.7%	8.6%
Debt/EBITDA	1.7x	2.5x	1.7x
EBITDA/Interest	18.8x	16.8x	7.0x
FCF/Debt	36.0%	21.1%	49.8%
Debt/Capital	29.4%	32.5%	23.6%

Johnson & Johnson's Credit Ratios	2008	2009	2010
Operating margin	25.1%	25.2%	26.8%
Debt/EBITDA	0.6x	0.8x	0.9x
EBITDA/Interest	43.3x	40.7x	42.8x
FCF/Debt	58.1%	61.1%	48.9%
Debt/Capital	21.8%	22.3%	22.9%

5. By the five credit ratios shown in the tables, Watson has a higher and less volatile operating margin than ArcelorMittal, lower leverage (except debt/capital in 2009), and higher interest coverage. Based on the volatility of its cash flow and operating margin, Arcelor appears to be a much more cyclical credit. Coupled with its higher debt levels, one would expect Arcelor to have a lower credit rating. To mitigate the impact of its more volatile credit ratios, Arcelor might have very high levels of liquidity. Its size and global diversity may also be a "plus." In addition, it could have favorable supplier and customer contracts, and/or its profitability might be improving as, for example, competitors that are sub-scale and/or employing aggressively low pricing strategies are forced to retrench or exit the industry.

Watson Pharmaceuticals' Credit Ratios	2008	2009	2010
Operating margin	14.1%	13.7%	8.6%
Debt/EBITDA	1.7x	2.5x	1.7x
EBITDA/Interest	18.8x	16.8x	7.0x
FCF/Debt	36.0%	21.1%	49.8%
Debt/Capital	29.4%	32.5%	23.6%

ArcelorMittal's Credit Ratios	2008	2009	2010
Operating margin	10.2%	−2.4%	4.6%
Debt/EBITDA	2.0x	8.0x	3.3x
EBITDA/Interest	7.4x	1.1x	3.6x
FCF/Debt	20.0%	13.0%	−2.1%
Debt/Capital	36.5%	27.5%	28.2%

5.2.2 *Collateral*

Collateral, or asset value, analysis is typically emphasized more with weaker credit quality companies. As discussed earlier, credit analysts focus primarily on probability of default, which is mostly about an issuer's ability to generate sufficient cash flow to support its debt payments, as well as its ability to refinance maturing debt. Only when the default probability rises to a sufficient level do analysts typically consider asset or collateral value in the context of loss severity in the event of default.

Analysts do think about the value and quality of a company's assets; however, these are difficult to observe directly. Factors to consider include the nature and amount of intangible assets on the balance sheet. Some assets, such as patents, are clearly valuable and can be sold if necessary to cover liabilities. Goodwill, on the other hand, is not considered a high-quality asset. In fact, sustained weak financial performance most likely implies that a company's goodwill will be written down, reinforcing its poor quality. Another factor to consider is the amount of depreciation an issuer takes relative to its capital expenditures: Low capital expenditures relative to depreciation expense could imply that management is insufficiently investing in its business, which will lead to lower-quality assets, potentially reduced future operating cash flow, and higher loss severity in the event of default.

A market-based signal that credit analysts use to impute the quality of a publicly traded company's assets, and its ability to support its debt, is equity market capitalization. For instance, a company whose stock trades below book value may have lower-quality assets than is suggested by the amount reported on the balance sheet.

As economies become more service- and knowledge-based and those types of companies issue debt, it's important to understand that these issuers rely more on human and intellectual capital than on "hard assets." In generating profits and cash flow, these companies are not as asset intensive. One example would be software companies. Another example would be investment management firms. Human- and intellectual- capital-based companies may generate a lot of cash flow, but their collateral value is questionable, unless there are patents and other forms of intellectual property and "intangible capital" that may not appear directly on the balance sheet but could be valuable in the event of financial distress or default.

Regardless of the nature of the business, the key point of collateral analysis is to assess the value of the assets relative to the issuer's level—and seniority ranking—of debt.

5.2.3 *Covenants*

Covenants are meant to protect creditors while also giving management sufficient flexibility to operate its business on behalf of and for the benefit of the shareholders. They are integral to credit agreements, whether they are bonds or bank loans, and they spell out what the issuer's management is (1) obligated to do and (2) limited in doing. The former are called "affirmative covenants," whereas the latter are called "negative" or "restrictive covenants." Obligations would include such duties as making interest and principal payments and filing audited financial statements on a timely basis. Covenants might also require a company to redeem debt in the event of the company being acquired[26] or to keep the ratio of debt to EBITDA below some prescribed amount. The limitations might include a cap on the amount of cash that can be paid out to shareholders relative to earnings, or perhaps on the amount of additional secured debt that can be issued. Covenant violations can be an event of default unless they are cured in a short time or a waiver is granted.

For corporate bonds, covenants are described in the bond **prospectus**, the document that is part of a new bond issue. The prospectus describes the terms of the bond issue, as well as supporting financial statements, to help investors perform their

---

26 This is often referred to as a "change of control" covenant.

analyses and make investment decisions as to whether or not to submit orders to buy the new bonds. Actually, the **bond indenture** is the governing legal credit agreement and is typically incorporated by reference in the prospectus.

Covenants are an important but underappreciated part of credit analysis. Strong covenants protect bond investors from the possibility of management taking actions that would hurt an issuer's creditworthiness. For example, without appropriate covenants management might pay large dividends, undertake stock buybacks well in excess of free cash flow, sell the company in a leveraged buyout,[27] or take on a lot of secured debt that structurally subordinates unsecured bondholders. All of these actions would enrich shareholders at the expense of bondholders. Recall that management works for the shareholders and that bonds are contracts, with management's only real obligation to creditors being to uphold the terms of the contract. Weak covenants pose additional risks to bond investors.

The bond-buying investor base is very large and diverse, particularly for investment-grade debt. It includes insurance companies, investment management firms, pension funds, mutual funds, hedge funds, sovereign wealth funds, and so on. Although there are some very large investment firms, the buyer base is fragmented and does not—and legally cannot—act as a syndicate. Thus, bondholders are generally not able to negotiate strong covenants on most new bond issues. Therefore, covenants provide limited protection to investment-grade bondholders and often only somewhat stronger protection to high-yield investors. Covenants on new bond issues tend to be stronger during weak economic or market conditions because investors seek more protection during such times. There are a few organized institutional investor groups focused on strengthening covenants: the Credit Roundtable[28] in the United States and the European Model Covenant Initiative in the United Kingdom.

Covenant language is often very technical and written in "legalese," so it can be helpful to have an in-house person with a legal background to review and interpret the specific covenant terms and wording. One might also use a third-party service specializing in covenant analysis, such as Covenant Review.[29]

We will go into more detail on specific covenants in the section on special considerations for high-yield bonds.

5.2.4 *Character*

The character of a corporate borrower can also be difficult to observe. The analysis of character as a factor in credit analysis dates to when loans were made to companies owned by individuals. Most corporate bond issuers are now publicly owned by shareholders or privately owned by pools of capital, such as private equity firms. Management often has little ownership in a corporation, so analysis and assessment of character is different than it would be for owner-managed firms. Credit analysts can make judgments about management's character in the following ways:

- An assessment of the soundness of management's strategy.

- Management's track record in executing past strategies, particularly if they led to bankruptcy or restructuring. A company run by executives whose prior positions/ventures resulted in significant distress might still be able to borrow in the debt markets, but it would likely have to borrow on a secured basis and/or pay a higher rate of interest.

- Use of aggressive accounting policies and/or tax strategies. Examples might include using a significant amount of off-balance-sheet financing, capitalizing

---

27 A leveraged buyout (LBO) is an acquisition of a company by private investors using high levels of debt and relatively little equity.

28 See www.creditroundtable.org.

29 See www.covenantreview.com.

versus immediately expensing items, timing revenue recognition, and/ or frequently changing auditors. These are potential warning flags to other behaviors or actions that may adversely impact an issuer's creditworthiness.

■ Any history of fraud or malfeasance—a major warning flag to credit analysts.

■ Previous poor treatment of bondholders—for example, management actions that resulted in major credit rating downgrades. These actions might include a debt-financed acquisition, a large special dividend to shareholders, or a major debt-financed stock buyback program.

Example 7

The Four Cs

1. Which of the following would not be a bond covenant?

   A. The issuer must file financial statements with the bond trustee on a timely basis.

   B. The company can buy back as much stock as it likes.

   C. If the company offers security to any creditors, it must offer security to this bond issue.

2. Why should credit analysts be concerned if a company's stock trades below book value?

   A. It means the company is probably going bankrupt.

   B. It means the company will probably incur lots of debt to buy back its undervalued stock.

   C. It's a signal that the company's asset value on its balance sheet may be impaired and have to be written down, suggesting less collateral protection for creditors.

3. If management is of questionable character, how can investors incorporate this assessment into their credit analysis and investment decisions?

   A. They can choose not to invest based on the increased credit risk.

   B. They can insist on getting collateral (security) and/or demand a higher return.

   C. They can choose not to invest or insist on additional security and/or higher return.

Solution to 1:

B is correct. Covenants describe what the borrower is (1) obligated to do or (2) limited in doing. It's the absence of covenants that would permit a company to buy back as much stock as it likes. A requirement that the company offer security to this bond issue if it offers security to other creditors (answer C) is referred to as a "negative pledge."

Solution to 2:

C is correct.

Solution to 3:

C is correct. Investors can always say no if they are not comfortable with the credit risk presented by a bond or issuer. They may also decide to lend to a borrower with questionable character only on a secured basis and/or demand a higher return for the perceived higher risk.

CREDIT RISK VS. RETURN: YIELDS AND SPREADS[30]

As in other types of investing, taking more risk in credit offers higher potential return, but with more volatility and less certainty of earning that return. Using credit ratings as a proxy for risk, Exhibit 14 shows the composite yield to maturity[31] for bonds of all maturities within each rating category in the U.S. and European bond markets according to Barclays Capital, one of the largest providers of fixed-income market indices.

Exhibit 14	Corporate Yields by Rating Category as of 30 June 2011								
	Investment Grade				Non-Investment Grade				
Barclays Capital Indices	**AAA (%)**	**AA (%)**	**A (%)**	**BBB (%)**	**BB (%)**	**B (%)**	**CCC (%)**	**CC (%)**	**D (%)**
U.S.	3.09	3.10	3.64	4.35	6.50	7.93	10.27	14.11	22.73
Pan European	3.33	3.58	4.14	4.98	6.90	8.67	17.12	13.81	54.80

Source: Based on data from Barclays Capital.

Note that the lower the credit quality, the higher the quoted yield. The realized yield, or return, will almost always be different because of changes in interest rates and the various forms of credit risk discussed earlier. For example, in the aggregate credit losses will "eat up" some of the yield premium offered by lower-quality bonds versus higher-quality credits. Trailing 12-month returns by credit rating category, and the volatility (standard deviation) of those returns, are shown in Exhibit 15.

---

30 The material in this section applies to all bonds subject to credit risk. For simplicity, in what follows all such bonds are sometimes referred to as "corporate" bonds.

31 High-yield bonds are often quoted on a "yield to call" (YTC) or "yield to worst" (YTW) basis because so many of them are callable before maturity, whereas most investment-grade bonds are non-callable, or at least callable at such punitive premiums that issuers are not likely to exercise that option.

Exhibit 15	**U.S. Trailing 12-Month Returns by Rating Category, 31 December 1996–30 June 2011**

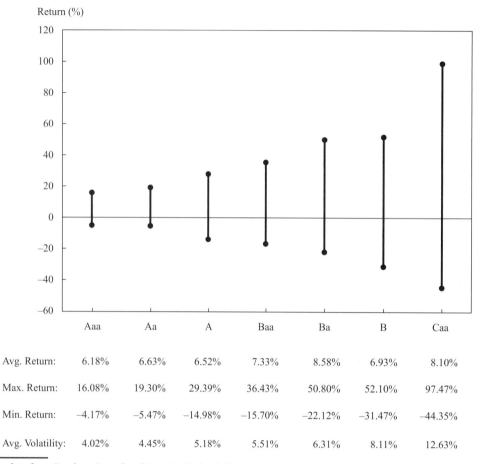

	Aaa	Aa	A	Baa	Ba	B	Caa
Avg. Return:	6.18%	6.63%	6.52%	7.33%	8.58%	6.93%	8.10%
Max. Return:	16.08%	19.30%	29.39%	36.43%	50.80%	52.10%	97.47%
Min. Return:	−4.17%	−5.47%	−14.98%	−15.70%	−22.12%	−31.47%	−44.35%
Avg. Volatility:	4.02%	4.45%	5.18%	5.51%	6.31%	8.11%	12.63%

Source: Based on data from Barclays Capital and Loomis, Sayles & Company.

As shown in the exhibit, the higher the credit risk, the greater the return potential and the higher the volatility of that return. This pattern is consistent with other types of investing that involves risk and return (although average returns on single-B rated bonds appear anomalous in this example).

For extremely liquid bonds that are deemed to have virtually no default risk (e.g., German government bonds, or *Bunds*), the yield is a function of real interest rates plus an expected inflation rate and a maturity premium. Of course, those factors are present in corporate bonds as well. In addition, the yield on corporate bonds will include a liquidity premium and a credit spread intended to compensate investors for these additional risks as well as for the expected level of credit losses. Thus, the yield on a corporate bond can be decomposed as

Yield on corporate bond = Real risk-free interest rate + Expected inflation rate + Maturity premium + Liquidity premium + Credit spread

Changes in any of these components will alter the yield, price, and return on the bond.

Investors in corporate bonds focus primarily on the yield spread relative to a comparable, default-free bond, which is composed of the liquidity premium and the credit spread:

Yield spread = Liquidity premium + Credit spread

The market's willingness to bear risk will affect each of these components. In general, however, it is not possible to directly observe the market's assessment of the components separately—analysts can only observe the total yield spread.

Spreads on all corporate bonds can be affected by a number of factors, with lower-quality issuers typically experiencing greater spread volatility. These factors, which are frequently linked, include the following:

- **Credit cycle.** As the credit cycle improves, credit spreads will narrow. Conversely, a deteriorating credit cycle will cause credit spreads to widen. Spreads are tightest at or near the top of the credit cycle, when financial markets believe risk is low, whereas they are widest at or near the bottom of the credit cycle, when financial markets believe risk is high.

- **Broader economic conditions.** Not surprisingly, weakening economic conditions will push investors to desire a greater risk premium and drive overall credit spreads wider. Conversely, a strengthening economy will cause credit spreads to narrow because investors anticipate credit metrics will improve due to rising corporate cash flow, thus reducing the risk of default.

- **Financial market performance overall, including equities.** In weak financial markets, credit spreads will widen, whereas in strong markets, credit spreads will narrow. In a steady, low-volatility environment, credit spreads will typically also narrow, as investors tend to "reach for yield."

- **Broker–dealers' willingness to provide sufficient capital for market making.** Bonds trade primarily over the counter, so investors need broker–dealers to commit capital for market-making purposes. During the financial crisis in 2008–2009, several large broker–dealer counterparties either failed or were taken over by another. This, combined with financial and regulatory stresses faced by virtually all the other broker–dealers, greatly reduced the total capital available for making markets and the willingness to buy/sell credit-risky bonds. Future regulatory reform may well lead to persistent or even permanent reductions in broker-provided capital.

- **General market supply and demand.** In periods of heavy new issue supply, credit spreads will widen if there is insufficient demand. In periods of high demand for bonds, spreads will move tighter.

Each of the first four factors played a role during the financial crisis of 2008–2009, causing spreads to widen dramatically, as shown in Exhibit 16, before narrowing sharply as governments intervened and markets stabilized. This is shown in two panels—one for investment grade, another for high yield—because of the much greater spread volatility in high-yield bonds, particularly CCC rated credits. This spread volatility is reflected in the different spread ranges on the y-axes. OAS is option-adjusted spread, which incorporates the value of the embedded call option in certain corporate bonds that issuers have the right to exercise before maturity.[32]

---

32 The details of valuing bonds with embedded options and the calculation of OAS are covered in Level II of the CFA curriculum.

| Exhibit 16 | U.S. Investment-Grade and High-Yield Corporate Spreads |

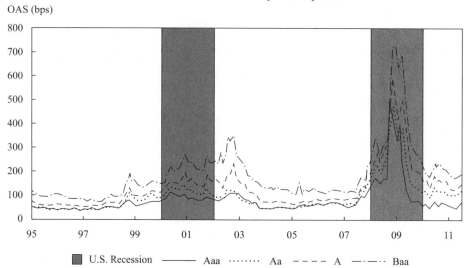

A. Investment-Grade Corporate Spreads

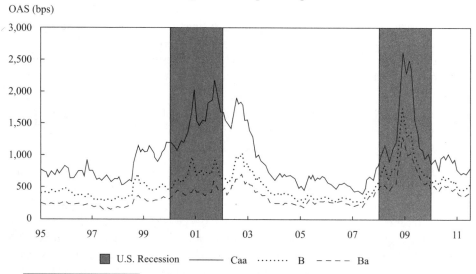

B. High-Yield Corporate Spreads

Sources: Based on data from Barclays Capital and Loomis Sayles & Company.

Example 8

Yield Spreads

1. Which bonds are likely to exhibit the greatest spread volatility?

   A. Bonds from issuers rated AA

   B. Bonds from issuers rated BB

   C. Bonds from issuers rated A

2. If investors become increasingly worried about the economy—say, as shown by declining stock prices—what is the *most likely* impact on credit spreads?

   A. There will be no change to credit spreads. They aren't affected by equity markets.

    B. Narrower spreads will occur. Investors will move out of equities into debt securities.

    C. Wider spreads will occur. Investors are concerned about weaker creditworthiness.

Solution to 1:

B is correct. Lower-quality bonds exhibit greater spread volatility than higher-quality bonds. All of the factors that affect spreads—the credit cycle, economic conditions, financial performance, market-making capacity, and supply/demand conditions—will tend to have a greater impact on the pricing of lower-quality credits.

Solution to 2:

C is correct. Investors will require higher yields as compensation for the greater credit losses that are likely to occur in a weakening economy.

We have discussed how yield spreads on credit-risky debt obligations, such as corporate bonds, can fluctuate based on a number of factors, including changes in the market's view of issuer-specific or idiosyncratic risk. The next question to ask is how these spread changes affect the price of and return on these bonds.

Although bond investors do concern themselves with default risks, recall that the probability of default for higher-quality bonds is typically very low: For investment-grade bonds, annual defaults are nearly always well below 1 percent (recall Exhibit 6). On the other hand, default rates can be very high for lower-quality issuers, although they can vary widely depending upon the credit cycle, among other things. What most investors in investment-grade debt focus on more than default risk is spread risk—that is, the effect on prices and returns from changes in spreads.

The return impact from spread changes is driven by two main factors: the modified duration (price sensitivity with respect to changes in interest rates) of the bond and the magnitude of the spread change. The effect on return to the bondholder depends on the holding period used for calculating the return.

The simplest example is that of a small, instantaneous change in the yield spread. In this case, the return impact, i.e., the percentage change in price (including accrued interest), can be approximated by

$$\text{Return impact} \approx -\text{MDur} \times \Delta\text{Spread}$$

where MDur is the modified duration. The negative sign in this equation reflects the fact that because bond prices and yields move in opposite directions, narrower spreads have a positive impact on bond prices and thus returns, whereas wider spreads have a negative impact on bond returns. Note that if the spread change is expressed in basis points, then the return impact will also be in basis points, whereas if the spread change is expressed as a decimal, the return impact will also be expressed as a decimal. Either way, the result is easily re-expressed as a percent.

For larger spread changes (and thus larger yield changes), the impact of convexity needs to be incorporated into the approximation:

$$\text{Return impact} \approx -(\text{MDur} \times \Delta\text{Spread}) + \tfrac{1}{2}\text{Cvx} \times (\Delta\text{Spread})^2$$

In this case, one must be careful to ensure that convexity (denoted by Cvx) is appropriately scaled to be consistent with the way the spread change is expressed. In general, for bonds without embedded options, one can scale convexity so that it has the same order of magnitude as the duration squared and then express the spread change as a decimal. For example, for a bond with duration of 5.0 and reported convexity of 0.235, one would re-scale convexity to 23.5 before applying the formula. For a 1 percent (i.e., 100 bps) increase in spread, the result would be

$$\text{Return impact} = (-5.0 \times 0.01) + \tfrac{1}{2} \times 23.5 \times (0.01)^2 = -0.04765 \text{ or } -4.765 \text{ percent}$$

The return impact of instantaneous spread changes is illustrated in Exhibit 17 using two bonds from British Telecom, the U.K. telecommunications company. The bonds, denominated in British pounds, are priced to provide a certain spread over British government bonds (gilts) of a similar maturity. From the starting spread, in increments of 25 bps and for both wider and narrower spreads, the new price and actual return for each spread change are calculated. In addition, the exhibit shows the approximate returns with and without the convexity term. As can be seen, the approximation using only duration is reasonably accurate for small spread changes but for larger changes, the convexity term generally provides a meaningful improvement.

Exhibit 17	Impact of Duration on Price for a Given Change in Spread

Issuer: British Telecom, 8.625%, maturing on 26 March 2020

Price: £129.475		Modified Duration: 6.084		Spread to Gilt Curve: 248 b.p.				
Accrued interest: 6.3		Convexity: 47.4		YTM: 4.31				
				Scenarios				
Spread Δ (b.p.)	−100	−75	−50	−25	0	25	50	75	100
Spread (b.p.)	148	173	198	223	248	273	298	323	348
New Price (£)	137.90	135.73	133.60	131.52	129.48	127.47	125.51	123.59	121.71
New Price + Accrued (£)	144.20	142.03	139.90	137.82	135.78	133.77	131.81	129.89	128.01
Price Δ (£)	8.43	6.26	4.13	2.05	0.00	−2.01	−3.96	−5.88	−7.77
Return (%)									
Actual	6.21%	4.61%	3.04%	1.51%	0.00%	−1.48%	−2.92%	−4.33%	−5.72%
Approx: Dur only	6.08%	4.56%	3.04%	1.52%	0.00%	−1.52%	−3.04%	−4.56%	−6.08%
Approx: Dur & Cvx	6.32%	4.70%	3.10%	1.54%	0.00%	−1.51%	−2.98%	−4.43%	−5.85%

Issuer: British Telecom, 6.375%, maturing on 23 June 2037

Price: £110.093		Modified Duration: 13.064		Spread to Gilt Curve: 247 b.p.				
Accrued interest: 3.117		Convexity: 253.5		YTM: 5.62				
				Scenarios				
Spread Δ (b.p.)	−100	−75	−50	−25	0	25	50	75	100
Spread (b.p.)	147	172	197	222	247	272	297	322	347
New Price (£)	125.99	121.72	117.65	113.78	110.09	106.58	103.23	100.04	97.00
New Price + Accrued (£)	129.11	124.84	120.77	116.90	113.21	109.70	106.35	103.16	100.11
Price Δ (£)	15.90	11.63	7.56	3.69	0.00	−3.51	−6.86	−10.05	−13.10
Return (%)									
Actual	14.04%	10.27%	6.68%	3.26%	0.00%	−3.10%	−6.06%	−8.88%	−11.57%
Approx: Dur only	13.06%	9.80%	6.53%	3.27%	0.00%	−3.27%	−6.53%	−9.80%	−13.06%
Approx: Dur & Cvx	14.33%	10.51%	6.85%	3.35%	0.00%	−3.19%	−6.22%	−9.09%	−11.80%

Source: Based on data from Bloomberg Finance, L.P. (settle date is 19 December 2011).

Note that the price change for a given spread change is higher for the longer-duration bond—in this case, the 2037 maturity British Telecom bond—than for the shorter-duration bond. Longer-duration corporate bonds are referred to as having "higher spread sensitivity"; that is, their prices, and thus returns, are more volatile with respect to changes in spread. It is essentially the same concept as duration for any bond: The longer the duration of a bond, the greater the price volatility for a given change in interest rates/yields.

In addition, investors want to be compensated for the fact that the further one is from a bond's maturity (i.e., the longer the bond), the greater the uncertainty about an issuer's future creditworthiness. Based on credit analysis, an investor might be confident that an issuer's risk of default is relatively low in the near term; however, looking many years into the future, the investor's uncertainty grows because of factors that are increasingly difficult, if not impossible, to forecast (e.g., poor management strategy or execution, technological obsolescence, natural or man-made disasters, corporate leveraging events). This increase in credit risk over time can be seen in Exhibit 18. Note that in this Standard & Poor's study,[33] one-year default rates for the 2010 issuance pool are 0 percent for all rating categories of B+ or higher. The three-year default rates for bonds issued in 2008 are materially higher, and the observed defaults include bonds originally rated up to BBB– (i.e., low investment grade). The 10-year default rates for bonds issued in 2001 are appreciably higher than the 3-year default rates, and the defaults include bonds initially rated as high as A+ (i.e., solid investment grade). In addition to the risk of default rising over time, the data also show quite conclusively that the lower the credit rating, the higher the risk of default. Finally, note the very high risk of default for bonds rated CCC or lower over all time horizons. This is consistent with Exhibit 7 earlier in the reading, which showed significant three-year ratings variability ("migration"), with much of the migration to lower credit ratings (i.e., higher risk of default).

Exhibit 18	Default Rate by Rating Category (%) (Non-financials)		
Credit Rating	**1 Year (2010 pool)**	**3 Year (2008 pool)**	**10 Year (2001 pool)**
AAA	0.00	0.00	0.00
AA+	0.00	0.00	0.00
AA	0.00	0.00	0.00
AA–	0.00	0.00	0.00
A+	0.00	0.00	1.76
A	0.00	0.00	1.70
A–	0.00	0.00	0.87
BBB+	0.00	0.00	5.03
BBB	0.00	0.00	4.55
BBB–	0.00	1.04	12.80
BB+	0.00	2.12	15.38
BB	0.00	3.53	19.91
BB–	0.00	6.14	26.84
B+	0.00	12.73	33.69
B	0.76	22.08	39.02
B–	2.07	25.23	55.83
CCC/C	21.99	56.63	65.31

Source: Based on data from S&P, "2010 Annual Global Corporate Default Study and Ratings Transitions," Standard & Poor's report (30 March 2011).

---

33 From S&P, "2010 Annual Global Corporate Default Study and Ratings Transitions," Standard & Poor's report (30 March 2011). Detailed descriptions of the underlying methodology are available in Appendix I of the report.

It is also worth noting that bid–ask spreads (in yield terms) translate into higher transaction costs for longer-duration bonds; investors want to be compensated for that as well. For these reasons, spread curves (often called **credit curves**), like yield curves, are typically upward sloping. That is, longer-maturity bonds of a given issuer typically trade at wider spreads than shorter-maturity bonds to their respective comparable-maturity government bonds.[34] Exhibit 19, using the U.S. telecommunications company AT&T as an example, shows the upward-sloping credit curve by plotting the yields of its bonds versus their maturity. (As a large and frequent issuer, AT&T has many bonds outstanding across the yield curve.)

Exhibit 19	AT&T Credit Curve vs. U.S. Treasury Curve

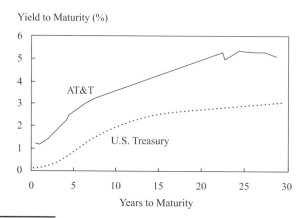

Source: Based on data from Bloomberg Finance, L.P., as of 5 October 2011.

Example 9

Return Impact

Calculate the return impact on a 10-year corporate bond with a 4.75 percent coupon priced at 100, with an instantaneous 50 bps widening in spread due to the issuer's announcement that it was adding substantial debt to finance an acquisition, resulting in a two-notch downgrade by the rating agencies. The bond has a modified duration of 7.9 and its convexity is 74.9.

Solution:

The impact from the 50 bps spread widening is:

Return impact

$$\approx -(\text{MDur} \times \Delta\text{Spread}) + \tfrac{1}{2}\,\text{Cvx} \times (\Delta\text{Spread})^2$$
$$= -(0.0050 \times 7.9) + (0.5 \times 74.9) \times (0.0050)^2$$
$$= -0.0386, \text{ or } -3.86 \text{ percent}$$

---

34 There are some exceptions to this—bonds that trade at a high premium price over par due to having coupons that are well above the bond's yield to maturity and bonds that trade at distressed levels due to credit concerns. Many investors are averse to paying high premium prices for bonds that have credit risk because of the greater potential price decline—towards a recovery price in the event of default—from a credit-adverse event. Thus, high-coupon intermediate-maturity bonds can trade at similar or wider spreads to longer-maturity bonds. For distressed credits, the high risk of default causes all bonds for a given issuer to migrate toward the same expected recovery price. In this case, the shorter-maturity and shorter-duration bonds will have a higher quoted yield to maturity, and wider spread, than the longer-maturity and longer-duration bonds. This follows from the return impact formulas. The shorter the duration, the higher the yield (including spread) must go to bring the price down to a given expected recovery price.

> Because yields and bond prices move in opposite directions, the wider spread caused the bond price to fall. Using a bond-pricing calculator, the exact return is −3.85 percent, so this approximation was very accurate.

In summary, spread changes can have a significant impact on the performance of credit-risky bonds over a given holding period, and the higher the modified duration of the bond(s), the greater the price impact from changes in spread. Wider spreads hurt bond performance, whereas narrower spreads help bond performance. For bond investors who actively manage their portfolios (i.e., don't just buy bonds and hold them to maturity), forecasting spread changes and expected credit losses on both individual bonds and their broader portfolios is an important strategy for enhancing investment performance.

SPECIAL CONSIDERATIONS OF HIGH-YIELD, SOVEREIGN, AND MUNICIPAL CREDIT ANALYSIS

7

Thus far, we have focused primarily on basic principles of credit analysis and investing with emphasis on higher-quality, investment-grade corporate bonds. Although many of these principles are applicable to other credit-risky segments of the bond market, there are some differences in credit analysis that need to be considered. This section focuses on special considerations in evaluating the credit of debt issuers from the following three market segments: high-yield corporate bonds, sovereign bonds, and municipal bonds.

7.1 High Yield

Recall that high-yield, or non-investment-grade, corporate bonds are those rated below Baa3/BBB– by the major rating agencies. These bonds are sometimes referred to as "junk bonds" because of the higher risk inherent in their weak balance sheets and/or poor or less-proven business prospects.

There are many reasons companies are rated below investment grade, including

- Highly leveraged capital structure
- Weak or limited operating history
- Limited or negative free cash flow
- Highly cyclical business
- Poor management
- Risky financial policies
- Lack of scale and/or competitive advantages
- Large off-balance-sheet liabilities
- Declining industry (e.g., newspaper publishing)

Companies with weak balance sheets and/or business profiles have lower margin for error and greater risk of default relative to higher-quality investment-grade names. And the higher risk of default means more attention must be paid to recovery analysis (or loss severity, in the event of default). Consequently, high-yield analysis typically is more in-depth than investment-grade analysis and thus has special considerations. This includes the following:

- Greater focus on issuer liquidity and cash flow
- Detailed financial projections

- Detailed understanding and analysis of the debt structure
- Understanding of an issuer's corporate structure
- Covenants
- Equity-like approach to high yield analysis

Liquidity. Liquidity—that is, having cash and/or the ability to generate or raise cash—is important to all issuers. It is absolutely critical for high-yield companies. Investment-grade companies typically have substantial cash on their balance sheets, generate a lot of cash from operations relative to their debt (or else they wouldn't be investment grade!), and/or are presumed to have alternate sources of liquidity, such as bank lines and commercial paper.[35] For these reasons, investment-grade companies can more easily roll over (refinance) maturing debt. On the other hand, high-yield companies may not have those options available. For example, there is no high-yield commercial paper market, and bank credit facilities often carry tighter restrictions for high-yield companies. Both bad company-specific news and difficult financial market conditions can lead to high-yield companies being unable to access the debt markets. And although the vast majority of investment-grade corporate debt issuers have publicly traded equity and can thus use that equity as a financing option, many high-yield companies are privately held and thus don't have access to public equity markets.

Thus, issuer liquidity is a key focus in high-yield analysis. Sources of liquidity, from strongest to weakest, are the following:

1. Cash on the balance sheet
2. Working capital
3. Operating cash flow
4. Bank credit facilities
5. Equity issuance
6. Asset sales

Cash on the balance sheet is easy to see and self-evident as a source for repaying debt.[36] As mentioned earlier in this reading, working capital can be a large source or use of liquidity, depending on its amount, its use in a company's cash-conversion cycle, and its role in a company's operations. Operating cash flow is a ready source of liquidity as sales turn to receivables, which turn to cash over a fairly short time period. Bank lines, or credit facilities, can be an important source of liquidity, though there may be some covenants relating to the use of the bank lines which are crucial to know and will be covered a little later. Equity issuance may not be a reliable source of liquidity because an issuer is private or because of poor market conditions if a company does have publicly traded equity. Asset sales are the least reliable source of liquidity because both the potential value and the actual time of closing can be highly uncertain.

The amount of these liquidity sources should be compared with the amount and timing of upcoming debt maturities. A large amount of debt coming due in the next 6–12 months alongside low sources of liquidity will be a warning flag for bond investors and could push an issuer into default because investors may choose not to

---

35 Commercial paper (CP) is short-term funding—fewer than 270 days—used by many large, investment-grade corporations on a daily basis. In practice, issuance of CP requires solid, long-term, investment-grade ratings, mostly A rated or better, with a much smaller market for BBB rated companies.
36 Note that some cash may be "trapped" in other countries for certain tax, business, or regulatory reasons, and may not be easily accessible, or repatriation—bringing the money back to the home country—could trigger cash tax payments.

buy new bonds intended to pay off the existing debt. Insufficient liquidity—that is, running out of cash or no longer having access to external financing to refinance or pay off existing debt—is the principal reason issuers default. Although liquidity is important for industrial companies, it is an absolute necessity for financial firms, as seen in the case of Lehman Brothers and other troubled firms during the financial crisis of 2008. Financial institutions are highly levered and often highly dependent on funding longer-term assets with short-term term liabilities.

Financial Projections. Because high-yield companies have less room for error, it's important to forecast, or project, future earnings and cash flow out several years, perhaps including several scenarios, to assess whether the issuer's credit profile is stable, improving, or declining and thus whether it needs other sources of liquidity or is at risk of default. Ongoing capital expenditures and working capital changes should be incorporated as well. Special emphasis should be given to realistic "stress" scenarios that could expose a borrower's vulnerabilities.

Debt Structure. High-yield companies tend to have many layers of debt in their capital structures, with varying levels of seniority and, therefore, different potential recovery rates in the event of default. (Recall the historical table of default recovery rates based on seniority in Exhibit 2.) A high-yield issuer will often have at least some of the following types of obligations in its debt structure:

- (Secured) Bank debt[37]
- Second lien debt
- Senior unsecured debt
- Subordinated debt, which may include convertible bonds[38]
- Preferred stock[39]

The lower the ranking in the debt structure, the lower the credit rating and the lower the expected recovery in the event of default. In exchange for these associated higher risks, investors will normally demand higher yields.

As discussed in Section 5, the standard leverage calculation used by credit analysts is debt/EBITDA and is quoted as a multiple (e.g., "5.2x levered"). For an issuer with several layers of debt with different expected recovery rates, high-yield analysts should calculate leverage at each level of the debt structure.

Example 10

Debt Structure and Leverage

Freescale Semiconductor specializes in semiconductors that are used in autos, communication equipment, and industrial machinery. This high-yield-rated company's debt structure is complicated because of the many levels of seniority that resulted from the company's 2006 leveraged buyout by a consortium of private equity firms. Exhibit 20 is a simplified depiction of the company's debt structure, as well as some key credit-related statistics.

---

37 Because of the higher risk of default, in most instances bank debt will be secured for high-yield issuers.
38 Convertible bonds are debt instruments that give holders the option to convert to a fixed number of shares of common stock. They can be at any level of the capital structure but are frequently issued as senior subordinated debt.
39 Preferred stock has elements of both debt and equity. It typically receives a fixed payment like a bond does and has higher priority of claims than common stock. As a type of equity, however, it is subordinated to all forms of debt.

Exhibit 20	Freescale Semiconductor Debt and Leverage Structure as of Year-End 2010

Financial Information ($ millions)

Cash	$ 1,050
Total debt	$ 7,611
Net debt	$ 6,561
Interest expense	$ 590
EBITDA	$ 990

Debt Structure ($ millions)

Secured debt (bank loan and bonds)	$ 4,899
Senior unsecured bonds	$ 1,948
Subordinated bonds	$ 764
TOTAL DEBT	$ 7,611

Source: Company Filings, Loomis Sayles & Company.

Using the information provided, address the following:

1. Calculate the total financial leverage through each level of debt, including total gross leverage.
2. Calculate the net leverage through the total debt structure.
3. Why might Freescale have so much secured debt relative to unsecured debt (both senior and subordinated)? (Note: This question draws on concepts from earlier sections.)

Solutions to 1 and 2:

	Gross Leverage	Net Leverage
	(Debt/EBITDA)	(Debt – Cash)/EBITDA
Secured debt leverage		
(Total secured debt/EBITDA)		
4899/990	4.9x	
Senior unsecured leverage		
(Secured debt + Senior unsecured debt)/EBITDA		
(4899 + 1948)/990	6.9x	
Total leverage (includes subordinated)		
(Total debt/EBITDA)		
7611/990	7.7x	

	Gross Leverage	Net Leverage
	(Debt/EBITDA)	(Debt – Cash)/EBITDA
Net leverage (leverage net of cash through entire debt structure) (Total debt – Cash)/EBITDA		6.6x

Solution to 3:

Freescale might have that much secured debt because (1) it was less expensive than issuing more unsecured debt on which investors would have demanded a higher yield and/or (2) given the riskiness of the business (semiconductors that are sold into cyclical industries, such as autos), the operating leverage of the business model, and the riskiness of the balance sheet (lots of debt from a leveraged buyout), investors would only lend the company money on a secured basis.

High-yield companies that have a lot of secured debt (typically bank debt) relative to unsecured debt are said to have a "top-heavy" capital structure. With this structure, there is less capacity to take on more bank debt in the event of financial stress. Along with the often more stringent covenants associated with bank debt and its generally shorter maturity compared with other forms of debt, this means that these issuers are more susceptible to default, as well as to lower recovery for the various less secured creditors.

Corporate Structure. Many debt-issuing corporations, including high-yield companies, utilize a holding company structure with a parent and several operating subsidiaries. Knowing where an issuer's debt resides (parent versus subsidiaries) and how cash can move from subsidiary to parent ("upstream") and vice versa ("downstream") should be key components of the analysis of high-yield issuers.

In a holding company structure, the parent owns stock in its subsidiaries. Typically, the parent doesn't generate much of its own earnings or cash flow but instead receives funds from its subsidiaries in the form of dividends from their earnings. And the subsidiaries' dividends are generally paid out of earnings after they satisfy of all their other obligations, such as debt payments. To the extent that their earnings and cash flow are weak, subsidiaries may be limited in their ability to pay dividends to the parent. Moreover, subsidiaries that carry a lot of their own debt may have restrictions or limitations on how much cash they can provide to the parent via dividends or another form, such as an intercompany loan. These restrictions and limitations on cash moving between parent and subsidiaries can have a major impact on their respective abilities to meet their debt obligations. The parent's reliance on cash flow from its subsidiaries means the parent's debt is structurally subordinated to the subsidiaries' debt and thus will usually have a lower recovery rating in default.

For companies with very complex holding companies, there may also be one or more intermediate holding companies, each carrying their own debt, and in some cases, they may not own 100 percent of the subsidiaries' stock. This structure is sometimes seen in high-yield companies that have been put together through many mergers and acquisitions or that were part of a leveraged buyout.[40]

Exhibit 21 returns to United Rentals, Inc. (URI), a high-yield company highlighted earlier as an example of the credit rating agency notching process. URI has a capital

---

[40] For holding companies with complex corporate structures, such as multiple subsidiaries with their own capital structures, a default in one subsidiary may not trigger a cross-default. Astute analysts will look for that in indentures and other legal documentation.

structure consisting of a parent company that has debt—in this case, convertible senior notes—as well as subsidiaries with outstanding debt. And in the case of URI's United Rentals North America subsidiary, it has several layers of debt by seniority.

Exhibit 21　　URI's Capital Structure

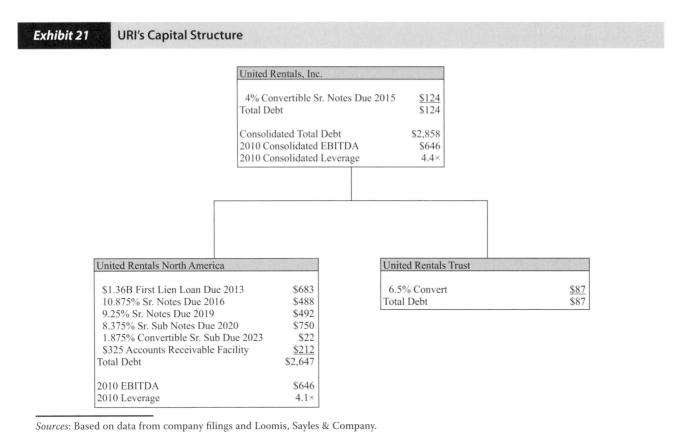

Sources: Based on data from company filings and Loomis, Sayles & Company.

Thus, high-yield investors should analyze and understand an issuer's corporate structure, including the distribution of debt between the parent and its subsidiaries. Leverage ratios should be calculated at each of the debt-issuing entities, as well as on a consolidated basis.

Also important is that although the debt of an operating subsidiary may be "closer to" and better secured by particular assets of the subsidiary, the credit quality of a parent company might still be superior. The parent company could, while being less directly secured by any particular assets, still benefit from the diversity and availability of all the cash flows in the consolidated system. In short, credit quality is not simply an automatic analysis of debt provisions and liens.

Covenant Analysis. As discussed earlier, analysis of covenants is very important for all bonds. It is especially important for high-yield credits because of their reduced margin of safety. Key covenants for high-yield issuers may include the following:

■ Change of control put

■ Restricted payments

■ Limitations on liens and additional indebtedness

■ Restricted versus unrestricted subsidiaries

Under the **change of control put**, in the event of an acquisition (a "change of control"), bondholders have the right to require the issuer to buy back their debt (a "put option"), often at par or at some small premium to par value. This covenant is intended to protect creditors from being exposed to a weaker, more indebted borrower as a result of acquisition. For investment-grade issuers, this covenant typically has a two-pronged test: acquisition of the borrower and a consequent downgrade to a high-yield rating.

The **restricted payments** covenant is meant to protect creditors by limiting how much cash can be paid out to shareholders over time. The restricted payments "basket" is typically sized relative to an issuer's cash flow and debt outstanding—or is being raised—and is an amount that can grow with retained earnings or cash flow, giving management more flexibility to make pay-outs.

The **limitations on liens** covenant is meant to put limits on how much secured debt an issuer can have. This covenant is important to unsecured creditors who are structurally subordinated to secured creditors; the higher the amount of debt that is layered ahead of them, the less they stand to recover in the event of default.

With regard to **restricted versus unrestricted subsidiaries**, issuers may classify certain of their subsidiaries as restricted and others as unrestricted as it pertains to offering guarantees for their holding company debt. These subsidiary guarantees can be very useful to holding company creditors because they put their debt on equal standing (pari passu) with debt at the subsidiaries instead of with structurally subordinated debt. Restricted subsidiaries should be thought of as those that are designated to help service parent-level debt, typically through guarantees. They tend to be an issuer's larger subsidiaries and have significant assets, such as plants and other facilities, and/or cash flow. There may be tax or legal (e.g., country of domicile) reasons why certain subsidiaries are restricted while others are not. Analysts should carefully read the definitions of restricted versus unrestricted subsidiaries in the indenture because sometimes the language is so loosely written that the company can reclassify subsidiaries from one type to another with a simple vote by a board of directors or trustees.

For high-yield investors, it is also important to know what covenants are in an issuer's bank credit agreements. These agreements are typically filed with the securities commission in the country where the loan document was drafted. Bank covenants can be more restrictive than bond covenants and may include so-called **maintenance covenants**, such as leverage tests, whereby the ratio of, say, debt/EBITDA may not exceed "x" times. In the event a covenant is breached, the bank is likely to block further loans under the agreement until the covenant is cured. If not cured, the bank may accelerate full payment of the facility, triggering a default.

Equity-like approach to high-yield analysis. High-yield bonds are sometimes thought of as a "hybrid" between higher-quality bonds, such as investment-grade corporate debt, and equity securities. Their more volatile price and spread movements are less influenced by interest rate changes than are higher-quality bonds, and they show greater correlation with movements in equity markets. Indeed, as shown in Exhibit 22, historical returns on high-yield bonds and the standard deviation of those returns fall somewhere between investment-grade bonds and equities.

Exhibit 22	U.S. Trailing 12-Month Returns by Asset Class, 31 December 1988–30 June 2011

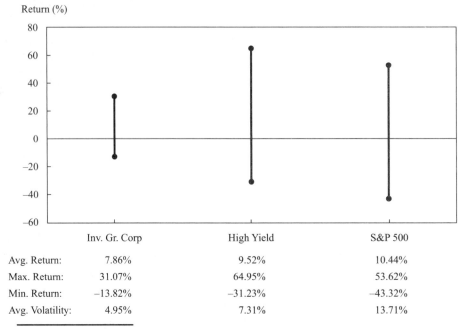

	Inv. Gr. Corp	High Yield	S&P 500
Avg. Return:	7.86%	9.52%	10.44%
Max. Return:	31.07%	64.95%	53.62%
Min. Return:	−13.82%	−31.23%	−43.32%
Avg. Volatility:	4.95%	7.31%	13.71%

Sources: Based on data from Barclays, Haver Analytics, and Loomis, Sayles & Company.

Consequently, an equity market-like approach to analyzing a high-yield issuer can be useful. One approach is to calculate an issuer's enterprise value. Enterprise value (EV) is usually calculated by adding equity market capitalization and total debt and then subtracting excess cash.[41,42] Enterprise value is a measure of what a business is worth (before any takeover premium) because an acquirer of the company would have to either pay off or assume the debt and it would receive the acquired company's cash.

Bond investors like using EV because it shows the amount of equity "cushion" beneath the debt. It can also give a sense of (1) how much more leverage management might attempt to put on a company in an effort to increase equity returns or (2) how likely—and how expensive—a credit-damaging leveraged buyout might be. Similar to how stock investors look at equity multiples, bond investors may calculate and compare EV/EBITDA and debt/EBITDA across several issuers as part of their analysis. Narrow differences between the EV/EBITDA and debt/EBITDA ratios for a given issuer indicate a small equity cushion and, therefore, potentially higher risk for bond investors.

7.2 Sovereign Debt

Governments around the world issue debt to help finance their general operations, including current expenses such as wages for government employees, and investments in long-term assets such as infrastructure and education. Government bonds in developed countries (such as the United States) have traditionally been viewed as

---

41 Excess cash takes total cash and subtracts any negative working capital.
42 Unlike the vast majority of investment-grade companies, many high-yield issuers do not have publicly traded equity. For those issuers, one can use comparable public company equity data to estimate EV.

the default risk-free rate off of which all other credits are priced. Fiscal challenges in developed countries exacerbated by the 2008 crisis, however, have called into question the notion of a "risk-free rate," even for some of the highest-quality government borrowers. As their capital markets have developed, an increasing number of sovereigns have been able to issue both external debt (denominated in hard currency, often the U.S. dollar) as well as local debt (issued in the sovereign's own currency). Generally, weaker sovereigns can only access international (that is, non-local) debt markets by issuing bonds in foreign currencies that are viewed to be safer stores of value. Local—also known as internal—debt is somewhat easier to service because the debt is typically denominated in the country's own currency, subject to its own laws, and the central bank can print additional money to service the government's local debt. Twenty years ago, many emerging market countries[43] could only issue external debt. Today, many are able to issue local debt and have successfully built domestic yield curves of local bonds across the maturity spectrum. All sovereigns are best able to service both external and local debt if they run "twin surpluses"—that is, a government budget surplus as well as a current account surplus. Running a current account surplus means the country is a net exporter of capital to the world and is not dependent on external financing.

Despite ongoing financial globalization and the development of local bond markets, sovereign defaults continue. Defaults are often precipitated by such events as war, political upheaval, major currency devaluation, a sharp deterioration in trade, or dramatic price declines in a country's key commodity exports. But default risks for some developed countries escalated after 2009 as government revenues dropped precipitously following the financial crisis, expenditures surged, and financial markets focused on the long-term sustainability of public finances, given aging populations and rising social security needs. Some of the weaker and more highly indebted members of the eurozone became unable to access the debt markets at economical rates and had to seek loans from the International Monetary Fund (IMF) and the European Union. These weaker governments had previously been able to borrow at much lower rates because of their membership in the European Union and adoption of the euro. Intra-eurozone yield spreads widened and countries were shut out of markets, however, as the global financial crisis exacted a high toll on their public finances and, in some cases, their banking systems, which became contingent liabilities for the sovereigns. In Ireland, the government guaranteed most bank liabilities, causing the country's debt burden to increase dramatically.

Like corporate analysis, sovereign credit analysis is based on a combination of qualitative and quantitative factors. Ultimately, the two key issues for sovereign analysis are 1) a government's ability to pay and 2) its willingness to pay. Willingness to pay is important because, due to the principle of sovereign immunity, investors are generally unable to force a sovereign to pay its debts.

To illustrate the most important considerations in sovereign credit analysis, we present a basic framework for evaluating sovereign credit and assigning sovereign debt ratings.[44] The framework highlights the specific characteristics analysts should expect in a top-quality sovereign credit. Some of these are self-explanatory (e.g., absence of corruption). For others, a brief rationale and/or range of values is included to clarify interpretation. Most, but not all, of these items are included in rating agency Standard & Poor's methodology.

---

43 There is no commonly accepted definition of emerging market countries. The World Bank considers GDP/Capita to be a useful measure, with below-average GDP/Capita likely indicating an emerging market. Other factors include the degree of openness and maturity of the economy, as well as a country's political stability.

44 This outline was developed from the detailed exposition of Standard & Poor's methodology given in "Sovereign Government Rating Methodology and Assumptions," June 2011.

Political and economic profile

- *Institutional effectiveness and political risks*
  - *Effectiveness, stability, and predictability of policy making and institutions*
    - Successful management of past political, economic, and/or financial crises
    - Ability and willingness to implement reforms to address fiscal challenges
    - Predictable policy framework
    - Absence of challenges to political institutions
    - Checks and balances in the system
    - Absence of corruption
    - Unbiased law enforcement and respect for rule of law and property rights
    - Independent/ unfettered media and sources of economic data
  - *Perceived commitment to honor debts*
- *Economic structure and growth prospects*
  - Income per capita: More prosperous countries generally have a broader and deeper tax base with which to support debt.
  - Trend growth prospects: Trend GDP growth is primarily a reflection of productivity. Above-average trend growth indicates greater ability to service debt from future revenue and, therefore, greater creditworthiness.
  - Sources and stability of growth: Stable, broad-based growth and absence of excessive private sector credit expansion indicate stronger sovereign credit.
  - Size of the public sector relative to private sector: A smaller, leaner public sector is more likely to be able to enact necessary changes because it should be less beholden to special interest groups, including public employee unions.
  - Growth and age distribution of population: A relatively young and growing population contributes to trend GDP growth and an expanding tax base and mitigates the burden of social services, health care, and pensions, which are disproportionately costly for aging populations.

Flexibility and performance profile

- *External liquidity and international investment position*
  - Status of currency: Sovereigns that control a reserve currency or a very actively traded currency are able to use their own currency in many international transactions and are less vulnerable to adverse shifts in global investor portfolios.
  - External liquidity: Countries with a substantial supply of foreign exchange (foreign exchange reserves plus current account receipts) relative to projected external funding needs (current account payments plus debt maturities) are less vulnerable to interruption of external liquidity.
  - External debt: Countries with low external debt relative to current account receipts are better able to service their foreign currency debt. This is similar to that of a coverage ratio for a corporation.
- *Fiscal performance, flexibility, and debt burden*
  - Trend change in general government debt as a percent of GDP: Stable or declining debt as a percent of GDP indicates a strong credit; a rising ratio is ultimately unsustainable and is, therefore, a sign of diminishing creditworthiness.

- Perceived willingness and ability to increase revenue or cut expenditure to ensure debt service.

- General government interest expense as a percent of revenue: Less than 5 percent is good; greater than 15 percent is poor.

- Net general government debt as a percent of GDP: Less than 30 percent is good; more than 100 percent is poor.

- Contingent liabilities arising from financial sector, public enterprises, and guarantees: Less than 30 percent of GDP is good; more than 80 percent is very poor.

■ *Monetary flexibility*

- *Ability to use monetary policy to address domestic economic objectives* (e.g., growth)
  - Exchange rate regime: A freely floating currency allows maximum effectiveness for monetary policy. A fixed-rate regime limits effectiveness and flexibility. A hard peg, such as a currency board or monetary union, affords no independent monetary policy.

- *Credibility of monetary policy*
  - Operationally independent central bank: An independent central bank is less likely to "debase the currency" by excessive money creation (e.g., in order to fund government deficits).
  - Clear central bank mandate/objectives
  - Track record of low and stable inflation
  - Central government's ability to issue substantial long-term, fixed-rate debt in local currency: This is a sign of market confidence in the currency as a store of value.

- *Effectiveness of monetary policy transmission via domestic capital markets*
  - Well-developed banking system
  - Active money market and corporate bond market
  - Greater reliance on market-based policy tools (e.g., open market operations) and limited reliance on blunt, administrative policy tools (e.g., reserve requirements)

In light of a sovereign government's various powers—taxation, regulation, monetary policy, and ultimately, the sovereign's ability to "print money" to repay debt—within its own economy, it is virtually always at least as good a credit in its local currency as it is in foreign currency. Thus, credit rating agencies often distinguish between local and foreign currency bonds, with local currency ratings as much as two notches higher. Of course, if a sovereign were to rely heavily on printing money to repay debt, it would fuel high inflation or hyperinflation and increase default risk on local debt as well.[45]

Example 11

Sovereign Debt

Exhibit 23 shows several key sovereign statistics for Portugal.

---

45 According to Reinhart and Rogoff in their book *This Time is Different*, between 1800 and 2009 there have been more than 250 defaults on external sovereign debt and at least 68 defaults on internal debt. Reinhart and Rogoff use a broader definition of default that includes very high levels of inflation (more than 20 percent).

| **Exhibit 23** | **Key Sovereign Statistics for Portugal** | | | | | |

€ (billions), except where noted	2005	2006	2007	2008	2009	2010
Nominal GDP	153.7	160.3	169.3	171.2	168.6	172.6
Population (millions)	10.6	10.6	10.6	10.6	10.6	10.6
Unemployment (%)	8.6	8.6	8.9	8.5	10.6	12.0
Exports as share GDP (%)	20.3	22.2	22.6	22.6	18.8	21.3
Current account as share GDP (%)	−10.3	−10.7	−10.1	−12.6	−10.9	−10.0
Government revenues	61.3	64.8	69.7	70.7	67.0	71.8
Government expenditures	70.4	71.4	75.1	77.1	84.1	88.7
Budget balance (surplus/deficit)	−9.0	−6.5	−5.4	−6.4	−17.1	−16.9
Government interest payments	3.8	4.2	5.1	5.3	4.9	5.2
Primary balance (surplus/deficit)	−5.3	−2.2	−0.4	−1.1	−12.2	−11.7
Government debt	96.5	102.4	115.6	123.1	139.9	161.3
Interest rate on new debt (%)	3.4	3.9	4.4	4.5	4.2	5.4

Sources: Based on data from Haver Analytics, Eurostat, and Instituto Nacional de Estatistica (Portugal).

1. Calculate the government debt/GDP ratio for Portugal over the years 2005–2010.

2. Calculate GDP/Capita for the same period.

3. Based on those calculations, as well as other data from Exhibit 23, what can you say about Portugal's credit trend?

Solutions to 1 and 2:

	2005	2006	2007	2008	2009	2010
Gross government debt/GDP	63%	64%	68%	72%	83%	93%
GDP/Capita	14,500	15,123	15,972	16,151	15,906	16,283

Solution to 3:

The credit trend is deteriorating. Government debt/GDP is rising rapidly. The government is running a budget deficit, and the country is running a sizable current account deficit, which means it must attract funding from outside the country. Interest payments are generally rising, as is the interest rate on new debt.

7.3 Municipal Debt

While sovereigns are the largest issuers of government debt, non-sovereign—sometimes called sub-sovereign—government entities issue bonds as well. This would include state, provincial, and local governments (e.g., cities, towns, and counties, often referred to as municipalities) as well as the various agencies and authorities they create. For example, the City of Tokyo (Tokyo Metropolitan Government) has debt outstanding, as does the Lombardy region in Italy, the City of Buenos Aires in Argentina, and the State of California in the United States.

When people talk about municipal debt securities, however, they are usually referring to the U.S. municipal bond market because of its size. This market is approximately $3.7 trillion in size, roughly 10 percent of the total U.S. bond market,[46] and is composed of both tax-exempt[47] and, to a lesser extent, taxable bonds issued by state and local governments and their agencies. Municipal borrowers may also issue bonds on behalf of private entities, such as non-profit colleges or hospitals. Historically, for any given rating category, these bonds have much lower default rates than corporate bonds with the same ratings. For example, according to Moody's Investors Service, the 10-year average cumulative default rate from 1970 through 2009 was 0.09 percent for municipal bonds, compared with an 11.06 percent 10-year average cumulative default rate for all corporate debt.[48] The majority of municipal bonds are either general obligation bonds or revenue bonds.

General obligation (GO) bonds are unsecured bonds issued with the full faith and credit of the issuing government, typically a city, county, or state. These bonds are supported by the taxing authority of the issuer. The credit analysis of GO bonds has some similarities to sovereign debt analysis (e.g., the ability to levy and collect taxes and fees to help service debt). Almost without exception, however, municipalities must balance their operating budgets (i.e., exclusive of long-term capital projects) annually and they have no ability to use monetary policy the way many sovereigns can. The economic analysis focuses on employment, per capita income (and changes in it over time), per capita debt (and changes in it over time), the tax base (depth, breadth, diversification, stability, etc.), demographics, and net population growth, as well as an analysis of whether the state or municipality has the infrastructure and location to attract and support new jobs. Analysis should look at the volatility and variability of revenues during times of both economic strength and weakness. An overreliance on one or two types of tax revenue—particularly a volatile one, such as capital gains taxes or sales taxes—can signal increased credit risk. Pensions and other post-retirement obligations may not show up directly on the state or municipality's balance sheet, and many of these entities have underfunded pensions that need to be addressed. Adding the unfunded pension and post-retirement obligations to the debt reveals a more realistic picture of the issuer's debt and longer-term obligations. The relative ease or difficulty in managing the annual budgeting process and the government's ability to operate consistently within its budget are also important credit analysis considerations.

Disclosure by state and local governments varies widely, with some of the smaller issuers providing limited financial information. Reporting requirements are inconsistent, so the financial reports may not be available for six months or more after the closing of a reporting period.

Exhibit 24 compares several key debt statistics from two of the largest states in the United States: California and Texas. California has one of the lowest credit ratings of any of the states, whereas Texas has one of the highest. Note the higher debt burden (and ranking) across several measures: Total debt, Debt/Capita, Debt/Personal income, and debt as a percent of state GDP. What is not shown here is that California also has a higher tax burden and greater difficulty balancing its budget on an annual basis than Texas.

---

46 Securities Industry and Financial Markets Association (SIFMA), "Outstanding U.S. Bond Market Data," (Q3 2011).

47 Tax exempt refers to the fact that interest received on these bonds is not subject to U.S. federal income taxes and, in many cases, is exempt for in-state residents from state and local taxes as well.

48 Moody's Investors Service, "U.S. Municipal Bond Defaults and Recoveries, 1970–2009," Moody's Special Comment (February 2010).

Exhibit 24	Municipal Debt Comparison: California vs. Texas	
	California	Texas
Ratings:		
Moody's Investors Service	A1	Aaa
Standard & Poor's	A–	AA+
Fitch	A–	AAA
Unemployment rate (%)	12.40	8.20
Personal income per capita ($)	43,641	37,774
Debt burden, net ($/rank):		
Total (millions)	94,715 (1)	15,433 (9)
Per capita	2,542 (8)	612 (39)
As a percent of 2009 personal income	6.00 (9)	1.60 (40)
As a percent of 2010 GDP	4.73 (8)	1.05 (41)

Sources: Based on data from the U.S. Bureau of Labor Statistics (as of 2010), the U.S. Census Bureau (as of 2008), and Moody's Investors Service (as of 2010).

Revenue bonds are issued for specific project financing (e.g., financing for a new sewer system, a toll road, bridge, hospital, a sports arena, etc.). Revenue bonds have a higher degree of risk than GO bonds because they are dependent on a single source of revenue. The analysis of these bonds is a combination of an analysis of the project and the finances around the particular project. The project analysis focuses on the need and projected utilization of the project, as well as on the economic base supporting the project. The financial analysis has some similarities to the analysis of a corporate bond in that it is focused on operating results, cash flow, liquidity, capital structure, and the ability to service and repay the debt. A key credit metric for revenue-backed municipal bonds is the debt service coverage ratio (DSCR), which measures how much revenue is available to cover debt payments (principal and interest) after operating expenses. Many revenue bonds have a minimum DSCR covenant; the higher the DSCR, the stronger the creditworthiness.

8   CONCLUSION AND SUMMARY

In this reading, we introduced readers to the basic principles of credit analysis. We described the importance of the credit markets and the various types of credit risk. We discussed the role and importance of credit ratings and the methodology associated with assigning ratings, as well as the risks of relying on credit ratings. The reading covered the key components of credit analysis and the financial ratios used to help measure creditworthiness.

We also discussed risk versus return when investing in credit and how spread changes affect holding period returns. In addition, we addressed the special considerations to take into account when doing credit analysis of high-yield companies, sovereign borrowers, and municipal bonds.

■ Credit risk is the risk of loss resulting from the borrower failing to make full and timely payments of interest and/or principal.

- The key components of credit risk are risk of default and loss severity in the event of default. The product of the two is expected loss. Investors in higher-quality bonds tend not to focus on loss severity because default risk for those securities is low.

- Loss severity equals (1 − Recovery rate).

- Other forms of credit-related risk include downgrade risk (also called credit migration risk) and market liquidity risk. Either of these can cause yield spreads—yield premiums—to rise and bond prices to fall.

- Downgrade risk refers to a decline in an issuer's creditworthiness. Downgrades will cause its bonds to trade at wider yields and thus lower prices.

- Market liquidity risk refers to a widening of the bid–ask spread on an issuer's bonds. Lower-quality bonds tend to have greater market liquidity risk than higher-quality bonds, and during times of market or financial stress, market liquidity risk rises.

- The composition of an issuer's debt and equity is referred to as its "capital structure." Debt ranks ahead of all forms of equity with respect to priority of payment, and within the debt component of the capital structure, there can be varying levels of seniority.

- With respect to priority of claims, secured debt ranks ahead of unsecured debt, and within unsecured debt, senior debt ranks ahead of subordinated debt. In the typical case, all of an issuer's bonds have the same probability of default due to cross-default provisions in most indentures. Higher priority of claim means higher recovery rate—lower loss severity—in the event of default.

- For issuers with more complex corporate structures—for example, a parent holding company that has operating subsidiaries—debt at the holding company is structurally subordinated to the subsidiary debt, although the possibility of more diverse assets and earnings streams from other sources could still result in the parent having higher effective credit quality than a particular subsidiary.

- Recovery rates can vary greatly by issuer and industry. They are influenced by the composition of an issuer's capital structure, where in the economic and credit cycle the default occurred, and what the market's view of the future prospects are for the issuer and its industry.

- The priority of claims in bankruptcy is not always absolute. It can be influenced by several factors, including some leeway accorded to bankruptcy judges, government involvement, or a desire on the part of the more senior creditors to settle with the more junior creditors and allow the issuer to emerge from bankruptcy as a going concern, rather than risking smaller and delayed recovery in the event of a liquidation of the borrower.

- Credit rating agencies, such as Moody's, Standard & Poor's, and Fitch, play a central role in the credit markets. Nearly every bond issued in the broad debt markets carries credit ratings, which are opinions about a bond issue's creditworthiness. Credit ratings enable investors to compare the credit risk of debt issues and issuers within a given industry, across industries, and across geographic markets.

- Bonds rated Aaa to Baa3 by Moody's and AAA to BBB− by Standard & Poor's (S&P) and/or Fitch (higher to lower) are referred to as "investment grade." Bonds rated lower than that—Ba1 or lower by Moody's and BB+ or lower by S&P and/or Fitch—are referred to as "below investment grade" or "speculative grade." Below-investment-grade bonds are also called "high-yield" or "junk" bonds.

- The rating agencies rate both issuers and issues. Issuer ratings are meant to address an issuer's overall creditworthiness—its risk of default. Ratings for issues incorporate such factors as their rankings in the capital structure.

- The rating agencies will notch issue ratings up or down to account for such factors as capital structure ranking for secured or subordinated bonds, reflecting different recovery rates in the event of default. Ratings may also be notched due to structural subordination.

- There are risks in relying too much on credit agency ratings. Because creditworthiness is dynamic, initial/current ratings do not necessarily reflect the evolution of credit quality over an investor's holding period. Importantly, bond ratings do not always capture price risk because valuations often adjust before ratings change and the notching process may not adequately reflect the price decline of a bond that is lower ranked in the capital structure. Similarly, because ratings primarily reflect the probability of default but not necessarily the severity of loss given default, bonds with the same rating may have significantly different expected losses (default probability times loss severity). And like analysts, credit rating agencies may have difficulty forecasting certain credit-negative outcomes, such as adverse litigation, leveraging corporate transactions, and such low likelihood/high severity events as earthquakes and hurricanes.

- The role of corporate credit analysis is to assess the company's ability to make timely payments of interest and repay principal at maturity. Analysts focus on an issuer's ability to generate cash flow by doing an assessment of the company as well as the industry in which it operates.

- Credit analysis is similar to equity analysis. It is important to understand, however, that bonds are contracts and that management's duty to bondholders and other creditors is limited to the terms of the contract. In contrast, management's duty to shareholders is to act in their best interest by trying to maximize the value of the company—perhaps even at the expense of bondholders at times.

- Credit analysts tend to focus more on the downside risk given the asymmetry of risk/return, whereas equity analysts focus more on upside opportunity from earnings growth, and so on.

- The "4 Cs" of credit analysis—capacity, collateral, covenants, and character—provide a useful framework for evaluating credit risk.

- Credit analysis focuses on an issuer's ability to generate cash flow. The analysis starts with an industry assessment—structure and fundamentals—and continues with an analysis of an issuer's competitive position, management strategy, and track record. Key credit ratios focus on debt leverage and interest coverage and use such measures as EBITDA, free cash flow, funds from operations, balance sheet debt, and adjustments, such as leases, pensions, and other retiree benefits.

- Credit ratios are used to calculate an issuer's creditworthiness, as well as to compare its credit quality with peer companies.

- An issuer's ability to access liquidity is also an important consideration in credit analysis.

- The higher the credit risk, the greater the offered/required yield and potential return demanded by investors. Over time, bonds with more credit risk offer higher returns but with greater volatility of return than bonds with lower credit risk.

- The yield on a credit-risky bond comprises the yield on a default risk–free bond with a comparable maturity plus a yield premium, or "spread," that comprises a credit spread and a liquidity premium. That spread is intended to compensate investors for credit risk—risk of default and loss severity in the event of default—and the credit-related risks that can cause spreads to widen and prices to decline—downgrade or credit migration risk, as well as market liquidity risk.

Yield spread = Liquidity premium + Credit spread.

- In times of financial market stress, the liquidity premium can increase sharply, causing spreads to widen on all credit-risky bonds, with lower-quality issuers most affected. In times of credit improvement or stability, however, credit spreads can narrow sharply as well, providing attractive investment returns.

- Credit curves—the plot of yield spreads for a given bond issuer across the yield curve—are typically upward sloping, with the exception of high premium-priced bonds and distressed bonds, where credit curves can be inverted because of the fear of default, when all creditors at a given ranking in the capital structure will receive the same recovery rate without regard to debt maturity.

- The impact of spread changes on holding period returns for credit-risky bonds are a product of two primary factors: the basis point spread change and the sensitivity of price to yield as reflected by (end-of-period) modified duration and convexity. Spread narrowing enhances holding period returns, whereas spread widening has a negative impact on holding period returns. Longer-duration bonds have greater price and return sensitivity to changes in spread than shorter-duration bonds.

Return impact $\approx -(\text{MDur} \times \Delta\text{Spread}) + \frac{1}{2}\text{Cvx} \times (\Delta\text{Spread})^2$

- For high-yield bonds, with their greater risk of default, more emphasis should be placed on an issuer's sources of liquidity, as well as on its debt structure and corporate structure. Credit risk can vary greatly across an issuer's debt structure depending on the seniority ranking. Many high-yield companies often have complex capital structures, resulting in different levels of credit risk depending on where the debt resides.

- Covenant analysis is especially important for high-yield bonds. Key covenants include payment restrictions, limitation on liens, change of control, coverage maintenance tests (often limited to bank loans), and any guarantees from restricted subsidiaries. Covenant language can be very technical and legalistic, so it may help to seek legal or expert assistance.

- An equity-like approach to high-yield analysis can be helpful. Calculating and comparing enterprise value with EBITDA and debt/EBITDA can show a level of equity "cushion" or support beneath an issuer's debt.

- Sovereign credit analysis includes assessing both an issuer's ability and willingness to pay its debt obligations. Willingness to pay is important because, due to sovereign immunity, a sovereign government cannot be forced to pay its debts.

- In assessing sovereign credit risk, a helpful framework is to focus on five broad areas: (1) institutional effectiveness and political risks, (2) economic structure and growth prospects, (3) external liquidity and international investment position, (4) fiscal performance, flexibility, and debt burden, and (5) monetary flexibility.

- Among the characteristics of a high-quality sovereign credit are the absence of corruption and/or challenges to political framework; governmental checks and balances; respect for rule of law and property rights; commitment to honor debts; high per capita income with stable, broad-based growth prospects;

control of a reserve or actively traded currency; currency flexibility; low external debt and external financing needs relative to external receipts; stable or declining ratio of debt to GDP; low debt service as a percent of revenue; low ratio of net debt to GDP; operationally independent central bank; track record of low and stable inflation; and a well-developed banking system and active money market.

■ In the United States, there are two basic kinds of municipal debt: general obligation bonds and revenue-backed bonds.

■ General obligation (GO) bonds are backed by the taxing authority of the issuing municipality (e.g., state or city). The credit analysis of GO bonds has some similarities to sovereign analysis—debt burden per capita versus income per capita, tax burden, demographics, and economic diversity. Underfunded and "off-balance-sheet" liabilities, such as pensions for public employees and retirees, are debt-like in nature.

■ Revenue-backed bonds support specific projects, such as toll roads, bridges, airports, and other infrastructure. The creditworthiness comes from the revenues generated by usage fees and tolls levied.

PRACTICE PROBLEMS FOR READING 42

1. The risk that a bond's creditworthiness declines is *best* described by:
   A. credit migration risk.
   B. market liquidity risk.
   C. spread widening risk.

2. Stedsmart Ltd and Fignermo Ltd are alike with respect to financial and operating characteristics, except that Stedsmart Ltd has less publicly traded debt outstanding than Fignermo Ltd. Therefore, Stedsmart Ltd is *most likely* to have:
   A. no market liquidity risk.
   B. lower market liquidity risk.
   C. higher market liquidity risk.

3. In the event of default, debentures' claims will *most likely* rank:
   A. above that of secured debt holders.
   B. below that of secured debt holders.
   C. the same as that of secured debt holders.

4. In the event of default, the recovery rate of which of the following bonds would *most likely* be the highest?
   A. First mortgage debt
   B. Senior unsecured debt
   C. Junior subordinate debt

5. During bankruptcy proceedings of a firm, the priority of claims was not strictly adhered to. Which of the following is the *least likely* explanation for this outcome?
   A. Senior creditors compromised.
   B. The value of secured assets was less than the amount of the claims.
   C. The judge's order resulted in actual claims not adhering to strict priority of claims.

6. Although rating agencies assess the creditworthiness of debt issuers and issues, the *least likely* reason that a fixed income analyst should conduct an independent analysis of credit risk is because rating agencies:
   A. may at times mis-rate issues.
   B. often lag the market in pricing credit risk.
   C. cannot foresee future debt-financed acquisitions.

7. Jaco Meyer, a credit analyst, is analyzing the human capital of a company. Such an analysis will *most likely* give Meyer insight into the:
   A. quality of the company's management.
   B. strength of the company's balance sheet.
   C. power of the company's customers.

8. If goodwill makes up a large percentage of a company's total assets, this *most likely* indicates that:
   A. the company has low free cash flow before dividends.
   B. there is a low likelihood that the market price of the company's common stock is below book value.
   C. a large percentage of the company's assets are of low quality.

9. In order to analyze the **collateral** of a company a credit analyst should assess the:

   A. cash flows of the company.

   B. soundness of management's strategy.

   C. value of the company's assets in relation to the level of debt.

10. In order to determine the **capacity** of a company, it would be *most* appropriate to analyze the:

    A. company's strategy.

    B. growth prospects of the industry.

    C. aggressiveness of the company's accounting policies.

11. A credit analyst is evaluating the credit worthiness of three companies: a construction company, a travel and tourism company, and a beverage company. Both the construction and travel and tourism companies are cyclical, whereas the beverage company is non-cyclical. The construction company has the highest debt level of the three companies. The highest credit risk is *most likely* exhibited by the:

    A. construction company.

    B. beverage company.

    C. travel and tourism company.

12. Based on the information provided in Exhibit 1, the EBITDA interest coverage ratio of Adidas AG is *closest* to:

    A. 7.91x.

    B. 10.12x.

    C. 12.99x.

Exhibit 1	Adidas AG Excerpt from Consolidated Income Statement Year ending 31 December 2010 (€ in millions)
Gross profit	5,730
Royalty and commission income	100
Other operating income	110
Other operating expenses	5,046
Operating profit	894
Interest income	25
Interest expense	113
Income before taxes	806
Income taxes	238
Net income	568

Additional information:
Depreciation and amortization: €249 million

Source: Adidas AG Annual Financial Statements, December 2010

13. The following information is from the annual report of Adidas AG for December 2010:

    ● Depreciation and amortization: €249 million

    ● Total assets: €10,618 million

    ● Total debt: €1,613 million

    ● Shareholders' equity: €4,616 million

The debt/capital ratio of Adidas AG is *closest* to:

A. 15.19%.

B. 25.90%.

C. 34.94%.

14. Funds from operations (FFO) of Pay Handle Ltd increased in 2011. In 2011 the total debt of the company remained unchanged, while additional common shares were issued. Pay Handle Ltd's ability to service its debt in 2011, as compared to 2010, *most likely*:

A. improved.

B. worsened.

C. remained the same.

15. Based on the information in Exhibit 2, Grupa Zywiec SA's credit risk is *most likely*:

A. lower than the industry.

B. higher than the industry.

C. the same as the industry.

Exhibit 2	European Food, Beverage, and Tobacco Industry and Grupa Zywiec SA Selected Financial Ratios for 2010				
	Total debt/Total capital (%)	FFO/ Total debt (%)	Return on capital (%)	Total debt/ EBITDA (x)	EBITDA interest coverage (x)
Grupa Zywiec SA	47.1	77.5	19.6	1.2	17.7
Industry Median	**42.4**	**23.6**	**6.55**	**2.85**	**6.45**

16. Based on the information in Exhibit 3, the credit rating of Davide Campari-Milano S.p.A. is *most likely*:

A. lower than Associated British Foods plc.

B. higher than Associated British Foods plc.

C. the same as Associated British Foods plc.

Exhibit 3	European Food, Beverage, and Tobacco Industry; Associated British Foods plc; and Davide Campari-Milano S.p.A Selected Financial Ratios, 2010				
Company	Total debt/total capital (%)	FFO/ total debt (%)	Return on capital (%)	Total debt/ EBITDA (x)	EBITDA interest coverage (x)
Associated British Foods plc	0.2	84.3	0.1	1.0	13.9
Davide Campari-Milano S.p.A.	42.9	22.9	8.2	3.2	3.2
European Food, Beverage, and Tobacco Median	**42.4**	**23.6**	**6.55**	**2.85**	**6.45**

17. Holding all other factors constant, the *most likely* effect of low demand and heavy new issue supply on bond yield spreads is that yield spreads will:

   A. widen.

   B. tighten.

   C. not be affected.

18. A credit analyst is assessing a two-year, 13.5% coupon bond with a 1.77 duration. Because of a recent slump in operating revenue, the bond's yield to maturity has increased from 7.20% to 7.50%. The impact of the change in yield to maturity on the return of the bond is *closest* to:

   A. 0.53%.

   B. −0.53%.

   C. −0.60%.

SOLUTIONS FOR READING 42

1. A is correct. Credit migration risk or downgrade risk refers to the risk that a bond issuer's creditworthiness may deteriorate or migrate lower. The result is that investors view the risk of default to be higher, causing the spread on the issuer's bonds to widen.

2. C is correct. Market liquidity risk refers to the risk that the price at which investors transact may be different from the price indicated in the market. Market liquidity risk is increased by (1) less debt outstanding and/or (2) a lower issue credit rating. Because Stedsmart Ltd is comparable to Fignermo Ltd except for less publicly traded debt outstanding, it should have higher market liquidity risk.

3. B is correct. Secured debt holders have a direct claim on certain assets and their associated cash flows whereas unsecured debt holders only have a general claim on the issuer's assets and cash flow.

4. A is correct. First mortgage debt is the highest ranked debt in terms of priority of claims and is considered secured debt. First mortgage debt will also have the expected highest recovery rate. First mortgage debt refers to the pledge of specific property. Neither senior unsecured nor junior subordinate debt has any claims on specific assets.

5. B is correct. Whether or not secured assets are sufficient for the claims, this would not influence priority of claims. The difference between pledge assets and the claim becomes senior unsecured debt and still adheres to the guidelines of priority of claims.

6. C is correct. Neither an analyst nor ratings agencies can anticipate unexpected events.

7. B is correct. An analysis of the human capital of a company is the purpose of assessing the strength of its balance sheets or, stated differently, the value and quality of assets supporting the issuer's indebtedness (i.e., collateral).

8. C is correct. Goodwill is viewed as a lower quality asset compared with tangible assets that can be sold and more easily converted into cash.

9. C is correct. The value of assets in relation to the level of debt is important to assess the collateral of the company; that is, the quality and value of the assets that support the debt levels of the company.

10. B is correct. The growth prospects of the industry provide the analyst insight regarding the capacity of the company.

11. A is correct. The construction company is both highly leveraged which increases credit risk and in a highly cyclical industry which results in more volatile earnings. The beverage company is in a non-cyclical industry with less volatile earnings.

12. B is correct. The interest expense is €113 million and EBITDA = Operating profit + Depreciation and amortization = €894 + 249 million = €1,143 million. EBITDA interest coverage = EBITDA/Interest expense = 1,143/113 = 10.12 times.

13. B is correct. Total debt is €1,613 million with Total capital = Total debt + Shareholders' equity = €1,613 + 4,616 = €6,229 million. The Debt/Capital ratio = 1,613/6,229 = 25.90%.

14. A is correct. If the debt of the company remained unchanged but FFO increased, more cash is available to service debt compared to the previous

year. Additionally, the debt/capital ratio has improved. It would imply that the ability of Pay Handle Ltd to service their debt has improved.

15. A is correct. Based on four of the five credit ratios, Grupa Zywiec SA's credit quality is superior to that of the industry.

16. A is correct. Davide Campari-Milano S.p.A. has more financial leverage and less interest coverage than Associated British Foods plc, which implies greater credit risk.

17. A is correct. Low demand implies wider yield spreads, while heavy supply will widen spreads even further.

18. B is correct. Return impact $\approx -(\Delta \text{Spread} \times \text{Duration}_{\text{End}})$

Higher credit risk implies widening of the spread by 30 basis points and a lower return.

Return impact = −(30 basis points × 1.77 years) = −53.1 basis points = −0.531%

Term Structure and Volatility of Interest Rates

by Frank J. Fabozzi, CFA

LEARNING OUTCOMES

Mastery	The candidate should be able to:
☐	**a** explain parallel and nonparallel shifts in the yield curve;
☐	**b** describe factors that drive U.S. Treasury security returns, and evaluate the importance of each factor;
☐	**c** explain various universes of Treasury securities that are used to construct the theoretical spot rate curve, and evaluate their advantages and disadvantages;
☐	**d** explain the swap rate curve (LIBOR curve) and why market participants have used the swap rate curve rather than a government bond yield curve as a benchmark;
☐	**e** explain the pure expectations, liquidity, and preferred habitat theories of the term structure of interest rates and the implications of each for the shape of the yield curve;
☐	**f** calculate and interpret the yield curve risk of a security or a portfolio by using key rate duration;
☐	**g** calculate and interpret yield volatility, distinguish between historical yield volatility and implied yield volatility, and explain how to forecast yield volatility.

INTRODUCTION

1

Market participants pay close attention to yields on Treasury securities. An analysis of these yields is critical because they are used to derive interest rates which are used to value securities. Also, they are benchmarks used to establish the minimum yields that investors want when investing in a non-Treasury security. We distinguish between the on-the-run (i.e., the most recently auctioned Treasury securities) Treasury yield curve and the term structure of interest rates. The on-the-run Treasury yield curve shows the relationship between the yield for on-the-run Treasury issues and maturity. The term structure of interest rates is the relationship between the theoretical yield on zero-coupon Treasury securities and maturity. The yield on a zero-coupon Treasury security is called the Treasury spot rate. The term structure of interest rates is thus the relationship between Treasury spot rates and maturity. The importance of this distinction between the Treasury yield curve and the Treasury spot rate curve is that it is the latter that is used to value fixed-income securities.

We demonstrated how to derive the Treasury spot rate curve from the on-the-run Treasury issues using the method of bootstrapping and then how to obtain an arbitrage-free value for an option-free bond. In this reading we will describe other methods to derive the Treasury spot rates. In addition, we explained that another benchmark that is being used by practitioners to value securities is the swap curve. We discuss the swap curve in this reading.

Previously, the theories of the term structure of interest rates were explained. Each of these theories seeks to explain the shape of the yield curve. The concept of forward rates also was explained. In this reading, we explain the role that forward rates play in the theories of the term structure of interest rates. In addition, we critically evaluate one of these theories, the pure expectations theory, because of the economic interpretation of forward rates based on this theory.

We also mentioned the role of interest rate volatility or yield volatility in valuing securities and in measuring interest rate exposure of a bond. We will continue to see the importance of this measure. Specifically, we will see the role of interest rate volatility in valuing bonds with embedded options, valuing mortgage-backed and certain asset-backed securities, and valuing derivatives. Consequently, in this reading, we will explain how interest rate volatility is estimated and the issues associated with computing this measure.

In the opening sections of this reading we provide some historical information about the Treasury yield curve. In addition, we set the stage for understanding bond returns by looking at empirical evidence on some of the factors that drive returns.

2   HISTORICAL LOOK AT THE TREASURY YIELD CURVE

The yields offered on Treasury securities represent the base interest rate or minimum interest rate that investors demand if they purchase a non-Treasury security. For this reason market participants continuously monitor the yields on Treasury securities, particularly the yields of the on-the-run issues. In this reading we will discuss the historical relationship that has been observed between the yields offered on on-the-run Treasury securities and maturity (i.e., the yield curve).

A. Shape of the Yield Curve

Exhibit 1 shows some yield curves that have been observed in the U.S. Treasury market and in the government bond market of other countries. Four shapes have been observed. The most common relationship is a yield curve in which the longer the maturity, the higher the yield as shown in panel a. That is, investors are rewarded for holding longer maturity Treasuries in the form of a higher potential yield. This shape is referred to as a normal or positively sloped yield curve. A flat yield curve is one in which the yield for all maturities is approximately equal, as shown in panel b. There have been times when the relationship between maturities and yields was such that the longer the maturity the lower the yield. Such a downward-sloping yield curve is referred to as an inverted or a negatively sloped yield curve and is shown in panel c. In panel d, the yield curve shows yields increasing with maturity for a range of maturities and then the yield curve becoming inverted. This is called a humped yield curve.

Market participants talk about the difference between long-term Treasury yields and short-term Treasury yields. The spread between these yields for two maturities

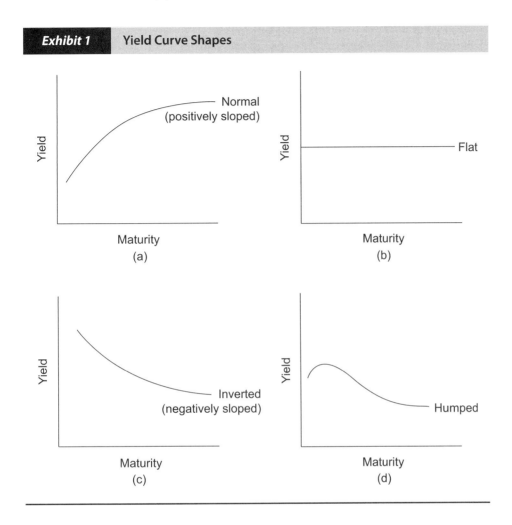

Exhibit 1   Yield Curve Shapes

is referred to as the steepness or slope of the yield curve. There is no industry-wide accepted definition of the maturity used for the long-end and the maturity used for the short-end of the yield curve. Some market participants define the slope of the yield curve as the difference between the 30-year yield and the 3-month yield. Other market participants define the slope of the yield curve as the difference between the 30-year yield and the 2-year yield. The more common practice is to use the spread between the 30-year and 2-year yield. In some markets, participants use the 10-year Treasury rate as a barometer of long-term interest rates.

It should be noted that not all sectors of the bond market view the slope of the yield curve in the same way. The mortgage sector of the bond—which we cover in the reading on the mortgage-backed sector of the bond market—views the yield curve in terms of the spread between the 10-year and 2-year Treasury yields. This is because it is the 10-year rates that affect the pricing and refinancing opportunities in the mortgage market.

Moreover, it is not only within the U.S. bond market that there may be different interpretations of what is meant by the slope of the yield curve, but there are differences across countries. In Europe, the only country with a liquid 30-year government market is the United Kingdom. In European markets, it has become increasingly common to measure the slope in terms of the swap curve (in particular, the euro swap curve) that we will cover later in this reading.

Some market participants break up the yield curve into a "short end" and "long end" and look at the slope of the short end and long end of the yield curve. Once again, there is no universal consensus that defines the maturity break points. In the United States, it is common for market participants to refer to the short end of the yield curve as up to the 10-year maturity and the long end as from the 10-year maturity to the 30-year maturity. Using the 2-year as the shortest maturity, the slope of the short end of the yield curve is then the difference between the 10-year Treasury yield and the 2-year Treasury yield. The slope of the long end of the yield curve is the difference between the 30-year Treasury yield and the 10-year Treasury yield. Historically, the long end of the yield curve has been flatter than the short-end of the yield curve. For example, in October 1992 when the slope of the yield curve was the greatest at 348 basis points, the slope of the long end of the yield curve was only 95 basis points.

Market participants often decompose the yield curve into three maturity sectors: short, intermediate, and long. Again, there is no consensus as to what the maturity break points are and those break points can differ by sector and by country. In the United States, a common breakdown has the 1–5 year sector as the short end (ignoring maturities less than 1 year), the 5–10 year sector as the intermediate end, and greater than 10-year maturities as the long end.[1] In Continental Europe where there is little issuance of bonds with a maturity greater than 10 years, the long end of the yield sector is the 10-year sector.

B. Yield Curve Shifts

A shift in the yield curve refers to the relative change in the yield for each Treasury maturity. A parallel shift in the yield curve refers to a shift in which the change in the yield for all maturities is the same. A nonparallel shift in the yield curve means that the yield for different maturities does not change by the same number of basis points. Both of these shifts are graphically portrayed in Exhibit 2.

Historically, two types of nonparallel yield curve shifts have been observed: 1) a twist in the slope of the yield curve and 2) a change in the humpedness or curvature

---

1 Index constructors such as Lehman Brothers when constructing maturity sector indexes define "short-term sector" as up to three years, the "intermediate sector" as maturities greater than three years but less than 10 years (note the overlap with the short-term sector), and the "long-term sector" as greater than 10 years.

Exhibit 2	Types of Yield Curve Shifts

(a) Parallel shifts

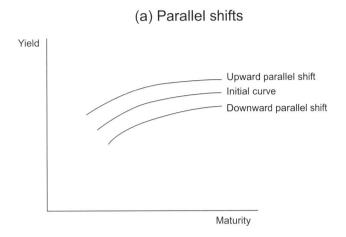

(b) Nonparallel shifts: Twists (steepening and flattening)

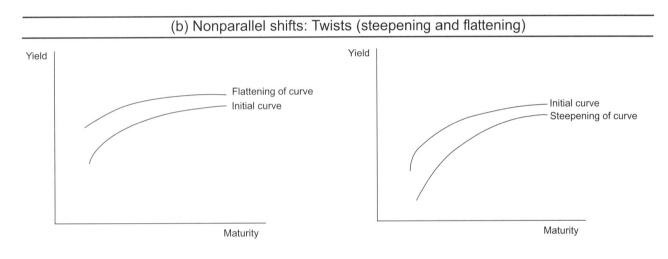

(c) Nonparallel shifts: Butterfly shifts (positive and negative)

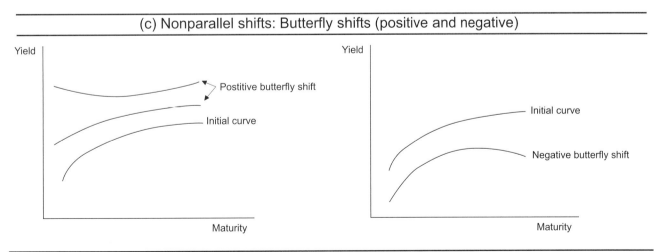

of the yield curve. A twist in the slope of the yield curve refers to a flattening or steepening of the yield curve. A flattening of the yield curve means that the slope of the yield curve (i.e., the spread between the yield on a long-term and short-term Treasury) has decreased; a steepening of the yield curve means that the slope of the yield curve has increased. This is depicted in panel b of Exhibit 2.

The other type of nonparallel shift is a change in the curvature or humpedness of the yield curve. This type of shift involves the movement of yields at the short maturity and long maturity sectors of the yield curve relative to the movement of yields in the intermediate maturity sector of the yield curve. Such nonparallel shifts in the yield curve that change its curvature are referred to as butterfly shifts. The name comes from viewing the three maturity sectors (short, intermediate, and long) as three parts of a butterfly. Specifically, the intermediate maturity sector is viewed as the body of the butterfly and the short maturity and long maturity sectors are viewed as the wings of the butterfly.

A positive butterfly means that the yield curve becomes less humped (i.e., has less curvature). This means that if yields increase, for example, the yields in the short maturity and long maturity sectors increase more than the yields in the intermediate maturity sector. If yields decrease, the yields in the short and long maturity sectors decrease less than the intermediate maturity sector. A negative butterfly means the yield curve becomes more humped (i.e., has more curvature). So, if yields increase, for example, yields in the intermediate maturity sector will increase more than yields in the short maturity and long maturity sectors. If, instead, yields decrease, a negative butterfly occurs when yields in the intermediate maturity sector decrease less than the short maturity and long maturity sectors. Butterfly shifts are depicted in panel c of Exhibit 2.

Historically, these three types of shifts in the yield curve have not been found to be independent. The two most common types of shifts have been 1) a downward shift in the yield curve combined with a steepening of the yield curve and 2) an upward shift in the yield curve combined with a flattening of the yield curve. Positive butterfly shifts tend to be associated with an upward shift in yields and negative butterfly shifts with a downward shift in yields. Another way to state this is that yields in the short-term sector tend to be more volatile than yields in the long-term sector.

3   TREASURY RETURNS RESULTING FROM YIELD CURVE MOVEMENTS

A yield measure is a promised return if certain assumptions are satisfied; but total return (return from coupons and price change) is a more appropriate measure of the potential return from investing in a Treasury security. The total return for a short investment horizon depends critically on how interest rates change, reflected by how the yield curve changes.

There have been several published and unpublished studies of how changes in the shape of the yield curve affect the total return on Treasury securities. The first such study by two researchers at Goldman Sachs (Robert Litterman and José Scheinkman) was published in 1991.[2] The results reported in more recent studies support the findings of the Litterman–Scheinkman study, so we will just discuss their findings. Litterman and Scheinkman found that three factors explained historical returns for zero-coupon Treasury securities for all maturities. The first factor was changes in the level of rates, the second factor was changes in the slope of the yield curve, and the third factor was changes in the curvature of the yield curve.

Litterman and Scheinkman employed regression analysis to determine the relative contribution of these three factors in explaining the returns on zero-coupon Treasury securities of different maturities. They determined the importance of each factor by its coefficient of determination, popularly referred to as the "R^2." In general, the R^2

---

[2] Robert Litterman and José Scheinkman, "Common Factors Affecting Bond Returns," *Journal of Fixed Income* (June 1991), pp. 54–61.

measures the percentage of the variance in the dependent variable (i.e., the total return on the zero-coupon Treasury security in their study) explained by the independent variables (i.e., the three factors).[3] For example, an R^2 of 0.8 means that 80% of the variation of the return on a zero-coupon Treasury security is explained by the three factors. Therefore, 20% of the variation of the return is not explained by these three factors. The R^2 will have a value between 0% and 100%. In the Litterman–Scheinkman study, the R^2 was very high for all maturities, meaning that the three factors had a very strong explanatory power.

The first factor, representing changes in the level of rates, holding all other factors constant (in particular, yield curve slope), had the greatest explanatory power for all the maturities, averaging about 90%. The implication is that the most important factor that a manager of a Treasury portfolio should control for is exposure to changes in the level of interest rates. For this reason it is important to have a way to measure or quantify this risk. Duration is in fact the measure used to quantify exposure to a parallel shift in the yield curve.

The second factor, changes in the yield curve slope, was the second largest contributing factor. The average relative contribution for all maturities was 8.5%. Thus, changes in the yield curve slope were, on average, about one-tenth as significant as changes in the level of rates. While the relative contribution was only 8.5%, this can still have a significant impact on the return for a Treasury portfolio, and a portfolio manager must control for this risk. We briefly explained how a manager can do this using key rate duration and will discuss this further in this reading.

The third factor, changes in the curvature of the yield curve, contributed relatively little to explaining historical returns for Treasury zero-coupon securities.

CONSTRUCTING THE THEORETICAL SPOT RATE CURVE FOR TREASURIES

4

Our focus thus far has been on the shape of the Treasury yield curve. In fact, often the financial press in its discussion of interest rates focuses on the Treasury yield curve. However, it is the default-free spot rate curve as represented by the Treasury spot rate curve that is used in valuing fixed-income securities. But how does one obtain the default-free spot rate curve? This curve can be constructed from the yields on Treasury securities. The Treasury issues that are candidates for inclusion are:

1. Treasury coupon strips
2. on-the-run Treasury issues
3. on-the-run Treasury issues and selected off-the-run Treasury issues
4. all Treasury coupon securities and bills

Once the securities that are to be included in the construction of the theoretical spot rate curve are selected, the methodology for constructing the curve must be determined. The methodology depends on the securities included. If Treasury coupon strips are used, the procedure is simple since the observed yields are the spot rates. If the on-the-run Treasury issues with or without selected off-the-run Treasury issues are used, then the methodology of bootstrapping is used.

Using an estimated Treasury par yield curve, bootstrapping is a repetitive technique whereby the yields prior to some maturity, same m, are used to obtain the spot rate

---

3 For a further explanation of the coefficient of determination, see Richard A. DeFusco, Dennis W. McLeavey, Jerald E. Pinto, and David E. Runkle, *Quantitative Methods for Investment Analysis* (Charlottesville, VA: Association for Investment Management and Research, 2002), pp. 388–390.

for year m. For example, suppose that the yields on the par yield curve are denoted by $y_1, \ldots, y_T$ where the subscripts denote the time periods. Then the yield for the first period, y_1, is the spot rate for the first period. Let the first period spot rate be denoted as s_1. Then y_2 and s_1 can be used to derive s_2 using arbitrage arguments. Next, y_3, s_1, and s_2 are used to derive s_3 using arbitrage arguments. The process continues until all the spot rates are derived, $s_1, \ldots, s_m$.

In selecting the universe of securities used to construct a default-free spot rate curve, one wants to make sure that the yields are not biased by any of the following: 1) default, 2) embedded options, 3) liquidity, and 4) pricing errors. To deal with default, U.S. Treasury securities are used. Issues with embedded options are avoided because the market yield reflects the value of the embedded options. In the U.S. Treasury market, there are only a few callable bonds so this is not an issue. In other countries, however, there are callable and putable government bonds. Liquidity varies by issue. There are U.S. Treasury issues that have less liquidity than bonds with a similar maturity. In fact, there are some issues that have extremely high liquidity because they are used by dealers in repurchase agreements. Finally, in some countries the trading of certain government bond issues is limited, resulting in estimated prices that may not reflect the true price.

Given the theoretical spot rate for each maturity, there are various statistical techniques that are used to create a continuous spot rate curve. A discussion of these statistical techniques is a specialist topic.

A. Treasury Coupon Strips

It would seem simplest to use the observed yield on Treasury coupon strips to construct an actual spot rate curve, but there are three problems with using the observed rates on Treasury strips. First, the liquidity of the strips market is not as great as that of the Treasury coupon market. Thus, the observed rates on strips reflect a premium for liquidity.

Second, the tax treatment of strips is different from that of Treasury coupon securities. Specifically, the accrued interest on strips is taxed even though no cash is received by the investor. Thus they are negative cash flow securities to taxable entities, and, as a result, their yield reflects this tax disadvantage.

Finally, there are maturity sectors where non-U.S. investors find it advantageous to trade off yield for tax advantages associated with a strip. Specifically, certain foreign tax authorities allow their citizens to treat the difference between the maturity value and the purchase price as a capital gain and tax this gain at a favorable tax rate. Some will grant this favorable treatment only when the strip is created from the principal rather than the coupon. For this reason, those who use Treasury strips to represent theoretical spot rates restrict the issues included to coupon strips.

B. On-the-Run Treasury Issues

The on-the-run Treasury issues are the most recently auctioned issues of a given maturity. In the U.S., these issues currently include the 1-month, 3-month, and 6-month Treasury bills, and the 2-year, 5-year, and 10-year Treasury notes and 30-year Treasury bond. Treasury bills are zero-coupon instruments; the notes are coupon securities.[4]

There is an observed yield for each of the on-the-run issues. For the coupon issues, these yields are not the yields used in the analysis when the issue is not trading at par. Instead, for each on-the-run coupon issue, the estimated yield necessary to make the issue trade at par is used. The resulting on-the-run yield curve is called the par coupon curve. The reason for using securities with a price of par is to eliminate the effect of

4 At one time, the Department of the Treasury issued 3-year notes, 7-year notes, 15-year bonds, and 20-year bonds.

the tax treatment for securities selling at a **discount** or premium. The differential tax treatment distorts the yield.

C. On-the-Run Treasury Issues and Selected Off-the-Run Treasury Issues

One of the problems with using just the on-the-run issues is the large gap between maturities, particularly after five years. To mitigate this problem, some dealers and vendors use selected off-the-run Treasury issues. Typically, the issues used are the 20-year issue and 25-year issue.[5] Given the par coupon curve including any off-the-run selected issues, a linear interpolation method is used to fill in the gaps for the other maturities. The bootstrapping method is then used to construct the theoretical spot rate curve.

D. All Treasury Coupon Securities and Bills

Using only on-the-run issues and a few off-the-run issues fails to recognize the information embodied in Treasury prices that are not included in the analysis. Thus, some market participants argue that it is more appropriate to use all outstanding Treasury coupon securities and bills to construct the theoretical spot rate curve. Moreover, a common practice is to filter the Treasury securities universe to eliminate securities that are on special (trading at a lower yield than their true yield) in the repo market.[6]

When all coupon securities and bills are used, methodologies more complex than bootstrapping must be employed to construct the theoretical spot rate curve since there may be more than one yield for each maturity. There are various methodologies for fitting a curve to the points when all the Treasury securities are used. The methodologies make an adjustment for the effect of taxes.[7] A discussion of the various methodologies is a specialist topic.

THE SWAP CURVE (LIBOR CURVE)   **5**

In the United States it is common to use the Treasury spot rate curve for purposes of valuation. In other countries, either a government spot rate curve is used (if a liquid market for the securities exists) or the swap curve is used (or as explained shortly, the *LIBOR curve*). LIBOR is the London interbank offered rate and is the interest rate which major international banks offer each other on Eurodollar certificates of deposit (CD) with given maturities. The maturities range from overnight to five years. So, references to "3-month LIBOR" indicate the interest rate that major international banks are offering to pay to other such banks on a CD that matures in three months. A swap curve can be constructed that is unique to a country where there is a swap market for converting fixed cash flows to floating cash flows in that country's currency.

---

5 See, for example, Philip H. Galdi and Shenglin Lu, *Analyzing Risk and Relative Value of Corporate and Government Securities*, Merrill Lynch & Co., Global Securities Research & Economics Group, Fixed Income Analytics, 1997, p. 11.

6 There must also be an adjustment for what is known as the "specials effect." This has to do with a security trading at a lower yield than its true yield because of its value in the repurchase agreement market. In a repurchase agreement, a security is used as collateral for a loan. If the security is one that is in demand by dealers, referred to as "hot collateral" or "collateral on special," then the borrowing rate is lower if that security is used as collateral. As a result of this favorable feature, a security will offer a lower yield in the market if it is on special so that the investor can finance that security cheaply. As a result, the use of the yield of a security on special will result in a biased yield estimate. The 10-year on-the-run U.S. Treasury issue is typically on special.

7 See Oldrich A. Vasicek and H. Gifford Fong, "Term Structure Modeling Using Exponential Splines," *Journal of Finance* (May 1982), pp. 339–358.

A. Elements of a Swap and a Swap Curve

To discuss a swap curve, we need the basics of a generic (also called a "plain vanilla" interest rate) swap. In a generic interest rate swap two parties are exchanging cash flows based on a notional amount where 1) one party is paying fixed cash flows and receiving floating cash flows and 2) the other party is paying floating cash flows and receiving fixed cash flows. It is called a "swap" because the two parties are "swapping" payments: 1) one party is paying a floating rate and receiving a fixed rate, and 2) the other party is paying a fixed rate and receiving a floating rate. While the swap is described in terms of a "rate," the amount the parties exchange is expressed in terms of a currency and determined by using the notional amount as explained below.

For example, suppose the swap specifies that 1) one party is to pay a fixed rate of 6%, 2) the notional amount is $100 million, 3) the payments are to be quarterly, and 4) the term of the swap is 7 years. The fixed rate of 6% is called the swap rate, or equivalently, the swap fixed rate. The swap rate of 6% multiplied by the notional amount of $100 million gives the amount of the annual payment, $6 million. If the payment is to be made quarterly, the amount paid each quarter is $1.5 million ($6 million/4) and this amount is paid every quarter for the next 7 years.[8]

The floating rate in an interest rate swap can be any short-term interest rate. For example, it could be the rate on a 3-month Treasury bill or the rate on 3-month LIBOR. The most common reference rate used in swaps is 3-month LIBOR. When LIBOR is the reference rate, the swap is referred to as a "LIBOR-based swap."

Consider the swap we just used in our illustration. We will assume that the reference rate is 3-month LIBOR. In that swap, one party is paying a fixed rate of 6% (i.e., the swap rate) and receiving 3-month LIBOR for the next 7 years. Hence, the 7-year swap rate is 6%. But entering into this swap with a swap rate of 6% is equivalent to locking in 3-month LIBOR for 7 years (rolled over on a quarterly basis). So, casting this in terms of 3-month LIBOR, the 7-year maturity rate for 3-month LIBOR is 6%.

So, suppose that the swap rates for the maturities quoted in the swap market are as shown below:

Maturity (years)	Swap Rate (%)
2	4.2
3	4.6
4	5.0
5	5.3
6	5.7
7	6.0
8	6.2
9	6.4
10	6.5
15	6.7
30	6.8

This would be the swap curve. But this swap curve is also telling us how much we can lock in 3-month LIBOR for a specified future period. By locking in 3-month LIBOR it is meant that a party that pays the floating rate (i.e., agrees to pay 3-month LIBOR) is locking in a borrowing rate; the party receiving the floating rate is locking in an amount to be received. Because 3-month LIBOR is being exchanged, the swap curve is also called the LIBOR curve.

---

[8] Actually the payments are slightly different each quarter because the amount of the quarterly payment depends on the actual number of days in the quarter.

Note that we have not indicated the currency in which the payments are to be made for our hypothetical swap curve. Suppose that the swap curve above refers to swapping U.S. dollars (i.e., the notional amount is in U.S. dollars) from a fixed to a floating (and vice versa). Then the swap curve above would be the U.S. swap curve. If the notional amount was for euros, and the swaps involved swapping a fixed euro amount for a floating euro amount, then it would be the euro swap curve.

Finally, let's look at how the terms of a swap are quoted. Rather than quote a swap rate for a given maturity, the convention in the swap market is to quote a **swap spread**. The spread can be over any benchmark desired, typically a government bond yield. The swap spread is defined as follows for a given maturity:

Swap spread = Swap rate − Government yield on a bond with the same maturity as the swap

For euro-denominated swaps (i.e., swaps in which the currency in which the payments are made is the euro), the government yield used as the benchmark is the German government bond with the same maturity as the swap.

For example, consider our hypothetical 7-year swap. Suppose that the currency of the swap payments is in U.S. dollars and the estimated 7-year U.S. Treasury yield is 5.4%. Then since the swap rate is 6%, the swap spread is:

Swap spread = 6% − 5.4% = 0.6% = 60 basis points

Suppose, instead, the swap was denominated in euros and the swap rate is 6%. Also suppose that the estimated 7-year German government bond yield is 5%. Then the swap spread would be quoted as 100 basis points (6% − 5%).

Effectively the swap spread reflects the risk of the counterparty to the swap failing to satisfy its obligation. Consequently, it primarily reflects credit risk. Since the counterparties in swaps are typically bank-related entities, the swap spread is a rough indicator of the credit risk of the banking sector. Therefore, the swap rate curve is not a default-free curve. Instead, it is an inter-bank or AA rated curve.

Notice that the swap rate is compared to a government bond yield to determine the swap spread. Why would one want to use a swap curve if a government bond yield curve is available? We answer that question next.

B. Reasons for Increased Use of Swap Curve

Investors and issuers use the swap market for hedging and arbitrage purposes, and the swap curve as a benchmark for evaluating performance of fixed income securities and the pricing of fixed income securities. Since the swap curve is effectively the LIBOR curve and investors borrow based on LIBOR, the swap curve is more useful to funded investors than a government yield curve.

The increased application of the swap curve for these activities is due to its advantages over using the government bond yield curve as a benchmark. Before identifying these advantages, it is important to understand that the drawback of the swap curve relative to the government bond yield curve could be poorer liquidity. In such instances, the swap rates would reflect a liquidity premium. Fortunately, liquidity is not an issue in many countries as the swap market has become highly liquid, with narrow bid–ask spreads for a wide range of swap maturities. In some countries swaps may offer better liquidity than that country's government bond market.

The advantages of the swap curve over a government bond yield curve are:[9]

1. There is almost no government regulation of the swap market. The lack of government regulation makes swap rates across different markets more

---

9 See Uri Ron, "A Practical Guide to Swap Curve Construction," Chapter 6 in Frank J. Fabozzi (ed.), *Interest Rate, Term Structure, and Valuation Modeling* (NY: John Wiley & Sons, 2002).

comparable. In some countries, there are some sovereign issues that offer various tax benefits to investors and, as a result, for global investors it makes comparative analysis of government rates across countries difficult because some market yields do not reflect their true yield.

2. The supply of swaps depends only on the number of counterparties that are seeking or are willing to enter into a swap transaction at any given time. Since there is no underlying government bond, there can be no effect of market technical factors[10] that may result in the yield for a government bond issue being less than its true yield.

3. Comparisons across countries of government yield curves is difficult because of the differences in sovereign credit risk. In contrast, the credit risk as reflected in the swaps curve are similar and make comparisons across countries more meaningful than government yield curves. Sovereign risk is not present in the swap curve because, as noted earlier, the swap curve is viewed as an inter-bank yield curve or AA yield curve.

4. There are more maturity points available to construct a swap curve than a government bond yield curve. More specifically, what is quoted in the swap market are swap rates for 2, 3, 4, 5, 6, 7, 8, 9, 10, 15, and 30 year maturities.

Thus, in the swap market there are 10 market interest rates with a maturity of 2 years and greater. In contrast, in the U.S. Treasury market, for example, there are only three market interest rates for on-the-run Treasuries with a maturity of 2 years or greater (2, 5, and 10 years) and one of the rates, the 10-year rate, may not be a good benchmark because it is often on special in the repo market. Moreover, because the U.S. Treasury has ceased the issuance of 30-year bonds, there is no 30-year yield available.

C. Constructing the LIBOR Spot Rate Curve

In the valuation of fixed income securities, it is not the Treasury yield curve that is used as the basis for determining the appropriate discount rate for computing the present value of cash flows but the Treasury spot rates. The Treasury spot rates are derived from the Treasury yield curve using the bootstrapping process.

Similarly, it is not the swap curve that is used for discounting cash flows when the swap curve is the benchmark but the spot rates. The spot rates are derived from the swap curve in exactly the same way—using the bootstrapping methodology. The resulting spot rate curve is called the LIBOR spot rate curve. Moreover, a forward rate curve can be derived from the spot rate curve. The same thing is done in the swap market. The forward rate curve that is derived is called the LIBOR forward rate curve. Consequently, if we understand the mechanics of moving from the yield curve to the spot rate curve to the forward rate curve in the Treasury market, there is no reason to repeat an explanation of that process here for the swap market; that is, it is the same methodology, just different yields are used.[11]

---

10 For example, a government bond issue being on "special" in the repurchase agreement market.

11 The question is what yields are used to construct the swap rate curve. Practitioners use yields from two related markets: the Eurodollar CD futures contract and the swap market. We will not review the Eurodollar CD futures contract here. For now, the only important fact to note about this contract is that it provides a means for locking in 3-month LIBOR in the future. In fact, it provides a means for doing so for an extended time into the future.

Practitioners use the Eurodollar CD futures rate up to four years to get 3-month LIBOR for every quarter. While there are Eurodollar CD futures contracts that settle further out than four years, for technical reasons (having to do with the convexity of the contract), analysts use only the first four years. (In fact, this actually varies from practitioner to practitioner. Some will use the Eurodollar CD futures from two years up to four years.) For maturities after four years, the swap rates are used to get 3-month LIBOR. As noted above, there is a swap rate for maturities for each year 10, and then swap rates for 15 years and 30 years.

EXPECTATIONS THEORIES OF THE TERM STRUCTURE OF INTEREST RATES

6

So far we have described the different types of curves that analysts and portfolio managers focus on. The key curve is the spot rate curve because it is the spot rates that are used to value the cash flows of a fixed-income security. The spot rate curve is also called the term structure of interest rates, or simply term structure. Now we turn to another potential use of the term structure. Analysts and portfolio managers are interested in knowing if there is information contained in the term structure that can be used in making investment decisions. For this purpose, market participants rely on different theories about the term structure.

We explained four theories of the term structure of interest rates—pure expectations theory, liquidity preference theory, preferred habitat theory, and market segmentation theory. Unlike the market segmentation theory, the first three theories share a hypothesis about the behavior of short-term forward rates and also assume that the forward rates in current long-term bonds are closely related to the market's expectations about future short-term rates. For this reason, the pure expectations theory, liquidity preference theory, and preferred habitat theory are referred to as expectations theories of the term structure of interest rates.

What distinguishes these three expectations theories is whether there are systematic factors other than expectations of future interest rates that affect forward rates. The pure expectations theory postulates that no systematic factors other than expected future short-term rates affect forward rates; the liquidity preference theory and the preferred habitat theory assert that there are other factors. Accordingly, the last two forms of the expectations theory are sometimes referred to as biased expectations theories. The relationship among the various theories is described below and summarized in Exhibit 3.

Exhibit 3	Expectations Theories of the Term Structure of Interest Rates

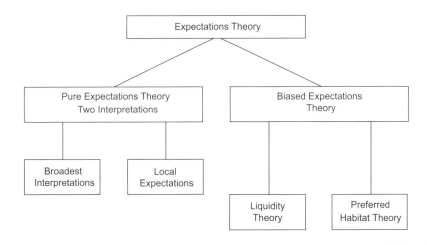

A. The Pure Expectations Theory

According to the pure expectations theory, forward rates exclusively represent expected future spot rates. Thus, the entire term structure at a given time reflects the market's current expectations of the family of future short-term rates. Under this view, a rising term structure must indicate that the market expects short-term rates to rise throughout the relevant future. Similarly, a flat term structure reflects an expectation that future short-term rates will be mostly constant, while a falling term structure must reflect an expectation that future short-term rates will decline.

1 Drawbacks of the Theory

The pure expectations theory suffers from one shortcoming, which, qualitatively, is quite serious. It neglects the risks inherent in investing in bonds. If forward rates were perfect predictors of future interest rates, then the future prices of bonds would be known with certainty. The return over any investment period would be certain and independent of the maturity of the instrument acquired. However, with the uncertainty about future interest rates and, therefore, about future prices of bonds, these instruments become risky investments in the sense that the return over some investment horizon is unknown.

There are two risks that cause uncertainty about the return over some investment horizon. The first is the uncertainty about the price of the bond at the end of the investment horizon. For example, an investor who plans to invest for five years might consider the following three investment alternatives:

Alternative 1	Invest in a 5-year zero-coupon bond and hold it for five years.
Alternative 2	Invest in a 12-year zero-coupon bond and sell it at the end of five years.
Alternative 3	Invest in a 30-year zero-coupon bond and sell it at the end of five years.

The return that will be realized in Alternatives 2 and 3 is not known because the price of each of these bonds at the end of five years is unknown. In the case of the 12-year bond, the price will depend on the yield on 7-year bonds five years from now; and the price of the 30-year bond will depend on the yield on 25-year bonds five years from now. Since forward rates implied in the current term structure for a 7-year bond five years from now and a 25-year bond five years from now are not perfect predictors of the actual future rates, there is uncertainty about the price for both bonds five years from now. Thus, there is interest rate risk; that is, the price of the bond may be lower than currently expected at the end of the investment horizon due to an increase in interest rates. An important feature of interest rate risk is that it increases with the length of the bond's maturity.

The second risk involves the uncertainty about the rate at which the proceeds from a bond that matures prior to the end of the investment horizon can be reinvested until the maturity date, that is, reinvestment risk. For example, an investor who plans to invest for five years might consider the following three alternative investments:

Alternative 1	Invest in a 5-year zero-coupon bond and hold it for five years.
Alternative 2	Invest in a 6-month zero-coupon instrument and, when it matures, reinvest the proceeds in 6-month zero-coupon instruments over the entire 5-year investment horizon.
Alternative 3	Invest in a 2-year zero-coupon bond and, when it matures, reinvest the proceeds in a 3-year zero-coupon bond.

The risk for Alternatives 2 and 3 is that the return over the 5-year investment horizon is unknown because rates at which the proceeds can be reinvested until the end of the investment horizon are unknown.

2 Interpretations of the Theory

There are several interpretations of the pure expectations theory that have been put forth by economists. These interpretations are not exact equivalents nor are they consistent with each other, in large part because they offer different treatments of the two risks associated with realizing a return that we have just explained.[12]

---

12 These formulations are summarized by John Cox, Jonathan Ingersoll, Jr., and Stephen Ross, "A Re-examination of Traditional Hypotheses About the Term Structure of Interest Rates," *Journal of Finance* (September 1981), pp. 769–799.

a. Broadest Interpretation The broadest interpretation of the pure expectations theory suggests that investors expect the return for any investment horizon to be the same, regardless of the maturity strategy selected.[13] For example, consider an investor who has a 5-year investment horizon. According to this theory, it makes no difference if a 5-year, 12-year, or 30-year bond is purchased and held for five years since the investor expects the return from all three bonds to be the same over the 5-year investment horizon. A major criticism of this very broad interpretation of the theory is that, because of price risk associated with investing in bonds with a maturity greater than the investment horizon, the expected returns from these three very different investments should differ in significant ways.[14]

b. Local Expectations Form of the Pure Expectations Theory A second interpretation, referred to as the local expectations form of the pure expectations theory, suggests that the return will be the same over a short-term investment horizon starting today. For example, if an investor has a 6-month investment horizon, buying a 1-year, 5-year or 10-year bond will produce the same 6-month return.

To illustrate this, we will use the hypothetical yield curve shown in Exhibit 4. We have previously used the yield curve in Exhibit 4 to show how to compute spot rates and forward rates. Exhibit 5 shows all the 6-month forward rates. We will focus on the 1-year, 5-year, and 10-year issues.

Exhibit 4	Hypothetical Treasury Par Yield Curve			
Period	**Years**	**Annual Yield to Maturity (BEY)(%)[a]**	**Price**	**Spot Rate (BEY)(%)**
1	0.5	3.00	—	3.0000
2	1.0	3.30	—	3.3000
3	1.5	3.50	100.00	3.5053
4	2.0	3.90	100.00	3.9164
5	2.5	4.40	100.00	4.4376
6	3.0	4.70	100.00	4.7520
7	3.5	4.90	100.00	4.9622
8	4.0	5.00	100.00	5.0650
9	4.5	5.10	100.00	5.1701
10	5.0	5.20	100.00	5.2772
11	5.5	5.30	100.00	5.3864
12	6.0	5.40	100.00	5.4976
13	6.5	5.50	100.00	5.6108
14	7.0	5.55	100.00	5.6643
15	7.5	5.60	100.00	5.7193
16	8.0	5.65	100.00	5.7755
17	8.5	5.70	100.00	5.8331
18	9.0	5.80	100.00	5.9584
19	9.5	5.90	100.00	6.0863
20	10.0	6.00	100.00	6.2169

[a] The yield to maturity and the spot rate are annual rates. They are reported as **bond-equivalent yields**. To obtain the semiannual yield or rate, one half the annual yield or annual rate is used.

---

13 F. Lutz, "The Structure of Interest Rates," *Quarterly Journal of Economics* (1940–41), pp. 36–63.
14 Cox, Ingersoll, and Ross, pp. 774–775.

Exhibit 5	Six-Month Forward Rates: The Short-Term Forward Rate Curve (Annualized Rates on a Bond-Equivalent Basis)		

Notation	Forward Rate	Notation	Forward Rate
$_1f_0$	3.00	$_1f_{10}$	6.48
$_1f_1$	3.60	$_1f_{11}$	6.72
$_1f_2$	3.92	$_1f_{12}$	6.97
$_1f_3$	5.15	$_1f_{13}$	6.36
$_1f_4$	6.54	$_1f_{14}$	6.49
$_1f_5$	6.33	$_1f_{15}$	6.62
$_1f_6$	6.23	$_1f_{16}$	6.76
$_1f_7$	5.79	$_1f_{17}$	8.10
$_1f_8$	6.01	$_1f_{18}$	8.40
$_1f_9$	6.24	$_1f_{19}$	8.72

Our objective is to look at what happens to the total return over a 6-month invest-ment horizon for the 1-year, 5-year, and 10-year issues if all the 6-month forward rates are realized. Look first at panel a in Exhibit 6. This shows the total return for the 1-year issue. At the end of 6 months, this issue is a 6-month issue. The 6-month forward rate is 3.6%. This means that if the forward rate is realized, the 6-month yield 6 months from now will be 3.6%. Given a 6-month issue that must offer a yield of 3.6% (the 6-month forward rate), the price of this issue will decline from 100 (today) to 99.85265 six months from now. The price must decline because if the 6-month forward rate is realized 6 months from now, the yield increases from 3.3% to 3.6%. The total dollars realized over the 6 months are coupon interest adjusted for the decline in the price. The total return for the 6 months is 3%.

Exhibit 6	Total Return over 6-Month Investment Horizon if 6-Month Forward Rates Are Realized

a: Total return on 1-year issue if forward rates are realized

Period	Cash Flow ($)	Six-Month Forward Rate (%)	Price at Horizon ($)
1	101.650	3.60	99.85265

Price at horizon: 99.85265   Total proceeds: 101.5027

Coupon: 1.65   Total return: 3.00%

b: Total return on 5-year issue if forward rates are realized

Period	Cash Flow ($)	Six-Month Forward Rate (%)	Present Value ($)
1	2.60	3.60	2.55403
2	2.60	3.92	2.50493
3	2.60	5.15	2.44205
4	2.60	6.54	2.36472
5	2.60	6.33	2.29217
6	2.60	6.23	2.22293
7	2.60	5.79	2.16039
8	2.60	6.01	2.09736

Exhibit 6	Continued

b: Total return on 5-year issue if forward rates are realized

Period	Cash Flow ($)	Six-Month Forward Rate (%)	Present Value ($)
9	102.60	6.24	80.26096
		Total	98.89954

Price at horizon: 98.89954   Total proceeds: 101.4995

Coupon: 2.60   Total return: 3.00%

c: Total return on 10-year issue if forward rates are realized

Period	Cash Flow ($)	Six-Month Forward Rate (%)	Present Value ($)
1	3.00	3.60	2.94695
2	3.00	3.92	2.89030
3	3.00	5.15	2.81775
4	3.00	6.54	2.72853
5	3.00	6.33	2.64482
6	3.00	6.23	2.56492
7	3.00	5.79	2.49275
8	3.00	6.01	2.42003
9	3.00	6.24	2.34681
10	3.00	6.48	2.27316
11	3.00	6.72	2.19927
12	3.00	6.97	2.12520
13	3.00	6.36	2.05970
14	3.00	6.49	1.99497
15	3.00	6.62	1.93105
16	3.00	6.76	1.86791
17	3.00	8.10	1.79521
18	3.00	8.40	1.72285
19	103.00	8.72	56.67989
		Total	98.50208

Price at horizon: 98.50208   Total proceeds: 101.5021

Coupon: 3.00   Total return: 3.00%

What the local expectations theory asserts is that over the 6-month investment horizon even the 5-year and the 10-year issues will generate a total return of 3% if forward rates are realized. Panels b and c show this to be the case. We need only explain the computation for one of the two issues. Let's use the 5-year issue. The 6-month forward rates are shown in the third column of panel b. Now we apply a few principles discussed previously. We demonstrate that to value a security each cash flow should be discounted at the spot rate with the same maturity. We also demonstrate that 6-month forward rates can be used to value the cash flows of a security and that the results will be identical using the forward rates to value a security. For example, consider the cash flow in period 3 for the 5-year issue. The cash flow is $2.60. The 6-month forward rates are 3.6%, 3.92%, and 5.15%. These are annual rates. So, half these rates are 1.8%, 1.96%, and 2.575%. The present value of $2.60 using the 6-month forward is:

$$\frac{\$2.60}{(1.018)(1.0196)(1.02575)} = \$2.44205$$

This is the present value shown in the third column of panel b. In a similar manner, all of the other present values in the third column are computed. The arbitrage-free value for this 5-year issue 6 months from now (when it is a 4.5-year issue) is 98.89954. The total return (taking into account the coupon interest and the loss due to the decline in price from 100) is 3%. Thus, if the 6-month forward rates are realized, all three issues provide a short-term (6-month) return of 3%.[15]

c. Forward Rates and Market Consensus We have already seen how various types of forward rates can be computed. That is, how to compute the forward rate for any length of time beginning at any future period of time. So, it is possible to compute the 2-year forward rate beginning 5 years from now or the 3-year forward rate beginning 8 years from now. We showed how, using arbitrage arguments, forward rates can be derived from spot rates.

Previously, no interpretation was given to the forward rates. The focus was just on how to compute them from spot rates based on arbitrage arguments. Let's provide two interpretations now with a simple illustration. Suppose that an investor has a 1-year investment horizon and has a choice of investing in either a 1-year Treasury bill or a 6-month Treasury bill and rolling over the proceeds from the maturing 6-month issue in another 6-month Treasury bill. Since the Treasury bills are zero-coupon securities, the rates on them are spot rates and can be used to compute the 6-month forward rate six months from now. For example, if the 6-month Treasury bill rate is 5% and the 1-year Treasury bill rate is 5.6%, then the 6-month forward rate six months from now is 6.2%. To verify this, suppose an investor invests $100 in a 1-year investment. The $100 investment in a zero-coupon instrument will grow at a rate of 2.8% (one-half 5.6%) for two 6-month periods to:

$$\$100(1.028)^2 = \$105.68$$

If $100 is invested in a six-month zero-coupon instrument at 2.5% (one-half 5%) and the proceeds reinvested at the 6-month forward rate of 3.1% (one-half 6.2%), the $100 will grow to:

$$\$100(1.025)(1.031) = \$105.68$$

Thus, the 6-month forward rate generates the same future dollars for the $100 investment at the end of 1 year.

One interpretation of the forward rate is that it is a "break-even rate." That is, a forward rate is the rate that will make an investor indifferent between investing for the full investment horizon and part of the investment horizon and rolling over the proceeds for the balance of the investment horizon. So, in our illustration, the forward rate of 6.2% can be interpreted as the break-even rate that will make an investment in a 6-month zero-coupon instrument with a yield of 5% rolled-over into another 6-month zero-coupon instrument equal to the yield on a 1-year zero-coupon instrument with a yield of 5.6%.

Similarly, a 2-year forward rate beginning four years from now can be interpreted as the break-even rate that will make an investor indifferent between investing in 1) a 4-year zero-coupon instrument at the 4-year spot rate and rolling over the investment for two more years in a zero-coupon instrument and 2) investing in a 6-year zero-coupon instrument at the 6-year spot rate.

A second interpretation of the forward rate is that it is a rate that allows the investor to lock in a rate for some future period. For example, consider once again our

---

15 It has been demonstrated that the local expectations formulation, which is narrow in scope, is the only interpretation of the pure expectations theory that can be sustained in equilibrium. See Cox, Ingersoll, and Ross, "A Re-examination of Traditional Hypotheses About the Term Structure of Interest Rates."

1-year investment. If an investor purchases this instrument rather than the 6-month instrument, the investor has locked in a 6.2% rate six months from now regardless of how interest rates change six months from now. Similarly, in the case of a 6-year investment, by investing in a 6-year zero-coupon instrument rather than a 4-year zero-coupon instrument, the investor has locked in the 2-year zero-coupon rate four years from now. That locked in rate is the 2-year forward rate four years from now. The 1-year forward rate five years from now is the rate that is locked in by buying a 6-year zero-coupon instrument rather than investing in a 5-year zero-coupon instrument and reinvesting the proceeds at the end of five years in a 1-year zero-coupon instrument.

There is another interpretation of forward rates. Proponents of the pure expectations theory argue that forward rates reflect the "market's consensus" of future interest rates. They argue that forward rates can be used to predict future interest rates. A natural question about forward rates is then how well they do at predicting future interest rates. Studies have demonstrated that forward rates do not do a good job at predicting future interest rates.[16] Then, why is it so important to understand forward rates? The reason is that forward rates indicate how an investor's expectations must differ from the "break-even rate" or the "lock-in rate" when making an investment decision.

Thus, even if a forward rate may not be realized, forward rates can be highly relevant in deciding between two alternative investments. Specifically, if an investor's expectation about a rate in the future is less than the corresponding forward rate, then he would be better off investing now to lock in the forward rate.

B. Liquidity Preference Theory

We have explained that the drawback of the pure expectations theory is that it does not consider the risks associated with investing in bonds. We know that the interest rate risk associated with holding a bond for one period is greater the longer the maturity of a bond. (Recall that duration increases with maturity.)

Given this uncertainty, and considering that investors typically do not like uncertainty, some economists and financial analysts have suggested a different theory—the liquidity preference theory. This theory states that investors will hold longer-term maturities if they are offered a long-term rate higher than the average of expected future rates by a risk premium that is positively related to the term to maturity.[17] Put differently, the forward rates should reflect both interest rate expectations and a "liquidity" premium (really a risk premium), and the premium should be higher for longer maturities.

According to the liquidity preference theory, forward rates will not be an unbiased estimate of the market's expectations of future interest rates because they contain a liquidity premium. Thus, an upward-sloping yield curve may reflect expectations that future interest rates either 1) will rise, or 2) will be unchanged or even fall, but with a liquidity premium increasing fast enough with maturity so as to produce an upward-sloping yield curve. That is, any shape for either the yield curve or the term structure of interest rates can be explained by the biased expectations theory.

C. The Preferred Habitat Theory

Another theory, known as the preferred habitat theory, also adopts the view that the term structure reflects the expectation of the future path of interest rates as well as a risk premium. However, the preferred habitat theory rejects the assertion that the risk premium must rise uniformly with maturity.[18] Proponents of the preferred habitat

---

16 Eugene F. Fama, "Forward Rates as Predictors of Future Spot Rates," *Journal of Financial Economics*, Vol. 3, No. 4, 1976, pp. 361–377.
17 John R. Hicks, *Value and Capital* (London: Oxford University Press, 1946), Second Ed., pp. 141–145.
18 Franco Modigliani and Richard Sutch, "Innovations in Interest Rate Policy," *American Economic Review* (May 1966), pp. 178–197.

theory say that the latter conclusion could be accepted if all investors intend to liquidate their investment at the shortest possible date while all borrowers are anxious to
borrow long. This assumption can be rejected since institutions have holding periods
dictated by the nature of their liabilities.

The preferred habitat theory asserts that if there is an imbalance between the supply and demand for funds within a given maturity range, investors and borrowers will
not be reluctant to shift their investing and financing activities out of their preferred
maturity sector to take advantage of any imbalance. However, to do so, investors must
be induced by a yield premium in order to accept the risks associated with shifting
funds out of their preferred sector. Similarly, borrowers can only be induced to raise
funds in a maturity sector other than their preferred sector by a sufficient cost savings
to compensate for the corresponding funding risk.

Thus, this theory proposes that the shape of the yield curve is determined by both
expectations of future interest rates and a risk premium, positive or negative, to induce
market participants to shift out of their preferred habitat. Clearly, according to this
theory, yield curves that slope up, down, or flat are all possible.

7   MEASURING YIELD CURVE RISK

We now know how to construct the term structure of interest rates and the potential
information content contained in the term structure that can be used for making
investment decisions under different theories of the term structure. Next we look at
how to measure exposure of a portfolio or position to a change in the term structure.
This risk is referred to as yield curve risk.

Yield curve risk can be measured by changing the spot rate for a particular key
maturity and determining the sensitivity of a security or portfolio to this change holding the spot rate for the other key maturities constant. The sensitivity of the change in
value to a particular change in spot rate is called rate duration. There is a rate duration
for every point on the spot rate curve. Consequently, there is not one rate duration,
but a vector of durations representing each maturity on the spot rate curve. The
total change in value if all rates change by the same number of basis points is simply
the effective duration of a security or portfolio to a parallel shift in rates. Recall that
effective duration measures the exposure of a security or portfolio to a parallel shift
in the term structure, taking into account any embedded options.

This rate duration approach was first suggested by Donald Chambers and Willard
Carleton in 1988,[19] who called it "duration vectors." Robert Reitano suggested a similar
approach in a series of papers and referred to these durations as "partial durations."[20]
The most popular version of this approach is that developed by Thomas Ho in 1992.[21]

Ho's approach focuses on 11 key maturities of the spot rate curve. These rate durations are called key rate durations. The specific maturities on the spot rate curve for
which a key rate duration is measured are 3 months, 1 year, 2 years, 3 years, 5 years,
7 years, 10 years, 15 years, 20 years, 25 years, and 30 years. Changes in rates between
any two key rates are calculated using a linear approximation.

The impact of any type of yield curve shift can be quantified using key rate durations. A level shift can be quantified by changing all key rates by the same number of

19 Donald Chambers and Willard Carleton, "A Generalized Approach to Duration," *Research in Finance*
7(1988).
20 See, for example, Robert R. Reitano, "Non-Parallel Yield Curve Shifts and Durational Leverage," *Journal
of Portfolio Management* (Summer 1990), pp. 62–67, and "A Multivariate Approach to Duration Analysis,"
ARCH 2(1989).
21 Thomas S.Y. Ho, "Key Rate Durations: Measures of Interest Risk," *The Journal of Fixed Income*
(September 1992), pp. 29–44.

basis points and determining, based on the corresponding key rate durations, the effect on the value of a portfolio. The impact of a steepening of the yield curve can be found by 1) decreasing the key rates at the short end of the yield curve and determining the positive change in the portfolio's value using the corresponding key rate durations, and 2) increasing the key rates at the long end of the yield curve and determining the negative change in the portfolio's value using the corresponding key rate durations.

To simplify the key rate duration methodology, suppose that instead of a set of 11 key rates, there are only three key rates—2 years, 16 years, and 30 years.[22] The duration of a zero-coupon security is approximately the number of years to maturity. Thus, the three key rate durations are 2, 16, and 30. Consider the following two $100 portfolios composed of 2-year, 16-year, and 30-year issues:

Portfolio	2-Year Issue ($)	16-Year Issue ($)	30-Year Issue ($)
I	50	0	50
II	0	100	0

The key rate durations for these three points will be denoted by $D(1)$, $D(2)$, and $D(3)$ and defined as follows:

$D(1)$ = key rate duration for the 2-year part of the curve
$D(2)$ = key rate duration for the 16-year part of the curve
$D(3)$ = key rate duration for the 30-year part of the curve

The key rate durations for the three issues and the duration are as follows:

Issue	$D(1)$	$D(2)$	$D(3)$	Crash Duration
2-year	2	0	0	2
16-year	0	16	0	16
30-year	0	0	30	30

A portfolio's key rate duration is the weighted average of the key rate durations of the securities in the portfolio. The key rate duration and the effective duration for each portfolio are calculated below:

Portfolio I

$$D(1) = (50/100) \times 2 + (0/100) \times 0 + (50/100) \times 0 = 1$$
$$D(2) = (50/100) \times 0 + (0/100) \times 16 + (50/100) \times 0 = 0$$
$$D(3) = (50/100) \times 0 + (0/100) \times 0 + (50/100) \times 30 = 15$$

Effective duration $= (50 / 100) \times 2 + (0 / 100) \times 16 + (50 / 100) \times 30 = 16$

Portfolio II

$$D(1) = (0/100) \times 2 + (100/100) \times 0 + (0/100) \times 0 = 0$$
$$D(2) = (0/100) \times 0 + (100/100) \times 16 + (0/100) \times 0 = 16$$
$$D(3) = (0/100) \times 0 + (100/100) \times 0 + (0/100) \times 30 = 0$$

Effective duration $= (0/100) \times 2 + (100/100) \times 16 + (0/100) \times 30 = 16$

---

22 This is the numerical example used by Ho, "Key Rate Durations," p. 33.

Thus, the key rate durations differ for the two portfolios. However, the effective duration for each portfolio is the same. Despite the same effective duration, the performance of the two portfolios will not be the same for a nonparallel shift in the spot rates. Consider the following three scenarios:

Scenario 1   All spot rates shift down 10 basis points.

Scenario 2   The 2-year key rate shifts up 10 basis points and the 30-year rate shifts down 10 basis points.

Scenario 3   The 2-year key rate shifts down 10 basis points and the 30-year rate shifts up 10 basis points.

Let's illustrate how to compute the estimated total return based on the key rate durations for Portfolio I for scenario 2. The 2-year key rate duration [D(1)] for Portfolio I is 1. For a 100 basis point increase in the 2-year key rate, the portfolio's value will decrease by approximately 1%. For a 10 basis point increase (as assumed in scenario 2), the portfolio's value will decrease by approximately 0.1%. Now let's look at the change in the 30-year key rate in scenario 2. The 30-year key rate duration [D(3)] is 15. For a 100 basis point decrease in the 30-year key rate, the portfolio's value will increase by approximately 15%. For a 10 basis point decrease (as assumed in scenario 2), the increase in the portfolio's value will be approximately 1.5%. Consequently, for Portfolio I in scenario 2 we have:

change in portfolio's value due to 2-year key rate change	−0.1%
change in portfolio's value due to 30-year key rate change	+1.5%
change in portfolio value	+1.4%

In the same way, the total return for both portfolios can be estimated for the three scenarios. The estimated total returns are shown below:

Portfolio	Scenario 1 (%)	Scenario 2 (%)	Scenario 3 (%)
I	1.6	1.4	−1.4
II	1.6	0	0

Thus, only for the parallel yield curve shift (scenario 1) do the two portfolios have identical performance based on their durations.

Key rate durations are different for ladder, barbell, and bullet portfolios. A ladder portfolio is one with approximately equal dollar amounts (market values) in each maturity sector. A barbell portfolio has considerably greater weights given to the shorter and longer maturity bonds than to the intermediate maturity bonds. A bullet portfolio has greater weights concentrated in the intermediate maturity relative to the shorter and longer maturities.

The key rate duration profiles for a ladder, a barbell, and a bullet portfolio are graphed in Exhibit 7.[23] All these portfolios have the same effective duration. As can be seen, the ladder portfolio has roughly the same key rate duration for all the key maturities from year 2 on. For the barbell portfolio, the key rate durations are much greater for the 5-year and 20-year key maturities and much smaller for the other key maturities. For the bullet portfolio, the key rate duration is substantially greater for the 10-year maturity than the duration for other key maturities.

---

23 The portfolios whose key rate durations are shown in Exhibit 7 were hypothetical Treasury portfolios constructed on April 23, 1997.

Exhibit 7	Key Rate Duration Profile for Three Treasury Portfolios (April 23, 1997): Ladder, Barbell, and Bullet

(a) Ladder Portfolio

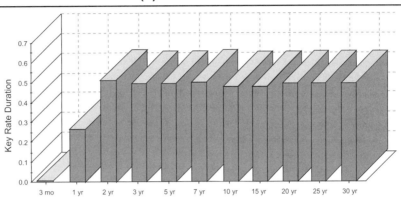

(b) Barbell Portfolio

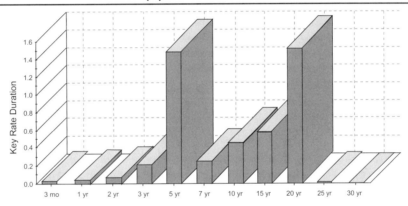

(c) Bullet Portfolio

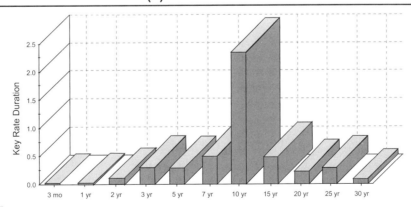

Source: Barra.

8   YIELD VOLATILITY AND MEASUREMENT

In assessing the interest rate exposure of a security or portfolio one should combine effective duration with yield volatility because effective duration alone is not sufficient to measure interest rate risk. The reason is that effective duration says that if interest rates change, a security's or portfolio's market value will change by approximately the percentage projected by its effective duration. However, the risk exposure of a portfolio to rate changes depends on how likely and how much interest rates may change, a parameter measured by yield volatility. For example, consider a U.S. Treasury security with an effective duration of 6 and a government bond of an emerging market country with an effective duration of 4. Based on effective duration alone, it would seem that the U.S. Treasury security has greater interest rate risk than the emerging market government bond. Suppose that yield volatility is substantial in the emerging market country relative to in the United States. Then the effective durations alone are not sufficient to identify the interest rate risk.

There is another reason why it is important to be able to measure yield or interest rate volatility: it is a critical input into a valuation model. An assumption of yield volatility is needed to value bonds with embedded options and structured products. The same measure is also needed in valuing some interest rate derivatives (i.e., options, caps, and floors).

In this section, we look at how to measure yield volatility and discuss some techniques used to estimate it. Volatility is measured in terms of the standard deviation or variance. We will see how yield volatility as measured by the daily percentage change in yields is calculated from historical yields. We will see that there are several issues confronting an investor in measuring historical yield volatility. Then we turn to modeling and forecasting yield volatility.

A. Measuring Historical Yield Volatility

Market participants seek a measure of yield volatility. The measure used is the standard deviation or variance. Here we will see how to compute yield volatility using historical data.

The sample variance of a random variable using historical data is calculated using the following formula:

$$\text{Variance} = \frac{\sum_{t=1}^{T}\left(X_t - \bar{X}\right)^2}{T - 1} \tag{1}$$

and then

$$\text{Standard deviation} = \sqrt{\text{Variance}}$$

where

X_t = observation t of variable X

$\bar{X}$ = the sample mean for variable X

T = the number of observations in the sample

Our focus is on yield volatility. More specifically, we are interested in the change in the daily yield relative to the previous day's yield. So, for example, suppose the yield on a zero-coupon Treasury bond was 6.555% on Day 1 and 6.593% on Day 2. The relative change in yield would be:

$$\frac{6.593\% - 6.555\%}{6.555\%} = 0.005797$$

This means if the yield is 6.555% on Day 1 and grows by 0.005797 in one day, the yield on Day 2 will be:

$$6.555\%(1.005797) = 6.593\%$$

If instead of assuming simple compounding it is assumed that there is continuous compounding, the relative change in yield can be computed as the natural logarithm of the ratio of the yield for two days. That is, the relative yield change can be computed as follows:

$$Ln(6.593\%/6.555\%) = 0.0057804$$

where "Ln" stands for the natural logarithm. There is not much difference between the relative change of daily yields computed assuming simple compounding and continuous compounding.[24] In practice, continuous compounding is used. Multiplying the natural logarithm of the ratio of the two yields by 100 scales the value to a percentage change in daily yields.

Therefore, letting y_t be the yield on day t and y_{t-1} be the yield on day $t - 1$, the percentage change in yield, X_t, is found as follows:

$$X_t = 100\left[Ln(y_t/y_{t-1})\right]$$

In our example, y_t is 6.593% and y_{t-1} is 6.555%. Therefore,

$$X_t = 100\left[Ln(6.593/6.555)\right] = 0.57804\%$$

To illustrate how to calculate a daily standard deviation from historical data, consider the data in Exhibit 8 which show the yield on a Treasury zero for 26 consecutive days. From the 26 observations, 25 days of percentage yield changes are calculated in Column 3. Column 4 shows the square of the deviations of the observations from the mean. The bottom of Exhibit 8 shows the calculation of the daily mean for 25 yield changes, the variance, and the standard deviation. The daily standard deviation is 0.6360%.

Exhibit 8	Calculation of Daily Standard Deviation Based on 26 Daily Observations for a Treasury Zero		
(1) t	(2) y_t	(3) $X_t = 100\left[Ln(y_t/y_{t-1})\right]$	(4) $\left(X_t - \bar{X}\right)^2$
0	6.6945		
1	6.699	0.06720	0.02599
2	6.710	0.16407	0.06660
3	6.675	−0.52297	0.18401
4	6.555	−1.81411	2.95875
5	6.583	0.42625	0.27066
6	6.569	−0.21290	0.01413
7	6.583	0.21290	0.09419
8	6.555	−0.42625	0.11038
9	6.593	0.57804	0.45164
10	6.620	0.40869	0.25270
11	6.568	−0.78860	0.48246

(continued)

---

[24] See DeFusco, McLeavey, Pinto, and Runkle, *Quantitative Methods for Investment Analysis*.

Exhibit 8	Continued		

(1) t	(2) y_t	(3) $X_t = 100\left[\text{Ln}\left(y_t/y_{t-1}\right)\right]$	(4) $\left(X_t - \bar{X}\right)^2$
12	6.575	0.10652	0.04021
13	6.646	1.07406	1.36438
14	6.607	−0.58855	0.24457
15	6.612	0.07565	0.02878
16	6.575	−0.56116	0.21823
17	6.552	−0.35042	0.06575
18	6.515	−0.56631	0.22307
19	6.533	0.27590	0.13684
20	6.543	0.15295	0.06099
21	6.559	0.24424	0.11441
22	6.500	−0.90360	0.65543
23	6.546	0.70520	0.63873
24	6.589	0.65474	0.56063
25	6.539	−0.76173	0.44586
	Total	−2.35020	9.7094094

$$\text{Sample mean} = \bar{X} = \frac{-2.35020\%}{25} = -0.09401\%$$

$$\text{Variance} = \frac{9.7094094\%}{25 - 1} = 0.4045587\%$$

$$\text{Std dev} = \sqrt{0.4045587\%} = 0.6360493\%$$

The daily standard deviation will vary depending on the 25 days selected. It is important to understand that the daily standard deviation is dependent on the period selected, a point we return to later in this reading.

1 Determining the Number of Observations

In our illustration, we used 25 observations for the daily percentage change in yield. The appropriate number of observations depends on the situation at hand. For example, traders concerned with overnight positions might use the 10 most recent trading days (i.e., two weeks). A bond portfolio manager who is concerned with longer term volatility might use 25 trading days (about one month). The selection of the number of observations can have a significant effect on the calculated daily standard deviation.

2 Annualizing the Standard Deviation

The daily standard deviation can be annualized by multiplying it by the square root of the number of days in a year.[25] That is,

$$\text{Daily standard deviation} \times \sqrt{\text{Number of days in a year}}$$

---

[25] For any probability distribution, it is important to assess whether the value of a random variable in one period is affected by the value that the random variable took on in a prior period. Casting this in terms of yield changes, it is important to know whether the yield today is affected by the yield in a prior period. The term *serial correlation* is used to describe the correlation between the yield in different periods. Annualizing the daily yield by multiplying the daily standard deviation by the square root of the number of days in a year assumes that serial correlation is not significant.

Market practice varies with respect to the number of days in the year that should be used in the annualizing formula above. Some investors and traders use the number of days in the year, 365 days, to annualize the daily standard deviation. Some investors and traders use only either 250 days or 260 days to annualize. The latter is simply the number of trading days in a year based on five trading days per week for 52 weeks. The former reduces the number of trading days of 260 for 10 non-trading holidays.

Thus, in calculating an annual standard deviation, the investor must decide on:

1. the number of daily observations to use.

2. the number of days in the year to use to annualize the daily standard deviation.

The annual standard deviation for the daily standard deviation based on the 25-daily yield changes shown in Exhibit 8 (0.6360493%) using 250 days, 260 days, and 365 days to annualize are as follows:

250 Days	260 Days	365 Days
10.06%	10.26%	12.15%

Now keep in mind that all of these decisions regarding the number of days to use in the daily standard deviation calculation, which set of days to use, and the number of days to use to annualize are not merely an academic exercise. Eventually, the standard deviation will be used in either the valuation of a security or in the measurement of risk exposure and can have a significant impact on the resulting value.

3 Using the Standard Deviation with Yield Estimation

What does it mean if the annual standard deviation for the *change in* the Treasury zero yield is 12%? It means that if the prevailing yield is 8%, then the annual standard deviation of the yield change is 96 basis points. This is found by multiplying the annual standard deviation of the yield change of 12% by the prevailing yield of 8%.

Assuming that yield volatility is approximately normally distributed, we can use the normal distribution to construct a confidence interval for the future yield.[26] For example, we know that there is a 68.3% probability that an interval between *one* standard deviation below and above the sample expected value will bracket the future yield. The sample expected value is the prevailing yield. If the annual standard deviation is 96 basis points and the prevailing yield is 8%, then there is a 68.3% probability that the range between 7.04% (8% minus 96 basis points) and 8.96% (8% plus 96 basis points) will include the future yield. For *three* standard deviations below and above the prevailing yield, there is a 99.7% probability. Using the numbers above, three standard deviations are 288 basis points (3 times 96 basis points). The interval is then 5.12% (8% minus 288 basis points) and 10.88% (8% plus 288 basis points).

Practice Question 1

A. The daily yields for 26 days are given below. Compute the daily percentage change in yield for each day assuming continuous compounding.

t	y_t
0	7.17400
1	7.19400

(continued)

26 See Chapter 4 in DeFusco, McLeavey, Pinto, and Runkle, *Quantitative Methods for Investment Analysis*.

t	y_t
2	7.21800
3	7.15100
4	7.02500
5	7.02400
6	7.03000
7	7.02000
8	6.96400
9	6.90400
10	6.89671
11	6.85300
12	6.87100
13	6.88300
14	6.87500
15	6.87800
16	6.80400
17	6.84300
18	6.79500
19	6.79500
20	6.85400
21	6.81000
22	6.77300
23	6.86700
24	6.88700
25	6.88100

B. Compute the daily standard deviation.

Practice Question 2

Based on the daily standard deviation computed in Practice Question 1, compute the annualized standard deviation based on the following number of days: a) 250, b) 260, and c) 365.

The interval or range constructed is called a "confidence interval."[27] Our first interval of 7.04% to 8.96% is a 68.3% confidence interval. Our second interval of 5.12% to 10.88% is a 99.7% confidence interval. A confidence interval with any probability can be constructed.

B. Historical versus Implied Volatility

Market participants estimate yield volatility in one of two ways. The first way is by estimating historical yield volatility. This is the method that we have thus far described in this reading. The resulting volatility is called historical volatility. The second way

---

27   See Chapter 6 in DeFusco, MacLeavey, Pinto, and Runkle, *Quantitative Methods for Investment Analysis.*

is to estimate yield volatility based on the observed prices of interest rate options and caps. Yield volatility calculated using this approach is called **implied volatility**.

The implied volatility is based on some option pricing model. One of the inputs to any option pricing model in which the underlying is a Treasury security or Treasury futures contract is expected yield volatility. If the observed price of an option is assumed to be the fair price and the option pricing model is assumed to be the model that would generate that fair price, then the implied yield volatility is the yield volatility that, when used as an input into the option pricing model, would produce the observed option price.

There are several problems with using implied volatility. First, it is assumed the option pricing model is correct. Second, option pricing models typically assume that volatility is constant over the life of the option. Therefore, interpreting an implied volatility becomes difficult.[28]

C. Forecasting Yield Volatility

As has been seen, the yield volatility as measured by the standard deviation can vary based on the time period selected and the number of observations. Now we turn to the issue of forecasting yield volatility. There are several methods. Before describing these methods, let's address the question of what mean value should be used in the calculation of the forecasted standard deviation.

Suppose at the end of Day 12 a trader was interested in a forecast for volatility using the 10 most recent days of trading and updating that forecast at the end of each trading day. What mean value should be used?

The trader can calculate a 10-day moving average of the daily percentage yield change. Exhibit 8 shows the daily percentage change in yield for the Treasury zero from Day 1 to Day 25. To calculate a moving average of the daily percentage yield change at the end of Day 12, the trader would use the 10 trading days from Day 3 to Day 12. At the end of Day 13, the trader will calculate the 10-day average by using the percentage yield change on Day 13 and would exclude the percentage yield change on Day 3. The trader will use the 10 trading days from Day 4 to Day 13.

Exhibit 9 shows the 10-day moving average calculated from Day 12 to Day 25. Notice the considerable variation over this period. The 10-day moving average ranged from −0.20324% to 0.07902%.

Exhibit 9	10-Day Moving Average of Daily Yield Change for Treasury Zero

10-Trading Days Ending	Daily Average (%)
Day 12	−0.20324
Day 13	−0.04354
Day 14	0.07902
Day 15	0.04396
Day 16	0.00913
Day 17	−0.04720
Day 18	−0.06121

(continued)

---

28 For a further discussion, see Frank J. Fabozzi and Wai Lee, "Measuring and Forecasting Yield Volatility," Chapter 16 in Frank J. Fabozzi (ed.), *Perspectives on Interest Rate Risk Management for Money Managers and Traders* (New Hope, PA: Frank J. Fabozzi Associates, 1998).

Exhibit 9	Continued

10-Trading Days Ending	Daily Average (%)
Day 19	−0.09142
Day 20	−0.11700
Day 21	−0.01371
Day 22	−0.11472
Day 23	−0.15161
Day 24	−0.02728
Day 25	−0.11102

Thus far, it is assumed that the moving average is the appropriate value to use for the expected value of the change in yield. However, there are theoretical arguments that suggest it is more appropriate to assume that the expected value of the change in yield will be zero.[29] In the equation for the variance given by Equation 1, the value of zero is used for $\bar{X}$ rather than the moving average. If zero is substituted into Equation 1, the equation for the variance becomes:

$$\text{Variance} = \frac{\sum_{t=1}^{T} X_t^2}{T-1} \qquad (2)$$

There are various methods for forecasting daily volatility. The daily standard deviation given by Equation 2 assigns an equal weight to all observations. So, if a trader is calculating volatility based on the most recent 10 days of trading, each day is given a weight of 0.10.

For example, suppose that a trader is interested in the daily volatility of our hypothetical Treasury zero yield and decides to use the 10 most recent trading days. Exhibit 10 reports the 10-day volatility for various days using the data in Exhibit 8 and the standard deviation derived from the formula for the variance given by Equation 2.

Exhibit 10	Moving Averages of Daily Standard Deviations Based on 10 Days of Observations

10-Trading Days Ending	Moving Average Daily Standard Deviation (%)
Day 12	0.75667
Day 13	0.81874
Day 14	0.58579
Day 15	0.56886
Day 16	0.59461
Day 17	0.60180
Day 18	0.61450
Day 19	0.59072
Day 20	0.57705

---

29 Jacques Longerstacey and Peter Zangari, *Five Questions about RiskMetrics*™, JP Morgan Research Publication 1995.

Exhibit 10	Continued

10-Trading Days Ending	Moving Average Daily Standard Deviation (%)
Day 21	0.52011
Day 22	0.59998
Day 23	0.53577
Day 24	0.54424
Day 25	0.60003

There is reason to suspect that market participants give greater weight to recent movements in yield or price when determining volatility. To give greater importance to more recent information, observations farther in the past should be given less weight. This can be done by revising the variance as given by Equation 2 as follows:

$$\text{Variance} = \frac{\sum\limits_{t=1}^{T} W_t X_t^2}{T - 1} \tag{3}$$

where W_t is the weight assigned to observation t such that the sum of the weights is equal to T (i.e., $\Sigma\ W_t = T$) and the farther the observation is from today, the lower the weight. The weights should be assigned so that the forecasted volatility reacts faster to a recent major market movement and declines gradually as we move away from any major market movement.

Finally, a time series characteristic of financial assets suggests that a period of high volatility is followed by a period of high volatility. Furthermore, a period of relative stability in returns appears to be followed by a period that can be characterized in the same way. This suggests that volatility today may depend upon recent prior volatility. This can be modeled and used to forecast volatility. The statistical model used to estimate this time series property of volatility is called an autoregressive conditional heteroskedasticity (ARCH) model.[30] The term "conditional" means that the value of the variance depends on or is conditional on the value of the random variable. The term heteroskedasticity means that the variance is not equal for all values of the random variable. The foundation for ARCH models is a specialist topic.[31]

SOLUTIONS FOR PRACTICE QUESTIONS

1. A. The daily percentage change in yield for each trading day is shown below in the next to the last column:

t	y_t	$X_t = 100\ [\text{Ln}\ (y_t/y_{t-1})]$	$(X_t - \bar{X})^2$
0	7.17400		
1	7.19400	0.27840	0.19820
2	7.21800	0.33306	0.24985

---

[30] See Robert F. Engle, "Autoregressive Conditional Heteroskedasticity with Estimates of Variance of U.K. Inflation," *Econometrica* 50 (1982), pp. 987–1008.

[31] See Chapter 9 in DeFusco, McLeavey, Pinto, and Runkle, *Quantitative Methods for Investment Analysis.*

t	y_t	$X_t = 100 [Ln (y_t/y_{t-1})]$	$(X_t - \bar{X})^2$
3	7.15100	−0.93257	0.58641
4	7.02500	−1.77770	2.59500
5	7.02400	−0.01424	0.02328
6	7.03000	0.08538	0.06360
7	7.02000	−0.14235	0.00060
8	6.96400	−0.80092	0.40211
9	6.90400	−0.86531	0.48792
10	6.89671	−0.10565	0.00374
11	6.85300	−0.63580	0.21996
12	6.87100	0.26231	0.18414
13	6.88300	0.17449	0.11648
14	6.87500	−0.11630	0.00255
15	6.87800	0.04363	0.04428
16	6.80400	−1.08172	0.83709
17	6.84300	0.57156	0.54517
18	6.79500	−0.70392	0.28850
19	6.79500	0.00000	0.02782
20	6.85400	0.86454	1.06365
21	6.81000	−0.64403	0.22775
22	6.77300	−0.54480	0.14289
23	6.86700	1.37832	2.38739
24	6.88700	0.29082	0.20942
25	6.88100	−0.08716	0.00634
	Total	−4.16994	10.91412

B. The daily standard deviation is computed as follows:

$$\text{Sample mean} = \bar{X} = \frac{-4.16994\%}{25} = -0.166798\%$$

$$\text{Variance} = \frac{10.91412\%}{25 - 1} = 0.4547550\%$$

$$\text{Std dev} = \sqrt{0.4547550\%} = 0.67436\%$$

2. The daily standard deviation is 0.67436% and the annualized standard deviation based on an assumed number of trading days in a year is:

250 days	260 days	365 days
10.66%	10.87%	12.88%

SUMMARY

■ Historically, four shapes have been observed for the yield curve: 1) normal or positively sloped (i.e., the longer the maturity, the higher the yield), 2) flat (i.e., the yield for all maturities is approximately equal), 3) inverted or negatively sloped (i.e., the longer the maturity, the lower the yield), and 4) a humped yield curve.

- The spread between long-term Treasury yields and short-term Treasury yields is referred to as the steepness or slope of the yield curve.

- Some investors define the slope of the yield curve as the spread between the 30-year yield and the 3-month yield and others as the spread between the 30-year yield and the 2-year yield.

- A shift in the yield curve refers to the relative change in the yield for each Treasury maturity.

- A parallel shift in the yield curve refers to a shift in which the change in the yield for all maturities is the same; a nonparallel shift in the yield curve means that the yield for all maturities does not change by the same number of basis points.

- Historically, the two types of nonparallel yield curve shifts that have been observed are a twist in the slope of the yield curve and a change in the curvature of the yield curve.

- A flattening of the yield curve means that the slope of the yield curve has decreased; a steepening of the yield curve means that the slope has increased.

- A butterfly shift is the other type of nonparallel shift—a change in the curvature or humpedness of the yield curve.

- Historically, the factors that have been observed to drive Treasury returns are 1) a shift in the level of interest rates, 2) a change in the slope of the yield curve, and 3) a change in the curvature of the yield curve.

- The most important factor driving Treasury returns is a shift in the level of interest rates. Two other factors, in decreasing importance, include changes in the yield curve slope and changes in the curvature of the yield curve.

- The universe of Treasury issues that can be used to construct the theoretical spot rate curve is 1) on-the-run Treasury issues, 2) on-the-run Treasury issues and selected off-the-run Treasury issues, 3) all Treasury coupon securities and bills, and 4) Treasury strips.

- There are three methodologies that have been used to derive the theoretical spot rate curve: 1) bootstrapping when the universe is on-the-run Treasury issues (with and without selected off-the-run issues), 2) econometric modeling for all Treasury coupon securities and bills, and 3) simply the observed yields on Treasury coupon strips.

- The problem with using Treasury coupon strips is that the observed yields may be biased due to a liquidity premium or an unfavorable tax treatment.

- The swap rate is the rate at which fixed cash flows can be exchanged for floating cash flows.

- In a LIBOR-based swap, the swap curve provides a yield curve for LIBOR.

- A swap curve can be constructed that is unique to a country where there is a swap market.

- The swap spread is primarily a gauge of the credit risk associated with a country's banking sector.

- The advantages of using a swap curve as the benchmark interest rate rather than a government bond yield curve are 1) there is almost no government regulation of the swap market making swap rates across different markets more comparable, 2) the supply of swaps depends only on the number of counterparties that are seeking or are willing to enter into a swap transaction at any given time, 3) comparisons across countries of government yield curves is difficult because of the differences in sovereign credit risk, and 4) there are more maturity points available to construct a swap curve than a government bond yield curve.

■ From the swap yield curve a LIBOR spot rate curve can be derived using the bootstrapping methodology and the LIBOR forward rate curve can be derived.

■ The three forms of the expectations theory (the pure expectations theory, the liquidity preference theory, and the preferred habitat theory) assume that the forward rates in current long-term bonds are closely related to the market's expectations about future short-term rates.

■ The three forms of the expectations theory differ on whether or not other factors also affect forward rates, and how.

■ The pure expectations theory postulates that no systematic factors other than expected future short-term rates affect forward rates.

■ Because forward rates are not perfect predictors of future interest rates, the pure expectations theory neglects the risks (interest rate risk and reinvestment risk) associated with investing in Treasury securities.

■ The broadest interpretation of the pure expectations theory suggests that investors expect the return for any investment horizon to be the same, regardless of the maturity strategy selected.

■ The local expectations form of the pure expectations theory suggests that the return will be the same over a short-term investment horizon starting today, and it is this narrow interpretation that economists have demonstrated is the only interpretation that can be sustained in equilibrium.

■ Two interpretations of forward rates based on arbitrage arguments are that they are 1) "break-even rates" and 2) rates that can be locked in.

■ Advocates of the pure expectations theory argue that forward rates are the market's consensus of future interest rates.

■ Forward rates have not been found to be good predictors of future interest rates; however, an understanding of forward rates is still extremely important because of their role as break-even rates and rates that can be locked in.

■ The liquidity preference theory and the preferred habitat theory assert that there are other factors that affect forward rates and these two theories are therefore referred to as biased expectations theories.

■ The liquidity preference theory states that investors will hold longer-term maturities only if they are offered a risk premium and therefore forward rates should reflect both interest rate expectations and a liquidity risk premium.

■ The preferred habitat theory, in addition to adopting the view that forward rates reflect the expectation of the future path of interest rates as well as a risk premium, argues that the yield premium need not reflect a liquidity risk but instead reflects the demand and supply of funds in a given maturity range.

■ A common approach to measure yield curve risk is to change the yield for a particular maturity of the yield curve and determine the sensitivity of a security or portfolio to this change holding all other key rates constant.

■ Key rate duration is the sensitivity of a portfolio's value to the change in a particular key rate.

■ The most popular version of key rate duration uses 11 key maturities of the spot rate curve (3 months, 1, 2, 3, 5, 7, 10, 15, 20, 25, and 30 years).

■ Variance is a measure of the dispersion of a random variable around its expected value.

■ The standard deviation is the square root of the variance and is a commonly used measure of volatility.

■ Yield volatility can be estimated from daily yield observations.

- The observation used in the calculation of the daily standard deviation is the natural logarithm of the ratio of one day's and the previous day's yield.
- The selection of the time period (the number of observations) can have a significant effect on the calculated daily standard deviation.
- A daily standard deviation is annualized by multiplying it by the square root of the number of days in a year.
- Typically, either 250 days, 260 days, or 365 days are used to annualize the daily standard deviation.
- Implied volatility can also be used to estimate yield volatility based on some option pricing model.
- In forecasting volatility, it is more appropriate to use an expectation of zero for the mean value.
- The simplest method for forecasting volatility is weighting all observations equally.
- A forecasted volatility can be obtained by assigning greater weight to more recent observations.
- Autoregressive conditional heteroskedasticity (ARCH) models can be used to capture the time series characteristic of yield volatility in which a period of high volatility is followed by a period of high volatility and a period of relative stability appears to be followed by a period that can be characterized in the same way.

PRACTICE PROBLEMS FOR READING 43

1. What are the four types of shapes observed for the yield curve?

2. How is the slope of the yield curve defined and measured?

3. Historically, how has the slope of the long end of the yield curve differed from that of the short end of the yield curve at a given point in time?

4. **A.** What are the three factors that have empirically been observed to affect Treasury returns?

   B. What has been observed to be the most important factor in affecting Treasury returns?

   C. Given the most important factor identified in Part B, justify the use of duration as a measure of interest rate risk.

   D. What has been observed to be the second most important factor in affecting Treasury returns?

   E. Given the second most important factor identified in Part D, justify the use of a measure of interest rate risk in addition to duration.

5. **A.** What are the limitations of using just the on-the-run Treasury issues to construct the theoretical spot rate curve?

   B. Why if all Treasury bills and Treasury coupon securities are used to construct the theoretical spot rate curve is it not possible to use the bootstrapping method?

6. **A.** What are the problems with using the yield on Treasury strips to construct the theoretical spot rate curve?

   B. Why, even if a practitioner decides to use the yield on Treasury strips to construct the theoretical spot rate curve despite the problems identified in Part A, will the practitioner restrict the analysis to Treasury coupon strips?

7. What are the advantages of using the swap curve as a benchmark of interest rates relative to a government bond yield curve?

8. How can a spot rate curve be constructed for a country that has a liquid swap market?

9. **A.** What is a swap spread?

   B. What is the swap spread indicative of?

10. **A.** What is the pure expectations theory?

    B. What are the shortcomings of the pure expectations theory?

11. Based on the broadest interpretation of the pure expectations theory, what would be the difference in the 4-year total return if an investor purchased a 7-year zero-coupon bond or a 15-year zero-coupon bond?

12. Based on the local expectations form of the pure expectations theory, what would be the difference in the 6-month total return if an investor purchased a 5-year zero-coupon bond or a 2-year zero-coupon bond?

13. Comment on the following statement made by a portfolio manager to a client:

    Proponents of the unbiased expectations theory argue that the forward rates built into the term structure of interest rates are the market's consensus of future interest rates. We disagree with the theory because studies suggest that forward rates are poor predictors of future interest rates. Therefore, the position that our investment management firm takes is that forward rates are irrelevant and provide no information to our managers in managing a bond portfolio.

14. Based on arbitrage arguments, give two interpretations for each of the following three forward rates:

    A. The 1-year forward rate seven years from now is 6.4%.

    B. The 2-year forward rate one year from now is 6.2%.

    C. The 8-year forward rate three years from now is 7.1%.

15. There are two forms of the "biased" expectations theory. Why are these two forms referred to as "biased" expectations?

16. You are the financial consultant to a pension fund. After your presentation to the trustees of the fund, you asked the trustees if they have any questions. You receive the two questions below. Answer each one.

    A. "The yield curve is upward-sloping today. Doesn't this suggest that the market consensus is that interest rates are expected to increase in the future and therefore you should reduce the interest rate risk exposure for the portfolio that you are managing for us?"

    B. "I am looking over one of the pages in your presentation that shows spot rates and I am having difficulty in understanding it. The spot rates at the short end (up to three years) are increasing with maturity. For maturities greater than three years but less than eight years, the spot rates are declining with maturity. Finally, for maturities greater than eight years the spot rates are virtually the same for each maturity. There is simply no expectations theory that would explain that type of shape for the term structure of interest rates. Is this market simply unstable?"

17. Below are the key rate durations for three portfolios of U.S. Treasury securities, all with the same duration for a parallel shift in the yield curve.

    A. For each portfolio describe the type of portfolio (barbell, ladder, or bullet).

Key Rate Maturity	Portfolio A	Portfolio B	Portfolio C
3-month	0.04	0.04	0.03
1-year	0.06	0.29	0.07
2-year	0.08	0.67	0.31
3-year	0.28	0.65	0.41
5-year	0.38	0.65	1.90
7-year	0.65	0.64	0.35
10-year	3.38	0.66	0.41
15-year	0.79	0.67	0.70
20-year	0.36	0.64	1.95
25-year	0.12	0.62	0.06
30-year	0.06	0.67	0.01

    B. Which portfolio will benefit the most if the spot rate for the 10-year decreases by 50 basis points while the spot rate for all other key maturities changes very little?

    C. What is the duration for a parallel shift in the yield curve for the three portfolios?

18. Compute the 10-day daily standard deviation of the percentage change in yield assuming continuous compounding and assuming the following daily yields.

t	y_t
0	5.854
1	5.843
2	5.774
3	5.719
4	5.726
5	5.761
6	5.797
7	5.720
8	5.755
9	5.787
10	5.759

19. For the daily yield volatility computed in the previous question, what is the annual yield volatility assuming the following number of days in the year?

    A. 250 days.

    B. 260 days.

    C. 365 days.

20. Comment on the following statement: "Two portfolio managers with the same set of daily yields will compute the same historical annual volatility."

21. Suppose that the annualized standard deviation for the change in the 2-year Treasury yield based on daily yields is 7% and the current level of the 2-year Treasury yield is 5%. Assuming that the probability distribution for the percentage change in 2-year Treasury yields is approximately normally distributed, how would you interpret the 7% annualized standard deviation?

22. A. What is implied volatility?

    B. What are the problems associated with using implied volatility as a measure of yield volatility?

23. A. In forecasting yield volatility, why would a manager not want to weight each daily yield change equally?

    B. In forecasting yield volatility, what is recommended for the sample mean in the formula for the variance or standard deviation?

The following information relates to Questions 24-26

Kate Campbell is the manager of a U.S. Treasury bond portfolio. She is considering increasing the portfolio's exposure to zero-coupon U.S. Treasury securities and asks her assistant, Naomi Moss, to investigate what determines the return on these bonds. Moss replies that three factors determine the return on zero-coupon U.S. Treasury bonds:

- the level of the yield curve;
- the slope of the yield curve;
- the curvature of the yield curve.

Intrigued by the role of the slope of yield curve, Campbell asks Moss for more information on the determinants of the term structure of interest rates. Moss replies:

> "The pure expectations theory and preferred habitat theory both assume that the forward rates in current long-term bonds are closely related to the market's expectations about future short-term rates."

Campbell learns that the investment mandate of her portfolio has been expanded to allow investments in asset-backed bonds, U.S. municipal revenue bonds, and non-dollar sovereign bonds. Campbell asks Moss to investigate the potential risks and credit rating issues involved with these bonds. Moss writes a report that makes the following statements:

1. "The role of the servicer in a securitization transaction is critical for asset-backed bonds. Therefore the rating agencies analyze servicing history and costs to the special purpose vehicle before assigning a credit rating."

2. "For U.S. municipal revenue bonds, the three areas that the legal opinion should address are: the flow-of-funds structure; limits of the basic security; and the stability of the excess spread."

3. "For non-dollar sovereign bonds, the key factors considered by S&P in assigning the local currency credit rating are a) the balance of payments, b) fiscal policy and budgetary flexibility, and c) monetary policy and inflation pressures."

After reading Moss's report, Campbell has decided to invest in the German government bond market. Campbell asks Moss to help structure this portfolio. Moss proposes the following alternative portfolios, each consisting solely of zero-coupon German government bonds:

Exhibit 1 Alternative Portfolio Weights

	Portfolio I (%)	Portfolio II (%)	Portfolio III (%)
2-year maturity	50	—	25
16-year maturity	—	100	50
30-year maturity	50	—	25
TOTAL	100	100	100

24. Which factor in Moss's list has the least impact on zero-coupon U.S. Treasury bond returns?
    A. The level of the yield curve.
    B. The slope of the yield curve.
    C. The curvature of the yield curve.

25. Is Moss's response regarding theories about the term structure of interest rates correct?
    A. Yes.
    B. No, preferred habitat theory does not make an assumption of market's expectations.
    C. No, pure expectations theory does not make an assumption of market's expectations.

26. If the 2-year key rate shifts up by 10 bps and the 30-year key rate shifts down by 20 bps, the difference in total return between portfolio III and portfolio I would be *closest* to:

    A. 1.45%.

    B. 2.90%.

    C. 4.35%.

SOLUTIONS FOR READING 43

1. Historically, four shapes have been observed for the yield curve. A positively sloping or normal yield curve is where the longer the maturity, the higher the yield. A flat yield curve is where the yield for all maturities is approximately the same. A negatively sloped or inverted yield curve is where yield decreases as maturity increases. A humped yield curve is where yield increases for a range of maturities and then decreases.

2. The slope of the yield curve is measured by the difference between long-term Treasury yields and short-term Treasury yields. While there is no industrywide accepted definition of the maturity used for the long-end and the maturity for the short-end of the yield curve, some market participants define the slope of the yield curve as the difference between the 30-year yield and the 3-month yield while other market participants define the slope of the yield curve as the difference between the 30-year yield and the 2-year yield. The more accepted measure is the latter. However, for some sectors of the bond market such as the mortgage sector, the slope of the yield curve is measured by the spread between the 10-year yield and 2-year yield.

3. Historically, the slope of the long end of the yield curve has been flatter than the slope of the short end of the yield curve.

4. **A.** Studies have shown that there have been three factors that affect Treasury returns: 1) changes in the level of yields, 2) changes in the slope of the yield curve, and 3) changes in the curvature of the yield curve.

   B. The most important factor is the change in the level of interest rates.

   C. The implication is that the manager of a Treasury portfolio should control for its exposure to changes in the level of interest rates. For this reason it is important to have a measure such as duration to quantify exposure to a parallel shift in the yield curve.

   D. The second most important factor is changes in the yield curve slope.

   E. The implication is that a measure such as duration must be supplemented with information about a portfolio's exposure to changes in the slope of the yield curve—a measure such as key rate duration.

5. **A.** One limitation is that there is a large gap between maturities for the on-the-run issues, and a linear extrapolation is used to get the yield for maturities between the on-the-runs. A second limitation is that information is lost about the yield on other Treasury securities. Finally, one or more of the on-the-run issues may be on special in the repo market and thereby distort the true yield for these issues.

   B. Since there may be more than one Treasury issue for a given maturity and since there are callable securities and securities trading at a price different from par (leading to tax issues), a methodology for handling these problems must be used. The bootstrapping methodology does not deal with such problems.

6. **A.** There are three problems with using the observed rates on Treasury strips: 1) there is a liquidity premium for the observed yields in the strips market because strips are not as liquid as Treasury coupon securities; 2) the tax treatment of strips is different from that of Treasury coupon securities—the accrued interest on strips is taxed even though no cash is received by the investor—resulting in the yield on strips reflecting this tax

disadvantage; and 3) there are maturity sectors where non-U.S. investors find it advantageous to trade off yield for tax advantages in their country that are associated with a strip.

B. A practitioner may restrict the use of Treasury strips to construct the theoretical spot rate curve to coupon strips because of the tax aspect mentioned in Part A. Specifically, certain foreign tax authorities allow their citizens to treat the difference between the maturity value and the purchase price as a capital gain and tax this gain at a favorable tax rate. Some will grant this favorable treatment only when the strip is created from the principal rather than the coupon. Any such bias can be avoided by just using coupon strips.

7. The advantages are that 1) there are typically more points available to construct a swap curve than a government bond yield curve; 2) there are no distortions in yields caused by bonds being on special in the repo market; and 3) comparisons across countries are easier because there is almost no government regulation and no distortions caused by tax benefits.

8. If the country has a liquid swap market with a wide spectrum of maturities, a swap curve can be developed. By the bootstrapping methodology, the spot rate curve for that country can be derived.

9. **A.** The convention in the swap market is to quote the fixed rate (i.e., the swap rate) as a spread over an estimated government yield for a bond with the same maturity as the swap. That spread is called the swap spread.

   B. Since the credit risk in a swap is that the counterparty will fail to make the contractual payments and typically the counterparty is a high credit quality bank, the swap spread is a gauge of the credit risk associated with the banking sector.

10. **A.** The pure expectations theory postulates that no systematic factors other than expected future short-term rates affect forward rates. According to the pure expectations theory, forward rates exclusively represent expected future rates. Thus, the entire term structure at a given time reflects the market's current expectations of the family of future short-term rates.

    B. The pure expectations theory neglects the risks inherent in investing in bonds. If forward rates were perfect predictors of future interest rates, then the future prices of bonds would be known with certainty. The return over any investment period would be certain and independent of the maturity of the instrument acquired. However, with the uncertainty about future interest rates and, therefore, about future prices of bonds, these instruments become risky investments in the sense that the return over some investment horizon is unknown.

11. The broadest interpretation of the pure expectations theory asserts that there is no difference in the 4-year total return if an investor purchased a 7-year zero-coupon bond or a 15-year zero-coupon bond.

12. The local expectations form of the pure expectations theory asserts that the total return over a 6-month horizon for a 5-year zero-coupon bond would be the same as for a 2-year zero-coupon bond.

13. The first sentence of the statement is correct. Moreover, it is correct that studies have shown that forward rates are poor predictors of future interest rates. However, the last sentence of the statement is incorrect. Forward rates should not be ignored because they indicate break-even rates and rates that can be locked in. So, they play an important role in investment decisions.

14. The two interpretations of forward rates are that they are break-even rates and they are rates that can be locked in.

   A. For the 1-year forward rate seven years from now of 6.4% the two interpretations are as follows:

   i. 6.4% is the rate that will make an investor indifferent between buying an 8-year zero-coupon bond or investing in a 7-year zero-coupon bond and when it matures reinvesting in a zero-coupon bond that matures in one year, and

   ii. 6.4% is the rate that can be locked in today by buying an 8-year zero-coupon bond rather than investing in a 7-year zero-coupon bond and when it matures reinvesting in a zero-coupon bond that matures in one year.

   B. For the 2-year forward rate one year from now of 6.2% the two interpretations are as follows:

   i. 6.2% is the rate that will make an investor indifferent between buying a 3-year zero-coupon bond or investing in a 1-year zero-coupon bond and when it matures reinvesting in a zero-coupon bond that matures in two years, and

   ii. 6.2% is the rate that can be locked in today by buying a 3-year zero-coupon bond rather than investing in a 1-year zero-coupon bond and when it matures reinvesting in a zero-coupon bond that matures in two years.

   C. For the 8-year forward rate three years from now of 7.1% the two interpretations are as follows:

   i. 7.1% is the rate that will make an investor indifferent between buying an 11-year zero-coupon bond or investing in a 3-year zero-coupon bond and when it matures reinvesting in a zero-coupon bond that matures in eight years, and

   ii. 7.1% is the rate that can be locked in today by buying an 11-year zero-coupon bond rather than investing in a 3-year zero-coupon bond and when it matures reinvesting in a zero-coupon bond that matures in eight years.

15. All expectations theories—the pure expectations theory, the liquidity preference theory, and the preferred habitat theory—share a hypothesis about the behavior of short-term forward rates and also assume that the forward rates in current long-term bonds are closely related to the market's expectations about future short-term rates. While the pure expectations theory postulates that no systematic factors other than expected future short-term rates affect forward rates, the liquidity preference theory and the preferred habitat theory postulate that there are other factors and therefore are referred to as biased expectations theories. The liquidity preference theory asserts that investors demand a liquidity premium for extending maturity so that the forward rates are biased by this premium. The preferred habitat theory asserts that investors must be induced by a yield premium in order to accept the risks associated with shifting funds out of their preferred sector and forward rates embody the premium for this inducement.

16. **A.** Proponents of the pure expectations theory would assert that an upward-sloping yield curve is a market's forecast of a rise in interest rates. If that is correct, an expected rise in interest rates would mean that the manager should shorten or reduce the duration (i.e., interest rate risk) of the portfolio. However, the pure expectations theory has serious pitfalls and the forward rates are not good predictors of future interest rates.

   B. The preferred habitat form of the biased expectations theory is consistent with the shape of the spot rate curve observed. The preferred habitat theory asserts that if there is an imbalance between the supply and demand for funds within a given maturity sector, market participants (i.e., borrowers and investors) will agree to shift their financing and investing activities out of their preferred maturity sector to take advantage of any such imbalance. However, participants will demand compensation for shifting out of their preferred maturity sector in the form of a yield premium. Consequently, any shape for the spot rate curve (and yield curve) can result, such as the one observed in the question. Therefore, the trustee's statement is incorrect.

(*Note*: The question only asked about *expectations* theories of the term structure of interest rates. Another theory, the market segmentation theory, asserts that when there are supply and demand imbalances within a maturity sector, market participants will not shift out of their preferred maturity sector. Consequently, different maturity sectors reflect supply and demand imbalances within each sector, and the type of yield curve observed in the question is possible.)

17. **A.** Portfolio A is the bullet portfolio because its 10-year key rate duration dominates by far the key rate duration for the other maturities. Portfolio B is the laddered portfolio because the key rate durations after year 2 are roughly equal. Portfolio C is the barbell portfolio with the short end of the barbell at 5 years and the long end of the barbell at 20 years.

B. The bullet portfolio has the highest 10-year key rate duration and will therefore increase the most if the 10-year spot rate decreases while the key rates for the other maturities do not change much.

C. Adding up the key rate durations for each portfolio gives 6.2. This is the duration of all three portfolios if the spot rate for all key maturities changes by the same number of basis points—that is, a parallel shift in the spot rate for the key maturities.

18. The information for computing the daily standard deviation for yield volatility is shown below:

t	y_t	$X_t = 100 [Ln (y_t/y_{t-1})]$	$(X_t - \bar{X})^2$
0	5.854		
1	5.843	−0.18808	0.00060
2	5.774	−1.18793	1.04922
3	5.719	−0.95711	0.62964
4	5.726	0.12232	0.08176
5	5.761	0.60939	0.59753
6	5.797	0.62295	0.61868
7	5.720	−1.33717	1.37724
8	5.755	0.61002	0.59851
9	5.787	0.55450	0.51568
10	5.759	−0.48502	0.10330
	Total	−1.63613	5.57216825

$$\text{Sample mean} = \bar{X} = \frac{-1.63613}{10} = -0.163613\%$$

$$\text{Variance} = \frac{5.57216825}{10 - 1} = 0.6191298$$

$$\text{Std dev} = \sqrt{0.6191298} = 0.786848\%$$

19. **A.** Using 250 days: $\sqrt{250}(0.786848\%) = 12.44\%$

B. Using 260 days: $\sqrt{260}(0.786848\%) = 12.69\%$

C. Using 365 days: $\sqrt{365}(0.786848\%) = 15.03\%$

20. This is not necessarily the case because with the same data there are still choices that the managers must make that may result in quite different estimates of historical volatility. These choices include the number of days to use and the annualization of the daily standard deviation.

21. Since the current level of the 2-year Treasury yield is 5%, then the annual standard deviation of 7% translates into a 35 basis point (5% times 7%) standard deviation. Assuming that yield volatility is approximately normally distributed, we can use the normal distribution to construct an interval or range for what the future yield will be. There is a 68.3% probability that the yield will be between one standard deviation below and above the expected value. The expected value is the prevailing yield. If the annual standard deviation is 35 basis points and the prevailing yield is 5%, then there is a 68.3% probability that the yield next year will be between 4.65% (5% minus 35 basis points) and 5.35% (5% plus 35 basis points). There is a 99.7% probability that the yield next year will be within three standard deviations. In our case, three standard deviations is 105 basis points. Therefore there is a 99.7% probability that the yield will be between 3.95% (5% minus 105 basis points) and 6.05% (5% plus 105 basis points).

22. **A.** Yield volatility can be estimated from the observed prices of interest rate options and caps. A yield volatility estimated in this way is called implied volatility and is based on some option pricing model. An input to any option pricing model in which the underlying is a Treasury security or Treasury futures contract is expected yield volatility. If the observed price of an option is assumed to be the fair price and the option pricing model is assumed to be the model that would generate that fair price, then the implied yield volatility is the yield volatility that when used as an input into the option pricing model would produce the observed option price.

B. The problems with using implied volatility are that 1) it is assumed the option pricing model is correct, and 2) since option pricing models typically assume that volatility is constant over the life of the option, interpreting an implied volatility becomes difficult.

23. **A.** There are reasons to believe that market participants give greater weight to recent movements in yield when determining volatility. To incorporate this belief into the estimation of historical volatility, different weights can be assigned to the observed changes in daily yields. More specifically, observations further in the past should be given less weight.

B. Some market practitioners argue that in forecasting volatility the expected value or mean that should be used in the formula for the variance is zero.

24. C is correct. The curvature of the yield has the least impact in explaining the return of zero-coupon bonds.

25. A is correct. Both theories assume that the forward rates in current long-term bonds are closely related to the market's expectations about future short-term rates.

26. A is correct. The return calculation for each bond is:

Bond duration × −Basis point change × % Weight in portfolio for each bond

We then add together the bond returns for each bond in the portfolio. The key rate durations are the same as the maturities because all bonds are zero-coupon bonds. This gives a return of:

Portfolio I: (2 × −0.10 × 50%) + (16 × 0.00 × 0%)
                                    + (30 × 0.20 × 50%) = +2.90%

Portfolio III: (2 × −0.10 × 25%) + (16 × 0.00 ×
                                    50%) + (30 × 0.20 × 25%) = +1.45%

Therefore the difference in return would be: 1.45% − 2.90% = −1.45%

44

Valuing Bonds with Embedded Options

by Frank J. Fabozzi, CFA

LEARNING OUTCOMES

Mastery	The candidate should be able to:
☐	**a** evaluate, using relative value analysis, whether a security is undervalued, fairly valued, or overvalued;
☐	**b** evaluate the importance of benchmark interest rates in interpreting spread measures;
☐	**c** describe the backward induction valuation methodology within the binomial interest rate tree framework;
☐	**d** calculate the value of a callable bond from an interest rate tree;
☐	**e** explain the relations among the values of a callable (putable) bond, the corresponding option-free bond, and the embedded option;
☐	**f** explain the effect of volatility on the arbitrage-free value of an option;
☐	**g** interpret an option-adjusted spread with respect to a nominal spread and to benchmark interest rates;
☐	**h** explain how effective duration and effective convexity are calculated using the binomial model;
☐	**i** calculate the value of a putable bond, using an interest rate tree;
☐	**j** describe and evaluate a convertible bond and its various component values;
☐	**k** compare the risk-return characteristics of a convertible bond with the risk-return characteristics of ownership of the underlying common stock.

INTRODUCTION

1

The presence of an embedded option in a bond structure makes the valuation of such bonds complicated. In this reading, we present a model to value bonds that have one or more embedded options and where the value of the embedded options depends on future interest rates. Examples of such embedded options are call and put provisions and caps (i.e., maximum interest rate) in floating-rate securities. While there are

Fixed Income Analysis for the Chartered Financial Analyst® Program, Second Edition, by Frank J. Fabozzi, CFA. Copyright © 2005 by CFA Institute.

several models that have been proposed to value bonds with embedded options, our focus will be on models that provide an "arbitrage-free value" for a security. At the end of this reading, we will discuss the valuation of convertible bonds. The complexity here is that these bonds are typically callable and may be putable. Thus, the valuation of convertible bonds must take into account not only embedded options that depend on future interest rates (i.e., the call and the put options) but also the future price movement of the common stock (i.e., the call option on the common stock).

In order to understand how to value a bond with an embedded option, there are several fundamental concepts that must be reviewed. We will do this in Sections 2, 3, 4, and 5. In Section 2, the key elements involved in developing a bond valuation model are explained. In Section 3, an overview of the bond valuation process is provided. Since the valuation of bonds requires benchmark interest rates, the various benchmarks are described in Section 4. In this section we also explain how to interpret spread measures relative to a particular benchmark. In Section 5, the valuation of an option-free bond is reviewed using a numerical illustration. The bond used in the illustration in this section to show how to value an option-free bond is then used in the remainder of the reading to show how to value that bond if there is one or more embedded options.

2   ELEMENTS OF A BOND VALUATION MODEL

The valuation process begins with determining benchmark interest rates. As will be explained later in this section, there are three potential markets where benchmark interest rates can be obtained:

- the Treasury market;
- a sector of the bond market;
- the market for the issuer's securities.

An arbitrage-free value for an option-free bond is obtained by first generating the spot rates (or forward rates). When used to discount cash flows, the spot rates are the rates that would produce a model value equal to the observed market price for each on-the-run security in the benchmark. For example, if the Treasury market is the benchmark, an arbitrage-free model would produce a value for each on-the-run Treasury issue that is equal to its observed market price. In the Treasury market, the on-the-run issues are the most recently auctioned issues. (Note that all such securities issued by the U.S. Department of the Treasury are option free.) If the market used to establish the benchmark is a sector of the bond market or the market for the issuer's securities, the on-the-run issues are estimates of what the market price would be if newly issued *option-free* securities with different maturities are sold.

In deriving the interest rates that should be used to value a bond with an embedded option, the same principle must be maintained. No matter how complex the valuation model, when each on-the-run issue for a benchmark security is valued using the model, the value produced should be equal to the on-the-run issue's market price. The on-the-run issues for a given benchmark are assumed to be fairly priced.[1]

The first complication in building a model to value bonds with embedded options is that the future cash flows will depend on what happens to interest rates in the future. This means that future interest rates must be considered. This is incorporated into a valuation model by considering how interest rates can change based on some assumed interest rate volatility. In the reading on term structure and volatility of interest rates,

---

[1] Market participants also refer to this characteristic of a model as one that "calibrates to the market."

we explained what interest rate volatility is and how it is estimated. Given the assumed interest rate volatility, an interest rate "tree" representing possible future interest rates consistent with the volatility assumption can be constructed. It is from the interest rate tree that two important elements in the valuation process are obtained. First, the interest rates on the tree are used to generate the cash flows taking into account the embedded option. Second, the interest rates on the tree are used to compute the present value of the cash flows.

For a given interest rate volatility, there are several interest rate models that have been used in practice to construct an interest rate tree. An interest rate model is a probabilistic description of how interest rates can change over the life of the bond. An interest rate model does this by making an assumption about the relationship between the level of short-term interest rates and the interest rate volatility as measured by the standard deviation. A discussion of the various interest rate models that have been suggested in the finance literature and that are used by practitioners in developing valuation models is beyond the scope of this reading.[2] What is important to understand is that the interest rate models commonly used are based on how short-term interest rates can evolve (i.e., change) over time. Consequently, these interest rate models are referred to as one-factor models, where "factor" means only one interest rate is being modeled over time. More complex models would consider how more than one interest rate changes over time. For example, an interest rate model can specify how the short-term interest rate and the long-term interest rate can change over time. Such a model is called a two-factor model.

Given an interest rate model and an interest rate volatility assumption, it can be assumed that interest rates can realize one of two possible rates in the next period. A valuation model that makes this assumption in creating an interest rate tree is called a **binomial model**. There are valuation models that assume that interest rates can take on three possible rates in the next period and these models are called trinomial models. There are even more complex models that assume in creating an interest rate tree that more than three possible rates in the next period can be realized. These models that assume discrete change in interest rates are referred to as "discrete-time option pricing models." It makes sense that option valuation technology is employed to value a bond with an embedded option because the valuation requires an estimate of what the value of the embedded option is worth. However, a discussion of the underlying theory of discrete-time pricing models in general and the binomial model in particular are beyond the scope of this reading.[3]

As we will see later in this reading, when a discrete-time option pricing model is portrayed in graph form, it shows the different paths that interest rates can take. The graphical presentation looks like a lattice.[4] Hence, discrete-time option pricing models are sometimes referred to as "lattice models." Since the pattern of the interest rate paths also look like the branches of a tree, the graphical presentation is referred to as an interest rate tree.

Regardless of the assumption about how many possible rates can be realized in the next period, the interest rate tree generated must produce a value for the securities in the benchmark that is equal to their observed market price—that is, it must produce an arbitrage-free value. Consequently, if the Treasury market is used for the benchmark interest rates, the interest rate tree generated must produce a value for each on-the-run Treasury issue that is equal to its observed market price. Moreover,

---

2 An excellent source for further explanation of many of these models is Gerald W. Buetow Jr. and James Sochacki, *Term Structure Models Using Binomial Trees: Demystifying the Process* (Charlottesville, VA: Association of Investment Management and Research, 2000).

3 For a discussion of the binomial model and the underlying theory, see Chapter 4 in Don M. Chance, *Analysis of Derivatives for the CFA Program* (Charlottesville, VA: Association for Investment Management and Research, 2003).

4 A lattice is an arrangement of points in a regular periodic pattern.

the intuition and the methodology for using the interest rate tree (i.e., the backward induction methodology described later) are the same. Once an interest rate tree is generated that 1) is consistent with both the interest rate volatility assumption and the interest rate model and 2) generates the observed market price for the securities in the benchmark, the next step is to use the interest rate tree to value a bond with an embedded option. The complexity here is that a set of rules must be introduced to determine, for any period, when the embedded option will be exercised. For a callable bond, these rules are called the "call rules." The rules vary from model builder to model builder.

While the building of a model to value bonds with embedded options is more complex than building a model to value option-free bonds, the basic principles are the same. In the case of valuing an option-free bond, the model that is built is simply a set of spot rates that are used to value cash flows. The spot rates will produce an arbitrage-free value. For a model to value a bond with embedded options, the interest rate tree is used to value future cash flows, and the interest rate tree is combined with the call rules to generate the future cash flows. Again, the interest rate tree will produce an arbitrage-free value.

Let's move from theory to practice. Only a few practitioners will develop their own model to value bonds with embedded options. Instead, it is typical for a portfolio manager or analyst to use a model developed by either a dealer firm or a vendor of analytical systems. A fair question is then: Why bother covering a valuation model that is readily available from a third party? The answer is that a valuation model should not be a black box to portfolio managers and analysts. *The models in practice share all of the principles described in this reading, but differ with respect to certain assumptions that can produce quite different values.* The reasons for these differences in valuation must be understood. Moreover, third-party models give the user a choice of changing the assumptions. A user who has not "walked through" a valuation model has no appreciation of the significance of these assumptions and therefore how to assess the impact of these assumptions on the value produced by the model. "Modeling risk" is the risk that the underlying assumptions of a model may be incorrect. Understanding a valuation model permits the user to effectively determine the significance of an assumption.

As an example of the importance of understanding the assumptions of a model, consider interest rate volatility. Suppose that the market price of a bond is $89. Suppose further that a valuation model produces a value for a bond with an embedded option of $90 based on a 12% interest rate volatility assumption. Then, according to the valuation model, this bond is cheap by one point. However, suppose that the same model produces a value of $87 if a 15% volatility is assumed. This tells the portfolio manager or analyst that the bond is two points rich. Which is correct? The answer clearly depends on what the investor believes interest rate volatility will be in the future.

In this reading, we will use the binomial model to demonstrate all of the issues and assumptions associated with valuing a bond with embedded options. This model is available on Bloomberg, as well as from other commercial vendors and several dealer firms.[5] We show how to create an interest rate tree (more specifically, a binomial interest rate tree) given a volatility assumption and how the interest rate tree can be used to value an option-free bond. Given the interest rate tree, we then show how to value several types of bonds with an embedded option—a callable bond, a putable bond, a step-up note, and a floating-rate note with a cap.

Once again, it must be emphasized that while the binomial model is used in this reading to demonstrate how to value bonds with embedded options, other

---

[5] The model described in this reading was first presented in Andrew J. Kalotay, George O. Williams, and Frank J. Fabozzi, "A Model for the Valuation of Bonds and Embedded Options," *Financial Analysts Journal* (May–June 1993), pp. 35–46.

models that allow for more than one interest rate in the next period all follow the same principles—they begin with on-the-run yields, they produce an interest rate tree that generates an arbitrage-free value, and they depend on assumptions regarding the volatility of interest rates and rules for when an embedded option will be exercised.

OVERVIEW OF THE BOND VALUATION PROCESS

3

In this section we review the bond valuation process and the key concepts that were previously introduced. This will help us tie together the concepts that have already been covered and how they relate to the valuation of bonds with embedded options.

Regardless if a bond has an embedded option, the following can be done:

1. Given a required yield to maturity, we can compute the value of a bond. For example, if the required yield to maturity of a 9-year, 8% coupon bond that pays interest semiannually is 7%, its price is 106.59.

2. Given the observed market price of a bond we can calculate its yield to maturity. For example, if the price of a 5-year, 6% coupon bond that pays interest semiannually is 93.84, its yield to maturity is 7.5%.

3. Given the yield to maturity, a yield spread can be computed. For example, if the yield to maturity for a 5-year, 6% coupon bond that pays interest semiannually is 7.5% and its yield is compared to a benchmark yield of 6.5%, then the yield spread is 100 basis points (7.5% minus 6.5%). We refer to the yield spread as the *nominal spread.*

The problem with using a single interest rate when computing the value of a bond (as in 1) on the preceding page) or in computing a yield to maturity (as in 2) on the preceding page) is that it fails to recognize that each cash flow is unique and warrants its own discount rate. Failure to discount each cash flow at an appropriate interest unique to when that cash flow is expected to be received results in an arbitrage opportunity.

It is at this point in the valuation process that the notion of theoretical spot rates are introduced to overcome the problem associated with using a single interest rate. The spot rates are the appropriate rates to use to discount cash flows. There is a theoretical spot rate that can be obtained for each maturity. The procedure for computing the spot rate curve (i.e., the spot rate for each maturity) was previously explained and discussed in the previous reading.

Using the spot rate curve, one obtains the bond price. However, how is the spot rate curve used to compute the yield to maturity? Actually, there is no equivalent concept to a yield to maturity in this case. Rather, there is a yield spread measure that is used to overcome the problem of a single interest rate. This measure is the zero-volatility spread. The zero-volatility spread, also called the Z-spread and the static spread, is the spread that when added to all of the spot rates will make the present value of the bond's cash flow equal to the bond's market price.

At this point, we have not introduced any notion of how to handle bonds with embedded options. We have simply dealt with the problem of using a single interest rate for discounting cash flows. But there is still a critical issue that must be resolved. When a bond has an embedded option, a portion of the yield, and therefore a portion of the spread, is attributable to the embedded option. When valuing a bond with an embedded option, it is necessary to adjust the spread for the value of the embedded option. The measure that does this is called the option-adjusted spread (OAS). In this reading, we show how this spread measure is computed for bonds with embedded options.

A. The Benchmark Interest Rates and Relative Value Analysis

Yield spread measures are used in assessing the relative value of securities. Relative value analysis involves identifying securities that can potentially enhance return relative to a benchmark. Relative value analysis can be used to identify securities as being overpriced ("rich"), underpriced ("cheap"), or fairly priced. A portfolio manager can use relative value analysis in ranking issues within a sector or sub-sector of the bond market or different issues of a specific issuer.

Two questions that need to be asked in order to understand spread measures were identified:

1. What is the benchmark for computing the spread? That is, what is the spread measured relative to?

2. What is the spread measuring?

The different spread measures begin with benchmark interest rates. The benchmark interest rates can be one of the following:

- the Treasury market;
- a specific bond sector with a given credit rating;
- a specific issuer.

A specific bond sector with a given credit rating, for example, would include single-A rated corporate bonds or double-A rated banks. The LIBOR curve discussed in the previous reading is an example, since it is viewed by the market as an inter-bank or AA rated benchmark.

Moreover, the benchmark interest rates can be based on either:

- an estimated yield curve,
- an estimated spot rate curve.

A yield curve shows the relationship between yield and maturity for coupon bonds; a spot rate curve shows the relationship between spot rates and maturity.

Consequently, there are six potential benchmark interest rates as summarized below:

	Treasury Market	Specific Bond Sector with a Given Credit Rating	Specific Issuer
Yield curve	Treasury yield curve	Sector yield curve	Issuer yield curve
Spot rate curve	Treasury spot rate curve	Sector spot rate curve	Issuer spot rate curve

We illustrated how the Treasury spot rate curve can be constructed from the Treasury yield curve. Rather than start with yields in the Treasury market as the benchmark interest rates, an estimated on-the-run yield curve for a bond sector with a given credit rating or a specific issuer can be obtained. To obtain a sector with a given credit rating or a specific issuer's on-the-run yield curve, an appropriate credit spread is added to each on-the-run Treasury issue. The credit spread need not be constant for all maturities. For example, the credit spread may increase with maturity. Given the on-the-run yield curve, the theoretical spot rates for the bond sector with a given credit rating or issuer can be constructed using the same methodology to construct the Treasury spot rates given the Treasury yield curve.

B. Interpretation of Spread Measures

Given the alternative benchmark interest rates, in this section we will see how to interpret the three spread measures that were previously described: nominal spread, zero-volatility spread, and option-adjusted spread.

1 Treasury Market Benchmark

In the United States, yields in the U.S. Treasury market are typically used as the benchmark interest rates. The benchmark can be either the Treasury yield curve or the Treasury spot rate curve. The nominal spread is a spread measured relative to the Treasury yield curve and the zero-volatility spread is a spread relative to the Treasury spot rate curve. As we will see in this reading, the OAS is a spread relative to the Treasury spot rate curve.

If the Treasury market rates are used, then the benchmark for the three spread measures and the risks for which the spread is compensating are summarized below:

Spread Measure	Benchmark	Reflects Compensation for...
Nominal	Treasury yield curve	Credit risk, option risk, liquidity risk
Zero-volatility	Treasury spot rate curve	Credit risk, option risk, liquidity risk
Option-adjusted	Treasury spot rate curve	Credit risk, liquidity risk

where "credit risk" is relative to the default-free rate since the Treasury market is viewed as a default-free market.

In the case of an OAS, if the computed OAS is greater than what the market requires for credit risk and liquidity risk, then the security is undervalued. If the computed OAS is less than what the market requires for credit risk and liquidity risk, then the security is overvalued. Only using the nominal spread or zero-volatility spread masks the compensation for the embedded option.

For example, assume the following for a non-Treasury security, Bond W, a triple B rated corporate bond with an embedded call option:

Benchmark: Treasury market
Nominal spread based on Treasury yield curve: 170 basis points
Zero-volatility spread based on Treasury spot rate curve: 160 basis points
OAS based on Treasury spot rate curve: 125 basis points

Suppose that in the market *option-free* bonds with the same credit rating, maturity, and liquidity as Bond W trade at a nominal spread of 145 basis points. It would seem, based solely on the nominal spread, Bond W is undervalued (i.e., cheap) since its nominal spread is greater than the nominal spread for comparable bonds (170 versus 145 basis points). Even comparing Bond W's zero-volatility spread of 160 basis points to the market's 145 basis point nominal spread for option-free bonds (not a precise comparison since the Treasury benchmarks are different), the analysis would suggest that Bond W is cheap. However, after removing the value of the embedded option—which as we will see is precisely what the OAS measure does—the OAS tells us that the bond is trading at a spread that is less than the nominal spread of otherwise comparable option-free bonds. Again, while the benchmarks are different, the OAS tells us that Bond W is overvalued.

C. Specific Bond Sector with a Given Credit Rating Benchmark

Rather than use the Treasury market as the benchmark, the benchmark can be a specific bond sector *with a given credit rating*. The interpretation for the spread measures would then be:

Spread Measure	Benchmark	Reflects Compensation for...
Nominal	Sector yield curve	Credit risk, option risk, liquidity risk
Zero-volatility	Sector spot rate curve	Credit risk, option risk, liquidity risk
Option-adjusted	Sector spot rate curve	Credit risk, liquidity risk

where "Sector" means the sector with a specific credit rating. "Credit risk" in this case means the *credit risk of a security under consideration relative to the credit risk of the sector used as the benchmark*, and "liquidity risk" is the *liquidity risk of a security under consideration relative to the liquidity risk of the sector used as the benchmark*.

Let's again use Bond W, a triple B rated corporate bond with an embedded call option to illustrate. Assume the following spread measures were computed:

Benchmark: double A rated corporate bond sector

Nominal spread based on benchmark: 110 basis points

Zero-volatility spread based benchmark spot rate curve: 100 basis points

OAS based on benchmark spot rate curve: 80 basis points

Suppose that in the market *option-free* bonds with the same credit rating, maturity, and liquidity as Bond W trade at a nominal spread *relative to the double A corporate bond sector* of 90 basis points. Based solely on the nominal spread as a relative yield measure using the same benchmark, Bond W is undervalued (i.e., cheap) since its nominal spread is greater than the nominal spread for comparable bonds (110 versus 90 basis points). Even naively comparing Bond W's zero-volatility spread of 100 basis points (relative to the double A corporate spot rate curve) to the market's 90 basis point nominal spread for option-free bonds relative to the double A corporate bond yield curve, the analysis would suggest that Bond W is cheap. However, the proper assessment of Bond W's relative value will depend on what its OAS is in comparison to the OAS (relative to the same double A corporate benchmark) of other triple B rated bonds. For example, if the OAS of other triple B rated corporate bonds is less than 80 basis points, then Bond W is cheap.

D. Issuer-Specific Benchmark

Instead of using as a benchmark the Treasury market or a bond market sector to measure relative value for a specific issue, one can use an estimate of the issuer's yield curve or an estimate of the issuer's spot rate curve as the benchmark. Then we would have the following interpretation for the three spread measures:

Spread Measure	Benchmark	Reflects Compensation for...
Nominal	Issuer yield curve	Option risk, liquidity risk
Zero-volatility	Issuer spot rate curve	Option risk, liquidity risk
Option-adjusted	Issuer spot rate curve	Liquidity risk

Note that there is no credit risk since it is assumed that the specific issue analyzed has the same credit risk as the embedded option in the issuer benchmark. Using the nominal spread, a value that is positive indicates that, ignoring any embedded option, the issue is cheap relative to how the market is pricing other bonds of the issuer. A negative value would indicate that the security is expensive. The same interpretation holds for the zero-volatility spread, ignoring any embedded option. For the OAS, a positive spread means that even after adjusting for the embedded option, the value of the security is cheap. If the OAS is zero, the security is fairly priced and if it is negative, the security is expensive.

Once again, let's use our hypothetical Bond W, a triple B rated corporate bond with an embedded call option. Assume this bond is issued by RJK Corporation. Then suppose for Bond W:

> Benchmark: RJK Corporation's bond issues
>
> Nominal spread based on RJK Corporation's yield curve: 30 basis points
>
> Zero-volatility spread based on RJK Corporation's spot rate curve: 20 basis points
>
> OAS based on RJK Corporation's spot rate curve: – 25 basis points

Both the nominal spread and the zero-volatility spread would suggest that Bond W is cheap (i.e., both spread measures have a positive value). However, once the embedded option is taken into account, the appropriate spread measure, the OAS, indicates that there is a negative spread. This means that Bond W is expensive and should be avoided.

E. OAS, the Benchmark, and Relative Value

Our focus in this reading is the valuation of bonds with an embedded option. While we have yet to describe how an OAS is calculated, here we summarize how to interpret OAS as a relative value measure based on the benchmark.

Consider first when the benchmark is the Treasury spot rate curve. A zero OAS means that the security offers no spread over Treasuries. Hence, a security with a zero OAS in this case should be avoided. A negative OAS means that the security is offering a spread that is less than Treasuries. Therefore, it should be avoided. A positive value alone does not mean a security is fairly priced or cheap. It depends on what spread relative to the Treasury market the market is demanding for comparable issues. Whether the security is rich, fairly priced, or cheap depends on the OAS for the security compared to the OAS for comparable securities. We will refer to the OAS offered on comparable securities as the "required OAS" and the OAS computed for the security under consideration as the "security OAS." Then,

> if security OAS is greater than required OAS, the security is cheap
>
> if security OAS is less than required OAS, the security is rich
>
> if security OAS is equal to the required OAS, the security is fairly priced

When a sector of the bond market with the same credit rating is the benchmark, the credit rating of the sector relative to the credit rating of the security being analyzed is important. In the discussion, *it is assumed that the credit rating of the bond sector that is used as a benchmark is higher than the credit rating of the security being analyzed.* A zero OAS means that the security offers no spread over the bond sector benchmark and should therefore be avoided. A negative OAS means that the security is offering a spread that is less than the bond sector benchmark and hence should be avoided. As with the Treasury benchmark, when there is a positive OAS, relative value depends on the security OAS compared to the required OAS. Here the required OAS is the OAS of comparable securities relative to the bond sector benchmark. Given the security OAS and the required OAS, then

> if security OAS is greater than required OAS, the security is cheap
>
> if security OAS is less than required OAS, the security is rich
>
> if security OAS is equal to the required OAS, the security is fairly priced

| Exhibit 1 | Relationship between the Benchmark, OAS, and Relative Value | | |

Benchmark	Negative OAS	Zero OAS	Positive OAS
Treasury market	Overpriced (rich) security	Overpriced (rich) security	Comparison must be made between security OAS and OAS of comparable securities (required OAS): if security OAS > required OAS, security is cheap if security OAS < required OAS, security is rich if security OAS = required OAS, security is fairly priced
Bond sector with a given credit rating (*assumes credit rating higher than security being analyzed*)	Overpriced (rich) security (*assumes credit rating higher than security being analyzed*)	Overpriced (rich) security (*assumes credit rating higher than security being analyzed*)	Comparison must be made between security OAS and OAS of comparable securities (required OAS): if security OAS > required OAS, security is cheap if security OAS < required OAS, security is rich if security OAS = required OAS, security is fairly priced
Issuer's own securities	Overpriced (rich) security	Fairly valued	Underpriced (cheap) security

The terms "rich," "cheap," and "fairly priced" are only relative to the benchmark. If an investor is a funded investor who is assessing a security relative to his or her borrowing costs, then a different set of rules exists. For example, suppose that the bond sector used as the benchmark is the LIBOR spot rate curve. Also assume that the funding cost for the investor is a spread of 40 basis points over LIBOR. Then the decision to invest in the security depends on whether the OAS exceeds the 40 basis point spread by a sufficient amount to compensate for the credit risk.

Finally, let's look at relative valuation when the issuer's spot rate curve is the benchmark. If a particular security by the issuer is fairly priced, its OAS should be equal to zero. Thus, unlike when the Treasury benchmark or bond sector benchmark is used, a zero OAS is a fairly valued security. A positive OAS means that the security is trading cheap relative to other securities of the issuer and a negative OAS means that the security is trading rich relative to other securities of the same issuer.

The relationship between the benchmark, OAS, and relative value is summarized in Exhibit 1.

4   REVIEW OF HOW TO VALUE AN OPTION-FREE BOND

Before we illustrate how to value a bond with an embedded option, we will review how to value an option-free bond. We will then take the same bond and explain how it would be valued if it has an embedded option.

We have previously explained how to compute an arbitrage-free value for an option-free bond using spot rates. We also showed the relationship between spot rates and forward rates, and then how forward rates can be used to derive the same arbitrage-free value as using spot rates. What we will review in this section is how to value an option-free bond using both spot rates and forward rates. We will use as our benchmark in the rest of this reading, the securities of the issuer whose bond we want to value. Hence, *we will start with the issuer's on-the-run yield curve.*

To obtain a particular issuer's on-the-run yield curve, an appropriate credit spread is added to each on-the-run Treasury issue. The credit spread need not be constant for all maturities. In our illustration, we use the following hypothetical *on-the-run issue for the issuer whose bond we want to value:*

Maturity (Years)	Yield to Maturity (%)	Market Price
1	3.5	100
2	4.2	100
3	4.7	100
4	5.2	100

Each bond is trading at par value (100) so the coupon rate is equal to the yield to maturity. We will simplify the illustration by assuming annual-pay bonds.

Using the bootstrapping methodology, the spot rates are given below:

Year	Spot Rate (%)
1	3.5000
2	4.2148
3	4.7352
4	5.2706

We will use the above spot rates shortly to value a bond.

We explained how to derive forward rates from spot rates. Recall that forward rates can have different interpretations based on the theory of the term structure to which one subscribes. However, in the valuation process, *we are not relying on any theory*. The forward rates below are mathematically derived from the spot rates and, as we will see, when used to value a bond will produce the same value as the spot rates. The 1-year forward rates are:

Current 1-year forward rate	3.500%
1-year forward rate one year from now	4.935%
1-year forward rate two years from now	5.784%
1-year forward rate three years from now	6.893%

Now consider an option-free bond with four years remaining to maturity and a coupon rate of 6.5%. The value of this bond can be calculated in one of two ways, both producing the same value. First, the cash flows can be discounted at the spot rates as shown below:

$$\frac{\$6.5}{(1.035)^1} + \frac{\$6.5}{(1.042148)^2} + \frac{\$6.5}{(1.047352)^3} + \frac{\$100 + \$6.5}{(1.052706)^4} = \$104.643$$

The second way is to discount by the 1-year forward rates as shown below:

$$\frac{\$6.5}{(1.035)} + \frac{\$6.5}{(1.035)(1.04935)} + \frac{\$6.5}{(1.035)(1.04935)(1.05784)}$$

$$+ \frac{\$100 + \$6.5}{(1.035)(1.04935)(1.05784)(1.06893)} = \$104.643$$

As can be seen, discounting by spot rates or forward rates will produce the same value for a bond.

Remember this value for the option-free bond, $104.643. When we value the same bond using the binomial model later in this reading, that model should produce a value of $104.643 or else our model is flawed.

5 | VALUING A BOND WITH AN EMBEDDED OPTION USING THE BINOMIAL MODEL

As explained in Section 2, there are various models that have been developed to value a bond with embedded options. The one that we will use to illustrate the issues and assumptions associated with valuing bonds with embedded options is the binomial model. The interest rates that are used in the valuation process are obtained from a binomial interest rate tree. We'll explain the general characteristics of this tree first. Then we see how to value a bond using the binomial interest rate tree. We will then see how to construct this tree from an on-the-run yield curve. Basically, the derivation of a binomial interest rate tree is the same in principle as deriving the spot rates using the bootstrapping method—that is, there is no arbitrage.

A. Binomial Interest Rate Tree

Once we allow for embedded options, consideration must be given to interest rate volatility. The reason is, the decision of the issuer or the investor (depending upon who has the option) will be affected by what interest rates are in the future. This means that the valuation model must explicitly take into account how interest rates may change in the future. In turn, this recognition is achieved by incorporating interest rate volatility into the valuation model. In the reading on term structure and volatility of interest rates, we explained what interest rate volatility is and how it can be measured.

Let's see how interest rate volatility is introduced into the valuation model. More specifically, let's see how this can be done in the binomial model using Exhibit 2. Look at panel a of the exhibit which shows the beginning or *root* of the interest rate tree. The time period shown is "Today." At the dot, denoted N, in the exhibit is an interest rate denoted by r_0, which represents the interest rate today.

Notice that there are two arrows as we move to the right of N. Here is where we are introducing interest rate volatility. The dot in the exhibit is referred to as a *node*. What takes place at a node is either a *random event* or a *decision*. We will see that in building a binomial interest rate tree, at each node there is a random event. The change in interest rates represents a random event. Later when we show how to use the binomial interest rate tree to determine the value of a bond with an embedded option, at each node there will be a decision. Specifically, the decision will be whether or not the issuer or bondholders (depending on the type of embedded option) will exercise the option.

Exhibit 2	Binomial Interest Rate Tree

Panel a: One-Year Binomial Interest Rate Tree   *Panel b: Two-Year Binomial Interest Rate Tree*

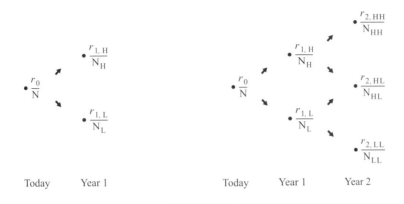

In the binomial model, it is assumed that the random event (i.e., the change in interest rates) will take on only two possible values. Moreover, it is assumed that the probability of realizing either value is equal. The two possible values are the interest rates shown by $r_{1,H}$ and $r_{1,L}$ in panel a.[6] If you look at the time frame at the bottom of panel a, you will notice that it is in years.[7] What this means is that the interest rate at r_0 is the current (i.e., today's) 1-year rate and at year 1, the two possible 1-year interest rates are $r_{1,H}$ and $r_{1,L}$. Notice the notation that is used for the two subscripts. The first subscript, 1, means that it is the interest rate starting in year 1. The second subscript indicates whether it is the higher (*H*) or lower (*L*) of the two interest rates in year 1.

Now we will grow the binomial interest rate tree. Look at panel b of Exhibit 2 which shows today, year 1, and year 2. There are two nodes at year 1 depending on whether the higher or the lower interest rate is realized. At both of the nodes a random event occurs. N_H is the node if the higher interest rate ($r_{1,H}$) is realized. In the binomial model, the interest rate that can occur in the next year (i.e., year 2) can be one of two values: $r_{2,HH}$ or $r_{2,HL}$. The subscript 2 indicates year 2. This would get us to either the node N_{HH} or N_{HL}. The subscript "*HH*" means that the path to get to node N_{HH} is the higher interest rate in year 1 and in year 2. The subscript "*HL*" means that the path to get to node N_{HL} is the higher interest rate in year 1 and the lower interest rate in year 2.

Similarly, N_L is the node if the lower interest rate ($r_{1,L}$) is realized in year 1. The interest rate that can occur in year 2 is either $r_{2,LH}$ or $r_{2,LL}$. This would get us to either the node N_{LH} or N_{LL}. The subscript "*LH*" means that the path to get to node N_{LH} is the lower interest rate in year 1 and the higher interest rate in year 2. The subscript "*LL*" means that the path to get to node N_{LL} is the lower interest rate in year 1 and in year 2.

Notice that in panel b, at year 2 only N_{HL} is shown but no N_{LH}. The reason is that if the higher interest rate is realized in year 1 and the lower interest rate is realized in year 2, we would get to the same node as if the lower interest rate is realized in year 1 and the higher interest rate is realized in year 2. Rather than clutter up the interest rate tree with notation, only one of the two paths is shown.

In our illustration of valuing a bond with an embedded option, we will use a 4-year bond. Consequently, we will need a 4-year binomial interest rate tree to value this bond. Exhibit 3 shows the tree and the notation used.

---

6 If we were using a trinomial model, there would be three possible interest rates shown in the next year.

7 In practice, much shorter time periods are used to construct an interest rate tree.

Exhibit 3	Four-Year Binomial Interest Rate Tree

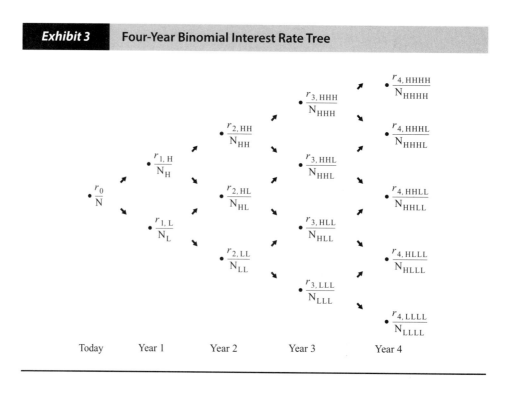

The interest rates shown in the binomial interest rate tree are actually forward rates. Basically, they are the one-period rates starting in period t. (A period in our illustration is one year.) Thus, in valuing an option-free bond we know that it is valued using forward rates, and we have illustrated this by using 1-period forward rates. For each period, there is a unique forward rate. When we value bonds with embedded options, we will see that we continue to use forward rates, but there is not just one forward rate for a given period but a set of forward rates.

There will be a relationship between the rates in the binomial interest rate tree. The relationship depends on the interest rate model assumed. Based on some interest rate volatility assumption, the interest rate model selected would show the relationship between:

$r_{1,L}$ and $r_{1,H}$ for year 1
$r_{2,LL}$, $r_{2,HL}$, and $r_{2,HH}$ for year 2
etc.

For our purpose of understanding the valuation model, it is not necessary that we show the mathematical relationships here.

B. Determining the Value at a Node

Now we want to see how to use the binomial interest rate tree to value a bond. To do this, we first have to determine the value of the bond at each node. To find the value of the bond at a node, we begin by calculating the bond's value at the high and low nodes to the right of the node for which we are interested in obtaining a value. For example, in Exhibit 3, suppose we want to determine the bond's value at node N_H. The bond's value at node N_{HH} and N_{HL} must be determined. Hold aside for now how we get these two values because, as we will see, the process involves starting from the last (right-most) year in the tree and working backwards to get the final solution we want. Because the procedure for solving for the final solution in any interest rate tree involves moving backwards, the methodology is known as backward induction.

Effectively what we are saying is that if we are at some node, then the value at that node will depend on the future cash flows. In turn, the future cash flows depend on 1) the coupon payment one year from now and 2) the bond's value one year from now. The former is known. The bond's value depends on whether the rate is the higher or lower rate reported at the two nodes to the right of the node that is the focus of our attention. So, the cash flow at a node will be either 1) the bond's value if the 1-year rate is the higher rate plus the coupon payment, or 2) the bond's value if the 1-year rate is the lower rate plus the coupon payment. Let's return to the bond's value at node N_H. The cash flow will be either the bond's value at N_{HH} plus the coupon payment, or the bond's value at N_{HL} plus the coupon payment.

In general, to get the bond's value at a node we follow the fundamental rule for valuation: the value is the present value of the expected cash flows. The appropriate discount rate to use is the 1-year rate at the node where we are computing the value. Now there are two present values in this case: the present value if the 1-year rate is the higher rate and one if it is the lower rate. Since it is assumed that the probability of both outcomes is equal (i.e., there is a 50% probability for each), an average of the two present values is computed. This is illustrated in Exhibit 4 for any node assuming that the 1-year rate is r^* at the node where the valuation is sought and letting:

> V_H = the bond's value for the higher 1-year rate
> V_L = the bond's value for the lower 1-year rate
> C = coupon payment

Using our notation, the cash flow at a node is either:

> $V_H + C$ for the higher 1-year rate
> $V_L + C$ for the lower 1-year rate

Exhibit 4   Calculating a Value at a Node

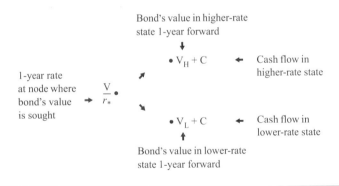

The present value of these two cash flows using the 1-year rate at the node, r^*, is:

$$\frac{V_H + C}{\left(1 + r^*\right)} = \text{present value for the higher 1-year rate}$$

$$\frac{V_L + C}{\left(1 + r^*\right)} = \text{present value for the lower 1-year rate}$$

Then, the value of the bond at the node is found as follows:

$$\text{Value at a node} = \frac{1}{2}\left[\frac{V_H + C}{\left(1 + r^*\right)} + \frac{V_L + C}{\left(1 + r^*\right)}\right]$$

C. Constructing the Binomial Interest Rate Tree

The construction of any interest rate tree is complicated, although the principle is simple to understand. This applies to the binomial interest rate tree or a tree based on more than two future rates in the next period. *The fundamental principle is that when a tree is used to value an on-the-run issue for the benchmark, the resulting value should be arbitrage free.* That is, the tree should generate a value for an on-the-run issue equal to its observed market value. Moreover, the interest rate tree should be consistent with the interest rate volatility assumed.

Here is a brief overview of the process for constructing the interest rate tree. It is not essential to know how to derive the interest rate tree; rather, it should be understood how to value a bond given the rates on the tree. The interest rate at the first node (i.e., the root of the tree) is the 1-year interest rate for the on-the-run issue. (This is because in our simplified illustration we are assuming that the length of the time between nodes is one year.) The tree is grown just the same way that the spot rates were obtained using the bootstrapping method based on arbitrage arguments.

The interest rates for year 1 (there are two of them and remember they are forward rates) are obtained from the following information:

1. the coupon rate for the 2-year on-the-run issue

2. the interest rate volatility assumed

3. the interest rate at the root of the tree (i.e., the current 1-year on-the-run rate)

Given the above, a *guess* is then made of the lower rate at node N_L, which is $r_{1,L}$. The upper rate, $r_{1,H}$, is not guessed at. Instead, it is determined by the assumed volatility of the 1-year rate ($r_{1,L}$). The formula for determining $r_{1,H}$ given $r_{1,L}$ is specified by the interest rate model used. Using the $r_{1,L}$ that was guessed and the corresponding $r_{1,H}$, the 2-year on-the-run issue can be valued. If the resulting value computed using the backward induction method is not equal to the market value of the 2-year on-the-run issue, then the $r_{1,L}$ that was tried is not the rate that should be used in the tree. If the value is too high, then a higher rate guess should be tried; if the value is too low, then a lower rate guess should be tried. The process continues in an iterative (i.e., trial and error) process until a value for $r_{1,L}$ and the corresponding $r_{1,H}$ produce a value for the 2-year on-the-run issue equal to its market value.

Exhibit 5	**Binomial Interest Rate Tree for Valuing an Issuer's Bond with a Maturity up to 4 Years (10% Volatility Assumed)**

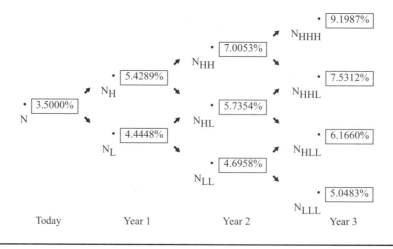

After this stage, we have the rate at the root of the tree and the two rates for year 1—$r_{1,L}$ and $r_{1,H}$. Now we need the three rates for year 2—$r_{2,LL}$, $r_{2,HL}$, and $r_{2,HH}$. These rates are determined from the following information:

1. the coupon rate for the 3-year on-the-run issue

2. the interest rate model assumed

3. the interest rate volatility assumed

4. the interest rate at the root of the tree (i.e., the current 1-year on-the-run rate)

5. the two 1-year rates (i.e., $r_{1,L}$ and $r_{1,H}$)

A guess is made for $r_{2,LL}$. The interest rate model assumed specifies how to obtain $r_{2,HL}$, and $r_{2,HH}$ given $r_{2,LL}$ and the assumed volatility for the 1-year rate. This gives the rates in the interest rate tree that are needed to value the 3-year on-the-run issue. The 3-year on-the-run issue is then valued. If the value generated is not equal to the market value of the 3-year on-the-run issue, then the $r_{2,LL}$ value tried is not the rate that should be used in the tree. An iterative process is again followed until a value for $r_{2,LL}$ produces rates for year 2 that will make the value of the 3-year on-the-run issue equal to its market value.

Exhibit 6	Demonstration That the Binomial Interest Rate Tree in Exhibit 5 Correctly Values the 3-Year 4.7% On-the-Run Issue

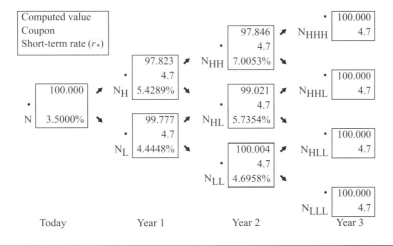

PRACTICE QUESTION 1

For the hypothetical issuer whose on-the-run yield was given in Section 4, the binomial interest rate tree below is based on 20% volatility. Using the 4-year on-the-run issue, show that the binomial interest tree below does produce a value equal to the price of the 4-year issue (i.e., par value).

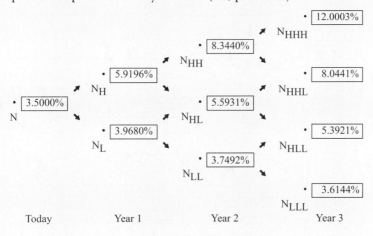

The tree is grown using the same procedure as described above to get $r_{1,L}$ and $r_{1,H}$ for year 1 and $r_{2,LL}$, $r_{2,HL}$, and $r_{2,HH}$ for year 2. Exhibit 5 shows the binomial interest rate tree for this issuer for valuing issues up to four years of maturity assuming volatility for the 1-year rate of 10%. The interest rate model used is not important. How can we be sure that the interest rates shown in Exhibit 5 are the correct rates? Verification involves using the interest rate tree to value an on-the-run issue and showing that the value obtained from the binomial model is equal to the observed market value. For example, let's just show that the interest rates in the tree for years 0, 1, and 2 in Exhibit 5 are correct. To do this, we use the 3-year on-the-run issue. The market value for the issue is 100. Exhibit 6 shows the valuation of this issue using the backward induction method. Notice that the value at the root (i.e., the value derived by the model) is 100. Thus, the value derived from the interest rate tree using the rates for the first two years produces the observed market value of 100 for the 3-year on-the-run issue. This verification is the same as saying that the model has produced an arbitrage-free value.

D. Valuing an Option-Free Bond with the Tree

To illustrate how to use the binomial interest rate tree shown in Exhibit 5, consider a 6.5% option-free bond with four years remaining to maturity. Also assume that the *issuer's on-the-run yield curve* is the one given earlier and hence the appropriate binomial interest rate tree is the one in Exhibit 5. Exhibit 7 shows the various values in the discounting process, and produces a bond value of $104.643.

PRACTICE QUESTION 2

Show that the value of an option-free bond with four years to maturity and a coupon rate of 6.5% is $104.643 if volatility is assumed to be 20%.

Exhibit 7	Valuing an Option-Free Bond with Four Years to Maturity and a Coupon Rate of 6.5% (10% Volatility Assumed)

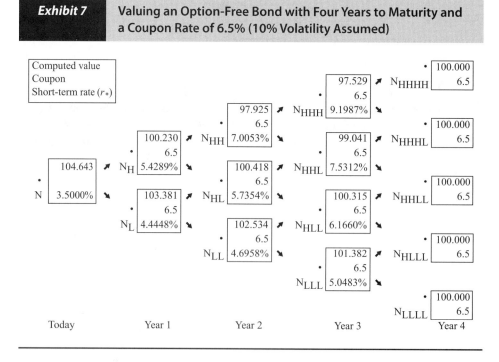

It is important to note that this value is identical to the bond value found earlier when we discounted at either the spot rates or the 1-year forward rates. We should expect to find this result since our bond is option free. This clearly demonstrates that the valuation model is consistent with the arbitrage-free valuation model for an option-free bond.

VALUING AND ANALYZING A CALLABLE BOND

6

Now we will demonstrate how the binomial interest rate tree can be applied to value a callable bond. The valuation process proceeds in the same fashion as in the case of an option-free bond, but with one exception: when the call option may be exercised by the issuer, the bond value at a node must be changed to reflect the lesser of its values if it is not called (i.e., the value obtained by applying the backward induction method described above) and the call price. As explained earlier, at a node either a random event or a decision must be made. In constructing the binomial interest rate tree, there is a random event at a node. When valuing a bond with an embedded option, at a node there will be a decision made as to whether or not an option will be exercised. In the case of a callable bond, the issuer must decide whether or not to exercise the call option.

For example, consider a 6.5% bond with four years remaining to maturity that is callable in one year at $100. Exhibit 8 shows two values at each node of the binomial interest rate tree. The discounting process explained above is used to calculate the first of the two values at each node. The second value is the value based on whether the issue will be called. For simplicity, let's assume that this issuer calls the issue if it exceeds the call price.

In Exhibit 9 two portions of Exhibit 8 are highlighted. Panel a of the exhibit shows nodes where the issue is not called (based on the simple call rule used in the illustration) in year 2 and year 3. The values reported in this case are the same as in the valuation of an option-free bond. Panel b of the exhibit shows some nodes where the issue is called in year 2 and year 3. Notice how the methodology changes the cash flows. In year 3, for example, at node N_{HLL} the backward induction method produces a value (i.e., cash flow) of 100.315. However, given the simplified call rule, this issue would be called. Therefore, 100 is shown as the second value at the node and it is this value that is then used in the backward induction methodology. From this we can see how the binomial method changes the cash flow based on future interest rates and the embedded option.

The root of the tree, shown in Exhibit 8, indicates that the value for this callable bond is $102.899.

Exhibit 8	Valuing a Callable Bond with Four Years to Maturity, a Coupon Rate of 6.5%, and Callable in One Year at 100 (10% Volatility Assumed)

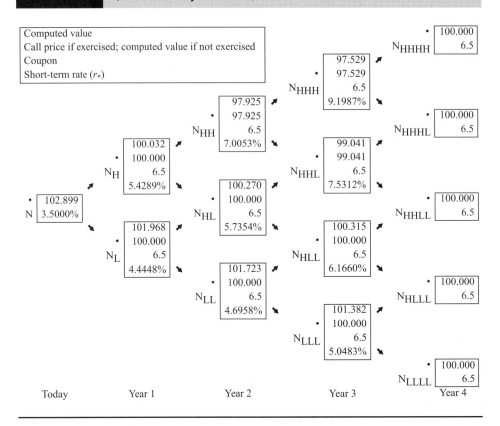

Today   Year 1   Year 2   Year 3   Year 4

Exhibit 9	Highlighting Nodes in Years 2 and 3 for a Callable Bond

(a) Nodes where call option is not exercised

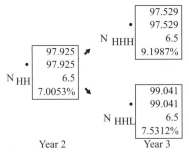

(b) Selected nodes where the call option is exercised

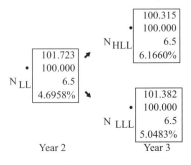

The question that we have not addressed in our illustration, which is nonetheless important, is the circumstances under which the issuer will actually call the bond. A detailed explanation of the call rule is beyond the scope of this reading. Basically, it involves determining when it would be economical for the issuer on an after-tax basis to call the issue.

Suppose instead that the call price schedule is 102 in year 1, 101 in year 2, and 100 in year 3. Also assume that the bond will not be called unless it exceeds the call price for that year. Exhibit 10 shows the value at each node and the value of the callable bond. The call price schedule results in a greater value for the callable bond, $103.942 compared to $102.899 when the call price is 100 in each year.

A. Determining the Call Option Value

The value of a callable bond is equal to the value of an option-free bond minus the value of the call option. This means that:

Value of a call option = Value of an option-free bond − Value of a callable bond

We have just seen how the value of an option-free bond and the value of a callable bond can be determined. The difference between the two values is therefore the value of the call option.

In our illustration, the value of the option-free bond is $104.643. If the call price is $100 in each year and the value of the callable bond is $102.899 assuming 10% volatility for the 1-year rate, the value of the call option is $1.744 (= $104.643 − $102.899).

Exhibit 10	**Valuing a Callable Bond with Four Years to Maturity, a Coupon Rate of 6.5%, and with a Call Price Schedule (10% Volatility Assumed)**

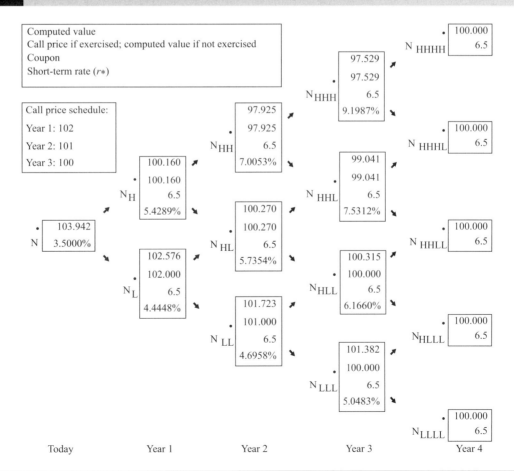

B. Volatility and the Arbitrage-Free Value

In our illustration, interest rate volatility was assumed to be 10%. The volatility assumption has an important impact on the arbitrage-free value. More specifically, the higher the expected volatility, the higher the value of an option. The same is true for an option embedded in a bond. Correspondingly, this affects the value of a bond with an embedded option.

For example, for a callable bond, a higher interest rate volatility assumption means that the value of the call option increases and, since the value of the option-free bond is not affected, the value of the callable bond must be lower.

We can see this using the on-the-run yield curve in our previous illustrations. In the previous illustrations, we assumed interest rate volatility of 10%. To show the effect of higher volatility, we will assume volatility of 20%. The solution to Practice Question 1 gives the corresponding binomial interest rate tree using the same interest rate model. The solution to Practice Question 2 verifies that the binomial interest rate tree provides the same value for the option-free bond, $104.643.

The solution to Practice Question 3 shows the calculation for the callable bond assuming interest rate volatility of 20%. For the callable bond it is assumed that the issue is callable at par beginning in year 1. The value of the callable bond is $102.108 if volatility is assumed to be 20% compared to $102.899 if volatility is assumed to be 10%. Notice that at the higher assumed volatility (20%), the callable bond has a lower value than at the lower assumed volatility (10%). The reason for this is that the value of an option increases with the higher assumed volatility. So, at 20% volatility the value of the embedded call option is higher than at 10% volatility. But the embedded call option is subtracted from the option-free value to obtain the value of the callable bond. Since a higher value for the embedded call option is subtracted from the option-free value at 20% volatility rather than at 10% volatility, the value of the callable bond is lower at 20% volatility.

Practice Question 3

Suppose that the volatility assumption is 20% rather than 10% and therefore the binomial interest rate tree is the one shown in Practice Question 1.

A. Compute the arbitrage-free value for the 4-year 6.5% coupon bond callable at par beginning Year 1 based on 20% volatility.

B. Compare the arbitrage-free value for this bond based on 20% volatility and 10% volatility as computed in Exhibit 8.

C. Option-Adjusted Spread

Suppose the market price of the 4-year 6.5% callable bond is $102.218 and the theoretical value assuming 10% volatility is $102.899. This means that this bond is cheap by $0.681 according to the valuation model. Bond market participants prefer to think not in terms of a bond's price being cheap or expensive in dollar terms but rather in terms of a yield spread—a cheap bond trades at a higher yield spread and an expensive bond at a lower yield spread.

The option-adjusted spread is the constant spread that when added to all the 1-year rates on the binomial interest rate tree will make the arbitrage-free value (i.e., the value produced by the binomial model) equal to the market price. In our illustration, if the market price is $102.218, the OAS would be the constant spread added to every rate in Exhibit 5 that will make the arbitrage-free value equal to $102.218. The solution in this case would be 35 basis points. This can be verified in Exhibit 11, which shows the value of this issue by adding 35 basis points to each rate.

As with the value of a bond with an embedded option, the OAS will depend on the volatility assumption. For a given bond price, the higher the interest rate volatility assumed, the lower the OAS for a callable bond. For example, if volatility is 20% rather than 10%, the OAS would be –6 basis points. This illustration clearly demonstrates the importance of the volatility assumption. Assuming volatility of 10%, the OAS is 35 basis points. At 20% volatility, the OAS declines and, in this case is negative and therefore the bond is overvalued relative to the model.

What the OAS seeks to do is remove from the nominal spread the amount that is due to the option risk. The measure is called an OAS because 1) it is a spread and 2) it adjusts the cash flows for the option when computing the spread to the benchmark interest rates. The second point can be seen from Exhibits 8 and 9. Notice that at each node the value obtained from the backward induction method is adjusted based on the call option and the call rule. Thus, the resulting spread is "option adjusted."

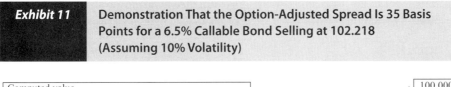

| Exhibit 11 | Demonstration That the Option-Adjusted Spread Is 35 Basis Points for a 6.5% Callable Bond Selling at 102.218 (Assuming 10% Volatility) |

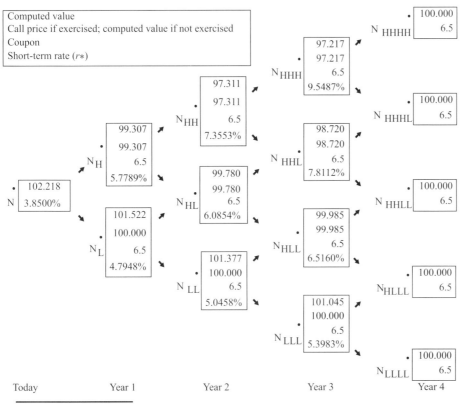

Note: Each 1-year rate is 35 basis points greater than in Exhibit 5.

What does the OAS tell us about the relative value for our callable bond? As explained in Section 3, the answer depends on the benchmark used. Exhibit 1 provides a summary of how to interpret the OAS. In valuing the callable bond in our illustration, the benchmark is the issuer's own securities. As can be seen in Exhibit 1, a positive OAS means that the callable bond is cheap (i.e., underpriced). At a 10% volatility, the OAS is 35 basis points. Consequently, assuming a 10% volatility, on a relative value basis the callable bond is attractive. However, and this is critical to remember, the OAS depends on the assumed interest rate volatility. When a 20% interest rate volatility is assumed, the OAS is–6 basis points. Hence, if an investor assumes that this is the appropriate interest rate volatility that should be used in valuing the callable bond, the issue is expensive (overvalued) on a relative value basis.

Practice Question 4

Show that if 20% volatility is assumed, the OAS is –6 basis points.

D. Effective Duration and Effective Convexity

We previously explained the meaning of duration and convexity measures and explained how these two measures can be computed. Specifically, duration is the approximate percentage change in the value of a security for a 100 basis point change in interest rates (assuming a parallel shift in the yield curve). The convexity measure allows for an adjustment to the estimated price change obtained by using duration. The formulas for duration and convexity are repeated below:

$$\text{Duration} = \frac{V_- - V_+}{2V_0(\Delta y)}$$

$$\text{Convexity} = \frac{V_+ + V_- - 2V_0}{2V_0(\Delta y)^2}$$

where

   Δy = change in rate used to calculate new values

   V_+ = estimated value if yield is increased by Δy

   V_- = estimated value if yield is decreased by Δy

   V_0 = initial price (per \$100 of par value)

We also made a distinction between "modified" duration and convexity and "effective" duration and convexity. **Modified duration** and convexity do not allow for the fact that the cash flows for a bond with an embedded option may change due to the exercise of the option. In contrast, effective duration and convexity do take into consideration how changes in interest rates in the future may alter the cash flows due to the exercise of the option. But, we did not demonstrate how to compute effective duration and convexity because they require a model for valuing bonds with embedded options and we did not introduce such models until this reading.

So, let's see how effective duration and convexity are computed using the binomial model. With effective duration and convexity, the values V_- and V_+ are obtained from the binomial model. Recall that in using the binomial model, the cash flows at a node are adjusted for the embedded call option as was demonstrated in Exhibit 8 and highlighted in the lower panel of Exhibit 9.

The procedure for calculating the value of V_+ is as follows:

Step 1   Given the market price of the issue calculate its OAS using the procedure described earlier.

Step 2   Shift the on-the-run yield curve up by a small number of basis points (Δy).

Step 3   Construct a binomial interest rate tree based on the new yield curve in Step 2.

Step 4   To each of the 1-year rates in the binomial interest rate tree, add the OAS to obtain an "adjusted tree." That is, the calculation of the effective duration and convexity assumes that the OAS will not change when interest rates change.

Step 5 Use the adjusted tree found in Step 4 to determine the value of the bond, which is V_+.

To determine the value of V_-, the same five steps are followed except that in Step 2, the on-the-run yield curve is shifted down by a small number of basis points (Δy).

To illustrate how V_+ and V_- are determined in order to calculate effective duration and effective convexity, we will use the same on-the-run yield curve that we have used in our previous illustrations assuming a volatility of 10%. The 4-year callable bond with a coupon rate of 6.5% and callable at par selling at 102.218 will be used in this illustration. The OAS for this issue is 35 basis points.

Exhibit 12 shows the adjusted tree by shifting the yield curve up by an arbitrarily small number of basis points, 25 basis points, and then adding 35 basis points (the OAS) to each 1-year rate. The adjusted tree is then used to value the bond. The resulting value, V_+, is 101.621. Exhibit 13 shows the adjusted tree by shifting the yield curve down by 25 basis points and then adding 35 basis points to each 1-year rate. The resulting value, V_-, is 102.765.

The results are summarized below:

$\Delta y = 0.0025$

$V_+ = 101.621$

$V_- = 102.765$

$V_0 = 102.218$

Exhibit 12 **Determination of V_+ for Calculating Effective Duration and Convexity[a]**

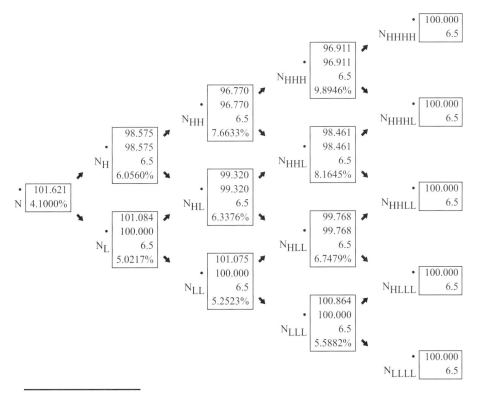

[a] +25 basis point shift in on-the-run yield curve.

Exhibit 13	Determination of V_ for Calculating Effective Duration and Convexity[a]

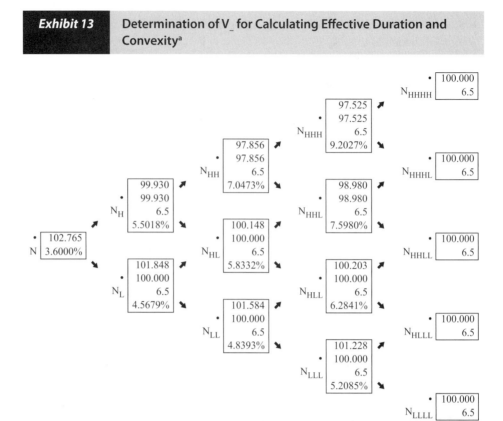

[a] −25 basis point shift in on-the-run yield curve.

Therefore,

$$\text{Effective duration} = \frac{102.765 - 101.621}{2(102.218)(0.0025)} = 2.24$$

$$\text{Effective convexity} = \frac{102.621 + 102.765 - 2(102.218)}{2(102.218)(0.0025)^2} = -39.1321$$

Notice that this callable bond exhibits negative convexity.

7 VALUING A PUTABLE BOND

A putable bond is one in which the bondholder has the right to force the issuer to pay off the bond prior to the maturity date. To illustrate how the binomial model can be used to value a putable bond, suppose that a 6.5% bond with four years remaining to maturity is putable in one year at par ($100). Also assume that the appropriate binomial interest rate tree for this issuer is the one in Exhibit 5, and the bondholder exercises the put if the bond's price is less than par.

Exhibit 14 shows the binomial interest rate tree with the values based on whether or not the investor exercises the option at a node. Exhibit 15 highlights selected nodes for year 2 and year 3 just as we did in Exhibit 9. The right side of the exhibit shows the nodes where the put option is not exercised, and therefore the value at each node is the same as when the bond is option free. In contrast, the left side of the exhibit shows where the value obtained from the backward induction method is overridden, and 100 is used because the put option is exercised.

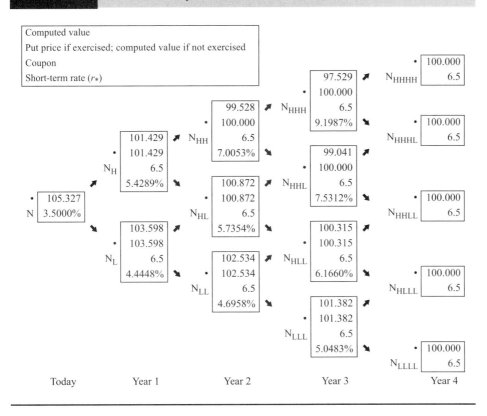

Exhibit 14 Valuing a Putable Bond with Four Years to Maturity, a Coupon Rate of 6.5%, and Putable in One Year at 100 (10% Volatility Assumed)

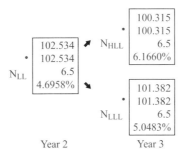

Exhibit 15 Highlighting Nodes in Years 2 and 3 for a Putable Bond

(a) Selected nodes where put option is exercised

(b) Nodes where put option is not exercised

The value of the putable bond is $105.327, a value that is greater than the value of the corresponding option-free bond. The reason for this can be seen from the following relationship:

Value of a putable bond = Value of an option-free bond
+Value of the put option

The reason for adding the value of the put option is that the investor has purchased the put option.

We can rewrite the above relationship to determine the value of the put option:

Value of the put option = Value of a putable bond

−Value of an option-free bond

In our example, since the value of the putable bond is $105.327 and the value of the corresponding option-free bond is $104.643, the value of the put option is −$0.684. The negative sign indicates the issuer has sold the option, or equivalently, the investor has purchased the option.

We have stressed that the value of a bond with an embedded option is affected by the volatility assumption. Unlike a callable bond, the value of a putable bond increases if the assumed volatility increases. It can be demonstrated that if a 20% volatility is assumed, the value of this putable bond increases from 105.327 at 10% volatility to 106.010.

| Exhibit 16 | Valuing a Putable/Callable Issue (10% Volatility Assumed) |

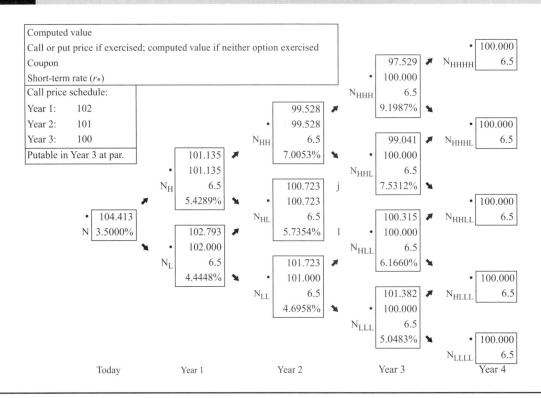

Suppose that a bond is both putable and callable. The procedure for valuing such a structure is to adjust the value at each node to reflect whether the issue would be put or called. To illustrate this, consider the 4-year callable bond analyzed earlier that had a call schedule. The valuation of this issue is shown in Exhibit 10. Suppose the issue is putable in year 3 at par value. Exhibit 16 shows how to value this callable/putable issue. At each node there are two decisions about the exercising of an option that must be made. First, given the valuation from the backward induction method at a node, the call rule is invoked to determine whether the issue will be called. If it is called, the value at the node is replaced by the call price. The valuation procedure then continues using the call price at that node. Second, if the call option is not exercised at a node, it must be determined whether or not the put option is exercised. If it is exercised, then the value from the backward induction method is overridden and the put price is substituted at that node and is used in subsequent calculations.

Practice Question 5

Using the binomial interest rate tree based on 20%, show that the value of this putable bond is 106.010. (Assume that the bond is noncallable.)

VALUING A STEP-UP CALLABLE NOTE

8

Step-up callable notes are callable instruments whose coupon rate is increased (i.e., "stepped up") at designated times. When the coupon rate is increased only once over the security's life, it is said to be a single step-up callable note. A multiple step-up callable note is a step-up callable note whose coupon is increased more than one time over the life of the security. Valuation using the binomial model is similar to that for valuing a callable bond except that the cash flows are altered at each node to reflect the coupon changing characteristics of a step-up note.

To illustrate how the binomial model can be used to value step-up callable notes, let's begin with a single step-up callable note. Suppose that a 4-year step-up callable note pays 4.25% for two years and then 7.5% for two more years. Assume that this note is callable at par at the end of Year 2 and Year 3. We will use the binomial interest rate tree given in Exhibit 5 to value this note.

Exhibit 17 shows the value of a corresponding single step-up *noncallable* note. The valuation procedure is identical to that performed in Exhibit 8 except that the coupon in the box at each node reflects the step-up terms. The value is $102.082. Exhibit 18 shows that the value of the single step-up callable note is $100.031. The value of the embedded call option is equal to the difference in the step-up noncallable note value and the step-up callable note value, $2.051.

The procedure is the same for a multiple step-up callable note. Suppose that a multiple step-up callable note has the following coupon rates: 4.2% in Year 1, 5% in Year 2, 6% in Year 3, and 7% in Year 4. Also assume that the note is callable at the end of Year 1 at par. Exhibit 19 shows that the value of this note if it *is* noncallable is $101.012. The value of the multiple step-up callable note is $99.996 as shown in Exhibit 20. Therefore, the value of the embedded call option is $1.016 (= 101.012 − 99.996).

Exhibit 17	Valuing a Single Step-Up Noncallable Note with Four Years to Maturity (10% Volatility Assumed)

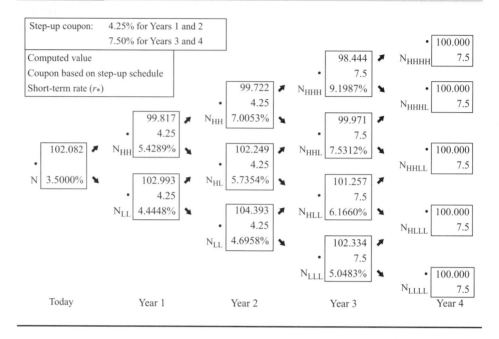

Exhibit 18	Valuing a Single Step-Up Callable Note with Four Years to Maturity, Callable in Two Years at 100 (10% Volatility Assumed)

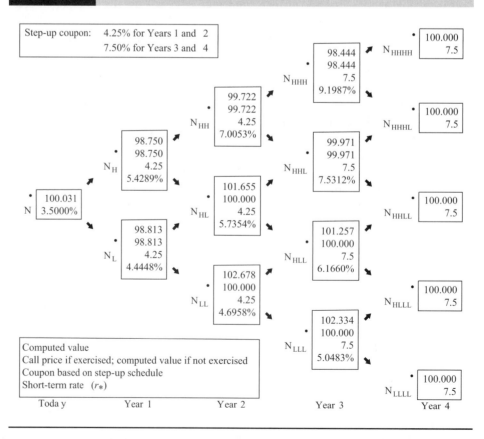

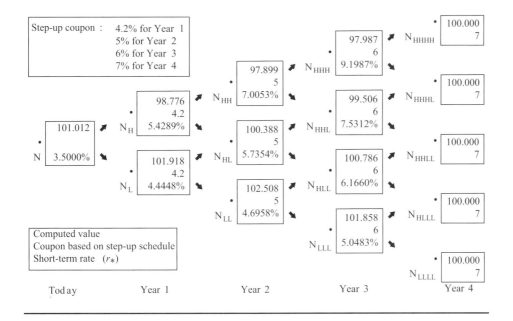

Exhibit 19 Valuing a Multiple Step-Up Noncallable Note with Four Years to Maturity (10% Volatility Assumed)

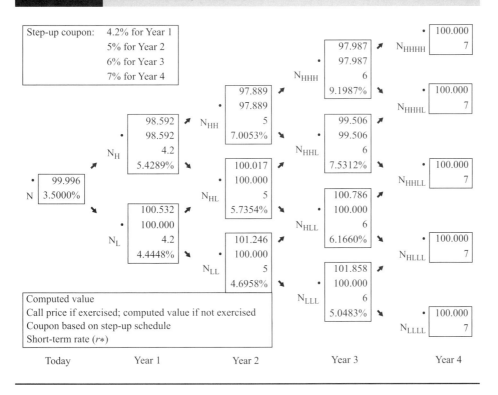

Exhibit 20 Valuing a Multiple Step-Up Callable Note with Four Years to Maturity, and Callable in One Year at 100 (10% Volatility Assumed)

VALUING A CAPPED FLOATER

The valuation of a floating-rate note with a cap (i.e., a capped floater) using the binomial model requires that the coupon rate be adjusted based on the 1-year rate (which is assumed to be the reference rate). Exhibit 21 shows the binomial tree and the relevant values at each node for a floater whose coupon rate is the 1-year rate flat (i.e., no margin over the reference rate) and in which there are no restrictions on the coupon rate.

What is important to recall about floaters is that the coupon rate is set at the beginning of the period but paid at the end of the period (i.e., beginning of the next period). That is, the coupon interest is paid in arrears.

The valuation procedure is identical to that for the other structures described above except that an adjustment is made for the characteristic of a floater that the coupon rate is set at the beginning of the year and paid in arrears. Here is how the payment in arrears characteristic affects the backward induction method. Look at the top node for year 2 in Exhibit 21. The coupon rate shown at that node is 7.0053% as determined by the 1-year rate at that node. Since the coupon payment will not be made until year 3 (i.e., paid in arrears), the value of 100 shown at the node is determined using the backward induction method but discounting the coupon rate shown at the node. For example, let's see how we get the value of 100 in the top box in year 2. The procedure is to calculate the average of the two present values of the bond value and coupon. Since the bond values and coupons are the same, the present value is simply:

$$\frac{100 + 7.0053}{1.070053} = 100$$

Exhibit 21   **Valuing a Floater with No Cap (10% Volatility Assumed)**

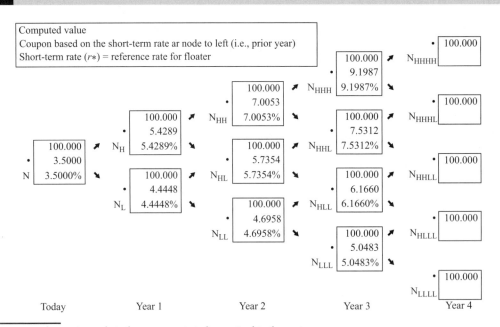

Note: The coupon rate shown at a node is the coupon rate to be received in the next year.

Suppose that the floater has a cap of 7.25%. Exhibit 22 shows how this floater would be valued. At each node where the 1-year rate exceeds 7.25%, a coupon of $7.25 is substituted. The value of this capped floater is 99.724. Thus, the cost of the cap is the difference between par and 99.724. If the cap for this floater was 7.75% rather than

7.25%, it can be shown that the value of this floater would be 99.858. That is, the higher the cap, the closer the capped floater will trade to par.

Thus, it is important to emphasize that the valuation mechanics are being modified slightly only to reflect the characteristics of the floater's cash flow. All of the other principles regarding valuation of bonds with embedded options are the same. For a capped floater there is a rule for determining whether or not to override the cash flow at a node based on the cap. Since a cap embedded in a floater is effectively an option granted by the investor to the issuer, it should be no surprise that the valuation model described in this reading can be used to value a capped floater.

Exhibit 22	**Valuing a Floating Rate Note with a 7.25% Cap (10% Volatility Assumed)**

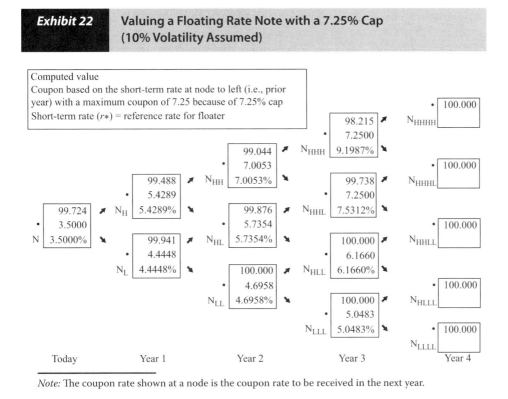

Note: The coupon rate shown at a node is the coupon rate to be received in the next year.

ANALYSIS OF CONVERTIBLE BONDS

10

A convertible bond is a security that can be converted into common stock at the option of the investor. Hence, it is a bond with an embedded option where the option is granted to the investor. Moreover, since a convertible bond may be callable and putable, it is a complex bond because the value of the bond will depend on both how interest rates change (which affects the value of the call and any put option) *and* how changes in the market price of the stock affects the value of the option to convert to common stock.

A. Basic Features of Convertible Securities

The conversion provision of a convertible security grants the securityholder the right to convert the security into a predetermined number of shares of common stock of the issuer. A convertible security is therefore a security with an embedded call option to buy the common stock of the issuer. An exchangeable security grants the securityholder the right to exchange the security for the common stock of a firm *other* than the issuer of the security. Throughout this reading we use the term convertible security to refer to both convertible and exchangeable securities.

In illustrating the calculation of the various concepts described below, we will use a hypothetical convertible bond issue. The issuer is the All Digital Component Corporation (ADC) 5¾% convertible issue due in 9 + years. Information about this hypothetical bond issue and the stock of this issuer is provided in Exhibit 23.

The number of shares of common stock that the securityholder will receive from exercising the call option of a convertible security is called the conversion ratio. The conversion privilege may extend for all or only some portion of the security's life, and the stated conversion ratio may change over time. It is always adjusted proportionately for stock splits and stock dividends. For the ADC convertible issue, the conversion ratio is 25.32 shares. This means that for each $1,000 of par value of this issue the securityholder exchanges for ADC common stock, he will receive 25.32 shares.

At the time of issuance of a convertible bond, the effective price at which the buyer of the convertible bond will pay for the stock can be determined as follows. The prospectus will specify the number of shares that the investor will receive by exchanging the bond for the common stock. The number of shares is called the conversion ratio. So, for example, assume the conversion ratio is 20. If the investor converts the bond for stock, the investor will receive 20 shares of common stock. Now, suppose that the par value for the convertible bond is $1,000 and is sold to investors at issuance at that price. Then effectively by buying the convertible bond for $1,000 at issuance, investors are purchasing the common stock for $50 per share ($1,000/20 shares). This price is referred to in the prospectus as the conversion price, and some investors refer to it as the stated conversion price. For a bond not issued at par (for example, a zero-coupon bond), the market or effective conversion price is determined by dividing the issue price per $1,000 of par value by the conversion ratio.

The ADC convertible was issued for $1,000 per $1,000 of par value and the conversion ratio is 25.32. Therefore, the conversion price at issuance for the ADC convertible issue is $39.49 ($1,000/25.32 shares).

Almost all convertible issues are callable. The ADC convertible issue has a non-call period of three years. The call price schedule for the ADC convertible issue is shown in Exhibit 23. There are some issues that have a provisional call feature that allows the issuer to call the issue during the non-call period if the price of the stock reaches a certain price.

Some convertible bonds are putable. Put options can be classified as "hard" puts and "soft" puts. A hard put is one in which the convertible security must be redeemed by the issuer for cash. In the case of a soft put, while the investor has the option to exercise the put, the *issuer* may select how the payment will be made. The issuer may redeem the convertible security for cash, common stock, subordinated notes, or a combination of the three.

Exhibit 23	**Information about All Digital Component Corporation (ADC) 5¾% Convertible Bond Due in 9 + Years and Common Stock**

Convertible bond

Current market price: $106.50   Maturity date: 9 + years

Non-call for 3 years

Call Price Schedule	
In Year 4	103.59
In Year 5	102.88
In Year 6	102.16
In Year 7	101.44

Exhibit 23	**Continued**

Call Price Schedule

In Year 8	100.72
In Year 9	100.00
In Year 10	100.00

Coupon rate: 5¾%

Conversion ratio: 25.320 shares of ADC shares per $1,000 par value

Rating: A3/A −

ADC common stock

| Expected volatility: 17% | Current dividend yield: 2.727% |
| Dividend per share: $0.90 per year | Stock price: $33 |

B. Traditional Analysis of Convertible Securities

Traditional analysis of convertible bonds relies on measures that do not attempt to directly value the embedded call, put, or common stock options. We present and illustrate these measures below and later discuss an option-based approach to valuation of convertible bonds.

1 Minimum Value of a Convertible Security

The conversion value or parity value of a convertible security is the value of the security if it is converted immediately.[8] That is,

Conversion value = Market price of common stock × Conversion ratio

The minimum price of a convertible security is the greater of[9]

1. Its conversion value, or

2. Its value as a security without the conversion option—that is, based on the convertible security's cash flows if not converted (i.e., a plain vanilla security). This value is called its straight value or investment value. The straight value is found by using the valuation model described earlier in this reading because almost all issues are callable.

If the convertible security does not sell for the greater of these two values, arbitrage profits could be realized. For example, suppose the conversion value is greater than the straight value, and the security trades at its straight value. An investor can buy the convertible security at the straight value and immediately convert it. By doing so, the investor realizes a gain equal to the difference between the conversion value and the straight value. Suppose, instead, the straight value is greater than the conversion

---

8 Technically, the standard textbook definition of conversion value given here is theoretically incorrect because as bondholders convert, the price of the stock will decline. The theoretically correct definition for the conversion value is that it is the product of the conversion ratio and the stock price *after* conversion.

9 If the conversion value is the greater of the two values, it is possible for the convertible bond to trade below the conversion value. This can occur for the following reasons: 1) there are restrictions that prevent the investor from converting, 2) the underlying stock is illiquid, and 3) an anticipated forced conversion will result in loss of accrued interest of a high coupon issue. See Mihir Bhattacharya, "Convertible Securities and Their Valuation," Chapter 51 in Frank J. Fabozzi (ed.), *The Handbook of Fixed Income Securities: Sixth Edition* (New York: McGraw Hill, 2001), p. 1128.

value, and the security trades at its conversion value. By buying the convertible at the conversion value, the investor will realize a higher yield than a comparable straight security.

Consider the ADC convertible issue. Suppose that the straight value of the bond is $98.19 per $100 of par value. Since the market price per share of common stock is $33, the conversion value per $1,000 of par value is:

Conversion value = $33 × 25.32 = $835.56

Consequently, the conversion value is 83.556% of par value. Per $100 of par value the conversion value is $83.556. Since the straight value is $98.19 and the conversion value is $83.556, the minimum value for the ADC convertible has to be $98.19.

2 *Market Conversion Price*

The price that an investor effectively pays for the common stock if the convertible bond is purchased and then converted into the common stock is called the market conversion price or conversion parity price. It is found as follows:

$$\text{Market conversion price} = \frac{\text{Marker price of convertible security}}{\text{Conversion ratio}}$$

The market conversion price is a useful benchmark because once the actual market price of the stock rises above the market conversion price, any further stock price increase is certain to increase the value of the convertible bond by at least the same percentage. Therefore, the market conversion price can be viewed as a break-even price.

An investor who purchases a convertible bond rather than the underlying stock, effectively pays a premium over the current market price of the stock. This premium per share is equal to the difference between the market conversion price and the current market price of the common stock. That is,

Market conversion premium per share = Market conversion price

−Current market price

The market conversion premium per share is usually expressed as a percentage of the current market price as follows:

$$\text{Market conversion premium ratio} = \frac{\text{Market conversion premium per share}}{\text{Market price of common stock}}$$

Why would someone be willing to pay a premium to buy the stock? Recall that the minimum price of a convertible security is the greater of its conversion value or its straight value. Thus, as the common stock price declines, the price of the convertible bond will not fall below its straight value. The straight value therefore acts as a floor for the convertible security's price. However, it is a moving floor as the straight value will change with changes in interest rates.

Viewed in this context, the market conversion premium per share can be seen as the price of a call option. The buyer of a call option limits the downside risk to the option price. In the case of a convertible bond, for a premium, the securityholder limits the downside risk to the straight value of the bond. The difference between the buyer of a call option and the buyer of a convertible bond is that the former knows precisely the dollar amount of the downside risk, while the latter knows only that the most that can be lost is the difference between the convertible bond's price and the straight value. The straight value at some future date, however, is unknown; the value will change as market interest rates change or if the issuer's credit quality changes.

The calculation of the market conversion price, market conversion premium per share, and market conversion premium ratio for the ADC convertible issue is shown below:

$$\text{Market conversion price} = \frac{\$1,065}{25.32} = \$42.06$$

Thus, if the investor purchased the convertible and then converted it to common stock, the effective price that the investor paid per share is $42.06.

Market conversion premium per share = $42.06 − $33 = $9.06

The investor is effectively paying a premium per share of $9.06 by buying the convertible rather than buying the stock for $33.

$$\text{Market conversion premium ratio} = \frac{\$9.06}{\$33} = 0.275 = 27.5\%$$

The premium per share of $9.06 means that the investor is paying 27.5% above the market price of $33 by buying the convertible.

3 Current Income of Convertible Bond versus Common Stock

As an offset to the market conversion premium per share, investing in the convertible bond rather than buying the stock directly, generally means that the investor realizes higher current income from the coupon interest from a convertible bond than would be received from common stock dividends based on the number of shares equal to the conversion ratio. Analysts evaluating a convertible bond typically compute the time it takes to recover the premium per share by computing the premium payback period (which is also known as the break-even time). This is computed as follows:

$$\text{Premium payback period} = \frac{\text{Market conversion premium per share}}{\text{Favorable income differential per share}}$$

where the favorable income differential per share is equal to the following:

$$\frac{\text{Coupon interest} - \left(\text{Conversion ratio} \times \text{Common stock dividend per share}\right)}{\text{Conversion ratio}}$$

The numerator of the formula is the difference between the coupon interest for the issue and the dividends that would be received if the investor converted the issue into common stock. Since the investor would receive the number of shares specified by the conversion ratio, then multiplying the conversion ratio by the dividend per share of common stock gives the total dividends that would be received if the investor converted. Dividing the difference between the coupon interest and the total dividends that would be received if the issue is converted by the conversion ratio gives the favorable income differential on a per share basis by owning the convertible rather than the common stock or changes in the dividend over the period.

Notice that the premium payback period does *not* take into account the time value of money or changes in the dividend over the period.

For the ADC convertible issue, the market conversion premium per share is $9.06. The favorable income differential per share is found as follows:

Coupon interest from bond = 0.0575 × $1,000 = $57.50

Conversion ratio × Dividend per share = 25.32 × $0.90 = $22.79

Therefore,

$$\text{Favorable income differential per share} = \frac{\$57.50 - \$22.79}{25.32} = \$1.37$$

and

$$\text{Premium payback period} = \frac{\$9.06}{\$1.37} = 6.6 \text{ years}$$

Without considering the time value of money, the investor would recover the market conversion premium per share assuming unchanged dividends in about 6.6 years.

4 Downside Risk with a Convertible Bond

Unfortunately, investors usually use the straight value as a measure of the downside risk of a convertible security, because it is assumed that the price of the convertible cannot fall below this value. Thus, some investors view the straight value as the floor for the price of the convertible bond. The downside risk is measured as a percentage of the straight value and computed as follows:

$$\text{Premium over straight value} = \frac{\text{Market price of convertible bond}}{\text{Straight value}} - 1$$

The higher the premium over straight value, all other factors constant, the less attractive the convertible bond.

Despite its use in practice, this measure of downside risk is flawed because the straight value (the floor) changes as interest rates change. If interest rates rise (fall), the straight value falls (rises) making the floor fall (rise). Therefore, the downside risk changes as interest rates change.

For the ADC convertible issue, since the market price of the convertible issue is 106.5 and the straight value is 98.19, the premium over straight value is

$$\text{Premium over straight value} = \frac{\$106.50}{\$98.19} - 1 = 0.085 = 8.5\%$$

5 The Upside Potential of a Convertible Security

The evaluation of the upside potential of a convertible security depends on the prospects for the underlying common stock. Thus, the techniques for analyzing common stocks discussed in books on equity analysis should be employed.

C. Investment Characteristics of a Convertible Security

The investment characteristics of a convertible bond depend on the common stock price. If the price is low, so that the straight value is considerably higher than the conversion value, the security will trade much like a straight security. The convertible security in such instances is referred to as a fixed income equivalent or a busted convertible.

When the price of the stock is such that the conversion value is considerably higher than the straight value, then the convertible security will trade as if it were an equity instrument; in this case it is said to be a common stock equivalent. In such cases, the market conversion premium per share will be small.

Between these two cases, fixed income equivalent and common stock equivalent, the convertible security trades as a hybrid security, having the characteristics of both a fixed income security and a common stock instrument.

D. An Option-Based Valuation Approach

In our discussion of convertible bonds, we did not address the following questions:

1. What is a fair value for the conversion premium per share?
2. How do we handle convertible bonds with call and/or put options?
3. How does a change in interest rates affect the stock price?

Consider first a noncallable/nonputable convertible bond. The investor who purchases this security would be effectively entering into two separate transactions: 1) buying a noncallable/nonputable straight security and 2) buying a call option (or warrant) on the stock, where the number of shares that can be purchased with the call option is equal to the conversion ratio.

The question is: What is the fair value for the call option? The fair value depends on the factors that affect the price of a call option. One key factor is the expected price volatility of the stock: the higher the expected price volatility, the greater the value of the call option. The theoretical value of a call option can be valued using the Black-Scholes option pricing model. This model will be discussed in the reading on option markets and contracts and is explained in more detail in investment textbooks. As a first approximation to the value of a convertible bond, the formula would be:

Convertible security value = Straight value + Value of the call option on the stock

The value of the call option is added to the straight value because the investor has purchased a call option on the stock.

Now let's add in a common feature of a convertible bond: the issuer's right to call the issue. Therefore, the value of a convertible bond that is callable is equal to:

Convertible bond value = Straight value + Value of the call option on the stock
−Value of the call option on the bond

Consequently, the analysis of convertible bonds must take into account the value of the issuer's right to call. This depends, in turn, on 1) future interest rate volatility and 2) economic factors that determine whether or not it is optimal for the issuer to call the security. The Black-Scholes option pricing model cannot handle this situation.

Let's add one more wrinkle. Suppose that the callable convertible bond is also putable. Then the value of such a convertible would be equal to:

Convertible bond value = Straight value + Value of the call option on the stock
−Value of the call option on the bond
+Value of the put option on the bond

To link interest rates and stock prices together (the third question we raise on the previous page), statistical analysis of historical movements of these two variables must be estimated and incorporated into the model.

Valuation models based on an option pricing approach have been suggested by several researchers.[10] These models can generally be classified as one-factor or multi-factor models. By "factor" we mean the stochastic (i.e., random) variables that are assumed to drive the value of a convertible or bond. The obvious candidates for factors are the price movement of the underlying common stock and the movement of interest rates. According to Mihir Bhattacharya and Yu Zhu, the most widely used convertible valuation model has been the one-factor model, and the factor is the price movement of the underlying common stock.[11]

E. The Risk/Return Profile of a Convertible Security

Let's use the ADC convertible issue and the valuation model to look at the risk/ return profile by investing in a convertible issue or the underlying common stock.

Suppose an investor is considering the purchase of either the common stock of ADC or the convertible issue. The stock can be purchased in the market for $33. By buying the convertible bond, the investor is effectively purchasing the stock for $42.06

---

10 See, for example: Michael Brennan and Eduardo Schwartz, "Convertible Bonds: Valuation and Optimal Strategies for Call and Conversion," *Journal of Finance* (December 1977), pp. 1699–1715; Jonathan Ingersoll, "A Contingent-Claims Valuation of Convertible Securities," *Journal of Financial Economics* (May 1977), pp. 289–322; Michael Brennan and Eduardo Schwartz, "Analyzing Convertible Bonds," *Journal of Financial and Quantitative Analysis* (November 1980), pp. 907–929; and, George Constantinides, "Warrant Exercise and Bond Conversion in Competitive Markets," *Journal of Financial Economics* (September 1984), pp. 371–398.
11 Mihir Bhattacharya and Yu Zhu, "Valuation and Analysis of Convertible Securities," Chapter 42 in Frank J. Fabozzi (ed.), *The Handbook of Fixed Income Securities: Fifth Edition* (Chicago: Irwin Professional Publishing, 1997).

(the market conversion price per share). Exhibit 24 shows the total return for both alternatives one year later assuming 1) the stock price does not change, 2) it changes by ±10%, and 3) it changes by ±25%. The convertible's theoretical value is based on some valuation model not discussed here.

If the ADC's stock price is unchanged, the stock position will underperform the convertible position despite the fact that a premium was paid to purchase the stock by acquiring the convertible issue. The reason is that even though the convertible's theoretical value decreased, the income from coupon more than compensates for the capital loss. In the two scenarios where the price of ADC stock declines, the convertible position outperforms the stock position because the straight value provides a floor for the convertible.

One of the critical assumptions in this analysis is that the straight value does not change except for the passage of time. If interest rates rise, the straight value will decline. Even if interest rates do not rise, the perceived credit-worthiness of the issuer may deteriorate, causing investors to demand a higher yield. The illustration clearly demonstrates that there are benefits and drawbacks of investing in convertible securities. The disadvantage is the upside potential give-up because a premium per share must be paid. An advantage is the reduction in downside risk (as determined by the straight value).

Keep in mind that the major reason for the acquisition of the convertible bond is the potential price appreciation due to the increase in the price of the stock. An analysis of the growth prospects of the issuer's earnings and stock price is beyond the scope of this book but is described in all books on equity analysis.

Exhibit 24	Comparison of 1-Year Return for ADC Stock and Convertible Issue for Assumed Changes in Stock Price

Beginning of horizon: October 7, 1993
End of horizon: October 7, 1994
Price of ADC stock on October 7, 1993: $33.00
Assumed volatility of ADC stock return: 17%

Stock Price Change (%)	ADC Stock Return (%)	Convertible's Theoretical Value	Convertible's Return (%)
−25	−22.27	100.47	−0.26
−10	−7.27	102.96	2.08
0	2.73	105.27	4.24
10	12.73	108.12	6.92
25	27.73	113.74	12.20

SOLUTIONS FOR PRACTICE QUESTIONS

1.

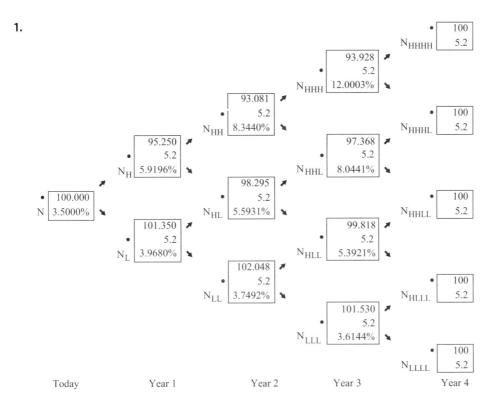

2. The binomial interest rate tree is the one in Practice Question 1. Below is the tree with the values completed at each node. As can be seen, the root of the tree is 104.643, the arbitrage-free value found in the reading for this option-free bond.

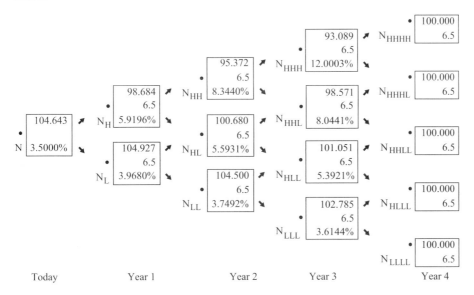

Fixed Income Analysis for the Chartered Financial Analyst Program, Second Edition, by Frank J. Fabozzi, CFA. Copyright© 2005 by CFA Institute.

3. A. The root of the binomial interest rate tree below shows that the arbitrage-free value of this bond is 102.108.

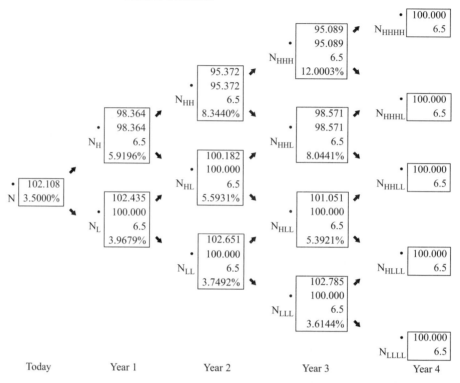

| Today | Year 1 | Year 2 | Year 3 | Year 4 |

B. The arbitrage-free value at 20% is less than the arbitrage-free value at 10% (102.108 versus 102.899). This is because the value of the embedded call option is greater the higher the volatility.

4. The tree below shows that the OAS is −6 basis points for the 6.5% callable bond assuming 20% volatility. (Each 1-year rate is 6 basis points less than in Practice Question 1.)

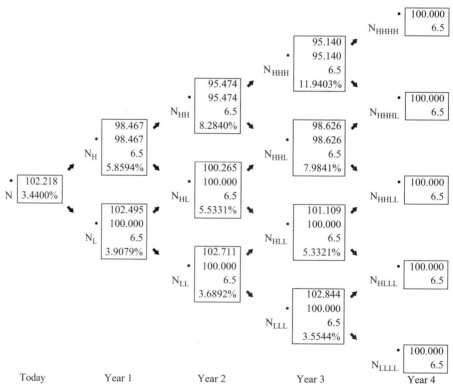

| Today | Year 1 | Year 2 | Year 3 | Year 4 |

5. The tree below shows the arbitrage-free value for a putable bond with four years to maturity, a coupon rate of 6.5%, and putable in one year at 100 assuming a 20% volatility is 106.010.

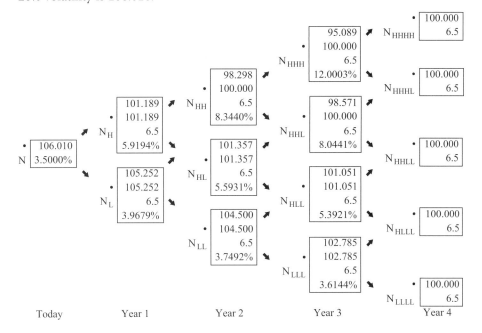

| Today | Year 1 | Year 2 | Year 3 | Year 4 |

SUMMARY

- The potential benchmark interest rates that can be used in bond valuation are those in the Treasury market, a specific bond sector with a given credit rating, or a specific issuer.

- Benchmark interest rates can be based on either an estimated yield curve or an estimated spot rate curve.

- Yield spread measures are used in assessing the relative value of securities.

- Relative value analysis is used to identify securities as being overpriced ("rich"), underpriced ("cheap"), or fairly priced relative to benchmark interest rates.

- The interpretation of a spread measure depends on the benchmark used.

- The option-adjusted spread is a spread after adjusting for the option risk.

- Depending on the benchmark interest rates used to generate the interest rate tree, the option-adjusted spread may or may not capture credit risk.

- The option-adjusted spread is not a spread off of one maturity of the benchmark interest rates; rather, it is a spread over the forward rates in the interest rate tree that were constructed from the benchmark interest rates.

- A valuation model must produce arbitrage-free values; that is, a valuation model must produce a value for each on-the-run issue that is equal to its observed market price.

- There are several arbitrage-free models that can be used to value bonds with embedded options, but they all follow the same principle—they generate a tree of interest rates based on some interest rate volatility assumption, they require rules for determining when any of the embedded options will be exercised, and they employ the backward induction methodology.

- A valuation model involves generating an interest rate tree based on 1) benchmark interest rates, 2) an assumed interest rate model, and 3) an assumed interest rate volatility.

- The assumed volatility of interest rates incorporates the uncertainty about future interest rates into the analysis.

- The interest rate tree is constructed using a process that is similar to bootstrapping but requires an iterative procedure to determine the interest rates that will produce a value for the on-the-run issues equal to their market value.

- At each node of the tree there are interest rates and these rates are effectively forward rates; thus, there is a set of forward rates for each year.

- Using the interest rate tree the arbitrage-free value of any bond can be determined.

- In valuing a callable bond using the interest rate tree, the cash flows at a node are modified to take into account the call option.

- The value of the embedded call option is the difference between the value of an option-free bond and the value of the callable bond.

- The volatility assumption has an important impact on the arbitrage-free value.

- The option-adjusted spread is the constant spread that when added to the short rates in the binomial interest rate tree will produce a valuation for the bond (i.e., arbitrage-free value) equal to the market price of the bond.

- The interpretation of the OAS, or equivalently, what the OAS is compensating an investor for, depends on what benchmark interest rates are used.

- The required values for calculating effective duration and effective convexity are found by shifting the on-the-run yield curve, calculating a new binomial interest rate tree, and then determining the required values after adjusting the tree by adding the OAS to each short rate.

- For a bond with any embedded option or options, application of the binomial model requires that the value at each node of the tree be adjusted based on whether or not the option will be exercised; the binomial model can be used to value bonds with multiple or interrelated embedded options by determining at each node of the tree whether or not one of the options will be exercised.

- With a putable bond, the option will be exercised if the value at a node is less than the price at which the bondholder can put the bond to the issuer.

- The value of a putable bond is greater than the value of an otherwise option-free bond.

- The binomial model can be used to value a single step-up callable note or a multiple step-up callable note.

- To value a floating-rate note that has a cap, the coupon at each node of the tree is adjusted by determining whether or not the cap is reached at a node; if the rate at a node does exceed the cap, the rate at the node is the capped rate rather than the rate determined by the floater's coupon formula.

- For a floating-rate note, the binomial method must be adjusted to account for the fact that a floater pays in arrears; that is, the coupon payment is determined in a period but not paid until the next period.

- Convertible and exchangeable securities can be converted into shares of common stock.

- The conversion ratio is the number of common stock shares for which a convertible security may be converted.

- Almost all convertible securities are callable and some are putable.

- The conversion value is the value of the convertible bond if it is immediately converted into the common stock.

- The market conversion price is the price that an investor effectively pays for the common stock if the convertible security is purchased and then converted into the common stock.

- The premium paid for the common stock is measured by the market conversion premium per share and market conversion premium ratio.

- The straight value or investment value of a convertible security is its value if there was no conversion feature.

- The minimum value of a convertible security is the greater of the conversion value and the straight value.

- A fixed income equivalent (or a busted convertible) refers to the situation where the straight value is considerably higher than the conversion value so that the security will trade much like a straight security.

- A common stock equivalent refers to the situation where the conversion value is considerably higher than the straight value so that the convertible security trades as if it were an equity instrument.

- A hybrid equivalent refers to the situation where the convertible security trades with characteristics of both a fixed income security and a common stock instrument.

- While the downside risk of a convertible security usually is estimated by calculating the premium over straight value, the limitation of this measure is that the straight value (the floor) changes as interest rates change.

- An advantage of buying the convertible rather than the common stock is the reduction in downside risk.

- The disadvantage of a convertible relative to the straight purchase of the common stock is the upside potential give-up because a premium per share must be paid.

- An option-based valuation model is a more appropriate approach to value convertible securities than the traditional approach because it can handle multiple embedded options.

- There are various option-based valuation models: one-factor and multiple-factor models.

- The most common convertible bond valuation model is the one-factor model in which the one factor is the stock price movement.

PRACTICE PROBLEMS FOR READING 44

1. Comment on the following statement:

    "There are several arbitrage-free models for valuing callable bonds. These models differ significantly in terms of how interest rates may change in the next period. There are models that allow the rate in the next period to take on only one of two values. Such a model is called a binomial model. There are models that allow the rate in the next period to take on more than two possible values. For example, there is a model that allows the rate in the next period to take on three possible values. Such a model is called a trinomial model. All these models represent a significantly different approach to valuation and involve different procedures for obtaining the arbitrage-free value."

2. Why is the procedure for valuing a bond with an embedded option called "backward induction"?

3. Why is the value produced by a binomial model and any similar models referred to as an "arbitrage-free value"?

4. **A.** When valuing an option-free bond, short-term forward rates can be used. When valuing a bond with an embedded option, there is not one forward rate for a period but a set of forward rates for a given period. Explain why.

    B. Explain why the set of forward rates for a given period depend on the assumed interest rate volatility.

5. The on-the-run issue for the Inc.Net Company is shown below:

Maturity (Years)	Yield to Maturity (%)	Market Price
1	7.5	100
2	7.6	100
3	7.7	100

Using the bootstrapping methodology, the spot rates are:

Maturity (Years)	Spot Rate (%)
1	7.500
2	7.604
3	7.710

Assuming an interest rate volatility of 10% for the 1-year rate, the binomial interest rate tree for valuing a bond with a maturity of up to three years is shown below:

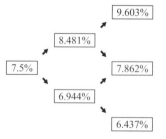

A. Demonstrate using the 2-year on-the-run issue that the binomial interest rate tree above is in fact an arbitrage-free tree.

B. Demonstrate using the 3-year on-the-run issue that the binomial interest rate tree above is in fact an arbitrage-free tree.

C. Using the spot rates given above, what is the arbitrage-free value of a 3-year 8.5% coupon issue of Inc.Net Company?

D. Using the binomial tree, determine the value of an 8.5% 3-year option-free bond.

E. Suppose that the 3-year 8.5% coupon issue is callable starting in year 1 at par (100) (that is, the call price is 100). Also assume that the following call rule is used: if the price exceeds 100, the issue will be called. What is the value of this 3-year 8.5% coupon callable issue?

F. What is the value of the embedded call option for the 3-year 8.5% coupon callable issue?

6. In discussing the approach taken by its investment management firm in valuing bonds, a representative of the firm made the following statement:

"Our managers avoid the use of valuation methodologies such as the binomial model or other fancier models because of the many assumptions required to determine the value. Instead, our managers are firm believers in the concept of option-adjusted spread."

Comment on this statement.

7. A portfolio manager must mark a bond position to market. One issue, a callable issue, has not traded in the market recently. So to obtain a price that can be used to mark a position to market, the manager requested a bid from a dealer and a value from a pricing service. The dealer bid's price was 92. The pricing service indicated a bid price of 93 would be a fair value. The manager could not understand the reason for the 1 point difference in the bid prices.

Upon questioning the trader at the dealer firm that gave a bid of 92, the manager found that the trader based the price on the dealer's valuation model. The model used is the binomial model and the benchmark interest rates the model uses are the on-the-run Treasury issues. The manager then contacted a representative from the pricing service and asked what type of valuation model it used. Again, the response was that the binomial model is used and that the on-the-run Treasury issues are used as the benchmark interest rates.

The manager is puzzled why there is a 1 point difference even though the dealer and the pricing service used the same model and the same benchmark interest rates. The manager has asked you to explain why. Provide an explanation to the manager.

8. The manager of an emerging market bond portfolio is approached by a broker about purchasing a new corporate bond issue in Brazil. The issue is callable, and the broker's firm estimates that the option-adjusted spread is 220 basis points. What questions would you ask the broker with respect to the 220 basis points OAS?

9. In explaining the option-adjusted spread to a client, a manager stated the following: "The option-adjusted spread measures the yield spread using the Treasury on-the-run yield curve as benchmark interest rates." Comment on this statement.

10. A. Explain why the greater the assumed interest rate volatility the lower the value of a callable bond?

B. Explain why the greater the assumed interest rate volatility the higher the value of a putable bond?

11. An assistant portfolio manager described the process for valuing a bond that is both callable and putable using the binomial model as follows:

> "The process begins by first valuing one of the embedded options, say the call option. Then the model is used to value the put option. The value of the corresponding option-free bond is then computed. Given the value of the call option, the value of the put option, and the value of the option-free bond, the value of the bond that is callable and putable is found by adding to the value of the option-free bond the value of the put option and then subtracting the value of the call option."

Explain why you agree or disagree with this assistant portfolio manager's description of the process for valuing a bond that is both callable and putable.

12. Explain why, when the binomial model is used to obtain the values to be used in the formula for computing duration and convexity, the measures computed are an effective duration and effective convexity.

13. An assistant portfolio manager is trying to find the duration of a callable bond of FeedCo Corp. One vendor of analytical systems reported the duration for the issue is 5.4. A dealer firm reported that the duration is 4.5. The assistant portfolio manager was confused by the difference in the reported durations for the FeedCo Corp. issue. He discussed the situation with the senior portfolio manager. In the discussion, the assistant portfolio manager commented: "I don't understand how such a difference could occur. After all, there is a standard formula for computing any duration." How should the senior portfolio manager respond?

14. In computing the effective duration and convexity of a bond with an embedded option, what assumption is made about the option-adjusted spread when rates change?

15. Four portfolio managers are discussing the meaning of option-adjusted spread. Here is what each asserted:

Manager 1   "The option-adjusted spread is a measure of the value of the option embedded in the bond. That is, it is the compensation for accepting option risk."

Manager 2   "The option-adjusted spread is a measure of the spread relative to the Treasury on-the-run yield curve and reflects compensation for credit risk."

Manager 3   "The option-adjusted spread is a measure of the spread relative to the Treasury on-the-run yield curve and reflects compensation for credit risk and liquidity risk."

Manager 4   "The option-adjusted spread is a measure of the spread relative to the issuer's on-the-run yield curve and reflects compensation for credit risk and liquidity risk."

Comment on each manager's interpretation of OAS.

16. Suppose that a callable bond is valued using as the benchmark interest rates the on-the-run yield curve of the issuer and that the yield for the 10-year issue is 6%. Suppose further that the option-adjusted spread computed for a 10-year callable bond of this issuer is 20 basis points. Is it proper to interpret the OAS as meaning that the 10-year callable bond is offering a spread of 20 basis points over the 6% yield on the 10-year on-the-run issue? If not, what is the proper interpretation of the 20 basis point OAS?

17. Suppose that a callable bond has an option-adjusted spread of zero. Does that mean the corporate bond is being overvalued in the market (i.e., trading rich)?

18. In valuing a floating rate note, it is necessary to make a modification to the backward induction method.

    A. Why is the adjustment necessary?

    B. What adjustment is made?

    C. If the floating rate note has a cap, how is that handled by the backward induction method?

19. A. In what sense does a convertible bond typically have multiple embedded options?

    B. Why is it complicated to value a convertible bond?

20. In the October 26, 1992, prospectus summary of the Staples 5% convertible subordinated debentures due 1999, the offering stated: "Convertible into Common Stock at a conversion price of $45 per share..." Since the par value is $1,000, what is the conversion ratio?

21. Consider the convertible bond by Miser Electronics:

    par value = $1,000

    coupon rate = 8.5%

    market price of convertible bond = $900

    conversion ratio = 30

    estimated straight value of bond = $700

    Assume that the price of Miser Electronics common stock is $25 and that the dividend per share is $1 per annum.

    Calculate each of the following:

    A. conversion value.

    B. market conversion price.

    C. conversion premium per share.

    D. conversion premium ratio.

    E. premium over straight value.

    F. favorable income differential per share.

    G. premium payback period.

22. Suppose that the price of the common stock of Miser Electronics whose convertible bond was described in the previous question increases from $25 to $54.

    A. What will be the approximate return realized from investing in the convertible bond if an investor had purchased the convertible for $900?

    B. What would be the return realized if $25 had been invested in the common stock?

    C. Why would the return be higher by investing in the common stock directly rather than by investing in the convertible bond?

23. Suppose that the price of the common stock declines from $25 to $10.

    A. What will be the approximate return realized from investing in the convertible bond if an investor had purchased the convertible for $900 *and* the straight value does not change?

    B. What would be the return realized if $25 had been invested in the common stock?

    C. Why would the return be higher by investing in the convertible bond rather than by investing in the common stock directly?

24. The following excerpt is taken from an article entitled "Caywood Looks for Convertibles," that appeared in the January 13, 1992 issue of *BondWeek*, p. 7:

> Caywood Christian Capital Management will invest new money in its $400 million high-yield portfolio in "busted convertibles," double- and triple-B rated convertible bonds of companies whose stock ..., said James Caywood, CEO. Caywood likes these convertibles as they trade at discounts and are unlikely to be called, he said.

    A. What is a "busted convertible"?

    B. What is the premium over straight value that these bonds would trade?

    C. Why does Mr. Caywood seek convertibles with higher investment grade ratings?

    D. Why is Mr. Caywood interested in call protection?

25. Explain the limitation of using premium over straight value as a measure of the downside risk of a convertible bond?

26. A. The valuation of a convertible bond using an options approach requires a two-factor model. What is meant by a two-factor model and what are the factors?

    B. In practice, is a two-factor model used to value a convertible bond?

The following information relates to Questions 27–32

Mary Merton is a fixed income analyst. She is considering three bonds: a callable bond issued by Wentz Electronics, a non-callable bond issued by AGP Foods Inc., and a convertible bond issued by Ashling Enterprises.

Merton has developed the binomial interest rate tree in Exhibit 1 to use in valuing the Wentz Electronics callable bond. In each non-empty cell of Exhibit 1, there is the one-year interest rate for that node and the expected value at that node of a *non-callable* bond with originally four years to maturity and annual coupons of 8%. The expected values show the ex-coupon price of the bond, the 8% coupon payment, and the cum-coupon price of the bond, each expressed as a percent of par. Some of the data is indicated as missing.

The Wentz Electronics callable bond has four years to maturity, pays an annual coupon of 8%, and is callable any time after today at par plus one-half of the annual coupon (i.e., callable at 104).

In applying the binomial tree to this problem, Merton assumes that the probability of an up move equals the probability of a down move. In other words, at every node of the tree, there is a 50% chance of moving to the higher interest rate node in the next period and a 50% chance of moving to the lower interest rate node in the next period. Merton uses annual compounding in all of her calculations.

The AGP Foods bond has ten years to maturity and pays an annual coupon of 8%. The yield-to-maturity of this bond is 8%.

Merton is also considering a convertible bond issued by Ashling Enterprises. The convertible bond has three years to maturity and a coupon rate of 5.75% with coupons paid annually. Par value of the bond is $1,000. The bond can be converted into 40 shares of Ashling stock. Ashling Enterprises stock closed today at $28.80 per share. Ashling has never paid cash dividends on its stock and does not plan to pay dividends in the near future. Non-convertible bonds of equivalent risk and maturity to the Ashling bond currently have a yield-to-maturity of 6%.

| Exhibit 1 | | Binomial Interest Rate Tree with Certain Prices of a Four-Year Non-Callable Bond with an 8% Coupon | | |

Today	Year 1	Year 2	Year 3	Year 4
				10% 100.00 + 8.00 108.00
			9.00% 99.0826 + 8.00 107.0826	
		8.00% 100.0079 + 8.00 108.0079		8.00% 100.00 + 8.00 108.00
	7.00% 102.6557 + 8.00 110.6557		7.00% 100.9346 + 8.00 108.9346	
6.00% missing		6.00% 103.6753 + 8.00 111.6753		6.00% 100.00 + 8.00 108.00
	5.00% missing + 8.00 missing		5.00% 102.8571 + 8.00 110.8571	
		4.00% missing + 8.00 missing		4.00% 100.00 + 8.00 108.00
			3.00% 104.8544 + 8.00 112.8544	
				2.00% 100.00 + 8.00 108.00

27. Today's ex-coupon price of a *non-callable* bond with four years to maturity and an 8% coupon rate like the Wentz bond is *closest* to:

   A. 99.4623.

   B. 107.0094.

   C. 107.0437.

28. Today's ex-coupon price of the *callable* Wentz bond is *closest* to:

   A. 96.0000.

   B. 104.5688.

   C. 105.0263.

29. Holding all other factors constant, if Merton revises her analysis and uses a higher estimate of the volatility of interest rates, the price of the callable Wentz bond:

    A. is likely to fall.

    B. will not change.

    C. is likely to increase.

30. Merton has calculated the price of the AGP Foods bond if its YTM increases to 9%. The price is $935.82. On the other hand, if the YTM of the bond falls to 7%, the price of the bond would be $1,070.24. Using these two prices, the price of the bond at an 8% YTM, and the 100bps change in interest rates, the effective duration of the AGP Foods bond is *closest* to:

    A. 6.72.

    B. 7.00.

    C. 7.25.

31. Today's minimum market price of the Ashling Enterprises convertible bond is *most likely*:

    A. $993.32.

    B. $1,006.72.

    C. $1,152.00.

32. Which of the following provides the best rationale for purchasing the Ashling Enterprises convertible bond rather than the common stock of Ashling?

    A. The convertible bond is more liquid than the common stock.

    B. The convertible bond provides current income; the common stock does not.

    C. The convertible bond is, in effect, a leveraged position in Ashling stock and therefore offers the opportunity for dramatically higher returns.

The following information relates to Questions 33–38 and is based on "General Principles of Credit Analysis" and this reading

Eero Jokinen is a portfolio manager at Northern Lights Pension Fund in Finland. Given the overall low level of interest rates currently in Europe, Jokinen is looking for ways to enhance the yield of Northern Lights' portfolio. The investment guidelines have recently been amended to allow investments in corporate bonds and bonds with embedded options. Jokinen is analyzing three different bonds as possible investments for Northern Lights: Thor Products bonds, France Telecom bonds, and a particular dual currency bond.

Thor Products Bonds

Selected financial data for Thor Products are provided in Exhibit 1.

Exhibit 1	Selected Financial Data for Thor Products (€ Thousands)		
Balance Sheet			
Current assets	230	Current liabilities	120
Property, plant, and equipment	1,039	Long-term debt	850
		Shareholders' equity	299
Total assets	1,269	Total debt and equity	1,269

Exhibit 1	Continued

Income Statement

Sales	2,000
Cost of sales and operating expenses	1,400
Depreciation expense	200
Income from operations	400
Interest expense	75
Income tax expense	98
Net income	227

The covenants on Thor's outstanding bonds require the company to maintain:

1. a dividend payout ratio below 30 percent.
2. timely interest and principal payments.
3. a total debt-to-capitalization ratio of no more than 60 percent.

Jokinen expects that the current environment of low interest rates and low interest rate volatility may not continue. So, he analyzes the effects of an increase in interest rates and volatility on the value of any callable bonds in the portfolio. Jokinen states:

■ "If interest rates rise and interest rate volatility remains unchanged, the value of callable bonds should decrease."

■ "If interest rate volatility increases and interest rates remain unchanged, the value of the callable bonds should increase."

Jokinen will use a binomial model to value a Thor Products bond with a 5.75 percent coupon and a maturity of 3 years. The bond is callable at par every year starting one year from now. Jokinen assumes that Thor would call the bonds if their price rose above par. A binomial interest rate tree for a *non-callable* Thor Products bond is shown in Exhibit 2. The probability of each interest rate move in the tree is 0.50.

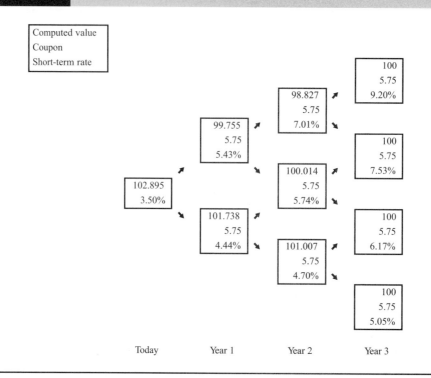

| Exhibit 2 | Option-Free Binomial Interest Rate Tree (10% Volatility Assumed) for Valuing a 3-Year Option-Free Bond with a 5.75% Coupon |

France Telecom Bonds

Jokinen is considering investing in a France Telecom (FRTEL) convertible bond because of the favorable outlook for the industry. His 12-month price forecast is €27.50 per FRTEL share. The convertible bond has the following characteristics:

- FRTEL 1.6% 01 January 2012;
- conversion ratio is 100 shares per bond;
- par value is €2,581;
- current price of the bond is €2,825;
- FRTEL common stock has a current price of €25.75 per share and pays no dividend;
- bond is callable at €2,581 on 31 December 2009.

Dual Currency Bond

Finally, Jokinen is considering a dual currency bond with coupon payments in euros and principal repayment in Turkish lira. He states that the bond would not have any currency exposure to the Turkish lira until it matured and the Turkish lira were actually paid.

33. The total debt-to-capitalization and the EBITDA interest coverage ratios for Thor Products are *closest* to:

	Total Debt-to-Capitalization	EBITDA Interest Coverage
A.	68.4%	5.3
B.	76.4%	8.0
C.	84.4%	2.7

34. Which of the three covenants on Thor's bonds is an affirmative covenant?

   A. #1.

   B. #2.

   C. #3.

35. Are Jokinen's statements regarding the effects on callable bonds of an increase in interest rates and an increase in interest rate volatility, respectively, correct?

	Interest Rates	Interest Rate Volatility
A.	No	No
B.	No	Yes
C.	Yes	No

36. From Exhibit 2, the current price of the Thor callable bond is *closest* to:

   A. 102.05.

   B. 102.17.

   C. 103.01.

37. The premium payback period (in years) for the France Telecom convertible bond is *closest* to:

   A. 1.60.

   B. 1.81.

   C. 6.05.

38. Is Jokinen's statement about the currency exposure to investing in the dual currency bond (euro and Turkish lira) correct?

   A. No, the bond has exposure to the Turkish lira from the date of purchase.

   B. Yes, the bond has appreciation exposure to the Turkish lira only at maturity.

   C. Yes, the bond has depreciation exposure to the Turkish lira only at maturity.

SOLUTIONS FOR READING 44

1. This statement is incorrect. While there are different models such as the binomial and trinomial models, the basic features of all these models are the same. They all involve assessing the cash flow at each node in the interest rate tree and determining whether or not to adjust the cash flow based on the embedded options. All these models require a rule for calling the issue and all require an assumption about the volatility of interest rates. The backward induction method is used for all these models.

2. The procedure for determining the value of a bond with an embedded option starts at the maturity date on the interest rate tree (i.e., the end of the tree) and values the bond moving backward to the root of the tree—which is today's value. Hence the procedure is called backward induction.

3. The reason is that in constructing the interest rate tree the on-the-run issues are used and interest rates on the tree must be such that if the on-the-run issue is valued using the tree, the model will produce the market value of the on-the-run issue. When a model produces the market value of the on-the-run issues, it is said to be "calibrated to the market" or "arbitrage free."

4. **A.** In the interest rate tree, the forward rates for a given period are shown at each node. (In the illustrations in the reading, each period is one year.) Since there is more than one node for each period (after the root of the tree), there is not one forward rate for a given period but several forward rates.

   B. The binomial interest rate tree is constructed based on an assumption about interest rate volatility. If a different volatility assumption is made, a new interest rate tree is constructed, and therefore there are different interest rates at the nodes for a given period and therefore a different set of forward rates.

5. **A.**

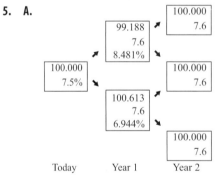

B.

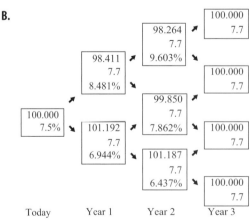

C. The value of an 8.5% coupon 3-year bond using the spot rates is as follows:

$$\frac{8.5}{(1.07500)} + \frac{8.5}{(1.07604)^2} + \frac{108.5}{(1.07710)^3} = \$102.076$$

D.

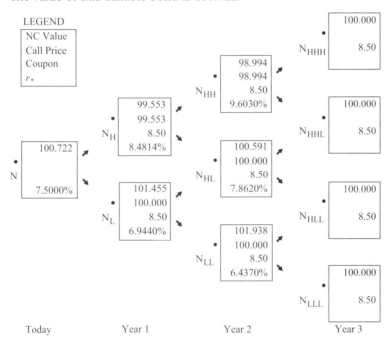

| Today | Year 1 | Year 2 | Year 3 |

E. The value of this callable bond is 100.722.

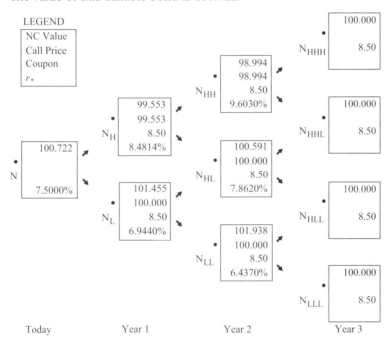

| Today | Year 1 | Year 2 | Year 3 |

F. The value of the embedded call option is $1.354, which is equal to the value of the option-free bond ($102.076) minus the value of the callable bond ($100.722).

6. The statement is wrong. The option-adjusted spread is a byproduct (i.e., is obtained from) of a valuation model. Any assumptions that must be made in a valuation model to obtain the arbitrage-value of a bond also apply to the option-adjusted spread. For example, if a valuation model assumes that interest rate volatility is x%, then the OAS is based on a volatility of x%.

7. Despite the fact that both the dealer and the pricing service used the same model and same benchmark, there are other inputs to the model that could cause a 1 point difference. The major reason is probably that the two may have used a different volatility assumption. A second reason is that the call rule used by the two may be quite different.

8. One of the first questions should be what is the benchmark that the spread is relative to. The other key question is what is the assumed interest rate volatility.

9. This statement is not necessarily correct. An OAS can be computed based on any benchmark interest rates. For example, the on-the-run rates for the issuer or the on-the-run rates for issuers in the same bond sector and having the same credit rating can be used.

10. **A.** The value of a callable bond is equal to the value of an otherwise option-free bond minus the value of the embedded call option. The value of the embedded call option is higher the greater the assumed interest rate volatility. Therefore, a higher value for the embedded call option is subtracted from the value of the option-free bond, resulting in a lower value for the callable bond.

   B. The value of a putable bond is equal to the value of an otherwise option-free bond plus the value of the embedded put option. The value of the embedded put option is higher the greater the assumed interest rate volatility. Therefore, a higher value for the embedded put option is added to the value of the option-free bond, resulting in a higher value of the putable bond.

11. While it is true that the value of a bond that is callable and putable is conceptually equal to the value of the option-free bond adjusted for the value of the put option and the value of the call option, this is not the procedure used in a model such as the binomial model that uses the backward induction method. The reason is that these embedded options exist simultaneously so that the exercise of one option would extinguish the value of the other option. What is done in the backward induction method is to value the callable/putable bond by simultaneously considering the two embedded options. The way this works is at each node it will be determined whether or not the call option will be exercised based on the call rule and then whether or not the put option will be exercised. If either option is exercised, the corresponding exercise value for the bond is used in subsequent calculations in the backward induction process.

12. There are two types of duration and convexity—modified and effective. Modified forms of duration and convexity assume that when interest rates change the cash flows do not change. In contrast, the effective forms assume that when interest rates change the cash flows may change. When the binomial model is used to determine the values when rates are increased and decreased, the new values reflect how the cash flows may change. That is, the cash flow at each node of the binomial interest tree when rates are shifted up and down are allowed to change depending on the rules for when an option will be exercised. Thus, the resulting duration and convexity are effective duration and convexity.

13. It is true that there is a standard formula for computing duration by shocking (i.e., changing) interest rates and substituting the values computed in the duration formula. However, for a bond with an embedded option, such as a callable bond, it is necessary to have a valuation model (such as the binomial model) to determine the value of the bond when interest rates are changed. Valuation models can give different values for the same bond depending on the assumptions used. For example, suppose that the vendor and the dealer use the same valuation model but employ 1) a different volatility assumption, 2) different benchmark interest rates, and 3) a different call rule. The values produced by the two models that are substituted into the (effective) duration formula can result in the difference of 5.4 versus 4.5.

14. It is assumed that the option-adjusted spread is constant when interest rates change.

15. The starting point is defining what the benchmark interest rates are that the spread is being measured relative to. It is based on the benchmark that one interprets what the option-adjusted spread is compensation for.

Manager 1 is wrong. The option-adjusted spread is adjusting any spread for the option risk. That is, it is netting out from the spread the option risk.

Manager 2 is partially correct. If the benchmark interest rates are the on-the-run Treasury issues, then the option-adjusted spread is indicating compensation for credit risk. But it also captures liquidity risk. Moreover, it is not necessarily true that the benchmark interest rates are the on-the-run Treasury rates.

Manager 3 is correct if the benchmark interest rates are the on-the-run Treasury issues. However, other benchmark interest rates have been used, and in such cases Manager 3's interpretation would be incorrect.

Manager 4 is incorrect. Even if the benchmark interest rates are the rates for the issuer's on-the-run issues, the spread would not reflect compensation for credit risk.

16. It is incorrect to state that the 20 basis point OAS is a spread over the issuer's 10-year on-the-run issue. That is, it is not a spread over one point on the yield curve. Rather, from the issuer's on-the-run yield curve, the rates at each node on the interest rate tree are determined. These rates are the one-period forward rates. The OAS is the spread that when added to all these forward rates will produce a value for the callable bond equal to the market price of the bond. So, it is a spread over the forward rates in the interest rate tree which are in turn generated from the benchmark interest rates.

17. Without knowing the benchmark interest rate used to compute the OAS, no statement can be made. If the benchmark is the Treasury sector or a corporate sector with a higher credit quality than the issue being analyzed, then the statement is correct. However, if the benchmark is the issuer's yield curve, then an OAS of zero means that the issue is fairly priced.

18. **A.** The coupon rate on a floater is paid in arrears. This means that for a floater the rate determined in the current period is not paid until the end of the period (or beginning of the next period). This requires that an adjustment be made to the backward induction method.

    B. The adjustment is made to the backward induction method by discounting the coupon payment to be made in the next period for a floater based on the beginning of the period reference rate.

    C. A cap on a floater is handled by determining at each node if the cap is reached. At a node where the coupon rate exceeds the cap, the coupon rate is replaced by the capped rate.

19. **A.** A convertible bond grants the investor the option to call the common stock of the issuer. Thus, a convertible bond has an embedded call option on the common stock. However, most convertible bonds are callable. That is, there is a second embedded call option granting the issuer the right to retire the bond.

    B. The complication that arises is that one of the options, the call on the common stock granted to the investor, depends on the future price of the common stock. However, the call on the bond granted to the issuer depends on future interest rates. Thus, valuing a callable convertible bond requires including in one valuation model both future stock price movements and future interest rate movements.

20. The conversion ratio is found by dividing the par value of $1,000 by the conversion price stated in the prospectus of $45 per share. The conversion ratio is then 22.22 ($1,000/$45).

21. **A.** Conversion value = Market price of common stock × Conversion ratio
    = $25 × 30 = $750

B. Market conversion price

$$= \frac{\text{Market price of convertible bond}}{\text{Conversion ratio}} = \frac{\$900}{30} = \$30$$

C. Conversion premium per share

= Market conversion price − Market price of common stock

= $30 − $25 = $5

D. Conversion premium ratio

$$= \frac{\text{Conversion premium per share}}{\text{Market price of common stock}} = \frac{\$5}{\$25} = 20\%$$

E. Premium over straight value $= \dfrac{\text{Market price of convertible bond}}{\text{Straight value}} - 1$

$$= \frac{\$900}{\$700} - 1 = 28.6\%$$

F. Favorable income differential per share

$$= \frac{\text{Coupon interest from bond} - \text{Conversion ratio} \times \text{Dividend per share}}{\text{Conversion ratio}}$$

$$= \frac{\$85 - (30 \times \$1)}{30} = \$1.833$$

G. Premium payback period $= \dfrac{\text{Market conversion premium per share}}{\text{Favorable income differential per share}}$

$$= \frac{\$5}{\$1.833} = 2.73 \text{ years}$$

22. A. If the price increases to $54, the conversion value will be

Conversion value = $54 × 30 = $1,620

Assuming that the convertible bond's price does not exceed the conversion value (that is why the question asked for an approximate return), then the return on the $900 investment in the convertible bond is:

$$\frac{\$1,620}{\$900} - 1 = 0.8 = 80\%$$

B. The return realized if $25 had been invested in the common stock is equal to:

$$\frac{\$54 - \$25}{\$25} = 1.16 = 116\%$$

C. The reason for the lower return by buying the convertible bond rather than the stock directly is that the investor has effectively paid $5 more for the stock.

23. A. If the price decreases to $10, the conversion value will be

Conversion value = $10 × 30 = $300

However, it is assumed in the question that the straight value is unchanged at $700. The convertible bond will trade at the greater of the straight value or the conversion value. In this case, it is $700. The return is then:

$$\frac{\$700}{\$900} - 1 = -0.22 = -22\%$$

B. The return realized if $25 had been invested in the common stock is equal to:

$$\frac{\$10 - \$25}{\$25} = -0.6 = -60\%$$

C. The return is greater for the convertible bond because of the assumption made that the straight value did not change. If the straight value did decline, the loss would be greater than −22% but it would still be probably less than the loss on the direct purchase of the stock. The key here is that the floor (straight value) is what cushions the decline—but it is a moving floor.

24. **A.** If the stock price is low so that the straight value is considerably higher than the conversion value, the bond will trade much like a straight bond. The convertible in such instances is referred to as a "busted convertible."

    B. Since the market value of a busted convertible is very close to that of a straight bond, the premium over straight value would be very small.

    C. By restricting the convertible bonds in which Mr. Caywood would invest to higher investment grade ratings, he is reducing credit risk.

    D. By seeking bonds not likely to be called, Mr. Caywood is reducing call risk that would result in a forced conversion to the common stock.

25. The measure assumes that the straight value does not decline.

26. **A.** A "factor" is the stochastic (or random) variable that is assumed to affect the value of a security. The two factors in valuing a convertible bond are the price movement of the underlying common stock (which affects the value of the embedded call option on the common stock) and the movement of interest rates (which affects the value of the embedded call option on the bond).

    B. In practice, models used to value convertible bonds have been one-factor models with the factor included being the price movement of the underlying common stock.

27. B is correct. To answer this question, you need to find the missing values. The ex-coupon missing value at Year 2 is ((110.8571 + 112.8544)/2)/1.04 = 107.5536. This is the expected value of the cash flows at the end of year 2 (beginning of year 3) discounted by the year 2 one-year interest rate of 4%. The cum-coupon value is 115.5536. Once the missing value for Year 2 is found, the missing value for Year 1 can be calculated. The missing ex-coupon value at Year 1 is ((111.6753 + (107.5536 + 8))/2)/1.05 = 108.2042. Add the coupon to get the cum-coupon value of 116.2042. The ex-coupon value of the non-callable bond today is then calculated as [(110.6557 + 116.2042)/2]/1.06 = 107.0094.

28. C is correct. At each node in Exhibit 1 where the ex-coupon value exceeds 104 the bond will be called. Therefore, at each node in Exhibit 1 where the ex-coupon value exceeds 104, replace that value with 104. Year 4 needs no adjustment. The first required adjustment occurs in the Year 3 column. Replace the ex-coupon value of 104.8544 with 104. The cum-coupon becomes 112. Since a Year 3 value changed, at least one Year 2 value must change. The ex-coupon missing value in Year 2 for a *callable* bond now becomes ((110.8571 + 112.0000)/2)/1.04 = 107.1428. As this value exceeds 104, replace it with 104 and add 8 to get a cum-coupon value of 112. No other year 2 value has to be adjusted (no other year 2 node has a cum-coupon value in excess of 104). The year 1 ex-coupon missing value is [(111.6753 + 112.0000)/2]/1.05 = 106.5120. As this value exceeds 104, replace it with 104 and add 8 to get a cum-coupon value of 112. The other year 1 node requires no adjustment. Finally, solve for the ex-coupon value of the bond today by [(110.6557 + 112.0000)/2]/1.06 = 105.0263.

29. A is correct. An increase in volatility, holding other factors constant, will increase the value of the call. Because the value of a callable bond equals the

value of an otherwise identical non-callable bond minus the value of the call, an increase in the value of the call decreases the value of the callable bond.

30. A is correct. Effective duration is a measure of the bond's price sensitivity to a change in interest rates. ED = $(BV_{-\Delta y} - BV_{+\Delta y})/(2 \times BV_0 \times \Delta y)$ = (1,070.24 – 935.82)/(2 × 1,000 × 0.01) = 6.72.

31. C is correct. The minimum market price of a convertible bond is the higher of its straight-debt value and its conversion value. The straight-debt value of the convertible bond is $993.32 (found using a financial calculator: N = 3, I/Y = 6, PMT = 57.50, FV = 1,000 and solve for PV). The conversion value of the bond is 40 × $28.80 = $1,152. $1,152 is the minimum value of the bond.

32. B is correct. Ashling common does not pay a dividend. Buying the convertible provides the investor with current income (the coupon) while allowing the investor to benefit from an increase in the price of Ashling common.

33. B is correct. Total debt to capitalization = (120 + 850)/(850 + 120 + 299) = 76.4%. EBITDA interest coverage = (2000 – 1400)/75 = 8.0.

34. B is correct. Covenant #2, to pay interest and principal, is an affirmative covenant requiring action. The other two covenants are negative covenants restricting actions.

35. C is correct. The value of a callable bond equals the value of an otherwise identical non-callable bond minus the value of the call. A rise in interest rates will reduce the value of the non-callable bond portion and thus reduce the value of the callable bond. Jokinen's first statement is correct. If volatility increases, the value of the call portion of the bond increases and the value of the callable bond decreases. Jokinen's second statement is incorrect.

36. A is correct. The bond will be called when the price exceeds par so replace all the bond values above par with 100 and recalculate the tree. The current price is [.5(99.748 + 5.75) + .5(100 + 5.75)]/1.035 = 102.05.

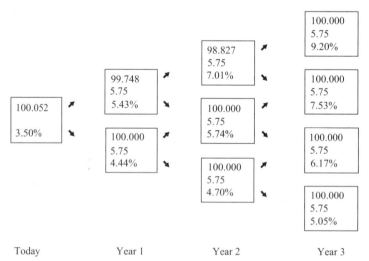

37. C is correct. The coupon interest = €2581 × 1.60% = €41.30

    Favorable income difference per share = [€41.30 – (100 × 0)]/100 = €0.413

    Market conversion price = (€2825)/100 = €28.25

    Market conversion premium per share = €28.25 – €25.75 = €2.50

    Then the premium payback period = €2.50/€0.413 = 6.05 years

38. A is correct. The bond has currency exposure to the Turkish lira from the date of purchase.

Fixed Income:

Structured Securities

This study session provides information on the knowledge and skills needed for valuing a unique segment of the fixed income market—structured securities. It begins with an in-depth study of the structure and characteristics of mortgage-backed and asset-backed markets and securities and concludes with a study of valuation techniques for these fixed income instruments.

READING ASSIGNMENTS

Reading 45 *Mortgage-Backed Sector of the Bond Market*

*Fixed Income Analysis for the Chartered Financial Analyst®
Program*, Second Edition, by Frank J. Fabozzi, CFA

Reading 46 *Asset-Backed Sector of the Bond Market*

*Fixed Income Analysis for the Chartered Financial Analyst®
Program*, Second Edition, by Frank J. Fabozzi, CFA

Reading 47 *Valuing Mortgage-Backed and Asset-Backed Securities*

*Fixed Income Analysis for the Chartered Financial Analyst®
Program*, Second Edition, by Frank J. Fabozzi, CFA

45

Mortgage-Backed Sector of the Bond Market

by Frank J. Fabozzi, CFA

LEARNING OUTCOMES

Mastery	The candidate should be able to:
☐	**a** describe a mortgage loan, and explain the cash flow characteristics of a fixed-rate, level payment, and fully amortized mortgage loan;
☐	**b** explain investment characteristics, payment characteristics, and risks of mortgage passthrough securities;
☐	**c** calculate the prepayment amount on a mortgage passthrough security for a month, given the single monthly mortality rate;
☐	**d** compare the conditional prepayment rate (CPR) with the Public Securities Association (PSA) prepayment benchmark;
☐	**e** explain why the average life of a mortgage-backed security is more relevant than the security's maturity;
☐	**f** explain factors that affect prepayments and the types of prepayment risks;
☐	**g** explain how a collateralized mortgage obligation (CMO) is created and how it provides a better matching of assets and liabilities for institutional investors;
☐	**h** distinguish among the sequential pay tranche, the accrual tranche, the planned amortization class tranche, and the support tranche in a CMO;
☐	**i** evaluate the risk characteristics and relative performance of each type of CMO tranche, given changes in the interest rate environment;
☐	**j** explain investment characteristics of stripped mortgage-backed securities;
☐	**k** compare agency and nonagency mortgage-backed securities;
☐	**l** compare credit risk analysis of commercial and residential nonagency mortgage-backed securities;
☐	**m** describe the basic structure of a commercial mortgage-backed security (CMBS), and explain the ways in which a CMBS investor may realize call protection at the loan level and by means of the CMBS structure.

Fixed Income Analysis for the Chartered Financial Analyst® Program, Second Edition, by Frank J. Fabozzi, CFA. Copyright© 2005 by CFA Institute.

1 INTRODUCTION

In this reading we will discuss securities backed by a pool of loans or receivables—mortgage-backed securities and asset-backed securities. The mortgage-backed securities sector, simply referred to as the **mortgage sector** of the bond market, includes securities backed by a pool of mortgage loans. There are securities backed by residential mortgage loans, referred to as **residential mortgage-backed securities**, and securities backed by commercial loans, referred to as **commercial mortgage-backed securities**.

In the United States, the securities backed by residential mortgage loans are divided into two sectors: 1) those issued by federal agencies (one federally related institution and two government sponsored enterprises) and 2) those issued by private entities. The former securities are called **agency mortgage-backed securities** and the latter **nonagency mortgage-backed securities**.

Securities backed by loans other than traditional residential mortgage loans or commercial mortgage loans and backed by receivables are referred to as **asset-backed securities**. There is a long and growing list of loans and receivables that have been used as collateral for these securities. Together, mortgage-backed securities and asset-backed securities are referred to as **structured financial products**.

It is important to understand the classification of these sectors in terms of bond market indexes. A popular bond market index, the Lehman Aggregate Bond Index, has a sector that it refers to as the "mortgage passthrough sector." Within the "mortgage passthrough sector," Lehman Brothers includes only agency mortgage-backed securities that are mortgage passthrough securities. To understand why it is essential to understand this sector, consider that the "mortgage passthrough sector" represents more than one-third of the Lehman Aggregate Bond Index. It is the largest sector in the bond market index. The commercial mortgage-backed securities sector represents about 2% of the bond market index. The mortgage sector of the Lehman Aggregate Bond Index includes the mortgage passthrough sector and the commercial mortgage-backed securities.

In this reading, our focus will be on the mortgage sector. Although many countries have developed a mortgage-backed securities sector, our focus in this reading is the U.S. mortgage sector because of its size and its important role in U.S. bond market indexes. Credit risk does not exist for agency mortgage-backed securities issued by a federally related institution and is viewed as minimal for securities issued by government sponsored enterprises. The significant risk is prepayment risk, and there are ways to redistribute prepayment risk among the different bond classes created. Historically, it is important to note that the agency mortgage-backed securities market developed first. The technology developed for creating agency mortgage-backed security was then transferred to the securitization of other types of loans and receivables. In transferring the technology to create securities that expose investors to credit risk, mechanisms had to be developed to create securities that could receive investment grade credit ratings sought by the issuer. We will discuss these mechanisms in the reading on the asset-backed sector of the market.

Outside the United States, market participants treat asset-backed securities more generically. Specifically, asset-backed securities include mortgage-backed securities as a subsector. While that is actually the proper way to classify these securities, it was not the convention adopted in the United States. The development of the asset-backed securities (including mortgage-backed securities) outside the United States will also be covered in the reading on the asset-backed sector of the market.

Residential mortgage-backed securities include 1) mortgage passthrough securities, 2) collateralized mortgage obligations, and 3) stripped mortgage-backed securities. The latter two mortgage-backed securities are referred to as derivative mortgage-backed securities because they are created from mortgage passthrough securities.

RESIDENTIAL MORTGAGE LOANS   **2**

A mortgage is a loan secured by the collateral of some specified real estate property which obliges the borrower to make a predetermined series of payments. The mortgage gives the lender the right to "foreclose" on the loan if the borrower defaults and to seize the property in order to ensure that the debt is paid off. The interest rate on the mortgage loan is called the mortgage rate or contract rate. Our focus in this section is on residential mortgage loans.

When the lender makes the loan based on the credit of the borrower and on the collateral for the mortgage, the mortgage is said to be a conventional mortgage. The lender may require that the borrower obtain mortgage insurance to guarantee the fulfillment of the borrower's obligations. Some borrowers can qualify for mortgage insurance which is guaranteed by one of three U.S. government agencies: the Federal Housing Administration (FHA), the Veteran's Administration (VA), and the Rural Housing Service (RHS). There are also private mortgage insurers. The cost of mortgage insurance is paid by the borrower in the form of a higher mortgage rate.

There are many types of mortgage designs used throughout the world. A mortgage design is a specification of the interest rate, term of the mortgage, and the manner in which the borrowed funds are repaid. In the United States, the alternative mortgage designs include 1) fixed-rate, level-payment fully amortized mortgages, 2) adjustable-rate mortgages, 3) balloon mortgages, 4) growing equity mortgages, 5) reverse mortgages, and 6) tiered payment mortgages. Other countries have developed mortgage designs unique to their housing finance market. Some of these mortgage designs relate the mortgage payment to the country's rate of inflation. Below we will look at the most common mortgage design in the United States—the fixed-rate, level-payment, fully amortized mortgage. All of the principles we need to know regarding the risks associated with investing in mortgage-backed securities and the difficulties associated with their valuation can be understood by just looking at this mortgage design.

A. Fixed-Rate, Level-Payment, Fully Amortized Mortgage

A fixed-rate, level-payment, fully amortized mortgage has the following features:

- the mortgage rate is fixed for the life of the mortgage loan;
- the dollar amount of each monthly payment is the same for the life of the mortgage loan (i.e., there is a "level payment");
- when the last scheduled monthly mortgage payment is made, the remaining mortgage balance is zero (i.e., the loan is fully amortized).

The monthly mortgage payments include principal repayment and interest. The frequency of payment is typically monthly. Each monthly mortgage payment for this mortgage design is due on the first of each month and consists of:

1. interest of $\frac{1}{12}$ of the fixed annual interest rate times the amount of the outstanding mortgage balance at the beginning of the previous month, and

2. a repayment of a portion of the outstanding mortgage balance (principal).

The difference between the monthly mortgage payment and the portion of the payment that represents interest equals the amount that is applied to reduce the outstanding mortgage balance. The monthly mortgage payment is designed so that after the last scheduled monthly mortgage payment is made, the amount of the outstanding mortgage balance is zero (i.e., the mortgage is fully repaid).

To illustrate this mortgage design, consider a 30-year (360-month), $100,000 mortgage with an 8.125% mortgage rate. The monthly mortgage payment would be

$742.50. Exhibit 1 shows for selected months how each monthly mortgage payment is divided between interest and scheduled principal repayment. At the beginning of month 1, the mortgage balance is $100,000, the amount of the original loan. The mortgage payment for month 1 includes interest on the $100,000 borrowed for the month. Since the interest rate is 8.125%, the monthly interest rate is 0.0067708 (0.08125 divided by 12). Interest for month 1 is therefore $677.08 ($100,000 times 0.0067708). The $65.41 difference between the monthly mortgage payment of $742.50 and the interest of $677.08 is the portion of the monthly mortgage payment that represents the scheduled principal repayment. It is also referred to as the scheduled amortization, and we shall use the terms scheduled principal repayment and scheduled amortization interchangeably throughout this reading. This $65.41 in month 1 reduces the mortgage balance.

The mortgage balance at the end of month 1 (beginning of month 2) is then $99,934.59 ($100,000 minus $65.41). The interest for the second monthly mortgage payment is $676.64, the monthly interest rate (0.0067708) times the mortgage balance at the beginning of month 2 ($99,934.59). The difference between the $742.50 monthly mortgage payment and the $676.64 interest is $65.86, representing the amount of the mortgage balance paid off with that monthly mortgage payment. Notice that the mortgage payment in month 360—the final payment—is sufficient to pay off the remaining mortgage balance.

As Exhibit 1 clearly shows, *the portion of the monthly mortgage payment applied to interest declines each month and the portion applied to principal repayment increases.* The reason for this is that as the mortgage balance is reduced with each monthly mortgage payment, the interest on the mortgage balance declines. Since the monthly mortgage payment is a fixed dollar amount, an increasingly larger portion of the monthly payment is applied to reduce the mortgage balance outstanding in each subsequent month.

Exhibit 1	Amortization Schedule for a Level-Payment, Fixed-Rate, Fully Amortized Mortgage

Mortgage loan:	$100,000	Monthly payment:	$742.50
Mortgage rate:	8.125%	Term of loan:	30 years (360 months)

Month	Beginning of Month Mortgage Balance ($)	Mortgage Payment ($)	Interest ($)	Scheduled Repayment ($)	End of Month Mortgage Balance ($)
1	100,000.00	742.50	677.08	65.41	99,934.59
2	99,934.59	742.50	676.64	65.86	99,868.73
3	99,868.73	742.50	676.19	66.30	99,802.43
4	99,802.43	742.50	675.75	66.75	99,735.68
...	...	...	...	...	...
25	98,301.53	742.50	665.58	76.91	98,224.62
26	98,224.62	742.50	665.06	77.43	98,147.19
27	98,147.19	742.50	664.54	77.96	98,069.23
...	...	...	...	...	...
74	93,849.98	742.50	635.44	107.05	93,742.93
75	93,742.93	742.50	634.72	107.78	93,635.15
76	93,635.15	742.50	633.99	108.51	93,526.64
...	...	...	...	...	...
141	84,811.77	742.50	574.25	168.25	84,643.52

| Exhibit 1 | Continued |

Month	Beginning of Month Mortgage Balance ($)	Mortgage Payment ($)	Interest ($)	Scheduled Repayment ($)	End of Month Mortgage Balance ($)
142	84,643.52	742.50	573.11	169.39	84,474.13
143	84,474.13	742.50	571.96	170.54	84,303.59
...	...	...	...	...	...
184	76,446.29	742.50	517.61	224.89	76,221.40
185	76,221.40	742.50	516.08	226.41	75,994.99
186	75,994.99	742.50	514.55	227.95	75,767.04
...	...	...	...	...	...
233	63,430.19	742.50	429.48	313.02	63,117.17
234	63,117.17	742.50	427.36	315.14	62,802.03
235	62,802.03	742.50	425.22	317.28	62,484.75
...	...	...	...	...	...
289	42,200.92	742.50	285.74	456.76	41,744.15
290	41,744.15	742.50	282.64	459.85	41,284.30
291	41,284.30	742.50	279.53	462.97	40,821.33
...	...	...	...	...	...
321	25,941.42	742.50	175.65	566.85	25,374.57
322	25,374.57	742.50	171.81	570.69	24,803.88
323	24,803.88	742.50	167.94	574.55	24,229.32
...	...	...	...	...	...
358	2,197.66	742.50	14.88	727.62	1,470.05
359	1,470.05	742.50	9.95	732.54	737.50
360	737.50	742.50	4.99	737.50	0.00

1 Servicing Fee

Every mortgage loan must be serviced. Servicing of a mortgage loan involves collecting monthly payments and forwarding proceeds to owners of the loan; sending payment notices to mortgagors; reminding mortgagors when payments are overdue; maintaining records of principal balances; initiating foreclosure proceedings if necessary; and, furnishing tax information to borrowers (i.e., mortgagors) when applicable.

The servicing fee is a portion of the mortgage rate. If the mortgage rate is 8.125% and the servicing fee is 50 basis points, then the investor receives interest of 7.625%. The interest rate that the investor receives is said to be the net interest or net coupon. The servicing fee is commonly called the servicing spread.

The dollar amount of the servicing fee declines over time as the mortgage amortizes. This is true for not only the mortgage design that we have just described, but for all mortgage designs.

2 Prepayments and Cash Flow Uncertainty

Our illustration of the cash flow from a level-payment, fixed-rate, fully amortized mortgage assumes that the homeowner does not pay off any portion of the mortgage balance prior to the scheduled due date. But homeowners can pay off all or part of their mortgage balance prior to the maturity date. A payment made in excess of the monthly mortgage payment is called a prepayment. The prepayment could be to pay off the entire outstanding balance or a partial paydown of the mortgage balance. When a prepayment is not for the entire outstanding balance it is called a curtailment.

The effect of prepayments is that the amount and timing of the cash flow from a mortgage loan are not known with certainty. This risk is referred to as prepayment risk. For example, all that the lender in a $100,000, 8.125% 30-year mortgage knows is that as long as the loan is outstanding and the borrower does not default, interest will be received and the principal will be repaid at the scheduled date each month; then at the end of the 30 years, the investor would have received $100,000 in principal payments. What the investor does not know—the uncertainty—is for how long the loan will be outstanding, and therefore what the timing of the principal payments will be. This is true for all mortgage loans, not just the level-payment, fixed-rate, fully amortized mortgage. Factors affecting prepayments will be discussed later in this reading.

Most mortgages have no prepayment penalty. The outstanding loan balance can be repaid at par. However, there are mortgages with prepayment penalties. The purpose of the penalty is to deter prepayment when interest rates decline. A prepayment penalty mortgage has the following structure. There is a period of time over which if the loan is prepaid in full or in excess of a certain amount of the outstanding balance, there is a prepayment penalty. This period is referred to as the lockout period or penalty period. During the penalty period, the borrower may prepay up to a specified amount of the outstanding balance without a penalty. Over that specified amount, the penalty is set in terms of the number of months of interest that must be paid.

3 MORTGAGE PASSTHROUGH SECURITIES

A mortgage passthrough security is a security created when one or more holders of mortgages form a collection (pool) of mortgages and sell shares or participation certificates in the pool. A pool may consist of several thousand or only a few mortgages. When a mortgage is included in a pool of mortgages that is used as collateral for a mortgage passthrough security, the mortgage is said to be securitized.

A. Cash Flow Characteristics

The cash flow of a mortgage passthrough security depends on the cash flow of the underlying pool of mortgages. As we explained in the previous section, the cash flow consists of monthly mortgage payments representing interest, the scheduled repayment of principal, and any prepayments.

Payments are made to security holders each month. However, neither the amount nor the timing of the cash flow from the pool of mortgages is identical to that of the cash flow passed through to investors. The monthly cash flow for a passthrough is less than the monthly cash flow of the underlying pool of mortgages by an amount equal to servicing and other fees. The other fees are those charged by the issuer or guarantor of the passthrough for guaranteeing the issue (discussed later). The coupon rate on a passthrough is called the passthrough rate. The passthrough rate is less than the mortgage rate on the underlying pool of mortgages by an amount equal to the servicing and guaranteeing fees.

The timing of the cash flow is also different. The monthly mortgage payment is due from each mortgagor on the first day of each month, but there is a delay in passing through the corresponding monthly cash flow to the security holders. The length of the delay varies by the type of passthrough security.

Not all of the mortgages that are included in a pool of mortgages that are securitized have the same mortgage rate and the same maturity. Consequently, when describing a passthrough security, a weighted average coupon rate and a weighted average maturity are determined. A weighted average coupon rate, or WAC, is found by weighting the mortgage rate of each mortgage loan in the pool by the percentage of the mortgage outstanding relative to the outstanding amount of all the mortgages in the pool. A weighted average maturity, or WAM, is found by weighting the remaining number of months to maturity for each mortgage loan in the pool by the amount of the outstanding mortgage balance.

For example, suppose a mortgage pool has just five loans and the outstanding mortgage balance, mortgage rate, and months remaining to maturity of each loan are as follows:

Loan	Outstanding Mortgage Balance ($)	Weight in Pool (%)	Mortgage Rate (%)	Months Remaining
1	125,000	22.12	7.50	275
2	85,000	15.04	7.20	260
3	175,000	30.97	7.00	290
4	110,000	19.47	7.80	285
5	70,000	12.39	6.90	270
Total	565,000	100.00	7.28	279

The WAC for this mortgage pool is:

$$0.2212(7.5\%) + 0.1504(7.2\%) + 0.3097(7.0\%) + 0.1947(7.8\%)$$
$$+ 0.1239(6.90\%) = 7.28\%$$

The WAM for this mortgage pool is

$$0.2212(275) + 0.1504(260) + 0.3097(290) + 0.1947(285)$$
$$+ 0.1239(270) = 279 \text{ months(rounded)}$$

B. Types of Mortgage Passthrough Securities

In the United States, the three major types of passthrough securities are guaranteed by agencies created by Congress to increase the supply of capital to the residential mortgage market. Those agencies are the Government National Mortgage Association (Ginnie Mae), the Federal Home Loan Mortgage Corporation (Freddie Mac), and the Federal National Mortgage Association (Fannie Mae).

While Freddie Mac and Fannie Mae are commonly referred to as "agencies" of the U.S. government, both are corporate instrumentalities of the U.S. government. That is, they are government sponsored enterprises; therefore, their guarantee does not carry the full faith and credit of the U.S. government. In contrast, Ginnie Mae is a federally related institution; it is part of the Department of Housing and Urban Development. As such, its guarantee carries the full faith and credit of the U.S. government. The passthrough securities issued by Fannie Mae and Freddie Mac are called conventional passthrough securities. However, in this reading we shall refer to those passthrough securities issued by all three entities (Ginnie Mae, Fannie Mae, and Freddie Mac) as agency passthrough securities. It should be noted, however, that market participants do reserve the term "agency passthrough securities" for those issued only by Ginnie Mae.[1]

---

1 The name of the passthrough issued by Ginnie Mae and Fannie Mae is a *Mortgage-Backed Security* or *MBS*. So, when a market participant refers to a Ginnie Mae MBS or Fannie Mae MBS, what is meant is a passthrough issued by these two entities. The name of the passthrough issued by Freddie Mac is a *Participation Certificate* or *PC*. So, when a market participant refers to a Freddie Mac PC, what is meant is a passthrough issued by Freddie Mac. Every agency has different "programs" under which passthroughs are issued with different types of mortgage pools (e.g., 30-year fixed-rate mortgages, 15-year fixed-rate mortgages, adjustable-rate mortgages). We will not review the different programs here.

In order for a loan to be included in a pool of loans backing an agency security, it must meet specified underwriting standards. These standards set forth the maximum size of the loan, the loan documentation required, the maximum loan-to-value ratio, and whether or not insurance is required. If a loan satisfies the underwriting standards for inclusion as collateral for an agency mortgage-backed security, it is called a conforming mortgage. If a loan fails to satisfy the underwriting standards, it is called a nonconforming mortgage.

Nonconforming mortgages used as collateral for mortgage passthrough securities are privately issued. These securities are called nonagency mortgage passthrough securities and are issued by thrifts, commercial banks, and private conduits. Private conduits may purchase nonconforming mortgages, pool them, and then sell passthrough securities whose collateral is the underlying pool of nonconforming mortgages. Nonagency passthrough securities are rated by the nationally recognized statistical rating organizations. These securities are supported by credit enhancements so that they can obtain an investment grade rating. We shall describe these securities in the next reading.

C. Trading and Settlement Procedures

Agency passthrough securities are identified by a pool prefix and pool number provided by the agency. The prefix indicates the type of passthrough. There are specific rules established by the Bond Market Association for the trading and settlement of mortgage-backed securities. Many trades occur while a pool is still unspecified, and therefore no pool information is known at the time of the trade. This kind of trade is known as a TBA trade (to-be-announced trade). In a TBA trade the two parties agree on the agency type, the agency program, the coupon rate, the face value, the price, and the settlement date. The actual pools of mortgage loans underlying the agency passthrough are not specified in a TBA trade. However, this information is provided by the seller to the buyer before delivery. There are trades where more specific requirements are established for the securities to be delivered. An example is a Freddie Mac with a coupon rate of 8.5% and a WAC between 9.0% and 9.2%. There are also specified pool trades wherein the actual pool numbers to be delivered are specified.

Passthrough prices are quoted in the same manner as U.S. Treasury coupon securities. A quote of 94-05 means 94 and 5 32nds of par value, or 94.15625% of par value. The price that the buyer pays the seller is the agreed upon sale price plus accrued interest. Given the par value, the dollar price (excluding accrued interest) is affected by the amount of the pool mortgage balance outstanding. The pool factor indicates the percentage of the initial mortgage balance still outstanding. So, a pool factor of 90 means that 90% of the original mortgage pool balance is outstanding. The pool factor is reported by the agency each month.

The dollar price paid for just the principal is found as follows given the agreed upon price, par value, and the month's pool factor provided by the agency:

Price × Par value × Pool factor

For example, if the parties agree to a price of 92 for $1 million par value for a passthrough with a pool factor of 0.85, then the dollar price paid by the buyer in addition to accrued interest is:

0.92 × $1,000,000 × 0.85 = $782,000

The buyer does not know what he will get unless he specifies a pool number. There are many seasoned issues of the same agency with the same coupon rate outstanding at a given point in time. For example, in early 2000 there were more than 30,000 pools of 30-year Ginnie Mae MBSs outstanding with a coupon rate of 9%. One passthrough may be backed by a pool of mortgage loans in which all the properties are located in California, while another may be backed by a pool of mortgage loans in which all the properties are in Minnesota. Yet another may be backed by a pool of mortgage loans in which the properties are from several regions of the country. So which pool are dealers referring to when they talk about Ginnie Mae 9s? They are not referring to any specific pool but instead to a generic security, despite the fact that the prepayment characteristics of passthroughs with underlying pools from different parts of the country are different. Thus, the projected prepayment rates for passthroughs reported by dealer firms (discussed later) are for generic passthroughs. A particular pool purchased may have a materially different prepayment rate from the generic. Moreover, when an investor purchases a passthrough without specifying a pool number, the seller has the option to deliver the worst-paying pools as long as the pools delivered satisfy good delivery requirements.

D. Measuring the Prepayment Rate

A prepayment is any payment toward the repayment of principal that is in excess of the scheduled principal payment. In describing prepayments, market participants refer to the prepayment rate or prepayment speed. In this section we will see how the historical prepayment rate is computed for a month. We then look at how to annualize a monthly prepayment rate and then explain the convention in the residential mortgage market for describing a pattern of prepayment rates over the life of a mortgage pool.

There are three points to keep in mind in the discussion in this section. First, we will look at how the actual or historical prepayment rate of a mortgage pool is calculated. Second, we will see later how in projecting the cash flow of a mortgage pool, an investor uses the same prepayment measures to project prepayments given a prepayment rate. The third point is that we are just describing the mechanics of calculating prepayment measures. The difficult task of projecting the prepayment rate is not discussed here. In fact, this task is beyond the scope of this reading. However, the factors that investors use in prepayment models (i.e., statistical models used to project prepayments) will be described in Section F.

1 Single Monthly Mortality Rate

Given the amount of the prepayment for a month and the amount that was available to prepay that month, a monthly prepayment rate can be computed. The amount available to prepay in a month is *not* the outstanding mortgage balance of the pool in the previous month. The reason is that there will be scheduled principal payments for the month and therefore by definition this amount cannot be prepaid. Thus, the amount available to prepay in a given month, say month t, is the beginning mortgage balance in month t reduced by the scheduled principal payment in month t.

The ratio of the prepayment in a month and the amount available to prepay that month is called the single monthly mortality rate[2] or simply SMM. That is, the SMM for month t is computed as follows

$$\text{SMM}_t = \frac{\text{Prepayment in month } t}{\text{Beginning mortgage balance for month } t - \text{Scheduled principal payment in month } t}$$

Let's illustrate the calculation of the SMM. Assume the following:

beginning mortgage balance in month 33	=	$358,326,766
scheduled principal payment in month 33	=	$297,825
prepayment in month 33	=	$1,841,347

---

2 It may seem strange that the term "mortality" is used to describe this prepayment measure. This term reflects the influence of actuaries who in the early years of the development of the mortgage market migrated to dealer firms to assist in valuing mortgage-backed securities. Actuaries viewed the prepayment of a mortgage loan as the "death" of a mortgage.

The SMM for month 33 is therefore:

$$\text{SMM}_{33} = \frac{\$1,841,347}{\$358,326,766 - \$297,825} = 0.005143 = 0.5143\%$$

The SMM_{33} of 0.5143% is interpreted as follows: In month 33, 0.5143% of the outstanding mortgage balance available to prepay in month 33 prepaid.

Let's make sure we understand the two ways in which the SMM can be used. First, given the prepayment for a month for a mortgage pool, an investor can calculate the SMM as we just did in our illustration to determine the SMM for month 33. Second given an *assumed* SMM, an investor will use it to project the prepayment for a month. The prepayment for a month will then be used to determine the cash flow of a mortgage pool for the month. We'll see this later in this section when we illustrate how to calculate the cash flow for a passthrough security. For now, it is important to understand that given an assumed SMM for month t, the prepayment for month t is found as follows:

$$\text{Prepayment for month } t = \text{SMM} \times (\text{Beginning mortgage balance for month } t - \text{Scheduled principal payment for month } t) \tag{1}$$

For example, suppose that an investor owns a passthrough security in which the remaining mortgage balance at the beginning of some month is $290 million and the scheduled principal payment for that month is $3 million. The investor believes that the SMM next month will be 0.5143%. Then the projected prepayment for the month is:

$$0.005143 \times (\$290,000,000 - \$3,000,000) = \$1,476,041$$

2 Conditional Prepayment Rate

Market participants prefer to talk about prepayment rates on an annual basis rather than a monthly basis. This is handled by annualizing the SMM. The annualized SMM is called the conditional prepayment rate or CPR.[3] Given the SMM for a given month, the CPR can be demonstrated to be:[4]

$$\text{CPR} = 1 - (1 - \text{SMM})^{12} \tag{2}$$

For example, suppose that the SMM is 0.005143. Then the CPR is

$$\text{CPR} = 1 - (1 - 0.005143)^{12}$$
$$= 1 - (0.994857)^{12} = 0.06 = 6\%$$

A CPR of 6% means that, ignoring scheduled principal payments, approximately 6% of the outstanding mortgage balance at the beginning of the year will be prepaid by the end of the year.

Given a CPR, the corresponding SMM can be computed by solving Equation 2 for the SMM:

$$\text{SMM} = 1 - (1 - \text{CPR})^{1/12} \tag{3}$$

To illustrate Equation 3, suppose that the CPR is 6%; then the SMM is

$$\text{SMM} = 1 - (1 - 0.06)^{1/12} = 0.005143 = 0.5143\%$$

---

3 It is referred to as a "conditional" prepayment rate because the prepayments in one year depend upon (i.e., are conditional upon) the amount available to prepay in the previous year. Sometimes market participants refer to the CPR as the "constant" prepayment rate.
4 The derivation of the CPR for a given SMM is beyond the scope of this chapter. The proof is provided in Lakhbir S. Hayre and Cyrus Mohebbi, "Mortgage Mathematics," in Frank J. Fabozzi (ed.), *Handbook of Mortgage-Backed Securities: Fifth Edition* (New York, NY: McGraw-Hill, 2001), pp. 844–845.

3 *PSA Prepayment Benchmark*

An SMM is the prepayment rate for a month. A CPR is a prepayment rate for a year. Market participants describe prepayment rates (historical/actual prepayment rates and those used for projecting future prepayments) in terms of a prepayment pattern or benchmark over the life of a mortgage pool. In the early 1980s, the Public Securities Association (PSA), later renamed the Bond Market Association, undertook a study to look at the pattern of prepayments over the life of a typical mortgage pool. Based on the study, the PSA established a prepayment benchmark which is referred to as the PSA prepayment benchmark. Although sometimes referred to as a "prepayment model," it is a convention and not a model to predict prepayments.

The PSA prepayment benchmark is expressed as a monthly series of CPRs. The PSA benchmark assumes that prepayment rates are low for newly originated mortgages and then will speed up as the mortgages become seasoned. The PSA benchmark assumes the following prepayment rates for 30-year mortgages: 1) a CPR of 0.2% for the first month, increased by 0.2% per year per month for the next 30 months until it reaches 6% per year, and 2) a 6% CPR for the remaining months.

This benchmark, referred to as "100% PSA" or simply "100 PSA," is graphically depicted in Exhibit 2. Mathematically, 100 PSA can be expressed as follows:

$$\text{if } t < 30 \text{ then CPR} = 6\%(t/30)$$

$$\text{if } t \geq 30 \text{ then CPR} = 6\%$$

where t is the number of months since the mortgages were originated.

Exhibit 2	**Graphical Depiction of 100 PSA**

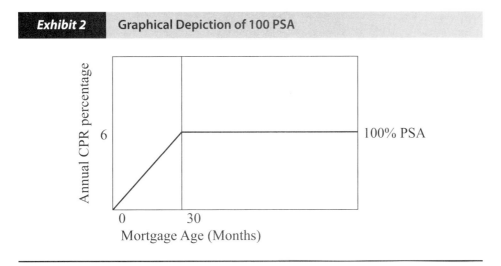

It is important to emphasize that the CPRs and corresponding SMMs apply to a mortgage pool *based on the number of months since origination*. For example, if a mortgage pool has loans that were originally 30-year (360-month) mortgage loans and the WAM is currently 357 months, this means that the mortgage pool is seasoned three months. So, in determining prepayments for the next month, the CPR and SMM that are applicable are those for month 4.

Slower or faster speeds are then referred to as some percentage of PSA. For example, "50 PSA" means one-half the CPR of the PSA prepayment benchmark; "150 PSA" means 1.5 times the CPR of the PSA prepayment benchmark; "300 PSA" means three times the CPR of the prepayment benchmark. A prepayment rate of 0 PSA means that no *prepayments* are assumed. While there are no prepayments at 0 PSA, there are scheduled principal repayments.

In constructing a schedule for monthly prepayments, the CPR (an annual rate) must be converted into a monthly prepayment rate (an SMM) using Equation 3. For example, the SMMs for month 5, month 20, and months 31 through 360 assuming 100 PSA are calculated as follows:

for month 5:

$$\text{CPR} = 6\%(5/30) = 1\% = 0.01$$

$$\text{SMM} = 1 - (1 - 0.01)^{1/12} = 1 - (0.99)^{0.083333} = 0.000837$$

for month 20:

$$\text{CPR} = 6\%(20/30) = 4\% = 0.04$$

$$\text{SMM} = 1 - (1 - 0.04)^{1/12} = 1 - (0.96)^{0.083333} = 0.003396$$

for months 31–360:

$$\text{CPR} = 6\%$$

$$\text{SMM} = 1 - (1 - 0.06)^{1/12} = 1 - (0.94)^{0.083333} = 0.005143$$

What if the PSA were 165 instead? The SMMs for month 5, month 20, and months 31 through 360 assuming 165 PSA are computed as follows:
for month 5:

$$\text{CPR} = 6\%(5/30) = 1\% = 0.01$$

$$165 \text{ PSA} = 1.65(0.01) = 0.0165$$

$$\text{SMM} = 1 - (1 - 0.0165)^{1/12} = 1 - (0.9835)^{0.08333} = 0.001386$$

for month 20:

$$\text{CPR} = 6\%(20/30) = 4\% = 0.04$$

$$165 \text{ PSA} = 1.65(0.04) = 0.066$$

$$\text{SMM} = 1 - (1 - 0.066)^{1/12} = 1 - (0.934)^{0.08333} = 0.005674$$

for months 31–360:

$$\text{CPR} = 6\%$$

$$165 \text{ PSA} = 1.65(0.06) = 0.099$$

$$\text{SMM} = 1 - (1 - 0.099)^{1/12} = 1 - (0.901)^{0.08333} = 0.008650$$

Notice that the SMM assuming 165 PSA is not just 1.65 times the SMM assuming 100 PSA. It is the CPR that is a multiple of the CPR assuming 100 PSA.

4 Illustration of Monthly Cash Flow Construction

As our first step in valuing a hypothetical passthrough given a PSA assumption, we must construct a monthly cash flow. For the purpose of this illustration, the underlying mortgages for this hypothetical passthrough are assumed to be fixed-rate, level-payment, fully amortized mortgages with a weighted average coupon (WAC) rate of 8.125%. It will be assumed that the passthrough rate is 7.5% with a weighted average maturity (WAM) of 357 months.

Exhibit 3 shows the cash flow for selected months assuming 100 PSA. The cash flow is broken down into three components: 1) interest (based on the passthrough rate), 2) the scheduled principal repayment (i.e., scheduled amortization), and 3) prepayments based on 100 PSA.

Exhibit 3	Monthly Cash Flow for a $400 Million Passthrough with a 7.5% Passthrough Rate, a WAC of 8.125%, and a WAM of 357 Months Assuming 100 PSA								
Months from Now (1)	Months Seasoned[a] (2)	Outstanding Balance ($) (3)	SMM (4)	Mortgage Payment ($) (5)	Net Interest ($) (6)	Scheduled Principal ($) (7)	Prepayment ($) (8)	Total Principal ($) (9)	Cash Flow ($) (10)
1	4	400,000,000	0.00067	2,975,868	2,500,000	267,535	267,470	535,005	3,035,005
2	5	399,464,995	0.00084	2,973,877	2,496,656	269,166	334,198	603,364	3,100,020
3	6	398,861,631	0.00101	2,971,387	2,492,885	270,762	400,800	671,562	3,164,447
4	7	398,190,069	0.00117	2,968,399	2,488,688	272,321	467,243	739,564	3,228,252
5	8	397,450,505	0.00134	2,964,914	2,484,066	273,843	533,493	807,335	3,291,401
6	9	396,643,170	0.00151	2,960,931	2,479,020	275,327	599,514	874,841	3,353,860
7	10	395,768,329	0.00168	2,956,453	2,473,552	276,772	665,273	942,045	3,415,597
8	11	394,826,284	0.00185	2,951,480	2,467,664	278,177	730,736	1,008,913	3,476,577
9	12	393,817,371	0.00202	2,946,013	2,461,359	279,542	795,869	1,075,410	3,536,769
10	13	392,741,961	0.00219	2,940,056	2,454,637	280,865	860,637	1,141,502	3,596,140
11	14	391,600,459	0.00236	2,933,608	2,447,503	282,147	925,008	1,207,155	3,654,658
27	30	364,808,016	0.00514	2,766,461	2,280,050	296,406	1,874,688	2,171,094	4,451,144
28	31	362,636,921	0.00514	2,752,233	2,266,481	296,879	1,863,519	2,160,398	4,426,879
29	32	360,476,523	0.00514	2,738,078	2,252,978	297,351	1,852,406	2,149,758	4,402,736
30	33	358,326,766	0.00514	2,723,996	2,239,542	297,825	1,841,347	2,139,173	4,378,715
100	103	231,249,776	0.00514	1,898,682	1,445,311	332,928	1,187,608	1,520,537	2,965,848
101	104	229,729,239	0.00514	1,888,917	1,435,808	333,459	1,179,785	1,513,244	2,949,052
102	105	228,215,995	0.00514	1,879,202	1,426,350	333,990	1,172,000	1,505,990	2,932,340
103	106	226,710,004	0.00514	1,869,538	1,416,938	334,522	1,164,252	1,498,774	2,915,712
104	107	225,211,230	0.00514	1,859,923	1,407,570	335,055	1,156,541	1,491,596	2,899,166

(continued)

Exhibit 3 *Continued*

Months from Now (1)	Months Seasoned[a] (2)	Outstanding Balance ($) (3)	SMM (4)	Mortgage Payment ($) (5)	Net Interest ($) (6)	Scheduled Principal ($) (7)	Prepayment ($) (8)	Total Principal ($) (9)	Cash Flow ($) (10)
105	108	223,719,634	0.00514	1,850,357	1,398,248	335,589	1,148,867	1,484,456	2,882,703
200	203	109,791,339	0.00514	1,133,751	686,196	390,372	562,651	953,023	1,639,219
201	204	108,838,316	0.00514	1,127,920	680,239	390,994	557,746	948,740	1,628,980
202	205	107,889,576	0.00514	1,122,119	674,310	391,617	552,863	944,480	1,618,790
203	206	106,945,096	0.00514	1,116,348	668,407	392,241	548,003	940,243	1,608,650
300	303	32,383,611	0.00514	676,991	202,398	457,727	164,195	621,923	824,320
301	304	31,761,689	0.00514	673,510	198,511	458,457	160,993	619,449	817,960
302	305	31,142,239	0.00514	670,046	194,639	459,187	157,803	616,990	811,629
303	306	30,525,249	0.00514	666,600	190,783	459,918	154,626	614,545	805,328
352	355	3,034,311	0.00514	517,770	18,964	497,226	13,048	510,274	529,238
353	356	2,524,037	0.00514	515,107	15,775	498,018	10,420	508,437	524,213
354	357	2,015,600	0.00514	512,458	12,597	498,811	7,801	506,612	519,209
355	358	1,508,988	0.00514	509,823	9,431	499,606	5,191	504,797	514,228
356	359	1,004,191	0.00514	507,201	6,276	500,401	2,591	502,992	509,269
357	360	501,199	0.00514	504,592	3,132	501,199	0	501,199	504,331

[a]Since the WAM is 357 months, the underlying mortgage pool is seasoned an average of three months, and therefore based on 100 PSA, the CPR is 0.8% in month 1 and the pool seasons at 6% in month 27.

Let's walk through Exhibit 3 column by column.

Column 1   This is the number of months from now when the cash flow will be received.

Column 2   This is the number of months of seasoning. Since the WAM for this mortgage pool is 357 months, this means that the loans are seasoned an average of 3 months (360 months–357 months) now.

Column 3   This column gives the outstanding mortgage balance at the beginning of the month. It is equal to the outstanding balance at the beginning of the previous month reduced by the total principal payment in the previous month.

Column 4   This column shows the SMM based on the number of months the loans are seasoned—the number of months shown in Column 2. For example, for the first month shown in the exhibit, the loans are seasoned three months going into that month. Therefore, the CPR used is the CPR that corresponds to four months. From the PSA benchmark, the CPR is 0.8% (4 times 0.2%). The corresponding SMM is 0.00067. The mortgage pool becomes fully seasoned in Column 1 corresponding to month 27 because by that time the loans are seasoned 30 months. When the loans are fully seasoned the CPR at 100 PSA is 6% and the corresponding SMM is 0.00514.

Column 5   The total monthly mortgage payment is shown in this column. Notice that the total monthly mortgage payment declines over time as prepayments reduce the mortgage balance outstanding. There is a formula to determine what the monthly mortgage balance will be for each month given prepayments.[5]

Column 6   The *net* monthly interest (i.e., amount available to pay bondholders after the servicing fee) is found in this column. This value is determined by multiplying the outstanding mortgage balance at the beginning of the month by the passthrough rate of 7.5% and then dividing by 12.

Column 7   This column gives the scheduled principal repayment (i.e., scheduled amortization). This is the difference between the total monthly mortgage payment (the amount shown in Column 5) and the gross coupon interest for the month. The gross coupon interest is found by multiplying 8.125% by the outstanding mortgage balance at the beginning of the month and then dividing by 12.

Column 8   The prepayment for the month is reported in this column. The prepayment is found by using Equation 1. For example, in month 100, the beginning mortgage balance is $231,249,776, the scheduled principal payment is $332,928, and the SMM at 100 PSA is 0.00514301 (only 0.00514 is shown in the exhibit to save space), so the prepayment is:

$$0.00514301 \times (\$231,249,776 - \$332,928) = \$1,187,608$$

Column 9   The total principal payment, which is the sum of columns 7 and 8, is shown in this column.

Column 10   The projected monthly cash flow for this passthrough is shown in this last column. The monthly cash flow is the sum of the interest paid (Column 6) and the total principal payments for the month (Column 9).

---

5 The formula is presented in Chapter 19 of Frank J. Fabozzi, *Fixed Income Mathematics* (Chicago: Irwin Professional Publishing, 1997).

Let's look at what happens to the cash flows for this passthrough if a different PSA assumption is made. Suppose that instead of 100 PSA, 165 PSA is assumed. Prepayments are assumed to be faster. Exhibit 4 shows the cash flow for this passthrough based on 165 PSA. Notice that the cash flows are greater in the early years compared to Exhibit 3 because prepayments are higher. The cash flows in later years are less for 165 PSA compared to 100 PSA because of the higher prepayments in the earlier years.

E. Average Life

It is standard practice in the bond market to refer to the maturity of a bond. If a bond matures in five years, it is referred to as a "5-year bond." However, the typical bond repays principal only once: at the maturity date. Bonds with this characteristic are referred to as "bullet bonds." We know that the maturity of a bond affects its interest rate risk. More specifically, for a given coupon rate, the greater the maturity the greater the interest rate risk.

For a mortgage-backed security, we know that the principal repayments (scheduled payments and prepayments) are made over the life of the security. While a mortgage-backed has a "legal maturity," which is the date when the last scheduled principal payment is due, the legal maturity does not tell us much about the characteristic of the security as its pertains to interest rate risk. For example, it is incorrect to think of a 30-year corporate bond and a mortgage-backed security with a 30-year legal maturity with the same coupon rate as being equivalent in terms of interest rate risk. Of course, duration can be computed for both the corporate bond and the mortgage-backed security. (We will see how this is done for a mortgage-backed security in the reading on valuing mortgage-backed and asset-backed securities.) Instead of duration, another measure widely used by market participants is the weighted average life or simply average life. This is the convention-based average time to receipt of principal payments (scheduled principal payments and projected prepayments).

Mathematically, the average life is expressed as follows:

$$\text{Average life} = \sum_{t=1}^{T} \frac{t \times \text{Projected principal received at time } t}{12 \times \text{Total principal}}$$

where T is the number of months.

The average life of a passthrough depends on the prepayment assumption. To see this, the average life is shown below for different prepayment speeds for the passthrough we used to illustrate the cash flow for 100 PSA and 165 PSA in Exhibits 3 and 4:

PSA Speed	50	100	165	200	300	400	500	600	700
Average Life (years)	15.11	11.66	8.76	7.68	5.63	4.44	3.68	3.16	2.78

F. Factors Affecting Prepayment Behavior

The factors that affect prepayment behavior are:

1. prevailing mortgage rate

2. housing turnover

3. characteristics of the underlying residential mortgage loans

The current mortgage rate affects prepayments. The spread between the prevailing mortgage rate in the market and the rate paid by the homeowner affects the incentive to refinance. Moreover, the path of mortgage rates since the loan was originated affects prepayments through a phenomenon referred to as refinancing burnout. Both the spread and path of mortgage rates affect prepayments that are the product of refinancing.

Exhibit 4 Monthly Cash Flow for a $400 Million Passthrough with a 7.5% Passthrough Rate, a WAC of 8.125%, and a WAM of 357 Months Assuming 165 PSA

Months (1)	Months Seasoned[a] (2)	Outstanding Balance ($) (3)	SMM (4)	Mortgage Payment ($) (5)	Net Interest ($) (6)	Scheduled Principal ($) (7)	Prepayment ($) (8)	Total Principal ($) (9)	Cash Flow ($) (10)
1	4	400,000,000	0.00111	2,975,868	2,500,000	267,535	442,389	709,923	3,209,923
2	5	399,290,077	0.00139	2,972,575	2,495,563	269,048	552,847	821,896	3,317,459
3	6	398,468,181	0.00167	2,968,456	2,490,426	270,495	663,065	933,560	3,423,986
4	7	397,534,621	0.00195	2,963,513	2,484,591	271,873	772,949	1,044,822	3,529,413
5	8	396,489,799	0.00223	2,957,747	2,478,061	273,181	882,405	1,155,586	3,633,647
6	9	395,334,213	0.00251	2,951,160	2,470,839	274,418	991,341	1,265,759	3,736,598
7	10	394,068,454	0.00279	2,943,755	2,462,928	275,583	1,099,664	1,375,246	3,838,174
8	11	392,693,208	0.00308	2,935,534	2,454,333	276,674	1,207,280	1,483,954	3,938,287
9	12	391,209,254	0.00336	2,926,503	2,445,058	277,690	1,314,099	1,591,789	4,036,847
10	13	389,617,464	0.00365	2,916,666	2,435,109	278,631	1,420,029	1,698,659	4,133,769
11	14	387,918,805	0.00393	2,906,028	2,424,493	279,494	1,524,979	1,804,473	4,228,965
27	30	347,334,116	0.00865	2,633,950	2,170,838	282,209	3,001,955	3,284,164	5,455,002
28	31	344,049,952	0.00865	2,611,167	2,150,312	281,662	2,973,553	3,255,215	5,405,527
29	32	340,794,737	0.00865	2,588,581	2,129,967	281,116	2,945,400	3,226,516	5,356,483
30	33	337,568,221	0.00865	2,566,190	2,109,801	280,572	2,917,496	3,198,067	5,307,869
100	103	170,142,350	0.00865	1,396,958	1,063,390	244,953	1,469,591	1,714,544	2,777,933
101	104	168,427,806	0.00865	1,384,875	1,052,674	244,478	1,454,765	1,699,243	2,751,916
102	105	166,728,563	0.00865	1,372,896	1,042,054	244,004	1,440,071	1,684,075	2,726,128
103	106	165,044,489	0.00865	1,361,020	1,031,528	243,531	1,425,508	1,669,039	2,700,567
104	107	163,375,450	0.00865	1,349,248	1,021,097	243,060	1,411,075	1,654,134	2,675,231

(continued)

Exhibit 4   Continued

Months (1)	Months Seasoned[a] (2)	Outstanding Balance ($) (3)	SMM (4)	Mortgage Payment ($) (5)	Net Interest ($) (6)	Scheduled Principal ($) (7)	Prepayment ($) (8)	Total Principal ($) (9)	Cash Flow ($) (10)
105	108	161,721,315	0.00865	1,337,577	1,010,758	242,589	1,396,771	1,639,359	2,650,118
200	203	56,746,664	0.00865	585,990	354,667	201,767	489,106	690,874	1,045,540
201	204	56,055,790	0.00865	580,921	350,349	201,377	483,134	684,510	1,034,859
202	205	55,371,280	0.00865	575,896	346,070	200,986	477,216	678,202	1,024,273
203	206	54,693,077	0.00865	570,915	341,832	200,597	471,353	671,950	1,013,782
300	303	11,758,141	0.00865	245,808	73,488	166,196	100,269	266,465	339,953
301	304	11,491,677	0.00865	243,682	71,823	165,874	97,967	263,841	335,664
302	305	11,227,836	0.00865	241,574	70,174	165,552	95,687	261,240	331,414
303	306	10,966,596	0.00865	239,485	68,541	165,232	93,430	258,662	327,203
352	355	916,910	0.00865	156,460	5,731	150,252	6,631	156,883	162,614
353	356	760,027	0.00865	155,107	4,750	149,961	5,277	155,238	159,988
354	357	604,789	0.00865	153,765	3,780	149,670	3,937	153,607	157,387
355	358	451,182	0.00865	152,435	2,820	149,380	2,611	151,991	154,811
356	359	299,191	0.00865	151,117	1,870	149,091	1,298	150,389	152,259
357	360	148,802	0.00865	149,809	930	148,802	0	148,802	149,732

[a]Since the WAM is 357 months, the underlying mortgage pool is seasoned an average of three months, and therefore based on 165 PSA, the CPR is 0.8% × 1.65 in month 1 and the pool seasons at 6% × 1.65 in month 27.

By far, the single most important factor affecting prepayments because of refinancing is the current level of mortgage rates relative to the borrower's contract rate. The greater the difference between the two, the greater the incentive to refinance the mortgage loan. For refinancing to make economic sense, the interest savings must be greater than the costs associated with refinancing the mortgage. These costs include legal expenses, origination fees, title insurance, and the value of the time associated with obtaining another mortgage loan. Some of these costs will vary proportionately with the amount to be financed. Other costs such as the application fee and legal expenses are typically fixed.

Historically it had been observed that mortgage rates had to decline by between 250 and 350 basis points below the contract rate in order to make it worthwhile for borrowers to refinance. However, the creativity of mortgage originators in designing mortgage loans such that the refinancing costs are folded into the amount borrowed has changed the view that mortgage rates must drop dramatically below the contract rate to make refinancing economic. Moreover, mortgage originators now do an effective job of advertising to make homeowners cognizant of the economic benefits of refinancing.

The historical pattern of prepayments and economic theory suggests that it is not only the level of mortgage rates that affects prepayment behavior but also the path that mortgage rates take to get to the current level. To illustrate why, suppose the underlying contract rate for a pool of mortgage loans is 11% and that three years after origination, the prevailing mortgage rate declines to 8%. Let's consider two possible paths of the mortgage rate in getting to the 8% level. In the first path, the mortgage rate declines to 8% at the end of the first year, then rises to 13% at the end of the second year, and then falls to 8% at the end of the third year. In the second path, the mortgage rate rises to 12% at the end of the first year, continues its rise to 13% at the end of the second year, and then falls to 8% at the end of the third year.

If the mortgage rate follows the first path, those who can benefit from refinancing will more than likely take advantage of this opportunity when the mortgage rate drops to 8% in the first year. When the mortgage rate drops again to 8% at the end of the third year, the likelihood is that prepayments because of refinancing will not surge; those who want to benefit by taking advantage of the refinancing opportunity will have done so already when the mortgage rate declined for the first time. This is the prepayment behavior referred to as the refinancing burnout (or simply, burnout) phenomenon. In contrast, the expected prepayment behavior when the mortgage rate follows the second path is quite different. Prepayment rates are expected to be low in the first two years. When the mortgage rate declines to 8% in the third year, refinancing activity and therefore prepayments are expected to surge. Consequently, the burnout phenomenon is related to the path of mortgage rates.

There is another way in which the prevailing mortgage rate affects prepayments: through its effect on the affordability of housing and housing turnover. The level of mortgage rates affects housing turnover to the extent that a lower rate increases the affordability of homes. However, even without lower interest rates, there is a normal amount of housing turnover. This is attributed to economic growth. The link is as follows: a growing economy results in a rise in personal income and in opportunities for worker migration; this increases family mobility and as a result increases housing turnover. The opposite holds for a weak economy.

Two characteristics of the underlying residential mortgage loans that affect prepayments are the amount of seasoning and the geographical location of the underlying properties. Seasoning refers to the aging of the mortgage loans. Empirical evidence suggests that prepayment rates are low after the loan is originated and increase after the loan is somewhat seasoned. Then prepayment rates tend to level off, in which case the loans are referred to as fully seasoned. This is the underlying theory for the PSA prepayment benchmark discussed earlier in this chapter. In some regions of the country the prepayment behavior tends to be faster than the average national prepayment rate, while other regions exhibit slower prepayment rates. This is caused by differences in local economies that affect housing turnover.

G. Contraction Risk and Extension Risk

An investor who owns passthrough securities does not know what the cash flow will be because that depends on actual prepayments. As we noted earlier, this risk is called prepayment risk.

To understand the significance of prepayment risk, suppose an investor buys a 9% coupon passthrough security at a time when mortgage rates are 10%. Let's consider what will happen to prepayments if mortgage rates decline to, say, 6%. There will be two adverse consequences. First, a basic property of fixed income securities is that the price of an option-free bond will rise. But in the case of a passthrough security, the rise in price will not be as large as that of an option-free bond because a fall in interest rates will give the borrower an incentive to prepay the loan and refinance the debt at a lower rate. This results in the same adverse consequence faced by holders of callable bonds. As in the case of those instruments, the upside price potential of a passthrough security is compressed because of prepayments. (This is the negative convexity characteristic.) The second adverse consequence is that the cash flow must be reinvested at a lower rate. Basically, the faster prepayments resulting from a decline in interest rates causes the passthrough to shorten in terms of the timing of its cash flows. Another way of saying this is that "shortening" results in a decline in the average life. Consequently, the two adverse consequences from a decline in interest rates for a passthrough security are referred to as contraction risk.

Now let's look at what happens if mortgage rates rise to 15%. The price of the passthrough, like the price of any bond, will decline. But again it will decline more because the higher rates will tend to slow down the rate of prepayment, in effect increasing the amount invested at the coupon rate, which is lower than the market rate. Prepayments will slow down, because homeowners will not refinance or partially prepay their mortgages when mortgage rates are higher than the contract rate of 10%. Of course this is just the time when investors want prepayments to speed up so that they can reinvest the prepayments at the higher market interest rate. Basically, the slower prepayments associated with a rise in interest rates that causes these adverse consequences are due to the passthrough lengthening in terms of the timing of its cash flows. Another way of saying this is that "lengthening" results in an increase in the average life. Consequently, the adverse consequence from a rise in interest rates for a passthrough security is referred to as extension risk.

Therefore, prepayment risk encompasses contraction risk and extension risk. Prepayment risk makes passthrough securities unattractive for certain financial institutions to hold from an asset/liability management perspective. Some institutional investors are concerned with extension risk and others with contraction risk when they purchase a passthrough security. This applies even for assets supporting specific types of insurance contracts. Is it possible to alter the cash flow of a passthrough so as to reduce the contraction risk or extension risk for institutional investors? This can be done, as we shall see, when we describe collateralized mortgage obligations.

4   COLLATERALIZED MORTGAGE OBLIGATIONS

As we noted, there is prepayment risk associated with investing in a mortgage passthrough security. Some institutional investors are concerned with extension risk and others with contraction risk. This problem can be mitigated by redirecting the cash flows of mortgage-related products (passthrough securities or a pool of loans) to different bond classes, called tranches,[6] so as to create securities that have different exposure to prepayment risk and therefore different risk/return patterns than the mortgage-related product from which they are created.

When the cash flows of mortgage-related products are redistributed to different bond classes, the resulting securities are called collateralized mortgage obligations (CMO). The mortgage-related products from which the cash flows are obtained are referred to as the collateral. Since the typical mortgage-related product used in a CMO is a pool of passthrough securities, sometimes market participants will use the terms "collateral" and "passthrough securities" interchangeably. The creation of a CMO cannot eliminate prepayment risk; it can only distribute the various forms of this risk among different classes of bondholders. The CMO's major financial innovation is that the securities created more closely satisfy the asset/liability needs of institutional investors, thereby broadening the appeal of mortgage-backed products.

There is a wide range of CMO structures.[7] We review the major ones below.

A. Sequential-Pay Tranches

The first CMO was structured so that each class of bond would be retired sequentially. Such structures are referred to as sequential-pay CMOs. The rule for the monthly distribution of the principal payments (scheduled principal plus prepayments) to the tranches would be as follows:

- Distribute all principal payments to Tranche 1 until the principal balance for Tranche 1 is zero. After Tranche 1 is paid off,

- distribute all principal payments to Tranche 2 until the principal balance for Tranche 2 is zero. After Tranche 2 is paid off,

- distribute all principal payments to Tranche 3 until the principal balance for Tranche 3 is zero. After Tranche 3 is paid off, …

  and so on.

To illustrate a sequential-pay CMO, we discuss FJF-01, a hypothetical deal made up to illustrate the basic features of the structure. The collateral for this hypothetical CMO is a hypothetical passthrough with a total par value of $400 million and the following characteristics: 1) the passthrough coupon rate is 7.5%, 2) the weighted average coupon (WAC) is 8.125%, and 3) the weighted average maturity (WAM) is 357 months. This is the same passthrough that we used in Section 3 to describe the cash flow of a passthrough based on some PSA assumption.

From this $400 million of collateral, four bond classes or tranches are created. Their characteristics are summarized in Exhibit 5. The total par value of the four tranches is equal to the par value of the collateral (i.e., the passthrough security).[8] In this simple structure, the coupon rate is the same for each tranche and also the same as the coupon rate on the collateral. There is no reason why this must be so, and, in fact, typically the coupon rate varies by tranche.

Now remember that a CMO is created by redistributing the cash flow—interest and principal—to the different tranches based on a set of payment rules. The payment rules at the bottom of Exhibit 5 describe how the cash flow from the passthrough (i.e., collateral) is to be distributed to the four tranches. There are separate rules for the

---

6 "Tranche" is from an old French word meaning "slice." In the case of a collateralized mortgage obligation it refers to a "slice of the cash flows."

7 The issuer of a CMO wants to be sure that the trust created to pass through the interest and principal payments is not treated as a taxable entity. A provision of the Tax Reform Act of 1986, called the Real Estate Mortgage Investment Conduit (REMIC), specifies the requirements that an issuer must fulfill so that the legal entity created to issue a CMO is not taxable. Most CMOs today are created as REMICs. While it is common to hear market participants refer to a CMO as a REMIC, not all CMOs are REMICs.

8 Actually, a CMO is backed by a pool of passthrough securities.

distribution of the coupon interest and the payment of principal (the principal being the total of the scheduled principal payment and any prepayments).

While the payment rules for the disbursement of the principal payments are known, the precise amount of the principal in each month is not. This will depend on the cash flow, and therefore principal payments, of the collateral, which depends on the actual prepayment rate of the collateral. An assumed PSA speed allows the cash flow to be projected. Exhibit 6 shows the cash flow (interest, scheduled principal repayment, and prepayments) assuming 165 PSA. Assuming that the collateral does prepay at 165 PSA, the cash flow available to all four tranches of FJF-01 will be precisely the cash flow shown in Exhibit 6.

Exhibit 5	FJF-01—A Hypothetical 4-Tranche Sequential-Pay Structure	
Tranche	**Par Amount ($)**	**Coupon Rate (%)**
A	194,500,000	7.5
B	36,000,000	7.5
C	96,500,000	7.5
D	73,000,000	7.5
Total	400,000,000	

Payment rules:

1. *For payment of monthly coupon interest:* Disburse monthly coupon interest to each tranche on the basis of the amount of principal outstanding for each tranche at the beginning of the month.
2. *For disbursement of principal payments:* Disburse principal payments to tranche A until it is completely paid off. After tranche A is completely paid off, disburse principal payments to tranche B until it is completely paid off. After tranche B is completely paid off, disburse principal payments to tranche C until it is completely paid off. After tranche C is completely paid off, disburse principal payments to tranche D until it is completely paid off.

Exhibit 6	Monthly Cash Flow for Selected Months for FJF-01 Assuming 165 PSA					
	Tranche A			**Tranche B**		
Month	**Balance ($)**	**Principal ($)**	**Interest ($)**	**Balance ($)**	**Principal ($)**	**Interest ($)**
1	194,500,000	709,923	1,215,625	36,000,000	0	225,000
2	193,790,077	821,896	1,211,188	36,000,000	0	225,000
3	192,968,181	933,560	1,206,051	36,000,000	0	225,000
4	192,034,621	1,044,822	1,200,216	36,000,000	0	225,000
5	190,989,799	1,155,586	1,193,686	36,000,000	0	225,000
6	189,834,213	1,265,759	1,186,464	36,000,000	0	225,000
7	188,568,454	1,375,246	1,178,553	36,000,000	0	225,000
8	187,193,208	1,483,954	1,169,958	36,000,000	0	225,000
9	185,709,254	1,591,789	1,160,683	36,000,000	0	225,000
10	184,117,464	1,698,659	1,150,734	36,000,000	0	225,000
11	182,418,805	1,804,473	1,140,118	36,000,000	0	225,000
12	180,614,332	1,909,139	1,128,840	36,000,000	0	225,000
75	12,893,479	2,143,974	80,584	36,000,000	0	225,000
76	10,749,504	2,124,935	67,184	36,000,000	0	225,000
77	8,624,569	2,106,062	53,904	36,000,000	0	225,000

Exhibit 6 *Continued*

Month	Tranche A Balance ($)	Principal ($)	Interest ($)	Tranche B Balance ($)	Principal ($)	Interest ($)
78	6,518,507	2,087,353	40,741	36,000,000	0	225,000
79	4,431,154	2,068,807	27,695	36,000,000	0	225,000
80	2,362,347	2,050,422	14,765	36,000,000	0	225,000
81	311,926	311,926	1,950	36,000,000	1,720,271	225,000
82	0	0	0	34,279,729	2,014,130	214,248
83	0	0	0	32,265,599	1,996,221	201,660
84	0	0	0	30,269,378	1,978,468	189,184
85	0	0	0	28,290,911	1,960,869	176,818
95	0	0	0	9,449,331	1,793,089	59,058
96	0	0	0	7,656,242	1,777,104	47,852
97	0	0	0	5,879,138	1,761,258	36,745
98	0	0	0	4,117,879	1,745,550	25,737
99	0	0	0	2,372,329	1,729,979	14,827
100	0	0	0	642,350	642,350	4,015
101	0	0	0	0	0	0

Month	Tranche C Balance ($)	Principal ($)	Interest ($)	Tranche D Balance ($)	Principal ($)	Interest ($)
1	96,500,000	0	603,125	73,000,000	0	456,250
2	96,500,000	0	603,125	73,000,000	0	456,250
3	96,500,000	0	603,125	73,000,000	0	456,250
4	96,500,000	0	603,125	73,000,000	0	456,250
5	96,500,000	0	603,125	73,000,000	0	456,250
6	96,500,000	0	603,125	73,000,000	0	456,250
7	96,500,000	0	603,125	73,000,000	0	456,250
8	96,500,000	0	603,125	73,000,000	0	456,250
9	96,500,000	0	603,125	73,000,000	0	456,250
10	96,500,000	0	603,125	73,000,000	0	456,250
11	96,500,000	0	603,125	73,000,000	0	456,250
12	96,500,000	0	603,125	73,000,000	0	456,250
95	96,500,000	0	603,125	73,000,000	0	456,250
96	96,500,000	0	603,125	73,000,000	0	456,250
97	96,500,000	0	603,125	73,000,000	0	456,250
98	96,500,000	0	603,125	73,000,000	0	456,250
99	96,500,000	0	603,125	73,000,000	0	456,250
100	96,500,000	1,072,194	603,125	73,000,000	0	456,250
101	95,427,806	1,699,243	596,424	73,000,000	0	456,250
102	93,728,563	1,684,075	585,804	73,000,000	0	456,250

(continued)

| Exhibit 6 | Continued |

	Tranche C			Tranche D		
Month	Balance ($)	Principal ($)	Interest ($)	Balance ($)	Principal ($)	Interest ($)
103	92,044,489	1,669,039	575,278	73,000,000	0	456,250
104	90,375,450	1,654,134	564,847	73,000,000	0	456,250
105	88,721,315	1,639,359	554,508	73,000,000	0	456,250
175	3,260,287	869,602	20,377	73,000,000	0	456,250
176	2,390,685	861,673	14,942	73,000,000	0	456,250
177	1,529,013	853,813	9,556	73,000,000	0	456,250
178	675,199	675,199	4,220	73,000,000	170,824	456,250
179	0	0	0	72,829,176	838,300	455,182
180	0	0	0	71,990,876	830,646	449,943
181	0	0	0	71,160,230	823,058	444,751
182	0	0	0	70,337,173	815,536	439,607
183	0	0	0	69,521,637	808,081	434,510
184	0	0	0	68,713,556	800,690	429,460
185	0	0	0	67,912,866	793,365	424,455
350	0	0	0	1,235,674	160,220	7,723
351	0	0	0	1,075,454	158,544	6,722
352	0	0	0	916,910	156,883	5,731
353	0	0	0	760,027	155,238	4,750
354	0	0	0	604,789	153,607	3,780
355	0	0	0	451,182	151,991	2,820
356	0	0	0	299,191	150,389	1,870
357	0	0	0	148,802	148,802	930

Note: The cash flow for a tranche in each month is the sum of the principal and interest.

To demonstrate how the payment rules for FJF-01 work, Exhibit 6 shows the cash flow for selected months assuming the collateral prepays at 165 PSA. For each tranche, the exhibit shows 1) the balance at the end of the month, 2) the principal paid down (scheduled principal repayment plus prepayments), and 3) interest. In month 1, the cash flow for the collateral consists of a principal payment of $709,923 and an interest payment of $2.5 million (0.075 times $400 million divided by 12). The interest payment is distributed to the four tranches based on the amount of the par value outstanding. So, for example, tranche A receives $1,215,625 (0.075 times $194,500,000 divided by 12) of the $2.5 million. The principal, however, is all distributed to tranche A. Therefore, the cash flow for tranche A in month 1 is $1,925,548. The principal balance at the end of month 1 for tranche A is $193,790,076 (the original principal balance of $194,500,000 less the principal payment of $709,923). No principal payment is distributed to the three other tranches because there is still a principal balance outstanding for tranche A. This will be true for months 2 through 80. The cash flow for tranche A for each month is found by adding the amounts shown in the "Principal" and "Interest" columns. So, for tranche A, the cash flow in month 8 is $1,483,954 plus $1,169,958 or $2,653,912. The cash flow from months 82 on is zero based on 165 PSA.

After month 81, the principal balance will be zero for tranche A. For the collateral, the cash flow in month 81 is $3,318,521, consisting of a principal payment of $2,032,197 and interest of $1,286,325. At the beginning of month 81 (end of month 80), the principal balance for tranche A is $311,926. Therefore, $311,926 of the $2,032,196 of the principal payment from the collateral will be disbursed to tranche A. After this payment is made, no additional principal payments are made to this tranche as the principal balance is zero. The remaining principal payment from the collateral, $1,720,271, is distributed to tranche B. Based on an assumed prepayment speed of 165 PSA, tranche B then begins receiving principal payments in month 81. The cash flow for tranche B for each month is found by adding the amounts shown in the "Principal" and "Interest" columns. For months 1 though 80, the cash flow is just the interest. There is no cash flow after month 100 for Tranche B.

Exhibit 6 shows that tranche B is fully paid off by month 100, when tranche C begins to receive principal payments. Tranche C is not fully paid off until month 178, at which time tranche D begins receiving the remaining principal payments. The maturity (i.e., the time until the principal is fully paid off) for these four tranches assuming 165 PSA would be 81 months for tranche A, 100 months for tranche B, 178 months for tranche C, and 357 months for tranche D. The cash flow for each month for tranches C and D is found by adding the principal and the interest for the month.

The principal paydown window or principal window for a tranche is the time period between the beginning and the ending of the principal payments to that tranche. So, for example, for tranche A, the principal paydown window would be month 1 to month 81 assuming 165 PSA. For tranche B it is from month 81 to month 100.[9] In confirmation of trades involving CMOs, the principal paydown window is specified in terms of the initial month that principal is expected to be received to the final month that principal is expected to be received.

Let's look at what has been accomplished by creating the CMO. Earlier we saw that the average life of the passthrough is 8.76 years assuming a prepayment speed of 165 PSA. Exhibit 7 reports the average life of the collateral and the four tranches assuming different prepayment speeds. Notice that the four tranches have average lives that are both shorter and longer than the collateral, thereby attracting investors who have a preference for an average life different from that of the collateral.

Exhibit 7	Average Life for the Collateral and the Four Tranches of FJF-01				
Prepayment Speed (PSA)	**Average Life (in Years) for**				
	Collateral	**Tranche A**	**Tranche B**	**Tranche C**	**Tranche D**
50	15.11	7.48	15.98	21.02	27.24
100	11.66	4.90	10.86	15.78	24.58
165	8.76	3.48	7.49	11.19	20.27
200	7.68	3.05	6.42	9.60	18.11
300	5.63	2.32	4.64	6.81	13.36
400	4.44	1.94	3.70	5.31	10.34
500	3.68	1.69	3.12	4.38	8.35
600	3.16	1.51	2.74	3.75	6.96
700	2.78	1.38	2.47	3.30	5.95

9 The window is also specified in terms of the length of the time from the beginning of the principal paydown window to the end of the principal paydown window For tranche A, the window would be stated as 81 months; for tranche B, 20 months.

There is still a major problem: there is considerable variability of the average life for the tranches. We'll see how this can be handled later on. However, there is some protection provided for each tranche against prepayment risk. This is because prioritizing the distribution of principal (i.e., establishing the payment rules for principal) effectively protects the shorter-term tranche A in this structure against extension risk. This protection must come from somewhere, so it comes from the three other tranches. Similarly, tranches C and D provide protection against extension risk for tranches A and B. At the same time, tranches C and D benefit because they are provided protection against contraction risk, the protection coming from tranches A and B.

B. Accrual Tranches

In our previous example, the payment rules for interest provided for all tranches to be paid interest each month. In many sequential-pay CMO structures, at least one tranche does not receive current interest. Instead, the interest for that tranche would accrue and be added to the principal balance. Such a tranche is commonly referred to as an accrual tranche or a Z bond. The interest that would have been paid to the accrual tranche is used to pay off the principal balance of earlier tranches.

To see this, consider FJF-02, a hypothetical CMO structure with the same collateral as our previous example and with four tranches, each with a coupon rate of 7.5%. The last tranche, Z, is an accrual tranche. The structure for FJF-02 is shown in Exhibit 8.

Exhibit 9 shows cash flows for selected months for tranches A and B. Let's look at month 1 and compare it to month 1 in Exhibit 6. Both cash flows are based on 165 PSA. The principal payment from the collateral is $709,923. In FJF-01, this is the principal paydown for tranche A. In FJF-02, the interest for tranche Z, $456,250, is not paid to that tranche but instead is used to pay down the principal of tranche A. So, the principal payment to tranche A in Exhibit 9 is $1,166,173, the collateral's principal payment of $709,923 plus the interest of $456,250 that was diverted from tranche Z.

Exhibit 8	FJF-02—A Hypothetical 4-Tranche Sequential-Pay Structure with an Accrual Tranche	

Tranche	Par Amount ($)	Coupon Rate (%)
A	194,500,000	7.5
B	36,000,000	7.5
C	96,500,000	7.5
Z (Accrual)	73,000,000	7.5
Total	400,000,000	

Payment rules:

1. *For payment of monthly coupon interest:* Disburse monthly coupon interest to tranches A, B, and C on the basis of the amount of principal outstanding for each tranche at the beginning of the month. For tranche Z, accrue the interest based on the principal plus accrued interest in the previous month. The interest for tranche Z is to be paid to the earlier tranches as a principal paydown.
2. *For disbursement of principal payments:* Disburse principal payments to tranche A until it is completely paid off. After tranche A is completely paid off, disburse principal payments to tranche B until it is completely paid off. After tranche B is completely paid off, disburse principal payments to tranche C until it is completely paid off. After tranche C is completely paid off, disburse principal payments to tranche Z until the original principal balance plus accrued interest is completely paid off.

The expected final maturity for tranches A, B, and C has shortened as a result of the inclusion of tranche Z. The final payout for tranche A is 64 months rather than 81 months; for tranche B it is 77 months rather than 100 months; and, for tranche C it is 113 months rather than 178 months.

The average lives for tranches A, B, and C are shorter in FJF-02 compared to our previous non-accrual, sequential-pay tranche example, FJF-01, because of the inclusion of the accrual tranche. For example, at 165 PSA, the average lives are as follows:

Structure	Tranche A	Tranche B	Tranche C
FJF-02	2.90	5.86	7.87
FJF-01	3.48	7.49	11.19

The reason for the shortening of the non-accrual tranches is that the interest that would be paid to the accrual tranche is being allocated to the other tranches. Tranche Z in FJF-02 will have a longer average life than tranche D in FJF-01 because in tranche Z the interest payments are being diverted to tranches A, B, and C.

Thus, shorter-term tranches and a longer-term tranche are created by including an accrual tranche in FJF-02 compared to FJF-01. The accrual tranche has appeal to investors who are concerned with reinvestment risk. Since there are no coupon payments to reinvest, reinvestment risk is eliminated until all the other tranches are paid off.

Exhibit 9 Monthly Cash Flow for Selected Months for Tranches A and B for FJF-02 Assuming 165 PSA

	Tranche A			Tranche B		
Month	Balance ($)	Principal ($)	Interest ($)	Balance ($)	Principal ($)	Interest ($)
1	194,500,000	1,166,173	1,215,625	36,000,000	0	225,000
2	193,333,827	1,280,997	1,208,336	36,000,000	0	225,000
3	192,052,829	1,395,531	1,200,330	36,000,000	0	225,000
4	190,657,298	1,509,680	1,191,608	36,000,000	0	225,000
5	189,147,619	1,623,350	1,182,173	36,000,000	0	225,000
6	187,524,269	1,736,446	1,172,027	36,000,000	0	225,000
7	185,787,823	1,848,875	1,161,174	36,000,000	0	225,000
8	183,938,947	1,960,543	1,149,618	36,000,000	0	225,000
9	181,978,404	2,071,357	1,137,365	36,000,000	0	225,000
10	179,907,047	2,181,225	1,124,419	36,000,000	0	225,000
11	177,725,822	2,290,054	1,110,786	36,000,000	0	225,000
12	175,435,768	2,397,755	1,096,474	36,000,000	0	225,000
60	15,023,406	3,109,398	93,896	36,000,000	0	225,000
61	11,914,007	3,091,812	74,463	36,000,000	0	225,000
62	8,822,195	3,074,441	55,139	36,000,000	0	225,000
63	5,747,754	3,057,282	35,923	36,000,000	0	225,000
64	2,690,472	2,690,472	16,815	36,000,000	349,863	225,000
65	0	0	0	35,650,137	3,023,598	222,813
66	0	0	0	32,626,540	3,007,069	203,916
67	0	0	0	29,619,470	2,990,748	185,122
68	0	0	0	26,628,722	2,974,633	166,430
69	0	0	0	23,654,089	2,958,722	147,838
70	0	0	0	20,695,367	2,943,014	129,346
71	0	0	0	17,752,353	2,927,508	110,952
72	0	0	0	14,824,845	2,912,203	92,655

(continued)

	Exhibit 9	Continued				

	Tranche A			Tranche B		
Month	**Balance ($)**	**Principal ($)**	**Interest ($)**	**Balance ($)**	**Principal ($)**	**Interest ($)**
73	0	0	0	11,912,642	2,897,096	74,454
74	0	0	0	9,015,546	2,882,187	56,347
75	0	0	0	6,133,358	2,867,475	38,333
76	0	0	0	3,265,883	2,852,958	20,412
77	0	0	0	412,925	412,925	2,581
78	0	0	0	0	0	0
79	0	0	0	0	0	0
80	0	0	0	0	0	0

C. Floating-Rate Tranches

The tranches described thus far have a fixed rate. There is a demand for tranches that have a floating rate. The problem is that the collateral pays a fixed rate and therefore it would be difficult to create a tranche with a floating rate. However, a floating-rate tranche can be created. This is done by creating from any fixed-rate tranche a floater and an inverse floater combination. We will illustrate the creation of a floating-rate tranche and an inverse floating-rate tranche using the hypothetical CMO structure—the 4-tranche sequential-pay structure with an accrual tranche (FJF-02).[10] We can select any of the tranches from which to create a floating-rate and inverse floating-rate tranche. In fact, we can create these two securities for more than one of the four tranches or for only a portion of one tranche.

In this case, we create a floater and an inverse floater from tranche C. A floater could have been created from any of the other tranches. The par value for this tranche is $96.5 million, and we create two tranches that have a combined par value of $96.5 million. We refer to this CMO structure with a floater and an inverse floater as FJF-03. It has five tranches, designated A, B, FL, IFL, and Z, where FL is the floating-rate tranche and IFL is the inverse floating-rate tranche. Exhibit 10 describes FJF-03. Any reference rate can be used to create a floater and the corresponding inverse floater. The reference rate for setting the coupon rate for FL and IFL in FJF-03 is 1-month LIBOR.

	Exhibit 10	FJF-03—A Hypothetical 5-Tranche Sequential-Pay Structure with Floater, Inverse Floater, and Accrual Bond Tranches

Tranche	Par Amount ($)	Coupon Rate (%)
A	194,500,000	7.50
B	36,000,000	7.50
FL	72,375,000	1-month LIBOR + 0.50
IFL	24,125,000	$28.50 - 3 \times (1\text{-month LIBOR})$
Z (Accrual)	73,000,000	7.50
Total	400,000,000	

Payment rules:

1. *For payment of monthly coupon interest:* Disburse monthly coupon interest to tranches A, B, FL, and IFL on the basis of the amount of principal outstanding at the beginning of the month.

---

[10] The same principle for creating a floating-rate tranche and inverse floating-rate tranche could have been accomplished using the 4-tranche sequential-pay structure without an accrual tranche (FJF-01).

For tranche Z, accrue the interest based on the principal plus accrued interest in the previous month. The interest for tranche Z is to be paid to the earlier tranches as a principal paydown. The maximum coupon rate for FL is 10%; the minimum coupon rate for IFL is 0%.

2. *For disbursement of principal payments:* Disburse principal payments to tranche A until it is completely paid off. After tranche A is completely paid off, disburse principal payments to tranche B until it is completely paid off. After tranche B is completely paid off, disburse principal payments to tranches FL and IFL until they are completely paid off. The principal payments between tranches FL and IFL should be made in the following way: 75% to tranche FL and 25% to tranche IFL. After tranches FL and IFL are completely paid off, disburse principal payments to tranche Z until the original principal balance plus accrued interest are completely paid off.

The amount of the par value of the floating-rate tranche will be some portion of the $96.5 million. There are an infinite number of ways to slice up the $96.5 million between the floater and inverse floater, and final partitioning will be driven by the demands of investors. In the FJF-03 structure, we made the floater from $72,375,000 or 75% of the $96.5 million. The coupon formula for the floater is 1-month LIBOR plus 50 basis points. So, for example, if LIBOR is 3.75% at the reset date, the coupon rate on the floater is 3.75% + 0.5%, or 4.25%. There is a cap on the coupon rate for the floater (discussed later).

Unlike a floating-rate note in the corporate bond market whose principal is unchanged over the life of the instrument, the floater's principal balance declines over time as principal payments are made. The principal payments to the floater are determined by the principal payments from the tranche from which the floater is created. In our CMO structure, this is tranche C.

Since the floater's par value is $72,375,000 of the $96.5 million, the balance is par value for the inverse floater. Assuming that 1-month LIBOR is the reference rate, the coupon formula for the inverse floater takes the following form:

$$K - L \times (1\text{-month LIBOR})$$

where K and L are constants whose interpretation will be explained shortly.

In FJF-03, K is set at 28.50% and L at 3. Thus, if 1-month LIBOR is 3.75%, the coupon rate for the month is:

$$28.50\% - 3 \times (3.75\%) = 17.25\%$$

K is the cap or maximum coupon rate for the inverse floater. In FJF-03, the cap for the inverse floater is 28.50%. The determination of the inverse floater's cap rate is based on 1) the amount of interest that would have been paid to the tranche from which the floater and the inverse floater were created, tranche C in our hypothetical deal, and 2) the coupon rate for the floater if 1-month LIBOR is zero.

We will explain the determination of K by example. Let's see how the 28.5% for the inverse floater is determined. The total interest to be paid to tranche C if it was not split into the floater and the inverse floater is the principal of $96,500,000 times 7.5%, or $7,237,500. The maximum interest for the inverse floater occurs if 1-month LIBOR is zero. In that case, the coupon rate for the floater is

$$1\text{-month LIBOR} + 0.5\% = 0.5\%$$

Since the floater receives 0.5% on its principal of $72,375,000, the floater's interest is $361,875. The remainder of the interest of $7,237,500 from tranche C goes to the inverse floater. That is, the inverse floater's interest is $6,875,625 (= $7,237,500 − $361,875). Since the inverse floater's principal is $24,125,000, the cap rate for the inverse floater is

$$\frac{\$6,875,625}{\$24,125,000} = 28.5\%$$

In general, the formula for the cap rate on the inverse floater, K, is

$$K = \frac{\text{Inverse floater interest when reference rate for floater is zero}}{\text{Principal for inverse floater}}$$

The L or multiple in the coupon formula to determine the coupon rate for the inverse floater is called the *leverage*. The higher the leverage, the more the inverse floater's coupon rate changes for a given change in 1-month LIBOR. For example, a coupon leverage of 3 means that a 1-basis point change in 1-month LIBOR will change the coupon rate on the inverse floater by 3 basis points.

As in the case of the floater, the principal paydown of an inverse floater will be a proportionate amount of the principal paydown of tranche C.

Because 1-month LIBOR is always positive, the coupon rate paid to the floater cannot be negative. If there are no restrictions placed on the coupon rate for the inverse floater, however, it is possible for its coupon rate to be negative. To prevent this, a floor, or minimum, is placed on the coupon rate. In most structures, the floor is set at zero. Once a floor is set for the inverse floater, a cap or ceiling is imposed on the floater.

In FJF-03, a floor of zero is set for the inverse floater. The floor results in a cap or maximum coupon rate for the floater of 10%. This is determined as follows. If the floor for the inverse floater is zero, this means that the inverse floater receives no interest. All of the interest that would have been paid to tranche C, $7,237,500, would then be paid to the floater. Since the floater's principal is $72,375,000, the cap rate on the floater is $7,237,500/$72,375,000, or 10%.

In general, the cap rate for the floater *assuming a floor of zero for inverse floater* is determined as follows:

$$\text{Cap rate for floater} = \frac{\text{Collateral tranche interest}}{\text{Principal for floater}}$$

The cap for the floater and the inverse floater, the floor for the inverse floater, the leverage, and the floater's spread are not determined independently. Any cap or floor imposed on the coupon rate for the floater and the inverse floater must be selected so that the weighted average coupon rate does not exceed the collateral tranche's coupon rate.

D. Structured Interest-Only Tranches

CMO structures can be created so that a tranche receives only interest. Interest only (IO) tranches in a CMO structure are commonly referred to as structured IOs to distinguish them from IO mortgage strips that we will describe later in this reading. The basic principle in creating a structured IO is to set the coupon rate below the collateral's coupon rate so that excess interest can be generated. It is the excess interest that is used to create one or more structured IOs.

Let's look at how a structured IO is created using an illustration. Thus far, we used a simple CMO structure in which all the tranches have the same coupon rate (7.5%), and that coupon rate is the same as the collateral. A structured IO is created from a CMO structure where the coupon rate for at least one tranche is different from the collateral's coupon rate. This is seen in FJF-04 shown in Exhibit 11. In this structure, notice that the coupon interest rate for each tranche is less than the coupon interest rate for the collateral. That means that there is excess interest from the collateral that is not being paid to all the tranches. At one time, all of that excess interest not paid to the tranches was paid to a bond class called a "residual." Eventually (due to changes in the tax law that do not concern us here), structures of CMO began allocating the excess interest to the tranche that receives only interest. This is tranche IO in FJF-04.

Notice that for this structure the par amount for the IO tranche is shown as $52,566,667 and the coupon rate is 7.5%. Since this is an IO tranche there is no par amount. The amount shown is the amount upon which the interest payments will be determined, not the amount that will be paid to the holder of this tranche. Therefore, it is called a notional amount. The resulting IO is called a notional IO.

Exhibit 11	FJF-04: A Hypothetical Five-Tranche Sequential Pay with an Accrual Tranche, an Interest-Only Tranche, and a Residual Class	
Tranche	**Par Amount ($)**	**Coupon Rate (%)**
A	194,500,000	6.00
B	36,000,000	6.50
C	96,500,000	7.00
Z	73,000,000	7.25
IO	52,566,667 (Notional)	7.50
Total	400,000,000	

Payment rules:

1. *For payment of monthly coupon interest:* Disburse monthly coupon interest to tranches A, B, and C on the basis of the amount of principal outstanding for each class at the beginning of the month. For tranche Z, accrue the interest based on the principal plus accrued interest in the previous month. The interest for tranche Z is to be paid to the earlier tranches as a principal pay-down. Disburse periodic interest to the IO tranche based on the notional amount for all tranches at the beginning of the month.
2. *For disbursement of principal payments:* Disburse monthly principal payments to tranche A until it is completely paid off. After tranche A is completely paid off, disburse principal payments to tranche B until it is completely paid off. After tranche B is completely paid off, disburse principal payments to tranche C until it is completely paid off. After tranche C is completely paid off, disburse principal payments to tranche Z until the original principal balance plus accrued interest is completely paid off.
3. *No principal is to be paid to the IO tranche:* The notional amount of the IO tranche declines based on the principal payments to all other tranches.

Let's look at how the notional amount is determined. Consider tranche A. The par value is $194.5 million and the coupon rate is 6%. Since the collateral's coupon rate is 7.5%, the excess interest is 150 basis points (1.5%). Therefore, an IO with a 1.5% coupon rate and a notional amount of $194.5 million can be created from tranche A. But this is equivalent to an IO with a notional amount of $38.9 million and a coupon rate of 7.5%. Mathematically, this notional amount is found as follows:

$$\text{Notional amount for 7.5\% IO} = \frac{\text{Original tranche's par value} \times \text{Excess interest}}{0.075}$$

where

Excess interest = Collateral tranche's coupon rate − Tranche coupon rate

For example, for tranche A:

Excess interest = 0.075 − 0.060 = 0.015

Tranche's par value = $194,500,000

$$\text{Notional amount for 7.5\% IO} = \frac{\$194,500,000 \times 0.015}{0.075} = \$38,900,000$$

Similarly, from tranche B with a par value of $36 million, the excess interest is 100 basis points (1%) and therefore an IO with a coupon rate of 1% and a notional amount of $36 million can be created. But this is equivalent to creating an IO with a notional amount of $4.8 million and a coupon rate of 7.5%. This procedure is shown in Exhibit 12 for all four tranches.

Exhibit 12	Creating a Notional IO Tranche		
Tranche	**Par Amount ($)**	**Excess Interest (%)**	**Notional Amount for a 7.5% Coupon Rate IO ($)**
A	194,500,000	1.50	38,900,000
B	36,000,000	1.00	4,800,000
C	96,500,000	0.50	6,433,333
Z	73,000,000	0.25	2,433,333

Notional amount for 7.5% IO = $52,566,667

E. Planned Amortization Class Tranches

The CMO structures discussed above attracted many institutional investors who had previously either avoided investing in mortgage-backed securities or allocated only a nominal portion of their portfolio to this sector of the bond market. While some traditional corporate bond buyers shifted their allocation to CMOs, a majority of institutional investors remained on the sidelines, concerned about investing in an instrument they continued to perceive as posing significant prepayment risk. This concern was based on the substantial average life variability, despite the innovations designed to mitigate prepayment risk.

In 1987, several structures came to market that shared the following characteristic: if the prepayment speed is within a specified band over the collateral's life, the cash flow pattern is known. The greater predictability of the cash flow for these classes of bonds, now referred to as planned amortization class (PAC) bonds, occurs because there is a principal repayment schedule that must be satisfied. PAC bondholders have priority over all other classes in the CMO structure in receiving principal payments from the collateral. The greater certainty of the cash flow for the PAC bonds comes at the expense of the non-PAC tranches, called the support tranches or companion tranches. It is these tranches that absorb the prepayment risk. Because PAC tranches have protection against both extension risk and contraction risk, they are said to provide two-sided prepayment protection.

To illustrate how to create a PAC bond, we will use as collateral the $400 million passthrough with a coupon rate of 7.5%, an 8.125% WAC, and a WAM of 357 months. The creation requires the specification of two PSA prepayment rates—a *lower PSA prepayment assumption* and an *upper PSA prepayment assumption*. In our illustration the lower PSA prepayment assumption will be 90 PSA and the upper PSA prepayment assumption will be 300 PSA. A natural question is: How does one select the lower and upper PSA prepayment assumptions? These are dictated by market conditions. For our purpose here, how they are determined is not important. The lower and upper PSA prepayment assumptions are referred to as the initial PAC collar or the initial PAC band. In our illustration the initial PAC collar is 90-300 PSA.

The second column of Exhibit 13 shows the principal payment (scheduled principal repayment plus prepayments) for selected months assuming a prepayment speed of 90 PSA, and the next column shows the principal payments for selected months assuming that the passthrough prepays at 300 PSA.

The last column of Exhibit 13 gives the minimum principal payment if the collateral prepays at 90 PSA or 300 PSA for months 1 to 349. (After month 349, the outstanding principal balance will be paid off if the prepayment speed is between 90 PSA and 300 PSA.) For example, in the first month, the principal payment would be $508,169 if the collateral prepays at 90 PSA and $1,075,931 if the collateral prepays at 300 PSA. Thus, the minimum principal payment is $508,169, as reported in the last column of Exhibit 13. In month 103, the minimum principal payment is also the amount if the prepayment speed is 90 PSA, $1,446,761, compared to $1,458,618 for 300 PSA. In month 104, however, a prepayment speed of 300 PSA would produce a principal payment of $1,433,539, which is less than the principal payment of $1,440,825 assuming 90 PSA. So, $1,433,539 is reported in the last column of Exhibit 13. From month 104 on, the minimum principal payment is the one that would result assuming a prepayment speed of 300 PSA.

In fact, if the collateral prepays at any one speed between 90 PSA and 300 PSA over its life, the minimum principal payment would be the amount reported in the last column of Exhibit 13. For example, if we had included principal payment figures assuming a prepayment speed of 200 PSA, the minimum principal payment would not change: from month 1 through month 103, the minimum principal payment is that generated from 90 PSA, but from month 104 on, the minimum principal payment is that generated from 300 PSA.

This characteristic of the collateral allows for the creation of a PAC tranche, assuming that the collateral prepays over its life at a speed between 90 PSA to 300 PSA. A schedule of principal repayments that the PAC bondholders are entitled to receive before any other tranche in the CMO structure is specified. The monthly schedule of principal repayments is as specified in the last column of Exhibit 13, which shows the minimum principal payment. That is, this minimum principal payment in each month is the principal repayment schedule (i.e., planned amortization schedule) for investors in the PAC tranche. While there is no assurance that the collateral will prepay at a constant speed between these two speeds over its life, a PAC tranche can be structured to assume that it will.

Exhibit 14 shows a CMO structure, FJF-05, created from the $400 million, 7.5% coupon passthrough with a WAC of 8.125% and a WAM of 357 months. There are just two tranches in this structure: a 7.5% coupon PAC tranche created assuming 90 to 300 PSA with a par value of $243.8 million, and a support tranche with a par value of $156.2 million.

Exhibit 15 reports the average life for the PAC tranche and the support tranche in FJF-05 assuming various *actual* prepayment speeds. Notice that between 90 PSA and 300 PSA, the average life for the PAC bond is stable at 7.26 years. However, at slower or faster PSA speeds, the schedule is broken, and the average life changes, extending when the prepayment speed is less than 90 PSA and contracting when it is greater than 300 PSA. Even so, there is much greater variability for the average life of the support tranche.

1 *Creating a Series of PAC Tranches*

Most CMO PAC structures have more than one class of PAC tranches. A sequence of six PAC tranches (i.e., PAC tranches paid off in sequence as specified by a principal schedule) is shown in Exhibit 16 and is called FJF-06. The total par value of the six PAC tranches is equal to $243.8 million, which is the amount of the single PAC tranche in FJF-05. The schedule of principal repayments for selected months for each PAC bond is shown in Exhibit 17.

Exhibit 13	Monthly Principal Payment for $400 Million, 7.5% Coupon Passthrough with an 8.125% WAC and a 357 WAM Assuming Prepayment Rates of 90 PSA and 300 PSA		

Month	At 90 PSA ($)	At 300 PSA ($)	Minimum Principal Payment Available to PAC Investors—the PAC Schedule ($)
1	508,169	1,075,931	508,169
2	569,843	1,279,412	569,843
3	631,377	1,482,194	631,377
4	692,741	1,683,966	692,741
5	753,909	1,884,414	753,909
6	814,850	2,083,227	814,850
7	875,536	2,280,092	875,536
8	935,940	2,474,700	935,940
9	996,032	2,666,744	996,032
10	1,055,784	2,855,920	1,055,784
11	1,115,170	3,041,927	1,115,170
12	1,174,160	3,224,472	1,174,160
13	1,232,727	3,403,265	1,232,727
14	1,290,844	3,578,023	1,290,844
15	1,348,484	3,748,472	1,348,484
16	1,405,620	3,914,344	1,405,620
17	1,462,225	4,075,381	1,462,225
18	1,518,274	4,231,334	1,518,274
101	1,458,719	1,510,072	1,458,719
102	1,452,725	1,484,126	1,452,725
103	1,446,761	1,458,618	1,446,761
104	1,440,825	1,433,539	1,433,539
105	1,434,919	1,408,883	1,408,883
211	949,482	213,309	213,309
212	946,033	209,409	209,409
213	942,601	205,577	205,577
346	618,684	13,269	13,269
347	617,071	12,944	12,944
348	615,468	12,626	12,626
349	613,875	12,314	3,432
350	612,292	12,008	0
351	610,719	11,708	0
352	609,156	11,414	0
353	607,603	11,126	0
354	606,060	10,843	0
355	604,527	10,567	0
356	603,003	10,295	0
357	601,489	10,029	0

Exhibit 14	FJF-05 CMO Structure with One PAC Tranche and One Support Tranche	

Tranche	Par Amount ($)	Coupon Rate (%)
P (PAC)	243,800,000	7.5
S (Support)	156,200,000	7.5
Total	400,000,000	

Payment rules:

1. *For payment of monthly coupon interest:* Disburse monthly coupon interest to each tranche on the basis of the amount of principal outstanding for each tranche at the beginning of the month.
2. *For disbursement of principal payments:* Disburse principal payments to tranche P based on its schedule of principal repayments. Tranche P has priority with respect to current and future principal payments to satisfy the schedule. Any excess principal payments in a month over the amount necessary to satisfy the schedule for tranche P are paid to tranche S. When tranche S is completely paid off, all principal payments are to be made to tranche P regardless of the schedule.

Exhibit 18 shows the average life for the six PAC tranches and the support tranche in FJF-06 at various prepayment speeds. From a PAC bond in FJF-05 with an average life of 7.26, six tranches have been created with an average life as short as 2.58 years (P-A) and as long as 16.92 years (P-F) if prepayments stay within 90 PSA and 300 PSA.

Exhibit 15	Average Life for PAC Tranche and Support Tranche in FJF-05 Assuming Various Prepayment Speeds (Years)	

Prepayment Rate (PSA)	PAC Bond (P)	Support Bond (S)
0	15.97	27.26
50	9.44	24.00
90	7.26	20.06
100	7.26	18.56
150	7.26	12.57
165	7.26	11.16
200	7.26	8.38
250	7.26	5.37
300	7.26	3.13
350	6.56	2.51
400	5.92	2.17
450	5.38	1.94
500	4.93	1.77
700	3.70	1.37

Exhibit 16	FJF-06: CMO Structure with Six PAC Tranches and a Support Tranche	

Tranche	Par Amount ($)	Coupon Rate (%)
P-A	85,000,000	7.5
P-B	8,000,000	7.5
P-C	35,000,000	7.5

(continued)

Exhibit 16	Continued	
Tranche	**Par Amount ($)**	**Coupon Rate (%)**
P-D	45,000,000	7.5
P-E	40,000,000	7.5
P-F	30,800,000	7.5
S	156,200,000	7.5
Total	400,000,000	

Payment rules:

1. *For payment of monthly coupon interest:* Disburse monthly coupon interest to each tranche on the basis of the amount of principal outstanding of each tranche at the beginning of the month.
2. *For disbursement of principal payments:* Disburse monthly principal payments to tranches P-A to P-F based on their respective schedules of principal repayments. Tranche P-A has priority with respect to current and future principal payments to satisfy the schedule. Any excess principal payments in a month over the amount necessary to satisfy the schedule for tranche P-A are paid to tranche S. Once tranche P-A is completely paid off, tranche P-B has priority, then tranche P-C, etc. When tranche S is completely paid off, all principal payments are to be made to the remaining PAC tranches in order of priority regardless of the schedule.

As expected, the average lives are stable if the prepayment speed is between 90 PSA and 300 PSA. Notice that even outside this range the average life is stable for several of the PAC tranches. For example, the PAC P-A tranche is stable even if prepayment speeds are as high as 400 PSA. For the PAC P-B, the average life does not vary when prepayments are in the initial collar until prepayments are greater than 350 PSA. Why is it that the shorter the PAC, the more protection it has against faster prepayments?

To understand this phenomenon, remember there are $156.2 million in support tranches that are protecting the $85 million of PAC P-A. Thus, even if prepayments are faster than the initial upper collar, there may be sufficient support tranches to assure the satisfaction of the schedule. In fact, as can be seen from Exhibit 18, even if prepayments are 400 PSA over the life of the collateral, the average life is unchanged.

Now consider PAC P-B. The support tranches provide protection for both the $85 million of PAC P-A and $93 million of PAC P-B. As can be seen from Exhibit 18, prepayments could be 350 PSA and the average life is still unchanged. From Exhibit 18 it can be seen that the degree of protection against contraction risk increases the shorter the PAC. Thus, while the initial collar may be 90 to 300 PSA, the effective collar is wider for the shorter PAC tranches.

2　PAC Window

The length of time over which expected principal repayments are made is referred to as the window. For a PAC tranche it is referred to as the PAC window. A PAC window can be wide or narrow. The narrower a PAC window, the more it resembles a corporate bond with a bullet payment. For example, if the PAC schedule calls for just one principal payment (the narrowest window) in month 120 and only interest payments up to month 120, this PAC tranche would resemble a 10-year (120-month) corporate bond.

| Exhibit 17 | Mortgage Balance ($) for Selected Months for FJF-06 Assuming 165 PSA |

				Tranche			
Month	A	B	C	D	E	F	Support
1	85,000,000	8,000,000	35,000,000	45,000,000	40,000,000	30,800,000	156,200,000
2	84,491,830	8,000,000	35,000,000	45,000,000	40,000,000	30,800,000	155,998,246
3	83,921,987	8,000,000	35,000,000	45,000,000	40,000,000	30,800,000	155,746,193
4	83,290,609	8,000,000	35,000,000	45,000,000	40,000,000	30,800,000	155,444,011
5	82,597,868	8,000,000	35,000,000	45,000,000	40,000,000	30,800,000	155,091,931
6	81,843,958	8,000,000	35,000,000	45,000,000	40,000,000	30,800,000	154,690,254
7	81,029,108	8,000,000	35,000,000	45,000,000	40,000,000	30,800,000	154,239,345
8	80,153,572	8,000,000	35,000,000	45,000,000	40,000,000	30,800,000	153,739,635
9	79,217,631	8,000,000	35,000,000	45,000,000	40,000,000	30,800,000	153,191,621
10	78,221,599	8,000,000	35,000,000	45,000,000	40,000,000	30,800,000	152,595,864
11	77,165,814	8,000,000	35,000,000	45,000,000	40,000,000	30,800,000	151,952,989
12	76,050,644	8,000,000	35,000,000	45,000,000	40,000,000	30,800,000	151,263,687
13	74,876,484	8,000,000	35,000,000	45,000,000	40,000,000	30,800,000	150,528,708
52	5,170,458	8,000,000	35,000,000	45,000,000	40,000,000	30,800,000	109,392,664
53	3,379,318	8,000,000	35,000,000	45,000,000	40,000,000	30,800,000	108,552,721
54	1,595,779	8,000,000	35,000,000	45,000,000	40,000,000	30,800,000	107,728,453
55	0	7,819,804	35,000,000	45,000,000	40,000,000	30,800,000	106,919,692
56	0	6,051,358	35,000,000	45,000,000	40,000,000	30,800,000	106,126,275
57	0	4,290,403	35,000,000	45,000,000	40,000,000	30,800,000	105,348,040
58	0	2,536,904	35,000,000	45,000,000	40,000,000	30,800,000	104,584,824
59	0	790,826	35,000,000	45,000,000	40,000,000	30,800,000	103,836,469
60	0	0	34,052,132	45,000,000	40,000,000	30,800,000	103,102,817
61	0	0	32,320,787	45,000,000	40,000,000	30,800,000	102,383,711
62	0	0	30,596,756	45,000,000	40,000,000	30,800,000	101,678,995
78	0	0	3,978,669	45,000,000	40,000,000	30,800,000	92,239,836
79	0	0	2,373,713	45,000,000	40,000,000	30,800,000	91,757,440
80	0	0	775,460	45,000,000	40,000,000	30,800,000	91,286,887
81	0	0	0	44,183,878	40,000,000	30,800,000	90,828,046
82	0	0	0	42,598,936	40,000,000	30,800,000	90,380,792
83	0	0	0	41,020,601	40,000,000	30,800,000	89,944,997
108	0	0	0	3,758,505	40,000,000	30,800,000	82,288,542
109	0	0	0	2,421,125	40,000,000	30,800,000	82,030,119
110	0	0	0	1,106,780	40,000,000	30,800,000	81,762,929
111	0	0	0	0	39,815,082	30,800,000	81,487,234
112	0	0	0	0	38,545,648	30,800,000	81,203,294
113	0	0	0	0	37,298,104	30,800,000	80,911,362
153	0	0	0	0	1,715,140	30,800,000	65,030,732
154	0	0	0	0	1,107,570	30,800,000	64,575,431

(continued)

| Exhibit 17 | Continued |

				Tranche			
Month	A	B	C	D	E	F	Support
155	0	0	0	0	510,672	30,800,000	64,119,075
156	0	0	0	0	0	30,724,266	63,661,761
157	0	0	0	0	0	30,148,172	63,203,587
158	0	0	0	0	0	29,582,215	62,744,644
347	0	0	0	0	0	29,003	1,697,536
348	0	0	0	0	0	16,058	1,545,142
349	0	0	0	0	0	3,432	1,394,152
350	0	0	0	0	0	0	1,235,674
351	0	0	0	0	0	0	1,075,454
352	0	0	0	0	0	0	916,910
353	0	0	0	0	0	0	760,026
354	0	0	0	0	0	0	604,789
355	0	0	0	0	0	0	451,182
356	0	0	0	0	0	0	299,191
357	0	0	0	0	0	0	148,801

PAC buyers appear to prefer tight windows, although institutional investors facing a liability schedule are generally better off with a window that more closely matches their liabilities. Investor demand dictates the PAC windows that dealers will create. Investor demand in turn is governed by the nature of investor liabilities.

3 Effective Collars and Actual Prepayments

The creation of a mortgage-backed security cannot make prepayment risk disappear. This is true for both a passthrough and a CMO. Thus, the reduction in prepayment risk (both extension risk and contraction risk) that a PAC offers investors must come from somewhere.

Where does the prepayment protection come from? It comes from the support tranches. It is the support tranches that defer principal payments to the PAC tranches if the collateral prepayments are slow; support tranches do not receive any principal until the PAC tranches receive the scheduled principal repayment. This reduces the risk that the PAC tranches will extend. Similarly, it is the support tranches that absorb any principal payments in excess of the scheduled principal payments that are made. This reduces the contraction risk of the PAC tranches. Thus, the key to the prepayment protection offered by a PAC tranche is the amount of support tranches outstanding. If the support tranches are paid off quickly because of faster-than-expected prepayments, then there is no longer any protection for the PAC tranches. *In fact, in FJF-06, if the support tranche is paid off, the structure effectively becomes a sequential-pay CMO.*

| Exhibit 18 | Average Life for the Six PAC Tranches in FJF-06 Assuming Various Prepayment Speeds | | | | | |

Prepayment Rate (PSA)	PAC Bonds					
	P-A	P-B	P-C	P-D	P-E	P-F
0	8.46	14.61	16.49	19.41	21.91	23.76
50	3.58	6.82	8.36	11.30	14.50	18.20
90	2.58	4.72	5.78	7.89	10.83	16.92
100	2.58	4.72	5.78	7.89	10.83	16.92
150	2.58	4.72	5.78	7.89	10.83	16.92
165	2.58	4.72	5.78	7.89	10.83	16.92
200	2.58	4.72	5.78	7.89	10.83	16.92
250	2.58	4.72	5.78	7.89	10.83	16.92
300	2.58	4.72	5.78	7.89	10.83	16.92
350	2.58	4.72	5.44	6.95	9.24	14.91
400	2.57	4.37	4.91	6.17	8.33	13.21
450	2.50	3.97	4.44	5.56	7.45	11.81
500	2.40	3.65	4.07	5.06	6.74	10.65
700	2.06	2.82	3.10	3.75	4.88	7.51

The support tranches can be thought of as bodyguards for the PAC bond-holders. When the bullets fly—i.e., prepayments occur—it is the bodyguards that get killed off first. The bodyguards are there to absorb the bullets. Once all the bodyguards are killed off (i.e., the support tranches paid off with faster-than-expected prepayments), the PAC tranches must fend for themselves: they are exposed to all the bullets. A PAC tranche in which all the support tranches have been paid off is called a busted PAC or broken PAC.

With the bodyguard metaphor for the support tranches in mind, let's consider two questions asked by investors in PAC tranches:

1. Will the schedule of principal repayments be satisfied if prepayments are faster than the initial upper collar?

2. Will the schedule of principal repayments be satisfied as long as prepayments stay within the initial collar?

a. Actual Prepayments Greater than the Initial Upper Collar Let's address the first question. The initial upper collar for FJF-06 is 300 PSA. Suppose that actual prepayments are 500 PSA for seven consecutive months. Will this disrupt the schedule of principal repayments? The answer is: It depends!

There are two pieces of information we will need to answer this question. First, when does the 500 PSA occur? Second, what has been the actual prepayment experience up to the time that prepayments are 500 PSA? For example, suppose six years from now is when the prepayments reach 500 PSA, and also suppose that for the past six years the actual prepayment speed has been 90 PSA every month. What this means is that there are more bodyguards (i.e., support tranches) around than were expected when the PAC was structured at the initial collar. In establishing the schedule of principal repayments, it is assumed that the bodyguards would be killed off at 300 PSA. (Recall that 300 PSA is the upper collar prepayment assumption used in creating

FJF-06.) But the actual prepayment experience results in them being killed off at only 90 PSA. Thus, six years from now when the 500 PSA is assumed to occur, there are more bodyguards than expected. In turn, a 500 PSA for seven consecutive months may have no effect on the ability of the schedule of principal repayments to be met.

In contrast, suppose that the actual prepayment experience for the first six years is 300 PSA (the upper collar of the initial PAC collar). In this case, there are no extra bodyguards around. As a result, any prepayment speeds faster than 300 PSA, such as 500 PSA in our example, jeopardize satisfaction of the principal repayment schedule and increase contraction risk. This does not mean that the schedule will be "busted"— the term used in the CMO market when the support tranches are fully paid off. What it does mean is that the prepayment protection is reduced.

It should be clear from these observations that the initial collars are not particularly useful in assessing the prepayment protection for a seasoned PAC tranche. This is most important to understand, as it is common for CMO buyers to compare prepayment protection of PACs in different CMO structures and conclude that the greater protection is offered by the one with the wider initial collar. This approach is inadequate because it is actual prepayment experience that determines the degree of prepayment protection, as well as the expected future prepayment behavior of the collateral.

The way to determine this protection is to calculate the effective collar for a seasoned PAC bond. An effective collar for a seasoned PAC is the lower and the upper PSA that can occur in the future and still allow maintenance of the schedule of principal repayments. For example, consider two seasoned PAC tranches in two CMO structures where the two PAC tranches have the same average life and the prepayment characteristics of the remaining collateral (i.e., the remaining mortgages in the mortgage pools) are similar. The information about these PAC tranches is as follows:

	PAC Tranche X	PAC Tranche Y
Initial PAC collar	180 PSA–350 PSA	170 PSA–410 PSA
Effective PAC collar	160 PSA–450 PSA	240 PSA–300 PSA

Notice that at issuance PAC tranche Y offered greater prepayment protection than PAC tranche X as indicated by the *wider* initial PAC collar. However, that protection is irrelevant for an investor who is considering the purchase of one of these two tranches today. Despite PAC tranche Y's greater prepayment protection at issuance than PAC tranche X, tranche Y has a much narrower effective PAC collar than PAC tranche X and therefore less prepayment protection.

The effective collar changes every month. An extended period over which actual prepayments are below the upper range of the initial PAC collar will result in an increase in the upper range of the effective collar. This is because there will be more bodyguards around than anticipated. An extended period of prepayments slower than the lower range of the initial PAC collar will raise the lower range of the effective collar. This is because it will take faster prepayments to make up the shortfall of the scheduled principal payments not made plus the scheduled future principal payments.

b. Actual Prepayments within the Initial Collar   The PAC schedule may not be satisfied even if the actual prepayments never fall outside of the *initial* collar. This may seem surprising since our previous analysis indicated that the average life would not change if prepayments are at either extreme of the initial collar. However, recall that all of our previous analysis has been based on a single PSA speed for the life of the structure.

The table below shows for FJF-05 what happens to the effective collar if prepayments are 300 PSA for the first 24 months but another prepayment speed for the balance of the life of the structure.

PSA from Year 2 On	Average Life
95	6.43
105	6.11
115	6.01
120	6.00
125	6.00
300	6.00
305	5.62

Notice that the average life is stable at six years if the prepayments for the subsequent months are between 115 PSA and 300 PSA. That is, the effective PAC collar is no longer the initial collar. Instead, the lower collar has shifted upward. This means that the protection from year 2 on is for 115 to 300 PSA, a narrower band than initially (90 to 300 PSA), even though the earlier prepayments did not exceed the initial upper collar.

F. Support Tranches

The support tranches are the bonds that provide prepayment protection for the PAC tranches. Consequently, support tranches expose investors to the greatest level of prepayment risk. Because of this, investors must be particularly careful in assessing the cash flow characteristics of support tranches to reduce the likelihood of adverse portfolio consequences due to prepayments.

The support tranche typically is divided into different tranches. All the tranches we have discussed earlier are available, including sequential-pay support tranches, floater and inverse floater support tranches, and accrual support tranches.

The support tranche can even be partitioned to create support tranches with a schedule of principal payments. That is, support tranches that are PAC tranches can be created. In a structure with a PAC tranche and a support tranche with a PAC schedule of principal payments, the former is called a PAC I tranche or Level I PAC tranche and the latter a PAC II tranche or Level II PAC tranche or scheduled tranche (denoted SCH in a prospectus). While PAC II tranches have greater prepayment protection than the support tranches without a schedule of principal repayments, the prepayment protection is less than that provided PAC I tranches.

The support tranche without a principal repayment schedule can be used to create any type of tranche. In fact, a portion of the non-PAC II support tranche can be given a schedule of principal repayments. This tranche would be called a PAC III tranche or a Level III PAC tranche. While it provides protection against prepayments for the PAC I and PAC II tranches and is therefore subject to considerable prepayment risk, such a tranche has greater protection than the support tranche without a schedule of principal repayments.

G. An Actual CMO Structure

Thus far we have presented some hypothetical CMO structures in order to demonstrate the characteristics of the different types of tranches. Now let's look at an actual CMO structure, one that we will look at further when we discuss how to analyze a CMO deal in the reading on valuing mortgage-backed and asset-backed securities.

The CMO structure we will discuss is the Freddie Mac (FHLMC) Series 1706 issued in early 1994. The collateral for this structure is Freddie Mac 7% coupon passthroughs. A summary of the deal is provided in Exhibit 19.

There are 17 tranches in this structure: 10 PAC tranches, three scheduled tranches, a floating-rate support tranche, and an inverse floating-rate support tranche.[11] There are also two "TAC" support tranches. We will explain a TAC tranche below. Let's look at all tranches.

First, we know what a PAC tranche is. There are 10 of them: tranches A, B, C, D, E, G, H, J, K, and IA. The initial collar used to create the PAC tranches was 95 PSA to 300 PSA. The PAC tranches except for tranche IA are simply PACs that pay off in sequence. Tranche IA is structured such that the underlying collateral's interest not allocated to the other PAC tranches is paid to the IO tranche. This is a notional IO tranche and we described earlier in this section how it is created. In this deal the tranches from which the interest is stripped are the PAC tranches. So, tranche IA is referred to as a PAC IO. (As of the time of this writing, tranches A and B had already paid off all of their principal.)

The prepayment protection for the PAC bonds is provided by the support tranches. The support tranches in this deal are tranches LA, LB, M, O, OA, PF, and PS. Notice that the support tranches have been carved up in different ways. First, there are scheduled (SCH) tranches. These are what we have called the PAC II tranches earlier in this section. The scheduled tranches are LA, LB, and M. The initial PAC collar used to create the scheduled tranches was 190 PSA to 250 PSA.

There are two support tranches that are designed such that they are created with a schedule that provides protection against contraction risk but not against extension. We did not discuss these tranches in this reading. They are called target amortization class (TAC) tranches. The support tranches O and OA are TAC tranches. The schedule of principal payments is created by using just a single PSA. In this structure the single PSA is 225 PSA.

Finally, the support tranche without a schedule (that must provide support for the scheduled bonds and the PACs) was carved into two tranches—a floater (tranche PF) and an inverse floater (tranche PS). In this structure the creation of the floater and inverse floater was from a support tranche.

Now that we know what all these tranches are, the next step is to analyze them in terms of their relative value and their price volatility characteristics when rates change. We will do this in the reading on valuing mortgage-backed and asset-backed securities.

Exhibit 19	Summary of Federal Home Loan Mortgage Corporation—Multiclass Mortgage Participation Certificates (Guaranteed), Series 1706		

| Total Issue: | $300,000,000 | Original Settlement Date: | 3/30/94 |
| Issue Date: | 2/18/94 | | |

Tranche	Original Balance ($)	Coupon (%)	Average Life (Yrs)
A (PAC Bond)	24,600,000	4.50	1.3
B (PAC Bond)	11,100,000	5.00	2.5
C (PAC Bond)	25,500,000	5.25	3.5
D (PAC Bond)	9,150,000	5.65	4.5
E (PAC Bond)	31,650,000	6.00	5.8
G (PAC Bond)	30,750,000	6.25	7.9

---

11 Actually there were two other tranches, R and RS, called "residuals." These tranches were not described in the reading. They receive any excess cash flows remaining after the payment of all the tranches. The residual is actually the equity part of the deal.

Exhibit 19	Continued		
Tranche	**Original Balance ($)**	**Coupon (%)**	**Average Life (Yrs)**
H (PAC Bond)	27,450,000	6.50	10.9
J (PAC Bond)	5,220,000	6.50	14.4
K (PAC Bond)	7,612,000	7.00	18.8
LA (SCH Bond)	26,673,000	7.00	3.5
LB (SCH Bond)	36,087,000	7.00	3.5
M (SCH Bond)	18,738,000	7.00	11.2
O (TAC Bond)	13,348,000	7.00	2.5
OA (TAC Bond)	3,600,000	7.00	7.2
IA (IO, PAC Bond)	30,246,000	7.00	7.1
PF (FLTR, Support Bond)	21,016,000	6.75[a]	17.5
PS (INV FLTR, Support Bond)	7,506,000	7.70[a]	17.5

[a] Coupon at issuance.

Structural Features:

Cash Flow Allocation: Commencing on the first principal payment date of the Class A Bonds, principal equal to the amount specified in the Prospectus will be applied to the Class A, B, C, D, E, G, H, J, K, LA, LB, M, O, OA, PF, and PS Bonds. After all other Classes have been retired, any remaining principal will be used to retire the Class O, OA, LA, LB, M, A, B, C, D, E, G, H, J, and K Bonds. The Notional Class IA Bond will have its notional principal amount retired along with the PAC Bonds.

Other: The PAC Range is 95% to 300% PSA for the A–K Bonds, 190% to 250% PSA for the LA, LB, and M Bonds, and 225% PSA for the O and OA Bonds.

STRIPPED MORTGAGE-BACKED SECURITIES

5

In a CMO, there are multiple bond classes (tranches) and separate rules for the distribution of the interest and the principal to the bond classes. There are mortgage-backed securities where there are only two bond classes and the rule for the distribution for interest and principal is simple: one bond class receives all of the principal and one bond class receives all of the interest. This mortgage-backed security is called a stripped mortgage-backed security. The bond class that receives all of the principal is called the principal-only class or PO class. The bond class that receives all of the interest is called the interest-only class or IO class. These securities are also called mortgage strips. The POs are called principal-only mortgage strips and the IOs are called interest-only mortgage strips.

We have already seen interest-only type mortgage-backed securities: the structured IO. This is a product that is created within a CMO structure. A structured IO is created from the excess interest (i.e., the difference between the interest paid on the collateral and the interest paid to the bond classes). There is no corresponding PO class within the CMO structure. In contrast, in a stripped mortgage-backed security, the IO class is created by simply specifying that all interest payments be made to that class.

A. Principal-Only Strips

A principal-only mortgage strip is purchased at a substantial discount from par value. The return an investor realizes depends on the speed at which prepayments are made. The faster the prepayments, the higher the investor's return. For example, suppose that a pool of 30-year mortgages has a par value of $400 million and the market value of the pool of mortgages is also $400 million. Suppose further that the market value of just the principal payments is $175 million. The dollar return from this investment is the difference between the par value of $400 million that will be repaid to the investor in the principal mortgage strip and the $175 million paid. That is, the dollar return is $225 million.

Since there is no interest that will be paid to the investor in a principal-only mortgage strip, the investor's return is determined solely by the speed at which he or she receives the $225 million. In the extreme case, if all homeowners in the underlying mortgage pool decide to prepay their mortgage loans immediately, PO investors will realize the $225 million immediately. At the other extreme, if all homeowners decide to remain in their homes for 30 years and make no prepayments, the $225 million will be spread out over 30 years, which would result in a lower return for PO investors.

Let's look at how the price of the PO would be expected to change as mortgage rates in the market change. When mortgage rates decline below the contract rate, prepayments are expected to speed up, accelerating payments to the PO investor. Thus, the cash flow of a PO improves (in the sense that principal repayments are received earlier). The cash flow will be discounted at a lower interest rate because the mortgage rate in the market has declined. The result is that the PO price will increase when mortgage rates decline. When mortgage rates rise above the contract rate, prepayments are expected to slow down. The cash flow deteriorates (in the sense that it takes longer to recover principal repayments). Couple this with a higher discount rate, and the price of a PO will fall when mortgage rates rise.

Exhibit 20 shows the general relationship between the price of a principal-only mortgage strip when interest rates change and compares it to the relationship for the underlying passthrough from which it is created.

B. Interest-Only Strips

An interest-only mortgage strip has no par value. In contrast to the PO investor, the IO investor wants prepayments to be slow. The reason is that the IO investor receives interest only on the amount of the principal outstanding. When prepayments are made, less dollar interest will be received as the outstanding principal declines. In fact, *if prepayments are too fast, the IO investor may not recover the amount paid for the IO even if the security is held to maturity.*

Let's look at the expected price response of an IO to changes in mortgage rates. If mortgage rates decline below the contract rate, prepayments are expected to accelerate. This would result in a deterioration of the expected cash flow for an IO. While the cash flow will be discounted at a lower rate, the net effect typically is a decline in the price of an IO. If mortgage rates rise above the contract rate, the expected cash flow improves, but the cash flow is discounted at a higher interest rate. The net effect may be either a rise or fall for the IO.

Exhibit 20	Relationship between Price and Mortgage Rates for a Passthrough, PO, and IO

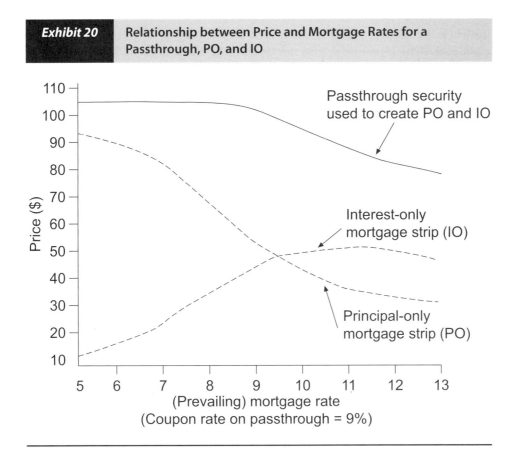

Thus, we see an interesting characteristic of an IO: its price tends to move in the same direction as the change in mortgage rates 1) when mortgage rates fall below the contract rate and 2) for some range of mortgage rates above the contract rate. Both POs and IOs exhibit substantial price volatility when mortgage rates change. The greater price volatility of the IO and PO compared to the passthrough from which they were created is due to the fact that the combined price volatility of the IO and PO must be equal to the price volatility of the passthrough.

Exhibit 20 shows the general relationship between the price of an interest-only mortgage strip when interest rates change and compares it to the relationship for the corresponding principal-only mortgage strip and underlying passthrough from which it is created.

An average life for a PO can be calculated based on some prepayment assumption. However, an IO receives no principal payments, so technically an average life cannot be computed. Instead, for an IO a cash flow average life is computed, using the projected interest payments in the average life formula instead of principal.

C. Trading and Settlement Procedures

The trading and settlement procedures for stripped mortgage-backed securities are similar to those set by the Public Securities Association for agency passthroughs described in Section 3.C. IOs and POs are extreme premium and discount securities and consequently are very sensitive to prepayments, which are driven by the specific characteristics (weighted average coupon, weighted average maturity, geographic concentration, average loan size) of the underlying loans. Therefore, almost all secondary trades in IOs and POs are on a specified pool basis rather than on a TBA basis.

All IOs and POs are given a trust number. For instance, Fannie Mae Trust 1 is a IO/PO trust backed by specific pools of Fannie Mae 9% mortgages. Fannie Mae Trust

2 is backed by Fannie Mae 10% mortgages. Fannie Mae Trust 23 is another IO/PO trust backed by Fannie Mae 10% mortgages. Therefore, a portfolio manager must specify which trust he or she is buying.

The total proceeds of a PO trade are calculated the same way as with a passthrough trade except that there is no accrued interest. The market trades IOs based on notional principal. The proceeds include the price on the notional amount and the accrued interest.

6   NONAGENCY RESIDENTIAL MORTGAGE-BACKED SECURITIES

In the previous sections we looked at agency mortgage-backed securities in which the underlying mortgages are 1- to 4-single-family residential mortgages. The mortgage-backed securities market includes other types of securities. These securities are called nonagency mortgage-backed securities (referred to as nonagency securities hereafter).

The underlying mortgage loans for nonagency securities can be for any type of real estate property. There are securities backed by 1- to 4-single family residential mortgages with a first lien (i.e., the lender has a first priority or first claim) on the mortgaged property. There are nonagency securities backed by other types of single family residential loans. These include home equity loan-backed securities and manufactured housing-loan backed securities. Our focus in this section is on nonagency securities in which the underlying loans are first-lien mortgages for 1- to 4-single-family residential properties.

As with an agency mortgage-backed security, the servicer is responsible for the collection of interest and principal. The servicer also handles delinquencies and foreclosures. Typically, there will be a master servicer and subservicers. The servicer plays a key role. In fact, in assessing the credit risk of a nonagency security, rating companies look carefully at the quality of the servicers.

A.   Underlying Mortgage Loans

The underlying loans for agency securities are those that conform to the underwriting standards of the agency issuing or guaranteeing the issue. That is, only conforming loans are included in pools that are collateral for an agency mortgage-backed security. The three main underwriting standards deal with

1. the maximum loan-to-value ratio
2. the maximum payment-to-income ratio
3. the maximum loan amount

The loan-to-value ratio (LTV) is the ratio of the amount of the loan to the market value or appraised value of the property. The *lower* the LTV, the *greater* the protection afforded the lender. For example, an LTV of 0.90 means that if the lender has to repossess the property and sell it, the lender must realize at least 90% of the market value in order to recover the amount lent. An LTV of 0.80 means that the lender only has to sell the property for 80% of its market value in order to recover the amount lent.[12] Empirical studies of residential mortgage loans have found that the LTV is a key determinant of whether a borrower will default: the higher the LTV, the greater the likelihood of default.

---

12 This ignores the costs of repossession and selling the property.

As mentioned earlier in this reading, a nonconforming mortgage loan is one that does not conform to the underwriting standards established by any of the agencies. Typically, the loans for a nonagency security are nonconforming mortgage loans that fail to qualify for inclusion because the amount of the loan exceeds the limit established by the agencies. Such loans are referred to as jumbo loans. Jumbo loans do not necessarily have greater credit risk than conforming mortgages.

Loans that fail to qualify because of the first two underwriting standards expose the lender to greater credit risk than conforming loans. There are specialized lenders who provide mortgage loans to individuals who fail to qualify for a conforming loan because of their credit history. These specialized lenders classify borrowers by credit quality. Borrowers are classified as A borrowers, B borrowers, C borrowers, and D borrowers. A borrowers are those that are viewed as having the best credit record. Such borrowers are referred to as prime borrowers. Borrowers rated below A are viewed as subprime borrowers. However, there is no industry-wide classification system for prime and subprime borrowers.

B. Differences between Agency and Nonagency Securities

Nonagency securities can be either passthroughs or CMOs. In the agency market, CMOs are created from pools of passthrough securities. In the nonagency market, CMOs are created from unsecuritized mortgage loans. Since a mortgage loan not securitized as a passthrough is called a whole loan, nonagency CMOs are commonly referred to as whole-loan CMOs.

The major difference between agency and nonagency securities has to do with guarantees. With a nonagency security there is no explicit or implicit government guarantee of payment of interest and principal as there is with an agency security. The absence of any such guarantee means that the investor in a nonagency security is exposed to credit risk. The nationally recognized statistical rating organizations rate nonagency securities.

Because of the credit risk, all nonagency securities are credit enhanced. By credit enhancement it means that additional support against defaults must be obtained. The amount of credit enhancement needed is determined relative to a specific rating desired for a security rating agency. There are two general types of credit enhancement mechanisms: external and internal. We describe each of these types of credit enhancement in the reading on the asset-backed sector of the bond market where we cover asset-backed securities.

COMMERCIAL MORTGAGE-BACKED SECURITIES | 7

Commercial mortgage-backed securities (CMBSs) are backed by a pool of commercial mortgage loans on income-producing property—multifamily properties (i.e., apartment buildings), office buildings, industrial properties (including warehouses), shopping centers, hotels, and health care facilities (i.e., senior housing care facilities). The basic building block of the CMBS transaction is a commercial loan that was originated either to finance a commercial purchase or to refinance a prior mortgage obligation.

There are two types of CMBS deal structures that have been of primary interest to bond investors: 1) multiproperty single borrower and 2) multiproperty conduit. Conduits are commercial-lending entities that are established for the sole purpose of generating collateral to securitize.

CMBS have been issued outside the United States. The dominant issues have been U.K. based (more than 80% in 2000), with the primary property types being retail and office properties. Starting in 2001, there was a dramatic increase in the number of CMBS deals issued by German banks. An increasing number of deals include multi-country properties. The first pan-European securitization was Pan European Industrial Properties in 2001.[13]

A. Credit Risk

Unlike residential mortgage loans where the lender relies on the ability of the borrower to repay and may have recourse to the borrower if the payment terms are not satisfied, commercial mortgage loans are nonrecourse loans. This means that the lender can only look to the income-producing property backing the loan for interest and principal repayment. If there is a default, the lender looks to the proceeds from the sale of the property for repayment and has no recourse to the borrower for any unpaid balance. The lender must view each property as a stand-alone business and evaluate each property using measures that have been found useful in assessing credit risk.

While fundamental principles of assessing credit risk apply to all property types, traditional approaches to assessing the credit risk of the collateral differs between CMBS and nonagency mortgage-backed securities and real estate-backed securities that fall into the asset-backed securities sector (those backed by home equity loans and manufactured housing loans). For mortgage-backed securities and asset-backed securities in which the collateral is residential property, typically the loans are lumped into buckets based on certain loan characteristics, and then assumptions regarding default rates are made regarding each bucket. In contrast, for commercial mortgage loans, the unique economic characteristics of each income-producing property in a pool backing a CMBS require that credit analysis be performed on a loan-by-loan basis not only at the time of issuance, but monitored on an ongoing basis.

Regardless of the type of commercial property, the two measures that have been found to be key indicators of the potential credit performance is the debt-to-service coverage ratio and the loan-to-value ratio.

The debt-to-service coverage ratio (DSC) is the ratio of the property's net operating income (NOI) divided by the debt service. The NOI is defined as the rental income reduced by cash operating expenses (adjusted for a replacement reserve). A ratio greater than 1 means that the cash flow from the property is sufficient to cover debt servicing. The higher the ratio, the more likely that the borrower will be able to meet debt servicing from the property's cash flow.

For all properties backing a CMBS deal, a weighted average DSC ratio is computed. An analysis of the credit quality of an issue will also look at the dispersion of the DSC ratios for the underlying loans. For example, one might look at the percentage of a deal with a DSC ratio below a certain value.

As explained in Section 6.A, in computing the LTV, the figure used for "value" in the ratio is either market value or appraised value. In valuing commercial property, it is typically the appraised value. There can be considerable variation in the estimates of the property's appraised value. Thus, analysts tend to be skeptical about estimates of appraised value and the resulting LTVs reported for properties.

B. Basic CMBS Structure

As with any structured finance transaction, a rating agency will determine the necessary level of credit enhancement to achieve a desired rating level. For example, if certain DSC and LTV ratios are needed, and these ratios cannot be met at the loan level, then "subordination" is used to achieve these levels. By subordination it is meant

---

13 Christopher Flanagan and Edward Reardon, *European Structures Products: 2001 Review and 2002 Outlook*, Global Structured Finance Research, J.P. Morgan Securities Inc. (January 11, 2002), pp. 12–13.

that there will be bond classes in the structure whose claims on the cash flow of the collateral are subordinated to that of other bond classes in the structure.

The rating agencies will require that the CMBS transaction be retired sequentially, with the highest-rated bonds paying off first. Therefore, any return of principal caused by amortization, prepayment, or default will be used to repay the highest-rated tranche.

Interest on principal outstanding will be paid to all tranches. In the event of a delinquency resulting in insufficient cash to make all scheduled payments, the transaction's servicer will advance both principal and interest. Advancing will continue from the servicer for as long as these amounts are deemed recoverable.

Losses arising from loan defaults will be charged against the principal balance of the lowest-rated CMBS tranche outstanding. The total loss charged will include the amount previously advanced as well as the actual loss incurred in the sale of the loan's underlying property.

1 Call Protection

A critical investment feature that distinguishes residential MBS and commercial MBS is the call protection afforded an investor. An investor in a residential MBS is exposed to considerable prepayment risk because the borrower has the right to prepay a loan, in whole or in part, before the scheduled principal repayment date. Typically, the borrower does not pay any penalty for prepayment. When we discussed CMOs, we saw how certain types of tranches (e.g., sequential-pay and PAC tranches) can be purchased by an investor to reduce prepayment risk.

With CMBS, there is considerable call protection afforded investors. In fact, it is this protection that results in CMBS trading in the market more like corporate bonds than residential MBS. This call protection comes in two forms: 1) call protection at the loan level and 2) call protection at the structure level. We discuss both below.

a. Protection at the Loan Level   At the commercial loan level, call protection can take the following forms:

1. prepayment lockout

2. defeasance

3. prepayment penalty points

4. yield maintenance charges

A prepayment lockout is a contractual agreement that prohibits any prepayments during a specified period of time, called the lockout period. The lockout period at issuance can be from 2 to 5 years. After the lockout period, call protection comes in the form of either prepayment penalty points or yield maintenance charges. Prepayment lockout and defeasance are the strongest forms of prepayment protection.

With defeasance, rather than loan prepayment, the borrower provides sufficient funds for the servicer to invest in a portfolio of Treasury securities that replicates the cash flows that would exist in the absence of prepayments. Unlike the other call protection provisions discussed next, there is no distribution made to the bondholders when the defeasance takes place. So, since there are no penalties, there is no issue as to how any penalties paid by the borrower are to be distributed amongst the bondholders in a CMBS structure. Moreover, the substitution of the cash flow of a Treasury portfolio for that of the borrower improves the credit quality of the CMBS deal.

Prepayment penalty points are predetermined penalties that must be paid by the borrower if the borrower wishes to refinance. (A point is equal to 1% of the outstanding loan balance.) For example, 5-4-3-2-1 is a common prepayment penalty point structure. That is, if the borrower wishes to prepay during the first year, the borrower must pay a 5% penalty for a total of $105 rather than $100 (which is the norm in the residential market). Likewise, during the second year, a 4% penalty would apply, and so on.

When there are prepayment penalty points, there are rules for distributing the penalty among the tranches. Prepayment penalty points are not common in new CMBS structures. Instead, the next form of call protection discussed, yield maintenance charges, is more commonly used.

Yield maintenance charge, in its simplest terms, is designed to make the lender indifferent as to the timing of prepayments. The yield maintenance charge, also called the make-whole charge, makes it uneconomical to refinance solely to get a lower mortgage rate. While there are several methods used in practice for calculating the yield maintenance charge, the key principle is to make the lender whole. However, when a commercial loan is included as part of a CMBS deal, there must be an allocation of the yield maintenance charge amongst the tranches. Several methods are used in practice for distributing the yield maintenance charge and, depending on the method specified in a deal, not all tranches may be made whole.

b. Structural Protection   The other type of call protection available in CMBS transactions is structural. Because the CMBS bond structures are sequential-pay (by rating), the AA-rated tranche cannot pay down until the AAA is completely retired, and the AA-rated bonds must be paid off before the A-rated bonds, and so on. However, principal losses due to defaults are impacted from the bottom of the structure upward.

2 Balloon Maturity Provisions

Many commercial loans backing CMBS transactions are balloon loans that require substantial principal payment at the end of the term of the loan. If the borrower fails to make the balloon payment, the borrower is in default. The lender may extend the loan, and in so doing may modify the original loan terms. During the workout period for the loan, a higher interest rate will be charged, called the default interest rate.

The risk that a borrower will not be able to make the balloon payment because either the borrower cannot arrange for refinancing at the balloon payment date or cannot sell the property to generate sufficient funds to pay off the balloon balance is called balloon risk. Since the term of the loan will be extended by the lender during the workout period, balloon risk is a type of "extension risk." This is the same risk that we referred to earlier in describing residential mortgage-backed securities.

Although many investors like the "bullet bond-like" paydown of the balloon maturities, it does present difficulties from a structural standpoint. That is, if the deal is structured to completely pay down on a specified date, an event of default will occur if any delays occur. However, how such delays impact CMBS investors is dependent on the bond type (premium, par, or discount) and whether the servicer will advance to a particular tranche after the balloon default.

Another concern for CMBS investors in multitranche transactions is the fact that all loans must be refinanced to pay off the most senior bondholders. Therefore, the balloon risk of the most senior tranche (i.e., AAA) may be equivalent to that of the most junior tranche (i.e., B).

SUMMARY

- The basic mortgage-backed security is the mortgage passthrough security created from a pool of mortgage loans.
- Agency passthrough securities are those issued/guaranteed by Ginnie Mae, Fannie Mae, and Freddie Mac.

- The cash flow of a passthrough includes net interest, scheduled principal repayments (i.e., scheduled amortization), and prepayments.

- Any amount paid in excess of the required monthly mortgage payment is a prepayment; the cash flow of a mortgage-backed security is unknown because of prepayments.

- A projection of prepayments is necessary to project the cash flow of a passthrough security.

- The single monthly mortality (SMM) rate is the ratio of the amount of prepayments divided by the amount available to prepay (i.e., outstanding mortgage balance at the beginning of the month minus the scheduled principal payment for the month).

- The PSA prepayment benchmark is a series of conditional prepayment rates and is simply a market convention that describes in general the pattern of prepayments.

- A measure commonly used to estimate the life of a passthrough is its average life.

- The prepayment risk associated with investing in mortgage passthrough securities can be decomposed into contraction risk and extension risk.

- Prepayment risk makes passthrough securities unattractive for certain financial institutions to hold from an asset/liability perspective.

- The three factors that affect prepayments are 1) the prevailing mortgage rate, 2) normal housing turnover, and 3) characteristics of the underlying mortgage pool.

- Collateralized mortgage obligations are bond classes created by redirecting the interest and principal from a pool of passthroughs or whole loans.

- The creation of a CMO cannot eliminate prepayment risk; it can only transfer the various forms of this risk among different classes of bonds called tranches.

- From a fixed-rate CMO tranche, a floating-rate tranche and an inverse floating-rate tranche can be created.

- A notional interest-only tranche (also called a structured IO) can be created from the excess interest available from other tranches in the structure; excess interest is the difference between the collateral's coupon rate and a tranche's coupon rate.

- The amortization schedule for a planned amortization class is structured based on a lower PSA prepayment assumption and an upper PSA prepayment assumption—called the initial PAC collar.

- A planned amortization class (PAC) tranche has reduced average life variability, the better prepayment protection provided by the support tranches.

- If the collateral from which a PAC bond is created pays at a constant PSA rate that is anywhere within the initial PAC collar, the amortization schedule will be satisfied.

- Over time, the prepayment collar that will be able to support the PAC tranches (i.e., provide the prepayment protection) changes as the amount of the support tranches change.

- The effective collar is the lower and upper PSA prepayment rates that can occur in the future and still be able to satisfy the amortization schedule for the PAC tranche.

- The key to the prepayment protection for the PAC tranches is the support tranches.

- The support tranches are exposed to the greatest prepayment risk of all the tranches in a CMO structure and greater prepayment risk than the collateral (i.e., passthrough securities) from which a deal is created.

- Support tranches with a PAC schedule can be created from the support tranches; these tranches are still support tranches but they have better prepayment protection than other support tranches in the structure that do not have a schedule.

- A stripped mortgage-backed security is a derivative mortgage-backed security that is created by redistributing the interest and principal payments to two different classes.

- A principal-only mortgage strip (PO) benefits from declining interest rates and fast prepayments.

- An interest-only mortgage strip (IO) benefits from rising interest rates and a slowing of prepayments; if rates fall instead, the investor in an interest-only security may not realize the amount invested even if the security is held to maturity.

- Nonagency securities are not backed by any federal government agency guarantee.

- The underlying loans for nonagency securities are nonconforming mortgage loans—loans that do not qualify for inclusion in mortgage pools that underlie agency mortgage-backed securities.

- Credit enhancement is needed to support nonagency mortgage-backed securities.

- Credit enhancement levels are determined relative to a specific rating desired for a security and there are two general types of credit enhancement structures—external and internal.

- Commercial mortgage-backed securities are backed by a pool of commercial mortgage loans—loans on income-producing property.

- Unlike residential mortgage loans where the lender relies on the ability of the borrower to repay and has recourse to the borrower if the payment terms are not satisfied, commercial mortgage loans are nonrecourse loans, and as a result the lender can only look to the income-producing property backing the loan for interest and principal repayment.

- Two measures that have been found to be key indicators of the potential credit performance of a commercial mortgage loan are the debt-to-service coverage ratio (i.e., the property's net operating income divided by the debt service) and the loan-to-value ratio.

- The degree of call protection available to a CMBS investor is a function of 1) call protection available at the loan level and 2) call protection afforded from the actual CMBS structure.

- At the commercial loan level, call protection can be in the form of a prepayment lockout, defeasance, prepayment penalty points, or yield maintenance charges.

- Many commercial loans backing CMBS transactions are balloon loans that require substantial principal payment at the end of the balloon term and therefore the investor faces balloon risk—the risk that the loan will extend beyond the scheduled maturity date.

PRACTICE PROBLEMS FOR READING 45

1. A. Complete the following schedule for a 30-year fully amortizing mortgage loan with a mortgage rate of 7.25% where the amount borrowed is $150,000. The monthly mortgage payment is $1,023.26.

Month	Beginning Mortgage ($)	Mortgage Payment ($)	Interest ($)	Sch. Prin. Repayment ($)	End-of-Month Balance ($)
1	150,000.00	1,023.26			
2		1,023.26			
3		1,023.26			
4		1,023.26			
5		1,023.26			
6		1,023.26			
7		1,023.26			
8		1,023.26			
9		1,023.26			
10		1,023.26			
11		1,023.26			
12		1,023.26			
13		1,023.26			
14		1,023.26			

B. Complete the following schedule for the mortgage loan in part A given the following information:

Month	Beginning Mortgage ($)	Mortgage Payment ($)	Interest ($)	Sch. Prin. Repayment ($)	End-of-Month Balance ($)
357	4,031.97	1,023.26			
358		1,023.26			
359		1,023.26			
360		1,023.26			

2. A. Suppose that the servicing fee for a mortgage loan is 0.5%. Complete the following schedule for the mortgage loan in the previous question. The column labeled "Servicing Fee" is the dollar amount of the servicing fee for the month. The column labeled "Net Interest" is the monthly interest after the servicing fee for the month.

Month	Beginning Mortgage ($)	Mortgage Payment ($)	Servicing Fee ($)	Net Interest ($)	Sch. Prin. Repayment ($)	End-of-Month Balance ($)
1						
2						
3						

(continued)

Practice Problems and Solutions: 1–41 taken from *Fixed Income Analysis for the Chartered Financial Analyst® Program*, Second Edition, by Frank J. Fabozzi, CFA. Copyright © 2005 by CFA Institute. All other problems and solutions copyright © CFA Institute.

Month	Beginning Mortgage ($)	Mortgage Payment ($)	Servicing Fee ($)	Net Interest ($)	Sch. Prin. Repayment ($)	End-of-Month Balance ($)
4						
5						
6						

   B. Determine for the first six months the cash flow for an investor who purchases this mortgage loan after the servicing fee is paid.

3. Explain why you agree or disagree with the following statement: "Since mortgage passthrough securities issued by Ginnie Mae are guaranteed by the full faith and credit of the U.S. government, there is no uncertainty about the cash flow for the security."

4. Consider the following mortgage pool.

Loan	Outstanding Mortgage Balance ($)	Mortgage Rate (%)	Months Remaining
1	215,000	6.75	200
2	185,000	7.75	185
3	125,000	7.25	192
4	100,000	7.00	210
5	200,000	6.50	180
Total	825,000		

   A. What is the weighted average coupon rate for this mortgage pool?

   B. What is the weighted average maturity for this mortgage pool?

5. Mr. Jamison is looking at the historical prepayment for a passthrough security. He finds the following:

   mortgage balance in month 42   = $260,000,000

   scheduled principal payment in month 42   = $1,000,000

   prepayment in month 42   = $2,450,000

   A. What is the SMM for month 42?

   B. How should Mr. Jamison interpret the SMM computed?

   C. What is the CPR for month 42?

   D. How should Mr. Jamison interpret the CPR computed?

6. Using the Public Securities Association Prepayment benchmark, complete the following table:

Month	PSA	CPR	SMM
5	100		
15	80		
20	175		
27	50		
88	200		
136	75		
220	225		

7. Explain why 30 months after the origination of a mortgage pool, discussing prepayments in terms of one CPR and a PSA are identical.

8. Suppose that in month 140 the mortgage balance for a mortgage pool underlying a passthrough security is $537 million and that the scheduled principal repayment for month 140 is $440,000. Assuming 175 PSA, what is the amount of the prepayment for month 140?

9. Comment on the following statement: "The PSA model is a prepayment model."

10. Robert Reed is an assistant portfolio manager who has been recently given the responsibility of assisting Joan Soprano, the portfolio manager for the mortgage-backed securities portfolio. Ms. Soprano gave Mr. Reed a copy of the Prudential Securities publication for November 1999 entitled *Mortgage and Asset-Backed Prepayment and Issuance*. An excerpt from the publication is given below:

		Projected PSA				
GNMA	30 Year	Dec	Jan	Feb	One Year	Long Term
6.0	1998	73	68	60	60	65
6.5	1998	113	102	92	91	90
7.0	1998	154	137	124	126	116
7.5	1993	181	166	150	155	138
8.0	1996	220	211	181	185	159
8.5	1994	283	272	223	205	173
9.0	1986	269	263	232	209	195

The mortgage rate at the time of the report was 8.13%.

Mr. Reed asks the following questions about the information in the above excerpt. Respond to each question.

A. What does "GNMA 30 YEAR" mean?

B. What does "8.5 1994" mean?

C. What do the numbers under "PROJECTED" mean?

D. Do the prepayment rates for "7.5 1993" apply to all GNMA issues in the market?

E. Why are the projected prepayments for "one year" and "long term" such that they increase with the coupon rate?

11. Suppose that you are analyzing prepayments of a passthrough security that was issued more than 15 years ago. The weighted average coupon (WAC) for the underlying mortgage pool was 13%. Suppose that the mortgage rate over the year of the analysis declined from 8% to 7% but prepayments for this mortgage pool you are analyzing did not increase. Explain why there is no increase in prepayments despite the lower mortgage rate relative to 13% being paid by borrowers and the decline in the mortgage rates over the year.

12. What type of prepayment risk is an investor interested in a short-term security concerned with when purchasing a mortgage-backed security?

13. Suppose that a portfolio manager is considering a collateralized mortgage obligation structure KMF-01. This structure has three tranches. The deal is a simple sequential pay and was issued several years ago. The tranches are A, B, and C with a coupon rate paid to each tranche each month and principal

payments are made first to tranche A, then to tranche B, and finally to tranche C. Here is the status of the deal as of the time of the analysis:

Tranche	Coupon Rate (%)	Par Amount Outstanding ($)
A	6	3 million
B	7	8 million
C	8	30 million

Based on some prepayment rate, the projected principal payments (prepayments plus scheduled principal repayment) for the next four years for the collateral underlying this deal are as follows:

Month	Sch. Principal Repayment + Prepayments ($)	Month	Sch. Principal Repayment + Prepayments ($)
1	520,000	25	287,000
2	510,000	26	285,000
3	490,000	27	283,000
4	450,000	28	280,000
5	448,000	29	278,000
6	442,000	30	275,000
7	410,000	31	271,000
8	405,000	32	270,000
9	400,000	33	265,000
10	396,000	34	260,000
11	395,000	35	255,000
12	390,000	36	252,000
13	388,000	37	250,000
14	385,000	38	245,000
15	380,000	39	240,000
16	377,000	40	210,000
17	375,000	41	200,000
18	370,000	42	195,000
19	369,000	43	190,000
20	366,000	44	185,000
21	300,000	45	175,000
22	298,000	46	170,000
23	292,000	47	166,000
24	290,000	48	164,000

A. Compute the principal, interest, and cash flow for tranche A for the 48 months.

B. Compute the principal, interest, and cash flow for tranche B for the 48 months.

C. Compute the principal, interest, and cash flow for tranche C for the 48 months.

D. Compute the average life for tranche A.

14. Suppose that in the previous CMO structure, KMF-01, that tranche C is an accrual tranche that accrues coupon interest monthly. We will refer to this new CMO structure as KMF-02.

    A. What is the principal repayment, interest, and cash flow for tranche A in KMF-02?

    B. What is the principal balance for tranche C for the first five months?

    C. What is the average life for tranche A in KMF-02 and contrast this with the average life for tranche A in KMF-01?

15. Explain why it is necessary to have a cap for the floater when a fixed-rate tranche is split into a floater and an inverse floater.

16. Suppose that a tranche from which a floater and an inverse floater are created has an average life of six years. What will be the average life of the floater and the inverse floater?

17. How does a CMO alter the cash flow from mortgages so as to redistribute the prepayment risk across various tranches in a deal?

18. "By creating a CMO, an issuer eliminates the prepayment risk associated with the underlying mortgages loans." Explain why you agree or disagree with this statement.

19. Ellen Morgan received a phone call from the trustee of a pension fund. Ms. Morgan is the portfolio manager for the pension fund's bond portfolio. The trustee expressed concerns about the inclusion of CMOs in the portfolio. The trustee's concern arose after reading several articles in the popular press where the CMO market was characterized as the sector of the mortgage-backed securities market with the greatest prepayment risk and the passthrough sector as the safest sector in terms of prepayment risk. What should Ms. Morgan say to this trustee regarding such statements made in the popular press?

20. What is the role of a support tranche in a CMO structure?

21. Suppose that the manager of a savings & loan association portfolio has decided to invest in mortgage-backed securities and is considering the following two securities: i) a Fannie Mae passthrough security with a WAM of 310 months or ii) a PAC tranche of a Fannie Mae CMO issue with an average life of 2 years. Which mortgage-backed security would probably be better from an asset/liability perspective?

22. Suppose that a PAC bond is created using prepayment speeds of 90 PSA and 240 PSA and the average life is 5 years. Will the average life for this PAC tranche be shorter than, longer than, or equal to 5 years if the collateral pays at 140 PSA over its life? Explain your answer.

23. Suppose that $1 billion of passthroughs are used to create a CMO structure, KMF-05. This structure includes a PAC tranche with a par value of $650 million and a support tranche with a par value of $350 million.

    A. Which of the following will have the least average life variability: i) the collateral, ii) the PAC tranche, or iii) the support tranche? Why?

    B. Which of the following will have the greatest average life variability: i) the collateral, ii) the PAC tranche, or iii) the support tranche? Why?

24. Suppose that the $1 billion of collateral in the CMO structure KMF-05 in the previous question was divided into a PAC tranche with a par value of $800 million and a support tranche with a par value of $200 million (instead of $650 million and $350 million). The new structure is KMF-06. Will the PAC tranche in KMF-06 have more or less protection than the PAC tranche in KMF-05?

25. Suppose that $500 million of passthroughs are used to create a CMO structure with a PAC tranche with a par value of $350 million (PAC I), a support tranche with a schedule (PAC II) with a par value of $100 million, and a support tranche without a schedule with a par value of $200 million.

    A. Will the PAC I or PAC II have less average life variability? Why?

    B. Will the support tranche without a schedule or the PAC II have the greater average life variability? Why?

26. In a CMO structure with several PAC tranches that pay off sequentially, explain what the structure effectively becomes once all the support tranches are paid off.

27. Suppose that for the first four years of a CMO, prepayments are well below the initial upper PAC collar and within the initial lower PAC collar. What will happen to the effective upper collar?

28. Consider the following CMO structure backed by 8% collateral:

Tranche	Par Amount ($)	Coupon Rate (%)
A	400,000,000	6.25
B	200,000,000	6.75
C	225,000,000	7.50
D	175,000,000	7.75

Suppose that the structurer of this CMO wants to create a notional IO tranche with a coupon rate of 8%. Calculate the notional amount for this notional IO tranche.

29. An issuer is considering the following two CMO structures: Structure I:

Tranche	Par Amount ($)	Coupon Rate (%)
A	150 million	6.50
B	100 million	6.75
C	200 million	7.25
D	150 million	7.75
E	100 million	8.00
F	500 million	8.50

Tranches A–E are a sequence of PAC Is, and F is the support tranche. Structure II:

Tranche	Par Amount ($)	Coupon Rate (%)
A	150 million	6.50
B	100 million	6.75
C	200 million	7.25
D	150 million	7.75
E	100 million	8.00
F	200 million	8.25
G	300 million	?????

Tranches A–E are a sequence of PAC Is, F is a PAC II, and G is a support tranche without a schedule.

    A. In Structure II tranche G is created from tranche F in Structure I. What is the coupon rate for tranche G assuming that the combined coupon rate for tranches F and G in Structure II should be 8.5%?

    B. What is the effect on the value and average life of tranches A–E by including the PAC II in Structure II?

    C. What is the difference in the average life variability of tranche G in Structure II and tranche F in Structure I?

30. What is a broken or busted PAC?

31. Assume that in FJF-01 (see Exhibit 5 in the reading), tranche C had been split to create a floater with a principal of $80,416,667 and an inverse floater with a principal of $16,083,333.

    A. What would be the cap rate for the inverse floater if the coupon rate for the floater is 1-month LIBOR plus 1%?

    B. Assuming that 1) the coupon formula for the floater is 1-month LIBOR plus 1% and 2) a floor is imposed on the inverse floater of zero, what would be the cap rate on the floater?

32. **A.** In assessing the prepayment protection offered by a seasoned PAC tranche, explain why the initial collars may provide limited insight?

    B. What measure provides better information about the prepayment protection offered by a seasoned PAC tranche?

33. **A.** For a mortgage loan, is a higher or lower loan-to-value ratio an indication of greater credit risk? Explain why.

    B. What is the empirical relationship between defaults and loan-to-value ratio observed by studies of residential mortgage loans?

34. **A.** What is a principal-only mortgage strip and an interest-only mortgage strip?

    B. How does an interest-only mortgage strip differ with respect to the certainty about the cash flow from a Treasury strip created from the coupon interest?

    C. How is the price of an interest-only mortgage strip expected to change when interest rates change?

35. **A.** An investor purchased $10 million par value of a 7% Ginnie Mae passthrough security agreeing to pay 102. The pool factor is 0.72. How much does the investor pay to the seller?

    B. Why would an investor who wants to purchase a principal-only mortgage strip not want to do so on a TBA basis?

36. Why can't all residential mortgage loans be securitized by either Ginnie Mae, Fannie Mae, or Freddie Mac?

37. Why is credit enhancement needed for a nonagency mortgage-backed security?

38. With respect to a default by the borrower, how does a residential mortgage loan differ from a commercial mortgage loan?

39. Why is the debt-to-service coverage ratio used to assess the credit risk of a commercial mortgage loan?

40. **A.** What types of provisions are usually included in a commercial loan to protect the lender against prepayment risk?

    B. In a commercial mortgage-backed securities deal, explain why the investor in a security may be afforded prepayment protection at the deal level.

41. What is balloon risk and how is it related to extension risk?

The following information relates to Questions 42–47

Ellen Hurst, a fixed income portfolio manager at a private foundation, is considering the purchase of a mortgage-backed security for the foundation's portfolio. The mortgage market has shown recent signs of turmoil due to a spike in mortgage rates and a decline in new and existing home sales, and Hurst believes that yields on MBS are at attractive levels.

Hurst is considering the two securities described in Exhibits 1 and 2. Both are specified-pool, seasoned issues. Security A is a non-conforming private-issue mortgage passthrough and Security B is a conventional Fannie Mae passthrough. Both are rated AAA.

Exhibit 1	MBS Descriptions					
	Par Value ($)	Passthrough Rate (%)	Pool Factor	Average Life (years)	WAC	WAM
Security A	1,175,000	5.60	0.72	10.44		
Security B	1,225,000	5.50	0.85	11.50	6.10%	136 months

Exhibit 2	Collateral Description Mortgage Pool Security A			
Loan	Outstanding Mortgage Balance ($)	Weight in Pool (%)	Mortgage Rate (%)	Months Remaining
1	152,000	17.88	5.80	156
2	86,000	10.12	6.32	169
3	92,000	10.82	6.15	150
4	128,000	15.06	6.20	175
5	185,000	21.77	6.00	187
6	101,000	11.88	5.75	162
7	106,000	12.47	6.25	157
Total	850,000	100.00		

42. In the prevailing economic environment, which of the following *best* describes the risk encountered by investors in mortgage passthrough securities?

   A. Extension risk, because prepayments are most likely to increase.

   B. Extension risk, because prepayments are most likely to decrease.

   C. Cycle risk, because prepayments are most likely to increase.

43. The WAC and WAM for Security A are *closest* to:

	WAC	WAM
A.	6.04%	167 months
B.	6.07%	165 months
C.	6.07%	167 months

44. Which of the securities is *most likely* subject to higher interest-rate risk?

   A. Security A, because it has a longer maturity.

   B. Security B, because it has a higher coupon.

   C. Security B, because it has a longer average life.

45. Given 150 PSA, the CPR (conditional prepayment rate) and SMM (single monthly mortality rate) for Security B for month 140 are *closest* to:

	CPR	SMM
A.	6.0%	0.5143%
B.	6.0%	0.7828%
C.	9.0%	0.7828%

46. The monthly mortgage-servicing fee for Security B is *closest* to:

A. 0.05%

B. 0.50%

C. 0.60%

47. Which of the two securities is *most likely* to have the lower credit risk?

A. Security A because it has the shortest average life.

B. Security B because it has an "agency" guarantee.

C. Security B because it has conventional mortgages.

SOLUTIONS FOR READING 45

1. A.

Month	Beginning Mortgage ($)	Mortgage Payment ($)	Interest ($)	Sch. Prin. Repayment ($)	End-of-Month Balance ($)
1	150,000.00	1,023.26	906.25	117.01	149,882.99
2	149,882.99	1,023.26	905.54	117.72	149,765.26
3	149,765.26	1,023.26	904.83	118.43	149,646.83
4	149,646.83	1,023.26	904.12	119.15	149,527.68
5	149,527.68	1,023.26	903.40	119.87	149,407.82
6	149,407.82	1,023.26	902.67	120.59	149,287.22
7	149,287.22	1,023.26	901.94	121.32	149,165.90
8	149,165.90	1,023.26	901.21	122.05	149,043.85
9	149,043.85	1,023.26	900.47	122.79	148,921.06
10	148,921.06	1,023.26	899.73	123.53	148,797.52
11	148,797.52	1,023.26	898.99	124.28	148,673.25
12	148,673.25	1,023.26	898.23	125.03	148,548.21
13	148,548.21	1,023.26	897.48	125.79	148,422.43
14	148,422.43	1,023.26	896.72	126.55	148,295.88

B.

Month	Beginning Mortgage ($)	Mortgage Payment ($)	Interest ($)	Sch. Prin. Repayment ($)	End-of-Month Balance ($)
357	4,031.97	1,023.26	24.36	998.90	3,033.07
358	3,033.07	1,023.26	18.32	1,004.94	2,028.13
359	2,028.13	1,023.26	12.25	1,011.01	1,017.12
360	1,017.12	1,023.26	6.15	1,017.12	0.00

2. A. The monthly servicing fee is found by dividing the servicing fee of 0.005 (50 basis points) by 12. The monthly servicing fee is therefore 0.0004167. Multiplying the monthly servicing fee by the beginning mortgage balance gives the servicing fee for the month.

Month	Beginning Mortgage ($)	Mortgage Payment ($)	Servicing Fee ($)	Net Interest ($)	Sch. Prin. Repayment ($)	End-of-Month Balance ($)
1	150,000.00	1,023.26	62.50	843.75	117.01	149,882.99
2	149,882.99	1,023.26	62.45	843.09	117.72	149,765.26
3	149,765.26	1,023.26	62.40	842.43	118.43	149,646.83
4	149,646.83	1,023.26	62.35	841.76	119.15	149,527.68
5	149,527.68	1,023.26	62.30	841.09	119.87	149,407.82
6	149,407.82	1,023.26	62.25	840.42	120.59	149,287.22

B. The investor's cash flow is the sum of the net interest and the scheduled principal repayment.

Month	Net Interest ($)	Sch. Prin. Repayment ($)	Investor Cash Flow ($)
1	843.75	117.01	960.76
2	843.09	117.72	960.81
3	842.43	118.43	960.86
4	841.76	119.15	960.91
5	841.09	119.87	960.96
6	840.42	120.59	961.01

3. The statement is incorrect. While the guarantee by the U.S. government means that there will not be a loss of principal and that interest payments will be made in full, there is uncertainty about the timing of the principal repayments because the borrower may prepay at any time, in whole or in part.

4. A and B. The weighted average coupon (WAC) and weighted average maturity (WAM) for the mortgage pool are computed below:

Loan	Outstanding Mortgage Balance ($)	Weight in Pool (%)	Mortgage Rate (%)	Months Remaining	WAC (%)	WAM
1	215,000	26.06	6.75	200	1.7591	52.12
2	185,000	22.42	7.75	185	1.7379	41.48
3	125,000	15.15	7.25	192	1.0985	29.09
4	100,000	12.12	7.00	210	0.8485	25.45
5	200,000	24.24	6.50	180	1.5758	43.64
Total	825,000	100.00			7.02	191.79

WAC = 7.02% WAM = 192 (rounded)

5. A. The SMM is equal to

$$\frac{\$2,450,000}{\$260,000,000 - \$1,000,000} = 0.009459 = 0.9459\%$$

B. Mr. Jamison should interpret the SMM as follows: 0.9459% of the mortgage pool available to prepay in month 42 prepaid in the month.

C. Given the SMM, the CPR is computed using Equation 2 in the reading:

$$CPR = 1 - (1 - SMM)^{12}$$

Therefore,

$$CPR = 1 - (1 - 0.009459)^{12} = 0.107790 = 10.78\%$$

D. Mr. Jamison should interpret the CPR as follows: ignoring scheduled principal payments, approximately 10.79% of the outstanding mortgage balance at the beginning of the year will be prepaid by the end of the year.

6. The CPR and SMM for each month are shown below:

Month	PSA	CPR	SMM
5	100	0.010	0.000837
15	80	0.024	0.002022

Month	PSA	CPR	SMM
20	175	0.070	0.006029
27	50	0.027	0.002278
88	200	0.120	0.010596
136	75	0.045	0.003829
220	225	0.135	0.012012

7. According to the PSA prepayment benchmark, after month 30 the CPR is constant over the life of the security. Specifically, it is equal to

$$\text{CPR} = 6\% \times (\text{PSA}/100)$$

So, for example, if the assumed PSA is 225, the CPR for the life of the security is

$$\text{CPR} = 6\% \times (225/100) = 13.5\%$$

Thus, the statement is correct that one CPR can be used to describe the PSA 30 months after the origination of the mortgages.

8. The amount of the prepayment for the month is determined as follows:

$$(\text{Beginning mortgage balance} - \text{Scheduled principal payment}) \times \text{SMM}$$

We know that

$$(\$537,000,000 - \$440,000) \times \text{SMM}$$

The CPR for month 140 assuming 175 PSA is

$$\text{CPR} = 6\% \times (175/100) = 10.5\%$$

The SMM is then

$$\text{SMM} = 1 - (1 - 0.105)^{0.08333} = 0.009201$$

Therefore, the prepayment in month 140 is

$$(\$537,000,000 - \$440,000) \times 0.009201 = \$4,936,889 (\text{rounded})$$

(Note: You will get a slightly different answer if you carried the SMM to more decimal places.)

9. The PSA model, or PSA prepayment benchmark, is not a prepayment model in that it does not predict prepayments for a mortgage-backed security. It is a generic benchmark that hypothesizes about what the pattern of prepayments will be over the life of a mortgage-backed security—that there is a prepayment ramp (that increases linearly) for 30 months, after which the CPR is assumed to be constant for the life of the security.

10. **A.** GNMA refers to passthrough securities issued by the Government National Mortgage Association. "30-YEAR" indicates that the mortgage loans were originated with 30-year terms.

B. This means GNMA 30-year passthrough securities with a coupon rate of 8.5% that were originated in 1994.

C. These are the prepayment rates that are projected for various periods. The prepayment rates are expressed in term of the PSA prepayment benchmark. There is a prepayment rate projection for each of the subsequent three months, a prepayment rate projection for one year, and a long-term prepayment rate.

D. First, the prepayments are only for 7.5% coupon GNMA issues originated in 1993. But there are many 7.5% coupon GNMA issues that were issued in 1993. The prepayments are for a generic issue. This means that when a specific Ginnie Mae 7.5% coupon originated in 1993 is delivered to the buyer, it can realize a prepayment rate quite different from the generic prepayment rate in the report, but on average, 1993 GNMA 7.5%'s are projected to have this prepayment rate.

E. One factor that affects prepayments is the prevailing mortgage rate relative to the rate that borrowers are paying on the underlying mortgages. As noted in the question, the mortgage rate at the time was 8.13%. The higher the coupon rate, the higher the rate that the borrowers in the underlying mortgage pool are paying and the greater the incentive to prepay. So, as the coupon rate increases, prepayments are expected to be greater because of the incentive to prepay.

11. Since the mortgage passthrough being analyzed has been outstanding for more than 15 years, there have been probably several opportunities for borrowers in the underlying mortgage pool to refinance at a lower rate than they are paying. Consequently, the low mortgage rate of 8% relative to 13% may not result in an increase in prepayments and the same is true for a further decline over the year to 7%. This characteristic of prepayments is referred to as "prepayment burnout."

12. An investor in a short-term security is concerned with extension risk. This is the risk that the security's average life will increase.

13. A. For tranche A:

Month	Sch. Principal Repayment/ Prepayments ($)	Beginning Principal ($)	Tranche A Principal Repayment ($)	Interest at 6% ($)	Cash Flow ($)
1	520,000	3,000,000	520,000	15,000	535,000
2	510,000	2,480,000	510,000	12,400	522,400
3	490,000	1,970,000	490,000	9,850	499,850
4	450,000	1,480,000	450,000	7,400	457,400
5	448,000	1,030,000	448,000	5,150	453,150
6	442,000	582,000	442,000	2,910	444,910
7	410,000	140,000	140,000	700	140,700
		Total	3,000,000		

From months 8 through 48, the principal repayment, interest, and cash flow are zero.

B. For tranche B:

Month	Sch. Principal Repayment/ Prepayments ($)	Beginning Principal ($)	Tranche B Principal Repayment($)	Interest at 7% ($)	Cash Flow ($)
1	520,000	8,000,000	0	46,667	46,667
2	510,000	8,000,000	0	46,667	46,667
3	490,000	8,000,000	0	46,667	46,667
4	450,000	8,000,000	0	46,667	46,667
5	448,000	8,000,000	0	46,667	46,667
6	442,000	8,000,000	0	46,667	46,667
7	410,000	8,000,000	270,000	46,667	316,667

(continued)

Month	Sch. Principal Repayment/ Prepayments ($)	Beginning Principal ($)	Tranche B Principal Repayment($)	Interest at 7% ($)	Cash Flow ($)
8	405,000	7,730,000	405,000	45,092	450,092
9	400,000	7,325,000	400,000	42,729	442,729
10	396,000	6,925,000	396,000	40,396	436,396
11	395,000	6,529,000	395,000	38,086	433,086
12	390,000	6,134,000	390,000	35,782	425,782
13	388,000	5,744,000	388,000	33,507	421,507
14	385,000	5,356,000	385,000	31,243	416,243
15	380,000	4,971,000	380,000	28,998	408,998
16	377,000	4,591,000	377,000	26,781	403,781
17	375,000	4,214,000	375,000	24,582	399,582
18	370,000	3,839,000	370,000	22,394	392,394
19	369,000	3,469,000	369,000	20,236	389,236
20	366,000	3,100,000	366,000	18,083	384,083
21	300,000	2,734,000	300,000	15,948	315,948
22	298,000	2,434,000	298,000	14,198	312,198
23	292,000	2,136,000	292,000	12,460	304,460
24	290,000	1,844,000	290,000	10,757	300,757
25	287,000	1,554,000	287,000	9,065	296,065
26	285,000	1,267,000	285,000	7,391	292,391
27	283,000	982,000	283,000	5,728	288,728
28	280,000	699,000	280,000	4,078	284,078
29	278,000	419,000	278,000	2,444	280,444
30	275,000	141,000	141,000	823	141,823
		Total	8,000,000		

For months 31 through 48 the principal payment, interest, and cash flow are zero.

C. For tranche C:

Month	Sch. Principal Repayment Prepayments ($)	Beginning Principal ($)	Tranche C Principal Repayment($)	Interest at 8% ($)	Cash Flow ($)
1	520,000	30,000,000	0	200,000	200,000
2	510,000	30,000,000	0	200,000	200,000
3	490,000	30,000,000	0	200,000	200,000
4	450,000	30,000,000	0	200,000	200,000
5	448,000	30,000,000	0	200,000	200,000
6	442,000	30,000,000	0	200,000	200,000
7	410,000	30,000,000	0	200,000	200,000
8	405,000	30,000,000	0	200,000	200,000
9	400,000	30,000,000	0	200,000	200,000
10	396,000	30,000,000	0	200,000	200,000
11	395,000	30,000,000	0	200,000	200,000
12	390,000	30,000,000	0	200,000	200,000
13	388,000	30,000,000	0	200,000	200,000

Month	Sch. Principal Repayment Prepayments ($)	Beginning Principal ($)	Tranche C Principal Repayment($)	Interest at 8% ($)	Cash Flow ($)
14	385,000	30,000,000	0	200,000	200,000
15	380,000	30,000,000	0	200,000	200,000
16	377,000	30,000,000	0	200,000	200,000
17	375,000	30,000,000	0	200,000	200,000
18	370,000	30,000,000	0	200,000	200,000
19	369,000	30,000,000	0	200,000	200,000
20	366,000	30,000,000	0	200,000	200,000
21	300,000	30,000,000	0	200,000	200,000
22	298,000	30,000,000	0	200,000	200,000
23	292,000	30,000,000	0	200,000	200,000
24	290,000	30,000,000	0	200,000	200,000
25	287,000	30,000,000	0	200,000	200,000
26	285,000	30,000,000	0	200,000	200,000
27	283,000	30,000,000	0	200,000	200,000
28	280,000	30,000,000	0	200,000	200,000
29	278,000	30,000,000	0	200,000	200,000
30	275,000	30,000,000	134,000	200,000	334,000
31	271,000	29,866,000	271,000	199,107	470,107
32	270,000	29,595,000	270,000	197,300	467,300
33	265,000	29,325,000	265,000	195,500	460,500
34	260,000	29,060,000	260,000	193,733	453,733
35	255,000	28,800,000	255,000	192,000	447,000
36	252,000	28,545,000	252,000	190,300	442,300
37	250,000	28,293,000	250,000	188,620	438,620
38	245,000	28,043,000	245,000	186,953	431,953
39	240,000	27,798,000	240,000	185,320	425,320
40	210,000	27,558,000	210,000	183,720	393,720
41	200,000	27,348,000	200,000	182,320	382,320
42	195,000	27,148,000	195,000	180,987	375,987
43	190,000	26,953,000	190,000	179,687	369,687
44	185,000	26,763,000	185,000	178,420	363,420
45	175,000	26,578,000	175,000	177,187	352,187
46	170,000	26,403,000	170,000	176,020	346,020
47	166,000	26,233,000	166,000	174,887	340,887
48	164,000	26,067,000	164,000	173,780	337,780

D. The average life for tranche A is computed as follows:

Month	Tranche A Principal Repayment ($)	Month × Principal Repayment ($)
1	520,000	520,000
2	510,000	1,020,000
3	490,000	1,470,000

(continued)

Month	Tranche A Principal Repayment ($)	Month × Principal Repayment ($)
4	450,000	1,800,000
5	448,000	2,240,000
6	442,000	2,652,000
7	140,000	980,000
Total	3,000,000	10,682,000

$$\text{Average life} = \frac{\$10,682,000}{12(\$3,000,000)} = 0.30$$

14. A. The coupon interest that would be paid to tranche C is diverted as principal repayment to tranche A. In the table below, the total principal paid to tranche A is tranche A's principal repayment as in KMF-01 plus the interest diverted from tranche C.

Month	Beginning Principal for Tranche A ($)	Principal Repayment before C int[a] ($)	Interest at 6% ($)	Principal for Tranche C ($)	Tranche C Diverted to Tranche A ($)	Principal Repayment for Tranche A ($)	Cash Flow ($)
1	3,000,000	520,000	15,000	30,000,000	200,000	720,000	735,000
2	2,280,000	510,000	11,400	30,200,000	201,333	711,333	722,733
3	1,568,667	490,000	7,843	30,401,333	202,676	692,676	700,519
4	875,991	450,000	4,380	30,604,009	204,027	654,027	658,407
5	221,964	448,000	1,110	30,808,036	205,387	221,964	223,074
					Total	3,000,000	

[a]This is the amount before the accrued interest from Tranche C is allocated to Tranche A.

B. The principal balance for tranche C is increased each month by the amount of interest diverted from tranche C to tranche A. The principal balance for the first five months is shown in the fifth column of the schedule for part A.

C.

Month	Principal Repayment for Tranche A ($)	Month × Principal ($)
1	720,000	720,000
2	711,333	1,422,667
3	692,676	2,078,027
4	654,027	2,616,107
5	221,964	1,109,822
	3,000,000	7,946,622

$$\text{Average life} = \frac{\$7,946,622}{12(\$3,000,000)} = 0.22$$

The average life is shorter for tranche A in KMF-02 relative to KMF-01 due to the presence of the accrual tranche.

15. There is typically a floor placed on an inverse floater to prevent the coupon rate from being negative. In order to fund this floor, the floater must be capped.

16. The principal payments that would have gone to the tranche used to create the floater and inverse floater are distributed proportionately to the floater and inverse floater based on their percentage of the par value. That is, if the floater's par value is 80% of the tranche from which it is created and the inverse floater 20%, then if $100 is received in principal payment, $80 is distributed to the floater and $20 to the inverse floater. The effect is that the average life for the floater and the inverse floater will be the same as the tranche from which they are created, six years in this example.

17. A CMO redistributes prepayment risk by using rules for the distribution of principal payments and interest payments from the collateral. The collateral for a CMO has prepayment risk and its cash flow consists of interest payments and principal payments (both scheduled principal and prepayments). Prepayment risk consists of contraction risk and extension risk. In a CMO there are different bond classes (tranches) which are exposed to different degrees of prepayment risk. The exposure to different degrees of prepayment risk relative to the prepayment risk for the collateral underlying a CMO is due to rules as to how the principal and the interest are to be redistributed to the CMO tranches—hence, redistributing prepayment risk amongst the tranches in the structure. In the simplest type of CMO structure—a sequential-pay structure—the rules for the distribution of the cash flow are such that some tranches receive some protection against extension risk while other tranches in the CMO have some protection against contraction risk. In a CMO with PAC tranches, the rules for the distribution of the cash flow result in the PAC tranches having protection against both contraction risk and extension risk while the support tranches (non-PAC tranches) have greater prepayment risk than the underlying collateral for the CMO.

18. By creating any mortgage-backed security, prepayment risk cannot ever be eliminated. Rather, the character of prepayment risk can be altered. Specifically, prepayment risk consists of contraction risk and extension risk. A CMO alters but does not eliminate the prepayment risk of the underlying mortgage loans. Therefore, the statement is incorrect.

19. Ms. Morgan should inform the trustee that the statement about the riskiness of the different sectors of the mortgage-backed securities market in terms of prepayment risk is incorrect. There are CMO tranches that expose an investor to less prepayment risk—in terms of extension or contraction risk— than the mortgage passthrough securities from which the CMO was created. There are CMO tranche types such as planned amortization classes that have considerably less prepayment risk than the mortgage passthrough securities from which the CMO was created. However, in order to create CMO tranches such as PACs, it is necessary to create tranches where there is considerable prepayment risk—prepayment risk that is greater than the underlying mortgage passthrough securities. These tranches are called support tranches.

20. A support tranche is included in a structure in which there are PAC tranches. The sole purpose of the support tranche is to provide prepayment protection for the PAC tranches. Consequently, support tranches are exposed to substantial prepayment risk.

21. The manager of an S&L portfolio is concerned with prepayment risk but more specifically extension risk. Moreover, to better match the average life of the investment to that of the S&L's funding cost, the manager will seek a shorter term investment. With the Fannie Mae PAC issue with an average life of 2 years the manager is buying a shorter term security and one with some protection against extension risk. In contrast, the Fannie Mae passthrough

is probably a longer term average life security because of its WAM of 310 months, and it will expose the S&L to substantial extension risk. Therefore, the Fannie Mae PAC tranche is probably a better investment from an asset/liability perspective.

22. Since the prepayments are assumed to be at a constant prepayment rate over the PAC tranche's life at 140 PSA, which is within the PSA collar in which the PAC was created, the average life will be equal to five years.

23. A. The PAC tranche will have the least average life variability. This is because the PAC tranche is created to provide protection against extension risk and contraction risk—the support tranches providing the protection.

   B. The support tranche will have the greatest average life variability. This is because it is designed to absorb the prepayment risk to provide protection for the PAC tranche.

24. The PAC structure in KMF-06 will have less prepayment protection than in KMF-05 because the support tranche is smaller ($200 million in KMF-06 versus $350 for KMF-05).

25. A. The PAC II is a support tranche and as a result will have more average life variability than the PAC I tranche. Consequently, PAC I has the less average life variability.

   B. The support tranche without a schedule must provide prepayment protection for both the PAC I and the PAC II. Therefore, the support tranche without a schedule will have greater average life variability than the PAC II.

26. In a PAC tranche structure in which the PAC tranches are paid off in sequence, the support tranches absorb any excess prepayments above the scheduled amount. Once the support tranches are paid off, any prepayments must go to the PAC tranche that is currently receiving principal payments. Thus, the structure effectively becomes a typical (plain vanilla) sequential-pay structure.

27. If the prepayments are well below the initial upper PAC collar, this means that there will be more support tranches available four years after the deal is structured than if prepayments were actually at the initial upper PAC collar. This means that there will be more support tranches to absorb prepayments. Hence, the effective upper collar will increase.

28. The notional amount of an 8% IO tranche is computed below:

Tranche	Par Amount ($)	Coupon Rate (%)	Excess Interest (%)	Excess Dollar Interest ($)	Notional Amount for an 8% Coupon Rate IO ($)
A	400,000,000	6.25	1.75	7,000,000	87,500,000
B	200,000,000	6.75	1.25	2,500,000	31,250,000
C	225,000,000	7.50	0.50	1,125,000	14,062,500
D	175,000,000	7.75	0.25	437,500	5,468,750
	Notional amount for 8% IO				138,281,250

29. A. The coupon rate for tranche G is found as follows:

$$\text{Coupon interest for tranche F in Structure I} = \$500,000,000 \times 0.085$$
$$= \$42,500,000$$

$$\text{Coupon interest for tranche F in Structure II} = \$200,000,000 \times 0.0825$$
$$= \$16,500,000$$

Coupon interest available to tranche G in Structure II

$$= \$42,500,000 - \$16,500,000 = \$26,000,000$$

$$\text{Coupon rate for tranche G} = \frac{\$26,000,000}{\$300,000,000} = 0.0867 = 8.67\%$$

B. There is no effect on the average life of the PAC tranches because the inclusion of the PAC II only impacts the support tranche in Structure I compared to Structure II.

C. There is greater average life variability for tranche G in Structure II than tranche F in Structure I because tranche G must provide prepayment protection in Structure II for not only the PACs but also tranche F.

30. A broken or busted PAC is a structure where all of the support tranches (the tranches that provide prepayment support for the PAC tranches in a structure) are completely paid off.

31. **A.** The formula for the cap rate on the inverse floater:

$$\frac{\text{Inverse floater interest when reference rate for floater is zero}}{\text{Principal for inverse floater}}$$

The total interest to be paid to tranche C if it was not split into the floater and the inverse floater is the principal of $96,500,000 times 7.5%, or $7,237,500. The maximum interest for the inverse floater occurs if 1-month LIBOR is zero. In that case, the coupon rate for the floater is

1-month LIBOR + 1% = 1%

Since the floater receives 1% on its principal of $80,416,667, the floater's interest is $804,167. The remainder of the interest of $7,237,500 from tranche C goes to the inverse floater. That is, the inverse floater's interest is $6,433,333 (= $7,237,500 − $804,167). Since the inverse floater's principal is $16,083,333.33, the cap rate for the inverse floater is

$$\frac{\$6,433,333}{\$16,083,333} = 40.0\%$$

B. Assuming a floor of zero for inverse floater, the cap rate is determined as follows:

$$\text{Cap rate for floater} = \frac{\text{Collateral tranche interest}}{\text{Principal for floater}}$$

The collateral tranche interest is $7,237,500. The floater principal is $80,416,667. Therefore,

$$\text{Cap rate for floater} = \frac{\$7,237,500}{\$80,416,667} = 9\%$$

32. **A.** The PAC collar indicates the prepayment protection afforded the investor in a PAC tranche. Prepayment protection means the ability of the collateral to satisfy the PAC tranche's schedule of principal payments. The initial PAC collar only indicates the protection at issuance. As prepayments occur over time, the amount of the support tranches decline and, as a result, the PAC collars change. In fact, in the extreme case, if the support tranches pay off completely, there is no longer a PAC collar since there is no longer prepayment protection for the PAC tranche.

B. To assess the prepayment protection at any given time for the PAC tranche, the effective PAC collar is computed. This measure is computed by determining the PSA prepayment rate range that given the current amount of the support tranche would be able to meet the remaining PAC schedule.

33. **A.** For a mortgage loan, the higher the loan-to-value ratio, the greater the credit risk faced by a lender. The reason is that if the property is repossessed and sold, the greater the ratio, the greater the required sale price necessary to recover the loan amount.

B. Studies of residential mortgage loans have found that the loan-to-value ratio is a key determinant of whether a borrower will default and that the higher the ratio, the greater the likelihood of default.

34. **A.** Mortgage strips are created when the principal (both scheduled principal repayments plus prepayments) and the coupon interest are allocated to different bond classes. The tranche that is allocated the principal payments is called the principal-only mortgage strip, and the tranche that is allocated the coupon interest is called the interest-only mortgage strip.

B. With an interest-only mortgage strip, there is no specific amount that will be received over time since the coupon interest payments depend on how prepayments occur over the security's life. In contrast, for a Treasury strip created from the coupon interest, the amount and the timing of the single cash flow is known with certainty.

C. Because prepayments increase when interest rates decrease and prepayments decrease when interest rates increase, the expected cash flow changes in the same direction as the change in interest rates. Thus, when interest rates increase, prepayments are expected to decrease and there will be an increase in the expected coupon interest payments since more of the underlying mortgages are expected to be outstanding. This will typically increase the value of an interest-only mortgage strip because the increase in the expected cash flow more than offsets the higher discount rates used to discount the cash flow. When interest rates decrease, the opposite occurs. So, an interest-only mortgage strip's value is expected to change in the same direction as the change in interest rates.

35. **A.** The purchase price per $100 par value is 1.02. Therefore

$$1.02 \times \$10,000,000 \times 0.72 = \$7,344,000$$

The investor pays $7,344,000 plus accrued interest.

B. Because the value and characteristics of a principal-only mortgage strip are highly sensitive to the underlying mortgage pool, an investor would not want the seller to have the option of which specific trust to deliver. If the trade is done on a TBA basis, the seller has the choice of the trust to deliver. To avoid this, a trade is done by the buyer specifying the trust that he or she is purchasing.

36. Ginnie Mae, Fannie Mae, and Freddie Mac have underwriting standards that must be met in order for a mortgage loan to qualify for inclusion in a mortgage pool underlying an agency mortgage-backed security. Mortgage loans that do qualify are called conforming loans. A loan may fail to be conforming because the loan balance exceeds the maximum permitted by the underwriting standard or the loan-to-value ratio is too high, or the payment-to-income ratio is too high. Loans that do not qualify are called nonconforming loans.

37. Since there is no implicit or explicit government guarantee for a nonagency mortgage-backed security, a mechanism is needed to reduce credit risk for bondholders when there are defaults. That is, there is a need to "enhance" the credit of the securities issued. These mechanisms are called credit enhancements, of which there are two types, internal and external.

38. With a residential mortgage loan the lender relies on the ability of the borrower to repay and has recourse to the borrower if the payment terms are not satisfied. In contrast, commercial mortgage loans are nonrecourse loans, which means that the lender can only look to the income-producing property backing the loan for interest and principal repayment. Should a default occur, the lender looks to the proceeds from the sale of the property for repayment and has no recourse to the borrower for any unpaid balance.

39. The figure used for "value" in the loan-to-value ratio is either market value or appraised value. In valuing commercial property, there can be considerable variance in the estimates of the property's market value. Thus, investors tend to be skeptical about estimates of market value and the resulting LTVs reported for properties in a pool of commercial loans. Therefore, the debt-to-service ratio is more objective, and a more reliable measure of risk.

40. A. Call protection at the loan level is provided in one or more of the following forms: 1) prepayment lockout, 2) defeasance, 3) prepayment penalty points, and 4) yield maintenance charges. A prepayment lockout is a contractual agreement that prohibits any prepayments during the lockout period (from 2 to 5 years). After the lockout period, call protection comes in the form of either prepayment penalty points or yield maintenance charges. With defeasance, rather than prepaying a loan, the borrower provides sufficient funds for the servicer to invest in a portfolio of Treasury securities that replicates the cash flows that would exist in the absence of prepayments. Prepayment penalty points are predetermined penalties that must be paid by the borrower if the borrower wishes to refinance. Yield maintenance charge provisions are designed to make the lender whole if prepayments are made.

B. A CMBS deal can be structured as a sequential-pay structure, thereby providing tranches some form of protection against prepayment risk at the structure level.

41. Typically commercial loans are balloon loans that require substantial principal payment at the end of the term of the loan. Balloon risk is the risk that a borrower will not be able to make the balloon payment because either the borrower cannot arrange for refinancing at the balloon payment date or cannot sell the property to generate sufficient funds to pay off the balloon balance. Since the term of the loan will be extended by the lender during the workout period, balloon risk is also referred to as extension risk.

42. B is correct. Extension risk describes the risk that mortgage prepayments will slow down more than the investor anticipates. Slow prepayments are associated with a rise in interest rates, declining housing turnover, or changing characteristics of underlying residential mortgage loans.

43. A is correct. The WAC is the weighted-average of the coupon rates for each mortgage in the pool, and the WAM is the weighted-average remaining months to maturity for each mortgage in the pool.

$$WAC = 0.1788(5.80\%) + 0.1012(6.32\%) + 0.1082(6.15\%) +$$
$$0.1506(6.20\%) + 0.2177(6.00\%) + 0.1188(5.75\%) +$$
$$0.1247(6.25\%) = 6.04\%$$
$$WAM = 0.1788(156) + 0.1012(169) + 0.1082(150) + 0.1506(175) +$$
$$0.2177(187) + 0.1188(162) + 0.1247(157) = 167.11 \approx 167\,months$$

44. C is correct. Security B has the longer average life and is considered to have the greater interest rate risk. In the bond market, for a given coupon, the greater the maturity, the greater the interest rate risk. For mortgage-backed securities, the legal maturity (the time until the last scheduled principal payment) does not give investors much information regarding the characteristics of the security as related to interest rate risk. Prepayments must be accounted for as well as scheduled payments. Therefore, for mortgage-backed securities, market participants generally use the weighted-average life (or simply average life) as the convention-based average time to receipt of principal payments or as the appropriate measure of maturity in evaluating interest-rate risk.

45. C is correct. Because the pool is seasoned more than 30 months, we use 6% as the CPR of the 100 PSA prepayment benchmark. The CPR of a mortgage pool is equal to the CPR of the PSA benchmark × (PSA of mortgage pool/100).

CPR of Security B = $6\% \times (150/100) = 9.0\%$. This is an annual rate.

The SMM is a monthly rate. $\text{SMM} = 1 - (1 - 0.09)^{1/12} = 1 - (0.91)^{0.08333} = 0.007828 = 0.7828\%$.

46. A is correct. The monthly mortgage servicing fee is the difference between the mortgage rate and the passthrough rate divided by 12.

Servicing fee = $(6.10\% - 5.50\%)/12 = 0.05\%$

47. B is correct. Security B has less credit risk since it is guaranteed by Fannie Mae, a corporate instrumentality of the U.S. government. Generally, nonagency securities are considered to be exposed to credit risk. The fact that Security A has non-conforming mortgages does not necessarily mean it has lower credit quality.

46

Asset-Backed Sector of the Bond Market

by Frank J. Fabozzi, CFA

LEARNING OUTCOMES

Mastery	The candidate should be able to:
☐	**a** describe the basic structural features of and parties to a securitization transaction;
☐	**b** explain and contrast prepayment tranching and credit tranching;
☐	**c** distinguish between the payment structure and collateral structure of a securitization backed by amortizing assets and non-amortizing assets;
☐	**d** distinguish among various types of external and internal credit enhancements;
☐	**e** describe cash flow and prepayment characteristics for securities backed by home equity loans, manufactured housing loans, automobile loans, student loans, SBA loans, and credit card receivables;
☐	**f** describe collateralized debt obligations (CDOs), including cash and synthetic CDOs;
☐	**g** distinguish among the primary motivations for creating a collateralized debt obligation (arbitrage and balance sheet transactions).

INTRODUCTION

1

As an alternative to the issuance of a bond, a corporation can issue a security backed by loans or receivables. Debt instruments that have as their collateral loans or receivables are referred to as asset-backed securities. The transaction in which asset-backed securities are created is referred to as a **securitization**.

While the major issuers of asset-backed securities are corporations, municipal governments use this form of financing rather than issuing municipal bonds and several European central governments use this form of financing. In the United States, the first type of asset-backed security (ABS) was the residential mortgage loan. We discussed the resulting securities, referred to as mortgage-backed securities, in the reading on the mortgage-backed sector of the bond market. Securities backed by other types of assets (consumer and business loans and receivables) have been issued throughout the

Fixed Income Analysis for the Chartered Financial Analyst Program, Second Edition, by Frank J. Fabozzi, CFA. Copyright © 2005 by CFA Institute.

world. The largest sectors of the asset-backed securities market in the United States are securities backed by credit card receivables, auto loans, home equity loans, manufactured housing loans, student loans, Small Business Administration loans, corporate loans, and bonds (corporate, emerging market, and structured financial products). Since home equity loans and manufactured housing loans are backed by real estate property, the securities backed by them are referred to as **real estate-backed asset-backed securities**. Other asset-backed securities include securities backed by home improvement loans, health care receivables, agricultural equipment loans, equipment leases, music royalty receivables, movie royalty receivables, and municipal parking ticket receivables. Collectively, these products are called **credit-sensitive structured products**.

In this reading, we will discuss the securitization process, the basic features of a securitization transaction, and the major asset types that have been securitized. In the last section of this reading, we look at collateralized debt obligations. While this product has traditionally been classified as part of the ABS market, we will see how the structure of this product differs from that of a typical securitization.

There are two topics not covered in this reading. The first is the valuation of an ABS. This topic is covered in the reading on valuing mortgage-backed and asset-backed securities. Second, the factors considered by rating agencies in rating an ABS transaction are not covered here.

2   THE SECURITIZATION PROCESS AND FEATURES OF ABS

The issuance of an asset-backed security is more complicated than the issuance of a corporate bond. In this section, we will describe the securitization process and the parties to a securitization. We will do so using a hypothetical securitization.

A. The Basic Securitization Transaction

Quality Home Theaters Inc. (QHT) manufactures high-end equipment for home theaters. The cost of one of QHT's home theaters ranges from $20,000 to $200,000. Some of its sales are for cash, but the bulk of its sales are by installment sales contracts. Effectively, an installment sales contract is a loan to the buyer of the home theater who agrees to repay QHT over a specified period of time. For simplicity we will assume that the loans are typically for four years. The collateral for the loan is the home theater purchased by the borrower. The loan specifies an interest rate that the buyer pays.

The credit department of QHT makes the decision as to whether or not to extend credit to a customer. That is, the credit department will request a credit loan application form be completed by a customer and based on criteria established by QHT will decide on whether to extend a loan. The criteria for extending credit are referred to as underwriting standards. Because QHT is extending the loan, it is referred to as the originator of the loan. Moreover, QHT may have a department that is responsible for servicing the loan. Servicing involves collecting payments from borrowers, notifying borrowers who may be delinquent, and, when necessary, recovering and disposing of the collateral (i.e., home theater equipment in our illustration) if the borrower does not make loan repayments by a specified time. While the servicer of the loans need not be the originator of the loans, in our illustration we are assuming that QHT will be the servicer.

Now let's see how these loans can be used in a securitization. We will assume that QHT has $100 million of installment sales contracts. This amount is shown on QHT's balance sheet as an asset. We will further assume that QHT wants to raise $100 million. Rather than issuing corporate bonds for $100 million, QHT's treasurer decides to raise the funds via a securitization. To do so, QHT will set up a legal entity referred to as a **special purpose vehicle** (SPV). In our discussion of asset-backed securities we described the critical role of this legal entity; its role will become clearer in our illustration. In our illustration, the SPV that is set up is called *Homeview Asset Trust* (HAT). QHT will then sell to HAT $100 million of the loans. QHT will receive from HAT $100 million in cash, the amount it wanted to raise. But where does HAT get $100 million? It obtains those funds by selling securities that are backed by the $100 million of loans. These securities are the asset-backed securities we referred to earlier and we will discuss these further in Section 2.C.

In the prospectus, HAT (the SPV) would be referred to as either the "issuer" or the "trust." QHT, the seller of the collateral to HAT, would be referred to as the "seller." The prospectus might then state: "The securities represent obligations of the issuer only and do not represent obligations of or interests in Quality Home Theaters Inc. or any of its affiliates."

The transaction is diagramed in panel A of Exhibit 1 on the next page. In panel B, the parties to the transaction are summarized.

The payments that are received from the collateral are distributed to pay servicing fees, other administrative fees, and principal and interest to the security holders. The legal documents in a securitization (prospectus or private placement memorandum) will set forth in considerable detail the priority and amount of payments to be made to the servicer, administrators, and the security holders of each bond class. The priority and amount of payments are commonly referred to as the "waterfall" because the flow of payments in a structure is depicted as a waterfall.

B. Parties to a Securitization

Thus far we have discussed three parties to a securitization: the seller of the collateral (also sometimes referred to as the originator), the special purpose vehicle (referred to in a prospectus or private placement memorandum as the issuer or the trust), and the servicer. There are other parties involved in a securitization: attorneys, independent accountants, trustees, underwriters, rating agencies, and guarantors. All of these parties plus the servicer are referred to as "third parties" to the transaction.

There is a good deal of legal documentation involved in a securitization transaction. The attorneys are responsible for preparing the legal documents. The first is the *purchase agreement* between the seller of the assets (QHT in our illustration) and the SPV (HAT in our illustration).[1] The purchase agreement sets forth the representations and warranties that the seller is making about the assets. The second is one that sets forth how the cash flows are divided among the bond classes (i.e., the structure's waterfall). Finally, the attorneys create the *servicing agreement* between the entity engaged to service the assets (in our illustration QHT retained the servicing of the loans) and the SPV.

---

1 There are concerns that both the creditors to the seller of the collateral (QHT's creditors in our illustration) and the investors in the securities issued by the SPV have about the assets. Specifically, QHT's creditors will be concerned that the assets are being sold to the SPV at less than fair market value, thereby weakening their credit position. The buyers of the asset-backed securities will be concerned that the assets were purchased at less than fair market value, thereby weakening their credit position. Because of this concern, the attorney will issue an opinion that the assets were sold at a fair market value.

Exhibit 1	Securitization Illustration for QHT

Panel A: Securitization Process

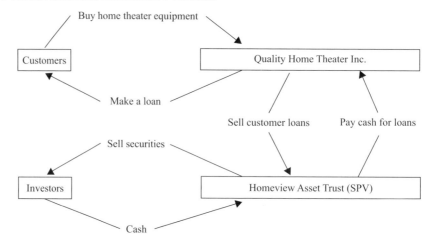

Panel B: Parties to the Securitization

Party	Description	Party in Illustration
Seller	Originates the loans and sells loans to the SPV	Quality Home Theaters Inc.
Issuer/Trust	The SPV that buys the loans from the seller and issues the asset-backed securities	Homeview Asset Trust
Servicer	Services the loans	Quality Home Theaters Inc.

An independent accounting firm will verify the accuracy of all numerical information placed in either the prospectus or private placement memorandum.[2] The result of this task results in a *comfort letter* for a securitization.

The trustee or trustee agent is the entity that safeguards the assets after they have been placed in the trust, receives the payments due to the bond holders, and provides periodic information to the bond holders. The information is provided in the form of *remittance reports* that may be issued monthly, quarterly or whenever agreed to by the terms of the prospectus or the private placement memorandum.

The underwriters and rating agencies perform the same function in a securitization as they do in a standard corporate bond offering. The rating agencies make an assessment of the collateral and the proposed structure to determine the amount of credit enhancement required to achieve a target credit rating for each bond class.

Finally, a securitization may have an entity that guarantees part of the obligations issued by the SPV. These entities are called guarantors and we will discuss their role in a securitization later.

C. Bonds Issued

Now let's take a closer look at the securities issued, what we refer to as the asset-backed securities.

---

2 The way this is accomplished is that a copy of the transaction's payment structure, underlying collateral, average life, and yield are supplied to the accountants for verification. In turn, the accountants reverse engineer the deal according to the deal's payment rules (i.e., the waterfall). Following the rules and using the same collateral that will actually generate the cash flows for the transaction, the accountants reproduce the yield and average life tables that are put into the prospectus or private placement memorandum.

A simple transaction can involve the sale of just one bond class with a par value of $100 million in our illustration. We will call this Bond Class A. Suppose HAT issues 100,000 certificates for Bond Class A with a par value of $1,000 per certificate. Then, each certificate holder would be entitled to 1/100,000 of the payment from the collateral after payment of fees and expenses. Each payment made by the borrowers (i.e., the buyers of the home theater equipment) consists of principal repayment and interest.

A structure can be more complicated. For example, there can be rules for distribution of principal and interest other than on a pro rata basis to different bond classes. As an example, suppose HAT issues Bond Classes A1, A2, A3, and A4 whose total par value is $100 million as follows:

Bond Class	Par Value ($ in Millions)
A1	40
A2	30
A3	20
A4	10
Total	100

As with a collateralized mortgage obligation (CMO) structure described in the reading on the mortgage-backed sector of the bond market, there are different rules for the distribution of principal and interest to these four bond classes or tranches. A simple structure would be a sequential-pay one. In a basic sequential-pay structure, each bond class receives periodic interest. However, the principal is repaid as follows: all principal received from the collateral is paid first to Bond Class A1 until it is fully paid off its $40 million par value. After Bond Class A1 is paid off, all principal received from the collateral is paid to Bond Class A2 until it is fully paid off. All principal payments from the collateral are then paid to Bond Class A3 until it is fully paid off, and then all principal payments are made to Bond Class A4.

The reason for the creation of the structure just described is to redistribute the prepayment risk among different bond classes. Prepayment risk is the uncertainty about the cash flow due to prepayments. This risk can be decomposed into contraction risk (i.e., the undesired shortening in the average life of a security) or extension risk (i.e., the undesired lengthening in the average life of a security). The creation of these bond classes is referred to as prepayment tranching or time tranching.

Now let's look at a more common structure in a transaction. As will be explained later, there are structures where there is more than one bond class, and the bond classes differ as to how they will share any losses resulting from defaults of the borrowers. In such a structure, the bond classes are classified as senior bond classes and subordinate bond classes. This structure is called a senior-subordinate structure. Losses are realized by the subordinate bond classes before there are any losses realized by the senior bond classes. For example, suppose that HAT issued $90 million par value of Bond Class A, the senior bond class, and $10 million par value of Bond Class B, the subordinate bond class. So the structure is as follows:

Bond Class	Par Value ($ in Millions)
A (senior)	90
B (subordinate)	10
Total	100

In this structure, as long as there are no defaults by the borrower greater than $10 million, then Bond Class A will be repaid fully its $90 million.

The purpose of this structure is to redistribute the credit risk associated with the collateral. This is referred to as credit tranching. As explained later, the senior-subordinate structure is a form of credit enhancement for a transaction.

There is no reason why only one subordinate bond class is created. Suppose that HAT issued the following structure:

Bond Class	Par Value ($ in Millions)
A (senior)	90
B (subordinate)	7
C (subordinate)	3
Total	100

In this structure, Bond Class A is the senior bond class while both Bond Classes B and C are subordinate bond classes from the perspective of Bond Class A. The rules for the distribution of losses would be as follows. All losses on the collateral are absorbed by Bond Class C before any losses are realized by Bond Classes A or B. Consequently, if the losses on the collateral do not exceed $3 million, no losses will be realized by Bond Classes A and B. If the losses exceed $3 million, Bond Class B absorbs the loss up to $7 million (its par value). As an example, if the total loss on the collateral is $8 million, Bond Class C loses its entire par value ($3 million) and Bond Class B realizes a loss of $5 million of its $7 million par value. Bond Class A does not realize any loss in this scenario. It should be clear that Bond Class A only realizes a loss if the loss from the collateral exceeds $10 million. The bond class that must absorb the losses first is referred to as the first loss piece. In our hypothetical structure, Bond Class C is the first loss piece.

Practice Question 1

Suppose that the structure for an asset-backed security structure is as follows:

senior bond class	$380 million
subordinated bond class 1	$40 million
subordinated bond class 2	$20 million

The value of the collateral for the structure is $440 million and subordinated bond class 2 is the first loss piece.

A. What is the amount of the loss for each bond class if losses due to defaults over the life of the structure total $15 million?

B. What is the amount of the loss for each bond class if losses due to defaults over the life of the structure total $50 million?

C. What is the amount of the loss for each bond class if losses due to defaults over the life of the structure total $90 million?

Now we will add just one more twist to the structure. Often in larger transactions, the senior bond class will be carved into different bond classes in order to redistribute the prepayment risk. For example, HAT might issue the following structure:

Bond Class	Par Value ($ in Millions)
A1 (senior)	35
A2 (senior)	28
A3 (senior)	15
A4 (senior)	12
B (subordinate)	7
C (subordinate)	3
Total	100

In this structure there is both prepayment tranching for the senior bond class (creation of Bond Classes A1, A2, A3, and A4) and credit tranching (creation of the senior bond classes and the two subordinate bond classes, Bond Classes B and C).

As explained in the reading on the mortgaged-backed sector of the bond market, a bond class in a securitization is also referred to as a "tranche." Consequently, throughout this reading the terms "bond class" and "tranche" are used interchangeably.

D. General Classification of Collateral and Transaction Structure

Later in this reading, we will describe some of the major assets that have been securitized. In general, the collateral can be classified as either amortizing or non-amortizing assets. Amortizing assets are loans in which the borrower's periodic payment consists of scheduled principal and interest payments over the life of the loan. The schedule for the repayment of the principal is called an amortization schedule. The standard residential mortgage loan falls into this category. Auto loans and certain types of home equity loans (specifically, closed-end home equity loans discussed later in this reading) are amortizing assets. Any excess payment over the scheduled principal payment is called a prepayment. Prepayments can be made to pay off the entire balance or a partial prepayment, called a curtailment.

In contrast to amortizing assets, non-amortizing assets require only minimum periodic payments with no scheduled principal repayment. If that payment is less than the interest on the outstanding loan balance, the shortfall is added to the outstanding loan balance. If the periodic payment is greater than the interest on the outstanding loan balance, then the difference is applied to the reduction of the outstanding loan balance. Since there is no schedule of principal payments (i.e., no amortization schedule) for a non-amortizing asset, the concept of a prepayment does not apply. A credit card receivable is an example of a non-amortizing asset.

The type of collateral—amortizing or non-amortizing—has an impact on the structure of the transaction. Typically, when amortizing assets are securitized, there is no change in the composition of the collateral over the life of the securities except for loans that have been removed due to defaults and full principal repayment due to prepayments or full amortization. For example, if at the time of issuance the collateral for an ABS consists of 3,000 four-year amortizing loans, then the same 3,000 loans will be in the collateral six months from now assuming no defaults and no prepayments. If, however, during the first six months, 200 of the loans prepay and 100 have defaulted, then the collateral at the end of six months will consist of 2,700 loans (3,000 – 200 – 100). Of course, the remaining principal of the 2,700 loans will decline because of scheduled principal repayments and any partial prepayments. All of the principal repayments from the collateral will be distributed to the security holders.

In contrast, for an ABS transaction backed by non-amortizing assets, the composition of the collateral changes. The funds available to pay the security holders are principal repayments and interest. The interest is distributed to the security holders. However, the principal repayments can be either 1) paid out to security holders or 2) reinvested by purchasing additional loans. What will happen to the principal repayments depends on the time since the transaction was originated. For a certain amount of time after issuance, all principal repayments are reinvested in additional loans. The period of time for which principal repayments are reinvested rather than paid out to the security holders is called the lockout period or revolving period. At the end of the lockout period, principal repayments are distributed to the security holders. The period when the principal repayments are not reinvested is called the principal amortization period. Notice that unlike the typical transaction that is backed by amortizing assets, the collateral backed by non-amortizing assets changes over time. A structure in which the principal repayments are reinvested in new loans is called a revolving structure.

While the receivables in a revolving structure may not be prepaid, all the bonds issued by the trust may be retired early if certain events occur. That is, during the lockout period, the trustee is required to use principal repayments to retire the securities rather than reinvest principal in new collateral if certain events occur. The most common trigger is the poor performance of the collateral. This provision that specifies the redirection of the principal repayments during the lockout period to retire the securities is referred to as the early amortization provision or rapid amortization provision.

Not all transactions that are revolving structures are backed by nonamortizing assets. There are some transactions in which the collateral consists of amortizing assets but during a lockout period, the principal repayments are reinvested in additional loans. For example, there are transactions in the European market in which the collateral consists of residential mortgage loans, but during the lockout period principal repayments are used to acquire additional residential mortgage loans.

E. Collateral Cash Flow

For an amortizing asset, projection of the cash flows requires projecting prepayments. One factor that may affect prepayments is the prevailing level of interest rates relative to the interest rate on the loan. In projecting prepayments it is critical to determine the extent to which borrowers take advantage of a decline in interest rates below the loan rate in order to refinance the loan.

As with nonagency mortgage-backed securities, described in the reading on the mortgage-backed sector of the bond market, modeling defaults for the collateral is critical in estimating the cash flows of an asset-backed security. Proceeds that are recovered in the event of a default of a loan prior to the scheduled principal repayment date of an amortizing asset represent a prepayment and are referred to as an involuntary prepayment. Projecting prepayments for amortizing assets requires an assumption about the default rate and the recovery rate. For a non-amortizing asset, while the concept of a prepayment does not exist, a projection of defaults is still necessary to project how much will be recovered and when.

The analysis of prepayments can be performed on a pool level or a loan level. In pool-level analysis it is assumed that all loans comprising the collateral are identical. For an amortizing asset, the amortization schedule is based on the gross weighted average coupon (GWAC) and weighted average maturity (WAM) for that single loan. We explained in the previous reading what the WAC and WAM of a pool of mortgage loans is and illustrated how it is computed. In this reading, we refer to the WAC as gross WAC. Pool-level analysis is appropriate where the underlying loans are homogeneous. Loan-level analysis involves amortizing each loan (or group of homogeneous loans).

The expected final maturity of an asset-backed security is the maturity date based on expected prepayments at the time of pricing of a deal. The legal final maturity can be two or more years after the expected final maturity. The average life, or weighted average life, was explained previously.

Also explained is a tranche's principal window, which refers to the time period over which the principal is expected to be paid to the bondholders. A principal window can be wide or narrow. When there is only one principal payment that is scheduled to be made to a bondholder, the bond is referred to as having a bullet maturity. Due to prepayments, an asset-backed security that is expected to have a bullet maturity may have an actual maturity that differs from that specified in the prospectus. Hence, asset-backed securities bonds that have an expected payment of only one principal are said to have a soft bullet.

F. Credit Enhancements

All asset-backed securities are credit enhanced. That means that support is provided for one or more of the bondholders in the structure. Credit enhancement levels are determined relative to a specific rating desired by the issuer for a security by each rating agency. Specifically, an investor in a triple A rated security expects to have "minimal" (virtually no) chance of losing any principal due to defaults. For example, a rating agency may require credit enhancement equal to four times expected losses to obtain a triple A rating or three times expected losses to obtain a double A rating. The amount of credit enhancement necessary depends on rating agency requirements.

There are two general types of credit enhancement structures: external and internal. We describe each type below.

1 External Credit Enhancements

In an ABS, there are two principal parties: the issuer and the security holder. The issuer in our hypothetical securitization is HAT. If another entity is introduced into the structure to guarantee any payments to the security holders, that entity is referred to as a "third party."

The most common third party in a securitization is a monoline insurance company (also referred to as a monoline insurer). A monoline insurance company is an insurance company whose business is restricted to providing guarantees for financial products such as municipal securities and asset-backed securities.[3] When a securitization has external credit enhancement that is provided by a monoline insurer, the securities are said to be "wrapped." The insurance works as follows. The monoline insurer agrees to make timely payment of interest and principal up to a specified amount should the issuer fail to make the payment. Unlike municipal bond insurance which guarantees the entire principal amount, the guarantee in a securitization is only for a percentage of the par value at origination. For example, a $100 million securitization may have only $5 million guaranteed by the monoline insurer.

Two less common forms of external credit enhancement are a letter of credit from a bank and a guarantee by the seller of the assets (i.e., the entity that sold the assets to the SPV—QHT in our hypothetical illustration).[4] The reason why these two forms of credit enhancement are less commonly used is because of the "weak link approach" employed by rating agencies when they rate securitizations. According to this approach, when rating a proposed structure, the credit quality of a security is

---

3 The major monoline insurance companies in the United States are Capital Markets Assurance Corporation (CapMAC), Financial Security Assurance Inc. (FSA), Financial Guaranty Insurance Corporation (FGIC), and Municipal Bond Investors Assurance Corporation (MBIA).

4 As noted earlier, the seller is not a party to the transaction once the assets are sold to the SPV who then issues the securities. Hence, if the seller provides a guarantee, it is viewed as a third-party guarantee.

only as good as the weakest link in its credit enhancement regardless of the quality of underlying assets. Consequently, if an issuer seeks a triple A rating for one of the bond classes in the structure, it would be unlikely to be awarded such a rating if the external credit enhancer has a rating that is less than triple A. Since few corporations and banks that issue letters of credit have a sufficiently high rating themselves to achieve the rating that may be sought in a securitization, these two forms of external credit enhancement are not as common as insurance.

There is credit risk in a securitization when there is a third-party guarantee because the downgrading of the third party *could* result in the downgrading of the securities in a structure.

2 Internal Credit Enhancements

Internal credit enhancements come in more complicated forms than external credit enhancements. The most common forms of internal credit enhancement are reserve funds, overcollateralization, and senior/subordinate structures.

Practice Question 2

Suppose that the collateral for an asset-backed securities structure has a gross weighted average coupon of 9.5%. The servicing fee is 75 basis points. The tranches issued have a weighted average coupon rate of 7.5%. What is the excess spread?

---

a. Reserve Funds   Reserve funds come in two forms:

■ cash reserve funds,

■ excess spread accounts.

Cash reserve funds are straight deposits of cash generated from issuance proceeds. In this case, part of the underwriting profits from the deal are deposited into a fund which typically invests in money market instruments. Cash reserve funds are typically used in conjunction with external credit enhancements.

Excess spread accounts involve the allocation of excess spread or cash into a separate reserve account after paying out the net coupon, servicing fee, and all other expenses on a monthly basis. The excess spread is a design feature of the structure. For example, suppose that:

1. gross weighted average coupon (gross WAC) is 8.00%—this is the interest rate paid by the borrowers

2. servicing and other fees are 0.25%

3. net weighted average coupon (net WAC) is 7.25%—this is the rate that is paid to all the tranches in the structure

So, for this hypothetical deal, 8.00% is available to make payments to the tranches, to cover servicing fees, and to cover other fees. Of that amount, 0.25% is paid for servicing and other fees and 7.25% is paid to the tranches. This means that only 7.50% must be paid out, leaving 0.50% (8.00% – 7.50%). This 0.50% or 50 basis points is called the excess spread. This amount is placed in a reserve account—the excess servicing account—and it will gradually increase and can be used to pay for possible future losses.

b. Overcollateralization   Overcollateralization in a structure refers to a situation in which the value of the collateral exceeds the amount of the par value of the outstanding securities issued by the SPV. For example, if $100 million par value of securities are issued and at issuance the collateral has a market value of $105, there is $5 million in overcollateralization. Over time, the amount of overcollateralization changes due to 1) defaults, 2) amortization, and 3) prepayments. For example, suppose that two years after issuance, the par value of the securities outstanding is $90 million and the value of the collateral at the time is $93 million. As a result, the overcollateralization is $3 million ($93 million − $90 million).

Overcollateralization represents a form of internal credit enhancement because it can be used to absorb losses. For example, if the liability of the structure (i.e., par value of all the bond classes) is $100 million and the collateral's value is $105 million, then the first $5 million of losses will not result in a loss to any of the bond classes in the structure.

c. Senior-Subordinate Structure   Earlier in this section we explained a senior-subordinate structure in describing the bonds that can be issued in a securitization. We explained that there are senior bond classes and subordinate bond classes. The subordinate bond classes are also referred to as junior bond classes or non-senior bond classes.

As explained earlier, the creation of a senior-subordinate structure is done to provide credit tranching. More specifically, the senior-subordinate structure is a form of internal credit enhancement because the subordinate bond classes provide credit support for the senior bond classes. To understand why, the hypothetical HAT structure with one subordinate bond class that was described earlier is reproduced below:

Bond Class	Par Value ($ in Millions)
A (senior)	90
B (subordinate)	10
Total	100

The senior bond class, A, is credit enhanced because the first $10 million in losses is absorbed by the subordinate bond class, B. Consequently, if defaults do not exceed $10 million, then the senior bond will receive the entire par value of $90 million.

Note that one subordinate bond class can provide credit enhancement for another subordinate bond class. To see this, consider the hypothetical HAT structure with two subordinate bond classes presented earlier:

Bond Class	Par Value ($ in Millions)
A (senior)	90
B (subordinate)	7
C (subordinate)	3
Total	100

Bond Class C, the first loss piece, provides credit enhancement for not only the senior bond class, but also the subordinate bond class B.

The basic concern in the senior-subordinate structure is that while the subordinate bond classes provide a certain level of credit protection for the senior bond class at the closing of the deal, the level of protection changes over time due to prepayments. Faster prepayments can remove the desired credit protection. Thus, the objective after the deal closes is to distribute any prepayments such that the credit protection for the senior bond class does not deteriorate over time.

In real-estate related asset-backed securities, as well as nonagency mortgage-backed securities, the solution to the credit protection problem is a well developed mechanism called the shifting interest mechanism. Here is how it works. The percentage of the mortgage balance of the subordinate bond class to that of the mortgage balance for the entire deal is called the level of subordination or the subordinate interest. The higher the percentage, the greater the level of protection for the senior bond classes. The subordinate interest changes after the deal is closed due to prepayments. That is, the subordinate interest shifts (hence the term "shifting interest"). The purpose of a shifting interest mechanism is to allocate prepayments so that the subordinate interest is maintained at an acceptable level to protect the senior bond class. In effect, by paying down the senior bond class more quickly, the amount of subordination is maintained at the desired level.

The prospectus will provide the shifting interest percentage schedule for calculating the senior prepayment percentage (the percentage of prepayments paid to the senior bond class). For mortgage loans, a commonly used shifting interest percentage schedule is as follows:

Year after Issuance	Senior Prepayment (%)
1–5	100
6	70
7	60
8	40
9	20
after year 9	0

So, for example, if prepayments in month 20 are $1 million, the amount paid to the senior bond class is $1 million and no prepayments are made to the subordinated bond classes. If prepayments in month 90 (in the seventh year after issuance) are $1 million, the senior bond class is paid $600,000 (60% × $1 million).

The shifting interest percentage schedule given in the prospectus is the "base" schedule. The set of shifting interest percentages can change over time depending on the performance of the collateral. If the performance is such that the credit protection for the senior bond class has deteriorated because credit losses have reduced the subordinate bond classes, the base shifting interest percentages are overridden and a higher allocation of prepayments is made to the senior bond class.

Performance analysis of the collateral is undertaken by the trustee for determining whether or not to override the base schedule. The performance analysis is in terms of tests, and if the collateral fails any of the tests, this will trigger an override of the base schedule.

It is important to understand that the presence of a shifting interest mechanism results in a trade-off between credit risk and contraction risk for the senior bond class. The shifting interest mechanism reduces the credit risk to the senior bond class. However, because the senior bond class receives a larger share of any prepayments, contraction risk increases.

G. Call Provisions

Corporate, federal agency, and municipal bonds may contain a call provision. This provision gives the issuer the right to retire the bond issue prior to the stated maturity date. The issuer motivation for having the provision is to benefit from a decline in interest rates after the bond is issued. Asset-backed securities typically have call provisions. The motivation is twofold. As with other bonds, the issuer (the SPV) will want to take advantage of a decline in interest rates. In addition, to reduce administrative fees, the trustee may want to call in the issue because the par value of a bond class is small and it is more cost-effective to pay off the one or more bond classes.

Typically, for a corporate, federal agency, and municipal bond the trigger event for a call provision is that a specified amount of time has passed.[5] In the case of asset-backed securities, it is not simply the passage of time whereby the trustee is permitted to exercise any call option. There are trigger events for exercising the call option based on the amount of the issue outstanding.

There are two call provisions where the trigger that grants the trustee to call in the issue is based on a date being reached: 1) call on or after specified date and 2) auction call. A call on or after specified date operates just like a standard call provision for corporate, federal agency, and municipal securities: once a specified date is reached, the trustee has the option to call all the outstanding bonds. In an auction call, at a certain date a call will be exercised if an auction results in the outstanding collateral being sold at a price greater than its par value. The premium over par value received from the auctioned collateral is retained by the trustee and is eventually distributed to the seller of the assets.

Provisions that allow the trustee to call an issue or a tranche based on the par value outstanding are referred to as optional clean-up call provisions. Two examples are 1) percent of collateral call and 2) percent of bond call. In a percent of collateral call, the outstanding bonds can be called at par value if the outstanding *collateral's* balance falls below a predetermined percent of the original collateral's balance. This is the most common type of clean-up call provision for amortizing assets and the predetermined level is typically 10%. For example, suppose that the value for the collateral is $100 million. If there is a percent of collateral call provision with a trigger of 10%, then the trustee can call the entire issue if the value of the call is $10 million or less. In a percent of bond call, the outstanding bonds can be called at par value if the outstanding *bond's* par value relative to the original par value of bonds issued falls below a specified amount.

There is a call option that combines two triggers based on the amount outstanding and date. In a latter of percent or date call, the outstanding bonds can be called if either 1) the collateral's outstanding balance reaches a predetermined level before the specified call date or 2) the call date has been reached even if the collateral outstanding is above the predetermined level.

In addition to the above call provisions which permit the trustee to call the bonds, there may be an insurer call. Such a call permits the insurer to call the bonds if the collateral's cumulative loss history reaches a predetermined level.

HOME EQUITY LOANS   **3**

A home equity loan (HEL) is a loan backed by residential property. At one time, the loan was typically a second lien on property that was already pledged to secure a first lien. In some cases, the lien was a third lien. In recent years, the character of a home equity loan has changed. Today, a home equity loan is often a first lien on property where the borrower has either an *impaired credit history* and/or the payment-to-income ratio is too high for the loan to qualify as a conforming loan for securitization by Ginnie Mae, Fannie Mae, or Freddie Mac. Typically, the borrower used a home equity loan to consolidate consumer debt using the current home as collateral rather than to obtain funds to purchase a new home.

Home equity loans can be either closed end or open end. A closed-end HEL is structured the same way as a fully amortizing residential mortgage loan. That is, it

---

5 The calling of a portion of the issue is permitted to satisfy any sinking fund requirement.

has a fixed maturity and the payments are structured to fully amortize the loan by the maturity date. With an open-end HEL, the homeowner is given a credit line and can write checks or use a credit card for up to the amount of the credit line. The amount of the credit line depends on the amount of the equity the borrower has in the property. Because home equity loan securitizations are predominately closed-end HELs, our focus in this section is securities backed by them.

There are both fixed-rate and variable-rate closed-end HELs. Typically, variable-rate loans have a reference rate of 6-month LIBOR and have periodic caps and lifetime caps. (A periodic cap limits the change in the mortgage rate from the previous time the mortgage rate was reset; a lifetime cap sets a maximum that the mortgage rate can ever be for the loan.) The cash flow of a pool of closed-end HELs is comprised of interest, regularly scheduled principal repayments, and prepayments, just as with mortgage-backed securities. Thus, it is necessary to have a prepayment model and a default model to forecast cash flows. The prepayment speed is measured in terms of a conditional prepayment rate (CPR).

A. Prepayments

As explained in the reading on the mortgage-backed sector of the bond market, in the agency MBS market the PSA prepayment benchmark is used as the base case prepayment assumption in the prospectus. This benchmark assumes that the conditional prepayment rate (CPR) begins at 0.2% in the first month and increases linearly for 30 months to 6% CPR. From month 30 to the last month that the security is expected to be outstanding, the CPR is assumed to be constant at 6%. At the time that the prepayment speed is assumed to be constant, the security is said to be seasoned. For the PSA benchmark, a security is assumed to be seasoned in month 30. When the prepayment speed is depicted graphically, the linear increase in the CPR from month 1 to the month when the security is assumed to be seasoned is called the prepayment ramp. For the PSA benchmark, the prepayment ramp begins at month 1 and extends to month 30. Speeds that are assumed to be faster or slower than the PSA prepayment benchmark are quoted as a multiple of the base case prepayment speed.

There are differences in the prepayment behavior for home equity loans and agency MBS. Wall Street firms involved in the underwriting and market making of securities backed by HELs have developed prepayment models for these deals. Several firms have found that the key difference between the prepayment behavior of HELs and agency residential mortgages is the important role played by the credit characteristics of the borrower.[6]

Borrower characteristics and the amount of seasoning (i.e., how long the loans have been outstanding) must be kept in mind when trying to assess prepayments for a particular deal. In the prospectus of an HEL, a base case prepayment assumption is made. Rather than use the PSA prepayment benchmark as the base case prepayment speed, issuer's now use a base case prepayment benchmark that is specific to that issuer. The benchmark prepayment speed in the prospectus is called the prospectus prepayment curve or PPC. As with the PSA benchmark, faster or slower prepayments speeds are quoted as a multiple of the PPC. Having an issuer-specific prepayment benchmark is preferred to a generic benchmark such as the PSA benchmark. The drawback for this improved description of the prepayment characteristics of a pool of mortgage loans is that it makes comparing the prepayment characteristics and investment characteristics of the collateral between issuers and issues (newly issued and seasoned issues) difficult.

---

6 Dale Westhoff and Mark Feldman, "Prepayment Modeling-Based Valuation of Home Equity Loan Securities," Chapter 18 in Frank J. Fabozzi, Chuck Ramsey, and Michael Marz (eds.), *The Handbook of Nonagency Mortgage-Backed Securities: Second Edition* (New Hope, PA: Frank J. Fabozzi Associates, 2000).

The base case prepayment for the Champion Home Equity Loan Trust 1996-1 is provided for the fixed-rate loans (referred to as Group One in the prospectus) and floating-rate loans (referred to as Group Two in the prospectus). The following is taken from the prospectus for the Group One loans:

> The model used with respect to the fixed rate certificates (the "prepayment ramp") assumes that the home equity loans in loan Group One prepay at a rate of 4% CPR in the first month after origination, and an additional 1.5% each month thereafter until the 14th month. Beginning in the 15th month and each month thereafter, the prepayment ramp assumes a prepayment rate of 25% CPR.

What is the CPR assuming 150% PPC for the fixed-rate collateral for the following months:

Month	CPR	Month	CPR	Month	CPR
1		11		30	
2		12		125	
3		13		150	
4		14		200	
5		15		250	
6		16		275	
7		17		300	
8		18		325	
9		19		350	
10		20		360	

Since HEL deals are backed by both fixed-rate and variable-rate loans, a separate PPC is provided for each type of loan. For example, in the prospectus for the Contimortgage Home Equity Loan Trust 1998-2, the base case prepayment assumption for the fixed-rate collateral begins at 4% CPR in month 1 and increases 1.45455% CPR per month until month 12, at which time it is 20% CPR. Thus, the collateral is assumed to be seasoned in 12 months. The prepayment ramp begins in month 1 and ends in month 12. If an investor analyzed the deal based on 200% PPC, this means doubling the CPRs cited and using 12 months for when the collateral seasons. For the variable-rate collateral in the ContiMortgage deal, 100% PPC assumes the collateral is seasoned after 18 months with the CPR in month 1 being 4% and increasing 1.82353% CPR each month. From month 18 on, the CPR is 35%. Thus, the prepayment ramp starts at month 1 and ends at month 18. Notice that for this issuer, the variable-rate collateral is assumed to season slower than the fixed-rate collateral (18 versus 12 months), but has a faster CPR when the pool is seasoned (35% versus 20%).

B. Payment Structure

As with nonagency mortgage-backed securities discussed in the reading on the mortgage-backed sector of the bond market, there are passthrough and paythrough home equity loan-backed structures.

Typically, home equity loan-backed securities are securitized by both closed-end fixed-rate and adjustable-rate (or variable-rate) HELs. The securities backed by the latter are called HEL floaters. The reference rate of the underlying loans typically is 6-month LIBOR. The cash flow of these loans is affected by periodic and lifetime caps on the loan rate.

Institutional investors that seek securities that better match their floating-rate funding costs are attracted to securities that offer a floating-rate coupon. To increase the attractiveness of home equity loan-backed securities to such investors, the securities typically have been created in which the reference rate is 1-month LIBOR. Because of 1) the mismatch between the reference rate on the underlying loans (6-month LIBOR) and that of the HEL floater and 2) the periodic and life caps of the underlying loans, there is a cap on the coupon rate for the HEL floater. Unlike a typical floater, which has a cap that is fixed throughout the security's life, the effective periodic and lifetime cap of an HEL floater is variable. The effective cap, referred to as the available funds cap, will depend on the amount of funds generated by the net coupon on the principal, less any fees.

Let's look at one issue, Advanta Mortgage Loan Trust 1995-2 issued in June 1995. At the offering, this issue had approximately $122 million closed-end HELs. There were 1,192 HELs consisting of 727 fixed-rate loans and 465 variable-rate loans. There were five classes (A-1, A-2, A-3, A-4, and A-5) and a residual. The five classes are summarized below:

Class	Paramount ($)	Passthrough Coupon Rate (%)
A-1	9,229,000	7.30
A-2	30,330,000	6.60
A-3	16,455,000	6.85
A-4	9,081,000	floating rate
A-5	56,917,000	floating rate

The collateral is divided into group I and group II. The 727 fixed-rate loans are included in group I and support Classes A-1, A-2, A-3, and A-4 certificates. The 465 variable-rate loans are in group II and support Class A-5.

Tranches have been structured in home equity loan deals so as to give some senior tranches greater prepayment protection than other senior tranches. The two types of structures that do this are the non-accelerating senior tranche and the planned amortization class tranche.

1 Non-Accelerating Senior Tranches

A non-accelerating senior tranche (NAS tranche) receives principal payments according to a schedule. The schedule is not a dollar amount. Rather, it is a principal schedule that shows for a given month the share of pro rata principal that must be distributed to the NAS tranche. A typical principal schedule for a NAS tranche is as follows:[7]

Months	Share of Pro Rata Principal (%)
1 through 36	0
37 through 60	45
61 through 72	80
73 through 84	100
After month 84	300

---

7 Charles Schorin, Steven Weinreich, and Oliver Hsiang, "Home Equity Loan Transaction Structures," Chapter 6 in Frank J. Fabozzi, Chuck Ramsey, and Michael Marz, *Handbook of Nonagency Mortgage-Backed Securities: Second Edition* (New Hope, PA: Frank J. Fabozzi Associates, 2000).

The average life for the NAS tranche is stable for a large range of prepayments because for the first three years all prepayments are made to the other senior tranches. This reduces the risk of the NAS tranche contracting (i.e., shortening) due to fast prepayments. After month 84, 300% of its pro rata share is paid to the NAS tranche, thereby reducing its extension risk.

The average life stability over a wide range of prepayments is illustrated in Exhibit 2. The deal analyzed is the ContiMortgage Home Equity Loan Trust 1997-2.[8] Class A-9 is the NAS tranche. The analysis was performed on Bloomberg shortly after the deal was issued using the issue's PPC. As can be seen, the average life is fairly stable between 75% to 200% PPC. In fact, the difference in the average life between 75% PPC and 200% PPC is slightly greater than one year.

In contrast, Exhibit 2 also shows the average life over the same prepayment scenarios for a non-NAS sequential-pay tranche in the same deal—Class A-7. Notice the substantial average life variability. While the average life difference between 75% and 200% PPC for the NAS tranche is just over 1 year, it is more than 9 years for the non-NAS tranche. Of course, the non-NAS in the same deal will be less stable than a regular sequential tranche because the non-NAS gets a greater share of principal than it would otherwise.

Exhibit 2	Average Life for NAS Tranche (Class A-9) and Non-NAS Tranche (Class A-7) for ContiMortgage Home Equity Loan Trust 1997-2 for a Range of Prepayments

| | % PPC | | | | | | | | | | | | Avg. Life Difference |
	0	50	75	100	120	150	200	250	300	350	400	500	75% to 200% PPC
Plateau CPR	0	10	15	20	24	30	40	50	60	70	80	100	
Avg. Life													
NAS Bond	11.71	7.81	7.06	6.58	6.30	6.06	5.97	3.98	2.17	1.73	1.38	0.67	1.09
Non-NAS Bond	21.93	14.54	11.94	8.82	6.73	4.71	2.59	1.96	1.55	1.25	1.03	0.58	9.35

Calculation: Bloomberg Financial Markets.
Reported in Charles Schorin, Steven Weinreich, and Oliver Hsiang, "Home Equity Loan Transaction Structures," Chapter 6 in Frank J. Fabozzi, Chuck Ramsey, and Michael Marz, *Handbook of Nonagency Mortgage-Backed Securities: Second Edition* (New Hope, PA: Frank J. Fabozzi Associates, 2000).

2 Planned Amortization Class Tranche

In our discussion of collateralized mortgage obligations issued by the agencies in the reading on the mortgage-backed sector of the bond market, we explained how a planned amortization class tranche can be created. These tranches are also created in HEL structures. Unlike agency CMO PAC tranches that are backed by fixed-rate loans, the collateral for HEL deals is both fixed rate and adjustable rate.

An example of an HEL PAC tranche in an HEL-backed deal is tranche A-6 in ContiMortgage 1998-2. We described the PPC for this deal in Section 3.A.1 above. There is a separate PAC collar for both the fixed-rate and adjustable-rate collateral. For the fixed-rate collateral the PAC collar is 125%–175% PPC; for the adjustable-rate collateral the PAC collar is 95%–130% PPC. The average life for tranche A-6 (a tranche backed by the fixed-rate collateral) is 5.1 years. As explained, the effective collar for shorter tranches can be greater than the upper collar specified in the prospectus. The effective upper collar for tranche A-6 is actually 180% PPC (assuming that the adjustable-rate collateral pays at 100% PPC).[9]

---

8 This illustration is from Schorin, Weinreich, and Hsiang, "Home Equity Loan Transaction Structures."
9 For a more detailed analysis of this tranche, see Schorin, Weinreich, and Hsiang, "Home Equity Loan Transaction Structures."

For shorter PACs, the effective upper collar is greater. For example, for tranche A-3 in the same deal, the initial PAC collar is 125% to 175% PPC with an average life of 2.02 years. However, the effective upper collar is 190% PPC (assuming the adjustable-rate collateral pays at 100% PPC).

The effective collar for PAC tranches changes over time based on actual prepayments and therefore based on when the support tranches depart from the initial PAC collar. For example, if for the next 36 months after the issuance of the ContiMortgage 1998-2 actual prepayments are a constant 150% PPC, then the effective collar would be 135% PPC to 210% PPC.[10] That is, the lower and upper collar will increase. If the actual PPC is 200% PPC for the 10 months after issuance, the support bonds will be fully paid off and there will be no PAC collateral. In this situation the PAC is said to be a broken PAC.

4   MANUFACTURED HOUSING-BACKED SECURITIES

Manufactured housing-backed securities are backed by loans for manufactured homes. In contrast to site-built homes, manufactured homes are built at a factory and then transported to a site. The loan may be either a mortgage loan (for both the land and the home) or a consumer retail installment loan.

Manufactured housing-backed securities are issued by Ginnie Mae and private entities. The former securities are guaranteed by the full faith and credit of the U.S. government. The manufactured home loans that are collateral for the securities issued and guaranteed by Ginnie Mae are loans guaranteed by the Federal Housing Administration (FHA) or Veterans Administration (VA).

Loans not backed by the FHA or VA are called conventional loans. Manufactured housing-backed securities that are backed by such loans are called conventional manufactured housing-backed securities. These securities are issued by private entities.

The typical loan for a manufactured home is 15 to 20 years. The loan repayment is structured to fully amortize the amount borrowed. Therefore, as with residential mortgage loans and HELs, the cash flow consists of net interest, regularly scheduled principal, and prepayments. However, prepayments are more stable for manufactured housing-backed securities because they are not sensitive to refinancing.

There are several reasons for this. First, the loan balances are typically small so that there is no significant dollar savings from refinancing. Second, the rate of depreciation of mobile homes may be such that in the earlier years depreciation is greater than the amount of the loan paid off. This makes it difficult to refinance the loan. Finally, typically borrowers are of lower credit quality and therefore find it difficult to obtain funds to refinance.

As with residential mortgage loans and HELs, prepayments on manufactured housing-backed securities are measured in terms of CPR and each issue contains a PPC.

The payment structure is the same as with nonagency mortgage-backed securities and home equity loan-backed securities.

5   RESIDENTIAL MBS OUTSIDE THE UNITED STATES

Throughout the world where the market for securitized assets has developed, the largest sector is the residential mortgage-backed sector. It is not possible to provide a discussion of the residential mortgage-backed securities market in every country. Instead, to provide a flavor for this market sector and the similarities with the U.S.

---

10 Schorin, Weinreich, and Hsiang, "Home Equity Loan Transaction Structures."

nonagency mortgage-backed securities market, we will discuss just the market in the United Kingdom and Australia.

A. U.K. Residential Mortgage-Backed Securities

In Europe, the country in which there has been the largest amount of issuance of asset-backed securities is the United Kingdom.[11] The largest component of that market is the residential mortgage-backed security market, which includes "prime" residential mortgage-backed securities and "nonconforming" residential mortgage-backed securities. In the U.S. mortgage market, a nonconforming mortgage loan is one that does not meet the underwriting standards of Ginnie Mae, Fannie Mae, or Freddie Mac. However, this does not mean that the loan has greater credit risk. In contrast, in the U.K. mortgage market, nonconforming mortgage loans are made to borrowers that are viewed as having greater credit risk—those that do not have a credit history and those with a history of failing to meet their obligations.

The standard mortgage loan is a variable rate, fully amortizing loan. Typically, the term of the loan is 25 years. As in the U.S. mortgage market, borrowers seeking a loan with a high loan-to-value ratio are required to obtain mortgage insurance, called a "mortgage indemnity guarantee" (MIG).

The deals are more akin to the nonagency market since there is no guarantee by a federally related agency or a government sponsored enterprise as in the United States. Thus, there is credit enhancement as explained below.

Because the underlying mortgage loans are floating rate, the securities issued are floating rate (typically, LIBOR is the reference rate). The cash flow depends on the timing of the principal payments. The deals are typically set up as a sequential-pay structure. For example, consider the Granite Mortgage 00-2 transaction, a typical structure in the United Kingdom.[12] The mortgage pool consists of prime mortgages. There are four bond classes. The two class A tranches, Class A-1 and Class A-2, are rated AAA. One is a dollar-denominated tranche and the other a pound sterling tranche. Class B is rated single A and tranche C is rated BBB. The sequence of principal payments is as follows: Class A-1 and Class A-2 are paid off on a pro rata basis, then Class B is paid off, and then Class C is paid off.

The issuer has the option to call the outstanding notes under the following circumstances:

■ a withholding tax is imposed on the interest payments to noteholders;

■ a clean-up call (if the mortgage pool falls to 10% or less of the original pool amount);

■ on a specified date (called the "step-up date") or dates in the future.

For example, for the Granite Mortgage 00-02 transaction, the step-up date is September 2007. The issuer is likely to call the issue because the coupon rate on the notes increases at that time. In this deal, as with most, the margin over LIBOR doubles.

Credit enhancement can consist of excess spread, reserve fund, and subordination. For the Granite Mortgage 00-2, there was subordination: Class B and C tranches for the two Class A tranche and Class C tranche for the Class B tranche. The reserve

---

11 Information about the U.K. residential mortgage-backed securities market draws from the following sources: Phil Adams, "UK Residential Mortgage-Backed Securities," and "UK Non-Conforming Residential Mortgage-Backed Securities," in *Building Blocks,* Asset-Backed Securities Research, Barclays Capital, January 2001; Christopher Flanagan and Edward Reardon, *European Structured Products: 2001 Review and 2002 Outlook,* Global Structured Finance Research, J.P. Morgan Securities Inc., January 11, 2002; and "UK Mortgages—MBS Products for U.S. Investors," *Mortgage Strategist,* UBS Warburg, February 27, 2001, pp. 15–21.
12 For a more detailed discussion of this structure, see Adams, "UK Residential Mortgage-Backed Securities," pp. 31–37.

was fully funded at the time of issuance, and the excess spread was used to build up the reserve fund. In addition, there is a "principal shortfall provision." This provision requires that if the realized losses for a period are such that the excess reserve for that period is not sufficient to cover the losses, as excess spread becomes available in future periods they are used to cover these losses. Also there are performance triggers that under certain conditions will provide further credit protection to the senior bonds by modifying the payment of principal. When the underlying mortgage pool consists of nonconforming mortgage loans, additional protections are provided for investors.

Since prepayments will reduce the average life of the senior notes in a transaction, typical deals have provisions that permit the purchase of substitute mortgages if the prepayment rate exceeds a certain rate. For example, in the Granite Mortgage 00-02 deal, this rate is 20% per annum.

B. Australian Mortgage-Backed Securities

In Australia, lending is dominated by mortgage banks, the larger ones being ANZ, Commonwealth Bank of Australia, National Australia Bank, Westpac, and St. George Bank.[13] Non-mortgage bank competitors who have entered the market have used securitization as a financing vehicle. The majority of the properties are concentrated in New South Wales, particularly the city of Sydney. Rating agencies have found that the risk of default is considerably less than in the U.S. and the U.K.

Loan maturities are typically between 20 and 30 years. As in the United States, there is a wide range of mortgage designs with respect to interest rates. There are fixed-rate, variable-rate (both capped and uncapped), and rates tied to a benchmark.

There is mortgage insurance for loans to protect lenders, called "lenders mortgage insurance" (LMI). Loans typically have LMI covering 20% to 100% of the loan. The companies that provide this insurance are private corporations.[14] When mortgage loans that do not have LMI are securitized, typically the issuer will purchase insurance for those loans.

LMI is important for securitized transactions since it is the first layer of credit enhancement in a deal structure. The rating agencies recognize this in rating the tranches in a structure. The amount that a rating agency will count toward credit enhancement for LMI depends on the rating agency's assessment of the mortgage insurance company.

When securitized, the tranches have a floating rate. There is an initial revolving period—which means that no principal payments are made to the tranche holders but instead reinvested in new collateral. As with the U.K. Granite Mortgage 00-02 deal, the issuer has the right to call the issue if there is an imposition of a withholding tax on note holders' interest payments, after a certain date, or if the balance falls below a certain level (typically, 10%).

Australian mortgage-backed securities have tranches that are U.S. dollar denominated and some that are denominated in euros.[15] These global deals typically have two or three AAA senior tranches and one AA or AA—junior tranche.

---

13 Information about the Australian residential mortgage-backed securities market draws from the following sources: Phil Adams, "Australian Residential Mortgage-Backed Securities," in *Building Blocks*; Karen Weaver, Eugene Xu, Nicholas Bakalar, and Trudy Weibel, "Mortgage-Backed Securities in Australia," Chapter 41 in *The Handbook of Mortgage-Backed Securities: Fifth Edition* (New York, NY: McGraw-Hill, 2001); and, "Australian Value Down Under," *Mortgage Strategist*, UBS Warburg, February 6, 2001, pp. 14–22.
14 The five major ones are Royal and Sun Alliance Lenders Mortgage Insurance Limited, CGU Lenders Mortgage Insurance Corporation Ltd., PMI mortgage insurance limited, GE Mortgage Insurance Property Ltd., and GE Mortgage Insurance Corporation.
15 The foreign exchange risk for these deals is typically hedged using various types of swaps (fixed/floating, floating/floating, and currency swaps).

For credit enhancement, there is excess spread (which in most deals is typically small), subordination, and, as noted earlier, LMI. To illustrate this, consider the Interstar Millennium Series 2000-3E Trust—a typical Australian MBS transaction. There are two tranches: a senior tranche (Class A) that was rated AAA and a subordinated tranche (Class B) that was AA–. The protection afforded the senior tranche is the subordinated tranche, LMI (all the properties were covered up to 100% and were insured by all five major mortgage insurance companies), and the excess spread.

AUTO LOAN-BACKED SECURITIES

6

Auto loan-backed securities represents one of the oldest and most familiar sectors of the asset-backed securities market. Auto loan-backed securities are issued by:

1. the financial subsidiaries of auto manufacturers

2. commercial banks

3. independent finance companies and small financial institutions specializing in auto loans

Historically, auto loan-backed securities have represented between 18% to 25% of the asset-backed securities market. The auto loan market is tiered based on the credit quality of the borrowers. "Prime auto loans" are of fundamentally high credit quality and originated by the financial subsidiaries of major auto manufacturers. The loans are of high credit quality for the following reasons. First, they are a secured form of lending. Second, they begin to repay principal immediately through amortization. Third, they are short-term in nature. Finally, for the most part, major issuers of auto loans have tended to follow reasonably prudent underwriting standards.

Unlike the sub-prime mortgage industry, there is less consistency on what actually constitutes various categories of prime and sub-prime auto loans. Moody's assumes the *prime* market is composed of issuers typically having cumulative losses of less than 3%; *near-prime* issuers have cumulative losses of 3–7%; and sub-prime issuers have losses exceeding 7%.

The auto sector was a small part of the European asset-backed securities market in 2002, about 5% of total securitization. There are two reasons for this. First, there is lower per capita car ownership in Europe. Second, there is considerable variance of tax and regulations dealing with borrower privacy rules in Europe, thereby making securitization difficult.[16] Auto deals have been done in Italy, the U.K., Germany, Portugal, and Belgium.

A. Cash Flow and Prepayments

The cash flow for auto loan-backed securities consists of regularly scheduled monthly loan payments (interest and scheduled principal repayments) and any prepayments. For securities backed by auto loans, prepayments result from 1) sales and trade-ins requiring full payoff of the loan, 2) repossession and subsequent resale of the automobile, 3) loss or destruction of the vehicle, 4) payoff of the loan with cash to save on the interest cost, and 5) refinancing of the loan at a lower interest cost.

Prepayments due to repossession and subsequent resale are sensitive to the economic cycle. In recessionary economic periods, prepayments due to this factor increase. While refinancings may be a major reason for prepayments of mortgage loans, they are of minor importance for automobile loans. Moreover, the interest rates for the

---

16 Flanagan and Reardon, *European Structures Products: 2001 Review and 2002 Outlook*, p. 9.

automobile loans underlying some deals are substantially below market rates since they are offered by manufacturers as part of a sales promotion.

B. Measuring Prepayments

For most asset-backed securities where there are prepayments, prepayments are measured in terms of the conditional prepayment rate, CPR. As explained in the reading on the mortgage-backed sector of the bond market, monthly prepayments are quoted in terms of the single monthly mortality (SMM) rate. The *convention* for calculating and reporting prepayment rates for auto loan-backed securities is different. Prepayments for auto loan-backed securities are measured in terms of the absolute prepayment speed, denoted by ABS.[17] The ABS is the monthly prepayment expressed as a percentage of the original collateral amount. The SMM (monthly CPR) expresses prepayments based on the prior month's balance.

There is a mathematical relationship between the SMM and the ABS measures. Letting M denote the number of months after loan origination, the SMM rate can be calculated from the ABS rate using the following formula:

$$SMM = \frac{ABS}{1 - \left[ABS \times (M - 1) \right]}$$

where the ABS and SMM rates are expressed in decimal form.

For example, if the ABS rate is 1.5% (i.e., 0.015) at month 14 after origination, then the SMM rate is 1.86%, as shown below:

$$SMM = \frac{0.015}{1 - \left[0.015 \times (14 - 1) \right]} = 0.0186 = 1.86\%$$

Practice Question 4

A. If the ABS for a security is 2% at month 11, what is the corresponding SMM?

B. If the SMM for a security is 1.7% at month 21, what is the corresponding ABS?

The ABS rate can be calculated from the SMM rate using the following formula:

$$ABS = \frac{SMM}{1 + \left[SMM \times (M - 1) \right]}$$

For example, if the SMM rate at month 9 after origination is 1.3%, then the ABS rate is:

$$ABS = \frac{0.013}{1 + \left[0.013 \times (9 - 1) \right]} = 0.0118 = 1.18\%$$

Historically, when measured in terms of SMM rate, auto loans have experienced SMMs that increase as the loans season.

---

17 The only reason for the use of ABS rather than SMM/CPR in this sector is historical. Auto loan-backed securities (which were popularly referred to at one time as CARS (Certificates of Automobile Receivables)) were the first non-mortgage assets to be developed in the market. (The first non-mortgage asset-backed security was actually backed by computer lease receivables.) The major dealer in this market at the time, First Boston (now Credit Suisse First Boston) elected to use ABS for measuring prepayments. You may wonder how one obtains "ABS" from "absolute prepayment rate." Again, it is historical. When the bond market first started, the ABS measure probably meant "asset-backed security" but over time to avoid confusion evolved to absolute prepayment rate.

STUDENT LOAN-BACKED SECURITIES

Student loans are made to cover college cost (undergraduate, graduate, and professional programs such as medical and law school) and tuition for a wide range of vocational and trade schools. Securities backed by student loans, popularly referred to as SLABS (student loan asset-backed securities), have similar structural features as the other asset-backed securities we discussed above.

The student loans that have been most commonly securitized are those that are made under the Federal Family Education Loan Program (FFELP). Under this program, the government makes loans to students via private lenders. The decision by private lenders to extend a loan to a student is not based on the applicant's ability to repay the loan. If a default of a loan occurs and the loan has been properly serviced, then the government will guarantee up to 98% of the principal plus accrued interest.[18]

Loans that are not part of a government guarantee program are called alternative loans. These loans are basically consumer loans, and the lender's decision to extend an alternative loan will be based on the ability of the applicant to repay the loan. Alternative loans have been securitized.

A. Issuers

Congress created Fannie Mae and Freddie Mac to provide liquidity in the mortgage market by allowing these government sponsored enterprises to buy mortgage loans in the secondary market. Congress created the Student Loan Marketing Association (nicknamed "Sallie Mae") as a government sponsored enterprise to purchase student loans in the secondary market and to securitize pools of student loans. Since its first issuance in 1995, Sallie Mae is now the major issuer of SLABS, and its issues are viewed as the benchmark issues.[19] Other entities that issue SLABS are either traditional corporate entities (e.g., the Money Store and PNC Bank) or non-profit organizations (Michigan Higher Education Loan Authority and the California Educational Facilities Authority). The SLABS of the latter typically are issued as tax-exempt securities and therefore trade in the municipal market. In recent years, several not-for-profit entities have changed their charter and applied for "for profit" treatment.

B. Cash Flow

Let's first look at the cash flow for the student loans themselves. There are different types of student loans under the FFELP including subsidized and unsubsidized Stafford loans, Parental Loans for Undergraduate Students (PLUS), and Supplemental Loans to Students (SLS). These loans involve three periods with respect to the borrower's payments—deferment period, grace period, and loan repayment period. Typically, student loans work as follows. While a student is in school, no payments are made by the student on the loan. This is the deferment period. Upon leaving school, the student is extended a grace period of usually six months when no payments on the loan must be made. After this period, payments are made on the loan by the borrower.

Student loans are floating-rate loans, exclusively indexed to the 3-month Treasury bill rate. As a result, some issuers of SLABs issue securities whose coupon rate is indexed to the 3-month Treasury bill rate. However, a large percentage of SLABS issued are indexed to LIBOR floaters.[20]

---

18 Actually, depending on the origination date, the guarantee can be up to 100%.

19 In 1997 Sallie Mae began the process of unwinding its status as a GSE; until this multi-year process is completed, all debt issued by Sallie Mae under its GSE status will be "grandfathered" as GSE debt until maturity.

20 This creates a mismatch between the collateral and the securities. Issuers have dealt with this by hedging with the risk by using derivative instruments such as interest rate swaps (floating-to-floating rate swaps) or interest rate caps.

Prepayments typically occur due to defaults or loan consolidation. Even if there is no loss of principal faced by the investor when defaults occur, the investor is still exposed to contraction risk. This is the risk that the investor must reinvest the proceeds at a lower spread and in the case of a bond purchased at a premium, the premium will be lost. Studies have shown student loan prepayments are insensitive to the level of interest rates. Consolidations of a loan occur when the student who has loans over several years combines them into a single loan. The proceeds from the consolidation are distributed to the original lender and, in turn, distributed to the bondholders.

8   SBA LOAN-BACKED SECURITIES

The Small Business Administration (SBA) is an agency of the U.S. government empowered to guarantee loans made by approved SBA lenders to qualified borrowers. The loans are backed by the full faith and credit of the government. Most SBA loans are variable-rate loans where the reference rate is the prime rate. The rate on the loan is reset monthly on the first of the month or quarterly on the first of January, April, July, and October. SBA regulations specify the maximum coupon allowable in the secondary market. Newly originated loans have maturities between 5 and 25 years.

The Small Business Secondary Market Improvement Act passed in 1984 permitted the pooling of SBA loans. When pooled, the underlying loans must have similar terms and features. The maturities typically used for pooling loans are 7, 10, 15, 20, and 25 years. Loans without caps are not pooled with loans that have caps.

Most variable-rate SBA loans make monthly payments consisting of interest and principal repayment. The amount of the monthly payment for an individual loan is determined as follows. Given the coupon formula of the prime rate plus the loan's quoted margin, the interest rate is determined for each loan. Given the interest rate, a level payment amortization schedule is determined. It is this level payment that is paid for the next month until the coupon rate is reset.

The monthly cash flow that the investor in an SBA-backed security receives consists of:

- the coupon interest based on the coupon rate set for the period;
- the scheduled principal repayment (i.e., scheduled amortization);
- prepayments.

Prepayments for SBA-backed securities are measured in terms of CPR. Voluntary prepayments can be made by the borrower without any penalty. There are several factors contributing to the prepayment speed of a pool of SBA loans. A factor affecting prepayments is the maturity date of the loan. It has been found that the fastest speeds on SBA loans and pools occur for shorter maturities.[21] The purpose of the loan also affects prepayments. There are loans for working capital purposes and loans to finance real estate construction or acquisition. It has been observed that SBA pools with maturities of 10 years or less made for working capital purposes tend to prepay at the fastest speed. In contrast, loans backed by real estate that are long maturities tend to prepay at a slow speed.

9   CREDIT CARD RECEIVABLE-BACKED SECURITIES

When a purchase is made on a credit card, the issuer of the credit card (the lender) extends credit to the cardholder (the borrower). Credit cards are issued by banks (e.g., Visa and MasterCard), retailers (e.g., Sears and Target Corporation), and travel

---

21 Donna Faulk, "SBA Loan-Backed Securities," in *Asset-Backed Securities*.

and entertainment companies (e.g., American Express). At the time of purchase, the cardholder is agreeing to repay the amount borrowed (i.e., the cost of the item purchased) plus any applicable finance charges. The amount that the cardholder has agreed to pay the issuer of the credit card is a receivable from the perspective of the issuer of the credit card. Credit card receivables are used as collateral for the issuance of an asset-backed security.

A. Cash Flow

For a pool of credit card receivables, the cash flow consists of finance charges collected, fees, and principal. Finance charges collected represent the periodic interest the credit card borrower is charged based on the unpaid balance after the grace period. Fees include late payments fees and any annual membership fees.

Interest to security holders is paid periodically (e.g., monthly, quarterly, or semiannually). The interest rate may be fixed or floating—roughly half of the securities are floaters. The floating rate is uncapped.

A credit card receivable-backed security is a nonamortizing security. For a specified period of time, the lockout period or revolving period, the principal payments made by credit card borrowers comprising the pool are retained by the trustee and reinvested in additional receivables to maintain the size of the pool. The lockout period can vary from 18 months to 10 years. So, during the lockout period, the cash flow that is paid out to security holders is based on finance charges collected and fees. After the lockout period, the principal is no longer reinvested but paid to investors. The principal-amortization period and the various types of structures are described next.

B. Payment Structure

There are three different amortization structures that have been used in credit card receivable-backed security deals: 1) passthrough structure, 2) controlled-amortization structure, and 3) bullet-payment structure. The latter two are the more common. One source reports that 80% of the deals are bullet structures and the balance are controlled amortization structures.[22]

In a passthrough structure, the principal cash flows from the credit card accounts are paid to the security holders on a pro rata basis. In a controlled-amortization structure, a scheduled principal amount is established, similar to the principal window for a PAC bond. The scheduled principal amount is sufficiently low so that the obligation can be satisfied even under certain stress scenarios, where cash flow is decreased due to defaults or slower repayment by borrowers. The security holder is paid the lesser of the scheduled principal amount and the pro rata amount. In a bullet-payment structure, the security holder receives the entire amount in one distribution. Since there is no assurance that the entire amount can be paid in one lump sum, the procedure is for the trustee to place principal monthly into an account that generates sufficient interest to make periodic interest payments and accumulate the principal to be repaid. These deposits are made in the months shortly before the scheduled bullet payment. This type of structure is also often called a soft bullet because the maturity is technically not guaranteed, but is almost always satisfied. The time period over which the principal is accumulated is called the accumulation period.

C. Performance of the Portfolio of Receivables

There are several concepts that must be understood in order to assess the performance of the portfolio of receivables and the ability of the issuer to meet its interest obligation and repay principal as scheduled.

---

22 Thompson, "MBNA Tests the Waters."

We begin with the concept of the gross portfolio yield. This yield includes finance charges collected and fees. Charge-offs represent the accounts charged off as uncollectible. Net portfolio yield is equal to gross portfolio yield minus charge-offs. The net portfolio yield is important because it is from this yield that the bondholders will be paid. So, for example, if the average yield (WAC) that must be paid to the various tranches in the structure is 5% and the net portfolio yield for the month is only 4.5%, there is the risk that the bondholder obligations will not be satisfied.

Delinquencies are the percentages of receivables that are past due for a specified number of months, usually 30, 60, and 90 days. They are considered an indicator of potential future charge-offs.

The monthly payment rate (MPR) expresses the monthly payment (which includes finance charges, fees, and any principal repayment) of a credit card receivable portfolio as a percentage of credit card debt outstanding in the previous month. For example, suppose a $500 million credit card receivable portfolio in January realized $50 million of payments in February. The MPR would then be 10% ($50 million divided by $500 million).

There are two reasons why the MPR is important. First, if the MPR reaches an extremely low level, there is a chance that there will be extension risk with respect to the principal payments on the bonds. Second, if the MPR is very low, then there is a chance that there will not be sufficient cash flows to pay off principal. This is one of the events that could trigger early amortization of the principal (described below).

At issuance, portfolio yield, charge-offs, delinquency, and MPR information are provided in the prospectus. Information about portfolio performance is then available from Bloomberg, the rating agencies, and dealers.

D. Early Amortization Triggers

There are provisions in credit card receivable-backed securities that require early amortization of the principal if certain events occur. Such provisions, which as mentioned earlier in this reading are referred to as early amortization or rapid amortization provisions, are included to safeguard the credit quality of the issue. The only way that the principal cash flows can be altered is by the triggering of the early amortization provision.

Typically, early amortization allows for the rapid return of principal in the event that the 3-month average excess spread earned on the receivables falls to zero or less. When early amortization occurs, the credit card tranches are retired sequentially (i.e., first the AAA bond, then the AA rated bond, etc.). This is accomplished by paying the principal payments made by the credit card borrowers to the investors instead of using them to purchase more receivables. The length of time until the return of principal is largely a function of the monthly payment rate. For example, suppose that a AAA tranche is 82% of the overall deal. If the monthly payment rate is 11%, then the AAA tranche would return principal over a 7.5-month period (82%/11%). An 18% monthly payment rate would return principal over a 4.5-month period (82%/18%).

10   COLLATERALIZED DEBT OBLIGATIONS

A collateralized debt obligation (CDO) is a security backed by a diversified pool of one or more of the following types of debt obligations:

■ U.S. domestic high-yield corporate bonds;

■ structured financial products (i.e., mortgage-backed and asset-backed securities);

- emerging market bonds;
- bank loans;
- special situation loans and distressed debt.

When the underlying pool of debt obligations are bond-type instruments (high-yield corporate, structured financial products, and emerging market bonds), a CDO is referred to as a collateralized bond obligation (CBO). When the underlying pool of debt obligations are bank loans, a CDO is referred to as a collateralized loan obligation (CLO).

A. Structure of a CDO

In a CDO structure, there is an asset manager responsible for managing the portfolio of debt obligations. There are restrictions imposed (i.e., restrictive covenants) as to what the asset manager may do and certain tests that must be satisfied for the tranches in the CDO to maintain the credit rating assigned at the time of issuance and determine how and when tranches are repaid principal.

The funds to purchase the underlying assets (i.e., the bonds and loans) are obtained from the issuance of debt obligations (i.e., tranches) and include one or more senior tranches, one or more mezzanine tranches, and a subordinate/equity tranche. There will be a rating sought for all but the subordinate/equity tranche. For the senior tranches, at least an A rating is typically sought. For the mezzanine tranches, a rating of BBB but no less than B is sought. As explained below, since the subordinate/equity tranche receives the residual cash flow, no rating is sought for this tranche.

The ability of the asset manager to make the interest payments to the tranches and pay off the tranches as they mature depends on the performance of the underlying assets. The proceeds to meet the obligations to the CDO tranches (interest and principal repayment) can come from 1) coupon interest payments of the underlying assets, 2) maturing assets in the underlying pool, and 3) sale of assets in the underlying pool.

In a typical structure, one or more of the tranches is a floating-rate security. With the exception of deals backed by bank loans which pay a floating rate, the asset manager invests in fixed-rate bonds. Now that presents a problem—paying tranche investors a floating rate and investing in assets with a fixed rate. To deal with this problem, the asset manager uses derivative instruments to be able to convert fixed-rate payments from the assets into floating-rate payments. In particular, interest rate swaps are used. This derivative instrument allows a market participant to swap fixed-rate payments for floating-rate payments or vice versa. Because of the mismatch between the nature of the cash flows of the debt obligations in which the asset manager invests and the floating-rate liability of any of the tranches, the asset manager must use an interest rate swap. A rating agency will require the use of swaps to eliminate this mismatch.

B. Family of CDOs

The family of CDOs is shown in Exhibit 3. While each CDO shown in the exhibit will be discussed in more detail below, we will provide an overview here.

The first breakdown in the CDO family is between cash CDOs and synthetic CDOs. A cash CDO is backed by a pool of cash market debt instruments. We described the range of debt obligations earlier. These were the original types of CDOs issued. A synthetic CDO is a CDO where the investor has the economic exposure to a pool of debt instrument, but this exposure is realized via a credit derivative instrument rather than the purchase of the cash market instruments. We will discuss the basic elements of a synthetic CDO later.

Exhibit 3	CDO Family Tree

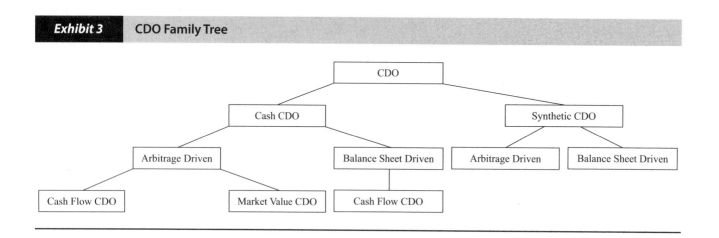

Both a cash CDO and a synthetic CDO are further divided based on the motivation of the sponsor. The motivation leads to balance sheet and arbitrage CDOs. As explained below, in a balance sheet CDO, the motivation of the sponsor is to remove assets from its balance sheet. In an arbitrage CDO, the motivation of the sponsor is to capture a spread between the return that it is possible to realize on the collateral backing the CDO and the cost of borrowing funds to purchase the collateral (i.e., the interest rate paid on the obligations issued).

Cash CDOs that are arbitrage transactions are further divided in cash flow and market value CDOs depending on the primary source of the proceeds from the underlying asset used to satisfy the obligation to the tranches. In a cash flow CDO, the primary source is the interest and maturing principal from the underlying assets. In a market value CDO, the proceeds to meet the obligations depend heavily on the total return generated from the portfolio. While cash CDOs that are balance sheet motivated transactions can also be cash flow or market value CDOs, only cash flow CDOs have been issued.

C. Cash CDOs

In this section, we take a closer look at cash CDOs. Before we look at cash flow and market value CDOs, we will look at the type of cash CDO based on the sponsor motivation: arbitrage and balance sheet transactions. As can be seen in Exhibit 3, cash CDOs are categorized based on the motivation of the sponsor of the transaction. In an arbitrage transaction, the motivation of the sponsor is to earn the spread between the yield offered on the debt obligations in the underlying pool and the payments made to the various tranches in the structure. In a balance sheet transaction, the motivation of the sponsor is to remove debt instruments (primarily loans) from its balance sheet. Sponsors of balance sheet transactions are typically financial institutions such as banks seeking to reduce their capital requirements by removing loans due to their higher risk-based capital requirements. Our focus in this section is on arbitrage transactions because such transactions are the largest part of the cash CDO sector.

1 Cash CDO Arbitrage Transactions

The key as to whether or not it is economic to create an arbitrage CDO is whether or not a structure can be created that offers a competitive return for the subordinate/equity tranche.

To understand how the subordinate/equity tranche generates cash flows, consider the following basic $100 million CDO structure with the coupon rate to be offered at the time of issuance as shown below:

Tranche	Par Value ($)	Coupon Rate
Senior	80,000,000	LIBOR + 70 basis points
Mezzanine	10,000,000	10-year Treasury rate plus 200 basis points
Subordinate/Equity	10,000,000	—

Suppose that the collateral consists of bonds that all mature in 10 years and the coupon rate for every bond is the 10-year Treasury rate plus 400 basis points. The asset manager enters into an interest rate swap agreement with another party with a notional amount of $80 million in which it agrees to do the following:

■ pay a fixed rate each year equal to the 10-year Treasury rate plus 100 basis points;

■ receive LIBOR.

The interest rate agreement is simply an agreement to periodically exchange interest payments. The payments are benchmarked off of a notional amount. This amount is not exchanged between the two parties. Rather it is used simply to determine the dollar interest payment of each party. This is all we need to know about an interest rate swap in order to understand the economics of an arbitrage transaction. Keep in mind, the goal is to show how the subordinate/equity tranche can be expected to generate a return.

Let's assume that the 10-year Treasury rate at the time the CDO is issued is 7%. Now we can walk through the cash flows for each year. Look first at the collateral. The collateral will pay interest each year (assuming no defaults) equal to the 10-year Treasury rate of 7% plus 400 basis points. So the interest will be:

Interest from collateral: $11\% \times \$100{,}000{,}000 = \$11{,}000{,}000$

Now let's determine the interest that must be paid to the senior and mezzanine tranches. For the senior tranche, the interest payment will be:

Interest to senior tranche: $\$80{,}000{,}000 \times (LIBOR + 70\,bps)$

The coupon rate for the mezzanine tranche is 7% plus 200 basis points. So, the coupon rate is 9% and the interest is:

Interest to mezzanine tranche: $9\% \times \$10{,}000{,}000 = \$900{,}000$

Finally, let's look at the interest rate swap. In this agreement, the asset manager is agreeing to pay some party (we'll call this party the "swap counterparty") each year 7% (the 10-year Treasury rate) plus 100 basis points, or 8%. But 8% of what? As explained above, in an interest rate swap payments are based on a notional amount. In our illustration, the notional amount is $80 million. The reason the asset manager selected the $80 million was because this is the amount of principal for the senior tranche which receives a floating rate. So, the asset manager pays to the swap counterparty:

Interest to swap counterparty: $8\% \times \$80{,}000{,}000 = \$6{,}400{,}000$

The interest payment received from the swap counterparty is LIBOR based on a notional amount of $80 million. That is,

Interest from swap counterparty: $\$80{,}000{,}000 \times LIBOR$

Now we can put this all together. Let's look at the interest coming into the CDO:

Interest from collateral	$11,000,000
Interest from swap counterparty	$80,000,000 × LIBOR
Total interest received	$11,000,000 + $80,000,000 × LIBOR

The interest to be paid out to the senior and mezzanine tranches and to the swap counterparty include:

Interest to senior tranche	$80,000,000 × (LIBOR + 70 bps)
Interest to mezzanine tranche	$900,000
Interest to swap counterparty	$6,400,000
Total interest paid	$7,300,000 + $80,000,000 × (LIBOR + 70 bps)

Netting the interest payments coming in and going out we have:

Total interest received	$11,000,000	+ $80,000,000	× LIBOR
Total interest paid	$7,300,000	+ $80,000,000	× (LIBOR + 70 bps)
Net interest	$3,700,000	− $80,000,000	× (70 bps)

Since 70 bps times $80 million is $560,000, the net interest remaining is $3,140,000 (= $3,700,000 – $560,000). From this amount any fees (including the asset management fee) must be paid. The balance is then the amount available to pay the subordinate/equity tranche. Suppose that these fees are $640,000. Then the cash flow available to the subordinate/equity tranche for the year is $2.5 million. Since the tranche has a par value of $10 million and is assumed to be sold at par, this means that the annual return is 25%.

Obviously, some simplifying assumptions have been made. For example, it is assumed that there are no defaults. It is assumed that all of the issues purchased by the asset manager are noncallable and therefore the coupon rate would not decline because issues are called. Moreover, as explained below, after some period the asset manager must begin repaying principal to the senior and mezzanine tranches. Consequently, the interest rate swap must be structured to take this into account since the entire amount of the senior tranche is not outstanding for the life of the collateral. Despite the simplifying assumptions, the illustration does demonstrate the basic economics of an arbitrage transaction, the need for the use of an interest rate swap, and how the subordinate/equity tranche will realize a return.

2 Cash Flow CDO Structure

In a cash flow CDO, the objective of the asset manager is to generate cash flow (primarily from interest earned and proceeds from bonds that have matured, have been called, or have amortized) to repay investors in the senior and mezzanine tranches. Because the cash flows from the structure are designed to accomplish the objective for each tranche, restrictions are imposed on the asset managers. The conditions for disposing of issues held are specified and are usually driven by credit risk considerations. Also, in assembling the portfolio, the asset manager must meet certain requirements set forth by the rating agency or agencies that rate the deal.

There are three relevant periods. The first is the *ramp-up period*. This is the period that follows the closing date of the transaction where the manager begins investing the proceeds from the sale of the debt obligations issued. This period is usually less than one year. The *reinvestment period* or *revolving period* is where principal proceeds are reinvested and is usually for five or more years. In the final period, the portfolio assets are sold and the debt holders are paid off as described below.

a. Distribution of Income   Income is derived from interest income from the underlying assets and capital appreciation. The income is then used as follows. Payments are first made to the trustee and administrators and then to the asset manager.[23] Once these fees are paid, then the senior tranches are paid their interest. At this point, before any other payments are made, there are certain tests that must be passed.

---

23 There are other management fees that are usually made based on performance. But these payments are made after payments to the mezzanine tranches.

These tests are called coverage tests and will be discussed later. If the coverage tests are passed, then interest is paid to the mezzanine tranches. Once the mezzanine tranches are paid, interest is paid to the subordinate/equity tranche.

In contrast, if the coverage tests are not passed, then there are payments that are made so as to protect the senior tranches. The remaining income after paying the fees and senior tranche interest is used to redeem the senior tranches (i.e., pay off principal) until the coverage tests are brought into compliance. If the senior tranches are paid off fully because the coverage tests are not brought into compliance, then any remaining income is used to redeem the mezzanine tranches. Any remaining income is then used to redeem the subordinate/equity tranche.

b. Distribution of Principal Cash Flow   The principal cash flow is distributed as follows after the payment of the fees to the trustees, administrators, and asset manager. If there is a shortfall in interest paid to the senior tranches, principal proceeds are used to make up the shortfall. Assuming that the coverage tests are satisfied, during the reinvestment period the principal is reinvested. After the reinvestment period or if the coverage tests are failed, the principal cash flow is used to pay down the senior tranches until the coverage tests are satisfied. If all the senior tranches are paid down, then the mezzanine tranches are paid off and then the subordinate/equity tranche is paid off.

c. Restrictions on Management   The asset manager in both a cash flow CDO and a market value CDO (discussed next) actively manage the portfolio. The difference is in the degree of active management. In a cash flow CDO, the asset manager initially structures and then rebalances the portfolio so that interest from the pool of assets plus repaid principal is sufficient to meet the obligations of the tranches. In contrast, the asset manager in a market value CDO seeks to generate trading profits to satisfy a portion of the obligations to the tranches.

The asset manager for both types of CDOs must monitor the collateral to ensure that certain tests imposed by the rating agencies are being met. For cash flow CDOs there are two types of tests: quality tests and coverage tests.

In rating a transaction, the rating agencies are concerned with the diversity of the assets. There are tests that relate to the diversity of the assets. These tests are called quality tests. An asset manager may not undertake a trade that will result in the violation of any of the quality tests. Quality tests include 1) a minimum asset diversity score,[24] 2) a minimum weighted average rating, and 3) maturity restrictions.

There are tests to ensure that the performance of the collateral is sufficient to make payments to the various tranches. These tests are called coverage tests. There are two types of coverage tests: par value tests and interest coverage ratio. Recall that if the coverage tests are violated, then income from the collateral is diverted to pay down the senior tranches.

3 *Market Value CDO*

As with a cash flow CDO, in a market value CDO there are debt tranches and a subordinate/equity tranche. However, because in a market value CDO the asset manager must sell assets in the underlying pool in order to generate proceeds for interest and repayment of maturing tranches, there is a careful monitoring of the assets and their price volatility. This is done by the frequent marking to market of the assets.

Because a market value CDO relies on the activities of the asset manager to generate capital appreciation and enhanced return to meet the obligations of the tranches in the structure, greater flexibility is granted to the asset manager with respect to some activities compared to a cash flow CDO. For example, while in a cash flow CDO the

---

24 Rating agencies have developed measures that quantify the diversity of a portfolio. These measures are referred to as "diversity scores."

capital structure is fixed, in a market value CDO the asset manager is permitted to utilize additional leverage after the closing of the transaction.

D. Synthetic CDOs

A synthetic CDO is so named because the CDO does not actually own the underlying assets on which it has risk exposure. That is, in a synthetic CDO the CDO debt holders absorb the economic risks, but not the legal ownership, of a pool of assets.

1 *Key Elements of a Synthetic CDO*

In a synthetic CDO there is credit risk exposure to a portfolio of assets, called the reference asset. The reference asset serves as the basis for a contingent payment as will be explained later. The reference asset can be a bond market index such as a high-yield bond index or a mortgage index. Or, the reference asset can be a portfolio of corporate loans that is owned by a bank.

The credit risk associated with the reference asset is divided into two sections: 1) senior section and 2) junior section. In a typical synthetic CDO structure, the senior section is about 90% and the junior section is about 10%. (We'll see what we mean by 90% and 10% shortly.) The losses that are realized from the reference are first realized by the junior section up to a notional amount and then after that full loss is realized, the senior section begins realizing losses.

For example, let's suppose that the reference asset is a high-yield corporate bond index. An amount of credit risk exposure in terms of market value must be determined. Suppose that it is $500 million. The $500 million is referred to as the notional amount. Suppose further that the credit risk associated with the $500 million credit exposure is divided into a $450 million senior section and $50 million junior section. The $450 million is the notional amount for the senior section and the $50 million is the notional amount for the junior section. The first $50 million of loss to the reference asset due to a credit event (explained later) is absorbed by the junior section. Only after the junior section absorbs the first $50 million in loss will the senior section realize any loss.

You may wonder why we refer to senior and junior "sections" rather than senior and junior "note holders." The reason is that in a synthetic CDO structure, no debt obligations are issued to fund the senior section. However, for the junior section, debt obligations are issued. In our illustration, $50 million of junior notes are issued. They are issued in the same way as in a cash CDO structure. That is, there are typically several tranches of junior notes issued by the special purpose vehicle (SPV). There will be the most senior tranche of the junior notes and there will be the subordinate/equity tranche.

The proceeds received from the issuance of the junior notes are then invested by the asset manager. However, the investments are restricted to high-quality debt instruments. This includes government securities, federal agency debentures, and corporate, mortgage-backed, and asset-backed securities rated triple A.

Now we introduce the key to a synthetic CDO—a credit derivative instrument. An interest rate derivative is used by an investor to protect against interest rate risk. (We actually illustrated the use of one type of interest rate derivative, an interest rate swap, earlier when we demonstrated the economics of an arbitrage CDO transaction.) A credit derivative, as the name indicates, is used to protect against credit risk. The type of credit derivative used in a synthetic CDO is a credit default swap. Here we discuss the essential elements of a credit default swap, just enough to understand its role in a synthetic CDO.

A credit default swap is conceptually similar to an insurance policy. There is a "protection buyer" who purchases protection against credit risk on the reference asset. In a synthetic CDO, the insurance buyer is the asset manager. The protection buyer (the asset manager in a synthetic CDO) pays a periodic fee (like an insurance premium) and receives, in return, payment from the protection seller in the event of a "credit event" affecting any asset included in the reference asset. Who is the protection seller? It is the SPV on behalf of the junior note holders.

As with an interest rate swap, a credit default swap has a notional amount. The notional amount will be equal to the senior section, $450 million in our example.

Let's clarify this by continuing with our earlier illustration and look at the return to the junior note holder in the structure. The junior note holders are getting payments that come from two sources:

1. the income from the high-quality securities purchased with the funds from the issuance of the junior debt obligations and

2. the insurance premium (premium from the credit default swap) paid by the asset manager to the SPV

Effectively, the junior note holders are receiving the return on a portfolio of high-quality assets subsidized by the insurance premium (i.e., the payment from the credit default swap). However, this ignores the obligation of the junior note holders with respect to the credit default swap. If there is a credit event (discussed below) that requires the junior note holders to make a payment to the protection buyer, then this reduces the return to the junior note holders. As noted earlier, the effect on a particular tranche of the junior section depends on its priority. That is, the subordinate/equity tranche is affected first before the most senior tranche, and the other tranches superior to the subordinate/equity tranche is affected.

So what becomes critical for the junior note holders' return is when it must make a payment. In credit derivatives, a payoff by the protection seller occurs when there is a credit event. Credit events are defined in the credit derivative documentation. On a debt instrument a credit event generally includes bankruptcy, failure to pay when due, cross default/cross acceleration, repudiation, and restructuring. This credit event applies to any of the assets within the reference asset. For example, if a high-yield corporate bond index is the reference asset and Company X is in the index, a credit event with respect to Company X results in a payment to the protection buyer. If a designated portfolio of bank loans to corporations is the reference asset and Corporation Y's loan is included, then a credit event with respect to Corporation Y results in a payment to the protection buyer.

How much must be paid by the protection seller (the junior tranches in our illustration) to the protection buyer (the asset manager)? Should a credit event occur, there is an intent that the protection buyer be made whole: The protection buyer should be paid the difference between par and the "fair value" of the securities. How this is determined is set forth in the credit derivative agreement.

What is the motivation for the creation of synthetic CDOs? There exist two types: synthetic balance sheet CDOs and synthetic arbitrage CDOs. In the case of a synthetic balance sheet CDO, by embedding a credit default swap within a CDO structure, a bank can shed the credit risk of a portfolio of bank loans without having to notify any borrowers that they are selling the loans to another party, a requirement in some countries. No consent is needed from borrowers to transfer the credit risk of the loans, as is effectively done in a credit default swap. This is the reason synthetic balance sheet CDOs were initially set up to accommodate European bank balance sheet deals.

For a synthetic arbitrage CDO, there are several economic advantages of using a synthetic CDO structure rather than a cash CDO structure. First, it is not necessary to obtain funding for the senior section, thus making it easier to do a CDO transaction.[25] Second, the ramp-up period is shorter than for a cash CDO structure since only the high-quality assets need be assembled, not all of the assets contained in the reference asset. Finally, there are opportunities in the market to be able to effectively acquire

---

25 It is for this reason that a nonsynthetic CDO structure is referred to as a "cash" CDO structure because cash is required to be raised to purchase all the collateral assets.

the assets included in the reference asset via a credit default swap at a cheaper cost than buying the assets directly.[26] It's because of these three advantages that issuance of synthetic CDO structures has increased dramatically since 2001 and is expected to continue to increase relative to cash CDO structures.

SOLUTIONS FOR PRACTICE QUESTIONS

1. Losses by bond class

Total Loss ($)	Senior Bond Class ($)	Subordinate Bond Class 1 ($)	Subordinate Bond Class 2 ($)
A. 15 million	zero	zero	15 million
B. 50 million	zero	30 million	20 million
C. 90 million	30 million	40 million	20 million

2. The excess servicing spread is determined as follows:

Gross weighted average coupon	=	9.50%
Servicing fee	=	0.75%
Spread available to pay tranches	=	8.75%
Net weighted average coupon	=	7.50%
Excess servicing spread	=	1.25%	= 125 basis points

3. For month 1 the CPR is 4% as per the prospectus. Since we are interested in 150% PPC, the CPR in month 1 is 6% (1.5 × 4%). For month 2, 1.5% is added to 4%, so 100% PPC is 5.5%. Then 150% PPC is a CPR of 8.3% (= 1.5 × 5.5%). In month 15, the CPR is 25% for 100% PPC and for 150% PPC, the CPR is 37.5% (1.5 × 25%). For all months after month 15, the CPR is 37.5%.

Month	CPR (%)	Month	CPR (%)	Month	CPR (%)
1	6.0	11	28.5	30	37.5
2	8.3	12	30.8	125	37.5
3	10.5	13	33.0	150	37.5
4	12.8	14	35.3	200	37.5
5	15.0	15	37.5	250	37.5
6	17.3	16	37.5	275	37.5
7	19.5	17	37.5	300	37.5
8	21.8	18	37.5	325	37.5
9	24.0	19	37.5	350	37.5
10	26.3	20	37.5	360	37.5

4. **A.** $$SMM = \frac{0.02}{1 - [0.02 \times (11 - 1)]} = 0.025 = 2.5\%$$

   B. $$ABS = \frac{0.017}{1 + [0.017 \times (21 - 1)]} = 0.0127 = 1.27\%$$

---

26 For a more detailed discussion of these advantages ▪ and how it impacts the economics of a CDO, see Laurie S.Goodman and Frank J. Fabozzi, *Collateralized Debt Obligations: Structures and Analysis* (New York, NY: John Wiley & Sons, 2002).

SUMMARY

- An entity that wants to raise funds via a securitization will sell assets to a special purpose vehicle and is referred to as the "seller" in the transaction.

- The buyer of assets in a securitization is a special purpose vehicle, and this entity, referred to as the issuer or trust, raises funds to buy the assets via the sale of securities (the asset-backed securities).

- There will be an entity in a securitization that will be responsible for servicing the loans or receivables.

- Third-party entities in the securitization are attorneys, independent accountants, trustee, rating agencies, servicer, and possibly a guarantor.

- The waterfall of a transaction describes how the distribution of the cash flow will be distributed to the bond classes after fees are paid.

- In a securitization structure, the bond classes issued can consist of a senior bond that is tranched so as to redistribute prepayment risk and one or more subordinate bonds; the creation of the subordinate bonds provides credit tranching for the structure.

- The collateral for an asset-backed security can be either amortizing assets (e.g., auto loans and closed-end home equity loans) or nonamortizing assets (e.g., credit card receivables).

- For amortizing assets, projection of the cash flow requires projecting prepayments.

- For non-amortizing assets, prepayments by an individual borrower do not apply since there is no schedule of principal repayments.

- When the collateral is amortizing assets, typically the principal repayments are distributed to the security holders.

- When the collateral consists of non-amortizing assets, typically there is a lockout period, a period where principal repayments are reinvested in new assets; after the lockout period, principal repayments are distributed to the security holders.

- A structure where there is a lockout for principal repayments is called a revolving structure.

- One factor that may affect prepayments is the prevailing level of interest rates relative to the interest rate on the loan.

- Since a default is a prepayment (an involuntary prepayment), prepayment modeling for an asset-backed security backed by amortizing assets requires a model for projecting the amount that will be recovered and when it will be recovered.

- Cash flow analysis can be performed on a pool level or a loan level.

- The expected final maturity of an asset-backed security is the maturity date based on expected prepayments at the time of pricing of a deal; the legal final maturity can be two or more years after the expected final maturity.

- Average life is commonly used as a measure for the length of time an asset-backed security will be outstanding.

- With an asset-backed security, due to prepayments a bond that is expected to have a bullet maturity may have an actual maturity that differs from that specified in the prospectus and is therefore referred to as a soft bullet.

- Asset-backed securities are credit enhanced; that is, there must be support from somewhere to absorb a certain amount of defaults.

- Credit enhancement levels are determined relative to a specific rating desired for a security.

- There are two general types of credit enhancement structures: external and internal.

- External credit enhancements come in the form of third-party guarantees that provide for first loss protection against losses up to a specified level.

- External credit enhancement includes insurance by a monoline insurer, a guarantee by the seller of the assets, and a letter of credit.

- The most common forms of internal credit enhancements are reserve funds and senior/subordinate structures.

- The senior/subordinated structure is the most widely used internal credit support structure with a typical structure having a senior tranche and one or more non-senior tranches.

- For mortgage-related asset-backed securities and nonagency mortgage-backed securities there is a concern that prepayments will erode the protection afforded by the non-senior (i.e., subordinated) tranches after the deal closes.

- A shifting interest structure is used to protect against a deterioration in the senior tranche's credit protection due to prepayments by redistributing the prepayments disproportionately from the non-senior tranches to the senior tranche according to a specified schedule.

- With an asset-backed security, one of the following call provisions may be granted to the trustee: 1) percent of collateral call, 2) percent of bonds, 3) percent of tranche, 4) call on or after specified date, 5) latter of percent or date, or 6) auction call.

- The collateral for a home equity loan is typically a first lien on residential property, and the loan fails to satisfy the underwriting standards for inclusion in a loan pool of Ginnie Mae, Fannie Mae, or Freddie Mac because of the borrower's impaired credit history or too high a payment-to-income ratio.

- Typically, a home equity loan is used by a borrower to consolidate consumer debt using the current home as collateral rather than to obtain funds to purchase a new home.

- Home equity loans can be either closed end (i.e., structured the same way as a fully amortizing residential mortgage loan) or open end (i.e., homeowner given a credit line).

- The monthly cash flow for a home equity loan-backed security backed by closed-end HELs consists of 1) net interest, 2) regularly scheduled principal payments, and 3) prepayments.

- Several studies by Wall Street firms have found that the key difference between the prepayment behavior of HELs and traditional residential mortgages is the important role played by the credit characteristics of the borrower.

- Studies strongly suggest that borrower credit quality is the most important determinant of prepayments, with the sensitivity of refinancing to interest rates being greater the higher the borrower's credit quality.

- The prospectus of an HEL offering contains a base case prepayment assumption regarding the initial speed and the amount of time until the collateral is expected to season.

- A prospectus prepayment curve is a multiple of the base case prepayments assumed in the prospectus (i.e., base case is equal to 100% PPC).

- Typically, home equity loan-backed securities are securitized by both closed-end fixed-rate and adjustable-rate (or variable-rate) HELs.

- Unlike a typical floater which has a cap that is fixed throughout the security's life, the available funds cap of a HEL floater is variable and depends on the amount of funds generated by the net coupon on the principal, less any fees.

- To provide stability to the average life of a senior tranche, closed-end home equity loan transactions will include either a non-accelerating senior (NAS) tranche or a planned amortization class (PAC) tranche.

- A NAS tranche receives principal payments according to a schedule based not on a dollar amount for a given month, but instead on a schedule that specifies for each month the share of pro rata principal that must be distributed to the NAS tranche.

- For a PAC tranche a schedule of the dollar amount for each month is specified.

- The structure of residential mortgage-backed securities outside the United States is similar to that of the nonagency mortgage market; there are internal and external credit enhancements.

- Auto loan-backed securities are issued by the financial subsidiaries of auto manufacturers, commercial banks, and independent finance companies and small financial institutions specializing in auto loans.

- The cash flow for auto loan-backed securities consists of regularly scheduled monthly loan payments (interest and scheduled principal repayments), and any prepayments.

- Prepayments on auto loans are not sensitive to interest rates.

- Prepayments on auto loan-backed securities are measured in terms of the absolute prepayment speed (denoted ABS) which measures monthly prepayments relative to the original collateral amount.

- Manufactured housing-backed securities are backed by loans on manufactured homes (i.e., homes built at a factory and then transported to a site).

- Manufactured housing-backed securities are issued by Ginnie Mae and private entities, the former being guaranteed by the full faith and credit of the U.S. government.

- A manufactured housing loan's cash flow consists of net interest, regularly scheduled principal, and prepayments.

- Prepayments are more stable for manufactured housing-backed securities because they are not sensitive to interest rate changes.

- SLABS are asset-backed securities backed by student loans.

- The student loans most commonly securitized are those that are made under the Federal Family Education Loan Program (FFELP), whereby the government makes loans to students via private lenders and the government guaranteeing up to 98% of the principal plus accrued interest.

- Alternative loans are student loans that are not part of a government guarantee program and are basically consumer loans.

- In contrast to government guaranteed loans, the lender's decision to extend an alternative loan is based on the ability of the applicant to repay the loan.

- Student loans involve three periods with respect to the borrower's payments—deferment period, grace period, and loan repayment period.

- Prepayments typically occur due to defaults or a loan consolidation (i.e., a loan to consolidate loans over several years into a single loan).

- Issuers of SLABs include the Student Loan Marketing Association (Sallie Mae), traditional corporate entities, and non-profit organizations.

- Student loan-backed securities offer a floating rate; for some issues the reference rate is the 3-month Treasury bill rate, but for most issues the reference rate is LIBOR.

- Small Business Administration (SBA) loans are backed by the full faith and credit of the U.S. government.

- Most SBA loans are variable-rate loans where the reference rate is the prime rate with monthly payments consisting of interest and principal repayment.

- Voluntary prepayments can be made by the SBA borrower without any penalty.

- Factors contributing to the prepayment speed of a pool of SBA loans are 1) the maturity date of the loan (it has been found that the fastest speeds on SBA loans and pools occur for shorter maturities), 2) the purpose of the loan, and 3) whether or not there is a cap on the loan.

- Credit card receivable-backed securities are backed by credit card receivables for credit cards issued by banks, retailers, and travel and entertainment companies.

- Credit card deals are structured as a master trust.

- For a pool of credit card receivables, the cash flow consists of finance charges collected, fees, and principal.

- The principal repayment of a credit card receivable-backed security is not amortized; instead, during the lockout period, the principal payments made by credit card borrowers are retained by the trustee and reinvested in additional receivables, and after the lockout period (the principal-amortization period), the principal received by the trustee is no longer reinvested but paid to investors.

- There are provisions in credit card receivable-backed securities that require early amortization of the principal if certain events occur.

- Since for credit card receivable-backed securities the concept of prepayments does not apply, participants look at the monthly payment rate (MPR) which expresses the monthly payment (which includes interest, finance charges, and any principal) of a credit card receivable portfolio as a percentage of debt outstanding in the previous month.

- The MPR for credit card receivable-backed securities is important because 1) if it reaches an extremely low level, there is a chance that there will be extension risk with respect to the principal payments and 2) if the MPR is very low, there is a chance that there will not be sufficient cash flows to pay off principal (which can trigger early amortization of the principal).

- To assess the performance of the portfolio of credit card receivables and the ability of the issuer to meet its interest obligation and repay principal as scheduled, an investor must analyze the gross portfolio yield (which includes finance charges collected and fees), charge-offs (which represents the accounts charged off as uncollectible), the net portfolio yield, gross portfolio yield minus charge-offs, and delinquencies (the percentage of receivable that are past due as specified number of months).

- There are three amortization structures that have been used in credit card receivable-backed security structures: 1) passthrough structure, 2) controlled-amortization structure, and 3) bullet-payment structure.

- A collateralized debt obligation is an asset-backed security backed by a diversified pool of debt obligations (high-yield corporate bonds, structured financial products, emerging market bonds, bank loans, and special situation loans and distressed debt).

- A collateralized bond obligation is a CDO in which the underlying pool of debt obligations consists of bond-type instruments (high-yield corporate and emerging market bonds).

- A collateralized loan obligation is a CDO in which the underlying pool of debt obligations consists of bank loans.

- In a CDO there is an asset manager responsible for managing the portfolio of assets.

- The tranches in a CDO include senior tranches, mezzanine tranches, and subordinate/equity tranches.

- The senior and mezzanine tranches are rated and the subordinate/equity tranche is unrated.

- The proceeds to meet the obligations to the CDO tranches (interest and principal repayment) can come from 1) coupon interest payments of the underlying assets, 2) maturing assets in the underlying pools, and 3) sale of assets in the underlying pool.

- CDOs are categorized based on the motivation of the sponsor of the transaction—arbitrage and balance sheet transactions.

- The motivation in an arbitrage transaction is for the sponsor to earn the spread between the yield offered on the debt obligations in the underlying pool and the payments made to the various tranches in the structure.

- In a balance sheet transaction the motivation of the sponsor is to remove debt instruments (primarily loans) from its balance sheet.

- The key as to whether or not it is economic to create an arbitrage transaction is whether or not a structure can offer a competitive return to the subordinated/equity tranche.

- Arbitrage transactions are classified as either cash flow CDOs or market value CDOs depending on where the primary source of the proceeds from the underlying asset is to come from to satisfy the obligation to the tranches.

- In a cash flow CDO the primary source is the interest and maturing principal from the underlying assets; in a market value CDO the proceeds to meet the obligations depend heavily on the total return generated from the portfolio.

- The three relevant periods in a CDO are the ramp-up period, the reinvestment period or revolving period, and the final period where the portfolio assets are sold and the debt holders are paid off.

- In a CDO transaction, senior tranches are protected against a credit deterioration by coverage tests; a failure of coverage tests results in the paying off of the senior tranches until the coverage tests are satisfied.

- The tests imposed in a cash flow structure are quality tests (e.g., minimum asset diversity score, a minimum weighted average rating, and maturity restrictions) and coverage tests.

- Coverage tests are tests to ensure that the performance of the collateral is sufficient to make payments to the various tranches and include par value tests and interest coverage ratio.

- In market value structures the focus is on monitoring of the assets and their price volatility by the frequent marking to market of the assets.

■ In a synthetic CDO a credit derivative instrument is used to allow the CDO issuer to transfer the economic risk, but not the legal ownership of a reference asset.

■ In a synthetic CDO, the credit derivative used is a credit default swap and this instrument allows the "protection buyer" (the asset manager in a synthetic CDO) to protect against default risk on a reference asset; the protection sellers are the tranches in the junior section of the CDO.

■ In a synthetic CDO, the return to the junior note holders is based on the return from a portfolio of high-quality debt instruments plus the premium received in the credit default swap, reduced by the payment that must be made as a result of a credit event.

■ There are synthetic balance sheet CDO transactions and synthetic arbitrage CDO transactions.

PRACTICE PROBLEMS FOR READING 46

1. Caterpillar Financial Asset Trust 1997-A is a special purpose vehicle. The collateral (i.e., assets) for the trust is a pool of fixed-rate retail installment sales contracts that are secured by new and used machinery manufactured primarily by Caterpillar Inc. The retail installment sales contracts were originated by the Caterpillar Financial Funding Corporation, a wholly owned subsidiary of Caterpillar Financial Services Corporation. Caterpillar Financial Services Corporation is a wholly owned subsidiary of Caterpillar Inc. The prospectus for the trust states that:

> "THE NOTES REPRESENT OBLIGATIONS OF THE ISSUER ONLY AND DO NOT REPRESENT OBLIGATIONS OF OR INTERESTS IN CATERPILLAR FINANCIAL FUNDING CORPORATION, CATERPILLAR FINANCIAL SERVICES CORPORATION, CATERPILLAR INC. OR ANY OF THEIR RESPECTIVE AFFILIATES."

The servicer of the retail installment sales contracts is Caterpillar Financial Services Corporation, a wholly owned finance subsidiary of Caterpillar Inc. and is referred to as the servicer in the prospectus. For servicing the collateral, Caterpillar Financial Services Corporation receives a servicing fee of 100 basis points of the outstanding loan balance.

The securities were issued on May 19, 1997 and had a par value of $337,970,000. In the prospectus the securities are referred to as "asset-backed notes." There were four rated bond classes:

Bond Class	Par Value ($)
Class A-1	88,000,000
Class A-2	128,000,000
Class A-3	108,100,000
Class B	13,870,000

A. In the prospectus, the term "Seller" is used. Who in this transaction would be the "Seller" and why?

B. In the prospectus, the term "Issuer" is used. Who in this transaction would be the "Issuer" and why?

C. Despite not having the waterfall for this structure, which bond classes do you think are the senior bonds?

D. Despite not having the waterfall for this structure, which bond classes do you think are the subordinate bonds?

E. Despite not having the waterfall for this structure, explain why there appears to be credit and prepayment tranching in this structure?

2. In the securitization process, what is the role played by the a) attorneys and b) independent accountants?

3. How are principal repayments from the collateral used by the trustee in a securitization transaction?

4. Suppose that the collateral for an asset-backed securities structure has a gross weighted average coupon of 8.6%. The servicing fee is 50 basis points. The tranches issued have a weighted average coupon rate of 7.1%. What is the excess servicing spread?

5. Suppose that the structure for an asset-backed security transaction is as follows:

senior tranche	$ 220 million
subordinate tranche 1	$ 50 million
subordinate tranche 2	$ 30 million

and that the value of the collateral for the structure is $320 million. Subordinate tranche 2 is the first loss tranche.

A. How much is the overcollateralization in this structure?

B. What is the amount of the loss for each tranche if losses due to defaults over the life of the structure total $15 million?

C. What is the amount of the loss for each tranche if losses due to defaults over the life of the structure total $35 million?

D. What is the amount of the loss for each tranche if losses due to defaults over the life of the structure total $85 million?

E. What is the amount of the loss for each tranche if losses due to defaults over the life of the structure total $110 million?

6. A. Explain why individual loans that are of a non-amortizing type are not subject to prepayment risk.

B. Explain why securities backed by collateral consisting of non-amortizing assets may expose an investor to prepayment risk.

7. An asset-backed security has been credit enhanced with a letter of credit from a bank with a single A credit rating. If this is the only form of credit enhancement, explain why this issue is unlikely to receive a triple A credit rating.

8. Why is it critical for monoline insurance companies that provide insurance for asset-backed security transactions to maintain a triple A credit rating?

9. What is the difference between a cash reserve fund and an excess servicing spread account?

10. Why is the assumption about how defaults may occur over the life of an asset-backed security transaction important in assessing the effectiveness of excess servicing spread as a form of internal credit enhancement?

11. A. Explain why a senior-subordinate structure is a form of internal credit enhancement.

B. Explain the need for a shifting interest mechanism in a senior-subordinate structure when the underlying assets are subject to prepayments.

12. A. What is meant by the "senior prepayment percentage" in a shifting interest mechanism of a senior-subordinate structure?

B. Why does a shifting interest mechanism affect the cash flow of the senior tranche and increase the senior tranche's exposure to contraction risk?

13. What is a "latter of percent or call date" call provision?

14. A. What is the cash flow of a closed-end home equity loan?

B. Indicate whether you agree or disagree with the following statement: "Typically, closed-end home equity loans are loans to borrowers of the highest credit quality."

15. The Izzobaf Home Equity Loan Trust 2000-1 is backed by fixed-rate closed-end home equity loans. The base case prepayment for this deal is specified in the prospectus as follows:

    The model used with respect to the loans (the "prepayment ramp") assumes that the home equity loans prepay at a rate of 5% CPR in the first month after origination, and an additional 1.8% each month thereafter until the 12th month. Beginning in the 12th month and each month thereafter, the prepayment ramp assumes a prepayment rate of 24.8% CPR.

    What is the CPR assuming 200% PPC for the following months?

Month	CPR	Month	CPR	Month	CPR
1		11		30	
2		12		125	
3		13		150	
4		14		200	
5		15		250	
6		16		275	
7		17		300	
8		18		325	
9		19		350	
10		20		360	

16. James Tellmen is an assistant portfolio manager for a mortgage-backed securities portfolio. Mr. Tellmen's responsibility is to analyze agency mortgage-backed securities. Recently, the portfolio manager has been given authorization to purchase closed-end home equity loan-backed securities. Mr. Tellmen is analyzing his first structure in this sector of the asset-backed securities market. Upon reading the prospectus he finds that the base case prepayment is specified and believes that this prepayment assumption is the benchmark used in all closed-end home equity loan-backed securities. Explain why you agree or disagree with Mr. Tellmen.

17. Why is there an available funds cap in an asset-backed security in which the collateral is adjustable-rate home equity loans?

18. Suppose that the base case shifting interest percentage schedule for a closed-end home equity loan-backed security is as follows:

Years after Issuance	Senior Prepayment Percentage (%)
1–4	100
5	90
6	80
7	50
8	20
after year 8	0

    A. If there are prepayments in month 36 of $100,000, how much of the prepayments is paid to the senior tranche? How much is paid to the subordinate tranches?

B. If there are prepayments in the 8th year after issuance of $100,000, how much of the prepayments is paid to the senior tranche? How much is paid to the subordinate tranches?

C. If there are prepayments in the 10th year after issuance of $100,000, how much of the prepayments is paid to the senior tranche? How much is paid to the subordinate tranches?

19. Larry Forest is an analyst reviewing for the first time a closed-end home equity loan-backed structure in order to determine whether or not to purchase the deal's senior tranche. He understands how the shifting interest percentage schedule is structured so as to provide the senior tranches with protection after the deal is closed. However, he is concerned that the schedule in the prospectus will not be adequate if the collateral's performance deteriorates (i.e., there is considerably greater losses for the collateral than expected). Explain to Mr. Forest what provision is included in the prospectus for protecting the senior tranches if the performance of the collateral deteriorates.

20. How is a non-accelerating senior tranche provided protection to reduce contraction risk and extension risk?

21. **A.** What are the components of the cash flow for a manufactured housing-backed security?

B. What are the reasons why prepayments due to refinancing are not significant for manufactured housing loans?

22. Why are residential mortgage-backed securities outside the United States structured more like transactions in the nonagency U.S. market than the agency market?

23. **A.** What are the components of the cash flow for an auto loan-backed security?

B. How important are prepayments due to refinancing for auto loans?

24. What is the difference between a single monthly mortality rate and an absolute prepayment speed?

25. **A.** If the ABS for a security is 1.5% at month 21, what is the corresponding SMM?

B. If the SMM for a security is 1.9% at month 11, what is the corresponding ABS?

26. A trustee for a pension fund is working with a consultant to develop investment guidelines for the fund's bond portfolio. The trustee states that the fund should be able to invest in securities backed by student loans because the loans are fully guaranteed by the U.S. government. How should the consultant respond?

27. For a student loan-backed security, what is the difference between the deferment period and the grace period?

28. **A.** What are the components of the cash flow for a Small Business Administration-backed security?

B. What reference rate is used for setting the coupon interest and how often is the coupon rate reset?

29. **A.** What is the cash flow for a credit card receivable-backed security during the lockout or revolving period?

B. How is the principal received from credit card borrowers handled during the lockout or revolving period?

C. Explain why you agree or disagree with the following statement: "After the lockout period, the principal is paid to bondholders in one lump sum amount at the maturity date of the security."

30. A manager of a corporate bond portfolio is considering the purchase of a credit card receivable-backed security. The manager believes that an advantage of such securities is that there is no contraction risk and no extension risk. Explain why you agree or disagree with this view.

31. **A.** What is meant by the monthly payment rate for a credit card deal?

    B. What is the significance of the monthly payment rate?

    C. How is the net portfolio yield determined for a credit card deal?

32. What is a typical cash CDO structure?

33. Explain why you agree or disagree with the following statement: "The asset manager for a CDO is free to actively manage the portfolio without any constraints."

34. Explain why you agree or disagree with the following statement: "By using an interest rate swap, the asset manager for a CDO increases the risk associated with meeting the obligations that must be paid to the senior tranche."

35. What is the key factor in determining whether or not an arbitrage CDO can be issued?

36. Consider the following CDO transaction:

    1. The CDO is a $200 million structure. That is, the assets purchased will be $200 million.

    2. The collateral consists of bonds that all mature in 8 years, and the coupon rate for every bond is the 8-year Treasury rate plus 600 basis points.

    3. The senior tranche comprises 75% of the structure ($150 million) and pays interest based on the following coupon formula: LIBOR plus 90 basis points.

    4. There is only one junior tranche ($30 million) with a coupon rate that is fixed. The coupon rate is the 8-year Treasury rate plus 300 basis points.

    5. The asset manager enters into an agreement with a counterparty in which it agrees to pay the counterparty a fixed rate each year equal to the 8-year Treasury rate plus 120 basis points and receive LIBOR. The notional amount of the agreement is $150 million.

    A. How much is the equity tranche in this CDO?

    B. Assume that the 8-year Treasury rate at the time the CDO is issued is 6%. Assuming no defaults, what is the cash flow for each year and how is it distributed?

    C. Ignoring the asset management fee, what is the amount available each year for the equity tranche?

37. What are the elements of the return for the junior note holders in a synthetic CDO structure?

38. Why have banks issued synthetic balance sheet CDOs?

The following information relates to Questions 39–44

Krista Boldon is the CFO of Whisper Spa, a company that sells high-quality spa and sauna equipment and accessories to homeowners through direct distribution. Approximately 76% of the company's sales are financed by direct-lending revolving credit card accounts funded internally by Whisper Spa. Boldon has recently proposed that the company raise cash to fund additional credit sales by securitizing Whisper Spa's existing credit card receivables. Boldon's proposal includes the multi-tranche, senior-subordinate structure with multiple internal credit enhancements shown in Exhibit 1. The total value of the collateral for the structure is $68.0 million, the lockout period is two years, and the B2 bond class is the first loss piece.

Exhibit 1	Proposed ABS Structure

Bond Class	Par Value ($ Millions)
A1	27
A2	23
A3	8
B1 (subordinate)	6
B2 (subordinate)	4
Total	68

Melvin Haggerty, Whisper Spa's CEO, reviewed Boldon's proposal and responded with the following statement:

> "I am concerned that the debt will not sell well in the market because Whisper Spa's credit rating is marginal."

39. The *primary* motivation for creating the three senior bond classes, represented by Class A in the structure shown in Exhibit 1, is:

   A. redistribution of credit risk.

   B. redistribution of prepayment risk.

   C. redistribution of interest rate risk.

40. The *primary* motivation for creating two different classes of bonds, A and B, in the structure in Exhibit 1 is:

   A. redistribution of credit risk.

   B. redistribution of prepayment risk.

   C. redistribution of interest rate risk.

41. If default losses over the life of the structure total $8.0 million, what is the loss to the class B1 bondholders?

   A. $2.0 million.

   B. $4.0 million.

   C. $6.0 million.

42. Which of the following credit enhancements is *most likely* to be incorporated into Whisper Spa's asset-backed securities?

   A. Letter of credit.

   B. Insurance "wrapping."

   C. Overcollateralization.

43. Haggerty's statement is *most likely*:

   A. justified, because the security will include internal credit enhancements.

   B. justified, because Whisper Spa has the ultimate responsibility for repaying the bondholders.

   C. not justified, because only internal credit enhancements are being used.

44. By the end of the fourteenth month after the securities were issued, the underlying credit card accounts have prepaid $30 million in principal in addition to regularly scheduled principal and interest payments. The amount of this principal prepaid to the holders of the A2 bond class is *closest* to:

   A. $0.

   B. $12.0 million.

   C. $23.0 million.

SOLUTIONS FOR READING 46

1. **A.** Since Caterpillar Financial Funding Corporation sold the retail installment sales contracts to Caterpillar Financial Asset Trust 1997-A, Caterpillar Financial Funding Corporation would be referred to in the prospectus as the "Seller."

    B. The special purpose vehicle in a securitization issues the securities and therefore is referred to as the "Issuer." In this transaction, Caterpillar Asset Financial Trust 1997-A is the "Issuer."

    C. Without having a full description of the waterfall for this structure, it appears that Bond Classes A-1, A-2, and A-3 are the senior classes.

    D. Without having a full description of the waterfall for this structure, it appears that Bond Class B is the subordinate class.

    E. Credit tranching in this structure was done by creating the senior and subordinate tranches. Prepayment tranching appears to have been done by offering three classes of the senior tranche.

2. **A.** In the securitization process, the attorneys prepare the legal documentation which includes i) the purchase agreement between the seller of the assets and the special purpose vehicle, ii) how the cash flows are divided among the bond classes, and iii) the servicing agreement between the entity engaged to service the assets and the special purpose vehicle.

    B. The independent accountant verifies the accuracy of all numerical information (e.g., yield and average life) placed in either the prospectus or private placement memorandum and then issues a comfort letter.

3. How the principal repayments from the collateral are used by the trustee in a securitization transaction depends on the waterfall which, in turn, is affected by the character of the collateral (amortizing versus non-amortizing). In a typical structure backed by amortizing assets, the principal repayments are distributed to the bond classes. In a typical structure backed by non-amortizing assets, the principal repayments for a specified period of time (the lockout period) are used to purchase new assets and after that period (assuming no early amortization provision is triggered), the principal repayments are distributed to the bond classes. This structure is referred to as a revolving structure.

4. The excess servicing spread is determined as follows:

	Gross weighted average coupon	=	8.60%	
−	Servicing fee	=	0.50%	
	Spread available to pay tranches	=	8.10%	
−	Net weighted average coupon	=	7.10%	
	Excess servicing spread	=	1.00%	= 100 basis points

5. **A.** The amount of overcollateralization is the difference between the value of the collateral, $320 million, and the par value for all the tranches, $300 million. In this structure it is $20 million.

    B. If the losses total $15 million, then the loss is entirely absorbed by the overcollateralization. No tranche will realize a loss.

C.–E.

Total Loss ($)	Senior Tranche ($)	Subordinate Tranche 1 ($)	Subordinate Tranche 2 ($)
C. 35 million	zero	zero	15 million
D. 85 million	zero	35 million	30 million
E. 110 million	10 million	50 million	30 million

6. **A.** For a non-amortizing loan, there is no schedule for repayment of principal. Consequently, for individual loans of this type there can be no prepayments.

   B. While there may be no prepayments for individual loans that are non-amortizing, the securities that are backed by these loans may be prepayable. For example, credit card receivable-backed securities can be prepaid under certain conditions. Such conditions are referred to as "early amortization" or "rapid amortization" events or triggers.

7. The rating agencies take the weak-link approach to credit enhancement. Typically a structure cannot receive a rating higher than the rating on any third party providing an external guarantee. Since the question specifies that the only form of credit enhancement is the letter of credit, then the rating will not exceed the single A rating of the bank providing the letter credit. Thus, a triple A rating is not likely.

8. Since credit agencies take the weak-link approach to credit enhancement, if an insurance company wants to offer bond insurance for an asset-backed security transaction where a triple A credit rating is sought, the insurance company must have a triple A credit rating.

9. Both a cash reserve fund and an excess servicing spread account are forms of internal credit enhancement. A cash reserve fund is provided by a deposit of cash at issuance. Excess servicing spread account is the cash available to absorb losses from the collateral after payment of interest to all the tranches and to the servicer.

10. The excess servicing spread account builds up over time in order to offset future losses. However, if losses occur early in the life of the collateral, there may not be enough time to accumulate the excess servicing spread to adequately cover future losses.

11. **A.** A senior-subordinate structure is a form of internal credit enhancement because it does not rely on the guarantee of a third party. Instead, the enhancement comes from within the structure by creating senior and subordinate tranches. The subordinate tranches provide credit protection for the senior tranche.

    B. Once a deal is closed, the percentage of the senior tranche and the percentage of the subordinate tranche change when the underlying assets are subject to prepayments. If the subordinate interest in a structure decreases after the deal is closed, the credit protection for the senior tranche decreases. The shifting interest mechanism seeks to prevent the senior tranche's credit protection provided by the subordinate tranche (or tranches) from declining by establishing a schedule that provides for a higher allocation of the prepayments to the senior tranche in the earlier years.

12. **A.** The senior prepayment percentage is the percentage of prepayments that are allocated to the senior tranche. The senior prepayment percentage is specified in the prospectus.

    B. Because the shifting interest mechanism results in a greater amount of the prepayments be paid to the senior tranche in the earlier years than in the absence of such a mechanism, the senior tranches are exposed to greater contraction risk.

13. The outstanding bonds in a structure can be called if either 1) the collateral outstanding reaches a predetermined level before the specified call date or 2) the call date has been reached even if the collateral outstanding is above the predetermined level.

14. **A.** The cash flow for a closed-end home equity loan is the same as for a standard mortgage loan: interest, regularly scheduled principal repayments (i.e., regular amortization), and prepayments.

    B. The statement is incorrect. Typically, a closed-end home equity loan borrower is a credit impaired borrower.

15. For month 1, the CPR for 100% PPC is 5%, so the CPR for 200% PPC is 10% (= 2 × 5%). For month 2, the CPR for 100% PPC is 5% plus 1.8%, which is 6.8%. Therefore, the CPR for 200% PPC for month 2 is 13.6% (2 × 6.8%).

In month 12, the CPR for 100% PPC is

$$5\% + 1.8\% \times 11 = 24.8\%$$

Therefore, the CPR for 200% PPC is 49.6% (2 × 24.8%). For all months after month 12, the CPR for 200% CPR is 49.6%.

Month	CPR (%)	Month	CPR (%)	Month	CPR (%)
1	10.0	11	46.0	30	49.6
2	13.6	12	49.6	125	49.6
3	17.2	13	49.6	150	49.6
4	20.8	14	49.6	200	49.6
5	24.4	15	49.6	250	49.6
6	28.0	16	49.6	275	49.6
7	31.6	17	49.6	300	49.6
8	35.2	18	49.6	325	49.6
9	38.8	19	49.6	350	49.6
10	42.4	20	49.6	360	49.6

16. The base case prepayment specified in the prospectus is called the prospectus prepayment curve (PPC). It is unique to each issuer and should be used instead of the generic PSA prepayment benchmark. However, it is not a generic prepayment benchmark for all closed-end home equity loan securities as Mr. Tellmen assumes.

17. For adjustable-rate HELs, the reference rate is typically 6-month LIBOR. However, the floating-rate securities that these loans back typically are referenced to 1-month LIBOR in order to make them attractive to investors who fund themselves based on 1-month LIBOR. As a result, there will be a mismatch between the reference rate on the floating-rate HELs used as collateral and the securities backed by that collateral that will prevent the cap from being fixed over the life of the securities. In addition, there are periodic caps and a lifetime cap.

18. **A.** Since month 36 is in the first five years after issuance, the schedule specifies that all prepayments are allocated to the senior tranche and none to the subordinate tranches. Thus, the prepayments of $100,000 are allocated only to the senior tranche.

B. According to the schedule, if prepayments occur 8 years after issuance, 20% is allocated to the senior tranche and the balance is paid to the subordinate tranches. Since the prepayments are assumed to be $100,000, the senior tranche receives $20,000 and the subordinate tranches $80,000.

C. All prepayments that occur 10 years after issuance are paid to the subordinate tranches. Thus, the $100,000 of prepayments some time in year 10 are paid to the subordinate tranches.

19. The schedule in the prospectus is the base schedule. The schedule can change so as to allocate less to the subordinate tranches if the collateral's performance deteriorates after the deal is closed. Determination of whether or not the base schedule should be overridden is made by the trustee based on tests that are specified in the prospectus.

20. The protection is provided by establishing a schedule for the allocation of principal payments (both regularly scheduled principal payments and prepayments) between the NAS tranche and the non-NAS tranches such that contraction risk and extension risk are reduced. For example, a schedule would specify a lockout period for the principal payments to the NAS tranche. This means that the NAS tranche would not receive any payments until the lockout period ends, and therefore contraction risk is mitigated. Extension risk is provided by allocating a large percentage to the NAS tranche in later years.

21. **A.** The cash flow is the same as for mortgage-backed securities backed by standard mortgage loans: 1) interest, 2) regularly scheduled principal repayments (amortization), and 3) prepayments.

B. The reasons why the securities backed by manufactured housing loans tend not to be sensitive to refinancing are:

   1. the loan balances are typically small so that there is no significant dollar savings from refinancing.

   2. the rate of depreciation of manufactured homes may be such that in the earlier years depreciation is greater than the amount of the loan paid off, making it difficult to refinance the loan.

   3. typically borrowers are of lower credit quality and therefore find it difficult to obtain funds to refinance.

22. The deals are more akin to the nonagency market since there is no guarantee by a federally related agency or a government sponsored enterprise as in the United States. As such, the deals must be rated and therefore require credit enhancement.

23. **A.** The cash flow for auto-loan backed securities consists of 1) interest, 2) regularly scheduled principal repayments (amortization), and 3) prepayments.

B. Prepayments due to refinancing on auto loans tend to be of minor importance.

24. A conditional prepayment rate measures prepayments relative to the amount outstanding in the previous year that could prepay. For a monthly CPR, called the single monthly mortality rate, SMM, prepayments are measured relative to the amount available in the previous month that was available to prepay.

The absolute prepayment speed, denoted ABS, is the monthly prepayment expressed as a percentage of the *original* collateral amount.

25. A. $SMM = \dfrac{0.015}{1 - \left[0.015 \times (21 - 1)\right]} = 0.0214 = 2.14\%$

B. $ABS = \dfrac{0.019}{1 + \left[0.019 \times (11 - 1)\right]} = 0.016 = 1.60\%$

26. The trustee is wrong. For certain student loans the government will guarantee up to 98% of the principal plus accrued interest (assuming the loans have been properly serviced). Moreover, there are securities backed by alternative student loans that carry no government guarantee.

27. While a student is in school, no payments are made by the student on the loan. This period is the deferment period. Upon leaving school, the student is extended a period of time (typically six months) when no payments on the loan must be made. This is called the grace period.

28. A. The cash flow for an SBA-backed security consists of 1) interest for the period, 2) the scheduled principal repayment, and 3) prepayments.

B. The interest is based on a coupon formula where the prime rate is the reference rate. The rate on the loan is reset monthly on the first of the month or quarterly on the first of January, April, July, and October.

29. A. During the lockout period, only finance charges and fees collected are distributed to the bondholders.

B. During the lockout period, principal paid by borrowers is reinvested in new receivables and not distributed to the bondholders.

C. The statement is incorrect because principal repayment can be made by either 1) a bullet payment structure (as stated in the question), 2) a controlled amortization structure, or 3) a passthrough structure.

30. While there is no schedule of principal repayments for credit card borrowers, there is the potential risk of contraction for the securities. This is because there is a provision for early or rapid amortization if certain triggers are reached.

There is also the potential for extension risk because principal repayment from the credit card borrowers and defaults and delinquencies may be such that the schedule specified for principal repayment of the security during the amortization period may not be adequate to completely pay off bondholders by the stated maturity.

While these are nontrivial risks, neither of these occurs frequently.

31. A. The monthly payment rate (MPR) expresses the monthly payment of a credit card receivable portfolio as a percentage of debt outstanding in the previous month. The monthly payment includes finance charges, fees, and any principal repayment collected.

B. There are two reasons why the MPR is important. First, if the MPR reaches an extremely low level, there is a chance that there will be extension risk with respect to the repayment of principal. The length of time until the return of principal is largely a function of the monthly payment rate. Second, if the MPR is very low, then there is a chance that there will not be sufficient cash flow to pay off principal. This is one of the events that could trigger early amortization of the principal.

C. The net portfolio yield for a credit card receivable portfolio is equal to the gross portfolio yield minus charge-offs. The gross portfolio yield includes finance charges collected and fees. From the gross portfolio yield charge-offs are deducted. Charge-offs represent the accounts charged off as uncollectible.

32. The typical structure of a CDO is as follows. There is 1) a senior tranche (between 70% and 80% of the deal) with a floating rate, 2) different layers of subordinate or junior debt tranches with a fixed rate, and 3) an equity tranche.

33. The statement is incorrect. The asset manager responsible for purchasing the debt obligations for the portfolio will have restrictions that are imposed by the rating agencies that rate the securities in the deal (coverage and quality tests). There will be certain tests that must be satisfied for the tranches in the CBO to maintain its credit rating at the time of issuance.

34. The statement is not correct. In fact, it is because of interest rate swaps that the risk is reduced for the senior tranche. This is because the collateral is typically fixed-rate bonds and the senior tranche must be paid a floating rate. An interest rate swap is used to convert the fixed-rate payments from the collateral into floating-rate payments that can be made to the senior tranche.

35. The key determinant is whether or not the CDO can be issued such that the subordinate/equity tranche can be offered a competitive return.

36. A. Given that the senior tranche is $150 million and the junior tranche is $30 million, the equity tranche is $20 million ($200 million minus $180 million).

B. The collateral will pay interest each year (assuming no defaults) equal to the 8-year Treasury rate of 6% plus 600 basis points. So the interest will be:

Interest from collateral: $12\% \times \$200{,}000{,}000 = \$24{,}000{,}000$

The interest that must be paid to the senior tranche is:

Interest to senior tranche: $\$150{,}000{,}000 \times (\text{LIBOR} + 90\text{ bps})$

The coupon rate for the junior tranche is 6% plus 300 basis points. So, the coupon rate is 9% and the interest is:

Interest to junior tranche: $9\% \times \$30{,}000{,}000 = \$2{,}700{,}000$

For the interest rate swap, the asset manager is agreeing to pay the swap counterparty each year 6% (the 8-year Treasury rate) plus 120 basis points, or 7.2%. Since the swap payments are based on a notional amount of $150 million, the asset manager pays to the swap counterparty:

Interest to swap counterparty: $7.2\% \times \$150{,}000{,}000 = \$10{,}800{,}000$

The interest payment received from the swap counterparty is LIBOR based on a notional amount of $150 million. That is,

Interest from swap counterparty: $\$150{,}000{,}000 \times \text{LIBOR}$

The interest for the CBO is:

Interest from collateral	$24,000,000	
Interest from swap counterparty	$150,000,000	× LIBOR
Total interest received	$24,000,000	+ $150,000,000 × LIBOR

The interest to be paid out to the senior and junior tranches and to the swap counterparty include:

Interest to senior tranche	$150,000,000	× (LIBOR + 90 bps)
Interest to junior tranche	$2,700,000	
Interest to swap counterparty	$10,800,000	
Total interest paid	$13,500,000	+ $150,000,000 × (LIBOR + 90 bps)

Netting the interest payments paid and received:

Total interest received	$24,000,000 + $150,000,000 × LIBOR
− Total interest paid	$13,500,000 + $150,000,000 × (LIBOR + 90 bps)
Net interest	$10,500,000 − $150,000,000 × (90 bps)

Since 90 bps times $150 million is $1,350,000, the net interest remaining is $9,150,000. This is the cash flow ignoring the asset management fee.

C. The amount available for the equity tranche is $9,150,000. This is the cash flow computed in Part B.

37. The return includes:

the return on a portfolio of high-quality debt instruments

plus

the payment from the asset manager as part of the credit default swap

minus

the payment that must be made by a junior tranche due to a credit event

38. By issuing a synthetic CDO, a bank can remove the economic risk of bank loans without having to notify any borrowers that they are selling the loans to another party. Thus, no consent would be needed from borrowers to transfer loans, a requirement in some countries.

39. B is correct. The primary motivation for the sequential-pay structure is to redistribute prepayment risk among the holders of different bond classes. This is known as a sequential pay structure.

40. A is correct. The primary motivation for the senior-subordinate structure is to redistribute credit risk (referred to as credit tranching), a form of internal credit enhancement for the senior bond classes.

41. B is correct. Given the sequential pay structure, the B2 bond class is the first-loss piece, and those bondholders would absorb the first $4.0 million in default losses. The remaining $4.0 million of losses would be absorbed by the B1 bond class. As long as the default losses do not exceed $10 million, the senior (A) classes would not suffer any default losses.

42. C is correct. Overcollateralization is a form of internal credit enhancement. Letters of credit and insurance wrapping are external credit enhancements.

43. C is correct. Whisper Spa's credit rating would not be taken into account when assigning a credit rating to the asset-backed securities unless they, as the seller, were to guarantee repayment on the bonds. Because Whisper Spa only plans to use internal credit enhancements, a guarantee would not apply, and Whisper Spa's credit rating would be irrelevant to the rating on the securities.

44. A is correct. Because the securities have a two-year lockout period, all principal prepayments within the first two years will be used to fund new loans. No security tranche will receive principal prepayments until after the 24-month lockout period. Credit card prepayments are usually just rolled into new loans (not repaid to bondholders).

Valuing Mortgage-Backed and Asset-Backed Securities

by Frank J. Fabozzi, CFA

LEARNING OUTCOMES

Mastery	The candidate should be able to:
☐	**a** explain the calculation, use, and limitations of the cash flow yield, nominal spread, and zero-volatility spread for a mortgage-backed security and an asset-backed security;
☐	**b** describe the Monte Carlo simulation model for valuing a mortgage-backed security;
☐	**c** describe path dependency in passthrough securities and the implications for valuation models;
☐	**d** explain how the option-adjusted spread is calculated using the Monte Carlo simulation model and how this spread measure is interpreted;
☐	**e** evaluate a mortgage-backed security using option-adjusted spread analysis;
☐	**f** explain why effective durations reported by various dealers and vendors may differ;
☐	**g** analyze the interest rate risk of a security, given the security's effective duration;
☐	**h** explain cash flow, coupon curve, and empirical measures of duration, and describe limitations of each in relation to mortgage-backed securities;
☐	**i** determine whether the nominal spread, zero-volatility spread, or option-adjusted spread should be used to evaluate a specific fixed income security.

INTRODUCTION

1

In previous readings, we looked at mortgage-backed and asset-backed securities. Our focus was on understanding the risks associated with investing in these securities, how they are created (i.e., how they are structured), and why the products are created. Specifically, in the case of agency mortgage-backed securities we saw how prepayment risk can be redistributed among different tranches to create securities

Fixed Income Analysis for the Chartered Financial Analyst® Program, Second Edition, by Frank J. Fabozzi, CFA. Copyright © 2005 by CFA Institute.

with a prepayment risk profile that is different from the underlying pool of mortgages. For asset-backed securities and nonagency mortgage-backed security, we saw how to create tranches with different degrees of credit risk.

What we did not discuss in describing these securities is how to value them and how to quantify their exposure to interest rate risk. That is, we know, for example, that a support tranche in a CMO structure has greater prepayment risk than a planned amortization class (PAC) tranche. However, how do we determine whether or not the price at which a support tranche is offered in the market adequately compensates for the greater prepayment risk? In this reading, we will describe and then apply a methodology for valuing mortgage-backed securities and some types of asset-backed securities—Monte Carlo simulation. A byproduct of a valuation model is the option-adjusted spread. We will see how the option-adjusted spread for a mortgage-backed or an asset-backed security is computed and applied. From a valuation model the effective duration and effective convexity of any security can be computed. We will explain how to compute effective duration and effective convexity using the Monte Carlo simulation model. However, in the case of mortgage-backed securities, there have been several alternative measures of duration used by practitioners. These measures will be identified along with their advantages and disadvantages.

Admittedly, the majority of this reading is devoted to the valuation of mortgage-backed securities and by extension to all real estate-related asset-backed securities. They are the most difficult asset-backed products to value and to quantify in terms of interest rate exposure. At the end of this reading, we provide a framework for determining which analytical measures discussed in this reading are appropriate for valuing any asset-backed security. In fact, the principles apply to all fixed income products.

2   CASH FLOW YIELD ANALYSIS

Let's begin with the traditional analysis of mortgage-backed and asset-backed securities—cash flow yield analysis. The yield on any financial instrument is the interest rate that makes the present value of the expected cash flow equal to its market price plus accrued interest. When applied to mortgage-backed and asset-backed securities, this yield is called a cash flow yield. The problem in calculating the cash flow yield of mortgage-backed and asset-backed securities is that the cash flow is unknown because of prepayments. Consequently, to determine a cash flow yield, some assumption about the prepayment rate must be made. And, in the case of all but agency mortgage-backed securities, an assumption about default rates and recovery rates must be made.

The cash flow for mortgage-backed and asset-backed securities is typically monthly. The convention is to compare the yield on mortgage-backed and asset-backed securities to that of a Treasury coupon security by calculating the security's *bond-equivalent yield*. The bond-equivalent yield for a Treasury coupon security is found by doubling the semiannual yield to maturity. However, it is incorrect to do this for a mortgage-backed or an asset-backed security because the investor has the opportunity to generate greater reinvestment income by reinvesting the more frequent (i.e., monthly) cash flows. The market convention is to calculate a yield so as to make it comparable to the yield to maturity on a bond-equivalent basis. The formula for annualizing the monthly cash flow yield for a monthly-pay product is therefore:

$$\text{Bond-equivalent yield} = 2\left[\left(1 + i_M\right)^6 - 1\right]$$

where i_M is the monthly interest rate that will equate the present value of the projected monthly cash flow equal to the market price (plus accrued interest) of the security.

To illustrate the calculation of the bond-equivalent yield, suppose that the monthly yield is 0.6%. That is, i_M is 0.006. Then

$$\text{Bond-equivalent yield} = 2\left[(1.006)^6 - 1\right] = 0.0731 = 7.31\%$$

A. Limitations of Cash Flow Yield Measure

All yield measures suffer from problems that limit their use in assessing a security's potential return. The yield to maturity has two major shortcomings as a measure of a bond's potential return. To realize the stated yield to maturity, the investor must:

1. reinvest the coupon payments at a rate equal to the yield to maturity, and

2. hold the bond to the maturity date.

The reinvestment of the coupon payments is critical and for long-term bonds can be as much as 80% of the bond's return. Reinvestment risk is the risk of having to reinvest the interest payments at less than the computed yield. Interest rate risk is the risk associated with having to sell the security before its maturity date at a price less than the purchase price.

These shortcomings are equally applicable to the cash flow yield measure:

1. the projected cash flows are assumed to be reinvested at the cash flow yield, and

2. the mortgage-backed or asset-backed security is assumed to be held until the final payout based on some prepayment assumption.

The importance of reinvestment risk, the risk that the cash flow will have to be reinvested at a rate less than the cash flow yield, is particularly important for many mortgage-backed and asset-backed securities because payments are monthly and both interest and principal must be reinvested. Moreover, an additional assumption is that the projected cash flow is actually realized. If the prepayment, default, and recovery experience is different from that assumed, the cash flow yield will not be realized.

B. Nominal Spread

Given the computed cash flow yield and the average life for a mortgage-backed or asset-backed security based on some prepayment, default, and recovery assumption, the next step is to compare the yield to the yield for a comparable Treasury security. "Comparable" is typically defined as a Treasury security with the same maturity as the security's average life. The difference between the cash flow yield and the yield on a comparable Treasury security is called the nominal spread.

Unfortunately, it is the nominal spread that some managers will use as a measure of relative value. However, this spread masks the fact that a portion of the nominal spread is compensation for accepting prepayment risk. For example, CMO support tranches have been offered at large nominal spreads. However, the nominal spread embodies the substantial prepayment risk associated with support tranches. The manager who buys solely on the basis of nominal spread fails to determine whether or not that nominal spread offered adequate compensation given the substantial prepayment risk faced by the holder of a support tranche.

Instead of nominal spread, managers need a measure that indicates the potential compensation after adjusting for prepayment risk. This measure is called the option-adjusted spread. We discussed this measure in the reading on valuing bonds with embedded options where we covered the valuation of corporate and agency bonds with embedded options. Before discussing this measure for structured products, we describe another spread measure commonly quoted for structured products called the zero-volatility spread.

3   ZERO-VOLATILITY SPREAD

The proper procedure to compare any security to a U.S. Treasury security is to compare it to a portfolio of Treasury securities that have the same cash flow. The value of the security is then equal to the present value of all of the cash flows. The security's value, assuming the cash flows are default-free, will equal the present value of the replicating portfolio of Treasury securities. In turn, these cash flows are valued at the Treasury spot rates.

The zero-volatility spread is a measure of spread that the investor would realize over the entire Treasury spot rate curve if the mortgage-backed or asset-backed security is held to maturity. It is not a spread off one point on the Treasury yield curve, as is the nominal spread. The zero-volatility spread (also called the Z-spread and the static spread) is the spread that will make the present value of the cash flows from the mortgage-backed or asset-backed security when discounted at the Treasury spot rate plus the spread equal to the price of the security. A trial and-error procedure (or search algorithm) is required to determine the zero-volatility spread.[1]

In general, the shorter the maturity or average life of a structured product, the less the zero-volatility spread will differ from the nominal spread. The magnitude of the difference between the nominal spread and the zero-volatility spread also depends on the shape of the yield curve. The steeper the yield curve, the greater the difference.

One of the objectives of this reading is to explain when it is appropriate to use the Z-spread instead of the OAS. What will be seen is that if a structured product has an option and the borrower tends to take advantage of that option when interest rates decline, then the OAS should be used. If the borrower has an option but tends not to take advantage of it when interest rates decline, then the Z-spread should be used.

4   MONTE CARLO SIMULATION MODEL AND OAS

In the reading on valuing bonds with embedded options, we discussed one model that is used to value callable agency debentures and corporate bonds, the binomial model. This valuation model accommodates securities in which the decision to exercise a call option is not dependent on how interest rates evolved over time. That is, the decision of an issuer to call a bond will depend on the level of the rate at which the issue can be refunded relative to the issue's coupon rate, and not the path interest rates took to get to that rate. In contrast, there are fixed-income securities and derivative instruments for which the periodic cash flows are "interest rate path-dependent." This means that the cash flow received in one period is determined not only by the current interest rate level, but also by the path that interest rates took to get to the current level.

For example, in the case of passthrough securities, prepayments are interest rate path-dependent because this month's prepayment rate depends on whether there have been prior opportunities to refinance since the underlying mortgages were originated. This phenomenon is referred to as "prepayment burnout." Pools of passthroughs are used as collateral for the creation of CMOs. Consequently, there are typically two sources of path dependency in a CMO tranche's cash flows. First, the collateral prepayments are path-dependent as discussed above. Second, the cash flows to be received in the current month by a CMO tranche depend on the outstanding balances of the other tranches in the deal. Thus, we need the history of prepayments to calculate these balances.

---

[1] Most common spreadsheet programs offer this type of algorithm.

Conceptually, the valuation of agency passthrough using the Monte Carlo model is simple. In practice, however, it is very complex. The simulation involves generating a set of cash flows based on simulated future mortgage refinancing rates, which in turn imply simulated prepayment rates.

Valuation modeling for agency CMOs is similar to valuation modeling for passthroughs, although the difficulties are amplified because the issuer has distributed both the prepayment risk and the interest rate risk into different tranches. The sensitivity of the passthroughs comprising the collateral to these two risks is not transmitted equally to every tranche. Some of the tranches wind up more sensitive to prepayment risk and interest rate risk than the collateral, while some of them are much less sensitive.

The objective is to figure out how the value of the collateral gets transmitted to the tranches in a deal. More specifically, the objective is to find out where the value goes and where the risk goes so that one can identify the tranches with low risk and high value: the tranches a manager wants to consider for purchase. The good news is that this combination usually exists in every deal. The bad news is that in every deal there are usually tranches with low value and high risk that managers want to avoid purchasing.

A. Simulating Interest Rate Paths and Cash Flows

To generate these random interest rate paths, the typical model used by Wall Street firms and commercial vendors takes as input today's term structure of interest rates and a volatility assumption. (We discussed these topics in the reading on valuing bonds with embedded options.) The term structure of interest rates is the theoretical spot rate (or zero coupon) curve implied by today's Treasury securities. The simulations should be calibrated so that the average simulated price of a zero-coupon Treasury bond equals today's actual price.

On-the-run Treasury issues are often used in the calibration process. Some dealers and vendors of analytical systems use the LIBOR curve instead of the Treasury curve—or give the user a choice to use either the Treasury curve or the LIBOR curve. The reason is that some investors are interested in spreads that they can earn relative to their funding costs, and LIBOR for many investors is a better proxy for that cost than Treasury rates.

As explained in the reading on valuing bonds with embedded options, every dealer and vendor of analytical systems employs an interest rate model. This is a model that assumes how interest rates will change over time. The interest rate models employed by most dealers and vendors of analytical systems are similar. However, one input to all interest rate models is the interest rate volatility assumption. It is that assumption that varies by dealer and vendor. As will be illustrated later in this reading, it is a critical input.

The volatility assumption determines the dispersion of future interest rates in the simulation. Today, many dealers and vendors do not use one volatility number for the yield of all maturities of the yield curve. Instead, they use either a short/long yield volatility or a term structure of yield volatility. A short/long yield volatility means that volatility is specified for maturities up to a certain number of years (short yield volatility) and a different yield volatility for longer maturities (long yield volatility). The short yield volatility is assumed to be greater than the long yield volatility. A term structure of yield volatilities means that a yield volatility is assumed for each maturity.

Based on the interest rate model and the assumed volatility, a series of interest rate paths will be generated. We will see shortly how a security is valued on each interest rate path. However, there is nothing that we have explained thus far that assures us that the values produced by the model will be arbitrage free. Recall from the reading on valuing bonds with embedded options that the binomial interest rate tree by design is constructed to be arbitrage free. That is, if any of the on-the-run issues that were used to construct the binomial interest rate tree are valued using the tree, the model would produce a value for that on-the-run issue equal to its market value. There is nothing we described so far about the Monte Carlo simulation to assure this.

More specifically, in the case of Monte Carlo simulation for valuing mortgage-backed and asset-backed securities, the on-the-run Treasury issues are typically used. What assurance is there that if an on-the-run Treasury issue is valued using the Monte Carlo simulation model it will be arbitrage free? That is, what assurance is there that the value produced by the model will equal the market price? Nothing. That's right, nothing. What the model builder must do is "adjust" the interest rate paths so that the model produces the correct values for the on-the-run Treasury issues. A discussion of this adjustment process is not important to us. In fact, there are very few published sources that describe how this is done. The key point here is that no such adjustment is necessary in a binomial model for valuing corporate and agency bonds with embedded options because the tree is built to be arbitrage free. In the case of the Monte Carlo simulation model, the builder must make an arbitrary adjustment to the interest rate paths to get the model to be arbitrage free.

The simulation works by generating many scenarios of future interest rate paths. As just explained, the "raw" interest rate paths that are simulated must be "adjusted" so as to make the model generate arbitrage-free values for whatever benchmark interest rates are used—typically, the on-the-run Treasury issues. So, *in the remainder of this reading, when we refer to interest rate paths it is understood that it is the "adjusted" interest rate paths where "adjusted" means that each interest rate path is adjusted so that the model will produce arbitrage-free values.*

In each month of the scenario (i.e., path), a monthly interest rate and a mortgage refinancing rate are generated. The monthly interest rates are used to discount the projected cash flows in the scenario. The mortgage refinancing rate is needed to determine the cash flows because it represents the opportunity cost the borrower (i.e., mortgagor) is facing at that time.

If the refinancing rates are high relative to the borrower's original coupon rate (i.e., the rate on the borrower's loan), the borrower will have less incentive to refinance, or even a disincentive (i.e., the homeowner will avoid moving in order to avoid refinancing). If the refinancing rate is low relative to the borrower's original coupon rate, the borrower has an incentive to refinance.

Prepayments are projected by feeding the refinancing rate and loan characteristics into a prepayment model. Given the projected prepayments, the cash flows along an interest rate path can be determined.

To make this more concrete, consider a newly issued mortgage passthrough security with a maturity of 360 months. Exhibit 1 shows N "adjusted" simulated interest rate path scenarios—adjusted to be arbitrage free. Each scenario consists of a path of 360 simulated 1-month future interest rates. (The number of paths generated is based on a well-known principle in simulation which will not be discussed here.) So, our first assumption that we make to get Exhibit 1 is the volatility of interest rates.

Exhibit 2 shows the paths of simulated mortgage refinancing rates corresponding to the scenarios shown in Exhibit 1. In going from Exhibit 1 to Exhibit 2, an assumption must be made about the relationship between the Treasury rates and refinancing rates. The assumption is that there is a constant spread relationship between the rate that the borrower will use to determine whether or not to refinance (i.e., the refinancing rate) and the 1-month interest rates shown in Exhibit 1. For example, for 30-year mortgage loans, model builders use the 10-year Treasury rate as a proxy for the refinancing rate.

| Exhibit 1 | "Adjusted" Simulated Paths of Arbitrage-Free 1-Month Future Interest Rates[a] |

	Interest Rate Path Number						
Month	1	2	3	...	n	...	N
1	$f_1(1)$	$f_1(2)$	$f_1(3)$	...	$f_1(n)$	...	$f_1(N)$
2	$f_2(1)$	$f_2(2)$	$f_2(3)$	...	$f_2(n)$	...	$f_2(N)$
3	$f_3(1)$	$f_3(2)$	$f_3(3)$	...	$f_3(n)$	...	$f_3(N)$
...	...	...	...	...	...	...	...
T	$f_t(1)$	$f_t(2)$	$f_t(3)$	...	$f_t(n)$	...	$f_t(N)$
...	...	...	...	...	...	...	...
358	$f_{358}(1)$	$f_{358}(2)$	$f_{358}(3)$	...	$f_{358}(n)$	...	$f_{358}(N)$
359	$f_{359}(1)$	$f_{359}(2)$	$f_{359}(3)$	...	$f_{359}(n)$	...	$f_{359}(N)$
360	$f_{360}(1)$	$f_{360}(2)$	$f_{360}(3)$	...	$f_{360}(n)$	...	$f_{360}(N)$

Notation:

$f_t(n)$ = 1-month future interest rate for month t on path n

N = total number of interest rate paths

[a]As explained in the reading, the "raw" interest rate paths that are simulated must be "adjusted" so as to make the model generate arbitrage-free values for whatever benchmark interest rates are used—typically, the on-the-run Treasury issues. The interest rates shown in the exhibit are the "adjusted" arbitrage-free interest rates.

| Exhibit 2 | Simulated Paths of Mortgage Refinancing Rates |

	Interest Rate Path Number						
Month	1	2	3	...	n	...	N
1	$r_1(1)$	$r_1(2)$	$r_1(3)$	...	$r_1(n)$	...	$r_1(N)$
2	$r_2(1)$	$r_2(2)$	$r_2(3)$	...	$r_2(n)$	...	$r_2(N)$
3	$r_3(1)$	$r_3(2)$	$r_3(3)$	...	$r_3(n)$	...	$r_3(N)$
...	...	...	...	...	...	...	...
T	$r_t(1)$	$r_t(2)$	$r_t(3)$	...	$r_t(n)$	...	$r_t(N)$
...	...	...	...	...	...	...	...
358	$r_{358}(1)$	$r_{358}(2)$	$r_{358}(3)$	...	$r_{358}(n)$	...	$r_{358}(N)$
359	$r_{359}(1)$	$r_{359}(2)$	$r_{359}(3)$	...	$r_{359}(n)$	...	$r_{359}(N)$
360	$r_{360}(1)$	$r_{360}(2)$	$r_{360}(3)$	...	$r_{360}(n)$	...	$r_{360}(N)$

Notation:

$r_t(n)$ = mortgage refinancing rate for month t on path n

N = total number of interest rate paths

Given the mortgage refinancing rates, the cash flows on each interest rate path can be generated. For agency mortgage-backed securities, this requires a prepayment model. For asset-backed securities and nonagency mortgage-backed securities, this requires both a prepayment model and a model of defaults and recoveries. So, our next assumption is that the outputs of these models (prepayments, defaults, and recoveries) are correct. The resulting cash flows are depicted in Exhibit 3.

Exhibit 3	Simulated Cash Flows on Each of the Interest Rate Paths						
	Interest Rate Path Number						
Month	**1**	**2**	**3**	**...**	**n**	**...**	**N**
1	$C_1(1)$	$C_1(2)$	$C_1(3)$	...	$C_1(n)$	...	$C_1(N)$
2	$C_2(1)$	$C_2(2)$	$C_2(3)$	...	$C_2(n)$	...	$C_2(N)$
3	$C_3(1)$	$C_3(2)$	$C_3(3)$	...	$C_3(n)$	...	$C_3(N)$
...	...	...	...	...	...	...	...
T	$C_t(1)$	$C_t(2)$	$C_t(3)$	...	$C_t(n)$	...	$C_t(N)$
...	...	...	...	...	...	...	...
358	$C_{358}(1)$	$C_{358}(2)$	$C_{358}(3)$	...	$C_{358}(n)$	...	$C_{358}(N)$
359	$C_{359}(1)$	$C_{359}(2)$	$C_{359}(3)$	...	$C_{359}(n)$	...	$C_{359}(N)$
360	$C_{360}(1)$	$C_{360}(2)$	$C_{360}(3)$	...	$C_{360}(n)$	...	$C_{360}(N)$

Notation:

$C_t(n) =$ cash flow for month t on path n

$N \;=\;$ total number of interest rate paths

B. Calculating the Present Value for an Interest Rate Path

Given the cash flows on an interest rate path, the path's present value can be calculated. The discount rate for determining the present value is the simulated spot rate for each month on the interest rate path plus an appropriate spread. The spot rate on a path can be determined from the simulated future monthly rates. The relationship that holds between the simulated spot rate for month T on path n and the simulated future 1-month rates is:

$$z_T(n) = \left\{ \left[1 + f_1(n)\right]\left[1 + f_2(n)\right]\cdots\left[1 + f_T(n)\right] \right\}^{1/T} - 1$$

Where

$Z_T(n)$ = simulated spot rate for month T on path n

$f_T(n)$ = simulated future 1-month rate for month t on path n

We previously explained the relationship between spot rates and forward rates.

Consequently, the interest rate path for the simulated future 1-month rates can be converted to the interest rate path for the simulated monthly spot rates as shown in Exhibit 4. Therefore, the present value of the cash flows for month T on interest rate path n discounted at the simulated spot rate for month T plus some spread is:

Exhibit 4	"Adjusted" Simulated Paths of Monthly Arbitrage-Free Spot Rates						
	Interest Rate Path Number						
Month	**1**	**2**	**3**	**...**	**n**	**...**	**N**
1	$z_1(1)$	$z_1(2)$	$z_1(3)$	...	$z_1(n)$	...	$z_1(N)$
2	$z_2(1)$	$z_2(2)$	$z_2(3)$	...	$z_2(n)$	...	$z_2(N)$
3	$z_3(1)$	$z_3(2)$	$z_3(3)$	...	$z_3(n)$	...	$z_3(N)$
...	...	...	...	...	...	...	...
t	$z_t(1)$	$z_t(2)$	$z_t(3)$	...	$z_t(n)$	...	$z_t(N)$

| | Exhibit 4 | | Continued | | | | |

Interest Rate Path Number

Month	1	2	3	...	n	...	N
...	...	...	...	...	...	...	...
358	$z_{358}(1)$	$z_{358}(2)$	$z_{358}(3)$	...	$z_{358}(n)$	...	$z_{358}(N)$
359	$z_{359}(1)$	$z_{359}(2)$	$z_{359}(3)$	...	$z_{359}(n)$	...	$z_{359}(N)$
360	$z_{360}(1)$	$z_{360}(2)$	$z_{360}(3)$	...	$z_{360}(n)$	...	$z_{360}(N)$

Notation:

$z_t(n)$ = spot rate for month t on path n

N = total number of interest rate paths

$$PV\left[C_T(n)\right] = \frac{C_T(n)}{\left[1 + z_T(n) + K\right]^T}$$

where

$PV[C_T(n)]$ = present value of cash flows for month T on path n

$CT(n)$ = cash flow for month T on path n

$z_T(n)$ = spot rate for month T on path n

K = spread

The spread, K, reflects the risks that the investor feels are associated with realizing the cash flows.

The present value for path n is the sum of the present value of the cash flows for each month on path n. That is,

$$PV\left[Path(n)\right] = PV\left[C_1(n)\right] + PV\left[C_2(n)\right] + \ldots + PV\left[C_{360}(n)\right]$$

where $PV[Path(n)]$ is the present value of interest rate path n.

C. Determining the Theoretical Value

The present value of a given interest rate path can be thought of as the theoretical value of a passthrough if that path was actually realized. The theoretical value of the passthrough can be determined by calculating the average of the theoretical values of all the interest rate paths. That is, the theoretical value is equal to

$$\text{Theoretical value} = \frac{PV\left[Path(1)\right] + PV\left[Path(2)\right] + \ldots + PV\left[Path(N)\right]}{N}$$

where N is the number of interest rate paths. The theoretical value derived from the above equation is based on some spread, K. It follows the usual practice of discounting cash flows at spot rates plus a spread—in this case the spread is K.

This procedure for valuing a passthrough is also followed for a CMO tranche. The cash flow for each month on each interest rate path is found according to the principal repayment and interest distribution rules of the deal.

D. Selecting the Number of Interest Rate Paths

Let's now address the question of the number of scenario paths, N, needed to value a security. The number of interest rate paths determines how "good" the estimate is, not relative to the truth but relative to the model used. The more paths, the more the average value produced tends to converge. It is simply a statistical sampling problem.

Most models employ some form of variance reduction to cut down on the number of sample paths necessary to get a good statistical sample.[2] Several vendor firms have developed computational procedures that reduce the number of paths required but still provide the accuracy of a full Monte Carlo analysis. The procedure is to use statistical techniques to reduce the number of interest rate paths to sets of similar paths. These paths are called representative paths. For example, suppose that 2,000 sample paths are generated. Using a certain statistical technique, these 2,000 sample paths can be collapsed to, say, 16 representative paths. The security is then valued on each of these 16 representative paths. The theoretical value of the security is then the *weighted* average of the 16 representative paths. The weight for a path is the percentage of that representative path relative to the total sample paths. Vendors often give the investor or portfolio manager the choice of whether to use the "full Monte Carlo simulation" or to specify a number of representative paths.

E. Option-Adjusted Spread

In the reading on valuing bonds with embedded options, we explained the option-adjusted spread (OAS). Specifically, we explained 1) how to compute the OAS for corporate and agency bonds with embedded options and 2) how to interpret the OAS and apply it in relative analysis. Below we cover the same issues for the OAS computed for mortgage-backed securities.

1 Computing the OAS

In the Monte Carlo model, the OAS is the spread that when added to all the spot rates on all interest rate paths will make the average present value of the paths equal to the observed market price (plus accrued interest). Mathematically, OAS is the value for K (the spread) that will satisfy the following condition:

$$\frac{PV\big[Path(1)\big] + PV\big[Path(2)\big] + \ldots + PV\big[Path(N)\big]}{N} = \text{Market price}$$

where N is the number of interest rate paths. The left-hand side of the above equation looks identical to that of the equation for the theoretical value. The difference is that the objective is to determine what spread, K, will make the model produce a theoretical value equal to the market price.

The procedure for determining the OAS is straightforward and involves the same search algorithm explained for the zero-volatility spread. The next question, then, is how to interpret the OAS. Basically, the OAS is used to reconcile value with market price. On the **right**-hand side of the previous equation is the market's statement: the price of a structured product. The average present value over all the paths on the **left**-hand side of the equation is the model's output, which we refer to as the theoretical value.

2 Interpreting the OAS and Relative Value Application

What an investor or a portfolio manager seeks to do is to buy a mortgage-backed security where value is greater than price. By using a valuation model such as the Monte Carlo model, a portfolio manager could estimate the value of a security, which at this point would be sufficient in determining whether to buy a security. That is, the portfolio manager can say that this security is 1 point cheap or 2 points cheap, and so on. The model does not stop here. Instead, it converts the divergence between price

---

2 The variance reduction technique is described in books on management science and Monte Carlo simulation.

and value into some type of spread measure since most market participants find it more convenient to think about spreads than price differences.

The OAS was developed as a measure of the spread that can be used to convert dollar differences between value and price. As we explained in the reading on valuing bonds with embedded options, in the binomial model a spread is measured relative to the benchmark interest rates used to generate the interest rate tree and which is therefore used to make the tree arbitrage free. The same is true in the case of the Monte Carlo simulation model. The spread is measured relative to the benchmark interest rates that were used to generate the interest rate paths and to adjust the interest rate paths to make them arbitrage free. Typically, for a mortgage-backed security the benchmark interest rates are the on-the-run Treasury rates. The OAS is then measuring the average spread over the Treasury spot rate curve, not the Treasury yield as explained in the reading on valuing bonds with embedded options. It is an average spread since the OAS is found by averaging over the interest rate paths for the possible Treasury spot rate curves. Of course, if the LIBOR curve is used, the OAS is the spread over that curve.

This spread measure is superior to the nominal spread, which gives no recognition to the prepayment risk. As explained in the reading on valuing bonds with embedded options, the OAS is "option adjusted" because the cash flows on the interest rate paths are adjusted for the option of the borrowers to prepay. While we may understand the mechanics of how to compute the OAS and why it is appropriate to use the OAS rather than the nominal spread or Z-spread, the question is what does the spread represent? In the reading on valuing bonds with embedded options, a discussion of what compensation the OAS reflects for corporate and agency bonds with embedded options was presented. The compensation is for a combination of credit risk and liquidity risk. The compensation depends on the benchmark interest rates used in the analysis. For example, consider the use of Treasury interest rates and more specifically the Treasury spot rate curve since this is the benchmark typically used in the calculation of an OAS for a mortgage-backed security. If there is an OAS computed using the Treasury benchmark, then what is that OAS compensating?

Consider first Ginnie Mae mortgage passthrough securities. Ginnie Mae is an arm of the U.S. government. The securities it issues are backed by the full faith and credit of the U.S. government. Effectively, a Ginnie Mae mortgage-backed security is a Treasury security with prepayment risk. The OAS removes the prepayment risk (i.e., the option risk). Additionally, if the benchmark is Treasury rates, the OAS should not be compensation for credit risk. That leaves liquidity risk. While Ginnie Mae mortgage passthrough securities may not be as liquid as on-the-run Treasury issues, they are fairly liquid as measured by the bid-ask spread. Nevertheless, part of the OAS should reflect compensation for liquidity risk. There is one more risk that was not the focus of the reading on valuing bonds with embedded options, modeling risk. In our explanation of the Monte Carlo model, there were several critical assumptions and parameters required. If those assumptions prove incorrect or if the parameters are misestimated, the prepayment model will not calculate the true level of risk. Thus, probably a good part of the compensation for a Ginnie Mae mortgage passthrough security reflects payment for this model uncertainty.

If we consider CMOs issued by Ginnie Mae rather than the mortgage passthrough securities, the OAS would reflect the complexity associated with a particular tranche. For example, a planned amortization class (PAC) tranche would be less exposed to modeling risk than a support tranche in the same CMO structure. Hence, compensation for modeling risk would be greater for a support tranche than a PAC tranche in the same structure. Moreover, PAC tranches have greater liquidity than support tranches, so compensation is less for the former relative to the latter.

As we move from Ginnie Mae issued mortgage products to those issued by Freddie Mac and Fannie Mae, we introduce credit risk. Freddie Mac and Fannie Mae are government sponsored enterprises (GSEs). As such, there is no requirement that a GSE be bailed out by the U.S. government. The GSEs are viewed as triple A rated. Consequently, in addition to modeling risk and liquidity risk, a portion of the OAS reflects credit risk relative to Treasury securities.

Moving on to nonagency mortgage-backed securities and real estate backed asset-backed securities, the OAS is compensating for 1) credit risk (which varies depending on the credit rating for the tranche under consideration), 2) liquidity risk (which is greater than for Ginnie Mae, Fannie Mae, and Freddie Mac mortgage products), and 3) modeling risk.

F. Option Cost

The implied cost of the option embedded for a mortgage-backed or asset-backed security can be obtained by calculating the difference between the option-adjusted spread at the assumed volatility of interest rates and the zero-volatility spread. That is,

Option cost = Zero-volatility spread − Option-adjusted spread

The option cost measures the prepayment (or option) risk embedded in the security. Note that the cost of the option is a byproduct of the option-adjusted spread analysis, not valued explicitly with some option pricing model.

G. Illustrations

We will use two deals to show how CMOs can be analyzed using the Monte Carlo model/OAS procedure discussed above—a simple structure and a PAC/support structure.[3]

1 *Simple Structure*

The simple structure analyzed is Freddie Mac (FHLMC) 1915. It is a simple sequential-pay CMO bond structure. The structure includes eight tranches, A, B, C, D, E, F, G, and S. The focus of our analysis is on tranches A, B, and C. All three tranches were priced at a premium.

The top panel of Exhibit 5 shows the OAS, the option cost, and effective duration[4] for the collateral and the three tranches in the CMO structure. However, tranche A had the smallest effective duration and tranche C had the largest effective duration. The OAS for the collateral is 51 basis points. Since the option cost is 67 basis points, the zero-volatility spread is 118 basis points (51 basis points plus 67 basis points).

At the time this analysis was performed, March 10, 1998, the Treasury yield curve was not steep. When the yield curve is relatively flat, the zero-volatility spread will not differ significantly from the nominal spread. Thus, for the three tranches shown in Exhibit 5, the zero-volatility spread is 83 basis points for A, 115 basis points for B, and 116 basis points for C.

---

3 These illustrations are from Frank J. Fabozzi, Scott F. Richard, and David S. Horowitz, "Valuation of CMOs," Chapter 6 in Frank J. Fabozzi (ed.), *Advances in the Valuation and Management of Mortgage-Backed Securities* (New Hope, PA: Frank J. Fabozzi Associates, 1998).

4 We will explain how to compute the effective duration using the Monte Carlo methodology in Section 5A.

Exhibit 5	OAS Analysis of FHLMC 1915 Classes A, B, and C (as of 3/10/98)

All three tranches were trading at a premium as of the date of the analysis.

	Base Case (Assumes 13% Interest Rate Volatility)			
	OAS (in Basis Points)	Option Cost (in Basis Points)	Z-Spread (in Basis Points)	Effective Duration (in Years)
Collateral	51	67	118	1.2
Tranche				
A	32	51	83	0.9
B	33	82	115	2.9
C	46	70	116	6.7

	Prepayments at 80% and 120% of Prepayment Model (Assumes 13% Interest Rate Volatility)			
	New OAS (in Basis Points)		Change in Price per $100 Par (Holding OAS Constant)	
	80%	120%	80%	120%
Collateral	63	40	$0.45	−$0.32
Tranche				
A	40	23	0.17	−0.13
B	43	22	0.54	−0.43
C	58	36	0.97	−0.63

	Interest Rate of Volatility of 9% and 17%			
	New OAS (in Basis Points)		Change in Price per $100 Par (Holding OAS Constant)	
	9%	17%	9%	17%
Collateral	79	21	$1.03	−$0.94
Tranche				
A	52	10	0.37	−0.37
B	66	−3	1.63	− 1.50
C	77	15	2.44	− 2.08

Notice that the tranches did not share the OAS equally. The same is true for the option cost. Both the Z-spread and the option cost increase as the effective duration increases. Whether or not any of these tranches were attractive investments requires a comparison to other tranches in the market with the same effective duration. While not presented here, all three tranches offered an OAS similar to other sequential-pay tranches with the same effective duration available in the market. On a relative basis (i.e., relative to the other tranches analyzed in the deal), the only tranche where there appears to be a bit of a bargain is tranche C. A portfolio manager contemplating the purchase of this last cash flow tranche can see that

C offers a higher OAS than B and appears to bear less of the risk (i.e., has lower option cost), as measured by the option cost. The problem portfolio managers may face is that they might not be able to go out as long on the yield curve as tranche C because of effective duration, maturity, and average life constraints relative to their liabilities, for example.

Now let's look at modeling risk. Examination of the sensitivity of the tranches to changes in prepayments and interest rate volatility will help us to understand the interaction of the tranches in the structure and who is bearing the risk. How the deal behaves under various scenarios should reinforce and be consistent with the valuation (i.e., a tranche may look "cheap" for a reason).

We begin with prepayments. Specifically, we keep the same interest rate paths as those used to get the OAS in the base case (the top panel of Exhibit 5), but reduce the prepayment rate on each interest rate path to 80% of the projected rate. As can be seen in the second panel of Exhibit 5, slowing down prepayments increases the OAS and price for the collateral. The exhibit reports two results of the sensitivity analysis. First, it indicates the change in the OAS. Second, it indicates the change in the price, holding the OAS constant at the base case.

To see how a portfolio manager can use the information in the second panel, consider tranche A. At 80% of the prepayment speed, the OAS for this tranche increases from 32 basis points to 40 basis points. If the OAS is held constant, the panel indicates that the buyer of tranche A would gain $0.17 per $100 par value.

Notice that for all of the tranches reported in Exhibit 5 there is a gain from a slowdown in prepayments. This is because all of the sequential tranches in this deal are priced over par. (An investor in a tranche priced at a premium benefits from a slowdown in prepayments because the investor receives the higher coupon for a longer period and postpones the capital loss from a prepayment.) Also notice that while the changes in OAS are about the same for the different tranches, the changes in price are quite different. This arises because the shorter tranches have less duration. Therefore, their prices do not move as much from a change in OAS as a longer average life tranche. A portfolio manager who is willing to go to the long end of the yield curve, such as tranche C, would realize the most benefit from the slowdown in prepayments.

Also shown in the second panel of the exhibit is the second part of our experiment to test the sensitivity of prepayments: the prepayment rate is assumed to be 120% of the base case. The collateral loses money in this scenario because it is trading above par. This is reflected in the OAS of the collateral, which declines from 51 basis points to 40 basis points. Now look at the three tranches. They all lost money because the tranches were all at a premium and the speeding of prepayments adversely affects the tranche.

Before looking at the last panel that shows the effect of a change in interest rate volatility on the OAS, let's review the relationship between expected interest rate volatility and the value of a mortgage-backed security. Recall that the investor in a mortgage-backed security has sold an option to homeowners (borrowers). Thus, the investor is short an option. The value of an option depends on expected interest rate volatility. When expected interest rate volatility decreases, the value of the option embedded in a mortgage-backed security decreases and therefore the value of a mortgage-backed security increases. The opposite is true when expected interest rate volatility increases—the value of the embedded option increases and the value of a mortgage-backed security decreases.

Now let's look at the sensitivity to the interest rate volatility assumption, 13% in the base case. Two experiments are performed: reducing the volatility assumption to 9% and increasing it to 17%. These results are reported in the third panel of Exhibit 5.

Reducing the volatility to 9% increases the dollar price of the collateral by $1.03 and increases the OAS from 51 in the base case to 79 basis points. However, this $1.03 increase in the price of the collateral is not equally distributed among the three tranches. Most of the increase in value is realized by the longer tranches. The OAS gain for each of the tranches follows more or less the effective durations of those tranches. This makes sense, because the longer the duration, the greater the risk, and when volatility declines, the reward is greater for the accepted risk. At the higher level of assumed interest rate volatility of 17%, the collateral is severely affected. The longer the duration, the greater the loss. These results for a decrease and an increase in interest rate volatility are consistent with what we explained earlier.

Using the Monte Carlo simulation/OAS analysis, a fair conclusion that can be made about this simple structure is: what you see is what you get. The only surprise in this structure is the lower option cost in tranche C. In general, however, a portfolio manager willing to extend duration gets paid for that risk in this structure.

2 PAC/Support Tranche Structure

Now let's look at how to apply the methodology to a more complicated CMO structure, FHLMC Series 1706. The collateral (i.e., pool of passthroughs) for this structure is Freddie Mac 7s (7% coupon rate). A partial summary of the deal is provided in Exhibit 6. That is, only the tranches we will be discussing in this section are shown in the exhibit.[5]

While this deal looks complicated, it is relatively simple compared to many deals that have been issued. Nonetheless, it brings out all the key points about application of OAS analysis, specifically, the fact that most deals include cheap bonds, expensive bonds, and fairly priced bonds. The OAS analysis helps identify how a tranche should be classified. A more proper analysis would compare the OAS for each tranche to a similar duration tranche available in the market.

All of the tranches in Exhibit 6 were discussed in the reading on mortgage-backed sector of the bond market. At issuance, there were 10 PAC tranches, three scheduled tranches, a floating-rate support tranche, and an inverse floating-rate support. Recall that the "scheduled tranches" are support tranches with a schedule, referred to the reading on mortgage-backed sector of the bond market as "PAC II tranches."

The first two PAC tranches in the deal, tranche A and tranche B, were paid off at the time of the analysis. The other PAC tranches were still available at the time of the analysis. The prepayment protection for the PAC tranches is provided by the support tranches. The support tranches in this deal that are shown in Exhibit 6 are tranches LA, LB, and M. There were other support tranches not shown in Exhibit 6. LA is the shortest average life support tranche (a scheduled (SCH) bond).

The collateral for this deal was trading at a premium. That is, the homeowners (borrowers) were paying a higher mortgage rate than available in the market at the time of the analysis. This meant that the value of the collateral would increase if prepayments slow down but would decrease if prepayments increase. What is important to note, however, is that a tranche could be trading at a discount, par, or premium even though the collateral is priced at a premium. For example, PAC C had a low coupon rate at the time of the analysis and therefore was trading at a discount. Thus, while the collateral (which was selling at a premium) loses value from an increase in prepayments, a discount tranche such as tranche C would increase in value if prepayments increase. (Recall that in the simple structure analyzed earlier, the collateral and all the tranches were trading at a premium.)

---

5 This deal was described in the reading on the mortgage-backed sector of the bond market.

Exhibit 6	Summary of Federal Home Loan Mortgage Corporation—Multiclass Mortgage Participation Certificates (Guaranteed), Series 1706

| | Total Issue: | $300,000,000 | Issue Date: | 2/18/94 | |

				Original Issue Pricing (225% PSA Assumed)	
Tranche	Original Balance ($)	Coupon (%)	Stated Maturity	Average Life (Yrs)	Expected Maturity
PAC Tranches					
C (PAC Bond)	25,500,000	5.25	4/15/14	3.5	6/15/98
D (PAC Bond)	9,150,000	5.65	8/15/15	4.5	1/15/99
E (PAC Bond)	31,650,000	6.00	1/15/19	5.8	1/15/01
G (PAC Bond)	30,750,000	6.25	8/15/21	7.9	5/15/03
H (PAC Bond)	27,450,000	6.50	6/15/23	10.9	10/15/07
J (PAC Bond)	5,220,000	6.50	10/15/23	14.4	9/15/09
K (PAC Bond)	7,612,000	7.00	3/15/24	18.8	5/15/19
Support Tranches					
LA (SCH Bond)	26,673,000	7.00	11/15/21	3.5	3/15/02
LB (SCH Bond)	36,087,000	7.00	6/15/23	3.5	9/15/02
M (SCH Bond)	18,738,000	7.00	3/15/24	11.2	10/15/08

The top panel of Exhibit 7 shows the base case OAS, the option cost, and the effective duration for the collateral and tranches in Exhibit 7. The collateral OAS is 60 basis points, and the option cost is 44 basis points. The Z-spread of the collateral to the Treasury spot curve is 104 basis points.

Exhibit 7	OAS Analysis of FHLMC 1706 (as of 3/10/98)

	Base Case (Assumes 13% Interest Rate Volatility)			
	OAS (in Basis Points)	Option Cost (in Basis Points)	Z-Spread (in Basis Points)	Effective Duration (in Years)
Collateral	60	44	104	2.6
PAC Tranches				
C (PAC)	15	0	15	0.2
D (PAC)	16	4	20	0.6
E (PAC)	26	4	30	1.7
G (PAC)	42	8	50	3.3
H (PAC)	50	12	62	4.9
J (PAC)	56	14	70	6.8
K (PAC)	57	11	68	8.6
Support Tranches				
LA (SCH)	39	12	51	1.4
LB (SCH)	29	74	103	1.2
M (SCH)	72	53	125	4.9

Exhibit 7   *Continued*

Prepayments at 80% and 120% of Prepayment Model (Assumes 13% Interest Rate Volatility)

	Base Case OAS	New OAS (in Basis Points)		Change in Price per $100 Par (Holding OAS Constant)	
		80%	120%	80%	120%
Collateral	**60**	**63**	**57**	**$0.17**	**−$0.11**
PAC Tranches					
C (PAC)	15	15	15	0.00	0.00
D (PAC)	16	16	16	0.00	0.00
E (PAC)	26	27	26	0.01	−0.01
G (PAC)	42	44	40	0.08	−0.08
H (PAC)	50	55	44	0.29	−0.27
J (PAC)	56	63	50	0.50	−0.47
K (PAC)	57	65	49	0.77	−0.76
Support Tranches					
LA (SCH)	39	31	39	−0.12	0.00
LB (SCH)	29	39	18	0.38	−0.19
M (SCH)	72	71	76	−0.07	0.18

Interest Rate Volatility of 9% and 17%

	Base Case OAS	New OAS (in Basis Points)		Change in Price per $100 Par(Holding OAS Constant)	
		9%	17%	9%	17%
Collateral	**60**	**81**	**35**	**$0.96**	**−$0.94**
PAC Tranches					
C (PAC)	15	15	15	0.00	0.00
D (PAC)	16	16	16	0.00	0.00
E (PAC)	26	27	24	0.02	−0.04
G (PAC)	42	48	34	0.21	−0.27
H (PAC)	50	58	35	0.48	−0.72
J (PAC)	56	66	41	0.70	−1.05
K (PAC)	57	66	44	0.82	−1.19
Support Tranches					
LA (SCH)	39	47	24	0.09	−0.18
LB (SCH)	29	58	−4	0.80	−0.82
M (SCH)	72	100	41	1.80	−1.72

The 60 basis points of OAS did not get equally distributed among the tranches—as was the case with the simple structure analyzed earlier. Tranche LB, the scheduled support, did not realize a good OAS allocation, only 29 basis points, and had an extremely high option cost. Given the prepayment uncertainty associated with this tranche, its OAS would be expected to be higher. The reason for the low OAS is that this tranche was priced so that its cash flow yield is high. Using the Z-spread as a proxy for the nominal spread (i.e., spread over the Treasury yield curve), the 103 basis point spread for tranche LB is high given that this appears to be a short average life tranche. Consequently, "yield buyers" (i.e., investors with a preference for high nominal yield, who may not be attentive to compensation for prepayment risk) probably bid aggressively for this tranche and thereby drove down its OAS, trading off "yield" for OAS. From a total return perspective, however, tranche LB should be avoided. It is a rich, or expensive, tranche. The other support tranche analyzed, tranche M, had an OAS of 72 basis points and at the time of this analysis was similar to that offered on comparable duration tranches available in the market.

The analysis reported in the top panel of Exhibit 7 helps us identify where the cheap tranches are in the deal. The long average life and effective duration tranches in the deal are the PAC tranches G, H, J, and K. These tranches have high OAS relative to the other tranches and low option cost. They appear to be the cheap tranches in the deal. These PAC tranches had well-protected cash flows and exhibited positive convexity (i.e., these tranches lose less in an adverse scenario than they gain in a positive scenario).

The next two panels in Exhibit 7 show the sensitivity of the OAS and the price (holding OAS constant at the base case) to changes in the prepayment speed (80% and 120% of the base case) and to changes in volatility (9% and 17%). This analysis shows that the change in the prepayment speed does not affect the collateral significantly, while the change in the OAS (holding the price constant) and price (holding OAS constant) for each tranche can be significant.

Tranches C and D at the time of the analysis were priced at a discount with short average lives. The OAS and price of these two tranches were not affected by a slowing down or a speeding up of the prepayment model. Tranche H was a premium tranche with a medium-term average life at the time of the analysis. Because tranche H was trading at a premium, it benefits from a slowing in prepayments, as the bondholder will receive the coupon for a longer time. Faster prepayments represent an adverse scenario. The PAC tranches are quite well-protected. The longer average life PACs will actually benefit from a reduced prepayment rate because they will be earning the higher coupon interest longer. So, on an OAS basis, the earlier conclusion that the long PACs were allocated a good part of the deal's value holds up under our first stress test (i.e., changing prepayments).

The sensitivity of the collateral and the tranches to changes in volatility are shown in the third panel of Exhibit 7. A lower volatility increases the value of the collateral, while a higher volatility reduces its value (This is consistent with our option cost equation in Section 4.E.) The long average life PACs continue to be fairly well protected, whether the volatility is lower or higher. In the two volatility scenarios they continue to get a good OAS on a relative value basis, although not as much as in the base case if volatility is higher (but the OAS still looks like a reasonable value in this scenario). This reinforces the earlier conclusion concerning the investment merit of the long PACs in this deal. Note, however, that PAC tranches H, J, and K are more sensitive to the volatility assumption than tranches C, D, E, and G and therefore the investor is accepting greater volatility risk (i.e., the risk that volatility will change) with tranches H, J, and K relative to tranches C, D, E, and G.

MEASURING INTEREST RATE RISK

5

Duration and convexity can be used to estimate the interest rate exposure to parallel shifts in the yield curve (i.e., a measure of level risk). In this section we will discuss duration measures for mortgage-backed securities. There are several duration measures that are used in practice. Two researchers who have done extensive work in measuring duration, Lakhbir Hayre and Hubert Chang, conclude that "No single duration measure will consistently work well for mortgage securities."[6] To that conclusion should be added that there are some measures that do not work at all.

A. Duration Measures

Duration is a measure of the price sensitivity to changes in interest rates. We have seen how to compute the duration of a security by shocking rates up and down and determining how the price of the security changes. Duration is then computed as follows:

$$\text{Duration} = \frac{V_- - V_+}{2V_0(\Delta y)}$$

where

Δy = change in rate used to calculate new values (i.e., the interest rate shock)
V_+ = estimated value if yield is increased by Δy
V_- = estimated value if yield is decreased by Δy
V_0 = initial price (per \$100 of par value)

For bonds with embedded options such as mortgage-backed securities, the appropriate measure is effective duration, and to capture the negative convexity of a bond with an embedded option, effective convexity should be computed. We will see how to calculate the effective duration for a mortgage-backed security using the Monte Carlo simulation model. Then we will see how the assumptions of the model impact the duration estimate. Dealers and vendors use other measures of duration that will be described later.

1 Effective Duration

To calculate effective duration, the value of the security must be estimated when rates are shocked up and down a given number of basis points. In terms of the Monte Carlo model, the yield curve used (either the Treasury yield curve or LIBOR curve) is shocked up and down, and the new curve is used to generate the values to be used in the effective duration and effective convexity formulas. This is analogous to the process we used to compute effective duration and effective convexity using the binomial model in the reading on valuing bonds with embedded options.

In generating the prices when rates are shocked up and down, there is an assumption that the relationships assumed in generating the initial price do not change when rates are shocked up and down. Specifically, the yield volatility is assumed to be unchanged to derive the new interest rate paths for a given shock (i.e., the new Exhibit 1), the spread between the mortgage rate and the 10-year Treasury rate is assumed to be unchanged in constructing the new Exhibit 2 from the newly constructed Exhibit 1, and the OAS is assumed to be constant. The constancy of the OAS comes into play because when discounting the new cash flows (i.e., the cash flows in the new Exhibit 3), the current OAS that was computed is assumed to be the same and is added to the new rates in the new Exhibit 1.

---

[6] Lakhbir Hayre and Hubert Chang, "Effective and Empirical Duration of Mortgage Securities," *The Journal of Fixed Income* (March 1997), pp. 17–33.

We'll use an illustration by Lakhbir Hayre and Hubert Chang to explain the calculation of effective duration for a mortgage-backed security, a FNMA 7.5% TBA passthrough on May 1, 1996.[7] On that day, the base mortgage rate was 7.64%. The price of the issue at the time was 98.781 (i.e., 98-25). The OAS was 65 basis points. Based on a shock of 25 basis points, the estimated prices holding the OAS constant at 65 basis points were as follows:

V_- = 99.949 for a decrease in the yield curve of 25 basis points

V_+ = 97.542 for an increase in the yield curve of 25 basis points

The effective duration based on a Δy of 0.0025 is then

$$\frac{99.949 - 97.542}{2 \times 98.781 \times 0.0025} = 4.87$$

There are differences in the effective durations for a given mortgage-backed security reported by dealers and vendors of analytical systems. Several practitioners have explained and illustrated why there are differences in effective duration estimates reported by dealers and vendors. The differences result from, among others:[8]

1. differences in the amount of the rate shock used

2. differences in prepayment models

3. differences in option-adjusted spread

4. differences in the relationship between short-term interest rates and refinancing rates

We previously discussed the first reason. As explained, the rate shock is the amount interest rates are increased and decreased to obtain the two values that are inserted into the effective duration formula. If the change is too large, there is the problem with picking up the effect of convexity.

Prepayment models differ across dealers and vendors. Some dealer models consistently forecast slower prepayments relative to other dealer models and others the reverse.

The effective duration is dependent on the OAS computed. Recall that the calculation of the OAS is a byproduct of the Monte Carlo model. Therefore, the computed value for the OAS depends on all of the assumptions in the Monte Carlo model. Specifically, it depends on the yield volatility assumed and the prepayment model employed. Dealers and vendors make different assumptions regarding yield volatility and use proprietary prepayment models. These can result in differences in OAS. Since the OAS is added to the new simulated short-term rates to compute the new values for V_- and V_+, a different OAS will result in different effective durations.

Finally, recall that in explaining the Monte Carlo simulation model that we stated that in moving from Exhibit 1 (the simulated short-term rates) to Exhibit 2 (the refinancing rates), an assumption must be made about the relationship between short-term rates and the 10-year Treasury rate (i.e., the rate used as a proxy for refinancing). Differences in models about how large the spread between these rates will be affect the value of a mortgage-backed security and therefore the values used in the duration equation when rates are shocked.

2 Other Duration Measures

There have been other measures proposed for estimating the duration of a mortgage-backed security. These measures include cash flow duration, coupon curve duration,

---

7 Hayre and Chang, "Effective and Empirical Duration of Mortgage Securities."

8 Sam Choi, "Effective Durations for Mortgage-Backed Securities: Recipes for Improvement," *The Journal of Fixed Income* (March 1996), pp. 24–30; and, Hayre and Chang, "Effective and Empirical Duration of Mortgage Securities."

and empirical duration. The first two duration measures are forms of effective duration in that they do recognize that the values that should be used in the duration formula should take into account how the cash flows may change due to changes in prepayments when interest rates change. In contrast, empirical duration is a duration that is computed statistically using observed market prices. Below we describe how each of these duration measures is calculated, as well as the advantages and limitations of each.

a. Cash Flow Duration Recall from the general duration formula that there are two values that must be substituted into the numerator of the formula—the value if rates are decreased (V_-) and the value if rates are increased (V_+). With effective duration, these two values consider how changes in interest rates change the cash flow due to prepayments. This is done through the Monte Carlo simulation by allowing for the cash flows to change on the interest rate paths.

For cash flow duration, there is recognition that the cash flow can change but the analysis to obtain the cash flow is done following a static methodology. Specifically, the cash flow duration is calculated as follows:

Step 1   Calculate the cash flow based on some prepayment assumption.

Step 2   From the cash flow in Step 1 and the market price (V_0), compute the cash flow yield.

Step 3   Increase the cash flow yield by Δy and from a prepayment model determine the new prepayment rate at that higher cash flow yield. Typically, the prepayment rate will be lower than in Step 1 because of the higher yield level.

Step 4   Using the lower prepayment rate in Step 3 determine the cash flow and then value the cash flow using the higher cash flow yield as the discount rate. This gives the value (V_+).

Step 5   Decrease the cash flow yield by Δy and from a prepayment model determine the new prepayment rate at that lower cash flow yield. Typically, the prepayment rate will be higher than in Step 1 because of the lower yield level.

Step 6   Using the higher prepayment rate in Step 5 determine the cash flow and then value the cash flow using the lower cash flow yield as the discount rate. This gives the value (V_-).

From the change in basis points (Δy), the values for V_+ and V_- found in Steps 4 and 6, and the initial value V_0, the duration can be computed.

We can use the hypothetical CMO structure to illustrate how to calculate cash flow duration. Specifically, in FJF-2, there were four tranches, A, B, C, and Z. Let's focus on tranche C. Suppose that the price for this tranche is 100.2813. Then the cash flow duration is computed as follows:

Step 1   Suppose that the assumed prepayment rate for this tranche is 165 PSA.

Step 2   Based on the assumed prepayment rate of 165 PSA and the price of 100.2813, it can be demonstrated that the cash flow yield is 7%.

Step 3   Suppose that the cash flow yield is increased (i.e., shocked) by 25 basis points (from 7% to 7.25%) and suppose that some prepayment model projects a prepayment rate of 150 PSA. (Note that this is a slower prepayment rate than at 7%.)

Step 4   Based on 150 PSA, a new cash flow can be generated. The cash flow is then discounted at 7.25% (the new cash flow yield). It can be demonstrated that the value of this tranche based on these assumptions would be 98.3438. This is the value V_+.

Step 5   Suppose that the cash flow yield is decreased (i.e., shocked) by 25 basis points (from 7% to 6.75%) and suppose that some prepayment model projects a prepayment rate of 200 PSA. (Note that this is a faster prepayment rate than at 7%.)

Step 6   Based on 200 PSA, the new cash flow can be generated. The cash flow is then discounted at 6.75% (the new cash flow yield). It can be demonstrated that the value of this tranche based on these assumptions would be 101.9063. This is the value V_-.

Now we have the following information:

$$V_0 = 100.2813$$
$$V_+ = 98.3438$$
$$V_- = 101.9063$$
$$\Delta y = 0.0025$$

Then using the general form of duration, we obtain:

$$\text{Duration} = \frac{101.9063 - 98.3438}{2(100.2813)(0.0025)} = 7.11$$

What type of duration measure is the cash flow duration—effective duration or modified duration? Technically, it is a form of effective duration because notice that in Steps 3 and 5 when the rate is changed, the cash flow is allowed to change. However, as has been stressed throughout, the valuation model that is used to get the new values to substitute into the duration formula is critical. The valuation model in the case of the cash flow duration is based on the naive assumption that there is a single prepayment rate over the life of the mortgage-backed security for any given interest rate shock. This is in contrast to the values produced by the Monte Carlo simulation model that does more sophisticated analyses of how the cash flow can change when interest rates change.

Why bother discussing the cash flow duration if it is an inferior form of effective duration? The reason is that it is a commonly cited duration measure and practitioners should be aware of how it is computed. Likewise, we did discuss in detail yield calculations despite their limitations.

An interesting question is how does this form of duration compare to modified duration? Recall that modified duration does not assume that cash flows will change when rates are shocked. That is, in the steps discussed above to obtain cash flow duration, in Steps 3 and 5 it is assumed that the prepayment rate is the same as in Step 1.

To illustrate this, we'll once again use tranche C in FJF-2. In Step 3, the prepayment rate assumed is still 165 PSA despite the fact that rates are assumed to increase. That is, the cash flow is not assumed to change. Based on a cash flow yield of 7.25% and a prepayment rate of 165 PSA, the value of this tranche would decline to 98.4063. When the cash flow yield is assumed to decline to 6.75%, the prepayment rate is still assumed to be 165 PSA and the value of this tranche would be 102.1875. Then to calculate the modified duration we know:

$$V_0 = 100.2813$$
$$V_+ = 98.4063$$
$$V_- = 102.1875$$
$$\Delta y = 0.0025$$

The modified duration is then:

$$\text{Duration} = \frac{102.1875 - 98.4063}{2(100.2813)(0.0025)} = 7.54$$

Thus, the modified duration is greater than the cash flow duration for this tranche.

It is important to reiterate that the modified duration is inferior to the cash flow duration because the former gives absolutely no recognition to how repayments may change when interest rates change. While cash flow duration is commonly cited in practice, it is a form of effective duration that does give some recognition that prepayments and therefore cash flow may change when interest rates change, but it is based on a naive assumption about how prepayments may change. The effective duration as computed using Monte Carlo simulation is superior to cash flow duration.

b. Coupon Curve Duration   The coupon curve duration uses market prices to estimate the duration of a mortgage-backed security. This approach, first suggested by Douglas Breeden,[9] starts with the coupon curve of prices for similar mortgage-backed securities. The coupon curve represents generic passthrough securities of a particular issuer with different coupon rates. By rolling up and down the coupon curve of prices, the duration can be obtained. Because of the way it is estimated, this approach to duration estimation was referred to by Breeden as the "roll-up, roll-down approach." The prices obtained from rolling up and rolling down the coupon curve of prices are substituted into the duration formula.

To illustrate this approach, suppose that the coupon curve of prices for a passthrough security for some month is as follows:

Coupon (%)	Price ($)
6	85.19
7	92.06
8	98.38
9	103.34
10	107.28
11	111.19

Suppose that the coupon curve duration for the 8% coupon passthrough is sought. If the yield declines by 100 basis points, the assumption is that the price of the 8% coupon passthrough will increase to the price of the current 9% coupon passthrough. Thus, the price will increase from 98.38 to 103.34. Similarly, if the yield increases by 100 basis points, the assumption is that the price of the 8% coupon passthrough will decline to the price of the 7% coupon passthrough (92.06). Using the duration formula, the corresponding values are:

$V_0 = 98.38$

$V_+ = 92.06$

$V_- = 103.34$

$\Delta y = 0.01$

The estimated duration based on the coupon curve is then:

$$\text{Duration} = \frac{103.34 - 92.06}{2(98.38)(0.01)} = 5.73$$

---

[9] Douglas Breeden, "Risk, Return, and Hedging of Fixed-Rate Mortgages," *The Journal of Fixed Income* (September 1991), pp. 85–107.

Breeden tested the coupon curve durations and found them to be relatively accurate in estimating the interest rate risk of generic passthrough securities.[10] Bennett Golub reports a similar finding.[11]

While the advantages of the coupon curve duration are the simplicity of its calculation and the fact that current prices embody market expectations, there are disadvantages. The approach is limited to generic mortgage-backed securities and difficult to use for mortgage derivatives such as CMOs.

c. Empirical Duration   When computing effective duration and cash flow duration, the values to be substituted into the duration formula are those based on some valuation model. For coupon curve duration, the observed market prices are used in the duration formula. In contrast, empirical duration is estimated statistically using historical market prices and market yields.[12] Regression analysis is used to estimate the relationship. Some firms such as PaineWebber use empirical duration, also called implied duration, as their primary measure of the duration of an MBS.

There are three advantages to the empirical duration approach.[13] First, the duration estimate does not rely on any theoretical formulas or analytical assumptions. Second, the estimation of the required parameters is easy to compute using regression analysis. Finally, the only inputs that are needed are a reliable price series and Treasury yield series.

There are disadvantages.[14] First, a reliable price series for the mortgage security may not be available. For example, there may be no price series available for a thinly traded mortgage or the prices may be matrix priced (i.e., priced by a pricing service based on issues with similar characteristics) or model priced rather than actual transaction prices. Second, an empirical relationship does not impose a structure for the options embedded in a mortgage-backed security and this can distort the empirical duration. This may occur after a sharp and sustained shock to interest rates has been realized. Finally, the volatility of the spread to Treasury yields can distort how the price of a mortgage-backed security reacts to yield changes.

6   VALUING ASSET-BACKED SECURITIES

From the description of the Monte Carlo model, it can be seen that the valuation process is complex. Rather than build their own valuation model, portfolio managers typically use a model of a third-party vendor of analytical systems or a model of a dealer firm to value mortgage-backed securities. But mortgage-backed securities are only one type of structured product. Asset-backed securities are also structured products. Is it necessary to use the Monte Carlo model for all asset-backed securities? Below we will explain the circumstances as to when the Monte Carlo model must be used and when it is sufficient to use the Z-spread.

---

10 Breeden, "Risk, Return, and Hedging of Fixed-Rate Mortgages."

11 See Bennett W. Golub, "Towards a New Approach to Measuring Mortgage Duration," Chapter 32 in Frank J. Fabozzi (ed.), *The Handbook of Mortgage-Backed Securities* (Chicago: Probus Publishing, 1995), p. 673.

12 This approach was first suggested in 1986 in Scott M. Pinkus and Marie A. Chandoha, "The Relative Price Volatility of Mortgage Securities," *Journal of Portfolio Management* (Summer 1986), pp. 9–22 and then in 1990 by Paul DeRossa, Laurie Goodman, and Mike Zazzarino, "Duration Estimates on Mortgage-Backed Securities," *Journal of Portfolio Management* (Winter 1993), pp. 32–37, and more recently in Laurie S. Goodman and Jeffrey Ho, "Mortgage Hedge Ratios: Which One Works Best?" *The Journal of Fixed Income* (December 1997), pp. 23–33, and Laurie S. Goodman and and Jeffrey Ho, "An Integrated Approach to Hedging and Relative Value Analysis," Chapter 15 in Frank J. Fabozzi (ed.), *Advances in the Valuation and Management of Mortgage-Backed Securities* (New Hope, PA: Frank J. Fabozzi Associates, 1999).

13 Golub, "Towards a New Approach to Measuring Mortgage Duration," p. 672.

14 Golub, "Towards a New Approach to Measuring Mortgage Duration."

The model that should be used for valuing an asset-backed security (ABS) depends on the characteristic of the loans or receivables backing the deal. An ABS can have one of the following three characteristics:

Characteristic 1   The ABS does not have a prepayment option.

Characteristic 2   The ABS has a prepayment option but borrowers do not exhibit a tendency to prepay when refinancing rates fall below the loan rate.

Characteristic 3   The ABS has a prepayment option and borrowers do exhibit a tendency to prepay when refinancing rates fall below the loan rate.

An example of a Characteristic 1 type ABS is a security backed by credit card receivables. An example of a Characteristic 2 type ABS is a security backed by automobile loans. A security backed by closed-end home equity loans where the borrowers are high quality borrowers (i.e., prime borrowers) is an example of a Characteristic 3 type ABS. There are some real-estate backed ABS that we discussed in the reading on the asset-backed sector of the bond market, where the verdict is still out as to the degree to which borrowers take advantage of refinancing opportunities. Specifically, these include securities backed by manufactured housing loans and securities backed by closed-end home equity loans to borrowers classified as low-quality borrowers.

There are two possible approaches to valuing an ABS. They are the

1. zero-volatility spread (Z-spread) approach

2. option-adjusted spread (OAS) approach

For the Z-spread approach the interest rates used to discount the cash flows are the spot rates plus the zero-volatility spread. The value of an ABS is then the present value of the cash flows based on these discount rates. The Z-spread approach does not consider the prepayment option. Consequently, the Z-spread approach should be used to value Characteristic 1 type ABS. (In terms of the relationship between the Z-spread, OAS, and option cost discussed earlier in this reading, this means that the value of the option is zero and therefore the Z-spread is equal to the OAS.) Since the Z-spread is equal to the OAS, the Z-spread approach to valuation can be used.

The Z-spread approach can also be used to value Characteristic 2 type ABS because while the borrowers do have a prepayment option, the option is not typically exercised. Thus, as with Characteristic 1 type ABS, the Z-spread is equal to the OAS.

The OAS approach—which is considerably more computationally extensive than the Z-spread approach—is used to value securities where there is an embedded option and there is an expectation that the option is expected to be exercised if it makes economic sense for the borrower to do so. Consequently, the OAS approach is used to value Characteristic 3 type ABS. The choice is then whether to use the binomial model (or a comparable model) or the Monte Carlo simulation model. Since typically the cash flow for an ABS with a prepayment option is interest rate path dependent—as with a mortgage-backed security—the Monte Carlo simulation model is used.

VALUING ANY SECURITY   7

We conclude this reading with a summary of the approaches to valuing any fixed income security using the two approaches that we discussed in the previous section—the Z-spread approach and the OAS approach.

Below we match the valuation approach with the type of security.

1. For an *option-free bond* the correct approach is the Z-spread approach.

2. For a *bond with an embedded option where the cash flow is not interest rate path dependent* (such as a callable corporate or agency debenture bond or a putable

bond) the correct approach is the OAS approach. Since the backward induction method can be used for such bonds, the binomial model or its equivalent should be used.

3. For a bond with an embedded option where the cash flow is interest rate path dependent (such as a mortgage-backed security or certain real estate-backed ABS) the correct approach is the OAS approach. However, because of the interest rate path dependency of the cash flow, the Monte Carlo simulation model should be used.

SUMMARY

- The cash flow yield is the interest rate that makes the present value of the projected cash flow for a mortgage-backed or asset-backed security equal to its market price plus accrued interest.

- The convention is to compare the yield on mortgage-backed and asset-backed securities to that of a Treasury coupon security by calculating the security's bond-equivalent yield. This measure is found by computing an effective semiannual rate and doubling it.

- The cash flow yield is based on three assumptions that thereby limit its use as a measure of relative value: 1) a prepayment assumption and default/recovery assumption, 2) an assumption that the cash flows will be reinvested at the computed cash flow yield, and 3) an assumption that the investor will hold the security until the last loan in the pool is paid off.

- The nominal spread is commonly computed as the difference between the cash flow yield and the yield on a Treasury security with the same maturity as the mortgage-backed or asset-backed security's average life.

- The nominal spread masks the fact that a portion of the spread is compensation for accepting prepayment risk.

- An investor or portfolio manager who buys solely on the basis of nominal spread fails to determine whether or not that nominal spread offers an adequate compensation for prepayment risk.

- An investor or portfolio manager needs a measure that indicates the potential compensation after adjusting for prepayment risk, and this measure is the option-adjusted spread.

- The zero-volatility spread is a measure of the spread that the investor would realize over the entire Treasury spot rate curve if the mortgage-backed or asset-backed security is held to maturity.

- The zero-volatility spread is not a spread off one point on the Treasury yield curve, as is the nominal spread, but a spread that will make the present value of the cash flows from the mortgage-backed or asset-backed security when discounted at the Treasury spot rate plus the spread equal to the market price of the security plus accrued interest.

- The binomial model and other similar models that use the backward induction method can be used to value securities where the decision to exercise a call option is not dependent on how interest rates evolved over time—that is, the decision of an issuer to call a bond will depend on the level of the rate at which the issue can be refunded relative to the issue's coupon rate, and not the path interest rates took to get to that rate.

- Mortgage-backed securities and some types of asset-backed securities are products where the periodic cash flows are "interest rate path-dependent"—meaning that the cash flow received in one period is determined not only by the current interest rate level, but also by the path that interest rates took to get to the current level.

- The Monte Carlo simulation model for valuing mortgage-backed securities involves generating a set of cash flows based on simulated future mortgage refinancing rates, which in turn imply simulated prepayment rates.

- In the Monte Carlo simulation model there is nothing to assure that the simulated interest rates will generate arbitrage-free values of the benchmark securities used in the valuation process; consequently, the simulated interest rates must be adjusted so as to produce arbitrage-free values.

- The present value of a given interest rate path can be thought of as the theoretical value of a security if that path was actually realized.

- The theoretical value of a mortgage-backed security can be determined by calculating the average of the theoretical values of all the interest rate paths.

- In the Monte Carlo simulation model, the option-adjusted spread is the spread that when added to all the spot rates on all interest rate paths will make the average present value of the paths equal to the observed market price (plus accrued interest).

- The OAS is measured relative to the benchmark interest rates that were used to generate the interest rate paths and to adjust the interest rate paths to make them arbitrage free.

- Since typically for a mortgage-backed security the benchmark interest rates are the on-the-run Treasury rates, the OAS measures the average spread over the Treasury spot rate curve, not the Treasury yield curve.

- Depending on the mortgage product being valued, the OAS reflects credit risk, liquidity risk, and modeling risk.

- The OAS is superior to the nominal spread which gives no recognition to the prepayment risk.

- The implied cost of the option embedded in a mortgage-backed or an asset-backed security can be obtained by calculating the difference between the option-adjusted spread at the assumed interest rate volatility and the zero-volatility spread.

- The option cost measures the prepayment (or option) risk embedded in the security and is a byproduct of the option-adjusted spread analysis, not valued explicitly with some option pricing model.

- In valuation modeling of collateralized mortgage obligations, the objective is to figure out how the value and risks of the collateral get transmitted to the tranches in a deal.

- There are several duration measures for mortgage-backed securities that are used in practice—effective duration, cash flow duration, coupon curve duration, and empirical duration.

- For bonds with embedded options such as mortgage-backed securities, the appropriate measure is effective duration, and to capture negative convexity, effective convexity should be computed.

- Effective duration is computed using Monte Carlo simulation by shocking the short-term interest rates for each interest rate path generated up and down and obtaining the new value for the security; the new values determined when rates are shocked up and down are used in the duration formula.

- There are differences in the effective duration reported for a given mortgage-backed security by dealers and vendors of analytical systems primarily due to differences in 1) the amount of the rate shock used, 2) the prepayment model used, 3) the option-adjusted spread computed, and 4) the relationship between short-term interest rates and refinancing rates assumed.

- Cash flow duration and coupon curve duration measures are forms of effective duration in that they do recognize that the values that should be used in the duration formula should take into account how the cash flows may change due to changes in prepayments when interest rates change.

- Cash flow duration is based on an initial cash flow yield and initial prepayment rate and computes the new values when rates are shocked (i.e., when the cash flow yield is shocked) allowing the cash flow to change based on a new prepayment rate as determined by a prepayment model.

- Cash flow duration is superior to modified duration (which assumes that cash flows do not change when rates are shocked) but inferior to effective duration as computed using the Monte Carlo simulation model.

- The coupon curve duration begins with the coupon curve of prices for similar mortgage-backed securities and uses values in the duration formula found by rolling up and down the coupon curve of prices.

- Empirical duration is a duration measure that is computed statistically using regression analysis based on observed market prices and yields.

- Empirical duration imposes no structure on the embedded option.

- A limitation of empirical duration and coupon curve duration is that they are difficult to apply to CMOs because of a lack of valid market price data.

- The zero-volatility spread added to the spot rates can be used to value an asset-backed security if either 1) the security does not have a prepayment option or 2) the borrower has the right to prepay but it has been observed that the borrower does not tend to exercise that option if interest rates decline below the loan rate.

- The option-adjusted spread approach to valuation using the Monte Carlo simulation model is used for an asset-backed security if the borrower does have the right to prepay and it has been observed that the borrower does tend to refinance when interest rates decline below the loan rate.

- For any fixed income security, the valuation approaches that can be employed are the zero-volatility spread approach and the option-adjusted spread approach.

- For option-free bonds, the zero-volatility spread approach should be used.

- The choice of whether to use the binomial model (or a similar "nomial" model that uses the backward induction method) or the Monte Carlo simulation model for a security with an embedded option depends on the characteristics of the security.

- For corporate and agency debentures with an embedded option the binomial model or its equivalent should be used for valuation.

- For securities such as mortgage-backed and asset-backed securities (those where it is observed that borrowers do exercise the prepayment option) the Monte Carlo simulation model should be used since the cash flows are typically interest rate path dependent.

PRACTICE PROBLEMS FOR READING 47

1. Suppose that based on a prepayment assumption of 200 PSA the cash flow yield for a specific agency passthrough security is 7.5% and the stated maturity is 15 years. Suppose further that the average life of this security is 8 years. Assume the following yield curve for Treasuries:

Maturity	Yield (%)
6-year	6.2
8-year	6.3
10-year	6.4
15-year	6.6

A. What is the nominal spread for this agency passthrough security?

B. What must occur over the life of this agency passthrough security for the cash flow yield of 7.5% to be realized?

2. Suppose that the monthly cash flow yield is 0.74%. What is the cash flow yield on a bond-equivalent basis?

3. Jane Howard is a corporate bond analyst. Recently she has been asked to extend her responsibilities to mortgage-backed securities. In researching the methodology for valuing mortgage-backed securities she read that these securities are valued using the Monte Carlo simulation model. She was unfamiliar with this approach to valuation because in valuing callable corporate bonds she used the binomial model. Explain to Ms. Howard why the Monte Carlo simulation method is used to value mortgage-backed securities rather than the binomial method.

4. The following questions have to do with the Monte Carlo simulation model.

A. What assumption must be made in generating the path of short-term interest rates?

B. Why must the paths of short-term interest rates be adjusted?

C. In determining the path of refinancing rates, what assumption must be made?

5. Nat Hawthorne, a portfolio manager, discussed the valuation of a particular mortgage-backed security with his broker, Steven Ruthledge. Mr. Hawthorne is considering the purchase of the security and asked what valuation model the brokerage firm used. Mr. Ruthledge responded that the Monte Carlo simulation model was used. Mr. Hawthorne then asked about what prepayment assumption is used in the Monte Carlo simulation model. Mr. Ruthledge responded that for the particular security Mr. Hawthorne is considering, 175 PSA was assumed. Mr. Hawthorne was confused by the response because he did not believe that a particular PSA assumption was made in the Monte Carlo simulation model. Is Mr. Hawthorne correct? Explain your answer.

6. What interest rates are used to value a mortgage-backed security on each interest rate path when using the Monte Carlo simulation model?

7. Juan Rodriguez is the manager of a portfolio containing mortgage passthrough securities. He is reviewing output of his firm's analytical system for several passthrough securities that are in the portfolio. Below is a portion of the report for three passthrough securities:

| | Price Based on an Assumed Interest Rate Volatility of | | | |
Passthrough	11%	13%	15%	16%
Security 1	100	98	95	93
Security 2	92	90	88	87
Security 3	102	104	106	107

Mr. Rodriguez believes that there is an error in the analytical system. Why does he suspect that there is an error?

8. Suppose that the pool of passthroughs used as collateral for a collateralized mortgage obligation is selling at a premium. Also suppose that one tranche in the deal, Tranche X, is selling at a discount and another tranche, Tranche Y, is selling at a premium.

   A. Explain why a slowdown in prepayments will tend to increase the value of the collateral.

   B. Explain why a slowdown in prepayments will not affect the value of Tranches X and Y in the same way.

9. Assume for simplicity that only ten interest rate paths are used in the Monte Carlo simulation model to a value Tranche W of a CMO deal. Suppose further that based on a spread of 70 basis points, the present value of the interest rate paths is as follows:

Interest rate path	1	2	3	4	5	6	7	8	9	10
PV for path	80	90	84	88	94	92	86	91	99	87

   Based on the Monte Carlo simulation model and assuming a spread required by the market of 70 basis points, what is the theoretical value of Tranche W?

10. Jane Hubert is using an analytical system purchased by her firm to analyze mortgage-backed securities. The analytical system uses the Monte Carlo simulation model for valuation. She is given a choice when using the system to use either the "full Monte Carlo analysis" or "16 representative interest rate paths."

    A. What is meant by "16 representative interest rate paths"?

    B. How is the theoretical value of a mortgage-backed security determined when representative paths are used?

    C. What is the trade-off when using representative interest rate paths versus using the full Monte Carlo analysis?

11. A portfolio manager is using an analytical system to value Tranche K of a CMO deal. The Monte Carlo simulation model uses eight representative interest rate paths. The present value of each of the representative interest rate paths and the weight of each path are shown below:

Representative path	1	2	3	4	5	6	7	8
Weight of representative path	20%	18%	16%	12%	12%	12%	6%	4%
PV of representative path	70	82	79	68	74	86	91	93

What is the theoretical value of Tranche K?

12. Mr. Wacker is a bond analyst whose primary responsibility has been to manage the corporate bond portfolio. Recently, his firm's analyst responsible for the mortgage-backed securities portfolio left. Mr. Wacker was asked to monitor the mortgage-backed securities portfolio until a new analyst is hired. The portfolio contains only Ginnie Mae mortgage products. In reviewing the Ginnie Mae portfolio and the option-adjusted spread (OAS) for each security, he was troubled by the values he observed. He was told that the benchmark interest rates used in the calculation of the OAS are Treasury rates. Below are two questions raised by Mr. Wacker. Respond to each one.

   A. "I don't understand why the Ginnie Mae securities in my portfolio have a positive OAS. These securities are backed by the full faith and credit of the U.S. government, so there is no credit risk. Why is there a positive OAS?"

   B. "There are different types of Ginnie Mae mortgage products in the portfolio. There are passthroughs, sequential-pay CMO tranches, planned amortization class CMO tranches, and support CMO tranches. Why do they have different OASs?"

13. Suppose that 10 representative paths are used in the Monte Carlo simulation model and that each path has a weight of 10%. The present value for each representative path is based on discounting the cash flows on an interest rate path by the short-term interest rates on that path plus a spread. For the different spreads used, the present value of each representative path is shown below for Tranche L in a CMO deal:

| Representative Path | Present Value if the Spread Used Is | | | |
	70 bps	75 bps	80 bps	85 bps
1	77	72	70	68
2	82	80	77	72
3	86	84	81	78
4	89	86	83	81
5	74	70	68	65
6	88	86	82	80
7	96	92	88	86
8	92	90	86	84
9	74	71	67	65
10	68	64	61	59

   A. Suppose that the market price of Tranche L is 79.5. What is the option-adjusted spread?

   B. Suppose instead of a market price for Tranche L of 79.5 the market price is 73.8. What is the option-adjusted spread?

14. Below are the results of a Monte Carlo simulation analysis using eight representative paths for two tranches of a CMO deal, Tranches M and N:

Representative Path	1	2	3	4	5	6	7	8
PV of path for:								
Tranche M	60	55	90	105	110	50	48	70
Tranche N	86	85	89	91	84	92	87	86

One of the tranches is a PAC tranche and the other is a support tranche. Which tranche is probably the PAC tranche and which is probably the support tranche?

15. An analysis of an agency CMO structure using the Monte Carlo simulation model based on 12% volatility found the following:

	OAS (Basis Points)	Z-Spread (Basis Points)	Effective Duration
Collateral	90	130	8.0
Tranche			
PAC I A	50	60	1.5
PAC I B	70	80	3.0
PAC I C	30	120	5.0
PAC I D	30	150	9.0
PAC II A	80	150	4.0
PAC II B	20	280	6.0
Support S1	35	165	11.0
Support S2	50	190	14.0

A. What is the option cost for PAC I A, PAC II A, and Support S1?

B. Which of the PAC tranches appears to be expensive in the deal on a relative value basis?

C. PAC II tranches are support tranches with schedules. The four support tranches in the deal are therefore PAC II A, PAC II B, Support S1, and Support S2. Which of the support tranches appears to be expensive on a relative value basis?

D. Despite its low OAS of 20 basis points, why might a yield buyer be induced to purchase PAC II B?

16. How is the effective duration and effective convexity of a mortgage-backed security computed using the Monte Carlo simulation model? Be sure to explain what assumption is made regarding the option-adjusted spread when computing the effective duration and effective convexity.

17. Joel Winters is a junior portfolio manager of a corporate bond portfolio. A decision has been made to include mortgage-backed securities in the portfolio. Mr. Winters is considering the purchase of a CMO tranche called a support bond. Before he buys this tranche, he wants to know its effective duration. Because he does not have the use of an analytical system to compute effective duration, Mr. Winters contacts three dealers and inquires as to the effective duration for this tranche. He is given the following effective duration from the three dealer firms:

Dealer	1	2	3
Effective duration	8.1	4.6	11.6

Mr. Winters is puzzled by the significant variation in the effective durations, especially since all the dealers indicated that the Monte Carlo simulation model was used. In his experience with corporate bonds with embedded options he has never observed such a significant variation in the effective duration from dealer firm to dealer firm.

Explain to Mr. Winters why there is such a significant variation in the effective durations. Be sure to clearly identify the reasons for the variation in the effective durations.

18. Explain why you agree or disagree with the following statement: "If the collateral for a CMO deal has negative convexity, then all the tranches in the deal must have negative convexity. The only difference is the degree of negative convexity from one tranche to another."

19. A. What is the cash flow duration of a mortgage-backed security?

   B. What are the limitations of cash flow duration as a measure of the price sensitivity of a mortgage-backed security to changes in interest rates?

20. Suppose that the coupon curve of prices for a passthrough security for some month is as follows:

Coupon (%)	Price ($)
7	94.00
8	97.06
9	99.50
10	102.60
11	105.25
12	106.19

What is the coupon curve duration for the 9% coupon passthrough?

21. Karen Brown is considering alternative measures for estimating the duration of some complex CMO tranches. One measure she is considering is empirical duration. Explain to Ms. Brown the difficulties of using empirical duration for complex CMO tranches.

22. Thomas Larken is a portfolio manager who is considering investing in the asset-backed securities market. In particular, Mr. Larken is considering investing in either credit card receivables, auto loan-backed securities, or prime home equity loan-backed securities. Examination of the nominal spreads in these three sectors of the market indicates that the largest nominal spread for AAA and AA issues is home equity loan-backed securities. Based on this analysis, Mr. Larken believes that the best sector in which to invest is in home equity loan-backed securities because it offers the greatest relative value as measured by the nominal spread. Explain whether or not you agree with Mr. Larken's assessment of the relative attractiveness of home equity loan-backed securities.

23. An investment banker has created an asset-backed security in which the collateral is the future royalties of a songwriter. Which valuation approach do you think should be used to value this security, the zero-volatility spread or the option-adjusted spread?

24. Suppose that empirical evidence on prepayments for manufactured housing loans suggests that borrowers do not take advantage of refinancing when interest rates decline. Explain whether the zero-volatility spread approach or OAS approach is appropriate for valuing securities backed by manufacturing housing loans.

25. Evidence by Wall Street firms on home equity loans strongly suggests that high-quality borrowers do take advantage of a decline in interest rates to refinance a loan. In contrast, low-quality borrowers tend not to take advantage of a decline in interest rates to refinance.

A. What is the appropriate valuation approach (option-adjusted spread approach or zero-volatility spread approach) to value home equity loan-backed securities where the underlying pool of loans are those of high-quality borrowers? Explain why.

B. What is the appropriate valuation approach (option-adjusted spread approach or zero-volatility spread approach) to value home equity loan-backed securities where the underlying pool of loans are those of low-quality borrowers? Explain why.

The following information relates to Questions 26–31 and is based on "Mortgage-Backed Sector of the Bond Market" and this reading

Atul Gupta is a mortgage-backed securities analyst at a macro hedge fund. Although mortgage rates have been fairly constant in recent years, Gupta expects interest rates to be higher in the coming months. His analysis of mortgage-backed securities leads him to the following conclusions:

1. Contraction risk occurs when interest rates increase. Therefore, mortgage securities will prepay faster than expected.

2. A sequential-pay collateralized mortgage obligation (CMO) with an accrual tranche lowers the prepayment risk and shortens the average life of the sequential-pay tranches relative to a sequential-pay CMO without an accrual tranche.

3. A planned amortization class (PAC) bond with a very narrow PAC window resembles a corporate bond with a bullet payment.

4. In general, principal-only strips (POs) should underperform interest-only strips (IOs) if interest rates increase.

Gupta receives the dealer quotes on mortgage-backed securities given in Exhibit 1:

Exhibit 1	Dealer Quotes			
Tranche	**Option-Adjusted Spread (bps)**	**Zero-Volatility Spread (bps)**	**Nominal Spread (bps)**	**Effective Duration (Years)**
PAC 1	50	60	68	1.50
PAC 2	70	80	85	3.00
PAC 3	30	120	128	5.00
PAC II A	80	150	156	4.00
Support 1	35	165	178	11.00

Note: bps = basis points

26. Is Gupta's first conclusion correct?

A. Yes.

B. No, because contraction risk occurs when interest rates fall.

C. No, because contraction risk occurs when principal payments are received later than expected.

27. Is Gupta's second conclusion correct?

    A. Yes.

    B. No, because an accrual tranche increases prepayment risk.

    C. No, because an accrual tranche has an indeterminable effect on prepayment risk.

28. Is Gupta's third conclusion correct?

    A. Yes.

    B. No, because the PAC bond is an accrual tranche.

    C. No, because the PAC bond is a scheduled tranche.

29. Is Gupta's fourth conclusion correct?

    A. Yes.

    B. No, IOs should underperform POs.

    C. No, both POs and IOs should increase in value.

30. Given the data in Exhibit 1, the cost of the embedded option for the PAC 1 tranche, in basis points, is *closest* to:

    A. 8.

    B. 10.

    C. 18.

31. Given the data in Exhibit 1, which PAC tranche is likely to be the *most* expensive in terms of option cost?

    A. PAC 1.

    B. PAC 2.

    C. PAC 3.

SOLUTIONS FOR READING 47

1. **A.** The convention is to determine the nominal spread relative to the spread on a Treasury security with the same maturity as the average life of the mortgage-backed security. Since the average life is 8 years, the benchmark Treasury issue is the 8-year issue. The nominal spread is then 7.5% minus the 6.3% of the 8-year Treasury issue. So, the nominal spread is 120 basis points.

   B. For the 7.5% cash flow yield to be realized the following must occur:
   - actual prepayments must be 200 PSA over the life of the security;
   - the monthly cash flow (interest plus principal repayment) must be reinvested at a rate of 7.5%;
   - the security must be held until the last mortgage pays off.

2. The monthly cash flow yield, i_M, is 0.0074. Therefore,

   Bond-equivalent yield = $2[(1.0074)^6 - 1] = 0.0905 = 9.05\%$

3. The binomial model used to value a corporate bond with an embedded option can handle securities in which the decision to exercise a call option is not dependent on how interest rates evolved over time. That is, the decision of a corporate issuer to call a bond will depend on the level of the rate at which the issue can be refunded relative to the issue's coupon rate. The decision to call does not depend on the path interest rates took to get to that rate. Ms. Howard must understand that this is not a characteristic of mortgage-backed securities. These securities are "interest rate path-dependent," meaning that the cash flow received in one period is determined not only by the interest rate level at that period, but also by the path that interest rates took to get to that rate.

   For example, in the case of passthrough securities, prepayments are interest rate path-dependent because this month's prepayment rate depends on whether there have been prior opportunities to refinance since the underlying mortgages were originated. For CMOs there are typically two sources of path dependency in a CMO tranche's cash flows. First, the collateral prepayments are path-dependent as just described. Second, the cash flows to be received in the current month by a CMO tranche depend on the outstanding balances of the other tranches in the deal. Thus, we need the history of prepayments to calculate these balances.

4. **A.** To generate the path of short-term interest rates, an assumption about the volatility of short-term interest rates must be made.

   B. If the short-term interest rates on each path are used without an adjustment, there is no assurance that the Monte Carlo simulation model will correctly value the on-the-run Treasury issues. An adjustment to the short-term interest rates is required in order to have the model properly price on-the-run Treasury issues so that the model will provide arbitrage-free values.

   C. In moving from the short-term interest rates to the refinancing rates, it is necessary to make an assumption about the spread between these rates.

5. In the Monte Carlo simulation model, a prepayment *model* is used. The prepayment model provides a prepayment rate for each month on each interest rate path. Thus, no specific PSA prepayment assumption is made. Consequently, the statement by Mr. Ruthledge that a 175 PSA was made is inconsistent with the Monte Carlo simulation model. Therefore, Mr. Hawthorne should have been confused by Mr. Ruthledge's response.

6. On an interest rate path, the short-term interest rates are the forward rates. It is the forward rates plus an appropriate spread that is used to value a mortgage-backed security on an interest rate path.

7. The investor in a passthrough security has effectively sold a call option to borrowers (homeowners). The higher the assumed interest rate volatility the greater the value of this embedded call option and therefore the lower the price of a passthrough security. Securities 1 and 2 have the correct relationship between price and assumed interest rate volatility. Security 3 has the opposite relationship. Therefore, the error that Mr. Rodriguez discovered is with the relationship between assumed interest rate volatility and price for Security 3.

8. **A.** Since the collateral is trading at a premium, a slowdown in prepayments will allow the investor to receive the higher coupon for a longer period of time. This will increase the value of the collateral.

   B. Because Tranche Y is selling at a premium, its value will increase with a slowdown in prepayments. In contrast, because Tranche X is selling at a discount, a slowdown in prepayments will decrease its value. This is because for Tranche X, there will be less principal returned to be reinvested at the new, higher rates. Also, assuming that X was purchased when it was trading at a discount, there will be less of a capital gain realized (since principal is returned at par).

9. The theoretical value based on the ten interest rate paths is the average of the present value of the interest rate paths. The average value is 89.1.

10. **A.** Rather than sampling a large number of interest rate paths, some vendors of mortgage analytical systems have developed computational procedures that reduce the number of paths required. The procedure involves using statistical techniques to reduce the number of interest rate paths to sets of similar paths. These paths are called representative paths. The security is then valued on each of the representative interest rate paths—16 in the question.

    B. The theoretical value of a security when the representative interest rate paths are used is the weighted average of the 16 representative paths. The weight for a path is the percentage of that representative path relative to the total paths in a full Monte Carlo analysis.

    C. The trade-off between the full Monte Carlo analysis and the 16 representative paths is one of speed versus accuracy. The full Monte Carlo analysis provides the true value of the security—*true only based on all the assumptions of the model.* Using 16 representative samples is less accurate but requires less computational time.

11. The theoretical value is the weighted average of the present value of the representative interest rate paths. The weighted average of the present value of the representative interest rate paths is 77.94 as shown below:

Weight	PV	Weight × PV
0.20	70	14.00
0.18	82	14.76
0.16	79	12.64
0.12	68	8.16
0.12	74	8.88
0.12	86	10.32
0.06	91	5.46
0.04	93	3.72
Theoretical value		77.94

12. **A.** While there is no credit risk for a Ginnie Mae mortgage product, there is liquidity risk (relative to on-the-run Treasury issues) and modeling risk. The latter risk is due to the assumptions that must be made in valuing a mortgage-backed security. If those assumptions prove incorrect or if the parameters used as inputs are wrong, the valuation model will not calculate the true level of risk. A major portion of the compensation for a Ginnie Mae mortgage product reflects payment for this model uncertainty.

    B. The OAS should differ by the type of Ginnie Mae mortgage product. The more complex the security to model and value, the greater the OAS should be to reflect the associated modeling risk. Moreover, the more complex the security, the less liquid the security tends to be. Consequently, the OAS will also differ because of liquidity risk.

13. Using the representative interest rate paths, the theoretical value of a mortgage-backed security is the weighted average of the present value of the paths. Since it is assumed in the question that each path has the same weight, the theoretical value is the simple average of the present values of the interest rate paths. For the four spreads, the average PV is given below:

Representative Path	Present Value if the Spread Used Is			
	70 bps	75 bps	80 bps	85 bps
Average PV	82.6	79.5	76.3	73.8

    A. The option-adjusted spread is the spread that will make the theoretical value equal to the market price. Since the question assumes that Tranche L has a market price of 79.5, then a spread of 75 basis points will produce a theoretical value equal to the market price of 79.5. Therefore, the OAS is 75 basis points.

    B. If the price is 73.8 instead of 79.5, then the OAS is the spread that will make the theoretical value equal to 73.8. From the table above it can be seen that a spread of 85 basis points will produce a theoretical value equal to 73.8. Therefore, the OAS is 85 basis points.

14. Tranche M has a substantial variation in the present value for the paths. This is a characteristic of a support tranche since a support tranche is exposed to substantial prepayment risk. Tranche N has little variation in the present value for the paths and this is a characteristic of a PAC tranche. Therefore, Tranche M is probably the support tranche and Tranche N is probably the PAC tranche.

15. **A.** The option cost is the difference between the Z-spread and the OAS. Therefore,

         PAC I A: 60 – 50 = 10 basis points

         PAC II A: 150 – 80 = 70 basis points

         Support S1:   165 – 35 = 130 basis points

    B. Typically, the OAS increases with effective duration. The two longer PAC tranches, PAC I C and PAC I D, have lower OAS than the two shorter duration PACs. Therefore, the two longer duration PACs appear to be expensive.

    C. On a relative value basis, all but PAC II A appear to be expensive. PAC II B has a lower OAS than PAC II A even though it has a higher effective duration. The other two support tranches without a schedule have a low OAS relative to their effective durations.

   D. Investors who do not appreciate the significance of the option risk associated with a tranche can be induced to buy PAC II B because they look exclusively at the nominal spread. While the nominal spread is not provided as part of the information in the question, it can be estimated from the Z-spread. A Z-spread of 280 basis points is extremely appealing to investors for a security with no credit risk (since the deal is an agency CMO deal). Also, investors who do not realize that a PAC II is a support bond will believe that they have purchased a PAC tranche with a high "spread" to Treasuries.

16. The effective duration and effective convexity require the calculation of V_- and V_+. To calculate V_-, each path of short-term interest rates is decreased by a small number of basis points, say 25 basis points. Then, the cash flows are generated for each interest rate path. When the new cash flows are valued using the short-term interest rates plus a spread, the spread used is the original OAS. That is, it is assumed that the OAS does not change when interest rates are decreased. The same procedure is followed to compute V_+, but each path of short-term rates is increased by the same small number of basis points as was used to compute V_-. Again, it is assumed that the OAS does not change, so the new short-term interest rates plus the original OAS are used to discount the new cash flows on the interest rate paths.

17. First it is important to note that the CMO tranche is a support tranche and therefore has considerable prepayment risk. Despite Mr. Winters having been told that all the dealer firms used the Monte Carlo simulation model to compute the effective duration, there are assumptions in the model that can vary from dealer to dealer. This is the reason for the variation in the effective duration. These different assumptions in computing the value of a mortgage-backed security include:

   1. differences in the amount of the rate shock used

   2. differences in prepayment models

   3. differences in option-adjusted spread (recall that the OAS is held constant when rates are shocked)

   4. differences in the relationship between short-term interest rates and refinancing rates

18. This statement is incorrect. From a collateral with negative convexity, tranches with both positive and negative convexity can be created. For example, a PAC bond that is well protected will have little prepayment risk and therefore positive convexity—effectively the convexity of an option-free bond. However, one or more of the other tranches in the deal would have to have more negative convexity than the collateral itself, since the tranching of the collateral can only reallocate prepayment risk; it cannot eliminate it entirely.

19. **A.** Cash flow duration is computed assuming that if interest rates are changed, the prepayment rate will change when computing the new value.

   B. The problem is that this duration measure is based on one initial prepayment speed, and when rates are changed, it is assumed the prepayment speed will change to another prepayment speed. It is a static approach because it considers only one prepayment speed if rates change. It does not consider the dynamics that interest rates can change in the future and therefore there is not just one potential cash flow or prepayment rate that must be considered in valuing a mortgage-backed security.

20. To compute the coupon curve duration the assumption is that if the yield declines by 100 basis points, the price of the 9% coupon passthrough will increase to the price of the current 10% coupon passthrough. Thus, the price will increase from 99.50 to 102.60. Similarly, if the yield increases by 100 basis points, the assumption is that the price of the 9% coupon passthrough will decline to the price of the 8% coupon passthrough (97.06). Using the duration formula, the corresponding values are:

$$V_0 = 99.50$$
$$V_+ = 97.06$$
$$V_- = 102.60$$
$$\Delta y = 0.01$$

The estimated duration based on the coupon curve is then:

$$\frac{102.60 - 97.06}{2(99.50)(0.01)} = 2.78$$

21. Empirical duration is computed using statistical analysis. It requires good price data for the tranche whose empirical duration is to be computed. A major problem with applying empirical duration to complex CMO tranches is that a reliable series of price data is often not available for a thinly traded mortgage product or the prices may be matrix priced or model priced rather than actual transaction prices. The second problem is that an empirical relationship does not impose a structure for the options embedded in a mortgage-backed security, and this can distort the empirical duration. Finally, the volatility of the spread to Treasury yields can distort how the price of a mortgage-backed security reacts to yield changes.

22. The nominal spread of an asset-backed security hides the associated option or prepayment risk. For auto loan-backed securities, refinancing is not an important factor and therefore prepayment risk is not significant. For credit card receivables, there is prepayment risk only at the security level—that is, a credit card borrower cannot prepay because there is no schedule of payments, but a security can be prepaid if certain rapid or early amortization triggers are realized. However, prepayment risk is not significant. In contrast, for home equity loan-backed securities prepayment risk is significant and the nominal spread reflects that risk. Consequently, assessing relative value for these three types of asset-backed securities based on the nominal spread is incorrect because the spread is not adjusted for the prepayment risk. Home equity loan-backed securities offer a higher nominal spread because of the prepayment risk.

23. The appropriate valuation approach depends on whether or not the borrower has an option to prepay. Furthermore, even if the borrower has the right to prepay, it depends on whether or not the borrower will take advantage of this option to prepay when interest rates decline. Since the security involves future royalties, there is no prepayment option. Consequently, there is no option value and the appropriate valuation approach is the zero-volatility spread.

24. While there is an option to prepay, if the empirical evidence is correct that borrowers do not prepay when rates decline, then the option value is zero. Consequently, the zero-volatility spread approach is the appropriate approach since the OAS is equal to the zero-volatility spread.

25. A. Since high-quality borrowers are observed to take advantage of refinancing opportunities, there is a value to the prepayment option. Consequently, the option-adjusted spread approach is appropriate when the underlying pool of home equity loans are those of high-quality borrowers.

   B. Since low-quality borrowers may prepay but have been observed not to take advantage of refinancing opportunities, there is very little value to the prepayment option. Since the option cost has a value of zero, the zero-volatility spread is equal to the option-adjusted spread. Consequently, the zero-volatility spread approach can be used to value securities backed by a pool of home equity loans of low-quality borrowers.

However, there is a caveat here regarding the behavior of low-quality borrowers. The answer ignores the adverse selection impact of borrowers who upgrade their credit profile and refinance out, leaving a potentially longer average life, and worse credit, pool.

26. B is correct. Gupta's first conclusion is incorrect. When interest rates fall, prepayments rise due to refinancing and contraction risk occurs. When interest rates increase, prepayments fall and mortgage securities extend rather than contract.

27. C is correct. Gupta's second conclusion is incorrect. An accrual tranche (Z tranche) is paid only after all other tranches have been paid in full. The payments that would otherwise have been paid to the accrual tranche are used to pay off the principal balance of earlier tranches. This increases the contraction risk and decreases the extension risk of the earlier tranches. The effect on prepayment risk (contraction and extension) is thus not determinable.

28. A is correct. A planned amortization class (PAC) bond is a mortgage-backed security wherein the investor has greater assurance of the timing of the repayment of principal. The window of the PAC describes the width of the period of time for the repayment of principal. A very narrow window, in effect, provides a single repayment date (maturity date). Thus, such a PAC bond resembles a corporate bond.

29. A is correct. If interest rates increase, prepayments slow and mortgage securities extend. IO strips benefit from the extension in the number of interest payments. Further, the interest received can be reinvested at the new higher rates. PO strips must wait longer to receive repayment of principal as prepayments decrease. Further, the principal repayments are discounted at higher rates and worth less even without the extended time. The time extension and the higher discount rate together make PO strips very poor investments should interest rates increase.

30. B is correct. The zero-volatility spread (also called the static spread or the Z-spread) indicates the increased yield on a MBS above the Treasury spot rate curve. It incorporates credit risk, liquidity risk, and any option risk. The option-adjusted spread (OAS) takes prepayment into account and removes (adjusts for) the option risk. The OAS reflects credit risk and liquidity risk. The difference between the two spreads reflects the cost of the option. In this problem the cost of the embedded option is 60 − 50 = 10 basis points.

31. C is correct. To answer this question, trade off OAS versus effective duration. The lower the OAS, the lower the return offered by the security. A lower return might be acceptable if effective duration (risk) is less. Of the three selected tranches, PAC3 has the lowest OAS (lowest return), yet its risk (effective duration) is higher than either PAC1 or PAC2. Furthermore, the option cost of PAC3 is 90, which exceeds the option cost for the other choices.

Glossary

Abandonment option   The ability to terminate a project at some future time if the financial results are disappointing.

Abnormal earnings   See *Residual income*.

Abnormal return   The return on an asset in excess of the asset's required rate of return; the risk-adjusted return.

Absolute convergence   The idea that developing countries, regardless of their particular characteristics, will eventually catch up with the developed countries and match them in per capita output.

Absolute valuation model   A model that specifies an asset's intrinsic value.

Absolute version of PPP   The extension of the law of one price to the broad range of goods and services that are consumed in different countries.

Accounting estimates   Estimates of items such as the useful lives of assets, warranty costs, and the amount of uncollectible receivables.

Accrual basis   Method of accounting in which the effect of transactions on financial condition and income are recorded when they occur, not when they are settled in cash.

Acquirer   The company in a merger or acquisition that is acquiring the target.

Acquiring company   The company in a merger or acquisition that is acquiring the target.

Acquisition   The purchase of some portion of one company by another; the purchase may be for assets, a definable segment of another entity, or the purchase of an entire company.

Active factor risk   The contribution to active risk squared resulting from the portfolio's different-than-benchmark exposures relative to factors specified in the risk model.

Active portfolio   In the context of the Treynor-Black model, the portfolio formed by mixing analyzed stocks of perceived nonzero alpha values. This portfolio is ultimately mixed with the passive market index portfolio.

Active return   The return on a portfolio minus the return on the portfolio's benchmark.

Active risk   The standard deviation of active returns.

Active risk squared   The variance of active returns; active risk raised to the second power.

Active specific risk or asset selection risk   The contribution to active risk squared resulting from the portfolio's active weights on individual assets as those weights interact with assets' residual risk.

Add-on interest   A procedure for determining the interest on a bond or loan in which the interest is added onto the face value of a contract.

Adjusted beta   Historical beta adjusted to reflect the tendency of beta to be mean reverting.

Adjusted funds from operations   Funds from operations (FFO) adjusted to remove any non-cash rent reported under straight-line rent accounting and to subtract maintenance-type capital expenditures and leasing costs, including leasing agents' commissions and tenants' improvement allowances.

Adjusted present value   (APV)As an approach to valuing a company, the sum of the value of the company, assuming no use of debt, and the net present value of any effects of debt on company value.

Adjusted R^2   A measure of goodness-of-fit of a regression that is adjusted for degrees of freedom and hence does not automatically increase when another independent variable is added to a regression.

Administrative regulations or administrative law   Rules issued by government agencies or other regulators.

Agency costs   Costs associated with the conflict of interest present when a company is managed by non-owners. Agency costs result from the inherent conflicts of interest between managers and equity owners.

Agency costs of equity   The smaller the stake that managers have in the company, the less is their share in bearing the cost of excessive perquisite consumption or not giving their best efforts in running the company.

Agency issues   (also agency problems, or principal-agent problems) Conflicts of interest that arise when the agent in an agency relationship has goals and incentives that differ from the principal to whom the agent owes a fiduciary duty.

Agency problem   A conflict of interest that arises when the agent in an agency relationship has goals and incentives that differ from the principal to whom the agent owes a fiduciary duty.

Alpha   The return on an asset in excess of the asset's required rate of return; the risk-adjusted return.

American Depositary Receipt   A negotiable certificate issued by a depositary bank that represents ownership in a non-U.S. company's deposited equity (i.e., equity held in custody by the depositary bank in the company's home market).

American option   An option that can be exercised at any time until its expiration date.

Amortizing and accreting swaps   A swap in which the notional principal changes according to a formula related to changes in the underlying.

Analysis of variance (ANOVA)   The analysis of the total variability of a dataset (such as observations on the dependent variable in a regression) into components representing different sources of variation; with reference to regression, ANOVA provides the inputs for an *F*-test of the significance of the regression as a whole.

Arbitrage   1) The simultaneous purchase of an undervalued asset or portfolio and sale of an overvalued but equivalent asset or portfolio, in order to obtain a riskless profit on the price differential. Taking advantage of a market inefficiency in a risk-free manner. 2) The condition in a financial market in which equivalent assets or combinations of assets sell for two different prices, creating an opportunity to profit at no risk with no commitment of money. In a well-functioning financial market, few arbitrage opportunities are possible. 3) A risk-free operation that earns an expected positive net profit but requires no net investment of money.

Arbitrage opportunity   An opportunity to conduct an arbitrage; an opportunity to earn an expected positive net profit without risk and with no net investment of money.

Arbitrage portfolio   The portfolio that exploits an arbitrage opportunity.

Arrears swap   A type of interest rate swap in which the floating payment is set at the end of the period and the interest is paid at that same time.

Asset beta   The unlevered beta; reflects the business risk of the assets; the asset's systematic risk.

Asset purchase   An acquisition in which the acquirer purchases the target company's assets and payment is made directly to the target company.

Asset-based approach   Approach that values a private company based on the values of the underlying assets of the entity less the value of any related liabilities.

Asset-based valuation   An approach to valuing natural resource companies that estimates company value on the basis of the market value of the natural resources the company controls.

Asymmetric information   The differential of information between corporate insiders and outsiders regarding the company's performance and prospects. Managers typically have more information about the company's performance and prospects than owners and creditors.

At-the-money   An option in which the underlying value equals the exercise price.

Autocorrelation   The correlation of a time series with its own past values.

Autoregressive model (AR)   A time series regressed on its own past values, in which the independent variable is a lagged value of the dependent variable.

Available-for-sale investments   Debt and equity securities not classified as either held-to-maturity or held-for-trading securities. The investor is willing to sell but not actively planning to sell. In general, available-for-sale securities are reported at fair value on the balance sheet.

Backward integration   A merger involving the purchase of a target ahead of the acquirer in the value or production chain; for example, to acquire a supplier.

Backwardation   A condition in the futures markets in which the benefits of holding an asset exceed the costs, leaving the futures price less than the spot price.

Balance-sheet-based accruals ratio   The difference between net operating assets at the end and the beginning of the period compared to the average net operating assets over the period.

Balance-sheet-based aggregate accruals   The difference between net operating assets at the end and the beginning of the period.

Basic earnings per share   (EPS) Net earnings available to common shareholders (i.e., net income minus preferred dividends) divided by the weighted average number of common shares outstanding during the period.

Basis swap   1) An interest rate swap involving two floating rates. 2) A swap in which both parties pay a floating rate.

Bear hug   A tactic used by acquirers to circumvent target management's objections to a proposed merger by submitting the proposal directly to the target company's board of directors.

Benchmark   A comparison portfolio; a point of reference or comparison.

Benchmark value of the multiple   In using the method of comparables, the value of a price multiple for the comparison asset; when we have comparison assets (a group), the mean or median value of the multiple for the group of assets.

Bill-and-hold basis   Sales on a bill-and-hold basis involve selling products but not delivering those products until a later date.

Binomial model   A model for pricing options in which the underlying price can move to only one of two possible new prices.

Binomial tree   The graphical representation of a model of asset price dynamics in which, at each period, the asset moves up with probability p or down with probability $(1 - p)$.

Blockage factor   An illiquidity discount that occurs when an investor sells a large amount of stock relative to its trading volume (assuming it is not large enough to constitute a controlling ownership).

Bond indenture   A legal contract specifying the terms of a bond issue.

Bond option   An option in which the underlying is a bond; primarily traded in over-the-counter markets.

Bond yield plus risk premium method   An estimate of the cost of common equity that is produced by summing the before-tax cost of debt and a risk premium that captures the additional yield on a company's stock relative to its bonds. The additional yield is often estimated using historical spreads between bond yields and stock yields.

Bond-equivalent yield   The yield to maturity on a basis that ignores compounding.

Bonding costs   Costs borne by management to assure owners that they are working in the owners' best interest (e.g., implicit cost of non-compete agreements).

Book value   Shareholders' equity (total assets minus total liabilities) minus the value of preferred stock; common shareholders' equity.

Book value of equity   Shareholders' equity (total assets minus total liabilities) minus the value of preferred stock; common shareholders' equity.

Book value per share   The amount of book value (also called carrying value) of common equity per share of common stock, calculated by dividing the book value of shareholders' equity by the number of shares of common stock outstanding.

Bottom-up forecasting approach   A forecasting approach that involves aggregating the individual company forecasts of analysts into industry forecasts, and finally into macroeconomic forecasts.

Bottom-up investing   An approach to investing that focuses on the individual characteristics of securities rather than on macroeconomic or overall market forecasts.

Breakup value   The value derived using a sum-of-the-parts valuation.

Breusch–Pagan test   A test for conditional heteroskedasticity in the error term of a regression.

Broker   1) An agent who executes orders to buy or sell securities on behalf of a client in exchange for a commission. 2) *See* Futures commission merchants.

Brokerage   The business of acting as agents for buyers or sellers, usually in return for commissions.

Buy-side analysts   Analysts who work for investment management firms, trusts, and bank trust departments, and similar institutions.

Call   An option that gives the holder the right to buy an underlying asset from another party at a fixed price over a specific period of time.

Cannibalization   Cannibalization occurs when an investment takes customers and sales away from another part of the company.

Cap 1) A contract on an interest rate, whereby at periodic payment dates, the writer of the cap pays the difference between the market interest rate and a specified cap rate if, and only if, this difference is positive. This is equivalent to a stream of call options on the interest rate. 2) A combination of interest rate call options designed to hedge a borrower against rate increases on a floating-rate loan.

Cap rate See capitalization rate.

Capital allocation line (CAL) A graph line that describes the combinations of expected return and standard deviation of return available to an investor from combining the optimal portfolio of risky assets with the risk-free asset.

Capital asset pricing model (CAPM) An equation describing the expected return on any asset (or portfolio) as a linear function of its beta relative to the market portfolio.

Capital charge The company's total cost of capital in money terms.

Capital deepening An increase in the capital-to-labor ratio.

Capital market line (CML) The line with an intercept point equal to the risk-free rate that is tangent to the efficient frontier of risky assets; represents the efficient frontier when a risk-free asset is available for investment.

Capital rationing A capital rationing environment assumes that the company has a fixed amount of funds to invest.

Capital structure The mix of debt and equity that a company uses to finance its business; a company's specific mixture of long-term financing.

Capitalization of earnings method In the context of private company valuation, valuation model based on an assumption of a constant growth rate of free cash flow to the firm or a constant growth rate of free cash flow to equity.

Capitalization rate The divisor in the expression for the value of perpetuity. In the context of real estate, the divisor in the direct capitalization method of estimating value. The cap rate equals net operating income divided by value.

Capitalized cash flow method (capitalized cash flow model) In the context of private company valuation, valuation model based on an assumption of a constant growth rate of free cash flow to the firm or a constant growth rate of free cash flow to equity.

Capitalized cash flow model (method) In the context of private company valuation, valuation model based on an assumption of a constant growth rate of free cash flow to the firm or a constant growth rate of free cash flow to equity.

Capitalized income method In the context of private company valuation, valuation model based on an assumption of a constant growth rate of free cash flow to the firm or a constant growth rate of free cash flow to equity.

Caplet Each component call option in a cap.

Capped swap A swap in which the floating payments have an upper limit.

Carried interest A share of any profits that is paid to the general partner (manager) of an investment partnership, such as a private equity or hedge fund, as a form of compensation designed to be an incentive to the manager to maximize performance of the investment fund.

Carrying costs The costs of holding an asset, generally a function of the physical characteristics of the underlying asset.

Cash available for distribution Funds from operations (FFO) adjusted to remove any non-cash rent reported under straight-line rent accounting and to subtract maintenance-type capital expenditures and leasing costs, including leasing agents' commissions and tenants' improvement allowances.

Cash basis Accounting method in which the only relevant transactions for the financial statements are those that involve cash.

Cash offering A merger or acquisition that is to be paid for with cash; the cash for the merger might come from the acquiring company's existing assets or from a debt issue.

Cash settlement A procedure used in certain derivative transactions that specifies that the long and short parties engage in the equivalent cash value of a delivery transaction.

Cash-flow-statement-based accruals ratio The difference between reported net income on an accrual basis and the cash flows from operating and investing activities compared to the average net operating assets over the period.

Cash-flow-statement-based aggregate accruals The difference between reported net income on an accrual basis and the cash flows from operating and investing activities.

Cash-generating unit The smallest identifiable group of assets that generates cash inflows that are largely independent of the cash inflows of other assets or groups of assets.

Catalyst An event or piece of information that causes the marketplace to re-evaluate the prospects of a company.

Chain rule of forecasting A forecasting process in which the next period's value as predicted by the forecasting equation is substituted into the right-hand side of the equation to give a predicted value two periods ahead.

Cheapest-to-deliver A bond in which the amount received for delivering the bond is largest compared with the amount paid in the market for the bond.

Clean surplus accounting Accounting that satisfies the condition that all changes in the book value of equity other than transactions with owners are reflected in income. The bottom-line income reflects all changes in shareholders' equity arising from other than owner transactions. In the absence of owner transactions, the change in shareholders' equity should equal net income. No adjustments such as translation adjustments bypass the income statement and go directly to shareholders equity.

Clean surplus relation The relationship between earnings, dividends, and book value in which ending book value is equal to the beginning book value plus earnings less dividends, apart from ownership transactions.

Clientele effect The preference some investors have for shares that exhibit certain characteristics.

Club convergence The idea that only rich and middle-income countries sharing a set of favorable attributes (i.e., are members of the "club") will converge to the income level of the richest countries.

Cobb–Douglas production function A function of the form $Y = K^\alpha L^{1-\alpha}$ relating output (Y) to labor (L) and capital (K) inputs.

Cointegrated Describes two time series that have a long-term financial or economic relationship such that they do not diverge from each other without bound in the long run.

Commercial real estate properties Income-producing real estate properties, properties purchased with the intent to let, lease, or rent (in other words, produce income).

Common size statements Financial statements in which all elements (accounts) are stated as a percentage of a key figure such as revenue for an income statement or total assets for a balance sheet.

Company fundamental factors   Factors related to the company's internal performance, such as factors relating to earnings growth, earnings variability, earnings momentum, and financial leverage.

Company share-related factors   Valuation measures and other factors related to share price or the trading characteristics of the shares, such as earnings yield, dividend yield, and book-to-market value.

Comparables   (comps, guideline assets, guideline companies) Assets used as benchmarks when applying the method of comparables to value an asset.

Compiled financial statements   Financial statements that are not accompanied by an auditor's opinion letter.

Comprehensive income   All changes in equity other than contributions by, and distributions to, owners; income under clean surplus accounting; includes all changes in equity during a period except those resulting from investments by owners and distributions to owners; comprehensive income equals net income plus other comprehensive income.

Comps   Assets used as benchmarks when applying the method of comparables to value an asset.

Conditional convergence   The idea that convergence of per capita income is conditional on the countries having the same savings rate, population growth rate, and production function.

Conditional heteroskedasticity   Heteroskedasticity in the error variance that is correlated with the values of the independent variable(s) in the regression.

Conglomerate discount   The discount possibly applied by the market to the stock of a company operating in multiple, unrelated businesses.

Conglomerate merger   A merger involving companies that are in unrelated businesses.

Consolidation   The combining of the results of operations of subsidiaries with the parent company to present financial statements as if they were a single economic unit. The assets, liabilities, revenues and expenses of the subsidiaries are combined with those of the parent company, eliminating intercompany transactions.

Constant dividend payout ratio policy   A policy in which a constant percentage of net income is paid out in dividends.

Constant maturity swap   (or **CMT swap**) A swap in which the floating rate is the rate on a security known as a constant maturity treasury or CMT security.

Constant maturity treasury (CMT)   A hypothetical U.S. Treasury note with a constant maturity. A CMT exists for various years in the range of 2 to 10.

Constant returns to scale   The condition that if all inputs into the production process are increased by a given percentage, then output rises by that same percentage.

Contango   A situation in a futures market where the current futures price is greater than the current spot price for the underlying asset.

Contingent consideration   Potential future payments to the seller that are contingent on the achievement of certain agreed on occurrences.

Continuing earnings   Earnings excluding nonrecurring components.

Continuing residual income   Residual income after the forecast horizon.

Continuing value   The analyst's estimate of a stock's value at a particular point in the future.

Continuous time   Time thought of as advancing in extremely small increments.

Control premium   An increment or premium to value associated with a controlling ownership interest in a company.

Convenience yield   The nonmonetary return offered by an asset when the asset is in short supply, often associated with assets with seasonal production processes.

Conventional cash flow   A conventional cash flow pattern is one with an initial outflow followed by a series of inflows.

Conversion factor   An adjustment used to facilitate delivery on bond futures contracts in which any of a number of bonds with different characteristics are eligible for delivery.

Core earnings   Earnings excluding nonrecurring components.

Corporate governance   The system of principles, policies, procedures, and clearly defined responsibilities and accountabilities used by stakeholders to overcome the conflicts of interest inherent in the corporate form.

Corporate raider   A person or organization seeking to profit by acquiring a company and reselling it, or seeking to profit from the takeover attempt itself (e.g., greenmail).

Corporation   A legal entity with rights similar to those of a person. The chief officers, executives, or top managers act as agents for the firm and are legally entitled to authorize corporate activities and to enter into contracts on behalf of the business.

Cost approach   Approach that values a private company based on the values of the underlying assets of the entity less the value of any related liabilities. In the context of real estate, this approach estimates the value of a property based on what it would cost to buy the land and construct a new property on the site that has the same utility or functionality as the property being appraised.

Cost of carry   The cost associated with holding some asset, including financing, storage, and insurance costs. Any yield received on the asset is treated as a negative carrying cost.

Cost of debt   The cost of debt financing to a company, such as when it issues a bond or takes out a bank loan.

Cost of equity   The required rate of return on common stock.

Cost-of-carry model   A model for pricing futures contracts in which the futures price is determined by adding the cost of carry to the spot price.

Covariance stationary   Describes a time series when its expected value and variance are constant and finite in all periods and when its covariance with itself for a fixed number of periods in the past or future is constant and finite in all periods.

Covered interest arbitrage   A transaction executed in the foreign exchange market in which a currency is purchased (sold) and a forward contract is sold (purchased) to lock in the exchange rate for future delivery of the currency. This transaction should earn the risk-free rate of the investor's home country.

Covered interest rate parity   Relationship among the spot exchange rate, forward exchange rate, and the interest rates in two currencies that ensures that the return on a hedged (i.e., covered) foreign risk-free investment is the same as the return on a domestic risk-free investment.

Currency option   An option that allows the holder to buy (if a call) or sell (if a put) an underlying currency at a fixed exercise rate, expressed as an exchange rate.

Current credit risk   The risk associated with the possibility that a payment currently due will not be made.

Current exchange rate   For accounting purposes, the spot exchange rate on the balance sheet date.

Current rate method   Approach to translating foreign currency financial statements for consolidation in which all assets and liabilities are translated at the current exchange rate. The current rate method is the prevalent method of translation.

Cyclical businesses Businesses with high sensitivity to business- or industry-cycle influences.

DOWNREIT A variation of the UPREIT structure under which the REIT owns more than one partnership and may own properties at both the REIT level and the partnership level.

Daily settlement See *Marking to market*.

Data mining The practice of determining a model by extensive searching through a dataset for statistically significant patterns.

Day trader A trader holding a position open somewhat longer than a scalper but closing all positions at the end of the day.

"Dead-hand" provision A poison pill provision that allows for the redemption or cancellation of a poison pill provision only by a vote of continuing directors (generally directors who were on the target company's board prior to the takeover attempt).

Debt covenants Agreements between the company as borrower and its creditors.

Debt ratings An objective measure of the quality and safety of a company's debt based upon an analysis of the company's ability to pay the promised cash flows, as well as an analysis of any indentures.

Decision rule With respect to hypothesis testing, the rule according to which the null hypothesis will be rejected or not rejected; involves the comparison of the test statistic to rejection point(s).

Deep-in-the-money Options that are far in-the-money.

Deep-out-of-the-money Options that are far out-of-the-money.

Deferred revenue A liability account for money that has been collected for goods or services that have not yet been delivered; payment received in advance of providing a good or service.

Definition of value A specification of how "value" is to be understood in the context of a specific valuation.

Definitive merger agreement A contract signed by both parties to a merger that clarifies the details of the transaction, including the terms, warranties, conditions, termination details, and the rights of all parties.

Delivery A process used in a deliverable forward contract in which the long pays the agreed-upon price to the short, which in turn delivers the underlying asset to the long.

Delivery option The feature of a futures contract giving the short the right to make decisions about what, when, and where to deliver.

Delta The relationship between the option price and the underlying price, which reflects the sensitivity of the price of the option to changes in the price of the underlying.

Depreciated replacement cost In the context of real estate, the replacement cost of a building adjusted different types of depreciation.

Derivative A financial instrument whose value depends on the value of some underlying asset or factor (e.g., a stock price, an interest rate, or exchange rate).

Descriptive statistics The study of how data can be summarized effectively.

Diff swaps A swap in which the payments are based on the difference between interest rates in two countries but payments are made in only a single currency.

Diluted earnings per share (diluted EPS) Net income, minus preferred dividends, divided by the number of common shares outstanding considering all dilutive securities (e.g., convertible debt and options); the EPS that would result if all dilutive securities were converted into common shares.

Dilution A reduction in proportional ownership interest as a result of the issuance of new shares.

Diminishing marginal productivity When each additional unit of an input, keeping the other inputs unchanged, increases output by a smaller increment.

Direct capitalization method In the context of real estate, this method estimates the value of an income-producing property based on the level and quality of its net operating income.

Direct financing leases A type of finance lease, from a lessor perspective, where the present value of the lease payments (lease receivable) equals the carrying value of the leased asset. The revenues earned by the lessor are financing in nature.

Dirty surplus accounting Accounting in which some income items are reported as part of stockholders' equity rather than as gains and losses on the income statement; certain items of comprehensive income bypass the income statement and appear as direct adjustments to shareholders' equity.

Dirty-surplus items Items that affect comprehensive income but which bypass the income statement.

Discount To reduce the value of a future payment in allowance for how far away it is in time; to calculate the present value of some future amount. Also, the amount by which an instrument is priced below its face value.

Discount for lack of control An amount or percentage deducted from the pro rata share of 100 percent of the value of an equity interest in a business to reflect the absence of some or all of the powers of control.

Discount for lack of marketability An amount of percentage deducted from the value of an ownership interest to reflect the relative absence of marketability.

Discount interest A procedure for determining the interest on a loan or bond in which the interest is deducted from the face value in advance.

Discount rate Any rate used in finding the present value of a future cash flow.

Discounted abnormal earnings model A model of stock valuation that views intrinsic value of stock as the sum of book value per share plus the present value of the stock's expected future residual income per share.

Discounted cash flow (DCF) analysis In the context of merger analysis, it is an estimate of a target company's value found by discounting the company's expected future free cash flows to the present.

Discounted cash flow method Income approach that values an asset based on estimates of future cash flows discounted to present value by using a discount rate reflective of the risks associated with the cash flows. In the context of real estate, this method estimates the value of an income-producing property based by discounting future projected cash flows.

Discounted cash flow model A model of intrinsic value that views the value of an asset as the present value of the asset's expected future cash flows.

Discrete time Time thought of as advancing in distinct finite increments.

Discriminant analysis A multivariate classification technique used to discriminate between groups, such as companies that either will or will not become bankrupt during some time frame.

Diversified REITs REITs that own and operate in more than one type of property; they are more common in Europe and Asia than in the United States.

Divestiture   The sale, liquidation, or spin-off of a division or subsidiary.

Dividend coverage ratio   The ratio of net income to dividends.

Dividend discount model   (also DDM) A present value model of stock value that views the intrinsic value of a stock as present value of the stock's expected future dividends.

Dividend displacement of earnings   The concept that dividends paid now displace earnings in all future periods.

Dividend imputation tax system   A taxation system which effectively assures that corporate profits distributed as dividends are taxed just once, at the shareholder's tax rate.

Dividend payout ratio   The ratio of cash dividends paid to earnings for a period.

Dividend policy   The strategy a company follows with regard to the amount and timing of dividend payments.

Dividend rate   The most recent quarterly dividend multiplied by four.

Double taxation system   Corporate earnings are taxed twice when paid out as dividends. First, corporate earnings are taxed regardless of whether they will be distributed as dividends or retained at the G-13 corporate level, and second, dividends are taxed again at the individual shareholder level.

Downstream   A transaction between two affiliates, an investor company and an associate company such that the investor company records a profit on its income statement. An example is a sale of inventory by the investor company to the associate.

Due diligence   Investigation and analysis in support of a recommendation; the failure to exercise due diligence may sometimes result in liability according to various securities laws.

Dummy variable   A type of qualitative variable that takes on a value of 1 if a particular condition is true and 0 if that condition is false.

Duration   A measure of an option-free bond's average maturity. Specifically, the weighted average maturity of all future cash flows paid by a security, in which the weights are the present value of these cash flows as a fraction of the bond's price. A measure of a bond's price sensitivity to interest rate movements.

Dutch disease   A situation in which currency appreciation driven by strong export demand for resources makes other segments of the economy (particularly manufacturing) globally uncompetitive.

Dynamic hedging   A strategy in which a position is hedged by making frequent adjustments to the quantity of the instrument used for hedging in relation to the instrument being hedged.

Earnings expectations management   Attempts by management to encourage analysts to forecast a slightly lower number for expected earnings than the analysts would otherwise forecast.

Earnings game   Management's focus on reporting earnings that meet consensus estimates.

Earnings management activity   Deliberate activity aimed at influencing reporting earnings numbers, often with the goal of placing management in a favorable light; the opportunistic use of accruals to manage earnings.

Earnings surprise   The difference between reported earnings per share and expected earnings per share.

Earnings yield   Earnings per share divided by price; the reciprocal of the P/E ratio.

Economic obsolescence   In the context of real estate, a reduction in value due to current economic conditions.

Economic profit   See *Residual income.*

Economic sectors   Large industry groupings.

Economic value added   (EVA®) A commercial implementation of the residual income concept; the computation of EVA® is the net operating profit after taxes minus the cost of capital, where these inputs are adjusted for a number of items.

Economies of scale   In reference to mergers, it is the savings achieved through the consolidation of operations and elimination of duplicate resources.

Edwards–Bell–Ohlson model   A model of stock valuation that views intrinsic value of stock as the sum of book value per share plus the present value of the stock's expected future residual income per share.

Efficient frontier   The portion of the minimum-variance frontier beginning with the global minimum-variance portfolio and continuing above it; the graph of the set of portfolios offering the maximum expected return for their level of variance of return.

Efficient portfolio   A portfolio offering the highest expected return for a given level of risk as measured by variance or standard deviation of return.

Enterprise value   (EV) Total company value (the market value of debt, common equity, and preferred equity) minus the value of cash and investments.

Enterprise value multiple   A valuation multiple that relates the total market value of all sources of a company's capital (net of cash) to a measure of fundamental value for the entire company (such as a pre-interest earnings measure).

Entry price   The price paid to buy an asset.

Equilibrium   The condition in which supply equals demand.

Equity REIT   A REIT that owns, operates, and/or selectively develops income-producing real estate.

Equity carve-out   A form of restructuring that involves the creation of a new legal entity and the sale of equity in it to outsiders.

Equity charge   The estimated cost of equity capital in money terms.

Equity forward   A contract calling for the purchase of an individual stock, a stock portfolio, or a stock index at a later date at an agreed-upon price.

Equity options   Options on individual stocks; also known as stock options.

Error autocorrelation   The autocorrelation of the error term.

Eurodollar   A dollar deposited outside the United States.

European option   An option that can only be exercised on its expiration date.

Ex ante version of PPP   Hypothesis that expected changes in the spot exchange rate are equal to expected differences in national inflation rates. An extension of relative purchasing power parity to expected future changes in the exchange rate.

Ex-dividend   Trading ex-dividend refers to shares that no longer carry the right to the next dividend payment.

Ex-dividend date   The first date that a share trades without (i.e., "ex") the dividend.

Ex-dividend price   The price at which a share first trades without (i.e., "ex") the right to receive an upcoming dividend.

Excess earnings method   Income approach that estimates the value of all intangible assets of the business by capitalizing future earnings in excess of the estimated return requirements associated with working capital and fixed assets.

Exchange for physicals (EFP)   A permissible delivery procedure used by futures market participants, in which the long and short arrange a delivery procedure other than the normal procedures stipulated by the futures exchange.

Exchange ratio   The number of shares that target stockholders are to receive in exchange for each of their shares in the target company.

Exercise   (also **exercising the option**) The process of using an option to buy or sell the underlying.

Exercise price   (also **strike price**, **striking price**, or **strike**) The fixed price at which an option holder can buy or sell the underlying.

Exercise rate   (also **strike rate**) The fixed rate at which the holder of an interest rate option can buy or sell the underlying.

Exercise value   (also **intrinsic value**) The value of an asset given a hypothetically complete understanding of the asset's investment characteristics; the value obtained if an option is exercised based on current conditions.

Exercising the option   (also **exercise**) The process of using an option to buy or sell the underlying.

Exit price   The price received to sell an asset or transfer a liability.

Expanded CAPM   An adaptation of the CAPM that adds to the CAPM a premium for small size and company-specific risk.

Expected holding-period return   The expected total return on an asset over a stated holding period; for stocks, the sum of the expected dividend yield and the expected price appreciation over the holding period.

Expenses   Outflows of economic resources or increases in liabilities that result in decreases in equity (other than decreases because of distributions to owners); reductions in net assets associated with the creation of revenues.

Expiration date   The date on which a derivative contract expires.

Exposure to foreign exchange risk   The risk of a change in value of an asset or liability denominated in a foreign currency due to a change in exchange rates.

External growth   Company growth in output or sales that is achieved by buying the necessary resources externally (i.e., achieved through mergers and acquisitions).

External sustainability approach   An approach to assessing the equilibrium exchange rate that focuses on exchange rate adjustments required to ensure that a country's net foreign-asset/GDP ratio or net foreign-liability/GDP ratio stabilizes at a sustainable level.

Externalities   Spillover effects of production and consumption activities onto others who did not consent to participate in the activity.

Externality   The effect of an investment on other things besides the investment itself.

FX carry trade   An investment strategy that involves taking on long positions in high-yield currencies and short positions in low-yield currencies.

Factor   A common or underlying element with which several variables are correlated.

Factor betas   An asset's sensitivity to a particular factor; a measure of the response of return to each unit of increase in a factor, holding all other factors constant.

Factor loadings   See *factor betas*.

Factor price   The expected return in excess of the risk-free rate for a portfolio with a sensitivity of 1 to one factor and a sensitivity of 0 to all other factors.

Factor risk premium   (or factor price) The expected return in excess of the risk-free rate for a portfolio with a sensitivity of 1 to one factor and a sensitivity of 0 to all other factors.

Factor risk premium   See *factor price*.

Factor sensitivity   See *factor betas*.

Fair market value   The market price of an asset or liability that trades regularly.

Fair value   The amount at which an asset (or liability) could be bought (or incurred) or sold (or settled) in a current transaction between willing parties, that is, other than in a forced or liquidation sale; the price that would be received to sell an asset or paid to transfer a liability in an orderly transaction between market participants at the measurement date.

Fiduciary call   A combination of a European call and a risk-free bond that matures on the option expiration day and has a face value equal to the exercise price of the call.

Finance lease   (capital lease) Essentially, the purchase of some asset by the buyer (lessee) that is directly financed by the seller (lessor).

Financial contagion   A situation where financial shocks spread from their place of origin to other locales; in essence, a faltering economy infects other, healthier economies.

Financial distress   Heightened uncertainty regarding a company's ability to meet its various obligations because of lower or negative earnings.

Financial futures   Futures contracts in which the underlying is a stock, bond, or currency.

Financial reporting quality   The accuracy with which a company's reported financials reflect its operating performance and their usefulness for forecasting future cash flows.

Financial risk   The risk that environmental, social, or governance risk factors will result in significant costs or other losses to a company and its shareholders; the risk arising from a company's obligation to meet required payments under its financing agreements.

Financial transaction   A purchase involving a buyer having essentially no material synergies with the target (e.g., the purchase of a private company by a company in an unrelated industry or by a private equity firm would typically be a financial transaction).

First-differencing   A transformation that subtracts the value of the time series in period $t-1$ from its value in period t.

First-in, first-out (FIFO)   The first in, first out, method of accounting for inventory, which matches sales against the costs of items of inventory in the order in which they were placed in inventory.

First-order serial correlation   Correlation between adjacent observations in a time series.

Fixed-rate perpetual preferred stock   Nonconvertible, non-callable preferred stock with a specified dividend rate that has a claim on earnings senior to the claim of common stock, and no maturity date.

Flip-in pill   A poison pill takeover defense that dilutes an acquirer's ownership in a target by giving other existing target company shareholders the right to buy additional target company shares at a discount.

Flip-over pill   A poison pill takeover defense that gives target company shareholders the right to purchase shares of the acquirer at a significant discount to the market price, which has the effect of causing dilution to all existing acquiring company shareholders.

Floor   A combination of interest rate put options designed to hedge a lender against lower rates on a floating-rate loan.

Floor traders   Market makers that buy and sell by quoting a bid and an ask price. They are the primary providers of liquidity to the market.

Floored swap   A swap in which the floating payments have a lower limit.

Floorlet   Each component put option in a floor.

Flotation cost   Fees charged to companies by investment bankers and other costs associated with raising new capital.

Foreign currency transactions   Transactions that are denominated in a currency other than a company's functional currency.

Forward P/E   A P/E calculated on the basis of a forecast of EPS; a stock's current price divided by next year's expected earnings.

Forward contract   An agreement between two parties in which one party, the buyer, agrees to buy from the other party, the seller, an underlying asset at a later date for a price established at the start of the contract.

Forward dividend yield   A dividend yield based on the anticipated dividend during the next 12 months.

Forward integration   A merger involving the purchase of a target that is farther along the value or production chain; for example, to acquire a distributor.

Forward price or forward rate   The fixed price or rate at which the transaction scheduled to occur at the expiration of a forward contract will take place. This price is agreed on at the initiation date of the contract.

Forward rate agreement (FRA)   A forward contract calling for one party to make a fixed interest payment and the other to make an interest payment at a rate to be determined at the contract expiration.

Forward swap   A forward contract to enter into a swap.

Franking credit   A tax credit received by shareholders for the taxes that a corporation paid on its distributed earnings.

Free cash flow   The actual cash that would be available to the company's investors after making all investments necessary to maintain the company as an ongoing enterprise (also referred to as free cash flow to the firm); the internally generated funds that can be distributed to the company's investors (e.g., shareholders and bondholders) without impairing the value of the company.

Free cash flow hypothesis   The hypothesis that higher debt levels discipline managers by forcing them to make fixed debt service payments and by reducing the company's free cash flow.

Free cash flow method   Income approach that values an asset based on estimates of future cash flows discounted to present value by using a discount rate reflective of the risks associated with the cash flows.

Free cash flow to equity   The cash flow available to a company's common shareholders after all operating expenses, interest, and principal payments have been made, and necessary investments in working and fixed capital have been made.

Free cash flow to equity model   A model of stock valuation that views a stock's intrinsic value as the present value of expected future free cash flows to equity.

Free cash flow to the firm   The cash flow available to the company's suppliers of capital after all operating expenses (including taxes) have been paid and necessary investments in working and fixed capital have been made.

Free cash flow to the firm model   A model of stock valuation that views the value of a firm as the present value of expected future free cash flows to the firm.

Friendly transaction   A potential business combination that is endorsed by the managers of both companies.

Functional currency   The currency of the primary economic environment in which an entity operates.

Functional obsolescence   In the context of real estate, a reduction in value due to a design that differs from that of a new building constructed for the intended use of the property.

Fundamental beta   A beta that is based at least in part on fundamental data for a company.

Fundamental factor models   A multifactor model in which the factors are attributes of stocks or companies that are important in explaining cross-sectional differences in stock prices.

Fundamentals   Economic characteristics of a business such as profitability, financial strength, and risk.

Funds available for distribution   Funds from operations (FFO) adjusted to remove any non-cash rent reported under straight-line rent accounting and to subtract maintenance-type capital expenditures and leasing costs, including leasing agents' commissions and tenants' improvement allowances.

Funds from operations   Accounting net earnings excluding (1) depreciation charges on real estate, (2) deferred tax charges, and (3) gains or losses from sales of property and debt restructuring.

Futures commission merchants (FCMs)   Individuals or companies that execute futures transactions for other parties off the exchange.

Futures contract   A variation of a forward contract that has essentially the same basic definition but with some additional features, such as a clearinghouse guarantee against credit losses, a daily settlement of gains and losses, and an organized electronic or floor trading facility.

Gamma   A numerical measure of how sensitive an option's delta is to a change in the underlying.

Generalized least squares   A regression estimation technique that addresses heteroskedasticity of the error term.

Going-concern assumption   The assumption that the business will maintain its business activities into the foreseeable future.

Going-concern value   A business's value under a going-concern assumption.

Goodwill   An intangible asset that represents the excess of the purchase price of an acquired company over the value of the net assets acquired.

Gross domestic product   A money measure of the goods and services produced within a country's borders over a stated time period.

Gross lease   A lease under which the tenant pays a gross rent to the landlord who is responsible for all operating costs, utilities, maintenance expenses, and real estate taxes relating to the property.

Growth accounting equation   The production function written in the form of growth rates. For the basic Cobb–Douglas production function, it states that the growth rate of output equals the rate of technological change plus α times the growth rate of capital plus $(1-\alpha)$ times the growth rate of labor.

Growth option   (expansion option) The ability to make additional investments in a project at some future time if the financial results are strong.

Guideline assets   Assets used as benchmarks when applying the method of comparables to value an asset.

Guideline companies   Assets used as benchmarks when applying the method of comparables to value an asset.

Guideline public companies   Public-company comparables for the company being valued.

Guideline public company method   A variation of the market approach; establishes a value estimate based on the observed multiples from trading activity in the shares of public companies viewed as reasonably comparable to the subject private company.

Guideline transactions method   A variation of the market approach; establishes a value estimate based on pricing multiples derived from the acquisition of control of entire public or private companies that were acquired.

Harmonic mean   A type of weighted mean computed by averaging the reciprocals of the observations, then taking the reciprocal of that average.

Health care REITs   REITs that invest in skilled nursing facilities (nursing homes), assisted living and independent residential facilities for retired persons, hospitals, medical office buildings, or rehabilitation centers.

Hedge ratio   The relationship of the quantity of an asset being hedged to the quantity of the derivative used for hedging.

Hedging   A general strategy usually thought of as reducing, if not eliminating, risk.

Held for trading investments   Debt or equity securities acquired with the intent to sell them in the near term.

Held-to-maturity investments   Debt (fixed-income) securities that a company intends to hold to maturity; these are presented at their original cost, updated for any amortization of discounts or premiums.

Herfindahl–Hirschman Index (HHI)   A measure of market concentration that is calculated by summing the squared market shares for competing companies in an industry; high HHI readings or mergers that would result in large HHI increases are more likely to result in regulatory challenges.

Heteroskedastic   With reference to the error term of regression, having a variance that differs across observations.

Heteroskedasticity   The property of having a nonconstant variance; refers to an error term with the property that its variance differs across observations.

Heteroskedasticity-consistent standard errors   Standard errors of the estimated parameters of a regression that correct for the presence of heteroskedasticity in the regression's error term.

Historical exchange rates   For accounting purposes, the exchange rates that existed when the assets and liabilities were initially recorded.

Holding period return   The return that an investor earns during a specified holding period; a synonym for total return.

Homoskedasticity   The property of having a constant variance; refers to an error term that is constant across observations.

Horizontal merger   A merger involving companies in the same line of business, usually as competitors.

Hostile transaction   An attempt to acquire a company against the wishes of the target's managers.

Hotel REITs   REITs that own hotel properties but, similar to health care REITs, in many countries they must refrain from operating their properties themselves to maintain their tax-advantaged REIT status.

Human capital   The accumulated knowledge and skill that workers acquire from education, training, or life experience.

Hybrid REITs   REITs that own and operate income-producing real estate and invest in mortgages as well; REITs that have positions in both real estate assets and real estate debt.

Illiquidity discount   See *Liquidity discount.*

Impairment   Diminishment in value as a result of carrying (book) value exceeding fair value and/or recoverable value.

Impairment of capital rule   A legal restriction that dividends cannot exceed retained earnings.

Implied repo rate   The rate of return from a cash-and-carry transaction implied by the futures price relative to the spot price.

Implied volatility   The volatility that option traders use to price an option, implied by the price of the option and a particular option-pricing model.

In-process research and development   Research and development costs relating to projects that are not yet completed, such as have been incurred by a company that is being acquired.

In-sample forecast errors   The residuals from a fitted time-series model within the sample period used to fit the model.

In-the-money   Options that, if exercised, would result in the value received being worth more than the payment required to exercise.

Income approach   Valuation approach that values an asset as the present discounted value of the income expected from it. In the context of real estate, this approach estimates the value of a property based on an expected rate of return; the estimated value is the present value of the expected future income from the property, including proceeds from resale at the end of a typical investment holding period.

Incremental cash flow   The cash flow that is realized because of a decision; the changes or increments to cash flows resulting from a decision or action.

Indenture   A written contract between a lender and borrower that specifies the terms of the loan, such as interest rate, interest payment schedule, maturity, etc.

Independent projects   Independent projects are projects whose cash flows are independent of each other.

Independent regulators   Regulators recognized and granted authority by a government body or agency. They are not government agencies per se and typically do not rely on government funding.

Index amortizing swap   An interest rate swap in which the notional principal is indexed to the level of interest rates and declines with the level of interest rates according to a predefined schedule. This type of swap is frequently used to hedge securities that are prepaid as interest rates decline, such as mortgage-backed securities.

Indexing   An investment strategy in which an investor constructs a portfolio to mirror the performance of a specified index.

Industrial REITs   REITs that hold portfolios of single-tenant or multi-tenant industrial properties that are used as warehouses, distribution centers, light manufacturing facilities, and small office or "flex" space.

Industry structure   An industry's underlying economic and technical characteristics.

Information ratio   (also IR)Mean active return divided by active risk; or alpha divided by the standard deviation of diversifiable risk.

Informational frictions   Forces that restrict availability, quality, and/or flow of information and its use.

Initial margin requirement   The margin requirement on the first day of a transaction as well as on any day in which additional margin funds must be deposited.

Initial public offering   (also IPO) The initial issuance of common stock registered for public trading by a formerly private corporation.

Instability in the minimum-variance frontier   The characteristic of minimum-variance frontiers that they are sensitive to small changes in inputs.

Interest rate call   An option in which the holder has the right to make a known interest payment and receive an unknown interest payment.

Interest rate cap   A series of call options on an interest rate, with each option expiring at the date on which the floating loan rate will be reset, and with each option having the same exercise rate. A cap in general can have an underlying other than an interest rate.

Interest rate collar   A combination of a long cap and a short floor, or a short cap and a long floor. A collar in general can have an underlying other than an interest rate.

Interest rate floor   (also **floor**) A series of put options on an interest rate, with each option expiring at the date on which the floating loan rate will be reset, and with each option having the same exercise rate. A floor in general can have an underlying other than the interest rate.

Interest rate option   An option in which the underlying is an interest rate.

Interest rate parity   A formula that expresses the equivalence or parity of spot and forward rates, after adjusting for differences in the interest rates.

Interest rate put   An option in which the holder has the right to make an unknown interest payment and receive a known interest payment.

Internal rate of return   (IRR) Rate of return that discounts future cash flows from an investment to the exact amount of the investment; the discount rate that makes the present value of an investment's costs (outflows) equal to the present value of the investment's benefits (inflows).

International Fisher effect   Proposition that nominal interest rate differentials across currencies are determined by expected inflation differentials.

Intrinsic value   The value of an asset given a hypothetically complete understanding of the asset's investment characteristics; the value obtained if an option is exercised based on current conditions.

Inverse price ratio   The reciprocal of a price multiple, e.g., in the case of a P/E ratio, the "earnings yield" E/P (where P is share price and E is earnings per share).

Investment objectives   Desired investment outcomes; includes risk objectives and return objectives.

Investment strategy   An approach to investment analysis and security selection.

Investment value   The value to a specific buyer, taking account of potential synergies based on the investor's requirements and expectations.

Judicial law   Interpretations of courts.

Justified (fundamental) P/E   The price-to-earnings ratio that is fair, warranted, or justified on the basis of forecasted fundamentals.

Justified price multiple   The estimated fair value of the price multiple, usually based on forecasted fundamentals or comparables.

***k*th order autocorrelation**   The correlation between observations in a time series separated by *k* periods.

Labor force   Everyone of working age (ages 16 to 64) that either is employed or is available for work but not working.

Labor force participation rate   The percentage of the working age population that is in the labor force.

Labor productivity   The quantity of real GDP produced by an hour of labor. More generally, output per unit of labor input.

Labor productivity growth accounting equation   States that potential GDP growth equals the growth rate of the labor input plus the growth rate of labor productivity.

Lack of marketability discount   An extra return to investors to compensate for lack of a public market or lack of marketability.

Last-in, first-out (LIFO)   The last in, first out, method of accounting for inventory, which matches sales against the costs of items of inventory in the reverse order the items were placed in inventory (i.e., inventory produced or acquired last are assumed to be sold first).

Law of one price   Hypothesis that (1) identical goods should trade at the same price across countries when valued in terms of a common currency, or (2) two equivalent financial instruments or combinations of financial instruments can sell for only one price. The latter form is equivalent to the principle that no arbitrage opportunities are possible.

Leading P/E   A P/E calculated on the basis of a forecast of EPS; a stock's current price divided by next year's expected earnings.

Leading dividend yield   Forecasted dividends per share over the next year divided by current stock price.

Legal risk   The risk that failures by company managers to effectively manage a company's environmental, social, and governance risk exposures will lead to lawsuits and other judicial remedies, resulting in potentially catastrophic losses for the company; the risk that the legal system will not enforce a contract in case of dispute or fraud.

Legislative and regulatory risk   The risk that governmental laws and regulations directly or indirectly affecting a company's operations will change with potentially severe adverse effects on the company's continued profitability and even its long-term sustainability.

Lessee   The party obtaining the use of an asset through a lease.

Lessor   The owner of an asset that grants the right to use the asset to another party.

Leveraged buyout   (also LBO) A transaction whereby the target company management team converts the target to a privately held company by using heavy borrowing to finance the purchase of the target company's outstanding shares.

Leveraged recapitalization   A post-offer takeover defense mechanism that involves the assumption of a large amount of debt that is then used to finance share repurchases; the effect is to dramatically change the company's capital structure while attempting to deliver a value to target shareholders in excess of a hostile bid.

Limit down   A limit move in the futures market in which the price at which a transaction would be made is at or below the lower limit.

Limit move   A condition in the futures markets in which the price at which a transaction would be made is at or beyond the price limits.

Limit up   A limit move in the futures market in which the price at which a transaction would be made is at or above the upper limit.

Linear trend   A trend in which the dependent variable changes at a constant rate with time.

Liquidation To sell the assets of a company, division, or subsidiary piecemeal, typically because of bankruptcy; the form of bankruptcy that allows for the orderly satisfaction of creditors' claims after which the company ceases to exist.

Liquidation value The value of a company if the company were dissolved and its assets sold individually.

Liquidity discount A reduction or discount to value that reflects the lack of depth of trading or liquidity in that asset's market.

Liquidity risk The risk that a financial instrument cannot be purchased or sold without a significant concession in price due to the size of the market.

Local currency The currency of the country where a company is located.

Locals Market makers that buy and sell by quoting a bid and an ask price. They are the primary providers of liquidity to the market.

Locational obsolescence In the context of real estate, a reduction in value due to decreased desirability of the location of the building.

Locked limit A condition in the futures markets in which a transaction cannot take place because the price would be beyond the limits.

Log-linear model With reference to time-series models, a model in which the growth rate of the time series as a function of time is constant.

Log-log regression model A regression that expresses the dependent and independent variables as natural logarithms.

Logit model A qualitative-dependent-variable multiple regression model based on the logistic probability distribution.

London Interbank Offer Rate (LIBOR) The Eurodollar rate at which London banks lend dollars to other London banks; considered to be the best representative rate on a dollar borrowed by a private, high-quality borrower.

Long The buyer of a derivative contract. Also refers to the position of owning a derivative.

Long-term equity anticipatory securities (also **LEAPS**) Options originally created with expirations of several years.

Look-ahead bias A bias caused by using information that was not available on the test date.

Lower bound The lowest possible value of an option.

Macroeconomic balance approach An approach to assessing the equilibrium exchange rate that focuses on exchange rate adjustments needed to close the gap between the medium-term expectation for a country's current account balance and that country's normal (or sustainable) current account balance.

Macroeconomic factor A factor related to the economy, such as the inflation rate, industrial production, or economic sector membership.

Macroeconomic factor model A multifactor model in which the factors are surprises in macroeconomic variables that significantly explain equity returns.

Maintenance margin requirement The margin requirement on any day other than the first day of a transaction.

Managerialism theories Theories that posit that corporate executives are motivated to engage in mergers to maximize the size of their company rather than shareholder value.

Margin The amount of money that a trader deposits in a margin account. The term is derived from the stock market practice in which an investor borrows a portion of the money required to purchase a certain amount of stock. In futures markets, there is no borrowing so the margin is more of a down payment or performance bond.

Marginal investor An investor in a given share who is very likely to be part of the next trade in the share and who is therefore important in setting price.

Mark-to-market The revaluation of a financial asset or liability to its current market value or fair value.

Market approach Valuation approach that values an asset based on pricing multiples from sales of assets viewed as similar to the subject asset.

Market efficiency A finance perspective on capital markets that deals with the relationship of price to intrinsic value. The **traditional efficient markets formulation** asserts that an asset's price is the best available estimate of its intrinsic value. The **rational efficient markets formulation** asserts that investors should expect to be rewarded for the costs of information gathering and analysis by higher gross returns.

Market price of risk The slope of the capital market line, indicating the market risk premium for each unit of market risk.

Market risk premium The expected excess return on the market over the risk-free rate.

Market timing Asset allocation in which the investment in the market is increased if one forecasts that the market will outperform T-bills.

Market value The estimated amount for which a property should exchange on the date of valuation between a willing buyer and a willing seller in an arm's-length transaction after proper marketing wherein the parties had each acted knowledgeably, prudently, and without compulsion.

Market value of invested capital The market value of debt and equity.

Marking to market A procedure used primarily in futures markets in which the parties to a contract settle the amount owed daily. Also known as the *daily settlement*.

Markowitz decision rule A decision rule for choosing between two investments based on their means and variances.

Mature growth rate The earnings growth rate in a company's mature phase; an earnings growth rate that can be sustained long term.

Mean reversion The tendency of a time series to fall when its level is above its mean and rise when its level is below its mean; a mean-reverting time series tends to return to its long-term mean.

Mean–variance analysis An approach to portfolio analysis using expected means, variances, and covariances of asset returns.

Merger The absorption of one company by another; two companies become one entity and one or both of the pre-merger companies ceases to exist as a separate entity.

Method based on forecasted fundamentals An approach to using price multiples that relates a price multiple to forecasts of fundamentals through a discounted cash flow model.

Method of comparables An approach to valuation that involves using a price multiple to evaluate whether an asset is relatively fairly valued, relatively undervalued, or relatively overvalued when compared to a benchmark value of the multiple.

Minimum-variance frontier The graph of the set of portfolios that have minimum variance for their level of expected return.

Minimum-variance portfolio The portfolio with the minimum variance for each given level of expected return.

Minority Interest The proportion of the ownership of a subsidiary not held by the parent (controlling) company.

Mispricing   Any departure of the market price of an asset from the asset's estimated intrinsic value.

Mixed factor models   Factor models that combine features of more than one type of factor model.

Mixed offering   A merger or acquisition that is to be paid for with cash, securities, or some combination of the two.

Model specification   With reference to regression, the set of variables included in the regression and the regression equation's functional form.

Modified duration   A measure of a bond's price sensitivity to interest rate movements. Equal to the Macaulay duration of a bond divided by one plus its yield to maturity.

Molodovsky effect   The observation that P/Es tend to be high on depressed EPS at the bottom of a business cycle, and tend to be low on unusually high EPS at the top of a business cycle.

Momentum indicators   Valuation indicators that relate either price or a fundamental (such as earnings) to the time series of their own past values (or in some cases to their expected value).

Monetary assets and liabilities   Assets and liabilities with value equal to the amount of currency contracted for, a fixed amount of currency. Examples are cash, accounts receivable, mortgages receivable, accounts payable, bonds payable, and mortgages payable. Inventory is not a monetary asset. Most liabilities are monetary.

Monetary/nonmonetary method   Approach to translating foreign currency financial statements for consolidation in which monetary assets and liabilities are translated at the current exchange rate. Nonmonetary assets and liabilities are translated at historical exchange rates (the exchange rates that existed when the assets and liabilities were acquired).

Moneyness   The relationship between the price of the underlying and an option's exercise price.

Monitoring costs   Costs borne by owners to monitor the management of the company (e.g., board of director expenses).

Mortgage REITs   REITs that invest the bulk of their assets in interest-bearing mortgages, mortgage securities, or short-term loans secured by real estate.

Mortgage-backed securities   Asset-backed securitized debt obligations that represent rights to receive cash flows from portfolios of mortgage loans.

Mortgages   Loans with real estate serving as collateral for the loans.

Multi-family/residential REITs   REITs that invest in and manage rental apartments for lease to individual tenants, typically using one-year leases.

Multicollinearity   A regression assumption violation that occurs when two or more independent variables (or combinations of independent variables) are highly but not perfectly correlated with each other.

Multiple linear regression   Linear regression involving two or more independent variables.

Multiple linear regression model   A linear regression model with two or more independent variables.

Mutually exclusive projects   Mutually exclusive projects compete directly with each other. For example, if Projects A and B are mutually exclusive, you can choose A or B, but you cannot choose both.

NTM P/E   Next twelve months P/E: current market price divided by an estimated next twelve months EPS.

Negative serial correlation   Serial correlation in which a positive error for one observation increases the chance of a negative error for another observation, and vice versa.

Net asset balance sheet exposure   When assets translated at the current exchange rate are greater in amount than liabilities translated at the current exchange rate. Assets exposed to translation gains or losses exceed the exposed liabilities.

Net asset value   The difference between assets and liabilities, all taken at current market values instead of accounting book values.

Net asset value per share   Net asset value divided by the number of shares outstanding.

Net lease   A lease under which the tenant pays a net rent to the landlord as well as an additional amount based on the tenant's pro rata share of the operating costs, utilities, maintenance expenses, and real estate taxes relating to the property.

Net liability balance sheet exposure   When liabilities translated at the current exchange rate are greater than assets translated at the current exchange rate. Liabilities exposed to translation gains or losses exceed the exposed assets.

Net operating assets   The difference between operating assets (total assets less cash) and operating liabilities (total liabilities less total debt).

Net operating income   Gross rental revenue minus operating costs, but before deducting depreciation, corporate overhead, and interest expense. In the context of real estate, a measure of the income from the property after deducting operating expenses for such items as property taxes, insurance, maintenance, utilities, repairs, and insurance but before deducting any costs associated with financing and before deducting federal income taxes. It is similar to earnings before interest, taxes, depreciation, and amortization (EBITDA) in a financial reporting context.

Net operating profit less adjusted taxes (NOPLAT)   A company's operating profit with adjustments to normalize the effects of capital structure.

Net present value (NPV)   The present value of an investment's cash inflows (benefits) minus the present value of its cash outflows (costs).

Net realisable value   Estimated selling price in the ordinary course of business less the estimated costs necessary to make the sale.

Net regulatory burden   The private costs of regulation less the private benefits of regulation.

Net rent   A rent that consists of a stipulated rent to the landlord and a further amount based on their share of common area costs for utilities, maintenance, and property taxes.

Netting   When parties agree to exchange only the net amount owed from one party to the other.

Network externalities   The impact that users of a good, a service, or a technology have on other users of that product; it can be positive (e.g., a critical mass of users makes a product more useful) or negative (e.g., congestion makes the product less useful).

No-growth company   A company without positive expected net present value projects.

No-growth value per share   The value per share of a no-growth company, equal to the expected level amount of earnings divided by the stock's required rate of return.

Node   Each value on a binomial tree from which successive moves or outcomes branch.

Non-cash rent   An amount equal to the difference between the average contractual rent over a lease term (the straight-line rent) and the cash rent actually paid during a period. This figure is one of the deductions made from FFO to calculate AFFO.

Non-convergence trap A situation in which a country remains relative poor, or even falls further behind, because it fails to implement necessary institutional reforms and/or adopt leading technologies.

Non-renewable resources Finite resources that are depleted once they are consumed; oil and coal are examples.

Nonconventional cash flow In a nonconventional cash flow pattern, the initial outflow is not followed by inflows only, but the cash flows can flip from positive (inflows) to negative (outflows) again (or even change signs several times).

Nondeliverable forwards (NDFs) Cash-settled forward contracts, used predominately with respect to foreign exchange forwards.

Nonearning assets Cash and investments (specifically cash, cash equivalents, and short-term investments).

Nonmonetary assets and liabilities Assets and liabilities that are not monetary assets and liabilities. Nonmonetary assets include inventory, fixed assets, and intangibles, and nonmonetary liabilities include deferred revenue.

Nonstationarity With reference to a random variable, the property of having characteristics such as mean and variance that are not constant through time.

Normal EPS The earnings per share that a business could achieve currently under mid-cyclical conditions.

Normal backwardation The condition in futures markets in which futures prices are lower than expected spot prices.

Normal contango The condition in futures markets in which futures prices are higher than expected spot prices.

Normalized EPS The earnings per share that a business could achieve currently under mid-cyclical conditions.

Normalized P/E P/Es based on normalized EPS data.

Normalized earnings Earnings adjusted for nonrecurring, noneconomic, or other unusual items to eliminate anomalies and/or facilitate comparisons.

n-Period moving average The average of the current and immediately prior $n - 1$ values of a time series.

Off-market FRA A contract in which the initial value is intentionally set at a value other than zero and therefore requires a cash payment at the start from one party to the other.

Office REITs REITs that invest in and manage multi-tenanted office properties in central business districts of cities and suburban markets.

Offsetting A transaction in exchange-listed derivative markets in which a party re-enters the market to close out a position.

Operating lease An agreement allowing the lessee to use some asset for a period of time; essentially a rental.

Operating risk The risk attributed to the operating cost structure, in particular the use of fixed costs in operations; the risk arising from the mix of fixed and variable costs; the risk that a company's operations may be severely affected by environmental, social, and governance risk factors.

Operational risk The risk of loss from failures in a company's systems and procedures, or from external events.

Opportunity cost The value that investors forgo by choosing a particular course of action; the value of something in its best alternative use.

Opportunity set The set of assets available for investment.

Optimal capital structure The capital structure at which the value of the company is maximized.

Optimizer A specialized computer program or a spreadsheet that solves for the portfolio weights that will result in the lowest risk for a specified level of expected return.

Option A financial instrument that gives one party the right, but not the obligation, to buy or sell an underlying asset from or to another party at a fixed price over a specific period of time. Also referred to as contingent claims.

Option premium The amount of money a buyer pays and seller receives to engage in an option transaction.

Option price The amount of money a buyer pays and seller receives to engage in an option transaction.

Orderly liquidation value The estimated gross amount of money that could be realized from the liquidation sale of an asset or assets, given a reasonable amount of time to find a purchaser or purchasers.

Organic growth Company growth in output or sales that is achieved by making investments internally (i.e., excludes growth achieved through mergers and acquisitions).

Orthogonal Uncorrelated; at a right angle.

Other comprehensive income Changes to equity that bypass (are not reported in) the income statement; the difference between comprehensive income and net income.

Out-of-sample forecast errors The differences between actual and predicted value of time series outside the sample period used to fit the model.

Out-of-the-money Options that, if exercised, would require the payment of more money than the value received and therefore would not be currently exercised.

Overnight index swap (OIS) A swap in which the floating rate is the cumulative value of a single unit of currency invested at an overnight rate during the settlement period.

PEG The P/E-to-growth ratio, calculated as the stock's P/E divided by the expected earnings growth rate.

Pairs trading An approach to trading that uses pairs of closely related stocks, buying the relatively undervalued stock and selling short the relatively overvalued stock.

Partial regression coefficients or **partial slope coefficients** The slope coefficients in a multiple regression.

Partial slope coefficients or **partial regression coefficients** The slope coefficients in a multiple regression.

Partnership A business owned and operated by more than one individual.

Passive portfolio A market index portfolio.

Payer swaption A swaption that allows the holder to enter into a swap as the fixed-rate payer and floating-rate receiver.

Payoff The value of an option at expiration.

Payout policy The principles by which a company distributes cash to common shareholders by means of cash dividends and/or share repurchases.

Pecking order theory The theory that managers take into account how their actions might be interpreted by outsiders and thus order their preferences for various forms of corporate financing. Forms of financing that are least visible to outsiders (e.g., internally generated funds) are most preferable to managers and those that are most visible (e.g., equity) are least preferable.

Perfect capital markets Markets in which, by assumption, there are no taxes, transactions costs, or bankruptcy costs, and in which all investors have equal ("symmetric") information.

Performance appraisal The evaluation of risk-adjusted performance; the evaluation of investment skill.

Periodic inventory system An inventory accounting system in which inventory values and costs of sales are determined at the end of the accounting period.

Perpetual inventory system An inventory accounting system in which inventory values and costs of sales are continuously updated to reflect purchases and sales.

Perpetuity   A perpetual annuity, or a set of never-ending level sequential cash flows, with the first cash flow occurring one period from now.

Persistent earnings   Earnings excluding nonrecurring components.

Pet projects   Projects in which influential managers want the corporation to invest. Often, unfortunately, pet projects are selected without undergoing normal capital budgeting analysis.

Physical deterioration   In the context of real estate, a reduction in value due to wear and tear.

Plain vanilla swap   An interest rate swap in which one party pays a fixed rate and the other pays a floating rate, with both sets of payments in the same currency.

Poison pill   A pre-offer takeover defense mechanism that makes it prohibitively costly for an acquirer to take control of a target without the prior approval of the target's board of directors.

Poison puts   A pre-offer takeover defense mechanism that gives target company bondholders the right to sell their bonds back to the target at a pre-specified redemption price, typically at or above par value; this defense increases the need for cash and raises the cost of the acquisition.

Pooling of interests accounting method   A method of accounting in which combined companies were portrayed as if they had always operated as a single economic entity. Called pooling of interests under U.S. GAAP and uniting of interests under IFRS. (No longer allowed under U.S. GAAP or IFRS).

Portfolio balance approach   A theory of exchange rate determination that emphasizes the portfolio investment decisions of global investors and the requirement that global investors willingly hold all outstanding securities denominated in each currency at prevailing prices and exchange rates.

Portfolio performance attribution   The analysis of portfolio performance in terms of the contributions from various sources of risk.

Portfolio possibilities curve   A graphical representation of the expected return and risk of all portfolios that can be formed using two assets.

Position trader   A trader who typically holds positions open overnight.

Positive serial correlation   Serial correlation in which a positive error for one observation increases the chance of a positive error for another observation, and a negative error for one observation increases the chance of a negative error for another observation.

Potential GDP   The maximum amount of output an economy can sustainably produce without inducing an increase in the inflation rate. The output level that corresponds to full employment with consistent wage and price expectations.

Potential credit risk   The risk associated with the possibility that a payment due at a later date will not be made.

Premise of value   The status of a company in the sense of whether it is assumed to be a going concern or not.

Premium   The amount of money a buyer pays and seller receives to engage in an option transaction.

Present value model   A model of intrinsic value that views the value of an asset as the present value of the asset's expected future cash flows.

Present value of growth opportunities   (or **value of growth**) The difference between the actual value per share and the nogrowth value per share.

Presentation currency   The currency in which financial statement amounts are presented.

Price limits   Limits imposed by a futures exchange on the price change that can occur from one day to the next.

Price momentum   A valuation indicator based on past price movement.

Price multiples   The ratio of a stock's market price to some measure of value per share.

Price-setting option   The operational flexibility to adjust prices when demand varies from forecast. For example, when demand exceeds capacity, the company could benefit from the excess demand by increasing prices.

Priced risk   Risk for which investors demand compensation for bearing (e.g., equity risk, company-specific factors, macroeconomic factors).

Principal-agent problem   A conflict of interest that arises when the agent in an agency relationship has goals and incentives that differ from the principal to whom the agent owes a fiduciary duty.

Prior transaction method   A variation of the market approach; considers actual transactions in the stock of the subject private company.

Private market value   The value derived using a sum-of-the-parts valuation.

Probit model   A qualitative-dependent-variable multiple regression model based on the normal distribution.

Procedural law   The body of law that focuses on the protection and enforcement of the substantive laws.

Production-flexibility   The operational flexibility to alter production when demand varies from forecast. For example, if demand is strong, a company may profit from employees working overtime or from adding additional shifts.

Project sequencing   To defer the decision to invest in a future project until the outcome of some or all of a current project is known. Projects are sequenced through time, so that investing in a project creates the option to invest in future projects.

Prospective P/E   A P/E calculated on the basis of a forecast of EPS; a stock's current price divided by next year's expected earnings.

Protective put   An option strategy in which a long position in an asset is combined with a long position in a put.

Proxy fight   An attempt to take control of a company through a shareholder vote.

Proxy statement   A public document that provides the material facts concerning matters on which shareholders will vote.

Prudential supervision   Regulation and monitoring of the safety and soundness of financial institutions to promote financial stability, reduce system-wide risks, and protect customers of financial institutions.

Purchased in-process research and development costs   Costs of research and development in progress at an acquired company; often, part of the purchase price of an acquired company is allocated to such costs.

Purchasing power gain   A gain in value caused by changes in price levels. Monetary liabilities experience purchasing power gains during periods of inflation.

Purchasing power loss   A loss in value caused by changes in price levels. Monetary assets experience purchasing power losses during periods of inflation.

Purchasing power parity (PPP)   The idea that exchange rates move to equalize the purchasing power of different currencies.

Pure factor portfolio   A portfolio with sensitivity of 1 to the factor in question and a sensitivity of 0 to all other factors.

Put   An option that gives the holder the right to sell an underlying asset to another party at a fixed price over a specific period of time.

Put–call parity   An equation expressing the equivalence (parity) of a portfolio of a call and a bond with a portfolio of a put and the underlying, which leads to the relationship between put and call prices.

Put–call–forward parity   The relationship among puts, calls, and forward contracts.

Qualifying special purpose entity   Under U.S. GAAP, a special purpose entity structured to avoid consolidation that must meet qualification criteria.

Qualitative dependent variables   Dummy variables used as dependent variables rather than as independent variables.

Quality of earnings analysis   The investigation of issues relating to the accuracy of reported accounting results as reflections of economic performance; quality of earnings analysis is broadly understood to include not only earnings management, but also balance sheet management.

Random walk   A time series in which the value of the series in one period is the value of the series in the previous period plus an unpredictable random error.

Rational efficient markets formulation   See *Market efficiency.*

Real estate investment trusts   Tax-advantaged entities (companies or trusts) that typically own, operate, and—to a limited extent—develop income-producing real estate property.

Real estate operating companies   Regular taxable real estate ownership companies that operate in the real estate industry in countries that do not have a tax-advantaged REIT regime in place or are engaged in real estate activities of a kind and to an extent that do not fit within their country's REIT framework.

Real exchange rate   The relative purchasing power of two currencies, defined in terms of the *real* goods and services that each can buy at prevailing national price levels and nominal exchange rates. Measured as the ratio of national price levels expressed in a common currency.

Real interest rate parity   The proposition that real interest rates will converge to the same level across different markets.

Real options   Options that relate to investment decisions such as the option to time the start of a project, the option to adjust its scale, or the option to abandon a project that has begun.

Receiver swaption   A swaption that allows the holder to enter into a swap as the fixed-rate receiver and floating-rate payer.

Regime   With reference to a time series, the underlying model generating the times series.

Regression coefficients   The intercept and slope coefficient(s) of a regression.

Regulatory arbitrage   Entities identify and use some aspect of regulations that allows them to exploit differences in economic substance and regulatory interpretation or in foreign and domestic regulatory regimes to their (the entities) advantage.

Regulatory burden   The costs of regulation for the regulated entity.

Regulatory capture   Theory that regulation often arises to enhance the interests of the regulated.

Regulatory competition   Regulators may compete to provide a regulatory environment designed to attract certain entities.

Relative valuation models   A model that specifies an asset's value relative to the value of another asset.

Relative version of PPP   Hypothesis that changes in (nominal) exchange rates over time are equal to national inflation rate differentials.

Relative-strength indicators   Valuation indicators that compare a stock's performance during a period either to its own past performance or to the performance of some group of stocks.

Renewable resources   Resources that can be replenished, such as a forest.

Rental price of capital   The cost per unit of time to rent a unit of capital.

Replacement cost   In the context of real estate, the value of a building assuming it was built today using current construction costs and standards.

Replacement value   The market value of a swap.

Reporting unit   An operating segment or one level below an operating segment (referred to as a component).

Reputational risk   The risk that a company will suffer an extended diminution in market value relative to other companies in the same industry due to a demonstrated lack of concern for environmental, social, and governance risk factors.

Required rate of return   The minimum rate of return required by an investor to invest in an asset, given the asset's riskiness.

Residential properties   Properties that provide housing for individuals or families. Single-family properties may be owner-occupied or rental properties, whereas multi-family properties are rental properties even if the owner or manager occupies one of the units.

Residual autocorrelations   The sample autocorrelations of the residuals.

Residual dividend policy   A policy in which dividends are paid from any internally generated funds remaining after such funds are used to finance positive NPV projects.

Residual income   (or economic profit or abnormal earnings) Earnings for a given time period, minus a deduction for common shareholders' opportunity cost in generating the earnings.

Residual income method   Income approach that estimates the value of all intangible assets of the business by capitalizing future earnings in excess of the estimated return requirements associated with working capital and fixed assets.

Residual income model   (RIM) (also discounted abnormal earnings model or Edwards-Bell-Ohlson model) A model of stock valuation that views intrinsic value of stock as the sum of book value per share plus the present value of the stock's expected future residual income per share.

Residual loss   Agency costs that are incurred despite adequate monitoring and bonding of management.

Retail REITs   REITs that invest in such retail properties as regional shopping malls or community/neighborhood shopping centers.

Return on invested capital   (ROIC) The after-tax net operating profits as a percent of total assets or capital.

Revenue   The amount charged for the delivery of goods or services in the ordinary activities of a business over a stated period; the inflows of economic resources to a company over a stated period.

Reviewed financial statements   A type of non-audited financial statements; typically provide an opinion letter with representations and assurances by the reviewing accountant that are less than those in audited financial statements.

Rho   The sensitivity of the option price to the risk-free rate.

Risk reversal An option position that consists of the purchase of an out-of-the-money call and the simultaneous sale of an out-of-the-money put with the same "delta," on the same underlying currency or security, and with the same expiration date.

Risk-neutral probabilities Weights that are used to compute a binomial option price. They are the probabilities that would apply if a risk-neutral investor valued an option.

Risk-neutral valuation The process by which options and other derivatives are priced by treating investors as though they were risk neutral.

Robust standard errors Standard errors of the estimated parameters of a regression that correct for the presence of heteroskedasticity in the regression's error term.

Root mean squared error (RMSE) The square root of the average squared forecast error; used to compare the out-of-sample forecasting performance of forecasting models.

Sales comparison approach In the context of real estate, this approach estimates value based on what similar or comparable properties (comparables) transacted for in the current market.

Sales-type leases A type of finance lease, from a lessor perspective, where the present value of the lease payments (lease receivable) exceeds the carrying value of the leased asset. The revenues earned by the lessor are operating (the profit on the sale) and financing (interest) in nature.

Sampling distribution The distribution of all distinct possible values that a statistic can assume when computed from samples of the same size randomly drawn from the same population.

Scaled earnings surprise Unexpected earnings divided by the standard deviation of analysts' earnings forecasts.

Scalper A trader who offers to buy or sell futures contracts, holding the position for only a brief period of time. Scalpers attempt to profit by buying at the bid price and selling at the higher ask price.

Screening The application of a set of criteria to reduce a set of potential investments to a smaller set having certain desired characteristics.

Seats Memberships in a derivatives exchange.

Sector neutralizing Measure of financial reporting quality by subtracting the mean or median ratio for a given sector group from a given company's ratio.

Securities offering A merger or acquisition in which target shareholders are to receive shares of the acquirer's common stock as compensation.

Security market line (SML) The graph of the capital asset pricing model.

Self-regulating organizations Private, non-governmental organizations that both represent and regulate their members. Some self-regulating organizations are also independent regulators.

Sell-side analysts Analysts who work at brokerages.

Sensitivity analysis Analysis that shows the range of possible outcomes as specific assumptions are changed.

Serially correlated With reference to regression errors, errors that are correlated across observations.

Settlement date (or **payment date**) The date on which the parties to a swap make payments.

Settlement period The time between settlement dates.

Settlement price The official price, designated by the clearinghouse, from which daily gains and losses will be determined and marked to market.

Shareholders' equity Total assets minus total liabilities.

Shark repellents A pre-offer takeover defense mechanism involving the corporate charter (e.g., staggered boards of directors and supermajority provisions).

Sharpe's measure Reward-to-volatility ratio; ratio of portfolio excess return to standard deviation.

Shopping center REITs that invest in such retail properties as regional shopping malls or community/neighborhood shopping centers.

Short The seller of a derivative contract. Also refers to the position of being short a derivative.

Sole proprietorship A business owned and operated by a single person.

Special purpose vehicle (also special purpose entity or variable interest entity) A non-operating entity created to carry out a specified purpose, such as leasing assets or securitizing receivables; can be a corporation, partnership, trust, limited liability, or partnership formed to facilitate a specific type of business activity.

Speculative value (also **time value**) The difference between the market price of the option and its intrinsic value, determined by the uncertainty of the underlying over the remaining life of the option.

Spin-off A form of restructuring in which shareholders of a parent company receive a proportional number of shares in a new, separate entity; shareholders end up owning stock in two different companies where there used to be one.

Split-off A form of restructuring in which shareholders of the parent company are given shares in a newly created entity in exchange for their shares of the parent company.

Split-rate tax system In reference to corporate taxes, a split-rate system taxes earnings to be distributed as dividends at a different rate than earnings to be retained. Corporate profits distributed as dividends are taxed at a lower rate than those retained in the business.

Stabilized NOI In the context of real estate, the expected NOI when a renovation is complete.

Stable dividend policy A policy in which regular dividends are paid that reflect long-run expected earnings. In contrast to a constant dividend payout ratio policy, a stable dividend policy does not reflect short-term volatility in earnings.

Standard deviation The positive square root of the variance; a measure of dispersion in the same units as the original data.

Standard of value A specification of how "value" is to be understood in the context of a specific valuation.

Standardized beta With reference to fundamental factor models, the value of the attribute for an asset minus the average value of the attribute across all stocks, divided by the standard deviation of the attribute across all stocks.

Standardized unexpected earnings (SUE) Unexpected earnings per share divided by the standard deviation of unexpected earnings per share over a specified prior time period.

Static trade-off theory of capital structure A theory pertaining to a company's optimal capital structure; the optimal level of debt is found at the point where additional debt would cause the costs of financial distress to increase by a greater amount than the benefit of the additional tax shield.

Statistical factor models A multifactor model in which statistical methods are applied to a set of historical returns to determine portfolios that best explain either historical return covariances or variances.

Statistical inference   Making forecasts, estimates, or judgments about a larger group from a smaller group actually observed; using a sample statistic to infer the value of an unknown population parameter.

Statutes   Laws enacted by legislative bodies.

Statutory merger   A merger in which one company ceases to exist as an identifiable entity and all its assets and liabilities become part of a purchasing company.

Steady state rate of growth   The constant growth rate of output (or output per capita) which can or will be sustained indefinitely once it is reached. Key ratios, such as the capital–output ratio, are constant on the steady-state growth path.

Sterilized intervention   A policy measure in which a monetary authority buys or sells its own currency to mitigate undesired exchange rate movements and simultaneously offsets the impact on the money supply with transactions in other financial instruments (usually money market instruments).

Stock purchase   An acquisition in which the acquirer gives the target company's shareholders some combination of cash and securities in exchange for shares of the target company's stock.

Storage REITs   REITs that own and operate self-storage properties, sometimes referred to as mini-warehouse facilities.

Storage costs   The costs of holding an asset, generally a function of the physical characteristics of the underlying asset.

Straight-line rent   The average annual rent under a multi-year lease agreement that contains contractual increases in rent during the life of the lease. For example if the rent is $100,000 in Year 1, $105,000 in Year 2, and $110,000 in Year 3, the average rent to be recognized each year as revenue under straight-line rent accounting is ($100,000 + $105,000 + $110,000)/3 = $105,000.

Straight-line rent adjustment   *See* Non-cash rent.

Strategic transaction   A purchase involving a buyer that would benefit from certain synergies associated with owning the target firm.

Strike   See *exercise price.*

Strike price   See *exercise price.*

Strike rate   (also **exercise rate**) The fixed rate at which the holder of an interest rate option can buy or sell the underlying.

Striking price   See *exercise price.*

Subsidiary merger   A merger in which the company being purchased becomes a subsidiary of the purchaser.

Substantive law   The body of law that focuses on the rights and responsibilities of entities and relationships among entities.

Sum-of-the-parts valuation   A valuation that sums the estimated values of each of a company's businesses as if each business were an independent going concern.

Sunk cost   A cost that has already been incurred.

Supernormal growth   Above average or abnormally high growth rate in earnings per share.

Surprise   The actual value of a variable minus its predicted (or expected) value.

Survivorship bias   Bias that may result when failed or defunct companies are excluded from membership in a group.

Sustainable growth rate   The rate of dividend (and earnings) growth that can be sustained over time for a given level of return on equity, keeping the capital structure constant and without issuing additional common stock.

Swap spread   The difference between the fixed rate on an interest rate swap and the rate on a Treasury note with equivalent maturity; it reflects the general level of credit risk in the market.

Swaption   An option to enter into a swap.

Synthetic call   The combination of puts, the underlying, and risk-free bonds that replicates a call option.

Synthetic forward contract   The combination of the underlying, puts, calls, and risk-free bonds that replicates a forward contract.

Synthetic lease   A lease that is structured to provide a company with the tax benefits of ownership while not requiring the asset to be reflected on the company's financial statements.

Synthetic put   The combination of calls, the underlying, and risk-free bonds that replicates a put option.

Systematic factors   Factors that affect the average returns of a large number of different assets.

Systemic risk   The risk of failure of the financial system.

Takeover   A merger; the term may be applied to any transaction, but is often used in reference to hostile transactions.

Takeover premium   The amount by which the takeover price for each share of stock must exceed the current stock price in order to entice shareholders to relinquish control of the company to an acquirer.

Tangible book value per share   Common shareholders' equity minus intangible assets from the balance sheet, divided by the number of shares outstanding.

Target   The company in a merger or acquisition that is being acquired.

Target capital structure   A company's chosen proportions of debt and equity.

Target company   The company in a merger or acquisition that is being acquired.

Target payout ratio   A strategic corporate goal representing the long-term proportion of earnings that the company intends to distribute to shareholders as dividends.

Technical indicators   Momentum indicators based on price.

Temporal method   A variation of the monetary/nonmonetary translation method that requires not only monetary assets and liabilities, but also nonmonetary assets and liabilities that are measured at their current value on the balance sheet date to be translated at the current exchange rate. Assets and liabilities are translated at rates consistent with the timing of their measurement value. This method is typically used when the functional currency is other than the local currency.

Tender offer   A public offer whereby the acquirer invites target shareholders to submit ("tender") their shares in return for the proposed payment.

Terminal price multiples   The price multiple for a stock assumed to hold at a stated future time.

Terminal share price   The share price at a particular point in the future.

Terminal value of the stock   (or continuing value of the stock) The analyst's estimate of a stock's value at a particular point in the future.

Termination date   The date of the final payment on a swap; also, the swap's expiration date.

Theta   The rate at which an option's time value decays.

Time series   A set of observations on a variable's outcomes in different time periods.

Time to expiration   The time remaining in the life of a derivative, typically expressed in years.

Time value   (also **speculative value**) The difference between the market price of the option and its intrinsic value, determined by the uncertainty of the underlying over the remaining life of the option.

Time value decay The loss in the value of an option resulting from movement of the option price towards its payoff value as the expiration day approaches.

Tobin's q The ratio of the market value of debt and equity to the replacement cost of total assets.

Top-down forecasting approach A forecasting approach that involves moving from international and national macroeconomic forecasts to industry forecasts and then to individual company and asset forecasts.

Top-down investing An approach to investing that typically begins with macroeconomic forecasts.

Total factor productivity (TFP) A multiplicative scale factor that reflects the general level of productivity or technology in the economy. Changes in total factor productivity generate proportional changes in output for any input combination.

Total invested capital The sum of market value of common equity, book value of preferred equity, and face value of debt.

Total return swap A swap in which one party agrees to pay the total return on a security. Often used as a credit derivative, in which the underlying is a bond.

Tracking error (tracking risk) The standard deviation of the differences between a portfolio's returns and its benchmark's returns; a synonym of active risk.

Tracking portfolio A portfolio having factor sensitivities that are matched to those of a benchmark or other portfolio.

Tracking risk (tracking error) The standard deviation of the differences between a portfolio's returns and its benchmark's returns; a synonym of active risk.

Trailing P/E (or current P/E) A stock's current market price divided by the most recent four quarters of earnings per share.

Trailing dividend yield Current market price divided by the most recent quarterly per-share dividend multiplied by four.

Transaction exposure The risk of a change in value between the transaction date and the settlement date of an asset or liability denominated in a foreign currency.

Trend A long-term pattern of movement in a particular direction.

Triangular arbitrage An arbitrage transaction involving three currencies which attempts to exploit inconsistencies among pair wise exchange rates.

UPREITs An umbrella partnership REIT under which the REIT owns an operating partnership and serves as the general partner of the operating partnership. All or most of the properties are held in the operating partnership.

Unconditional heteroskedasticity Heteroskedasticity of the error term that is not correlated with the values of the independent variable(s) in the regression.

Uncovered interest rate parity The proposition that the expected return on an uncovered (i.e., unhedged) foreign currency (risk-free) investment should equal the return on a comparable domestic currency investment.

Underlying An asset that trades in a market in which buyers and sellers meet, decide on a price, and the seller then delivers the asset to the buyer and receives payment. The underlying is the asset or other derivative on which a particular derivative is based. The market for the underlying is also referred to as the spot market.

Underlying earnings Earnings excluding nonrecurring components.

Unearned revenue A liability account for money that has been collected for goods or services that have not yet been delivered; payment received in advance of providing a good or service.

Unexpected earnings The difference between reported earnings per share and expected earnings per share.

Unit root A time series that is not covariance stationary is said to have a unit root.

Uniting of interests method A method of accounting in which combined companies were portrayed as if they had always operated as a single economic entity. Called pooling of interests under U.S. GAAP and uniting of interests under IFRS. (No longer allowed under U.S. GAAP or IFRS).

Unlimited funds An unlimited funds environment assumes that the company can raise the funds it wants for all profitable projects simply by paying the required rate of return.

Unsterilized intervention A policy measure in which a monetary authority buys or sells its own currency to mitigate undesired exchange rate movements and does not offset the impact on the money supply with transactions in other financial instruments.

Upstream A transaction between two affiliates, an investor company and an associate company such that the associate company records a profit on its income statement. An example is a sale of inventory by the associate to the investor company.

Valuation The process of determining the value of an asset or service on the basis of variables perceived to be related to future investment returns, or on the basis of comparisons with closely similar assets.

Value at risk (VAR) A money measure of the minimum value of losses expected during a specified time period at a given level of probability.

Value of growth The difference between the actual value per share and the nogrowth value per share.

Variance The expected value (the probability-weighted average) of squared deviations from a random variable's expected value.

Variation margin Additional margin that must be deposited in an amount sufficient to bring the balance up to the initial margin requirement.

Vega The relationship between option price and volatility.

Venture capital investors Private equity investors in development-stage companies.

Vertical merger A merger involving companies at different positions of the same production chain; for example, a supplier or a distributor.

Visibility The extent to which a company's operations are predictable with substantial confidence.

Weighted average cost An inventory accounting method that averages the total cost of available inventory items over the total units available for sale.

Weighted average cost of capital (WACC) A weighted average of the after-tax required rates of return on a company's common stock, preferred stock, and long-term debt, where the weights are the fraction of each source of financing in the company's target capital structure.

Weighted harmonic mean See *Harmonic mean.*

White knight A third party that is sought out by the target company's board to purchase the target in lieu of a hostile bidder.

White squire A third party that is sought out by the target company's board to purchase a substantial minority stake in the target—enough to block a hostile takeover without selling the entire company.

White-corrected standard errors A synonym for robust standard errors.

Winner's curse The tendency for the winner in certain competitive bidding situations to overpay, whether because of overestimation of intrinsic value, emotion, or information asymmetries.

Write-down A reduction in the value of an asset as stated in the balance sheet.

Zero-cost collar A transaction in which a position in the underlying is protected by buying a put and selling a call with the premium from the sale of the call offsetting the premium from the purchase of the put. It can also be used to protect a floating-rate borrower against interest rate increases with the premium on a long cap offsetting the premium on a short floor.

Index